CW01496170

THE DIOCESE *of* KILMORE
c.1100–1800

First published in 2017 by
coιumвα press
23 Merrion Square North,
Dublin 2, Co. Dublin.
www.columba.ie

Copyright © 2017 Liam Kelly.

All rights reserved. Without limiting the rights under
copyright reserved alone, no part of this publication may
be reproduced, stored in or introduced into a retrieval
system, or transmitted, in any form or by any means
(electronic, mechanical, photocopying, recording or
otherwise) without the prior written permission of both
the copyright owner and the above publisher of the book.

ISBN: 978 1 78218 331 0

Set in Palatino 10/13
Cover design by Alba Esteban | Columba Press
Origination by Chenai Publishing
Print managed by Jellyfish. Printed in Turkey

THE DIOCESE

of

KILMORE

c.1100–1800

LIAM KELLY

columba press

In memory

Of

My parents

Thomas & Mary B. Kelly

	DIOCESAN BOUNDARIES
	PROVINCIAL BOUNDARIES

Foreword

I warmly welcome the publication of *The Diocese of Kilmore c.*1100-1800 by Fr Liam Kelly. It is a very comprehensive and thoroughly researched history of the diocese from its very beginnings in the twelfth-century up to 1800. Thus it provides a companion volume to the history of the post-1800 period by the late Fr Dan Gallogly that was published in 1999. It also realises the dream of my predecessor, the late Bishop Francis MacKiernan, who was the inspiration for this project, to have a history of the diocese which would take account of the new historical material that has become available since Philip O'Connell published his history of the diocese in 1937.

In his letter to the people of Ireland in 2010, Pope Benedict XVI encouraged us, in the words of the prophet Isaiah, to 'remember the rock from which you are hewn'. He was asking us to turn to the history of our Church in Ireland to find inspiration for renewal at a time of crisis. In this time of great change in the Church in Ireland, when many of the old certainties have been shattered and an uncertain future lies ahead, it is very important to remember the past and to remember it accurately. We need to see the present crisis in the perspective of a long history which saw many crises and many new beginnings. This new history of the diocese will, I believe, enable us in the diocese of Kilmore to achieve a more balanced and more hopeful perspective on our present painful experience through being more aware of the ebb and flow of Church life in the centuries before us, not just in the Church in general, but more specifically in our own diocese of Kilmore - the rock from which we were hewn.

Fr Kelly has many publications on historical subjects to his credit but this will surely rank as his *magnum opus*. It covers a period of seven centuries and contains a large amount of original research and new insights on many topics. He generously acknowledges all those who assisted him in the course of researching and writing this book. However, without his own hard work, diligent research and sheer commitment and stamina, as well as his talents as a historian and a writer, this volume could never have seen the light of day. We are greatly indebted to him and I thank him sincerely for his work and congratulate him warmly on his achievement.

Leo O'Reilly,
Bishop of Kilmore,
1 May 2017.

Acknowledgments

Back in the year 2001 Bishop Leo O'Reilly invited me to call in to see him. When I got there Francis MacKiernan, the retired bishop of the diocese, was also present. I quickly learned that the purpose of the meeting was to ask me to write a history of the diocese and, rather rashly, I agreed on the spot. Two years earlier Fr Dan Gallogly had completed his history *The diocese of Kilmore 1800-1950* and the bishops saw the need for a history of the diocese to cover an unspecified period pre-dating 1800. So I am indebted to Bishop Leo O'Reilly and the late Bishop Francis MacKiernan for asking me to write this history because without their intervention I would not have done so. I am also grateful to Bishop O'Reilly for granting me a sabbatical year, starting in September 2013, so that I could carry out the research for this book.

Philip O'Connell's *The diocese of Kilmore, its history and antiquities*, which was published in 1937, is still held in high regard. However, research in recent decades has unearthed a great deal of information and provided new insights into the ecclesiastical history of Ireland and that of the diocese of Kilmore. The *Bréifne* journal, which has been publishing high-quality articles on local history since 1958, and many other local history publications such as Francis MacKiernan's *Diocese of Kilmore, priests and bishops 1136-1988* (1989), the Raymond Gillespie edited *Cavan, essays on the history of an Irish county* (1995), the Brendan Scott edited *Culture and society in early modern Breifne/Cavan* (2009) and *Cavan history and society* (2014) which was jointly edited by Jonathan Cherry and Brendan Scott – all these books have provided me with information and insights not available to Philip O'Connell when he was writing his history of the diocese eighty-years ago. My debt of gratitude to so many historians who have contributed to these and other publications will be obvious throughout this book.

Agreeing to write a history of the diocese was the easy part. Getting time to research and write it was proving more difficult. Doing the MA in local history in Maynooth University (2002-04) was a good way to start. The history department in Maynooth has made an immense contribution to the study of local history in Ireland and I am just one of many people who have been privileged to study there. Raymond Gillespie, who headed up our local history studies in Maynooth, has advised, encouraged and supported me at every stage throughout the researching and writing of this history and I am deeply indebted to him. I am also grateful to the other members of the history department in Maynooth University, particularly Marian Lyons and Thomas O'Connor, who have encouraged and helped along the way. Were it not for the generous spirit of these and other historians I would not have been able to complete this task.

Francis MacKiernan had a life-long interest in the history of the diocese of Kilmore and during our two-week stay in Rome in 2002 (much of it spent in the Propaganda Fide archives) we unearthed many documents relating to Kilmore. Shortly before he died in 2005 he donated his large collection of books on Irish ecclesiastical history to Cavan County Library. Having access to this remarkable and under-used resource has left my task researching and writing this book so much easier. It helped greatly that Tom Sullivan, the county librarian, was welcoming, helpful and accommodating whenever I arrived, usually unannounced, at the library. I thank him and Carmel Ní Chíosóg Mhic Gahbann (who procured several rare books for me on inter-library loan), Susan Hough, Teresa Treacy, Jonathan Smith and all the other library staff who were patient, courteous and helpful at all times.

Mary Conefrey and the staff in the local history section of Leitrim County Library, Tom McKiernan, the Kilmore diocesan archivist and Noelle Dowling, the archivist in the Dublin diocesan archive, came to the rescue several times as did Desmond McCabe in the Public Records Office of Northern Ireland, Leanne Harrington in the Manuscripts and Archives Research Library of Trinity College Dublin, Bernadette Cunningham in the Royal Irish Academy and various members of the staff in both the National Archives and the National Library in Dublin. I am also indebted to the library staff in NUIG who gave me access to a number of theses not otherwise available. All these libraries and archives have great resources but without the expertise, courtesy and human-kindness of their staff, my task, and that of other historians, would be much more difficult.

I thank Brendan Scott, a gifted historian with an intimate knowledge of the history of early modern Ireland and of his native County Cavan, who has helped, supported and advised me at several stages along the way. He read the text, corrected errors and suggested numerous changes.

Others who read either all of the text or portions of it were Rory Masterson, Brian MacCuarta, Colmán Ó Clabaigh, Paul MacCotter and Raymond Gillespie. I am also grateful to Nollaig Ó Muraíle, who helped with the spelling of some Irish place-names and personal-names, and my thanks to Pádraig Ó Riain, who advised me on some of the local saints. However, I must stress that any mistakes or omissions in the final draft are my sole responsibility. The errors would have been greater and more numerous were it not for these scholars who, despite living busy lives, generously took time to read the text and recommend changes.

My thanks to Columba Press for agreeing to publish this book and for doing so in a such a professional and efficient manner. All of the staff have been a joy to work with, being both helpful and courteous at all times. In particular I want to thank Garry O'Sullivan the managing director at Columba Press and Alba Esteban who designed the cover of the book. I am also indebted to my fellow priests and all the parishes in Kilmore whose help in getting this book into print has been invaluable.

Finally, and most importantly, I thank my family, friends and parishioners whose kindness, love and care make all the difference.

Contents

List of Illustrations

List of Abbreviations

AC	*Annals of Connacht.*
ACL	*Annals of Clonmacnoise.*
AFM	*Annals of the Four Masters.*
AGOP	General archive of the Order of Preachers, Rome.
AHN	Archivo Histórico Nacional, Madrid.
AICR	Archive of the Irish College, Rome.
ALC	*Annals of Loch Cé.*
Anal. Hib.	*Analecta Hibernica.*
APF	Archive of Propaganda Fide, Rome.
Arch. Hib.	*Archivium Hibernicum.*
ASV	Archivo segreto Vaticano, Rome.
AT	*Annals of Tigernach.*
AU	*Annals of Ulster.*
BL	British Library, London.
BM	British Museum, London.
CDA	Clogher diocesan archive.
Coll. Hib.	*Collectanea Hibernica.*
Comm. Rinucc.	R. O'Ferrall and R. O'Connell, *Commentarius Rinuccinianus de sedis ... per annos 1645–9.* Ed. by S. Kavanagh, 6 vols (Dublin, 1932–49).
CP	Congregazioni particolari, Propaganda Fide archives, Rome.
CPL	Calendar of Papal Letters.
CSPI	Calendar of State papers of Ireland.
DDA	Dublin diocesan archives.
Dep.	Deposition.
DIB	*Dictionary of Irish biography*, (eds), James Maguire and James Quinn, (Cambridge, 2009).
IER	*Irish Ecclesiastical Record.*
IHS	*Irish Historical Studies.*
IJA	Irish Jesuit archive.
JACAS	*Journal of Ardagh and Clonmacnois Antiquarian Society.*
JBAHS	*Journal of Breifny Antiquarian and Historical Society.*
JCLAS	*Journal of County Louth Archaeological Society.*

JRSAI	*Journal of the Royal Society of Antiquaries of Ireland.*
KDA	Kilmore diocesan archive.
MCA	Maynooth College archive.
NAI	National Archive of Ireland, Dublin.
NLI	National Library of Ireland, Dublin.
NUIG	National University of Ireland, Galway.
NUIM	Maynooth University.
OFM	Order of Friars Minor.
OP	Order of Preachers.
OPW	Office of Public Works.
PRIA	*Proceedings of the Royal Irish Academy.*
PRONI	Public Records Office of Northern Ireland, Belfast.
RIA	Royal Irish Academy, Dublin.
RP	Rebellion papers.
SC	*Scritture riferite nei Congressi (Irlanda).*
SCAR	Archive of San Clemente, Rome.
SOCG	*Scritture riferite nella Congregazioni Generali.*
SP	State papers.
Spic. Ossor.	P.F Moran (ed.), *Spicilegium Ossoriense,* (Dublin, 1874).
TCD	Trinity College, Dublin.
TNA	The National Archives, London.
TSC	The Schools Folklore collection.
UJA	*Ulster Journal of Archaeology.*

Chapter 1

An Emerging Diocese: *c.*1100–1300

The present-day diocese of Kilmore is a long diocese, stretching north-west from Kilmainhamwood in County Meath to Tullaghan on Leitrim's Atlantic coastline. It consists of most of County Cavan, half of County Leitrim, three parishes in Fermanagh and a half parish in both Meath and Sligo. Kilmore, like most other dioceses in Ireland, emerged out of the great European-inspired Church reform that took place in Ireland in the twelfth-century.

The leaders of the reform in Europe were Pope Gregory VII (1073–85) and the Cistercian abbot, Bernard of Clairvaux (1090–1153), while the leading reformers in Ireland were Archbishop Malachy of Armagh (1094/5–1148)[1] and Bishop Gillebertus of Limerick (*c.*1070–1145).[2] The synods of Ráith Breasail (1111) and of Kells/Mellifont (1152) were part of that reform and these synods set about dividing the island into dioceses and archdioceses with the result that during the course of the twelfth-century most of the dioceses of Ireland were established and, with a few exceptions, have remained largely unchanged since then. The origins of the diocese of Kilmore are less clear than those of other dioceses, principally because it was, at first, considerably larger than it is today and then over time its boundaries and the location of its See changed. It did not help matters that the diocese would be known by

---

1. His personal name Máel-M'aedóc suggests a family devotion to St Maodhóg. For information on Malachy see Donnchadh Ó Corráin, *The Irish Church, its reform and the English invasion* (Dublin, 2017), pp 76–90; Marie Therese Flanagan, 'Malachy, St Bernard of Clairvaux, and the Cistercian order' in *Arch. Hib.* lxviii (2015), pp 294–311; Pádraig Ó Riain, *A dictionary of Irish saints* (Dublin, 2011), pp 442–4; Ailbhe Mac Shamhráin, 'Malachy (Máel-M'áedóc Ua Morgair) in *DIB*, vi, pp 308–11.
2. For information on Gillebertus see John Fleming, *Gille of Limerick (c.1070–1145): Architect of a medieval church* (Dublin, 2001); Marie Therese Flanagan, *The transformation of the Irish church in the twelfth century* (Suffolk, 2013); Ó Corráin, *The Irish Church, its reform and the English invasion*, pp 70–1; Aidan Breen, 'Gilbert' in *DIB*, 4, pp 75–6.

a variety of different names such as 'Bréifne', 'Kells', 'Tír Briúin'[3] and finally 'Kilmore'. It was not until the middle of the fifteenth-century, when Bishop Andrew MacBrady had established his cathedral in the parish of Kilmore, that the diocese would be named 'Kilmore', a name it retains to this day.

The synod of Ráith Breasail in 1111, which was attended by approximately sixty bishops and more than three hundred priests, was presided over by Gillebertus who was both papal legate and bishop of Limerick.[4] This synod proposed that the island be divided into the two ecclesiastical provinces of Armagh and Cashel with twelve dioceses in each of these provinces. There was, however, no mention of a diocese corresponding to the kingdom of Bréifne at the Ráith Breasail synod even though it is likely that at least one of the many bishops present was from there. Despite this omission it is clear that not long after the synod of Ráith Breasail the territory of Bréifne was regarded as a bishopric since it was recorded that in 1136 Aedh Ua Finn, 'airdespuc na Brefne' died on the island of Iniscothron on Lough Ree.[5] The Annals of the Four Masters describe him both as bishop and *airdfer leighinn* or high man of learning in Bréifne.[6] Eoghan Ó Mórdha has suggested that the learned Aed Ua Finn, bishop of Bréifne, may be the one responsible for re-writing the early genealogy of the Ó Ruairc family linking it to the Ua Briúin of Connacht in an attempt to support the Ó Ruairc claims to the kingship of Connacht in the late eleventh and early twelfth centuries.[7]

If Aed Ua Finn was indeed the one responsible for re-writing the Ó Ruairc genealogies then the emergence both of the Ó Ruairc dynasty and the diocese of Bréifne are more closely intertwined than hitherto believed. Aedh Ua Finn's successor as 'bishop of Uí Briúin Bréifne'[8] was Muirchertach Ua Mael Mocheirge, a member of the Ó Maolmochéirghe

3.   The name Tír Briúin - in Latin *Triburnen* or some variation of that spelling - takes its name from the Uí Briúin sept from which both the O'Rourke's and O'Reilly's were said to be descended. More recent research suggests that this linking of Bréifne with the Uí Briúin may be a late eleventh or early twelfth-century fabrication. However, the jury is still out on that issue. See Paul MacCotter, 'The early history and sub-divisions of the kingdom of Bréifne' in Jonathan Cherry and Brendan Scott (eds), *Cavan history and society* (Dublin, 2014), pp 35–42; Eoghan Ó Mórdha, 'The Uí Briúin Bréifni genealogies and the origins of Bréifne' in *Peritia, Journal of the Medieval Academy of Ireland*, 16 (2002), pp 444–50.
4.   *AU*, 1111; *ALC* 1111. See also David Comyn & Patrick S. Dineen (eds) of Geoffrey Keating's, *Foras feasa ar Éirinn*, 4 vols (London, 1902–14), iii, 298–307; John Mac Erlean, 'Synod of Ráith Breasail' in *Arch. Hib.*, iii (1914), pp 1–33; Benignus Millett, O.F.M., 'Dioceses in Ireland up to the 15th century' in *Seanchas Ard Mhacha*, xii, 1 (1986), pp 1–42.
5.   *AT*, 1136.
6.   *AFM*, 1136, 1137.
7.   Ó Mórdha, 'The Uí Briúin Bréifni genealogies and the origins of Bréifne', pp 444–50.
8.   *AFM*, 1149; *AT*, 1149.

family, the coarbal[9] family in Drumreilly for much of the medieval period.[10] It is possible that in pre-medieval times several other members of this family were bishops since The Martyrology of Donegal and the Martyrology of Tallaght both mention 'seven bishops of Druim-airbhealaigh' and these bishops may be the reason why *Baile na gCléireach* (the place or townland of the clergy), which was in the medieval parish of Drumreilly, is so called.[11] Muirchertach Ó Maolmochéirghe died in 1149. The entries in the annals of the twelfth-century relating to Aed Ua Finn and Muirchertach Ó Maolmochéirghe, both bishops of Bréifne, suggest that the diocese was in existence for at least two decades before it was officially recognised and re-named 'Kells' at the synod of Kells in 1152.

Tighearnán Mór Ó Ruairc

The gradual evolution of diocesan boundaries in Ireland coincided with the reign of Tighearnán Mór Ó Ruairc who was king of Bréifne from 1122 to 1172. He was described as 'a man of great power for a long time'.[12] His chequered career came to an abrupt end in 1172 when he was defeated in battle by Hugh de Lacy and some of his own kinsmen. Following his capture he was beheaded and his body was brought to Dublin and ignominiously hanged upside down on the north side of the city.[13] Tighearnán Ó Ruairc had been a wily ruler and, even though his fortunes ebbed and flowed throughout his life, he succeeded in expanding the kingdom of Bréifne to include part of Sligo, Fermanagh, Westmeath and a considerable portion of Meath, including Kells where the synod was held in 1152. Because of his successes on the battlefield,

9. The coarb or *comharba* in Irish was either a cleric or layperson nominated by the bishop who was regarded as the heir or successor to the founder of an abbey. This ecclesiastical office, which was usually kept within a particular family, entitled the individual to the tenancy of the termon lands attached to the church and carried the responsibility of providing hospitality. Having a coarb attached to a particular church was usually an indication that the church was, or at least had been, a high status church.

10. William Hennessy (ed.), *Chronicum Scotorum, a chronicle of Irish affairs from the earliest times to A.D. 1135* (London, 1866), p. 347. For information on the Ó Maolmochéirghe family see Joseph E. Earley and Leonard Boyle, 'Conflict over the rectory of Cinel Luachain during the 15th century' in *Bréifne*, ix, 35 (1999), pp 103–11; MacCotter, 'The early history and sub-divisions of the kingdom of Bréifne', pp 51–2; idem, 'The comharba family of Ó Maolmochéirghe' in Brendan Scott & Liam Kelly (eds), *Leitrim history and society* (forthcoming).

11. J.H. Todd & W. Reeves (eds), John O'Donovan (trans.), *The Martyrology of Donegal* (Dublin, 1864), p. 17; O'Connell, *The diocese of Kilmore*, p. 115. This reference to the 'seven bishops' is formulaic and is to be found in several sources. It points towards Drumreilly being an episcopal seat, perhaps in the ninth or tenth century. My thanks to Paul MacCotter for this observation.

12. *ALC*, 1172.

13. *AFM*, 1172. For information on Tighearnán Ó Ruairc see Domhnall Mac an Gallóglaigh, 'Bréifne and its chieftains 940–1300' in *Bréifne*, 26, vii (1988), pp 531–45. According to *The Book of Fenagh* he was drawn 'at horses' tails after his death.' See W.M. Hennessy & D.H. Kelly (eds), *The Book of Fenagh* (Dublin, 1875), p. 67.

the early diocese, which was coterminous with the kingdom of Bréifne, was considerably larger than the present-day diocese of Kilmore. Aubrey Gwynn suggests that the deanery of Kells in Meath and that of Fore in Westmeath were, at first, part of the diocese of Bréifne. He believed that the churches of Westmeath (most likely in what was later the deanery of Fore) were returned to Clonmacnois in 1174, with Kells becoming a rural deanery of Meath in 1216.[14] However, the pushing back of the boundaries of the diocese may have been more gradual and somewhat later than he suggests. The Annals of the Four Masters refer to this diocese which stretched from 'Kells to Drumcliff' in its entries for 1258, 1296 and even as late as 1355. Besides, in the ecclesiastical taxation lists of 1302–6 'the Abbot de Kenles' [Kells] and 'the Prior Favorie' [Fore] are listed under the 'diocese of Tirbrunensis'.[15] What is clear is that as the power of the Anglo-Normans in Meath and the O'Connors in Sligo increased, the boundaries of the kingdom and diocese of Bréifne contracted, reducing the diocese in size to what is today.[16]

The Diocese of Kells

The synod of Kells/Mellifont in 1152 continued the process of establishing the dioceses of Ireland which was begun at Ráith Breasail.[17] The synod meeting in Kells took place in the extended kingdom of Bréifne and it listed 'Kells' as a new diocese. Tuathal Ó Connachtaigh, bishop of Tír Briúin, was present at the synod[18] and possibly was the bishop of Ceanannus/Kells which was listed as a diocese by Cardinal John Paparo, the pope's special legate at the synod.[19] Aubrey Gwynn suggested that 'Darnth', one of the others Sees listed by Paparo, referred to Dairinis, an island on Lough Uachtair, and that this was the See of the diocese of Bréifne at this time.[20] It seems unlikely that a diocesan See would be located on an island and more recent research confirms that

14.   Aubrey Gwynn, *The Irish Church in the eleventh and twelfth centuries*, ed. by Gerard O'Brien (Dublin, 1992), pp 251, 256.
15.   H.S. Sweetman & G.F. Handcock (eds), *Calendar of documents relating to Ireland 1302–1307* (London, 1886), p. 213.
16.   The existence of the Kilmore half parishes of Kilmainhamwood in Meath and Ballintrillick in Sligo are relics of the larger diocese that existed in early medieval times.
17.   Ó Corráin, *The Irish Church, its reform and the English invasion*, pp 91–6.
18.   Comyn & Dineen (eds), *Foras feasa ar Éirinn*, iii, p. 316.
19.   G. MacNiocaill (ed.), *Notititae as Leabhar Cheanannais* (Cló Morainn, 1961), p. 14.
20.   This view was also accepted by John Watt. See John Watt, *The Church in medieval Ireland* (Dublin, 1972), pp 24–5. See Aubrey Gwynn, 'The origins of the diocese of Kilmore' in *Bréifne*, i, 4 (1961), pp 293–307; idem, *The Irish Church in the eleventh and twelfth centuries*, pp 253–6; idem, *The twelfth century reform* (Dublin, 1968), p. 56.

Figure 1.1: Twelfth-century Romanesque doorway at Kilmore cathedral.

the diocese of Kells listed at the synod in 1152 was coterminous with the extended kingdom of Bréifne.[21]

Tuathal Ua Connachtaigh, the bishop of Uí Briúin, died in 1179.[22] After his death there is no further reference to a bishop of Bréifne until 1231 when his kinsman Flann Ua Connachtaig, *espuc na Bréifne*, dies.[23] From 1179 until 1211 the bishops of the diocese are referred to as bishops of Kells. It is clear that this arrangement, which had the diocese of Bréifne stretching into Meath and incorporating the town of Kells, did not sit easily and was not going to last because *c*.1185, Bishop Eugenius Echtigern of Meath tried to expel a Cistercian monk of good repute who had recently been elected bishop of Kells by the clergy and people, even though the appointment had been ratified by the pope, hoping that he could annex the diocese of Kells to his own diocese of Meath. His efforts failed.[24] Following the death in 1211 of M. Ua Doibhailen, the bishop of Kells, there is no more mention of the diocese of Kells .[25] The power of the Ó Ruairc's had waned considerably by this time and the Anglo-Normans were firmly established in Meath. In 1216, five years after the death of the last bishop of Kells, a special diocesan synod held in Trim, designates Kells as a rural deanery of the diocese of Meath.[26]

Kells, despite being an important ecclesiastical centre, was not a suitable location for the See of Bréifne since it was situated at the south-eastern end of an elongated diocese which stretched northwest as far as the Atlantic Ocean. There is some evidence to suggest that soon after Kells was named a diocese in 1152 there were efforts to establish a diocesan See more centrally in the kingdom of Bréifne. The building of the twelfth-century Romanesque doorway, now used as an entrance to the sacristy in the Church of Ireland cathedral at Kilmore, coincided with the creation of an elaborate bishop's crosier, both of which have been dated to *c*.1170. The creation of these elaborate ecclesiastical works of art at this time suggests both a wealthy patron and a concerted effort to

21. Katharine Simms, 'The origins of the diocese of Clogher' in *Clogher Record*, x, 2 (1980), pp 193–4; Flanagan, *The transformation of the Irish Church in the twelfth century*, p. 165, n. 247. Charles Doherty, wrote that 'by the mid-twelfth century Kells in Co. Meath became Ua Ruairc's capital' and he traces the rise of the cult of St Maodhóg to the increase in the power of the Ó Ruaircs from the mid eleventh-century onwards. See Charles Doherty, 'The transmission of the cult of St Máedhóg' in Próinséas Ní Chatháin and Michael Richter (eds), *Ireland and Europe in the early middle ages* (Dublin, 2002), p. 274.
22. Francis J. MacKiernan, *Diocese of Kilmore, bishops and priests 1136–1988* (Cavan, 1989), p. 11.
23. *AU*, 1231; *AC*, 1231.
24. Gwynn, *The Irish church in the eleventh and twelfth centuries*, p. 256; John T. Gilbert (ed.), *Chartularies of St Mary's abbey, Dublin*, ii (Dublin, 1884), p. 22.
25. *ALC*, 1211.
26. Gwynn, *The Irish church in the eleventh and twelfth centuries*, pp 250–6.

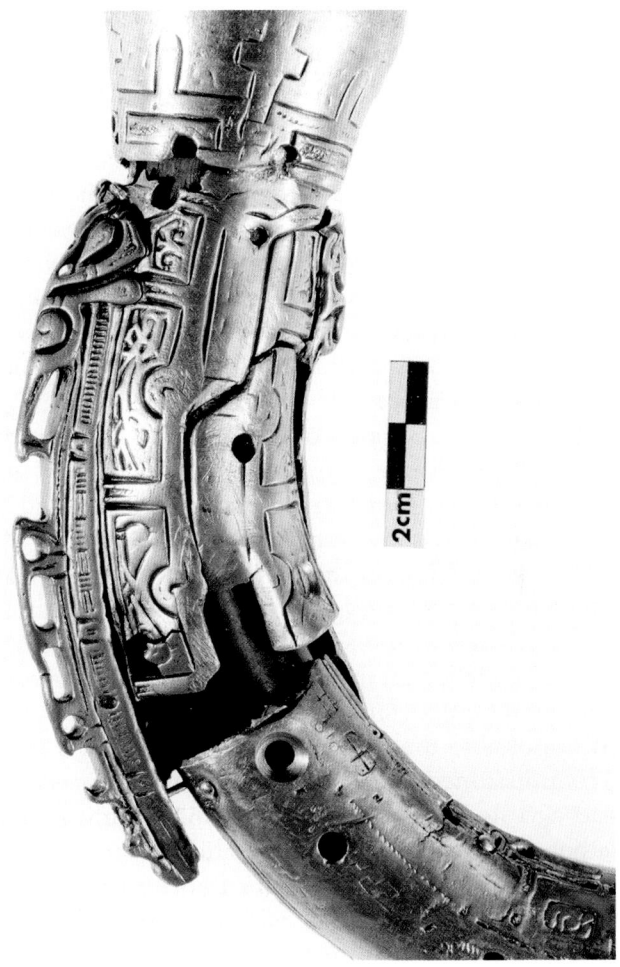

Figure 1.2: The twelfth-century Bréifne crosier. (*Courtesy of the National Museum of Ireland*).

establish a diocesan See in the Lough Uachtair/Kilmore area of Bréifne in the decades immediately after the synod of Kells/Mellifont.

Romanesque Doorway and Bishop's Crosier

The highly ornate Romanesque architecture which was introduced into Ireland from continental Europe in the twelfth-century was not just a result of the Church reform of that century but was also an integral part of that reform. The Kilmore doorway which has been described a s'one of only a few relics of Romanesque architecture to survive in Ulster and one of the finer examples of a twelfth-century doorway on the island of Ireland'[27] has been compared with the Romanesque portal of the Nun's church in Clonmacnois[28] which was completed in 1167 and was financed, at least in part, by Derbforgaill, wife of Tighearnán Ó Ruairc.[29] The Kilmore Romanesque portal which was commissioned at this time is one of the most outstanding pieces of ecclesiastical art in the diocese and is the best evidence of an attempt to establish a diocesan cathedral in the parish of Kilmore at this time. The bishop's crosier, another elaborate piece of artwork which was commissioned in Bréifne at this time, has become known as the 'crosier of the O'Bradys' and is now on display in the National Museum of Ireland. This crosier was created as a staff of ecclesiastical office, most likely for the bishops of Bréifne, and it was probably used by successive bishops of the diocese. Possibly sometime after the death of Bishop Andrew MacBrady, who died in 1455, the MacBrady sept became hereditary keepers of the crosier and it came to have relic status being associated with St Brighid[30] whose cult was strong in the MacBrady territory of Cúil Brighdín. More significantly for our understanding of the diocese in the twelfth-century it has been linked to the same period and the same location as the Romanesque doorway at Kilmore and some of the decoration on the crosier is said to have been modelled on the lozenge- shaped artwork that decorates the inner arch of that portal.[31]

It is possible that Tighearnán Ó Ruairc was the wealthy patron who commissioned these two elaborate works of ecclesiastical art since he had a vested interest in helping the fledgling diocese of Bréifne/ Kells get established. However, in his early life, Ó Ruairc was more likely to be found attacking clerics and church property than being their protector and patron. His father, Aedh Ua Ruairc, and the Uí Briúin had attacked the monastery of Kells in 1117, killing the superior, Mael-Brighte Mac Ronain, and several others in the community.[32]

27.   Rachel Moss, 'The old portal and cathedral of Kilmore' in *Bréifne*, xii, 46 (2011), p. 203; H.G. Leask, *Irish churches and monastic buildings* (Dundalk, 1955), i, p. 146. For the Romanesque stone fragments of Devenish see Claire Foley & Ronan McHugh, *An archaeological survey of County Fermanagh* (Belfast, 2014), i, part 2, pp 720–1.
28.   Liam de Paor states that the Kilmore doorway and the Nun's church doorway at Clonmacnois are so close in style that the same craftsman must have worked on both of them. See Gwynn, *The Irish church in the eleventh and twelfth centuries*, p. 358, n. 74.
29.   *AFM*, 1167.
30.   There are number of different ways to spell this saint's name. I favour the one used by Pádraig Ó Riain in *A dictionary of Irish saints*, pp 123–5.
31.   For a detailed description of the crosier see Griffin Murray, 'The crosier of the O'Bradys' in *Bréifne*, xii, 47 (2012), pp 420–40. For the significance of the lozenge and its association with Christ see Hilary Richardson, 'Biblical imagery and the heavenly Jerusalem' in Ní Chatháin & Richter (eds), *Ireland and Europe in the early middle ages*, pp 208–9.
32.   *AU*, 1117.

Tighearnán seemed intent on emulating his father and it was reported that in the year 1128:

> An ugly, ruthless, unprecedented deed, which earned the malediction of the men of Eirinn, both lay and clerical – for which no equal was found previously in Eirinn – was committed by Tighernan Ua Ruairc … The comarb of Patrick[33] was openly profaned in his own presence, and his retinue were plundered, and a number of them slain … this contempt was like the contempt of the Lord.[34]

Tighearnán Ó Ruairc may have been trying to make amends for his father's attack on the monastery of Kells or for his own disrespect to the archbishop of Armagh and his retinue and the relics they carried, when he gave lands in the vicinity of Kells 'to God and to Colum Cille as a perpetual grant for ever for the service of Int Ednén'.[35] This church of Int Ednén was consecrated by Máel Ciaráin, the priest of Kells, sometime between 1122 and 1148.[36] This dating would suggest that it may have been an act of reparation by O'Rourke soon after his attack on the archbishop of Armagh.

Derbforgaill: Saint or Sinner?

Tighearnán Ó Ruairc must have been on good terms with the bishops and other clergy of Ireland by 1152 as in that year he hosted the synod of Kells and five years later was again present at Mellifont when the archbishop of Armagh consecrated the church of the Cistercian monastery.[37] Derbforgaill, the wife of Tighearnán Ó Ruairc and daughter of Murchad Ua Máel Sechlainn the king of Meath, was also present at the consecration in Mellifont. She had donated sixty ounces of gold, a gold chalice for the altar of Mary and nine altar cloths for the other altars in the newly

---

33. This is a reference to Cellach, the archbishop of Armagh, who died in 1129.
34. *ALC*, 1128; *AU*, 1128.
35. This information about Ó Ruairc granting the lands to the church of Int Ednén is contained in one of the *notitiae* written into the *Book of Kells* in the twelfth-century. The original pages of the book which contained these *notitiae* have been lost though two later copies exist. One of these is in the British Library (Add. MS 4971) and the other is in the Royal Irish Academy (MS 934). Denis Casey has identified Int Ednén as Inan in south-west County Meath. See Denis Casey, 'Tigernán Ua Ruairc and the Book of Kells' in Katharine Simms (ed.), *Gaelic Ireland (c.600-c.1700): politics, culture and landscapes* (Dublin, 2013), pp 3–10. See also Donnchadh Ó Corráin, *The Irish Church, its reform and the English invasion*, pp 25–6.
36. Casey, 'Tigernán Ua Ruairc and the Book of Kells', pp 4–5.
37. *AU*, 1157. The abbey had been founded in 1142. It was the first Cistercian foundation in Ireland. This consecration was a seminal event in the twelfth-century church reform in Ireland. See Bridget M. Lynch, 'A monastic landscape: The Cistercians in Medieval Leinster', PhD thesis (NUIM, 2008), pp 23–5; Bernadette Williams (ed.), *The 'Annals of Multyfarnham': Roscommon and Connacht provenance* (Dublin, 2012), p. 132.

established abbey. Derbforgaill has been treated unfairly by history. She is best remembered as the woman who either willingly eloped with Diarmait Mac Murchada, the king of Leinster, or else was kidnapped by him.[38] She was an ardent supporter of Church reform and her kinswoman Agnes, who died in 1196, was recognised as a great abbess in the newly established convent of Arroasian nuns at Clonard.[39] Derbforgaill was a wealthy woman who supported church building and the establishing of new religious orders – both of which were key components of the twelfth-century Church reform. She retired to the abbey of Mellifont[40] in 1186 and died there in 1193 'in the eighty fifth year of her age'.[41] Derbforgaill had been a generous patron of the Church and it is possible that it was she, and not her husband, who commissioned not only the Nun's church portal at Clonmacnois, but also the similarly styled Kilmore Romanesque doorway.[42]

The Kilmore Doorway

Many of the dioceses of Ireland which were established in the twelfth-century were named after the early Christian foundations where the diocesan cathedral was located. When the diocese of Kells was established in 1152 it was hoped that the bishop would reside in Kells which had an early Christian foundation. For reasons stated above Kells did not continue for long as the name of the diocese or the location of the See. It appears that *c.*1170, especially with the commissioning of the Romanesque doorway, a new centre for the diocese of Bréifne, somewhere in the parish

---

38.   Paul Walsh, 'The Ua Maelechlainn kings of Meath' in Nollaig Ó Muráile (ed.), *Irish leaders and learning through the ages* (Dublin, 2003), p. 98; Denis Murphy (ed.), *The Annals of Clonmacnoise* (Dublin, 1896), pp 199–200; In 1693 Tadhg Ó Rodaighe blamed Derbforgaill, along with Diarmaid Na nGall, for being the 'cause from which came the destruction of Ireland' and she is referred to as 'Tighernan's wife of many crimes.' See Hennessy and Kelly (eds), *The Book of Fenagh*, p. 64, n. 1 and p. 65. For a more positive view of Derbforgaill see E.M. Greenwood, 'The Ulster cycle and the place of Armagh in the tradition' in A.J. Hughes & William Nolan (eds), *Armagh history and society* (Dublin, 2001), pp 106–7.
39.   *ALC*, 1196.
40.   Mary Ann Lyons writes that 'Many female benefactors, usually widows, retired to religious houses that they had endowed and lived there for several years before their deaths.' See Mary Ann Lyons, 'Lay female piety and church patronage in late medieval Ireland' in Brendan Bradshaw & Dáire Keogh (eds), *Christianity in Ireland: revisiting the story* (Blackrock, 2002), p. 62.
41.   *AFM*, 1193.
42.   For Derbforgaill see Jenifer Ní Ghrádaigh, 'But what exactly did she give?: Derforgaill and the nun's church at Clonmacnois' in Heather A. King (ed.), *Clonmacnoise studies* (Dublin, 1998), ii, pp 175–207; Dianne Hall, *Women and the church in medieval Ireland, c.1140–1540* (Dublin, 2003), pp 43, 72 & 79; Elizabeth McKenna, 'The gift of a lady: women as patrons of the arts in medieval Ireland' in Christine Meek (ed.), *Women in Renaissance and early modern Europe* (Dublin, 2000), p. 90; Flanagan, *The transformation of the Irish church in the twelfth century*, p. 201; Anthony Candon, 'Power, politics and polygamy: women and marriage in late pre-Norman Ireland' in Damian Bracken & Dag Ó Riain-Raedel (eds), *Ireland and Europe in the Twelfth century, reform and renewal* (Dublin, 2006), p. 126; Helen Perros-Walton, 'Church reform in Connacht' in Seán Duffy (ed.), *Princes, prelates and poets in medieval Ireland* (Dublin, 2013), p. 283.

of Kilmore, was being planned, although it is not clear where exactly the magnificent doorway was first placed. Samuel Lewis, who may have got his information from George de la Poer Beresford, the then Church of Ireland bishop of Kilmore, wrote that the doorway had been removed from Trinity Island, a view that has been repeated many times since then.[43] It is possible, that the doorway was removed from the Premonstratensian priory on Trinity Island, however, this view poses several difficulties. The doorway has been dated to *c.*1170 and work on the Trinity Island priory did not begin until 1237. Besides, it appears that the priory was not habitable until 1250 when the first of the white canons of the Premonstratensian Order moved into it.[44] This fact raises further questions: if the Romanesque doorway was incorporated into Holy Trinity priory on Lough Uachtair, where was it before work began on building Holy Trinity priory in 1237 and why would the elaborate doorway, which possibly was commissioned for a cathedral for the diocese of Bréifne, be given to the Premonstratensian Order less than eighty years after the doorway was created?

Recent scholarship suggests that the Kilmore doorway was never part of Holy Trinity priory but was incorporated from the beginning into the church of St Feidhlimidh at Kilmore.[45] This is a more likely viewpoint if for no other reason than it involves fewer moves for the doorway and it remaining in a small area of the townland of Kilmore Upper from the twelfth-century until the present day. Jim Higgins, who carried out an archaeological survey of Trinity Island *c.*1980, concluded that 'there is nothing to show where the Romanesque doorway which is now at Kilmore might have come from at this [Holy Trinity] site. It certainly did not belong to the present west gable'.[46] This ornate doorway is the best surviving ecclesiastical stonework in the diocese and while Rachel Moss states that it was 'a high status piece of architecture' she goes on to say that it was not unique in Ulster - pointing to carved stones at Tomregan, Drumlane and at Devenish as well as other locations in the Erne basin as evidence for the 'one-time presence of buildings which incorporated Romanesque sculpture'.[47] Apart from the high status portal there are no other surviving

---

43.   Samuel Lewis, *Topographical dictionary of Ireland* (London, 1837), ii, p. 185. For another negative view of Derbforgaill see Richard Stanihurst's, *De Rebus in Hibernia Gestis*, in John Barry & Hiram Morgan (eds), *Great deeds in Ireland* (Cork, 2013), p. 147.
44.   *ALC*, 1237, 1250.
45.   For this viewpoint see Moss, 'The old portal and cathedral of Kilmore', p. 221; Murray, 'The crosier of the O'Bradys', p. 438.
46.   Unpublished report by Jim Higgins, titled *Trinity Island church and graveyard, Lough Uachtair, Co. Cavan. A preliminary archaeological description and assessment.*
47.   Moss, 'The old portal and Cathedral of Kilmore', p. 212.

Romanesque stone fragments at Kilmore and all the indications are that the medieval church of St Feidhlimidh was otherwise a relatively small and plain structure which did not achieve the status of a cathedral until 1455.[48] Even at the time it was elevated to a cathedral it was deemed to be inadequate because in 1461 bishop Thady Mag Dhuibhne 'began to build [it] anew' at his own expense and then persuaded Rome to grant indulgences to all penitents who would give alms 'for the completion and conservation' of the newly established cathedral of Kilmore.[49]

The Romanesque portal of Kilmore has remained an enigma for archaeologists and historians for many years. It may have been that it was intended as a doorway for a new cathedral of the diocese, the plans for which came to an abrupt end. Tighearnán and Derbforgaill O'Rourke were wealthy and generous patrons of the Church and supporters of the twelfth-century Church reform and one or both of them may have commissioned the bishop's crosier and the Romanesque doorway *c*.1170. The catastrophic defeat of Tighearnán Ó Ruairc in 1172 was followed by chaos in Bréifne as various factions of the Ó Ruairc's vied for power and Hugh de Lacy, who was already established in Meath, made inroads in the kingdom.[50] It may well be that Ó Ruairc's death abruptly halted the building of a cathedral at Kilmore and that the ensuing chaos and the eventual division of the lordship into east and west Bréifne deprived the diocese of the unity, stability and patronage necessary to complete such a task.

---

48. In 1455 Bishop Andrew MacBrady wrote to Rome stating that he 'was without a cathedral church'. See *CPL*, xi, p. 240.
49. *CPL*, xii, p. 131.
50. Mac An Gallóglaigh, 'Bréifne and its chieftains 940–1300', pp 544–5.

Chapter 2

Monasteries: *c*.1140–1534

The marking out of diocesan boundaries and the establishment of a See in each diocese were important elements of the twelfth-century Church reform. Another important aspect of that reform was the introduction from the continent of the new religious Orders into Ireland. St Malachy of Armagh may have already learned about the Augustinian canons of Guisborough before his travels to and from Rome in 1139-40, when he visited the Cistercian abbey in Clairvaux and the abbey of the Augustinian canons in Arrouaise, both of which were leading the way in reviving religious life in Europe at this time. He was so impressed by their discipline, asceticism and spirituality that he became intent on introducing both the Cistercians and Augustinians into Ireland and quite a few communities of both these Orders had been introduced into Ireland by the time of his death in 1148.[1] Despite the fact that Derbforgaill and Tighearnán Ó Ruairc both admired and supported the newly founded Cistercian abbey at Mellifont, no Cistercian abbey was established in Bréifne.[2] The Cistercians were monks while the Augustinians were canons, one of the key differences being that the canons were all ordained priests while some of the monks were not.[3] Sometime after 1140 and before the death of Malachy of Armagh in 1148, St Mary's abbey, a community of Augustinian canons, was established at Kells, which was then part of the kingdom of Bréifne.[4]

---

1.   Marie Thérése Flanagan, 'St Malachy, St Bernard of Clairvaux, and the Cistercian order' in *Arch. Hib.*, lxviii (2015), pp 294–311.
2.   Each Cistercian monastery was expected to have a community of one abbot and at least twelve monks. The Augustinians on the other hand could have considerably smaller communities which suited less-wealthy patrons outside the Anglo-Norman controlled areas.
3.   Flanagan, *The transformation of the Irish Church in the twelfth century*, pp 137–8.
4.   Aubrey Gwynn & R. Neville Hadcock, *Medieval Religious houses in Ireland* (Dublin, 1970), p. 181. Derbforgaill may have had a role in establishing St Mary's abbey in Kells as it had close connections with the Arroasian abbey of nuns in Clonard where her kinswoman Agnes was abbess.

St Mary's Abbey, Kells

The location of Kells in the borderland marches between Gaelic Ireland and Anglo-Norman Pale meant that the abbey there was always vulnerable to attack. It was plundered by Dermot MacMurrough in 1171 and even though it was endowed by Hugh de Lacy in 1173[5] the instability of the region resulted in it being attacked by the Anglo-Normans three years later.[6] The Augustinians had the support of the native Irish from the beginning[7] and even though different generations of the de Lacy family were patrons of St Mary's abbey the Augustinian canons there were, for the most part, native Irish and the abbey 'was almost always ruled by a Gaelic abbot from Bréifne'.[8] Braen Ó Maolmochéirghe, the abbot of Kells who died in 1277, was probably one of the Ó Maolmochéirghe clerical family from the parish of Drumreilly.[9] Mauricius, who became abbot shortly after Braen Ó Maolmochéirghe's death, was appointed bishop of Tír Briúin in 1286, a position he held until his death in 1307.[10] Cormac and Renaldus, both members of the Magauran family from Tullyhaw, were abbots of Kells in the early 1400s.[11] However, it was the Ó Raghallaigh sept, by now the dominant family in east Bréifne, which supplied the greatest number of abbots to the monastery in Kells throughout the fifteenth-century. In some instances they controlled the abbey by handing on the position of abbot from father to son. In 1418 John Ó Raghallaigh, having been ordained a priest, made his profession in the Augustinian order and then two years later was appointed abbot of St Mary's in Kells.[12] John was replaced by his son and namesake in 1445 and twenty years later, on 17 May 1465, this son was appointed bishop of Kilmore.[13]

5.   In 1173 Hugh de Lacy, having endowed St Mary's abbey, stipulated 'that one of the canons of the abbey should be constantly retained as a chaplain to say Mass for the health of his soul and the souls of his ancestors and successors.' See Mervyn Archdall, *Monasticon Hibernicum* (Dublin, 1786), p. 544.

6.   *AFM*, 1171; *AU*, 1176.

7.   Tadhg O'Keefe, 'Augustinian Regular Canons in twelfth and thirteenth-century Ireland: history, architecture and identity' in Janet Burton & Karen Stober (eds), *The Regular Canons in the medieval British Isles* (Belgium, 2011), p. 476.

8.   D.B. Quinn & K.W. Nicholls, 'Ireland in 1534' in T.W. Moody, F.X. Martin & F.J. Byrne (eds), *A new history of Ireland*, iii (Oxford, 1976), p. 5.

9.   *ALC*, 1277. The links between this coarb family from Drumreilly and the Augustinian order were intermittent. Another member of the family, Hugh Ó Maolmochéirghe, an Augustinian prior of Drumlane, was drowned in 1512. See *AFM*, 1512.

10.   MacKiernan, *Diocese of Kilmore*, p. 11; H.S. Sweetman (ed.), *Calendar of documents relating to Ireland 1285–1292* (London, 1879), pp 128, 134; James Ware, *The antiquities and history of* Ireland (London, 1705), p. 59.

11.   *CPl*, viii, p. 157.

12.   *CPl*, vii, pp 62, 192.

13.   MacKiernan, *Diocese of Kilmore*, p. 13; *CPl, Lateran Regesta*, dcxvii, pp 430–1; He was usually referred to as John O'Raghallaigh II to distinguish him from an earlier bishop of the same name.

Philip Ó Raghallaigh, a son of Bishop John Ó Raghallaigh, was abbot of St Mary's in 1494 and retained that position, despite an attempt by Carbry MacBradaigh, a Kilmore diocesan priest, to unseat him in that year.[14] Philip Ó Raghallaigh died of the plague in 1504.[15] Diarmaid Ó Raghallaigh was the abbot of Kells when he was appointed bishop of Kilmore on 28 January 1512.[16] It is possible that he retained his position as abbot of Kells after being appointed bishop as someone of the same name was abbot in 1523.[17]

The Ó Raghallaigh clerical family held the abbey of Kells for much of the fifteenth-century and helped maintain strong links between the abbey and the diocese of Kilmore. The regular communication and travel between the Augustinian priory of Drumlane and its mother-house in Kells, further strengthened those links. There were also important economic ties between the abbey and the diocese as the parishes of Killann, Knockbride, Castlerahan, Lurgan, Munterconnacht, Templeport and the large rectory of Dartry in west Bréifne paid a portion of their tithes, known as rectorial tithes, to the abbey in Kells. This arrangement caused resentment within these parishes and despite several attempts to end it St Mary's abbey in Kells continued to receive revenues from the diocese of Kilmore until its dissolution in November 1539.[18]

St Mary's Priory, Drumlane[19]

St Mary's Augustinian priory at Drumlane, which was a daughter house of St Mary's abbey in Kells, was also established in the period 1140 to 1148, with Kells being founded nearer the earlier date and Drumlane closer to the later one. There had been an earlier monastery at Drumlane which was already in existence some time before the end of the sixth-century when it was restored by St Maodhóg.[20] By choosing old monastic sites for their twelfth-century foundations the Augustinians felt that they were renewing the church both materially and spiritually.[21] The priory at Drumlane was dedicated to St Mary, just like its mother house, even though the cult of St Maodhóg was promoted by the Augustinians of Drumlane from the

14. *CPI*, xv, p. 444.
15. Archdall, *Monasticon Hibernicum*, p. 546.
16. MacKiernan, *Diocese of Kilmore*, p. 13.
17. Archdall, *Monasticon Hibernicum*, p. 546.
18. 'Inquisition taken at Cavan' (1609) in *Calendar of Irish patent rolls of James I* (Dublin, 1966), p. 386.
19. Drumlane priory was situated near the town of Belturbet in County Cavan.
20. *Calendar of Irish patent rolls of James I*, p. 386. For an aerial view of Drumlane priory and cloictheach round tower see Fig. 5.2.
21. Flanagan, *The transformation of the Irish church in the twelfth century*, p. 120.

beginning.[22] The writing of the earliest Latin Life of St Maodhóg in the second half of the twelfth-century shows all the hallmarks of an Augustinian hand at work. It promoted not just the cult of Maodhóg but also the new Augustinian foundation at Drumlane and their houses elsewhere in Ireland.[23] The high-status reliquary known as the *Breac Maodhóg* was created in the late eleventh or early twelfth-century, and even though Rossinver[24] claimed it was rightfully theirs, it was held by either the Augustinian canons or coarbs at Drumlane. Later the reliquary was kept in a fifteenth-century satchel and these items became objects of veneration which helped to pro-mote the cult of St Maodhóg and re-establish Drumlane as an important ecclesiastical foundation in the medieval diocese of Kilmore.[25]

The Ó Farrellys were the hereditary erenaghs[26] of Drumlane even before the Augustinians settled there. In 1025 Dubhinnsi Ó Faircheallaigh (Farrelly) 'herenagh of Druim-lethan ... fell asleep in Christ'.[27] Thirty-four years later, Conaing Ó Farrelly, the erenagh of Drumlane and coarb of the churches of St Maodhóg in Connacht and Leinster, died.[28] Following the arrival of the Augustinians to Drumlane the Ó Farrellys held the more prestigious title of coarb of St Maodhóg and numerous members of the family became Augustinian canons and priors in Drumlane. Muiredhach Ó Farrelly, the 'coarb of St Maog ... abbot of Drumlane and archdeacon of Brefney' died in 1368.[29] He was described as 'a man full of the gifts of the Holy Ghost'.[30] His successor as prior of Drumlane and archdeacon of Kilmore, William Ó Farrelly, died just one year later.[31] In 1401, David

22.   The patron saint of the medieval parish church of Drumlane was St Maodhóg. See *CPL*, viii, p. 589.

23.   Ó Riain, *A dictionary of Irish saints*, p. 433; Raymond Gillespie, 'A sixteenth-century saint's life: the second Irish life of St Maedoc' in *Bréifne*, x, 40 (2004), pp 147–54; Griffin Murray, 'A note on the provenance of the Breac Maodhóg' in *JRSAI*, 135 (2005), pp 136–7; Charles Doherty, 'The transmission of the cult of St Máedhóg', pp 268–83.

24.   There was a church at Rossinver from early Christian times and a cross-inscribed grave slab in the adjacent graveyard is thought to have been created 'in the first quarter of the 9th century'. See P.J. Hartnett, 'Rossinver church and graveyard, Co. Leitrim' in *JRSAI*, 84, 2(1954), pp 180–1.

25.   The *Breac Maodhóg* and the fifteenth-century satchel it was held in are both in the National Museum of Ireland. The fragmentary remains of the *Clog Mogue* are to be found in Armagh Public Library.

26.   The erenagh (*airchinneach* in Irish) was the superior or guardian of a parish church and the termon lands attached to it. The erenagh was usually a layman, though some were in minor orders. One of their functions was to provide hospitality for the traveller, the sick, the pilgrim and the poor. The office usually remained within a particular family and it was similar, though of a lower status, to the office of coarb.

27.   *AU*, 1025.

28.   *AU*, 1059; Ó Corráin, *The Irish Church, its reform and the English invasion*, p. 21.

29.   *AFM*, 1368.

30.   Ibid.

31.   *AFM*, 1369; *AU*, 1369. It appears that William was a brother of Muiredhach. See *AU*, 1369, footnote 12.

Figure 2.1: Detail from the Breac Maodhóg reliquary which was created *c.*1100 and held at Drumlane. (*Courtesy of the National Museum of Ireland*).

Ó Farrelly, a 'clerk of the diocese of Kilmore' and coarb of Drumlane replaced Maurice Ó Farrelly as perpetual vicar of St Maodhóg's (parish) church of Drumlane.[32] Then *c.*1408 he was appointed bishop of Kilmore by Gregory XII, one of the claimants to the papacy during the Great Western Schism.[33] Patrick Ó Farrelly, who was already perpetual vicar of St Brighid's church in Urney, was mandated by the pope to be received as an Augustinian canon in Drumlane in 1431.[34] It was claimed that the priory had been 'unduly detained' by Cormac Magauran from 1431 until 1435 when he was removed and Patrick Ó Farrelly was appointed prior in his place.[35] When Patrick Ó Farrelly died in 1445[36] he was replaced by Thady Magivney, the perpetual vicar of Kilmore and Urney, who would, in 1455, be

32.   *CPL*, v, p. 452. In another papal letter of 1401 (*CPL*, v, p. 450) he was described as a 'deacon of the diocese of Kilmore'.
33.   St John D. Seymour, 'The coarb in the medieval Irish church' in *PRIA*, 41 (1932–4), pp 225–6; MacKiernan, *Diocese of Kilmore*, p. 12.
34.   This parish church may have been situated on the site of an earlier oratory since 'Urney' is a translation of the Irish *An Urnaí* (the oratory). There is another townland of the same name in the parish of Kilmore, near Ballinagh. The earliest Ordnance survey map shows a Caldragh or burial ground in this second Urney townland.
35.   *CPL*, viii, pp 384, 585; Costello, *De Annatis Hiberniae*, i, 234, 235.
36.   Costello, *De Annatis Hiberniae*, i, p. 251.

appointed bishop of Kilmore.[37] John Ó Farrelly 'canon of the community of Druim-lethan'[38] died in the summer of 1484. Brian Mór Ó Farrelly - 'he that began to build the anchorite's cell at the great church of Druim-lethan'[39] - died in that same summer. Donald Ó Farrelly, an Augustinian canon, was not based at Drumlane but in the far-off Augustinian monastery of St Martin in Siena. He was unhappy there and in March 1463/4 he sent a letter to the pope stating that:

> He cannot with a quiet mind remain there [in Siena], and that he desires to migrate to the monastery of St Mary, Drumllican, of the said order in the diocese of Kilmore, of which his ancestors were the founders.[40]

His request was granted. John Macculmartayn and Cormac O'Sheridan, both canons of Kilmore, and an un-named dean[41] of the diocese were mandated to have him received as a canon in St Mary's priory in Drumlane.

The Magauran family of Tullyhaw was also very involved with the Augustinian community at Drumlane. The cult of St Maodhóg, which flourished at the Magauran stronghold in Templeport and in the Augustinian priory of Drumlane, may explain this involvement. This clerical lineage family provided priests for the vicarage of Templeport and canons for priory of Drumlane. Cormac Magauran, the son of Piaras Magauran a prior of Drumlane was himself the prior there before being appointed bishop of Ardagh in 1444 and his son Cormac Magauran was prior of Drumlane for ten years before he was controversially appointed bishop of Kilmore in 1476.[42] In 1503, Fergal Magauran, a priest of the diocese and a son of Cormac Magauran who was still claiming to be the rightful bishop of Kilmore, was appointed to the perpetual vicarage of Templeport. What is clear from the example of the Magauran clerical lineage is that twelfth-century reform had failed to establish a celibate clergy as the norm in Ireland and that this situation was tolerated both in Ireland and in Rome with the papacy granting dispensations to the sons

37.   Ibid., pp 234–6;
38.   *AU*, 1484; *AFM*, 1484.
39.   Ibid. Presumably it was this reference which caused John Richardson (1668/9–1747), who was rector of the parish of Annagh, to make the erroneous claim that the round tower at Drumlane was built as an anchorite's cell. See George Petrie, *The ecclesiastical architecture of Ireland, an essay on the origin and uses of the Round Towers of Ireland* (Dublin, 1845), pp 109–16; Oliver Davies, 'The churches of County Cavan' reprinted in *Bréifne*, xiii, 48 (2013), p. 112.
40.   *CPL*, xii, p. 200.
41.   The dean was the archpriest or vicar forane of a particular deanery. There were three deaneries in the medieval diocese – Kilmore, Drumlane and Dartry.
42.   *CPL*, ix, p. 436, xiii, p. 154.

of priests whenever required. The priory of Drumlane provided leaders within the Augustinian order and for Kilmore and other neighbouring dioceses and throughout the fifteenth-century the priors of Drumlane were held in high esteem and often mandated by Rome to help resolve disputes that arose in several dioceses around.

Drumlane priory was situated strategically along the main route linking east and west Bréifne and the priory was sometimes used for negotiating peace between local warring factions as was the case in 1391 when a peace settlement was concluded there between Ó Ruairc and Ó Raghallaigh.[43] However, because of its location it was also used as a battle ground and the Annals of Loch Cé reported that in 1261 'A great depredation was committed by Aedh O'Conchobhair in the Bréifne, until he reached Druim-lethan, when a portion of his routs were defeated and a great number of them slain'. Over fifty years later, in 1314, Drumlane was the battle-ground when Ruaidhri Ó Conchobhair defeated the Ó Raghallaighs there.[44] No doubt the priory suffered in these wars although when it was burned in 1246 it appears that the fire started accidentally.[45] Drumlane priory also became a high status burial ground. For example in 1407, John the 'son of Tadg Ó Ruairc, heir to the sovereignty of Bréifne' was buried there even though he had died a considerable distance away in Magh Luirg in Roscommon.[46] Ferghal Ó Raghallaigh, who in the early months of 1487 had helped to capture the 'fortress of Loch-uachtar' died on 22 December of that year and he too was buried at Drumlane.[47]

The ruins of the priory and round tower at Drumlane are the most substantial surviving ecclesiastical ruins from the medieval period in the diocese of Kilmore and while most of these ruins are from the later medieval period they do point to a large and relatively wealthy Augustinian foundation there.[48] The 'great church'[49] at Drumlane was considerably larger than the late medieval cathedral church of

---

43.   *AU*, 1391; *ALC*, 1391. Ua Ruairc who went to Drumlane with a retinue of 'one and twenty' was waylaid by the Clan of Muircertach Ua Concobuir at Belach-in crinaigh but Ua Ruairc by 'his good fortune broke through the pass' and inflicted several casualties on the Ua Concobuir party. See *AU*, 1391.
44.   *AU*,1314; *ALC*, 1314.
45.   *ALC*, 1246.
46.   *ALC*, 1406.
47.   *AU*, 1487.
48.   Davies, 'The churches of County Cavan', pp 101–12; Tadhg O'Keefe, *Ireland's Round Towers* (Stroud, 2004), p. 143. The surviving ruins of Creevelea friary in west Bréifne are considerably greater than those at Drumlane. However, Creevelea friary is situated just across the River Bonet in the diocese of Ardagh.
49.   *AU*, 1484.

Figure 2.2: Round tower at Drumlane.

St Feidhlimidh at Kilmore.[50] Besides, Drumlane had thirty-two cartrons of land valued at thirty-two shillings annually while St Feidhlimidh's church at Kilmore had only six cartrons valued at six shillings.[51] Drumlane priory 'from ancient times held to their own use the perpetual vicarage of St Medocius's [Maodhóg's parish church]' thereby giving the priory access to the vicar's portion of the tithes collected in the parish of Drumlane.[52] The vicarage of Drumlane was valued at eight marks although the bishops of the diocese did for a period grant this vicarage to secular priests before it was restored to the Augustinians by Bishop Nicholas MacBrady who was bishop of Kilmore from *c.*1395-1421. When you compare the size and income of St Feidhlimidh's cathedral church at Kilmore with St Mary's priory at Drumlane you realise where the wealth, and possibly the power, lay in the medieval diocese of Kilmore.

The Augustinians communities, wherever they were situated, were subject to the diocesan bishop and the priory of Drumlane was no exception. However, the priory at Drumlane had the advantage of being established and having a fixed base and income approximately 300 years before the impoverished diocese of Kilmore had a recognised cathedral or

---

50.   Kilmore medieval cathedral measured 26m x 8m while the church at Drumlane measured 32.7m x 7.46m. See Patrick F. O'Donovan, *Archaeological inventory of County Cavan* (Dublin, 1995), pp 197, 201.

51.   Archdall, *Monasticon Hibernicum*, pp 784–5.

52.   *CPL*, vi, p. 159. St Mary's priory Drumlane also held the rectory of Killeshandra for a time in the late 1300s. See Costello, *De Annatis Hiberniae*, i, p. 242.

cathedral chapter. For a period of almost one hundred years, starting in 1455, the bishops of Kilmore were, with one exception, Augustinians and for a time it seemed not so much that Drumlane priory was located in the diocese of Kilmore but rather that the diocese was an appendage to the priory of Drumlane. Regularly the prior of Drumlane was mandated by the pope, along with one or two others, to resolve disputes that had arisen in the diocese and on 16 May 1470, John Bole, the archbishop of Armagh, even mandated the prior 'to carry out a metropolitan visitation of the city, church and diocese of Kilmore'.[53] Yet it would be wrong to see St Mary's priory and the diocese of Kilmore in a great power struggle given that both the diocesan priests and the canons of St Mary's tended to come from the same local clerical families. Besides, it was not unusual for a diocesan priest to become a canon in or prior of Drumlane nor was it unusual for the prior of Drumlane to become the bishop of Kilmore.

The Knights Hospitaller, Kilmainhamwood

In the twelfth-century, as conflict began between Christians and their Muslim and other non-Christian neighbours, there emerged new military orders whose members combined monastic life with the seemingly in-compatible life of active soldiering and hospital service. Their main focus was not ministry in Ireland but rather supporting, both financially and militarily, the Christians in the Holy Land. The Anglo-Norman invaders brought two of these Orders - the Knights Hospitaller and the Knights Templar - into Ireland with foundations of both being established in Ireland in the late twelfth and early thirteenth centuries.

The Hospitaller foundation at Kilmainham in Dublin established two preceptories or outlying houses in Meath and maintained the link with their mother house by naming one Kilmainhamwood and the oth-er Kilmainhambeg.[54] The small foundation of the Knights Hospitaller in Kilmainhamwood at the eastern end of the diocese of Tír Briúin was probably founded in the early decades of the thirteenth-century. It would appear that both of these Meath foundations had substantial buildings with the chapels being separate from the living quarters and thereby able to serve as parish churches. It also seems likely that they had large dining halls, although on a smaller scale than their mother-house in Kilmainham, which were suitable for meetings.[55] When Milo Sweteman,

53. See Anthony Lynch 'A Calendar of the reassembled register of John Bole, Archbishop of Armagh, 1457–71' in *Seanchas Ard Mhacha*, xv, 1 (1992), p. 167.
54. Helen J. Nicholson,'A long way from Jerusalem: the Templars and Hospitallers in Ireland, *c.*1172–1348' in Martin Browne & Colmán Ó Clabaigh (eds), *Soldiers of Christ, the Knights Hospi-taller and the Knights Templar in medieval Ireland* (Dublin, 2016), p. 8.
55. Tadhg O'Keeffe & Pat Grogan, 'Building a frontier? The architecture of the military orders in medieval Ireland' in Browne & Ó Clabaigh (eds), *Soldiers of Christ*, pp 88, 90–1.

the archbishop of Armagh, met Richard Ó Raghallaigh, the recalcitrant bishop of Tír Briúin, in June 1366 he did so in Kilmainhambeg[56] and when he met Ó Raghallaigh and his clergy for a two-day gathering in November 1368 he did so in Kilmainhamwood.[57] Both Kilmainhamwood and Kilmainhambeg were frontier foundations situated strategically between the English Pale and Gaelic Ireland and clearly Archbishop Sweteman felt safer meeting with the clergy of Tír Briúin in these military order frontier foundations than in any other location within the diocese of Tír Briúin.

The Kilmainhamwood Hospitallers made little impact on the diocese of Tír Briúin, a diocese which was virtually all *inter Hibernicos* (among the Irish) and was, for the most part, beyond the influence of the Anglo-Normans. Besides, virtually all the members of these foundations were English or Welsh and would, even if they wanted to, have found it difficult to relate to Gaelic Ireland. Because of this cultural divide 'these orders received little or nothing from the native Irish'.[58] The Kilmainhamwood Hospitaller foundation had a relatively short existence and may have already ceased functioning by the late 1300s or early 1400s.[59] When, following the Reformation, the king's commissioners surveyed the preceptory at Kilmainhamwood on 15 May 1541 all that remained on the site was 'an old castle in ruins and 4 messuages, of no value above repairs' and the whole property was estimated to be worth only £6 13s 4d per annum.[60] Kilmainhambeg preceptory, which was surveyed the following day, was said to have 'a capital messuage with a barn' and a water mill and was clearly more valuable than Kilmainhamwood being valued at £47 4s 8d.[61] A report in 1588 states that Kilmainhambeg had, possibly after some re-building had been carried out, a chapel with one lower and two upper lofts, a hall with battlements, a castle, a stone barn, a gatehouse and a mill.[62] The Knights Hospitaller foundations

56.   Brendan Smith, *The register of Milo Sweteman archbishop of Armagh 1361–1380* (Dublin, 1996), p. 7.
57.   Ibid., p. 72.
58.   Nicholson, 'A long way from Jerusalem', p. 9.
59.   Danny Cusack, *Kilmainham of the woody hollow* (Kilmainhamwood, 1998), p. 8.
60.   Newport B. White, *Extents of Irish monastic possessions, 1540–1541* (Dublin, 1943), p. 111.
61.   Ibid., pp 111–12. Gerald Keating, 'one of the brethren of the Hospital of St John of Jerusalem in Ireland' who had been parson of Kilmainham, was granted this annual income of £6 13s 4d from Kilmainhamwood on 6 September 1541. See Brendan Scott, 'The Knights Hospitaller in Tudor Ireland: their dissolution and attempted revival' in Browne & Ó Clabaigh (eds), *Soldiers of Christ*, pp 53–4. Peter Talbot had been granted a portion of the lands of Kilmainhambeg manor by 1547. See *CSPI, 1547–1553*, p. 4.
62.   See Charles McNeill (ed.), *Registrum de Kilmainham: register of chapter acts of the hospital of St John of Jerusalem in Ireland* (Dublin, 1932), p. 166; Eamonn Cotter, 'The archaeology of the Irish Hospitaller preceptories of Mourneabbey and Hospital in context' in Browne & Ó Clabaigh (eds), *Soldiers of Christ*, p. 106.

at Kilmainhamwood and Kilmainhambeg looked eastwards to their mother house in Dublin and to Jerusalem and the Holy Land and seldom glanced westwards or northwards into the diocese of Tír Briúin. Their impact on the diocese of Tír Briúin, unlike that of some of the other monastic orders established in the diocese in this period, was negligible.

Priory of St Féichín and Taurin, Fore

The Benedictine priory of St Féichín and St Taurin was established by Hugh de Lacy between 1180 and 1186 at Fore, which had been a short time earlier within the diocese of Tír Briúin.[63] The two patron saints of the foundation, one Irish and one French, were reminders that Féichín[64] had founded a monastery at Fore in the seventh-century and that the newly established priory was a daughter house of St Taurin's Benedictine abbey at Évreux in France.[65] Archbishop Malachy of Armagh favoured the Cistercians and Augustinians and not the Benedictines with the result that few Benedictine houses were established in Ireland and Fore was exceptional in being the only one set up in the English lordship.[66] The Benedictine priory of Fore was one of just two priories set up in Ireland which had their mother house in France and in that sense it was seen as an alien priory.[67] It was established at a turbulent time and in borderland territory which was often the battleground for disputes between the Gaelic chieftains and the Anglo-Normans in their quest for supremacy. The defeat and death of Tighearnán Ó Ruairc in 1172 brought instability to the area and in 1176 'the abbeys of Fabhar [Fore] and Ceanannus [Kells] were laid waste by the English and the people of Hy Briúin [Bréifne]'.[68] However, less than a decade later Hugh de Lacy felt secure enough to establish the Benedictine community at Fore.

---

63. It will be clear from this segment on the priory of Fore that the research of Rory Masterson has proved invaluable. For founding charter of Hugh de Lacy see J. Horace Round, *Calendar of documents preserved in France illustrative of the history of Great Britain and Ireland*, i (London, 1899), p. 105. For grants to Fore by Hugh and Walter de Lacy and Herbert de Matre see J.H. Round pp 105–7 and Muiris P. Mac Síthigh, 'Cairteacha Meán-aoiseacha do Mhainistir Fhohbair (XII –XII Céad)' in *Seanchas Ard Mhacha*, iv, no. 1 (1960–61), pp 172–5.
64. Ó Riain, *A dictionary of Irish saints*, pp 309–11. Féichín died of the plague in 667/668; *AU*, 667.
65. For an explanation as to why Hugh de Lacy choose to link the priory at Fore to the Benedictine abbey of Évreux see J.A. Howlett, 'The Benedictines in Ireland' in *The Irish Monthly*, vol. 19, no. 219 (Sept. 1891), pp 458–9. See also W.E. Wightman, *The Lacy family in England and Normandy 1066–1194* (Oxford, 1966), p. 214.
66. O'Keefe, 'Augustinian Regular Canons in twelfth and thirteenth-century Ireland: history, architecture and identity', p. 470.
67. The other alien priory was in Ards. See Rory Masterson, *Medieval Fore, County Westmeath* (Dublin, 2014), p. 7; for a list of the Benedictine foundations in medieval Ireland see Martin Browne & Colmán Ó Clabaigh (eds), *The Irish Benedictines, a history* (Dublin, 2005), p. 78.
68. *AFM*, 1176.

The Benedictines would remain at Fore for approximately three hundred and sixty years and had to endure attacks and violence at regular intervals, though in this they were little different to other religious houses in medieval Ireland. In 1329:

> Cathal, son of Donal O'Rourke, a worthy heir to the lordship of Brefney, was slain by the sons of John O'Ferrall and the English of Meath, and many others with them, in the house of Richard Tuite, at the monastery of Fobhar.[69]

The first half of the fifteenth-century was a particularly difficult time for the priory of Fore. In 1412 'O'Fergail made war on the Galls and they burned Fore and killed and captured many people'.[70] It was burned again five years later, this time by 'O'Fergail and the Clann Seain'.[71] The attack by 'Shan O'Reilly' and his followers in 1428 was particularly devastating:

> 8 yoke of horses, 2 cows, 6 sheep and other goods outside the lands of the prior and his convent [were] plundered from William Englonde, Prior of Fore … and the plunderers also killed 5 men of the prior and his convent.[72]

Primate John Swayne instructed Domhnall Ó Gabhann the bishop of Tír Briúin and other clergy of the diocese to ensure that the perpetrators made restitution for these deeds.[73] Twenty-four years later Cathal O'Ferrall was killed by 'the cast of a dart [an arrow] after the burning of Fore'.[74]

This priory, unlike the Augustinian communities at Kells and Drumlane, consisted mostly of men of French or Anglo-Irish backgrounds and the clerical families of Tír Briúin seemed to have little affinity with them. The community at Fore was always a small one - a cell rather than an abbey - and in 1343 when William Tessone was prior his community consisted of just five monks and a servant. It appears that no novices were trained at Fore but rather the monks were sent to and removed from Fore at the whim of the abbot of St Taurin's Benedictine abbey at

69.   *AFM*, 1329.
70.   *AC*, 1412.
71.   Ibid.,1417.
72.   D.A. Chart (ed.), *The register of John Swayne, archbishop of Armagh and primate of Ireland 1418–1439* (Belfast, 1935), p. 88.
73.   Ciaran Parker, 'Cavan, a medieval border area' in Raymond Gillespie (ed.), *Cavan, essays on the history of an Irish county* (Dublin, 1995), p. 45.
74.   *AFM*, 1452.

Évreux.[75] In 1174, just two years after the death of Tighearnán Ó Ruairc, the ancient See of Fore was annexed to Clonmacnois by a general decree of the clergy of Ireland.[76] Because of this decision the priory of Fore was no longer part of the diocese of Tír Briúin but it must be included in this volume because Fore had been part of the extended diocese of Tír Briuin a short time before the Benedictines arrived there and because a number of parishes in east Bréifne supported it financially throughout its existence. Hugh de Lacy, in his founding charter for the priory of Fore, stated that:

> he gives to God and St Taurin, and the monks there [in Évreux], the churches of Fore and the tithes of the honour of that town, and tithes of Tyrebegan and all Tyrefeihred in his demesne, and the mill of Fore, called St Fisquin's mill, and the wood near the town called 'Seculum Nemus' for the habitation of the monks.[77]

The new priory of Fore would be a gift, financial and otherwise, to the abbey of Évreux and the monks at Fore were expected to send any surplus revenue they had gathered to their mother house.[78] During the first fifty years of their stay in Fore the Benedictine monks were given several grants of land by Hugh and Walter de Lacy and Herbert de Matre.[79] Then, sometime between 1205 and 1212, Hugh de Lacy granted the priory of Fore the rectorial tithes from twelve present-day east Bréifne parishes and other isolated townlands in east Bréifne.[80] In contrast the Augustinian abbey of Kells, which had a great deal more interaction with the diocese, had an income from the tithes of just six parishes in east Bréifne and the large rectory of Dartry in west Bréifne. See Fig. 3.1. In the early 1300s the tithes going from the diocese of Tír Briúin to the priory of Fore were valued at eleven marks while those going to the

75.   See Rory Masterson, 'The alien priory of Fore, Co. Westmeath, in the middle ages' in *Arch. Hib.*, 53 (1999), p. 73.
76.   *AFM*, 1174. The early abbey of Fore had strong links with Clonmacnois. See Gwynn and Hadcock, *Medieval Religious houses Ireland*, p. 36.
77.   Round, *Calendar of documents preserved in France*, p. 105.
78.   For a detailed account of the financial and other woes of the Benedictine monks of Fore see Masterson, 'The alien priory of Fore' pp 73–8; idem, *Medieval Fore, County Westmeath*, pp 52–64.
79.   For information on the Fore priory lands see Masterson, *Medieval Fore, County Westmeath*, pp 16–17.
80.   Rory Masterson, 'The diocese of Kilmore and the priory of Fore: 1000–1540' in *Bréifne*, x, 39 (2003), p. 4. The parishes which paid tithes to the priory of Fore were Kilmore, Urney, Laragh, Lavey, Annagelliff, Drung, Denn, Ballintemple, Kildrumferton, Mullagh/Killinkere and Kilsherdany. See 'Inquisition taken at Cavan, 25 Sept. 1609' in *Calendar of Irish patent rolls of James I*, pp 385–7.

abbey of Kells were valued at just five marks. At the same time the priory of Drumlane had an income of only three marks while the total rent and revenue of the bishop of Kilmore was ten marks, one mark less than that going from the diocese to the priory of Fore.[81]

It would appear that the priory at Fore made little or no contribution to the pastoral care or sacramental life of the diocese of Tír Briúin because of its personnel, its location and the fact that the tithes they collected were 'without cure'. In any case, the Benedictines, unlike the Augustinians, did not work in parishes. During the 1400s several attempts were made by both laity and clergy of the diocese to claw back the tithes going to Fore. In 1375, John Ó Raghallaigh I, the bishop of Tír Briúin, wrote to Archbishop Milo Sweteman of Armagh complaining that John Croysse, the 'pretended prior' of St Féichín of Fore, had cited him to appear before the archbishop at Dromiskin, presumably for trying to prevent some of the tithes going from his diocese to Fore. The archbishop sided with John Croysse and cited the bishop to appear before him. Eventually Bishop John Ó Raghallaigh I agreed to meet the archbishop 'in the church of Armagh or in any place among the Irish to which he shall have safe access'.[82] In 1401 David Ó Farrelly, a deacon of the diocese and vicar of Drumlane, sought to have rectorial tithes of several townlands, mostly in the parishes of Kilsherdany, Laragh and Lavey, removed from the priory of Fore.[83] In 1401/2 Nicholas MacBradaigh, a clerk of the diocese of Kilmore, petitioned Rome to:

> Remove from the Benedictine prior and convent of St Feighin's, Fowr … who have detained it from time immemorial … the tithe without cure of the three townlands of Balichyllinnyllean, Balindrinug and Balinicarchi, in different parishes in the said diocese.[84]

Presumably this is the 'N. Mcbrady' that Nicholas Fleming, the archbishop of Armagh, summoned, together with Andrew MacBradaigh, Patrick Magauran and the bishop of Kilmore Nicholas MacBrady, to appear before him at a hearing in St Peter's church in Drogheda on 1 October 1408.[85] The issue must not have been resolved because in the autumn of

81. 'Ecclesiastical taxation of Ireland, 1302–6' in H.S. Sweetman (ed.), *Calendar of documents relating to Ireland 1302–1307* (London, 1886), p. 213.
82. Smith, *The register of Milo Sweteman*, p. 143.
83. *CPL*, v, p. 450.
84. Ibid., p. 366.
85. H.J. Lawlor, 'A calendar of the register of Archbishop Fleming' in *PRIA*, 30 (1912–13), p. 120.

1410, Archbishop Fleming wrote a rather sharp letter to Bishop Nicholas MacBrady stating that:

> The prior and convent of Faouria … complain that certain clerks and laymen of the diocese of Kilmore detain the tithes, oblations and obventions of churches appropriated and united to the priory … The bishop is therefore to admonish all who have done so to restore such tithes within twelve days … or if this is not done to excommunicate them.[86]

Archbishop Fleming added that if Bishop MacBrady did not carry out his orders he personally 'will do justice to the prior and convent'.[87]

When Donatus Ogowan, the perpetual vicar of Kilsherdany and later to become the bishop of Kilmore, tried to prevent some of the Kilsherdany tithes going to Fore in 1411 he too received a letter from Archbishop Fleming ruling in favour of the priory of Fore.[88] These early attempts to wrest the tithes from the priory of Fore took place during the Great Western Schism when Walter Prendergast, 'an illegal interloper' had seized the priory of Fore and their claim to the tithes seemed less secure.[89] It was, however, an issue that would not go away. In 1419 Augustine MacBradaigh, 'the perpetual vicar of the united churches of Drong and Leatrach' wrote to Rome stating that the tithes and 'the greater part of the fruits of his parish 'are received by the Benedictine prior and convent of Fore' and he applied to have the vicar's portion of the tithes increased because his income is 'insufficient for his support and for the repair of the said churches, hospitality and other burdens'.[90]

The canons appointed in 1455 to the newly established cathedral chapter were searching for incomes to support themselves in their new position and in 1461/2 Cormac Ó Sheridan wrote to Rome stating that his canonry had no prebend.[91] He requested that the rectorial tithes of

86.   Ibid., p. 134.
87.   Ibid.
88.   MacKiernan, *Diocese of Kilmore*, pp 12, 143, 139; Brendan Smith (ed.), *The register of Nicholas Fleming archbishop of Armagh 1404–1416* (Dublin, 2003), p. 153. The priory of Fore had the backing of the archbishop of Armagh from the early thirteenth-century. In a charter dated *c*.1206 Eugene Mac Gilla Uidir the archbishop of Armagh stated that 'he confirms to the abbey of St Taurin and Fechin at Favoria, and the monks there serving God and the saints the churches of Favores and all the tithes or ecclesiastical endowments which the charter of Hugh de Lacy confirms to them, with all other ecclesiastical profits that may arise from those churches, and the land which the said Hugh or other good men may have bestowed on that abbey.' See Round (ed.), *Calendar of documents preserved in France*, p. 107.
89.   Masterson, 'The diocese of Kilmore and the priory of Fore: 1000–1540', p. 13.
90.   *CPL*, vii, 116; Costello, *De Annatis Hiberniae*, i, p. 245.
91.   A prebend is the stipend or endowment given to a canon of the cathedral chapter.

the rural lands belonging to the parish of Kilmore, which did not belong to the episcopal *mensa* of Kilmore, be taken from the prior of Fore who, he claimed had long and wrongfully detained possession without any right of title, and be given to him.[92] Ten years later he requested Rome to grant him the perpetual rectory of 'the rural lands within the bounds of the parish churches of St Felimy, Kyllmore and St Patrick, Balleintempaill'[93] which had long been detained by the prior and convent of Fore. These attempts to recover the tithes from Fore usually ended in failure and by the time the priory was dissolved in November 1539 most of their claims to tithes in east Bréifne were still intact.

The links, apart from the monetary ones, between the diocese of Kilmore and the priory of Fore were tenuous, and yet from the mid-1400s onwards both the priory and its links with the diocese were changing. William Croys [Crose], who had been appointed prior in 1440, had previously 'built at his own costs, divers noble castles upon the lands of the said priory on the frontiers of the march, to the great relief and succour of the liege people of our said lord, the King'.[94] As a reward for helping to secure this borderland territory of the Pale he was appointed prior by the king and the priory was declared independent from St Taurin's abbey in Évreux. Further change came in 1454, when Edmund Fyztsimond, an acolyte from the diocese of Meath, having accused William Croys of perjury and simony, dilapidating, alienating and uselessly consuming the moveables and immoveables of the priory, was duly appointed prior in his stead.[95] The Fitzsimons family, which had branches in east Bréifne, continued to provide priors and monks to the convent of Fore.[96] In 1484 when Christopher Fuysymun [Fitzsimon], a monk of the priory, brought an accusation of simony against Roger Macregnet, another monk at Fore, he nominated three priests - the prior of Lough Uachtair together with John Ó Maolmochéirghe and Malachy Macachlerich - all clergy from the diocese of Kilmore - to adjudicate in the case, presumably because he knew them and felt confident that they

92.   *CPL* xi, p. 435.
93.   Ibid., xiii,p. 11.
94.   Henry F. Berry (ed.), *Statute Rolls of the Parliament of Ireland, reign of King Henry the sixth*,(Dublin, 1910), p. 144. This strengthening of the defences at Fore caused Patrick Corish to describe the priory as 'much more like a fortress than a monastery.' See Patrick Corish, *The Irish Catholic Experience, a historical survey* (Dublin, 1985), p. 60.
95.   *CPL*, x, p. 675. Edmund Fitzsimons was dead by 1484. See Costello, *De Annatis Hiberniae*, pp 72–3.
96.   Francis J. MacKiernan listed thirteen Fitzsimons priests (including Thomas Fitzsimons a controversial vicar-general of Kilmore), who had served in the diocese between 1614 and 1929. See MacKiernan, *Diocese of Kilmore*, p. 286. See also, Pádraig Ó Fiannachta, 'Do Chlainn tSiomuinn' appendix to Francis J. MacKiernan, 'Thomas Fitzsimons (1614–80)' in *Bréifne*, ix, 37 (2001), pp 336–40.

would decide in his favour.[97] The Annals of Ulster *sub anno* 1505 record-ed the death of 'Edmund the Dark' Fitzsimons, the prior of Fore.

The Nugent family of Delvin in Westmeath had an even more im-portant role in strengthening the links between the priory of Fore and the diocese of Kilmore. During the 1500s several members of the Nu-gent family helped to forge links by marrying one of the O'Reilly's of east Bréifne.[98] Besides, by the early 1500s, they had also managed to gain control of Multyfarnham Franciscan friary, Tristernagh Augus-tinian abbey and the Benedictine priory of Fore. William Nugent was the prior of Fore in 1539 when he surrendered it and their tithes in east Bréifne to Richard Nugent, the thirteenth baron of Delvin. The link between the Nugent family and Kilmore was copper-fastened in 1530 when Edmund Nugent, the prior of Tristernagh, was appoint-ed bishop of Kilmore.[99] The relationship between the Benedictines of Fore and the diocese of Kilmore, which had been both tenuous and fractious, was strongest from 1500 onwards. Less than four decades later, following the dissolution of the priory on 27 November 1539, the Benedictines left Fore. However, the monetary links between the prio-ry and the diocese of Kilmore continued after the closure of the priory and twelve east Bréifne parishes continued to pay tithes to the new owners, including the barons of Delvin, until relatively modern times.

Holy Trinity Priory, Lough Uachtair

During the twelfth-century many continental-based religious Orders established monasteries in Ireland, thereby contributing greatly to the Church reform at that time. Much of this development bypassed the di-ocese of Bréifne/Kells and it was not until the year 1237, approximately fifty years after the priory of Fore was set up, that another religious Or-der established a house in the diocese. In that year the Premonstratensian Order began building a priory on Trinity Island in Lough Uachtair, a site just over five miles south of the Augustinian priory at Drumlane and only separated from it by a series of small lakes.[100] Norbert, who founded the Premonstratensian order at Prémontré in northern France in 1120, was a friend of Bernard of Clairvaux and both were commit-ted to Church reform.[101] Even though Norbert died in 1134, just thirteen

97.   *CPL*, xiii, pp 170–1. See also Costello, *De Annatis Hiberniae*, p. 72.
98.   Bernadette Cunningham, 'The Anglicisation of east Bréifne' in Gillespie (ed.), *Cavan, essays on the history of an Irish county*, pp 57–8.
99.   Colm Lennon, 'The Nugent family and the diocese of Kilmore in the sixteenth and early seventeenth centuries' in *Bréifne*, ix, 37 (2001), pp 361–2. For information on the early history of the Nugent family see, Basil Iske, *The Green Cockatrice* (Dublin, 1978).
100.   *AC*, 1237.
101.   Williams (ed.), *The 'Annals of Multyfarnham': Roscommon and Connacht provenance*, p. 126.

years after the Order was founded, the Premonstratensians flourished. New Premonstratensian houses were established throughout Europe, especially in France, Belgium and Germany with the result that it became the second most prolific reformed religious Order (after the Cistercians) in the medieval Latin Church.[102] The first England Premonstratensian community was established in 1143.[103] However, it was the Premonstratensians from Dryburgh in Scotland who founded Carrickfergus, the first Premonstratensian community in Ireland, *c.*1183. Carrickfergus was the first of eight conventual houses and two hospitals set up by the Premonstratensians in the north-east of Ulster and Connacht between *c.*1180 and 1242.[104] The two Premonstratensian houses in north-east Ulster were Anglo-Norman foundations while those in Connacht, including Lough Uachtair, were Gaelic foundations.

Trinity Island priory on Lough Uachtair was founded by Clarus MacMailin, the archdeacon of Elphin diocese. He had already established the mother house on Trinity Island in Lough Cé *c.*1220[105] and The Annals of Loch Cé *sub anno* 1237 recorded that:

> The erection of a monastery for canons was commenced by Clarus MacMailin, in Trinity Island on Loch-Uachtair, through the gift of Cathal Ó Raghallaigh, *in hoc anno*.

Following the defeat and death of Tighearnán Mór Ó Ruairc in 1172, the power base in Bréifne changed considerably. The Anglo-Norman de Lacy family of Meath made inroads into east Bréifne, constructing a motte and bailey at Kilmore in 1211 and building Clogh Uachtair castle *c.*1220. Then they were defeated by Cathal Ó Raghallaigh, who had by then established himself as leader of this increasingly powerful family in east Bréifne. The decision in 1237 to build the priory on Lough Uachtair may have resulted from a devastating incursion into Bréifne by Domhnall Ó Domhnaill and Aengus Mac Gilla Finnéin six years earlier when they attacked Cathal Ó Raghallaigh and raided what may have been a small religious settlement or hermitage on Eonish

102.   Miriam Clyne, 'The founders and patrons of Premonstratensian houses in Ireland' in Burton & Stober (eds), *The Regular Canons in the medieval British Isles*, p. 145. It will be clear from this section that I am indebted to the research and writing of Miriam Clyne.
103.   For the Premonstratensian Order in England see Joseph A. Gribbin, *The Premonstratensian Order in late medieval England* (Suffolk, 2001).
104.   Clyne, 'The founders and patrons of Premonstratensian houses in Ireland', pp 148, 171.
105.   John Lynch (ed.), *De Praesulibus Hiberniae* (Dublin, 1944), ii, pp 301–2. Clarus Mac Mailin was a member of the learned Ó Maoilchonaire family. See Miriam Clyne, 'Medieval Irish Premonstratensian monasteries and their European context', unpublished PhD thesis (NUIG, 2010), i, p. 93.

Island in Lough Uachtair and carrying 'off the precious objects and the wealth and treasure and good things there'.[106] The building of the priory on Trinity Island 'under the recommendation and patronage of Cathal O'Reilly'[107] may have been intended as a religious settlement to replace either the one on Eonish island or another nearby in Slanore townland in the parish of Kilmore.[108] The location chosen for the Premonstratensian priory on Holy Trinity Island was directly north of the sixth-century monastery of Slanore (*Snámh Luthair*) and was separated by only a small expanse of water from it. Slanore had been founded by Saint Colmán the son of Eachaidh from Midhíseal in Carlow.[109] Colmán's sister, Comaigh, and his brothers Fiontan, Lughaidh and Muireadhach, together with Ruadhán of Lorrha, are among the saints associated with Slanore.[110] Slanore's best days were over before the twelfth-century reformation of the Irish Church began, though it is possible that it continued to be a bishop's seat after that time.

The new Premonstratensian priory on Holy Trinity Island was located on the same lake and between the older religious settlements of Eonish and Slanore in the parish of Kilmore. And even though the building work on the priory started in 1237 it slowed for some reason - possibly because of the turbulent times in Bréifne and Magh Luirg[111] or because of lack of funds. For whatever reason, the canons did not move

---

106.   *AC*, 1231; *AFM*, 1231; Aidan O'Sullivan, *The archaeology of lake settlement in Ireland* (Dublin, 1998), p. 165. Eonish Island has links with St Cuana who led the life of an anchorite there and, by the time of his death in 778 had built up a reputation for wisdom. See *AU*, 778. His feast day was on 14 November: Micheál Ó Cléirigh, *The Martyrology of Donegal*, ed. & trans. by John O'Donovan (Dublin, 1864), p. 309. St Fergna was also associated with Eonish and both his and Cuana's remains were buried in Clogher. See Ó Riain, *A dictionary of Irish saints*, pp 240, 308. A circular graveyard and nearby holy well dedicated to St Patrick are listed in O'Donovan's, *Archaeological inventory of County Cavan*, pp, 215, 219.

107.   *AFM*, 1237.

108.   Slanore is a promontory townland surrounded on three sides by water, the river Erne, Carr's Lough and Lough Uachtair. The earliest Ordnance survey map shows the 'abbey field' though only a few ashlar stones now mark the site of the church and graveyard. Oliver Davies argued, though not convincingly, that the twelfth-century Kilmore Romanesque doorway came from Slanore. See Davies, 'A summary of the archaeology of Ulster, Part II' in *UJA*, xii (1949), p. 55; Davies, 'The churches of County Cavan', p. 133; O'Donovan, *Archaeological inventory of County Cavan*, p. 208.

109.   Ó Riain, *A dictionary of Irish saints*, p. 198.

110.   Ibid., pp 215, 342–3, 409, 504. For Slanore see Martin Comey, 'The monastery at Slanore' in *The Breifny Antiquarian Journal*, i, 2 (1921), pp 166–73; Philip O'Connell, *The diocese of Kilmore, its history and antiquities* (Dublin, 1937), pp 25–6, 34; Ó Riain, *A dictionary of Irish saints*, p. 543.

111.   The Premonstratensian abbey in Lough Cé had mixed fortunes during these years. Their endowments increased in both 1237 and 1239 and it was plundered in 1249. See *ALC*, 1237, 1239; *AC*, 1249; Gwynn and Hadcock, *Medieval Religious Houses*, p. 205; Miriam Clyne, 'Archaeological excavations at Holy Trinity Abbey, Lough Key, Co. Roscommon' in *Proceedings of the Royal Irish Academy*, 105C, 2 (2005), pp 23–98.

into the new priory until the end of 1250.[112] The Annals of Connacht recorded that:

> The white Canons of the Premonstrant Order were taken shortly before Christmas by Clarus Mac Mailin from Trinity Island in Loch Key to Trinity Island in Loch Uachtair in Brefne, and canons of the Order were instituted there by permission of Cathal O Raghillig, who presented the site as an absolute and perpetual alms in honour of the Holy Trinity. And Clarus so acted, in the name of God, for this reason – that the Premonstratensians enjoy a privilege similar to that of the monks, in that they can pass [from their own] to any other house.

The island which Cathal Ó Raghallaigh gave to the white canons for their priory was, according to the earliest Ordnance survey map, just over 122 acres in size.[113] It provided farmland for the canons to support themselves and while working the land in silence the canons were carrying out the manual-labour required by their austere Order. The priory also had a considerable amount of land in other townlands on the south shore of Lough Uachtair. In an inquisition held in 1570 it was recorded that the priory had 'four parcels of land called Polle Drumore, Polle in Yllane and Dyrre, Polle Snaveloghher, Drumore alias Dromorore and their tithes'.[114]

A second inquisition, taken in 1609, adds the townlands of Bleancup and Killyvally to those owned by the 'late abbey or priory of Trinity Island situate near the Toagher'.[115] The priory had to pay 3s. 4d. to the bishop of the diocese out of the half poll of Snaulugher (Slanore).[116] Miriam Clyne has calculated that the priory owned 1,574 acres in total, with only the Lough Cé and Annaghdown Irish Premonstratensian houses having larger temporal estates.[117] All lands attached to Premonstratensian houses were meant to provide for the

112.   For other possible explanations see Clyne, 'Medieval Irish Premonstratensian monasteries', i, pp 101–2. Gwynn and Hadcock suggest that there may have been an earlier religious community in residence on Trinity Island in Lough Uachtair which delayed the arrival of the white canons. However, this seems unlikely.

113.   For an aerial view of Holy Trinity priory and the surrounding Lough Uachtair see *An introduction to the Architectural heritage of County Cavan*, p. 11.

114.   *The Irish Fiants of the Tudor sovereigns*, ii (1570), no. 1681.

115.   *Calendar of Irish patent rolls of James I*, p. 386. A number of toghers have been identified in the area but the one referred to here may be the one linking the townlands of Derries Lower and Kinkeel.

116.   *Calendar of Irish patent rolls of James I*, p. 386.

117.   Clyne, 'Medieval Irish Premonstratensian monasteries', i, Table 5:1, p. 189.

needs of the canons and also to help them provide hospitality, food, alms and clothing for travellers, pilgrims and the poor and to pay for the medical needs of the sick and the elderly.[118] There was a landing place for boats near the priory which could be used by the canons and by laity going to the priory to pray. There was also a causeway linking the island to the mainland in Killyvally which could be used to get to and from the island when the water levels of the lake were low. According to tradition there was a fishing stand which was used by the canons on a nearby island.[119]

The Premonstratensians were not monks but rather canons regular. The white canons[120] in adopting the rule of St Augustine and abiding by some of the stricter observances of the Cistercians, were very much part of the twelfth-century reform in Europe. They built their abbeys and priories on islands and other remote places as they tried to combine a monastic spirituality with manual labour. It was St Norbert's wish that the Premonstratensians would not 'live in towns but rather in desolate, wild and lonely places' and the island on Lough Uachtair, isolated yet accessible by boat, seemed an ideal location for their community in east Bréifne.[121] The priory was hoping to create a contemplative haven for the white canons which would also allow them to have an outreach of pastoral ministry in nearby parishes. The Premonstratensians were ministry-minded priests who lived in community. Later some of the white canons would live away from the abbeys and priories in small dependent rural cells in order to better serve the parish pastoral needs, though it seems that some of this pastoral outreach may have been done out of financial necessity.[122]

The establishment of monasteries in medieval times required not just wealthy but also powerful patrons who would protect them from attack and provide the stability necessary for them to survive. Part of the difficulty facing the Premonstratensians settling in Lough Uachtair was the volatile situation in east Bréifne, particularly in the Lough Uachtair area, in the thirteenth-century. The de Lacys who were leaders of the Anglo-Normans in Meath, had made inroads into east Bréifne

118.   Ibid., p. 40.
119.   Ibid., p. 242.
120.   They wore tunics of unbleached wool which, with time, became white after repeated washing.
121.   T.J. Antry & C. Neel, *Norbert and early Norbertine spirituality* (Mahwah, 2007), pp 11, 138, quoted in Clyne, 'The founders and patrons of Premonstratensian houses', p. 152.
122.   Gribbin, *The Premonstratensian Order in late medieval England*, pp 1–2. For the rural cells in north Connacht which were dependant on Lough Cé see Miriam Clyne, 'The Rental of Holy Trinity abbey, Lough Cé' in Thomas Finan (ed.), *Medieval Lough Cé, history, archaeology and landscape* (Dublin, 2010), p. 74.

and succeeded in building a fortress castle on an island in Lough Uachtair *c*.1220.[123] In 1226 Cathal Ó Raghallaigh captured 'the castle of Kilmore'[124] and seven years later, in 1233, defeated William de Lacy and the 'English of Meath' in a decisive battle at Móin Crandchain and 'they were driven from the country without prisoner or plunder'.[125] It was on the back of this victory and his increased status in east Bréifne that Cathal Ó Raghallaigh invited the Premonstratensian order to establish a community near his power base at Lough Uachtair. In doing so he was providing a chaplaincy, a place of worship and possibly a burial place for his family. It was also an important strategic move because Clarus MacMailin, who like some of the other Premonstratensians from Connacht, had direct links with Prémontré in France, and so, by bridging the two cultures, could be a useful negotiator in Gaelic/ Norman disputes in Bréifne just as he had been in Magh Luirg.[126]

Clarus MacMailin died in 1251, just one year after they the Premonstratensian canons came to Lough Uachtair.[127] Five years later Cathal O Raghallaigh was killed along with his brother and two sons in a battle on the slopes of Sliabh-an-Iarainn. Within six years of setting up at Lough Uachtair the Premonstratensians had lost both their founder and patron. These changes and subsequent local wars created instability for the canons. The nearby Clogh Uachtair castle, which was acting both as prison and fortress, was a magnet for regular attacks, and the priory, although never a place of great wealth, inevitably suffered during these raids.[128] In 1272, Donal Óg Ó Domhnaill retraced his father's steps by leading an incursion into Ó Raghallaigh territory in east Bréifne:

> [He] collected his vessels and boats on Lough Erne, with which he proceeded to Lough Uachtar, and seized on the property of the adjoining places (namely on the islands of that lake), which he carried away, plundered the people,

123.   Conleth Manning, *Clogh Oughter Castle, Co. Cavan, archaeology, history and architecture* (Dublin, 2013), p. vii.
124.   *AFM*, 1226.
125.   *AFM*, 1233; Colin Veach & Freya Verstraten Veach, 'William Gorm de Lacy: chiefest champion in these parts of Europe.' in Duffy (ed.), *Princes, Prelates and poets*, pp 78–9.
126.   Clyne, 'Medieval Irish Premonstratensian monasteries', i, pp 68, 93.
127.   Clarus MacMailin was buried at Lough Cé. See *AC*, 1251; *ALC*, 1251.
128.   One example of these raids was in 1369 when 'a naval expedition was made by Philip Mag Uidhir ... to Loch-uachtair and the Rock of the Loch was captured by them'. See *AU*, 1369.

and reduced them in all the neighbouring parts under his sway and subjection.[129]

This devastating attack was a great set-back for the recently founded priory. This second successful naval attack on Lough Uachtair proved to the Ó Raghallaigh sept that they were vulnerable to such attacks and may have influenced their decision to move their headquarters from Lough Uachtair to their purpose-built castle at Tullachmongan overlooking Cavan town. This move may have coincided with the Ó Raghallaigh's withdrawing their patronage from the Premonstratensians canons on Trinity Island and transferring it to the newly-established Franciscan friary in Cavan town. When records resume for Lough Uachtair priory early in the 1400s we discover that it is the O'Sheridan and not the Ó Raghallaigh family who are its main supporters.

Despite the attack in 1272 and the loss of the Ó Raghallaigh patronage, it appears that some limited alterations were carried out on the priory church in the early 1300s since a tracery bar in the Decorated Style of the time, which may have been part of the east window of the church, has survived.[130] Holy Trinity priory was not included in the ecclesiastical taxation list of the early 1300s and little is known about the fate of the Premonstratensians in Ireland throughout that century as virtually no records have survived. However, what is clear is that it was generally a period of decline for the Order, a decline which may have been caused by the ongoing local wars, bad weather, famine and the bubonic plague which affected much of Europe. There were also internal problems because the Premonstratensians, just like some other religious of the period, were becoming more materialistic and less disciplined. Some of the Premonstratensians white canons owned private property, ignored the rule of celibacy and gradually became independent from and out of touch with the idealism of the founding monastery in Prémontré. The Annals of Lough Cé for the year 1270 state that there was 'great Famine and scarcity in all Erinn *in hoc anno*' and then adds that a son named Cathal was born to Liathanach Ó Conchobhair, the Premonstratensian abbot of Lough Cé.[131] These entries gives an indication of the external difficulties and the internal indiscipline which were, even at that early stage, weakening the order in Loch Cé and presumably having a knock-on effect on its daughter-house in Lough Uachtair.

129.   *AFM*, 1272.
130.   Clyne, 'Medieval Irish Premonstratensian monasteries', i, pp 150–1, 160.
131.   He had at least two other sons: Diarmait who was killed and buried on Holy Trinity island in Lough Cé and Gilla Isa, who later became bishop of Elphin. See *AC*, 1284, 1294.

The priory of Lough Uachtair was ruinous and impoverished in 1411. In that year it was reported that it was:

> without cure, is not a dignity, is not conventual nor elective, depends on the said monastery [Lough Cé] and is wont to be governed by canons thereof, removed and recalled to their cloister at the sole pleasure of the abbot, and whose value does not exceed 5 marks.[132]

John O'Sheridan, a canon of Lough Cé, returned to Lough Uachtair and was appointed prior there in 1411. His appointment points towards an attempt to establish control over the priory by the O'Sheridan family whose power base was close by in the parish of Kilmore, the parish in which the priory was situated. John O'Sheridan was appointed prior in June of 1411 and by August of that year he was complaining that he had not obtained possession of the priory, and even if he had, the fruits of it would be insufficient to sustain him.[133] He made further representations to Rome in 1412 stating that 'the income of the aforesaid priory [Lough Uachtair] is so meagre ... that it would not suffice for his decent support'[134] and so he was granted 'in commendam for life' the perpetual vicarage of Tuaimregayn (Tomregan) which was valued at four marks[135] and the rectory of Kedy valued at six marks.[136] He either resigned this rectory or was deprived of it by Bishop Nicholas MacBradaigh and it was held by Andrew MacBradaigh for four years before it was, in 1427, granted to Patrick O'Sheridan, who was vicar of Kilmore and a man who had studied both canon and civil law at Oxford.[137]

Araltheus Ocathaalan was appointed prior of Lough Uachtair *c.*1421 and held that position for approximately six years.[138] He was appointed prior by Congallus, the abbot of Lough Cé. Congallus was later deprived of the abbacy of Lough Cé for extorting '10 shillings of silver ... worth about 3 florins in gold' from Ocathaalan before appointing him prior of Lough Uachtair and for extorting a similar amount from two others who wished to become canons in the Premonstratensian abbey

---

132.   *CPL*, vi, p. 231; In contrast the Premonstratensian abbey in Lough Cé was valued at twenty-four marks. See *CPL*, viii, pp 50–1.
133.   *CPL*, vi, p. 271.
134.   Costello, *De Annatis Hiberniae*, i, p. 244.
135.   *CPL*, vi, p. 271.
136.   Costello, *De Annatis Hiberniae*, i, p. 247.
137.   Ibid., pp 247–8.
138.   P. Norberto Backmund, *Monasticon Premonstratense*, 3 vols, (Strauhing, 1952). My thanks to Fr Kilian Mitchell, O. Praem., for giving me Backmund's three-volume history of the Order.

of Lough Cé.[139] By the beginning of 1428 John O'Sheridan, presumably a relation and not the same person as the prior appointed in 1411, had replaced Araltheus Ocathaalan as prior. The priory had progressed since 1411 and had, by 1428, a community of canons with a pastoral outreach to neighbouring parishes even though it was still only valued at five marks per annum. The new prior appealed to Rome for another benefice and was told that he could have:

> a benefice, with or without cure, value not exceeding 25 [with cure] or 18 marks [without cure] accordingly, in the common or several gift of the bishop and the dean and chapter of Kilmore, provided that it be not a canonry and prebend of a cathedral church.[140]

John O'Sheridan also wrote to Pope Martin V about the deplorable condition of their priory and the pope, having learned that:

> the church of the monastery of the Holy Trinity of Lough Uachtair of the Premonstratensian order was much in need of repairs … granted a relaxation of three years and as many quarantines of enjoyed penance to all who being truly penitent and confessed, shall devoutly visit the said church on the feast of the Assumption and give helping hands towards its repair.[141]

The Premonstratensian Order had particular devotion to the Virgin Mary and from 1428 onwards we can safely conclude there was a increased number of penitents visiting the priory of Lough Uachtair each year on the feast of the Assumption and while there making donations to the repair fund.[142] The ruined remains of the west gable and portions of the south and north walls of this church have survived and virtually all these ruins date from this period. The bell-cote and pointed west window can be dated to the early fifteenth-century, though the upper section of the late Gothic window in the west wall of the church dates to the period after the white canons had left the priory, which suggests that the church and perhaps the

139. *CPL*, vii, p. 50. Congallus was entitled to receive five marks from the prior.
140. *CPL*, vii, p. 516; Costello, *De Annatis Hiberniae*, i, p. 247.
141. Costello, *De Annatis Hiberniae*, i, p. 247; *CPL*, vii, p. 505.
142. Norbert's church at Premontré was dedicated to the Virgin Mary. When Msgr Massari visited the derelict priory in July 1646 among the items he found scattered in a corner was a statue of the 'blessed Virgin and child in her arms.' See 'My Irish campaign' in *The Catholic bulletin and book review*, ix (1919), p. 247.

domestic quarters of the priory continued to be used, possibly until the mid-seventeenth-century.[143] See Fig. 2.3. The several fragments of ornate cut stone which were found in the adjoining graveyard are, according to Oliver Davies, clearly derived from 'complex windows of about the 15th century'.[144] A grotesque stone head, now in the National Museum of Ireland and another, now in the nearby townland of Lisnamandra, are said to be from the priory and they too were sculpted in this period.[145] All this elaborate stonework points to major re-construction and intricate stone-work being carried out on Holy Trinity priory in the fifteenth-century - sometime after 1428 and possibly before 1450.

Being a daughter-house of Lough Cé, the priory of Lough Uachtair was dependent on and governed by the abbot of Holy Trinity Island in Lough Cé. When the abbot of Lough Cé appointed a prior to Lough Uachtair he was given five marks and then three marks and a bell-rope each subsequent year.[146] Since the abbey on Lough Cé was the headquar-ters of the Premonstratensians in Ireland the prior of Lough Uachtair was bound to report to the chapter at Lough Cé twice a year unless he has a legitimate excuse and if he fails to do so he could be deprived of his benefices.[147] It would appear that some of the priors of Lough Uachtair - such as Maurice Oduilinean who died *c.*1411 - came from the Lough Cé community. John O'Sheridan, who was a Premonstratensian canon in Lough Cé, most likely went there from Lough Uachtair before retracing his steps to become prior in Lough Uachtair in 1411.[148] Ruaidhrí Mac Diarmada lord of Magh Luirg, who lived for almost eighty years, was reputed to have been abbot of Lough Cé and Lough Uachtair and when he died in 1568 he was said to:

> have earned the blessings of patrons and ecclesiastics, poets and doctors, the poor and widows, strangers and orphans, the infirm and pilgrims, martyrs and victims of heavy sick-ness, guests and exiles.[149]

143.   Clyne, 'Medieval Irish Premonstratensian monasteries', i, p. 153; *An Introduction to the architectural heritage of County Cavan*, p. 11. The Lough Uachtair synod of 1651 was probably held in the priory church. The death of Archbishop Hugh O'Reilly on Holy Trinity Island in February 1653 was followed by the capture of the island by the Cromwellian forces less than a month later.
144.   Oliver Davies, 'The churches of County Cavan' reprinted in *Bréifne*, xiii, 48 (2013), pp 123–4.
145.   O'Donovan, *Archaeological Inventory of County Cavan*, pp 204, 210.
146.   Coolavin MS 142, translated and printed in Finan, *Medieval Lough Cé*, pp 94–6.
147.   Ibid.
148.   *CPL*, vi, p. 231.
149.   *ALC*, 1568.

Figure 2.3: The west wall and bellcote of Holy Trinity Premonstratensian priory, Lough Uachtair.

Although the Lough Uachtair priory was founded by the Ó Raghallaigh sept it was the O'Sheridans who became more closely associated with it from at least 1400 onwards if not earlier.[150] This family provided canons for the priory and priests for the diocese of Kilmore. The O'Sheridan diocesan priests were usually placed in the medieval vicarages of Urney, Kilmore and Kilsherdany. Some members of the family were rectors of Kedy (Keadew) and in 1471 Cormac O'Sheridan sought the 'perpetual rectory of the rural lands within the bounds of the parish churches of St Felimy, Kyllmore and St Patrick Balleintempaill' without cure, which the prior and convent of Fore had 'long detained without title'.[151] Francis J. MacKiernan in his book *Diocese of Kilmore, bishops and priests* lists ten fifteenth-century O'Sheridan diocesan priests[152] and while none of them became bishop of the diocese many of them held prominent positions

150. For Eoghan Ó Raghallaigh's 1703 legendary account of how the O'Sheridans came to east Bréifne *c.*1290 see James Carney (ed.), *A genealogical history of the O'Reillys written in the eighteenth century by Eóghan Ó Raghallaigh and incorporating portion of the earlier work of Dr Thomas Fitzsimons …* (Cavan, 1959), pp 116–7 and Donald M. Schlegel, 'The Sheridans untangled' in *Bréifne*, xiii, 51 (2016), pp 816–33. Some of the Sheridans also became Franciscans: James Sheridan was listed as guardian of the dissolved Cavan Franciscan friary in 1694; Francis J. MacKiernan, *St Mary's abbey Cavan* (Cavan, 2000), p. 25.

151. *CPL*, xiii, p. 11.

152. MacKiernan, *Diocese of Kilmore*, p. 293. He lists a further eleven Sheridan priests of the diocese between 1619 and 1914.

in it.[153] Patrick O'Sheridan, who had studied canon and civil law at Oxford,[154]was granted the perpetual vicarage of Kilmore in 1411 and, in 1427, the rectory and vicarage of 'Kedi'.[155] Andrew O'Sheridan, who was dean of Kilmore [deanery] and vicar of the church of St Feidhlimidh in Kilmore, was deprived of his position in 1460 because, according to John Ogoband (O'Gowan), a canon of both Ardagh and Kilmore, he had 'incurred simony and perjury to the shame of the clerical order'.[156] Malachy O'Sheridan, a priest of the diocese of Kilmore, became prior of Lough Uachtair in 1466.[157] The O'Sheridan family, by supplying priests for the diocese and canons for the priory in Lough Uachtair, provided an important link between the priory and the surrounding parishes in the diocese of Kilmore.

It would appear that during the period 1250 to 1411 the community on Trinity Island was small and impoverished and with little pastoral duties beyond the priory.[158] In 1411 the priory was said to be 'without cure' meaning that it had no pastoral care obligations and it was valued at a mere five marks. Through the efforts of the prior John O'Sheridan and others the status of the priory improved considerably during the course of the fifteenth-century. The priory, which was only valued at five marks annually in 1411 had increased to eight marks in 1466 and by 1491 was valued at ten marks, double what it had been eighty years earlier. Another sign of the increased status of the priory was that regularly throughout the fifteenth-century the prior of Lough Uachtair was mandated by the pope to help resolve disputes in various parishes in the diocese.[159] The white canons also had increased pastoral care re-sponsibilites most notably in the parishes of Tomregan, Kilmore, Urney, and from 1491, Killeshandra.

The priory of Lough Uacthair was controlled for much of the 1400s by the O'Sheridan family and in some instances was handed on in hereditary succession from one generation to the next. In 1466, Malachy O'Sheridan, a priest of the diocese of Kilmore, accused Fergal O'Sheridan who was the son of a Premonstratensian canon and the

---

153.   Hugh O'Sheridan, who was bishop of Kilmore from 1560 to 1579, was a priest of the dio-cese of Raphoe and may not have been a native of Kilmore. MacKiernan, *Diocese of Kilmore*, p. 13.
154.   *CPL*, vii, p. 483.
155.   Ibid.
156.   *CPL*, xii, pp 67–8.
157.   Ibid., p. 511.
158.   Backmund wrote: *Quae consuetudo certe etiam in Loch Uachtair, ac probabilius etiam in aliis prioratibus adhibita, in decursu saeculi XIV paulatim erat desueta, ex penuria sacerdotum.Tantum in Loch Uachtair, forte adhuc saeculo XV erat parva communitas ad nutum abbatis de Loch Ce.* Back-mund, *Monasticon Premonstratense*, ii, pp 124–5.
159.   For examples of this see *CPL*, viii, p. 428, *CPL*, x, p. 637 and xiv, p. 234.

prior of Lough Uachtair since 1444,[160] of being a notorious fornicator, guilty of simony and dilapidating 'the goods of the said priory, so that unless remedy be quickly taken it will soon be reduced to naught'.[161] Malachy was not a disinterested witness, however, since he hoped to succeed Fergal as prior. John Ó Raghallaigh II, the bishop of Kilmore, together with John Ogoband and John Macubuartayn, both canons of the diocese, were nominated to adjudicate on the case. They obviously found in favour of Malachy because he entered the Order, received the regular habit and made his profession in the monastery of Lough Cé before being appointed prior in Lough Uachtair, a position he held for twenty-five years.

In 1491, William O'Sheridan, who stated that he was a son of Malachy O'Sheridan, reported to Rome that his father unlawfully claimed to be the prior of Lough Uachtair, and that he himself wished to enter the Order and become the prior there. The abbot of the monastery of Kells, together with Donald Ó Floinn and John Ó Maolmochéirghe, canons of the diocese of Kilmore, were nominated to adjudicate with the result that William O'Sheridan became prior in that year.[162] This pernicious system, where the one who made the accusations and nominated those who would adjudicate in the matter stood to benefit most, means that the allegations in the surviving one-sided papal registers need to be treated with caution. However, in two instances in the fifteenth-century these allegations resulted in the replacing of an O'Sheridan prior of Lough Uachtair by another cleric from that family. Throughout much of the fifteenth-century the O'Sheridan clerical lineage family controlled the priory of Lough Uachtair and supplied it with canons and priors and 'as far as can be determined, son succeeded father'.[163]

The Ó Raghallaighs were the original patrons of the priory of Lough Uachtair though that patronage may not have extended beyond giving them the island site for the priory and providing them with protection from outside attack. Throughout the 1300s the priory seems to have been both small and impoverished[164] and it is possible that the transition to the O'Sheridans becoming patrons in the early 1400s may not have gone

160. Costello, *De Annatis Hiberniae*, i, p. 250. In 1444/5 there is a reference in the calendar of papal registers to Eugene '*dilecto filio Fergallo Osiredean, priori monasterii sancte Trinitatis de Lochwactair.*' See also *CPL*, x, p. 729.
161. *CPL*, xii, p. 511.
162. *CPl*, xiv, pp 359–60. He was still prior in 1494. See Costello, *De Annatis Hiberniae*, p. 240.
163. Clyne, 'Medieval Irish Premonstratensian monasteries', i, p. 111. In 1590 William Óg MacPrior O Sheridan was listed as a gentleman in the vicinity of Cavan. See Joseph B. Meehan, 'Termon or Hospital land in Cavan, 1590' in *Breifny antiquarian society Journal*, i, 2 (1921), p. 219.
164. Lough Uachtair priory did not merit inclusion in the ecclesiastical taxation list of 1302–7. See *Calendar of documents relating to Ireland, 1302–1307*, p. 213.

smoothly. There was no love lost between these two families with disputes starting between them over lands in the townlands of Breandrum and Tonymore in 1428. The dispute erupted again in 1452 and this time Archbishop John Swayne of Armagh was called on to intervene.[165] The O'Sheridans continued to control the priory in the early decades of the 1500s and, being situated *inter Hibernicos* in east Bréifne, the priory managed to survive the early decades of the Tudor Reformation. It was not until *c*.1582 that the white canons finally vacated their Trinity island base on Lough Uachtair.[166]

The Franciscan Friary, Cavan

The setting up of the Augustinian priory at Drumlane in the 1140s and the apparent attempt to establish a cathedral at Kilmore *c*.1170 are the earliest signs of the twelfth-century reform in the diocese of Tír Briúin. However, the impact of this twelfth-century reform continued long after the century was over and the founding of the Premonstratensian priory in Lough Uachtair in 1250 and the Franciscan friary in Cavan *circa* fifty years later were a continuation of that reform. Francis of Assisi (1181–1226) founded the Franciscan Order of Friars minor in 1209 and the Irish province of Friars minor was set up in 1230, just four years after his death, though it seems likely that there were already Friars minor in Ireland before that date. Virtually all of the early Franciscan foundations in Ireland were set up in towns controlled by the Anglo-Normans to the south and east of the island. All the early minister provincials were English friars and it was not until the middle of the fifteenth-century that William O'Reilly, a Franciscan friar from east Bréifne, was elected as the first Gaelic minister provincial of the order.[167]

There has been a long held view that the Franciscan friary in Cavan, usually referred to as St Mary's abbey, was founded in 1300. Francis J. MacKiernan in his *St Mary's abbey Cavan* quotes various seventeenth-century sources, including Brother Micheál Ó Cléirigh and Fr Thomas Fitzsimons, to make a strong case for the Cavan friary being founded in that year. This early date poses some problems, however. Cavan Franciscan friary is not named in a 1325 list of Franciscan foundations in Ireland[168] and is named in one compiled for a general chapter meeting in

165.   Chart (ed.), *The register of John Swayne*, pp 97, 198.
166.   Clyne, 'Medieval Irish Premonstratensian monasteries', i, p. 104.
167.   Colmán Ó Clabaigh, *The Friars in Ireland 1224–1540* (Dublin, 2012), pp 26, 70–72. Another Franciscan called Uilliam Ó Raghallaigh died in 1407. See Éamonn de hÓir, 'Annala as Bréifne' in *Bréifne*, iv, 13 (1970), p. 67. The head of the Irish province of the Franciscans, just like the head of Franciscan provinces elsewhere in Europe, was known as the minister provincial.
168.   Francis O'Mahony, '*Brevis synopsis provinciae Hiberniae FF. Minorum*' in *Anal. Hib.*, vi (1934), pp 142–3.

Perpignan in France in 1331[169] - leading Colmán Ó Clabaigh to conclude that the friary was built 'possibly after 1325' and before 1330.[170] The entry in the Bréifne annals for the year 1315 states that:

> Giolla Íosa Ó Raghallaigh … céadfhunduir mhainstreach an Chabháin … ar ndul is na bráithribh a ndeireadh a aoise agas a aimsire dhó; agus bás dfhagháil is an aibíd ar mbreith buadha ó dheamhan agas ó dhomhan. [Giolla Íosa Ó Raghallaigh … founder of the monastery of Cavan … joined the fraternity at the end of his age and reign; and he died in the abbey having achieved victory over the devil and the world.][171]

This entry supports the earlier date of 1300 for the foundation of the friary although fifteen years seems an exceptionally long time for Giolla Íosa to have spent in retirement there since he did not die until 1330.[172] Chevalier Thomas O'Gorman, in his eighteenth-century genealogy of the O'Reillys, a less than reliable source, states that Giolla Íosa founded the friary in 1300 and retired to it in 1326, spending the last four years of his life there.[173] We are on firmer ground when it comes to the death of Giolla Íosa Ó Raghallaigh. The Annals of the Four Masters, under the year 1330 state that:

> Giolla Íosa Roe O'Reilly, lord of Muintir Maolmordha, and of all Brefney for a long period, died at an advanced age, after gaining the palm of victory over the world and the devil, and was buried in the habit of a Franciscan friar in the monastery of Cavan, of which he was the original founder.

Cathal Ó Raghallaigh, grandfather to Giolla Íosa,[174] had founded the Premonstratensian priory at Lough Uachtair and the founding of the Franciscan friary in Cavan points towards a transference of the

169. E.B. Fitzmaurice & A.G. Little (eds), *Materials for the history of the Franciscan province in Ireland*, (Manchester, 1920), pp 133–4.
170. Ó Clabaigh, *The Friars in Ireland 1224–1540*, p. 14.
171. de hÓir, 'Annala as Bréifne', p. 65.
172. Katharine Simms accepts that the 1315 date for Giolla Íosa entering the friary 'may well be accurate'. See Katharine Simms, 'Gaelic lordships in Ulster in the later Middle Ages' (unpublished PhD thesis, TCD, 1976), i, p. 407. However, this entry in 'Annala as Bréifne' may not be reliable since it appears to indicate that Giolla Íosa died in 1315.
173. Thomas O'Gorman, *The genealogy of the very ancient and illustrious House of O'Reilly formerly princes and dynasts of Brefny O'Reilly now called the County of Cavan in the Kingdom of Ireland* (Dublin, *c.*1789), p. 56. A copy of this may be found in Cavan Central Library.
174. Carney (ed.), *A genealogical history of the O'Reillys*, p. 110.

Ó Raghallaigh patronage from the Premonstratensians to the Franciscans. Perhaps they wished to have a religious foundation nearer their new Tullachmongan castle which overlooked the friary in Cavan town.[175] In founding the Franciscan friary at Cavan the Ó Raghallaighs provided themselves with a centre of education, priests to celebrate the sacraments and a fitting place to bury their dead. The Ó Raghallaighs continued to support the friary and many of their menfolk became Franciscans, including Cuchonnacht Ó Raighallaigh who resigned as chieftain and 'for the sake of God' joined the Franciscan Order, possibly the Third Order, in 1365 and died in Cavan friary two years later.[176]

The friary in Cavan was within view of the Ó Raghallaigh stronghold on Tullachmongan hill and yet, despite appearing to be securely located, it was attacked many times. In 1390 'a great war'[177] broke out between east and west Bréifne which continued intermittently for more than a decade and in 1401 the sons of Ó Ruairc and Mag Samhradáin attacked Cavan and the Annals of Connacht state that 'it is hard to estimate the destruction [that they] wrought there'.[178] The friary needed to be rebuilt and in 1405 indulgences were granted to all penitents who:

> on the feast of the Exaltation of Holy Cross visit and give alms for the repair and conservation of the church of the house of Friars Minors of Caravallis in the diocese of Kilmore, which house and its habitations on account of the long and fierce wars in those parts, have been burned, and very many of the members of the house serving in its church slain, so that the church suffers very many defects, and is threatened with almost final ruin.[179]

The friary was again burned in 1451, this time by one of their own community. Friar Ua Mothlain 'he being inebriate after drinking wine … [and] the candle he took to his chamber was left lighting and he himself fell asleep and the chamber took fire and the whole monastery afterwards'.[180] In 1468, the friary and 'the town of O'Reilly' were burned,

175.   This transference of the O'Reilly patronage from the Premonstratensians to the Franciscans may help account, at least in part, for the relative poverty and obscurity of the Holy Trinity priory at Lough Uachtair throughout the fourteenth-century, though it seems likely that the priory also suffered greatly during the local wars.
176.   *ALC*, 1365, 1367; *AFM*, 1365.
177.   *AC*, 1390.
178.   Ibid., 1401.
179.   *CPL*, vi, p. 66.
180.   *AU*, 1451.

this time by 'the English and the Saxon [John Tiptoft]'.[181] Three years earlier, in 1465, William O'Reilly, the Franciscan minister provincial, in a futile bid to protect friaries from attack, petitioned Archbishop John Bole of Armagh for a copy of the papal bull *In quibusdam locis* – a bull which excommunicated anyone who occupied or damaged a church belonging to the friars.[182] In 1575 Mary, the granddaughter of the baron of Delvin and the second wife of Aodh Connallach Ó Raghallaigh, set fire to a house in Cavan, resulting in 'the great monastery of Cavan, and the entire town of Cavan itself, from the great castle downwards to the river' being burned and it was said 'there was not so much destroyed in any of the Irish towns as there had been there'.[183] The 'Annala as Bréifne' excuses her for this deed, explaining that she was deranged.[184]

Virtually none of the medieval ruins of Cavan Franciscan friary have survived though it appears that it compared unfavourably with some of the other large quadrangled, cloistered stone friaries elsewhere in the country.[185] The friary church in Cavan, which had 'very many defects' and was 'threatened with almost final ruin' in 1405, was, despite many devastating attacks on it in the intervening years, in relatively good shape c.1590. A detailed map of 'The Towne of the Cavan'[186] completed in the early 1590s, shows the church to be a large rectangular building with east-west orientation and crosses mounted on each gable end. A square-based external bell-tower is shown centrally situated on and adjacent to the south wall of the church.[187] Another building, of similar size to most of the houses in the town, is shown just west of the friary church. The cemetery and abbey lands were separated from the present-day Bridge Street by a long dog-legged wall which runs from the centre of the town to the Spanish style archway entrance to the friary grounds. What is striking in this beautifully crafted map is, apart

181. *AFM*, 1468.
182. Anthony Lynch, 'The administration of John Bole, archbishop of Armagh, 1457–71', *Seanchas Ard Mhacha*, xiv, 2 (1991), p. 127; Ó Clabaigh, *The Friars in Ireland, 1224–1540*, p. 166. Some interpreted this move as an attempt to prevent the Observant friars taking over Conventual friaries.
183. Ibid., 1576.
184. de hÓir, 'Annala as Bréifne', pp 73–4; MacKiernan, *St Mary's abbey Cavan*, p. 10.
185. Michael O'Neill 'Irish Franciscan friary architecture: late medieval and early modern' in Edel Bhreathnach, Joseph MacMahon & John McCafferty (eds), *The Irish Franciscans 1534–1990* (Dublin, 2009), pp 305–27. See also Canice Mooney, 'Franciscan architecture in pre-Reformation Ireland' in *RSAI*, lxxxv, 2 (1955), pp 133–73.
186. TNA, HO, Mp f. 1/81.
187. The bell-tower which has survived on the site of the Franciscan friary is not the one shown in this late sixteenth-century map but rather one which was built, or re-built, c.1750 for the Church of Ireland parish church. See *An introduction to the architectural heritage of County Cavan*, p. 39.

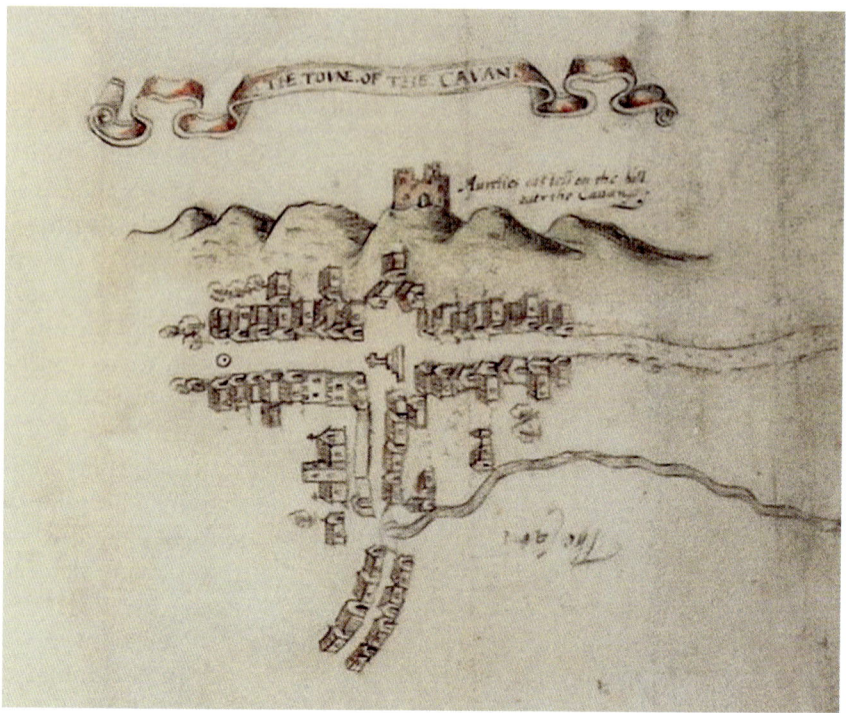

Figure 2.4: Map of Cavan town *c.*1591 showing Ó Raghaillaigh's castle and the
Franciscan friary. (*Courtesy of the National Archives, Kew*).

from the friary church and the one building to the west of it, the scarcity
of other friary buildings, though it is possible that a row of buildings
depicted west of the Kinnypottle river, also belonged to the friary.
See Fig. 2.4. Perhaps all the attacks, especially the devastating fire in
1575, less than twenty years before this map was drawn, had taken their
toll.

The Ó Raghallaigh sept, which had ceased to be patrons of the
Premonstratensian priory on Lough Uachtair *c.*1300, remained as patrons
of the Franciscan friary in Cavan throughout its three hundred year history and it was their place of choice for burying their dead.[188] Giolla Íosa
Ó Raghallaigh was buried there in 1330 and his son Cú Connacht, was

---

188. The involvement of the O'Reillys with the Franciscans continued long after the Cavan
friary was closed. Various members of the family are listed as guardians of the friary on eighteen different occasions between 1647 and 1787. See Canice Mooney, 'Some Cavan Franciscans
of the past' in *Bréifne*, i, 1 (1958), pp 25–7. Cornelius O'Reilly donated 120 *escudos* to the Irish
Franciscans at Louvain in 1616. See Mary Ann Lyons, 'The role of St Anthony's College, Louvain in establishing the Irish Franciscan college network, 1607–60' in Bhreathnach, MacMahon
& McCafferty (eds), *The Irish Franciscans 1534–1990*, p. 30.

buried there in 1367.[189] John Ó Raghallaigh, a grandson of Giolla Íosa, who died in 1401 'of a fit in his own bed in Tulach Mongain' was buried that same night in Cavan.[190] Eogan Ó Raghallaigh 'king of the two Breifni' died 'about the feast of Patrick' with 'victory of penance and was buried in the monastery of Cavan' in 1449.[191] When Aodh Conallach Ó Raghallaigh and his third wife, Isabella Barnwell, died at the same time in 1583 they were buried in the friary cemetery.[192] Edmund O'Reilly of Kilnacrott 'an aged, grey-haired man of strong memory of remote times' died at Tullachmongan in 1601 and was buried 'in the monastery of St Francis'.[193] When Captain Hugh O'Reilly, from Lisgannon in the parish of Drung, died on 10 February 1628, he too was buried in the 'Abby of Cavan'.[194] Colonel Roger Maguire was killed in 1648 as the Ulster army captured Carrick-on-Shannon from the crown forces and 'his corps was interred in S. Francis of Cavan'.[195] The Franciscan friary in Cavan provided a high-status burial ground not just for the Ó Raghallaigh family, but for other noble families of the region.

By the early fifteenth-century, less than two hundred years after the death of Francis of Assisi, a new reform movement was growing among the friars in Europe and in Ireland. This was part of a wider current that re-invigorated late medieval religious life in Europe and in Ireland the mendicant friars were its most enthusiastic proponents. The reformers felt that the Franciscans friars had drifted away from the stricter elements of their founder's rule by becoming the owners of land and accepting personal gifts from wealthy donors. In 1415 the Council of Florence took the wishes of the reformers on board and approved of the *Fratres Regularis Observantiae* or the Friars of Strict Observance. From 1460 onwards, largely due to the leadership of Friar Nehemias O'Donohoe, new Observant friaries were founded in Ireland and some of the already established Conventual friaries began to adopt the new reforms. It would appear that the Cavan friary was slow to accept the new reforms and in 1502 the reforms were imposed on the community by John Ó Raghallaigh, lord of east Bréifne, who had been empowered by Rome to do so.[196] The fact that the two

189. *AFM*, 1365, 1367.
190. *AU*, 1401.
191. Ibid., 1449. Throughout Ireland members of local aristocratic families, especially those who were patrons of the Franciscans, were given the privilege of being buried inside the friary church. See Ó Clabaigh, *The Friars in Ireland 1224–1540*, pp 108–10.
192. *AFM*, 1583.
193. Ibid., 1601.
194. Quoted in Eoghan Moore, 'Captain Hugh O'Reilly of Lisgannon' in *Bréifne*, xiii, 51(2016), p. 781.
195. Gilbert, *A contemporary history*, i, p. 281.
196. *AFM*, 1502 & *AU*, 1502. See also *AFM*, 1510 which reports the death of John O'Reilly who was 'the first to establish the order of friars *de observantia* at Cavan by the authority of the pope'.

earlier dates of 1492 and 1495 were also given for this reform in Cavan friary suggests that the change may have been strongly resisted and even temporarily reversed.[197]

Tragedy struck the Cavan friary in 1516 when it was reported that 'a large party of Friars of Cavan were drowned upon Loch-Erne and two Friars of [Stricter] Observance [were] in it, namely John Mag Craith … and Nicholas O'Cathain and other persons with them'.[198] This report suggests that the others were Conventual friars and so it seems that Conventual and Observant friars lived alongside one another in Cavan for some considerable time after 1502. Judging by their names it would appear that the two Observant friars who drowned in 1516 came from friaries in north-east Ulster, perhaps Downpatrick or Carrickfergus. There must have been considerable movement between the various Franciscan friaries in Ulster because in 1495 Toirdelbach Ua Neill, a friar minor of the community of Ard-Macha, was killed in Cavan by a kick from his own horse[199] and Patrick Brady, possibly from east Bréifne, was guardian of Monaghan Franciscan friary when it was attacked by English soldiers in 1589.[200]

Many members of the Ó Raghallaigh and other east Bréifne families entered the novitiate in Cavan and rose to positions of leadership in the Order in Ireland and in the Irish Franciscan colleges which were later established throughout Europe. William O'Reilly, a man of 'Irrysche blode, name and nacion'[201] had studied at Oxford and was a professor of theology before he was appointed the first Gaelic Franciscan minister provincial in 1445.[202] His appointment exacerbated the existing tensions in Ireland between the friars from Anglo Irish and Gaelic backgrounds. This resulted in objections and complaints against O'Reilly from the former group to both the king and to Pope Nicholas V. Among the charges made against William O'Reilly were that he was a rebel and was 'unfaithful and disobedient' to the king.[203] He was summoned to Clonmel to answer these charges before the bishop of Lismore and the dean of Cashel. He declined to go 'on account of wars, notoriously raging in those parts and of a writ to arrest him obtained under false

197.   Colmán Ó Clabaigh, *The Franciscans in Ireland, 1400–1534, from reform to reformation* (Dublin, 2002), p. 65.
198.   *AU*, 1516.
199.   Ibid., 1495.
200.   *Brevis synopsis*, p. 176.
201.   Bodleian Library, Rawlinson MS B 484, f. 18.
202.   Benignus Millet states that he was made minister provincial in 1446. See Millett, 'The Irish Franciscans and education in late medieval times and the early Counter-Reformation, 1230–1630', p. 12.
203.   *CPL*, x, p. 620.

pretences'.[204] Because of his failure to go to Clonmel two friars of Anglo Irish background were appointed in his place. William O'Reilly successfully appealed this decision to Rome and was restored as minister provincial in 1454. He showed considerable resilience by remaining in that position until *c*.1471, despite continued opposition. His period as minister provincial was a watershed for the Franciscan friars in Ireland with Gaelic friars gaining ascendancy and he facilitated both Observant and Conventual friaries being set up in previously neglected Gaelic areas.[205] However, it was not until 1508, approximately 200 years after the Cavan friary was established, that the Observant Franciscan friary of Creevelea was founded by Margaret and Eoghan Ó Ruairc, ensuring a strong Franciscan presence in west as well as east Bréifne.

During the period 1140 to 1300 six religious communities, Kells, Drumlane, Fore, Kilmainhamwood, Lough Uachtair and Cavan were set up in the extended diocese of Tír Briúin/Kells. From *c*.1300 onwards two of these - Kells and Fore - would no longer be within the borders of the contracted diocese, though links, financial and otherwise, would remain. And since the Kilmainhamwood foundation was on the periphery of the diocese and had virtually no impact on it, there were, in effect, just three religious communities in Kilmore, all grouped together in a small triangle less than eight miles apart, in lake-land country in the middle of east Bréifne. Large sections of the diocese, particularly west Bréifne, were untouched by the setting up of the new continental style religious communities, a development which was such an important aspect of the twelfth-century Church reform in Ireland. The religious communities set up in Ireland in the twelfth and thirteenth centuries were mostly located in the south and east of Ireland with large swathes of the diocese of Tír Briúin and much of the north west of Ireland being left without any religious community at all.[206] The Augustinians of Drumlane, the Premonstratensians of Lough Uachtair and the Franciscans of Cavan town, all played a role in the twelfth-century inspired reform and in the sacramental life and pastoral care of the people of the diocese.[207] However, because of their

204. Ibid.
205. For information on William O'Reilly see Ó Clabaigh, *The Friars in Ireland 1224–1540*, pp 70–2; Mooney, 'Some Cavan Franciscans of the past' pp 18–9. For details of the expansion of Franciscan friaries into Gaelic areas see map in Bhreathnach, MacMahon & McCafferty (eds), *The Irish Franciscans 1534–1990*, p. 306; Lynch, 'The administration of John Bole, Archbishop of Armagh, 1457–71', p. 127; Watt, *The church in medieval Ireland*, pp 184–5.
206. For distribution of religious communities throughout Ireland see OPW *Map of Monastic Ireland* (Dublin, 1959).
207. Other religious communities based nearby in the neighbouring diocese of Ardagh also had an impact on the medieval and early modern diocese of Kilmore. This is particularly true of Fenagh and to a lesser extent the Augustinians of Inismór island in Lough Gowna.

small number and their geographical location adjacent to one another, the impact of the religious orders in medieval Tír Briúin was less than their impact in many other dioceses of Ireland, particularly those to the south and the east.

Creevelea Franciscan Friary

This Franciscan friary, which was founded in Creevelea by the Ó Ruaircs in 1508, was situated just across the River Bonet from Dromahair in the diocese of Ardagh. It merits inclusion in this volume because it was an Ó Ruairc foundation and because of the great contribution the Franciscans made in west Bréifne for a period of more than 300 years. Towards the end of the fifteenth-century the Observant church reform, which advocated a stricter observance of the rule of St Francis, was gaining considerable momentum among the Franciscan friars in the north west of Ireland. The establishment of the Observant Franciscan friary in Donegal in 1474 by Fionnguala Ó Brien and her husband Aedh Ó Domhnaill was an important development in this process.[208] Fionnguala's sister, Margaret, who was married to Eoghan Ó Ruairc, was instrumental in setting up the Observant Franciscan friary at Creevelea thirty-four years later and this cooperation between the two sisters resulted in the first friars being brought to Creevelea from the Franciscan house in Donegal.[209] The annals are quite specific about both the location and the founders of the friary at Creevelea:

> The monastery of the town of O'Rourke, which is called Carrickpatrick, in Connacht in the diocese of Ardagh, was founded by O'Rourke, [that is] Eoghan and by his wife Margaret, the daughter of Conor O'Brien.[210]

Three years after it was founded, Thomas MacBradaigh the 'bishop and archdeacon of the two Breffnys' went to Creevelea to dedicate the friary chapel and died while there.

When Aedh Rua O'Domhnaill and his wife Fionnguala founded the Franciscan house in Donegal in 1474 they 'wanted it to be dedicated to God and the friars of St Francis for the benefit of their souls and for the purpose of forming a burying place for themselves and their posterity'.[211]

---

208.   *AFM*, 1474.
209.   Brendan Jennings (ed.), 'Brussels MS 3947: Donatus Moneyus de Provincia Hiberniae S. Francisci', *Anal. Hib.*, vi (1934), pp 48–9.
210.   *AFM*, 1508. For an aerial view of the substantial ruins of the Franciscan friary at Creevelea see Michael J. Moore, *An introduction to the architectural heritage of County Leitrim* (Dublin, 2004), p. 8.
211.   Ibid., 1474.

The Ó Ruaircs had similar motives for setting up the new friary at Creevelea because, with a scarcity of religious houses and high status burial grounds in west Bréifne, they tended to bury their dead in the Dominican friary in Sligo. When Áine, wife of Tighearnán Ó Ruairc, the 'most excellent of the women of Leth Chuinn' died at Garadice Lake in 1386 her body was taken the long distance to Sligo for burial.[212] Margaret Uí Ruairc, in founding the friary of Creevelea had created a fitting burial place for the Ó Ruaircs and she was buried there just five years after the friary was founded:

> Mairgrec, daughter of Conchobar O Briain and wife of O Ruairc, radiant paragon of the Gaels, to whom God gave prosperity and royal state and great wealth; hearth of hospitality and maintenance, humanity and charitable entertainment for scholars and ollavs, the weak and the wretched and all, whether mighty or outcast, who stood in need thereof; one who never as long as she lived denied any man craving a boon; died after Unction and Penance and was buried in the monastery which she herself had built to the honour of God and St Francis, namely the monastery of Creevelea.[213]

The Annals of Ulster state that 'she was buried in a wooden church [which] she herself had built for the Friars Minor close by Druim-da-ethiar'[214] – presumably the church which Bishop Thomas MacBradaigh had consecrated two years earlier. Her husband Eoghan Ó Ruairc retired to the friary and in 1528 'died in the habit of St Francis after extreme unction and repentance' and was buried alongside his wife.[215]

In the early decades of its existence the friary at Creevelea, like many other religious houses in medieval times, was used as a sanctuary where people sought refuge and deposited their valuables for safe-keeping. It soon became clear that Creevelea friary was not a secure sanctuary because in 1532 Owen Ó Ruairc, 'a distinguished gentleman', was killed by O'Mulvey and his kinsmen in 'the monastery of Dromahaire'.[216] Four years later a fire started accidently during the night and much of the monastery was destroyed together with a considerable amount

212. *AC*, 1386.
213. *AC*, 1513. See also Lyons, 'Lay female piety and church patronage in late medieval Ireland', p. 60; McKenna, 'Women as patrons of the arts in medieval Ireland', p. 91.
214. *AU*, 1512.
215. *AFM*, 1528.
216. Ibid., 1532.

of property which had been stored there for safe-keeping.[217] Two friars, Ereman Ua Domnaill and Mael-Sechlainn Mag Samradháin, lost their lives in the fire.[218] The former may have been one of the founding friars from Donegal and the latter a more recent recruit from the diocese of Kilmore. The friary was rebuilt, presumably shortly after this fire, by Brian Ballach Ó Ruairc.[219] Substantial stone ruins of the rebuilt friary, with intricate carvings and tracery, have survived.[220] King Henry VIII's Reformation started in England just twenty six years after Creevelea friary was founded. However, being firmly established in the Gaelic territory of west Bréifne, Creevelea lay largely undisturbed for another half century.

217.   *ALC*, 1536; *AU*, 1536; Ó Clabaigh, *The Friars in Ireland 1224–1540*, p. 211; idem, *The Franciscans in Ireland, 1400–1534*, p. 63.

218.   *AU*, 1536. Donagh Mooney wrote that 'Heremon O'Donnell … perished in the flames whilst striving to save the sacred vessels.' See C.P. Meehan, *The rise and fall of the Irish Franciscan monasteries* (Dublin, 1872), pp 83–4.

219.   Gwynn & Hadcock, *Medieval religious houses in Ireland*, p. 248. Canice Mooney states that the building of Creevelea friary was 'never completed.' See Mooney 'Franciscan architecture in pre-Reformation Ireland', p. 168 and Archdall, *Monasticon Hibernicum*, p. 408.

220.   Moore, *Archaeological inventory of County Leitrim*, pp 177–8; Robert Cochrane *Creevelea abbey Co. Leitrim, National Monument No. 69* (Dublin, n.d.), pp 1–19; O'Neill, 'Irish Franciscan friary architecture', pp 316–8. For the plan of the friary see Tadhg O'Keefe, *Medieval Irish Buildings 1100–1600* (Dublin, 2015), p. 153.

Chapter 3

Rectories, Vicarages and Clerical Lineages

The Gregorian reform of the twelfth-century led to the introduction of new religious Orders in Ireland, the establishment of dioceses and the dividing up of those dioceses into vicarages or areas of pastoral care. Much research has been carried out in recent decades on the setting up of parishes and there are different views on when and how this happened. One perspective is that while parishes had been established in England by the middle of the tenth-century they were considerably later in Celtic countries with the parishes in Ireland being formed only in the second half of the twelfth and throughout much of the thirteenth centuries. Within Ireland this process was said to have happened much more quickly in Anglo-Norman controlled territories than it did in Gaelic Ireland.[1] Another perspective, which has been gaining traction in recent years, is that there was a pre-Norman network of parishes in Ireland with each tuath having its own church and fixed parochial boundaries.[2]

Both of these perspectives agree that the bishops, following the twelfth-century reform, placed great emphasis on having an adequate parish network within their newly established dioceses. However, as Paddy Duffy has pointed out:

> The erection of such parishes did not necessarily mean ex-
> tensive creation of parochial territories *de novo*. The reform

---

1.   K.W. Nicholls, 'Rectory, vicarage and parish in the western Irish dioceses' in *JRSAI*, 101 (1971), p. 53; Elizabeth Fitzpatrick & Raymond Gillespie (eds), *The parish in medieval and early modern Ireland* (Dublin, 2006), pp 15–16.
2.   For this perspective see Richard Sharpe, 'Churches and communities in early medieval Ireland: towards a pastoral care model' in J. Blair & R. Sharpe (eds), *Pastoral care before the parish* (Leicester, 1992), pp 81–109; P.J. Duffy, 'The shape of the parish' in Fitzpatrick & Gillespie (eds), *The parish in medieval and early modern Ireland*, pp 33–61; Paul MacCotter, 'Túath, manor and parish: the kingdom of Fír Maige, cantred of Fermoy' in *Peritia*, 22–23, pp 224–74; idem, 'Parish, pastoral care and tuath in the diocese of Limerick c.1201' in *JRSAI*, 2012, pp 86–98. My thanks to Paul MacCotter for his insights on rectories, vicarages and parishes.

of the parochial structures might more properly be seen as a regularisation of pre-existing territories into proto-parishes …[3]

In the diocese of Bréifne/Tír Briúin, all of which was *inter Hibernicos* and much of which was largely inaccessible, the setting up of par-ishes was previously thought to have been later than in many other dioceses. The survival into the later middle-ages of the large rectories of Muintir Eolais and Dartry in present-day County Leitrim and the almost complete absence of parishes in the Tír Briúin ecclesiastical taxation lists of 1302-1306 would seem to bolster this viewpoint.[4] However, it is obvious that the diocesan taxation list is incomplete and it is possible that a network of parishes, based on the earlier tuath divisions, was already in place by then.

There is general consensus that a parochial system, much like the modern-day parish network, was long-established by 1400. However, the records in the Calendar of Papal Registers for Tír Briúin/Kilmore during the period 1394–1503 and those in the Annates for the period 1400–1535 refer regularly, not to the parishes of the diocese, but rather to the rectories and vicarages in it and in this chapter we will take a closer look at these ecclesiastical territories and at some of the clerical families that controlled them.

Rectories

In modern times a rectory is understood to be the house in which a rector lives. In medieval times a rectory was a geographical area, varying greatly in size from place to place, which paid a portion of its tithes to a rector or to a religious house. The rector may or may not have been a priest and he, in some instances, had no obligation to care pastorally for the people within his rectory. This pastoral care was carried out by the vicar. Kenneth Nicholls describes how the system where every parish had both a sine-cure rector and a vicar evolved and how the tithes of the parishes came to be divided between them:

> Originally … the rector or parson had been the parish priest and had received the entire tithe; however, with the coming of the custom of impropriation, by which the parochial rev-enues were vested in a religious house, and with the increase

3.   Duffy, 'The shape of the parish', p. 55.
4.   H.S. Sweetman & G.F. Handcock (eds), *Calendar of documents relating to Ireland 1302–1307* (London, 1886), p. 213.

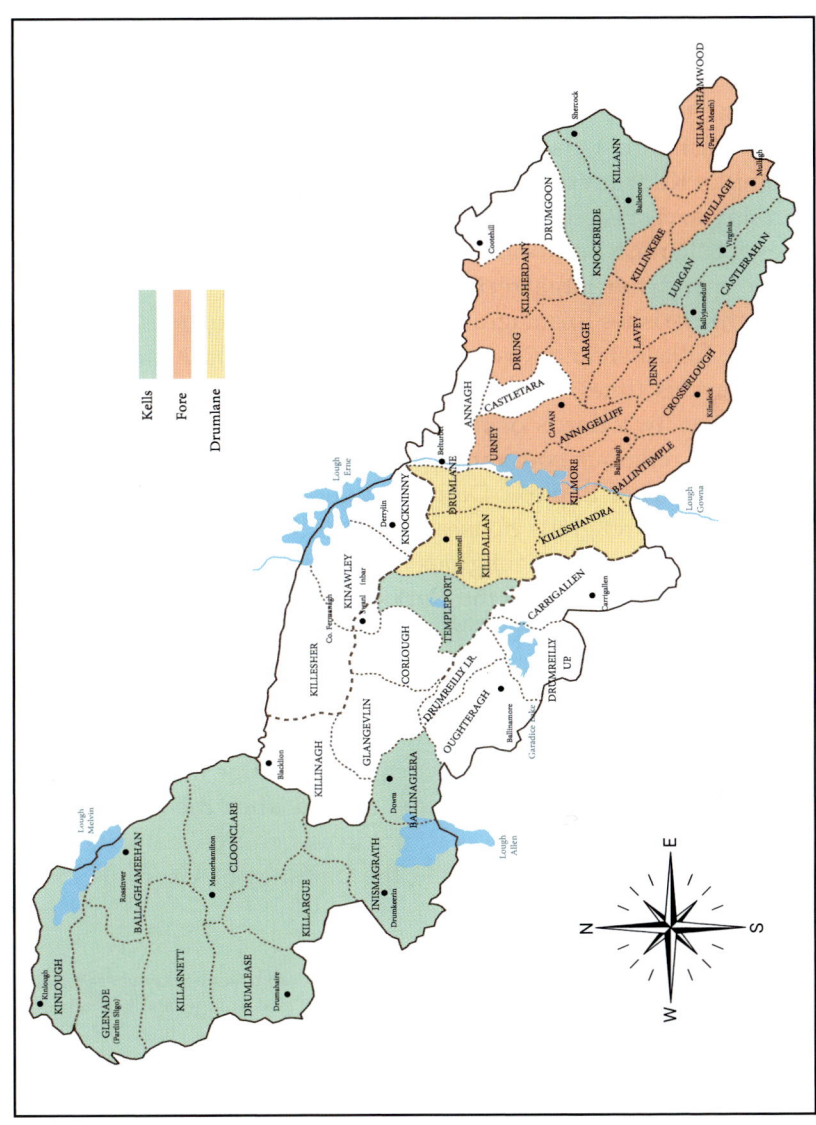

Figure 3.1: The parishes of Kilmore which paid tithes to the religious houses of Kells, Fore and Drumlane.

of the practice of granting rectories as benefices for the support of clerks who were actively engaged elsewhere, in study or in official work, it became necessary to provide vicars who would perform the actual duties of the cure.[5]

As we have already noted the rectorial tithes of a considerable portion of the diocese went to the abbey of Kells, the priory of Fore and, to a lesser extent, to the priory of Drumlane. Fore received tithes from the parishes of Kilmore, Urney, Annagelliff, Laragh, Lavey, Drung, Denn, Ballintemple, Kildrumferton (Crosserlough), Killinkere, Mullagh and Kilsherdany in east Bréifne.[6] The abbey of Kells received tithes from the parishes of Killann, Knockbride, Castlerahan, Lurgan, Munterconnacht, Templeport and the large rectory of Dartry in west Bréifne which included the parishes Inismagrath, Killargue, Cloonlogher, Cloonclare, Drumlease, Killasnett and Rossinver.[7] The priory of Drumlane received tithes, at various times, from Drumlane, Killeshandra and Kildallan.[8] Approximately two thirds of the diocese paid tithes to one or other of these three religious communities. This is in contrast to the other northern dioceses of Raphoe, Derry and Clogher where very little of the tithes went to religious houses.[9] Because so many of the rectories in the diocese paid tithes to religious houses there were fewer pickings or benefices without cure for the clerks or priests of the diocese. This resulted in greater competition for the rectories that were available, particularly the more lucrative ones such as Cinéal Luacháin in Leitrim and Kedy, a rectory near Cavan town.

The rectories in the diocese did not always correspond to parish boundaries nor were they always named after a church. Some of them such as the rectory of Kedy, named after the townland of Keadew in the parish of Urney, was 'not in any church'[10] and received tithes from particular townlands in the parishes of Urney, Kilmore

5. Nicholls, 'Rectory, vicarage and parish', p. 54.
6. Paul MacCotter dates the granting of these rectories to Fore to somewhere between 1211 and 1226, the short period of the de Lacy dominance in east Bréifne, and he suggests the granting of the rectories in west Bréifne to Kells took place between the years 1221 and 1226. See MacCotter, 'The early history and sub-division of the kingdom of Bréifne', pp 43–4.
7. Paul MacCotter, *Medieval Ireland, territorial, political and economic divisions* (Dublin, 2008), p. 220; Costello, *De Annatis Hiberniae*, i, p. 241; *Calendar of Irish patent rolls of James I*, pp 587–8.
8. *De Annatis Hiberniae*, i, p. 242; *Calendar of Irish patent rolls of James I*, p. 386.
9. See Nicholls, 'Rectory, vicarage and parish in western Irish dioceses' pp 55, 59.
10. *CPL*, vi, p. 121.

and Annagelliff.[11] Other rectories, such as Cinéal Luacháin, which included the churches of Drumreilly and Oughteragh and 'are wont to be governed by one rector only'[12] were considerably larger and in 1422 the rector, Maurice Ó Floinn, a priest of the diocese, was granted the additional rectory of Cúil Ó bhFloinn (Carrigallen) - bringing his income from both rectories to fourteen marks.[13] However, even these combined rectories were considerably smaller than the adjacent great rectory of Muintir Eolais which generally included all the parishes in present-day south Leitrim which are in the diocese of Ardagh. The rectory of 'Dartragie and Brefnichiar' in west Bréifne, 'which does not take its name from … any church, and whose holder receives tithes in diverse parishes'[14] consisted of a large portion of north Leitrim which is in the diocese of Kilmore. The rectorial tithes of Dartry were considerable, being valued at sixteen marks in 1412.[15] Most of modern-day County Leitrim was included in the two great rectories of Muintir Eolais and Dartry and all except one of the churches (Kiltrennan) in Muintir Eolais were parish churches as were both churches in Cinéal Luacháin.

Other rectories in the diocese, such as the rectory St Brighid and Fincheall in Kilsherdany[16] and St Patrick's rectory in Annagelliff[17] took their names from particular churches. The rectory of St Patrick's Drumgoon was to be granted in 1407 to Luke Oqueogan (Keogan) 'if he was found fit'.[18] He held the rectory for more than ten years before it was taken from him and apparently granted to Philip Macgillayssa, a priest of the diocese, who died in 1427. In that year the rectory was granted to David Omochan who, although not yet ordained a priest, had been granted the perpetual vicarage of the nearby parish of Kilsherdany in anticipation of his taking major orders.[19]

11.   1622 Visitation, TCD, MS 550, p. 144. William Dungan told an inquisition held in Cavan in 1736 that the rectory of Kedy 'consists of 39 ½ poles: Tirequin, with other lands belonging to the Cavan Free School; Drumboe, the two poles of Cullys, Latt and (?), Drumkeene, Lysdareene, Tullinlough, the two poles of Drimblish, Sweland with all its subdenominations, Derrycramps (?), Drumconwick, Shantorne, Killnevarra, Rosscolgan, Keadue and the abbey lands of the two Drimevanaghs, Drimalees and the green of Cavan with all the parks and gardens about the town (except Lurganboy).' See 'The Nugent papers' in *Anal. Hib.*, xx (1958), p. 182.
12.   *CPL*, vii, p. 228.
13.   Ibid., p. 229.
14.   Costello, *De Annatis Hiberniae*, i, p. 244; *CPL*, vi, p. 257.
15.   *CPL*, vi, pp 244, 257.
16.   Costello, *De Annatis Hiberniae*, i, p. 233–4.
17.   It was valued at only 3 marks in 1407. See *CPL*, vi, p. 121.
18.   *CPL*, vi, p. 120.
19.   MacKiernan, *Diocese of Kilmore*, p. 144; *CPL*, vii, pp 485–6.

The rectories were almost always *sine cure* (without a duty of pastoral care) and in lay patronage, while the vicars who looked after the pastoral needs of the people were appointed either by the bishop, the religious house to which the rectory paid tithes, or in certain circumstances by the archbishop of Armagh or even the pope. These sinecures, whether held by religious communities or by individual rectors, were highly prized and as such were a source of contention throughout the fifteenth-century. Some of the rectories which were not paying tithes to religious houses were held in successive generations by different members of clerical families. In 1407 Nemeas O'Fay, a priest of the diocese, was granted both the perpetual vicarage of St Maolán (Annagh)[20] valued at five marks and the perpetual benefice without cure of the rectory of Bali Mictonchabuil, a rectory in the Magherintemple area of the parish of Drung, which was valued at three marks.[21] Fourteen years later, in 1421, he was deprived of this rectory, now devalued to two marks, and it was granted to his son Adam O'Fay, a clerk.[22] Adam was granted the rectory 'provided that the fact that he is the illegitimate son of the said Nemeas (begotten, however, before his father took orders) shall not be a cause of scandal to the people there, and that no one else has a special right in the same'.[23] It would appear that both father and son were granted the rectory to help them with their studies before they took major orders. Adam held the rectory in 1423[24] and still retained it after 1450 by which time he too had been ordained a priest and appointed the perpetual vicar of Annagh.[25]

Cinéal Luacháin

The rectories were established before the vicarages and it appears that Drumreilly, a high status church in the townland of Cully beside Garadice Lake, was the principal church for the rectory of Cinéal Luacháin. Later the perpetual vicarage or parish of Oughteragh was carved out of the centre of Cinéal Luacháin, thereby dividing Drumreilly vicarage into two separate areas, both of which are still in the civil parish of Drumreilly. Later the northern portion would become known as Ballinaglera while the southern area continued to be known as Drumreilly.[26]

20.   For St Maolán of Annagh see Ó Riain, *A dictionary of Irish saints*, p. 447. His feast day was on 4 January. See also Todd and Reeves (eds), *The martyrology of Donegal*, p. 7.
21.   *CPL*, vi, 120.
22.   *CPL*, vii, p. 159.
23.   Costello, *De Annatis Hiberniae*, i, p. 245.
24.   Ibid., p. 230.
25.   *CPL*, x, p. 445. See also *CPL*, viii, pp 374–5. Interestingly, the O'Fay family, more than any other clerical family in the diocese, gave Old Testament names to their children.
26.   This southern portion of the parish would subsequently be divided into upper and lower Drumreilly.

The rectory of Cinéal Luacháin was controlled for much of the fifteenth-century by the Ó Maolmochéirghe (Earley) family, a clerical family based in the parish of Drumreilly who held the vicarages of Oughteragh and Drumreilly for considerable periods. However, two other clerical families from adjacent parishes, the Ó Floinns from Carrigallen and the Ó Rodocháins from Fenagh in the diocese of Ardagh, succeeding in wresting it from them at times, leading to considerable conflict between these families over both the rectory and vicarage.[27] Gelasius Ó Maolmochéirghe (Giolla Íosa Earley), a priest of the diocese of Tír Briúin, was in 1401 given the rectory, a benefice valued annually at ten marks, following the death of Robert Macneill.[28] He held the benefice untroubled until *c*.1409 when Luke O'Rodocháin, a clerk of the diocese of Ardagh, persuaded Alexander V, one of the claimants to the papacy during the Great Western Schism, that the rectory was unclaimed and so it was given to him. Gelasius appealed the decision and those mandated to hear the appeal 'granted the rectory to Luke and imposed perpetual silence on Gelasius'.[29] Following the protracted dispute between Gelasius Ó Maolmochéirghe and Luke Ó Rodocháin and the death of the latter *c*.1421, Maurice Ó Floinn, a priest of the diocese of Tír Briúin, sought and apparently was granted the rectories of both Cinéal Luacháin and Cúil Ó bhFloinn in 1422.[30]

The use of the rectorial tithes to subsidise students is exemplified in the case of Maurice Ó Maolmochéirghe who, having got a dispensation from the bishop of Kilmore as the son of unmarried parents, became 'a clerk' and took minor orders. He then set about getting an income from rectorial tithes and in 1445/6 was granted the rectory of Cinéal Luacháin.[31] He wrote to Rome, in that same year, complaining, and probably overstating, that:

> in divers rectories or churches and other rural benefices situate in the deaneries of Drumlaan [Drumlane] and Datraie [Dartry] in the said diocese [Kilmore] … through the fault of the clerks to whom the said rectories have been wont to be let … divine worship has almost entirely ceased;

27.   For a detailed account of this conflict see St John D. Seymour, 'Drumreilly and its clergy' in *JRSAI*, v, 2 (Dec. 1935), pp 245–53; Earley & Boyle, 'Conflict over the rectory of Cinel Luachain during the fifteenth-century', pp 103–13; Seymour, 'The coarb in the medieval Irish church' in *PRIA'*, pp 226–7, 230.
28.   *CPL*, v, p. 447.
29.   *CPL*, vi, p. 509.
30.   Costello, *De Annatis Hiberniae*, i, p. 230; *CPL*, vii, pp 228–9.
31.   *CPL*, ix, p. 506.

and that the hospitality which [he] ought to keep up by
reason of certain lands that he holds has become impossible
on account of the slenderness of the rents of the said lands
and of his other burdens.[32]

It may have been more difficult to obtain these 'divers rectories' as
these tithes went either to the bishop of Kilmore or the Augustinian
abbey of Kells. His attempts to secure the Cinéal Luacháin tithes
were successful, however, and by 1460, having completed his studies
he was not only a priest of the diocese of Kilmore but also a canon of
the recently established cathedral chapter.[33]

The Ó Maolmochéirghe family were coarbs of Drumreilly and
Maurice Ó Maolmochéirghe's reference to 'the hospitality which [he]
ought to keep up by reason of certain lands that he holds' points to
his obligation to provide a *teach aoidh* or house of hospitality for the
poor, by virtue of the fact that he held the termon lands of Drumreilly
parish church.[34] Obviously the income from the termon lands was
insufficient for him to provide this hospitality and Maurice used
the tithes he received to augment his income from the church lands
in order to provide it. Sometime before 1476 Maurice resigned the
rectory, giving it to John Ó Raghallaigh II who was bishop of Kilmore
from 1465 until 1476.[35] The bishop 'on realising that the fruits of the
said hospital were insufficient for the keeping of hospitality therein'
and with the consent of the cathedral chapter of Kilmore, united the
rectory of Cinéal Luacháin and the 'poor hospital [*hospitalis pauperum*]
of the place of Drumerlbelaid'.[36] This diocesan decision to unite
the rectory of Cinéal Luacháin and the hospital of Drumreilly was
confirmed by the pope in 1479 when John Ó Maolmochéirghe was
granted permission to take 'possession of it [the rectory] and convert
its fruits etc to the uses of the said hospital and poor forever'.[37] This
new arrangement seems to have worked and the Ó Maolmochéirghe
family flourished. In 1536 Cathal Ó Maolmochéirghe, 'a man of lasting
hospitality and affluence'[38] died and in 1579 'John O'Maelmocheirghe

---

32. Ibid, p. 478.
33. *CPL*, xii, pp 67–8; *CPL*, xiii, 2, p. 650.
34. Catherine Marie O'Sullivan, *Hospitality in medieval Ireland 900–1500* (Dublin, 2004),
p. 155; Gwynn & Hadcock, *Medieval religious houses*, p. 382.
35. MacKiernan, *Diocese of Kilmore*, p. 13; *CPL*, xiii, 2, p. 650.
36. *CPL*, xiii, 2, p. 650; Patrick Logan, 'Medieval hospital system in Bréifne' in *Bréifne*, iv,
13 (1970), p. 55.
37. *CPL*, xiii, 2, p. 650.
38. *AFM*, 1536; *ALC*, 1536.

Figure 3.2: Papal seal found at Clogh Uachtair castle in 1987. (*Courtesy of Conleth Manning*).

… coarb of Druim-Oirghialla [Drumreilly], the most eminent man in Eirinn for keeping a general house of hospitality for the men of Eirinn, and of the world (as many of them as he could supply) died'.[39] This period of prosperity came to an abrupt end in March 1590 when:

> The Saxons … [with] an immense army having being sent into Muinter Eolais to subdue O'Ruairc, stayed four nights at Druim Oiriallaigh and extracted 'the pledges of Cenel-Luachain … [and] pledges from the comarb of Druim-Oiriallaigh … both church and territory came with the Saxons on that occasion.[40]

The hospital of Rossinver, like the one in Drumreilly, was struggling to provide the care expected of it and in 1532 Bartholomew Ó Fergus, the rector of the hospital, petitioned Pope Clement VII to grant him the perpetual vicarage of the parish church of St Maodhóg stating that he exercised continual hospitality there and that if 'the said vicarage were united to the Hospital aforesaid, so long as he should possess it, the wants of Christ's poor as well as his own needs would be better' cared for.[41] The vicarage had been held without proper canonical title by Bartholomew Ó Mithín (Meehan), a clerk of the diocese. The pope allowed the vicarage and hospital of Rossinver to be joined, provided 'the said vicarage shall

39.   *ALC*, 1579.
40.   Ibid., 1590.
41.   Costello, *De Annatis Hiberniae*, i, p. 254.

not, on account of this union, be defrauded of its usual spiritual services nor the care of souls be therein in any way neglected'.[42]

Letters were being sent back and forth between the diocese of Kilmore and the Vatican throughout the late medieval and early modern period. The letters coming from Rome carried leaden papal seals 'with Saints Peter and Paul on one side and the name and number of the pope on the other'.[43] Half of one such seal was found during excavations, led by Conleth Manning, at Clogh Uachtair castle in 1987. The seal carries the name of one of the popes named Clement, perhaps Clement VII mentioned above who was pope from 1523–1534 or Clement VIII who was pope from 1592–1605.

The Rectory of Kedy

The rectory of Kedy, close by to Cavan town, was controlled for most of the fifteenth-century by the O'Sheridans in much the same way that the Ó Maolmochéirghe family controlled the rectory of Cinéal Luacháin. Thomas O'Sheridan held the rectory of Kedy and Denis O'Sheridan the vicarage of Urney in the late 1300s with both of them dying *c*.1400. Thomas O'Sheridan, a son of Denis the late vicar of Urney, was in 1401 granted the rectory 'to which the pope has recently annexed, united and incorporated the perpetual vicarage of St Brighid, Urnagy [Urney]' presumably in the expectation that the rector would, in the not too distant future, be ordained a priest.[44] However, Thomas O'Sheridan did not take major orders and in 1407 he resigned the rectory in favour of his son John, a move approved by Rome, and after which John took only minor orders, receiving the tonsure.[45] Approximately fifteen years later, however, John O'Sheridan either was deprived of the rectory by Nicholas MacBradaigh, the bishop of Kilmore who died in 1421, or else resigned it to John Swayne the archbishop of Armagh, while the See of Kilmore was vacant.[46] It is also possible that he was deprived of the rectory as the bishop and some of the O'Sheridans had been in dispute for some time.

In March 1427 Patrick O'Sheridan, a priest and perpetual vicar of Kilmore, having studied canon and civil law at Oxford, put his canon lawyer skills to use by writing to Rome, and asking that

42. Ibid.
43. Manning, *Clogh Oughter castle*, p. 99.
44. *CPL*, v, pp 453–4.
45. Ibid.,vi, 121. The vicarage of Urney was said to be held unlawfully at this time by Donald Omolbride, a priest of the diocese of Kilmore who had in 1394 been made a canon of the diocese of Ardagh 'in expectation of a prebend.' See *CPL*, iv, p. 470.
46. *CPL*, vii, p. 503.

Andrew MacBradaigh, a clerk of the diocese who he claimed unduly detained possession of the rectory of Kedy for more than four years, be deprived of it.[47] His efforts were unsuccessful and instead in December of 1427 Andrew MacBradaigh, who was now thirty-one years old, still in minor orders and dean of the rural deanery of Drumlane, was ratified by Rome as the rector of Kedy even though he already held the rectory of 'Bali Mcancobayl', in the nearby parish of Drung.[48]

The O'Sheridan Clerical Family

The O'Sheridans, just like the Ó Maolmochéirghe family in Drumreilly, held rectories and were the erenaghs of church or termon land. However, the termon land the O'Sheridans held in the parish of Kilmore was also being claimed by the O'Reillys. Patrick O'Sheridan was quarrelsome by nature. He not only brought accusations against his bishop but also, in his capacity as perpetual vicar of Kilmore and erenagh of the termon lands of Breandrum townland in that parish, wrote to John Swayne, the archbishop of Armagh, complaining that the O'Reillys were preventing him from getting certain tithes and other benefits he was entitled to. In response Archbishop Swayne wrote to the clergy of Kilmore diocese on 31 July 1428 telling them to:

> Admonish Owen Orayly, capt of his nation, Donald Orayly and other lay subjects of said diocese, who have obstructed said lands justly belonging to said herenach, and prevented him and his tenants there from their cultivation and peaceful inhabitation … and further to admonish certain sons of iniquity who detain and conceal certain tithes and other emoluments belonging to the said herenach, both by reason of said church of Kilmore and of said lands, and refuse to desist, to leave the said lands free, empty and unobstructed.[49]

The culprits were ordered by the archbishop to restore the tithes and other obventions within fifteen days, to refrain from interfering in the future and were told to make satisfaction or else face excommunication.[50] The actions of Patrick O'Sheridan in challenging both the ecclesiastical and secular powers in Bréifne demonstrate the

---

47. *CPL*, vii, p. 483. See also Chart (ed.), *The register of John Swayne*, p. 79.
48. Ibid., p. 503.
49. Ibid., p. 97.
50. Ibid.

increased status of the O'Sheridans and the overweening confidence
of an individual diocesan priest of that family who, with the benefit
a university education and qualifications in 'both laws', fought tooth
and nail to secure a sizeable income for himself.

The dispute between the O'Sheridans and the O'Reillys erupted
again twenty-four years later, this time over termon land in the
townland of Tonymore in the parish of Kilmore. In 1452 Cormac
O'Sheridan, a canon in the diocese and erenagh of lands in the parish
of Kilmore, wrote to Archbishop John Swayne complaining that the
O'Reillys and others were trespassing on his lands in Tonymore
and also that his bishop, Andrew MacBradaigh, despite repeated
requests, had refused to deal with the issue. O'Sheridan wrote to the
archbishop stating that:

> John Oragilly, capt. Of his nation, has vexed, perturbed …
> the said herenach and his bros., and put animals of oth-
> ers on said lands … and did cultivate them and stay and
> inhabit there, preventing them from peaceful possession
> and free disposition of said lands and herenachy. And that
> Hugh Oragilly with his accomplices, by the commands
> of Nellanus McGylrenan and Nolaic daughter of Oglyne,
> took, carried away and disposed 12 animals from tenants of
> said lands contrary to ecclesiastical liberty.[51]

As he had done in 1428, Primate John Swayne again wrote to
the bishop with a message for all clergy 'in cure and not in cure
throughout Kilmore diocese' asking them to admonish John and
Hugh O'Reilly and their accomplices, to impose sanctions on them
and to demand restitution. If the O'Reillys failed to cooperate they
were to be excommunicated. These measures were to remain in place
until the culprits merit absolution or the diocese receives different
instructions from the archbishop.

Thomas O'Sheridan, in replacing Andrew MacBradaigh as rector
of Kedy in 1436, recovered the tithes for the Sheridan family. However,
it is possible that he may have done so by foul means and in 1443 he
was accused by Cornelius Maconaing, the perpetual vicar of Drung
and Laragh, of being both 'a simoniac and a notorious fornicator'.[52]

---

51.   Chart (ed.), *The register of John Swayne*, pp 198–9.
52.   *CPL*, ix, p. 338.

Cornelius Maconaing was granted the rectory in 1443[53] and Thomas O'Sheridan was excommunicated, yet O'Sheridan was again rector of Kedy in 1466. In that year John Macculmartayn, a canon of the diocese, wrote to Rome stating that Thomas O'Sheridan:

> [The]rector of the parish church of St Bridget, Nurnagy, alias Kade ... has committed perjury and simony and being under sentence of excommunication for the said simony and publicly proclaimed excommunicate, has taken part in divine office in contempt of the Keys, thereby incurring irregularity.[54]

The prior of Lough Uachtair, the archdeacon of Kilmore and John O'Gowan, a canon of the diocese, were delegated by Rome to resolve the issue and they deprived O'Sheridan of the rectory and granted it to Canon Macculmartayn who already had a prebend valued at only three marks 'to which the parish church of Enagallib [Annagelliff] ... is annexed'.[55] He now had two benefices, in total worth eleven marks per annum, a fitting income for a canon of the relatively new cathedral chapter. John Macculmartayn acquired the rectory of Kedy by making a vicious accusation against the incumbent and being rewarded with the benefice for doing so. A similar strategy was used to deprive him of it in 1484. In that year Malachy Macachlerich, a clerk of the diocese, wrote to Rome stating that 'John Macmaelmactain, rector of Kedy ... has given a sum of money to the ordinaries[56] in order to obtain benefices for himself and his son, thereby committing simony'.[57]

The O'Sheridan family recovered the rectory of Kedy towards the end of the fifteenth-century. In 1501 Fergal O'Sheridan, a clerk of the diocese, stated that the rectory was vacant and requested that it be created into a simple prebend for his lifetime. This audacious request to be given the rectory and be created a canon was forwarded to the controversial pope Alexander VI (Borgia) who acceded to Fergal O'Sheridan's request that the case be heard by Gelasius O'Sheridan, a canon of the diocese, Corbanus Magmahuna, a canon of Clogher diocese and the unnamed prior of Drumlane – possibly Hugh Ó Maolmochéirghe who was

53.   Costello, *De Annatis Hiberniae*, i, p. 235.
54.   *CPL*, xii, p. 513.
55.   Ibid.
56.   There were two claimants to the bishopric of Kilmore at this time, Thomas Mac-Bradaigh who was bishop from 1480–1511, and Cormac Magauran, 'who was called the bishop of Bréifne'; *AFM*, 1511.
57.   *CPL*, xiii, 2, pp 173–4.

drowned in 1512. They adjudicated in Fergal's favour decreeing that 'Fergal (or his proctor) be received as a canon of the church of Kilmore, with plenitude of canon law, and the fruits etc, rights and obventions of the canonry be delivered to him'.[58] However, the rectory of Kedy and the vicarage of the parish church of St Brighid in Urney had already been granted to Nicholas MacBradaigh, a priest of the diocese, by 'the bishop of Kilmore, or his vicar general'.[59] Fergal O'Sheridan's petition to the pope requesting that he be given the rectory of Kedy as a prebend for his lifetime failed to mention that his father had held the rectory before him. When Rome discovered this, the decision to grant him the rectory and prebend was rescinded. Nicholas MacBradaigh remained as vicar of Urney[60] and the rectory of Kedy was separated from it and granted to Gilbert MacBradaigh, a cleric of the diocese of Kilmore.[61]

The patchwork quilt of rectories which existed in the diocese throughout the 1400s had evolved over a period of time. The rectories varied greatly in size, some consisting of one townland and others as large as eight parishes. In each rectory a portion of the tithes collected went either to a religious community or to an individual, who could be a lay person in minor orders who might or might not be preparing for ordination, or to a priest. Virtually all of the rectories were sinecures which carried no duty of pastoral care with them with the result that there had to be priests/vicars, usually, though not always, appointed by the bishop, who would celebrate the sacraments and pastorally care for the parishioners.[62]

Impoverished Clergy

The vicars, that is the priests who cared for people within the area of pastoral care known as a vicarage, received a portion of the tithes collected in the vicarage and their income was supplemented with altarages and offerings. Henry Jefferies, in his study of the diocese of Armagh *inter Hibernicos* in the sixteenth-century, identified a 'pervasive problem of clerical poverty' and went on to state that:

58.   *CPL*, xvii, 2, p. 347.
59.   Ibid., p. 505. A vicar-general is a priest appointed by the bishop to help him administer a diocese.
60.   Nicholas MacBradaigh had also been granted the rectory of Knockninny in Fermanagh. See Costello, *De Annatis Hiberniae*, i, p. 254.
61.   *CPL*, xvii, 2, pp 508–9. The fact that Thomas MacBradaigh was bishop of the diocese may help explain why the MacBradaigh family was able to claim the rectory from the O'Sheridans at the beginning of the sixteenth-century.
62.   See Paul MacCotter, *A history of the medieval diocese of Cloyne* (Dublin, 2013), pp 64–5.

Figure 3.3: Kilmore vicarages (parishes) listed in papal documents *c*.1300–1500.

Vicarage	Patron saint(s)	Clerical families	Annual value of Vicarage
Annagh	St Maolán	O Fay	4 marks
Ballintemple	St Patrick	O Gowan	5-4-5 marks*
Carrigallen		O Flynn	3 marks
Castletara	St Patrick	MacBrady	5-6 marks
Cloonclare			3 marks
Drumgoon	St Patrick	Macmaelmartayn	5 marks
Drumlane	St Maedhóg	O'Farrelly	8 marks
Drumlease	St Patrick		4 marks
Drumreilly		Ó Maolmochéirghe	3 marks
Drung	St Patrick	MacBrady	5 marks
Killasnett			6 marks
Kildallan	St Dallan		3 marks
Kildrumferton	St Patrick		7 marks
Killeshandra	St Brighid		6 marks
Killesher	St Lasair		4 marks
Killinagh		Magauran	3 marks
Killinkere	St Ultan		
Kilmore	St Feidhlimidh	O Sheridan	12 – 8 marks
Kilsherdany	St Brighid/Fincheall	O Sheridan/MacBrady	10 -12 marks
Kinawley	St Náile	O Droma	5 marks
Laragh	St Brighid	MacBrady	5 marks
Oughteragh		Ó Maolmochéirghe	3 marks
Rossinver	St Maodhóg	O Meehan/ O Ferguson	
Templeport	St Maodhóg	Magauran	3 marks
Tomregan			3 marks
Urney	St Brighid		4 marks

*The annual value of some vicarages varied throughout this period.

> Economic under-development, the dislocation which en-
> sued with war or more local conflicts and the difficulties in
> securing the full value of the tithes ... conspired to depress
> clerical incomes throughout the later middle ages.[63]

The clergy in Kilmore were also impoverished at this time. When Milo
Sweteman, the archbishop of Armagh, paid a two-day metropolitan
visitation to the diocese, which was held in Kilmainhamwood
church in November 1368, he demanded four marks from Richard Ó
Raghallaigh, the bishop of the diocese whom he had come to admonish, and he looked for only a combined total of four marks from all
the rest of the clergy of the diocese 'because they were poor'.[64] This
poverty persisted. In 1488, Arthur Macconrich, a canon of the cathedral church of Kilmore had a prebend of only three marks, an income
which was 'so meagre as to be insufficient to sustain him, so that he
is forced to beg to the disgrace of the clerical order'.[65] He was granted
the perpetual vicarage of Killesher, valued at four marks, in order
to increase his income. The great lengths the clergy of this period
went to - and sometimes the foul means they adopted in trying to
persuade the papacy to grant them benefices - were an indication
not so much of their greed and ambition but of their misery and
desperation.

The value of twenty-four of the fifteenth-century vicarages in the
diocese are given in the *Calendar of Papal Registers*. In these vicarages
the annual income of the vicars ranges from three to twelve marks.
Eight, or one third of all the vicarages, were valued at only three
marks and a further four vicarages were valued at four marks, with
the result that half of the vicarages whose values are listed were very
poor, being worth four marks or less. The vicarage of Kilmore had
the highest value of any in the diocese being valued at twelve marks
in 1411 though it had decreased to eight marks by 1444. The vicarage
of Kilsherdany was valued at ten marks in 1403 and had increased in
value to twelve marks in 1444. The vicarage of Drumlane, which was
usually held by the Augustinian priory there, was valued at eight
marks in 1409. Of the twenty-four vicarages whose value is given,
twenty-one of them were valued at six marks or less.

---

63.   Henry A. Jefferies, *Priests and prelates of Armagh in the age of Reformations 1518–1558*
(Dublin, 1997), p. 72.
64.   Smith, *The register of Milo Sweteman*, p. 72.
65.   *CPL*, xiv, p. 114.

The clergy who had a duty of care of the people of the diocese were paid a pittance, though the income of the clergy of the dioceses of Clogher, Armagh and Killaloe was broadly similar.[66] The parish clergy's low income in the diocese of Kilmore can be explained, at least in part, by the large amount of tithes which went to the religious houses in Fore, Kells and Drumlane, leaving only pickings to supplement the meagre income of vicars in the diocese. Despite the poverty of the majority of the priests, some of them proved quite adept at improving their incomes. For example, Augustine MacBradaigh,[67] the perpetual vicar of Drung and Laragh, wrote to Pope Martin V in 1419 outlining his impoverished state and his obligation to provide hospitality and contribute to the maintenance of the church buildings.[68] He stated that:

> he had not only the care of souls in these two parishes, but he was also bound to keep the two churches in repair, practice hospitality *juxta morem patrice,* and bear all the other burdens inherent in his office, and as the tithes and the greater part of the revenues from these two churches are payable to the Prior and convent of the monastery of Fore … what remains is so scanty and meagre, that it does not suffice for his fitting maintenance and for the discharge of his official obligations.[69]

The vicarages in the diocese of Kilmore were much more uniform in size than the rectories and were manageable areas for a single priest to exercise pastoral care of the people. Generally the vicarages were coterminous with the parishes though in some instances there were two parishes in the one vicarage. The above-mentioned Augustine MacBradaigh who was perpetual vicar of the united parish churches of St Patrick's in Drung and St Brighid's in Laragh

66.   See Henry A. Jefferies (ed.), *History of the diocese of Clogher* (Dublin, 2005), pp 91–96; Jefferies, *Priests and prelates of Armagh*, pp 70–73; Luke McInerney, *Clerical and learned lineages of medieval Co. Clare* (Dublin, 2014), pp 188–9. Some of the vicarages in Killaloe were valued as low as two marks with the majority of them being worth between two and five marks.

67.   Augustine MacBradaigh was made vicar of Drung and Laragh in 1396. He replaced Gilbert MacBrady who was appointed bishop of Ardagh that same year. *CPL*, iv, p. 529.

68.   It is not clear what portion of the costs of maintaining a church that the vicar had to pay. In east Bréifne 'the parson, vicar and herenagh are to repair and maintain their own parish church, at their own charge, out of their benefices and termon lands, in which work the parishioners did oftentimes voluntarily give their *bene volente* '. See 'Inquisition taken at Cavan on 25 Sept. 1609' in *Calendar of Irish patent rolls of James I*, p. 386.

69.   Costello, *De Annatis Hiberniae*, i, p. 245.

the union thereof [was] made by bishop John[70] on the ground that the fruits etc., value altogether not exceeding 10 marks, were insufficient for two vicars and that the two churches were near enough to be served by one.[71]

The chapel of ease of St Columba and St Canice, which was located in the townland of Magherintemple, was also in the parish of Drung though a long distance from its borders with Laragh and considerably nearer to the parish of Annagh. Nemeas O'Fay, the vicar of Annagh who held the rectory of 'Bali Mictonchabhuill' (Magherintemple), alleged that 'on account of the want of a stipend no ecclesiastic is willing to celebrate divine office in the said chapel'.[72] He was not a disinterested witness, however, as he hoped to have the chapel of ease added to his own vicarage of Annagh. He outlined his case in a letter to the pope in 1409:

> The chapel of SS Columba and Cannicus, Tulat,[73] ... situate within the bounds of the parish church of Drang, is more populous and more decent than the said parish church;[74] that between them flows a great river[75] which cannot at times be crossed without danger of drowning, wherefore the parishioners who dwell on the lands of the chapel cannot go to the church for divine office on the greater feasts of the year or others; that on account of the want of a stipend no ecclesiastic is willing to celebrate divine offices in the said chapel; and that he has decently repaired it at his own

70.   Possibly a reference to Bishop John Stokes. See MacKiernan, *Diocese of Kilmore*, p. 12.
71.   *CPL*, vi, p. 374. In 1453 John Ó Maolmochéirghe used a similar argument when he tried to persuade the pope to grant him the two vicarages of Oughteragh and Drumreilly, whose combined value was only six marks and which vicarages, he claimed, were 'so near that they can be served by one man.' See *CPL*, x, pp 617–8.
72.   *CPL*, vi, p. 153.
73.   Nemeas O'Fay incorrectly locates the chapel in the townland of Tullyalt, a townland adjacent to Magherintemple.
74.   The medieval parish church of Drung was situated just below the summit of a high hill in the townland of Drung. The baronial map of 1609 shows the church to be without a roof. A cemetery and substantial remains of a church, measuring 20m X 8m, have survived at the site, though Davies states that these ruins date 'at earliest from the 17th century'. See Davies, 'The churches of County Cavan', p. 113; O'Donovan, *Archaeological inventory of County Cavan*, p. 198.
75.   This is a reference to Annalee River. The risk of being drowned in the Annalee or other rivers in Ireland was very real since few bridges existed. Three years after this letter was written Catherine, a daughter of Maelechlainn MacDonnchaid, 'was drowned by a rushing flood whilst going to Sunday Mass from her own home'. See *ALC*, 1412.

expense, and in a house hard by keeps hospitality after the manner of the country.[76]

It appears that Nemeas O'Fay was successful in his bid and that he was granted the chapel, and all the tithes and oblations which went with it. The loss of this chapel of ease in his own vicarage of Drung and Laragh did not seem to deter Augustine MacBradaigh who was quite adept at getting benefices, both from inside and outside the diocese. At one time he held the treasurership of the diocese of Ferns, the archdeanery of the diocese of Elphin and the rectory of Telachgarve along with the vicarage of the parishes of Drung and Laragh.[77] Having, for more than a quarter of a century, successfully warded off attempts by bishop Nicholas MacBradaigh to remove him, he was eventually deprived of the vicarage of Drung and Laragh *c.*1427 by the combined efforts of Bishop Donatus O'Gowan, Thomas O'Sheridan, archdeacon of Kilmore and Andrew MacBradaigh, the rural dean of Drumlane.[78] Augustine MacBradaigh appealed to John Swayne, the archbishop of Armagh, stating that although he had canonically obtained the vicarage and had held it for some years the bishop had 'violently removed him'.[79] The archbishop of Armagh summoned the bishop of Kilmore and Cornelius Macconnayng, a priest of the diocese who had been appointed by the bishop to replace Augustine MacBradaigh as vicar of Drung and Laragh, to appear before him or his official in St Peter's parish church in Drogheda on 7 October 1427 to answer the charges made by Augustine MacBradaigh.[80] It appears that the bishop's dismissal of MacBradaigh was upheld. Augustine MacBradaigh died in 1428 leaving Cornelius Maconnayng as the undisputed vicar of Drung and Laragh.

Tithes

The method of paying tithes varied considerably throughout the diocese of Kilmore. In the parish of Drung, the vicar received one third of the tithes (which were paid in kind) and the prior of Fore received two thirds. The termon lands of Maghereholch (Magherintemple) and a portion of Ballemenchoell (Ballyhally?) townland paid one third of their tithes to the vicar and two thirds to the bishop of the

76. *CPL*, vi, p. 153.
77. Ibid., vi, pp 370–1.
78. He had been previously been deprived of the vicarage by bishop Nicholas MacBradaigh in 1398, but having been appointed to it by the pope in the first instance he successfully appealed to Rome and was re-instated. See *CPL*, v, p. 168.
79. Chart (ed.), *The Register of John Swayne*, p. 66.
80. Ibid.

diocese.[81] In Laragh parish one third of the tithes went to the vicar and two thirds to the prior of Fore. The bishop was paid two thirds of the tithes of 'the poll of land called Laragh' and 'one great acre of glebe land' belonging to the vicarage.[82] So both Drung and Laragh parishes, and the other parishes throughout east Bréifne, had broadly similar arrangements for paying their tithes, though some vicars, such as the vicar of Denn, also paid an agreed amount of money directly to the bishop.[83] In Templeport parish in west Cavan, where two thirds of the tithes were paid to the abbey of Kells and one third to the vicar, the payments to the bishop were slightly more complex:

> the said bushop of Kilmore hath of the vicar halfe a mark, proxies, and a third part of beofe [beef] for his visitacon …
> and the lord bushop of Killmore is seized in fee … out of the termon land of Templeport conteyninge six pooles, tenn shillings and two-third partes of a beofe per annum; and out of the other polles of termon land adjoyninge the chapple of Kilfert [Kilnavart] … twelve pence per annum.[84]

In Kinawley, a mensal parish contributing handsomely to the bishop's income, the bishop of Kilmore was to be paid '4 quarters of beef at his visitation or 40 groats in lieu thereof' out of the O'Droma erenagh lands. The bishop was also paid an unspecified sum of money out of the Blake erenagh lands in Killesher.[85]

The rectory of Kilmainhamwood paid the bishop of the diocese both in kind and with money, giving him sixteen shillings and four jars (*lagene*) of honey worth 13*s*. 4*d*. each year.[86] The parishes of Castlerahan, Lurgan, Munterconnacht, Knockbride and Killann in east Bréifne had a different arrangement in that both the rectory and vicarage paid all their tithes to the abbey of Kells. In these parishes 'the whole of the tithes are paid in kind and the said abbey [Kells] is to maintain curates [vicars]'.[87] These parishes appear to have belonged more to the abbey of Kells than they did to the diocese of Kilmore, although, the

81. 'Inquisition taken at Cavan on 25 Sept. 1609' in *Calendar of Irish patent rolls of James I*, p. 386.
82. Ibid., p. 385.
83. The vicar of the parish of Denn paid twelve shillings annually to the bishop.
84. Costello, *De Annatis Hiberniae*, i, p. 246.
85. Inquisition held in Enniskillen on 18 September 1609. *The Journal of the Breiffne Antiquarian society*, iii, 3 (1931–3), p. 382.
86. White (ed.), *Extents of Irish monastic possessions*, p. 111.
87. *Calendar of Irish patent rolls of James I*, p. 386.

Figure 3.4: East window of Killinagh medieval parish church, looking on to Lough MacNean, near Blacklion.

bishop of the diocese did receive rents from a small area or designated townland in each of these parishes.[88]

The majority of the parishes in east Bréifne paid two thirds of the tithes to the rector and one third to the vicar and this was similar to what happened in Armagh diocese *inter Hibernicos*.[89] However, in the parish of Killinagh and all the parishes in the deanery of Dartry in west Bréifne the tithes were divided in a different way, with one third going to the bishop, one third to the rector and one third to the vicar.[90] The vicar of Killinagh paid 3*s* 4*d* to the bishop each year and presumably the vicars in Dartry deanery also made an annual contribution to him. The tri-partition system which prevailed in Killinagh parish and in Dartry deanery in west Bréifne was similar to the way tithes were paid in the north-western dioceses of Derry and Raphoe.[91] All the tithes of fruits in the parishes of 'Cluayn Lochayr [Cloonlogher] and Fareli Cluayn [Cloonclare]' and those 'in the lands of Cuyl and Carrag and Letirchayn [?]' together with 'all the tithes of

88.   For Killann see Thomas Hall, 'Killan old church, County Cavan' in *JRSAI*, xxxviii, 4 (Dec.1908), pp 334–43.

89.   Nicholls, Rectory, vicarage and parish', p. 65.

90.   See *CPL*, vi (1404–1415), p. 319; *Calendar of Irish patent rolls of James I*, p. 386.

91.   Nicholls, 'Rectory, vicarage and parish', p. 65.

animals in the said parishes' also belonged to the episcopal *mensa* of Kilmore.[92]

Required Skills

The vicars were usually, though not always, priests. Some of them were young men still in minor orders who were appointed on the understanding that they would proceed quickly to ordination. This did not always happen, however. In 1398 John MacBradaigh, who was twenty-three years old, was to be granted the perpetual vicarage of Cúil Brighdín (Castletara) - made vacant by the consecration of Nicholas MacBradaigh as bishop of the diocese in 1395 - 'should it be found that the said John reads and construes Latin well and speaks it suitably, sings well and is otherwise fit for the said benefice'.[93] He was granted the vicarage but did not proceed to ordination and so in 1428 Philip MacBradaigh, a priest of the diocese, was given the vicarage which had been vacant for a long time because John MacBradaigh 'some time vicar of the said plebs or church' held it for more than a year without being ordained a priest.[94] Similarly, Cornelius O'Rourke was deprived of the vicarage of Cloonclare because he held it for more than a year without being ordained a priest and in 1455 it was given instead to William O'Curneen.[95] Vicars were required to be able to both read Latin and translate it and to be tolerably good singers. Lazarianus Macmulmartain was to be appointed vicar of Ballintemple in 1407 provided he can prove that he 'can read and translate Latin well, and speak it befittingly and sing well'. Obviously the ability to sing was an important requirement because his appointment was allowed to proceed 'even if he cannot sing well, provided he makes an oath that he will learn to do so within a year after this examination'.[96]

The fact that vicars needed to be proficient in Latin and able to sing suggests that their liturgical duties were seen as paramount. Other clerics were prevented from taking major orders because of the way they wore their hair. Malachy Macbrady and Donatus [ ], both clerics of the diocese or Kilmore, were excommunicated under an Armagh provincial statute dated 6 June 1460 which prohibited beneficed clergy and cathedral canons from wearing glibs and moustaches [*comas et barbas superiors*]. However, Archbishop John Bole dispensed them from this drastic punishment 'as long as they

92.   *CPL*, vii (1427–1447), p. 54.
93.   Costello, *De Annatis Hiberniae*, i, p. 242; *CPL*, iv, p. 167.
94.   *CPL*, viii, pp 74–5.
95.   *CPL*, xi, pp 217–8; MacKiernan, *Diocese of Kilmore*, p. 146.
96.   Costello, *De Annatis Hiberniae*, i, p. 243.

Figure 3.5: Doorway in west wall of St Brighid's church, Urney.

do not proceed in holy orders beyond first tonsure'.[97] This particular rule smacked of an attempt to impose an English or Anglo-Irish dress style on the native Irish clergy and does not appear to have been very successful because when Archbishop Bole commissioned 'Master Marcellus, chamberlain of the pope and counsellor of the archbishop' to carry out his first metropolitan visitation of Kilmore diocese in 1463 he granted him special powers 'to grant dispensations ... in the case of the provincial statute against clerics who grow glibs and moustaches'.[98] Physical disabilities did not seem to be a barrier to priests ministering in the vicarages. In 1401, John Maecmulmartam, the vicar of Ballintemple, who had been blind for some time was allowed, 'his said defect of sight notwithstanding, to receive and to hold the said vicarage for life'.[99] In the 1460s another John Macculmartayn, a canon of the diocese, continued to minister despite the fact that he lost his index finger and had part of his right hand paralysed in a shipwreck.[100]

Clerical Lineages

We learn from the fifteenth-century papal documents that many of the priests of the diocese of Kilmore and those of the religious orders based in it came from a relatively small number of clerical families. These families controlled certain vicarages, rectories and religious houses and, in some instances, handed on these benefices in hereditary succession from father to son. The Magaurans of Tullyhaw was one such family. This family supplied clergy for the diocese of Kilmore and for the Augustinians of Drumlane and Kells throughout the medieval period and had possession of the vicarages of Templeport and Killinagh for virtually all of the fifteenth-century. In 1393, Fergal Magauran 'a man of unbounded hospitality to the clergy', died.[101] Andrew Magauran was probably vicar of Templeport at this time and in 1414, following his death, was replaced by Magonius Magauran, a priest of Kilmore diocese.[102]

97.   Lynch, 'A Calendar of the reassembled register of John Bole, Archbishop of Armagh, 1457–71', p. 130.
98.   Ibid., p. 124.
99.   *CPL*, v, p. 447.
100.   Ibid., xii, p. 513. Eugene Marchameall, a priest of the neighbouring diocese of Clogher, got a papal dispensation 'on account of the loss and want of a small part of the little fingers of his left hand which he suffered in defence of the said church [Clogher]'. See *CPL*, xix, p. 2.
101.   *AFM*, 1393.
102.   *CPL*, vi, p. 175. MacKiernan, *Diocese of Kilmore*, p. 143. There are many variations in the spelling of Magauran in the papal letters.

In 1425, Rory Magauran, who claimed to be 'of a race of dukes', was appointed vicar of Templeport even though he was not yet a priest.[103] He was ordained sometime before 1430 and by then had secured, not just the vicarage of Templeport which was worth eight marks, but also the vicarage of Killinagh which was worth three marks *per annum*. The vicarage of Killinagh had been held at different times by Sitrinius Magauran and Luke Magauran, both priests of the diocese, and by Thomas Magauran who held it for more than a year without being ordained a priest.[104] Rory Magauran had a substantial income from the two vicarages and also considerable hardship trying to travel the hilly terrain between the two parish churches which were more than twenty-miles apart. He continued to seek other benefices and, early in 1431, he was given permission to hold another benefice not exceeding twenty marks with cure or fifteen marks without cure.[105] However, it was not until August 1433 that he succeeded in getting such a benefice, the rectory of Iniskaeynlachaherny in the diocese of Clogher, which was valued at sixteen marks and had become vacant by the appointment of the previous rector, Piaras Mag Uidhir, as bishop of Clogher.[106]

Many of the accusatory letters sent from the diocese to the pope during the fifteenth-century were attempts by younger men, usually clerks, to dislodge an older incumbent rector or vicar who may or may not be related to them, and thereby get the benefice for themselves. These accusatory and often vicious letters tried to prove that the incumbent either held the benefice illegally or else that he was such an immoral and notorious character that he was unfit for office. Nemeas O'Droma, a young clerk of the diocese, made a variety of accusations in August 1453 against Rory Magauran in an attempt to unseat and replace him in the vicarage of Templeport.[107] Three months earlier, and using virtually the same formulaic accusations, he tried to unseat Thomas Ocalmon who held the vicarage of Tomregan. In doing so O'Droma hoped to gain both vicarages which he said 'are so near that they can be conveniently served by one man ... [and in order] that he may better maintain and

103.   *CPL*, vii, p. 402.
104.   Ibid., viii, p. 152; Costello, *De Annatis Hiberniae*, i, p. 235.
105.   *CPL*, viii, p. 193.
106.   Ibid., pp 470–1. Piaras or Petrus Mag Uidhir was bishop of Clogher from 1433 to 1447.
107.   *CPL*, x, p. 634. The O'Droma family was a learned, clerical family based in Kinawley. Solamh Ó Droma was one of the compilers of the *Book of Ballymote*. John Ua Droma, 'vicar of Cell-Naaille', died in 1378 (*AU*, 1378). Raymond Gillespie has suggested that the O'Droma family may have moved northwards from Killenaule, near Cashel, and brought the cult of St Náile with them to Kinawley. See Raymond Gillespie, 'Traditional religion in sixteenth- century Ireland', in Tadhg Ó hAnnracháin & Robert Armstrong, *Christianities in the early modern Celtic world* (London, 2014), p. 36.

keep up the wonted hospitality'.[108] Rory Magauran was deprived of the vicarage and replaced, not by Nemeas O'Droma, but by Cristinus Magauran, a move which triggered off a vicious and prolonged dispute. In 1455 Rory Magauran had Cristinus Magauran removed from the vicarage by sending a litany of accusations against him to Rome and he became vicar of Templeport once more, a position he held until 1461.[109] In that year Cormac Magauran made specific, and therefore more credible, accusations against Rory, alleging that:

> Rory Magabraim … has wounded a clerk with an arrow and committed perjury, and thereby incurred sentence and excommunication … and being excommunicate and publicly proclaimed excommunicate has celebrated and taken part in masses and other divine offices, even in contempt of the Keys.[110]

The accusations held. Rory Magauran was excommunicated and Cormac, even though he was still a clerk and only about nineteen years old, was granted the vicarage of Templeport. Cormac Magauran was a son and namesake of the bishop of Ardagh and grandson of Piaras or Peter Magauran who had, in 1456, been appointed prior of Drumlane.[111] In 1467, he accused John MacBrien 'who behaves as prior of Drumlane' of simony - alleging that he paid a large sum of money to John[112] the abbot of Kells in order to be appointed to Drumlane. Pope Paul II ordered two canons of the diocese of Ardagh to investigate the allegations. John MacBrien was deprived of the priory and it was given to Cormac Magauran 'even before he receives the habit of the said [Augustinian] order and makes his final profession as a canon … [and that] as soon he has received the habit and made his profession he shall resign the said vicarage'.[113] Nicolanus Magauran, a clerk of the diocese, obtained the vicarage in 1471, while Cormac remained prior of Drumlane, even after he had been appointed bishop of Kilmore by Sixtus IV on 4 November 1476.[114] The appointment in 1503 of Fergal Magauran, a priest of the diocese and a son of Cormac

108.   *CPL*, x, pp 634, 637.
109.   Ibid., xi, p. 219.
110.   Ibid., xii, p. 142.
111.   Ibid., xi, p. 307; B.L., Egerton MS 1781, f. 128; Robin Flower, *Irish Manuscripts in the British Library*, ii (repr. Dublin, 1992), p. 539; *CPL*, viii, pp 585–6.
112.   This is probably a reference to 'John O'Raghallaigh II' who was appointed bishop of Kilmore in 1465.
113.   *CPL*, xii, p. 564.
114.   Costello, *De Annatis Hiberniae*, i, p. 257; *CPL*, xiii, 1, p. 277.

Magauran, who was still claiming to be the rightful bishop of Kilmore, to the perpetual vicarage of Templeport, provides an example of clerical lineages in the diocese. He was the fourth in a direct line of priests of the Magauran family who held a variety of ecclesiastical positions including the vicarage of Templeport, the priory of Drumlane, the abbey of Kells and the bishoprics of Ardagh and Kilmore.[115]

The hereditary succession of ecclesiastical positions was a regular occurrence in Ireland in the fifteenth-century. Young men regularly applied to the papacy for a dispensation as the son of a priest so that they themselves might be ordained priests.[116] The regularity of such applications and the granting of papal dispensations points towards the acceptance of hereditary succession by people in Ireland and a tacit acceptance if not approval of the practice by the papacy. Clerical lineages, where an ecclesiastical position was passed on from father to son or to another member of the extended family, were prevalent in Kilmore diocese as elsewhere in the country. Whenever a member of the O'Rourke, Magauran, MacBrady or O'Reilly families appealed to the pope to be granted a benefice they invariably stated that they were 'of noble race' or 'descended from dukes' in order to further their cause. In this way these noble families were able to consolidate their control over certain vicarages, rectories or religious houses within the sphere of their family's influence.

The Ó Ruaircs, who were in the ascendancy in both west and east Bréifne at a crucial time in the twelfth-century when the diocesan boundaries were being ironed out, continued to reign in west Bréifne until late in the sixteenth-century although the family ceased to wield influence in east Bréifne from the mid-1300s onwards. Simon Ó Ruairc had been bishop of the diocese for at least thirty-four years when he died in 1285 and, judging by their names, both Bishop Patraic O Cridecain who died in 1328 and Bishop Conchobhar MacConsnamha (Forde) who died in 1355 were natives of west Bréifne and may have depended on the support of the Ó Ruaircs.[117] With the appointment of Bishop Richard Ó Raghallaigh *c*.1356 the power base in the diocese switched to east Bréifne and for the remainder of the fourteenth-century and throughout the fifteenth-century, the bishops of the diocese would be selected from the Ó Raghallaigh,

115.   *CPL*, xvii, 2, p. 574.

116.   The celibacy rule for priests was ignored in many instances not just in Ireland but throughout much of Europe in medieval times. For example see the exploits of the French priest Pierre Clergue in Emmanuel Le Roy Ladurie's wonderful depiction of life in a medieval French village in *Montaillou* (English translation, London, 1980). See also Jefferies, *Priests and prelates of Armagh*, p. 80; Ó Corráin, *The Irish Church, its reform and the English invasion*, pp 2, 18–9.

117.   MacKiernan, *Diocese of Kilmore*, pp 11–12; *AFM*, 1328 & 1355.

MacBradaigh, Ó Faircheallaigh, Mac Givney, O'Gowan and Magauran families of east Bréifne. There were two exceptions, Thomas Rushook and John Stokes, both outsiders and both of whom held ecclesiastical positions in England even after being appointed to Kilmore and it seems neither of them ever resided in the diocese. Members of the Ó Ruairc family, however, continued to hold certain vicarages in the north-western part of the diocese.

Cornelius Ó Ruairc 'of noble race' and a clerk of the diocese of Kilmore, was in 1412 granted the perpetual vicarage of the parish church of Killasnett.[118] In that same year William Ó Mithín, an Augustinian canon from St Mary's abbey in Kells and posssibly a native of Bealach Uí Mhithín (Ballaghameehan) in west Bréifne, attempted to oust Cornelius Ó Ruairc from the vicarage of Cloonclare which he had held for more than a year without being ordained. William Ó Mithín was anxious escape from Kells because he said the abbey 'is so desolated by the long wars and other calamities in those parts that the inmates cannot be fitly sustained' and he felt he would be safer in the Gaelic controlled Ó Ruairc territory and close to the Ó Mithín sept in Ballaghameehan.[119] Cornelius Ó Ruairc did take major orders and in 1451 when his son, also named Cornelius, held the vicarage of Killasnett, Donald Ó Mithín tried to remove him from it because he held it for more than a year without being ordained. Cornelius the younger was later ordained and by 1459 was also canon in the newly established diocesan chapter.[120] The Ó Ruairc family continued to supply priests to the diocese and, following the founding of Creevelea friary by Margaret and Eoghan Ó Ruairc in 1508, they provided friars for the Franciscans. This dominant family in west Bréifne was a clerical family and the fifteenth-century father and son priests named Cornelius Ó Ruairc, suggests that there was an Ó Ruairc clerical lineage as in some other clerical families in the diocese. However, because of the dearth of letters from Dartry deanery in the *Calendar of Papal Registers* for this period, one cannot be certain about this.[121]

The MacBrady family of Cúil Brighdín regularly provided priests throughout the fifteenth century for the combined vicarages of Drung and Laragh and the vicarage of Castletara. All three vicarages were adjacent to one another in east Bréifne. In contrast, the O'Reillys did not seem to have hereditary succession in any one vicarage in the diocese although the family regularly provided Augustinian canons for Saint

---

118.   *CPL*, vi, p. 265; Costello, *De Annatis Hiberniae*, i, p. 243.
119.   Ibid., p. 396.
120.   Ibid., xii, p. 30.
121.   There are 165 letters relating to the diocese of Kilmore in the Calendar of Papal Registers between the years 1394 and 1503. Of this total 133 or 80.6% relate to east Bréifne and only eleven or 6.6% relate to Dartry deanery in present-day north Leitrim.

Mary's abbey in Kells and Franciscan friars in Cavan. Between 1356 and 1529 four of the Ó Raghallaigh sept were appointed bishops of the diocese and at least two of them had been Augustinian abbots in Kells before their translation to Kilmore.[122] As we have already noted, John Ó Raghallaigh, the abbot of Kells and the son of an Augustinian abbot of the same name, was appointed bishop of Kilmore on 17 May 1465.[123] Diarmaid Ó Raghallaigh, the bishop of the diocese from 1512 to 1529, had also been abbot of Kells before his appointment to Kilmore.[124] The Ó Raghallaigh clerical family, like those of the other noble families in the diocese, helped to keep certain ecclesiastical positions, both within the diocese and beyond, it under their control.

There were several other clerical families in the diocese who could not claim to be of royal lineage though even a tentative link to nobility appeared to help their cause. When Thady Magivney, a priest of the diocese and perpetual vicar of Urney, asked to be granted the adjacent lucrative vicarage of Kilmore in 1436 he claimed to have relations who were of royal stock.[125] His appeal was successful. He became an Augustinian canon in Drumlane in 1444 and the following year was made prior there before being appointed bishop of Kilmore in 1455.[126] The second Irish Life of St Maodhóg, which was written in Rossinver *c.*1536, lists the twelve coarb families of Maodhóg whose duty it was to crown the chieftains of Bréifne and it goes on to say that 'no one of the men of Bréifne till doom is either valid king or chief until this band of clerics are all ordaining him together'.[127] Listed among these twelve coarbal families are the Magivneys, the O'Fergus family, O'Farrellys, O'Connaghys, O'Trevors[128] and Maguarans - all clerical families which supplied priests to the medieval diocese of Tír Briúin and some of them, particularly the Magaurans and O'Farrellys, who supplied priests to the Augustinians in Drumlane and Kells.

John Macculmathayn and his son James were both priests of the diocese and both held rectories attached to St Brighid's church in Urney and St Patrick's church in Drumgoon.[129] Clerical families tended to hold

---

122. MacKiernan, *Diocese of Kilmore*, pp 12–13. Three of the MacBradaigh sept were bishops of the diocese between 1395 and 1511.
123. *CPL*, ix, p. 458.
124. MacKiernan, *Diocese of Kilmore*, p. 13.
125. *CPL*, viii, p. 599.
126. MacKiernan, *Diocese of Kilmore*, p. 13.
127. Charles Plummer (ed.), *Bethada Náem nÉrenn* (Oxford, 1922), ii, p. 200. The cult of St Maodhóg was strong in Rossinver and 'St Mogue's fair', a weeklong fair, was held in the first week of February each year at a crossroads between Rossinver and Garrison. See 'The school's folklore collection', vol.189, pp 164–5.
128. The O'Treabairs (Travers) were erenaghs of Killarga. See *AC*, 1416.
129. *CPL*, xv, p. 410.

certain vicarages and rectories from one generation to the next though it is important not to overstate this because the possession of some of the vicarages and rectories alternated between different families. Members of the Ó Mithín and Ó Fergus[130] families held Rossinver vicarage, members of both the Ó Maolmochéirghe and Ó Floinn families were vicars in Drumreilly and Oughteragh and members of the MacBrady and MacConnon families were vicars of Drung and Laragh. Sometimes the vicarages were the cause of bitter disputes between individuals and families and at other times the change of vicar from one generation to another within a family or from one family to another seemed to take place without incident. In disputed cases the vicars had no compunction about writing vicious condemnatory letters about their opponent either to the papal courts or to the archbishop of Armagh. Sometimes the disputes even turned violent. We have already noted above how Rory Magauran the vicar of Templeport had, sometime before 1461, wounded a clerk with an arrow - possibly a clerk who was trying to take the vicarage from him. In 1474 Eugene Ó Raghallaigh, the archdeacon of Kilmore, was accused of the more serious crime of having killed a layman, although there is no evidence to suggest that this death happened in a dispute over a vicarage or other ecclesiastical position.[131]

Because of the poverty of the diocese and the scarcity of rectories available as benefices, ecclesiastical benefices were much sought after. The unholy scrambling for benefices, the scurrilous and defamatory letters to Rome and the prevalence of some clerical lineage families suggests that the clerical order had lost its way. Benefices that had been set up to provide for the care of souls were in many instances sought after as sources of income 'that could be had by papal grace in return for payment of a fee'.[132] And yet, surprisingly, despite the many and varied denunciations of clergy forwarded to Rome, the charge that they neglected the pastoral care of people was notably absent. There was no shortage of priests and even though they were generally poorly educated and ill-equipped to preach it appears that the pastoral care of people was adequate or even good throughout the fifteenth-century.[133]

130.   John O'Donovan, writing in 1841, stated that 'O Fergus, the descendant of the ancient Erenachs of Rossinver, has, we are sorry to say, lately changed his named to Ferguson'. See *The Irish Penny Journal*, i, 50 (12 June 1841), p. 398.
131.   *CPL*, xiii, 1, p. 372.
132.   Patrick J. Corish, *The Catholic Community in the seventeenth and eighteenth centuries* (Dublin, 1981), p. 6.
133.   Henry A. Jefferies, 'Why the Reformation failed in Ireland' in *IHS* (2016), 40 (158), p. 155; idem, *Priests and prelates of Armagh*, p. 81.

Chapter 4

Bishops and their Troubles: *c.*1100–1455

When Bishop Aed Ua Finn died on the island of Inisclothron in 1136 he was described as 'Ardespoc of Bréifne' in the *Annals of Boyle* and the *Annals of Tighearnach*.[1] This suggests that not only was there a bishop in Bréifne before the diocesan boundaries were teased out at the synod of Kells but also that there may have been another deputy bishop or even bishops in Bréifne at the time. A major challenge for the twelfth-century reform in Ireland was not to appoint new bishops but rather to 'regulate the dioceses of the bishops of Ireland'.[2] The status or function of bishops prior to the twelfth-century reform is the subject of much debate, though at least in some instances they lived in the shadow of the abbots of the long established monasteries and their function was confined to ordaining priests, blessing the sacred oils and administering the sacrament of confirmation.[3] The twelfth-century reforming synods set about restoring a pastoral leadership role for bishops and defining the boundaries within which they were to carry out that role.

The late Bishop Francis MacKiernan, in his research on the clergy of the diocese of Kilmore, lists twenty-one bishops of the diocese for the period 1100–1455 although twenty would seem to be the correct figure since the bishop 'Johannes' 'and 'Seoan O Raghallaigh 1' in his list appear to be one and the same person.[4] Little is known about many of them except perhaps a single entry in one or other of the annals recording their death. Others receive a mention in the papal letters of the period or in the registers of the various archbishops of Armagh, though generally the historian is faced with a frustrating dearth of episcopal records. The most notorious of the bishops, particularly those who were mired in disputes and controversies, generated the greatest number of records which could skew the overall picture since the mundane lives of the more exemplary

---

1. MacKiernan, *Diocese of Kilmore*, p. 11.
2. Keating, *Foras Feasa ar Éirinn: the history of Ireland*, iii, pp 298–9.
3. For a discussion on this see Flanagan, *The transformation of the Irish Church in the twelfth century*, pp 34–91.
4. MacKiernan, *Diocese of Kilmore*, p. 12.

bishops often went unnoticed. Of the twenty bishops of this period we know only the first name of 'Mauricius' who was bishop from *c.*1286 to 1307 and we have no name at all for the Cistercian priest who was appointed bishop in 1185. However, we can learn quite a lot about where the power base was, both inside and outside the diocese, if we take a closer look at the names of the other eighteen bishops.

The papacy, the English monarch and local ecclesiastical and secular families all had an interest in the appointment of bishops. Eighteen of the twenty bishops in the diocese during this period appear to have been Irish and most of them, judging by their family name, seem to have come from within the diocese. This suggests that local factors predominated in the appointments of the bishops of the diocese. The Anglicisation of the episcopacy in Ireland, which began *c.*1178 and continued throughout the thirteenth-century, had virtually no impact on the diocese of Tír Briúin.[5] If the scholarly Aed Ua Finn was the scribe who wrote the early genealogy of the Ó Ruairc sept then his appointment as bishop may have been due to the dominance of Tighearnán Ó Ruairc in Bréifne at this time.[6] Muirchertach Ua Mael Mochéirge, a member of the Ó Maolmochéirghe family from Drumreilly, who succeeded Aedh Ua Finn as bishop and died in 1149,[7] was also from the Ó Ruairc power base in west Bréifne. The names of Tuathal Ua Connachtaig who was bishop from *c.*1152 to 1179 and Flann Ua Connachtaigh who died in 1231 would suggest that they too came from Connacht and possibly, though not certainly, from west Bréifne. The only Cistercian to be appointed bishop of the diocese was appointed in 1185 and even though we do not know his name, he was said to be 'a Cistercian monk of good repute [who] had been elected by the clergy and people of Kells [diocese] to be their bishop'.[8] The Cistercians had considerable influence on the Ó Ruaircs at this time, and the synod of Kells, which was held in Ó Ruairc controlled territory was said to be 'the high-water mark of Cistercian influence on Irish affairs'.[9] It is possible that the Cistercian bishop owed his appointment, not to the people and clergy of the diocese, but to the Ó Ruaircs or more precisely to Derbforgaill, wife of Tighearnán Ó Ruairc.

5.   Watt, *The Church in medieval Ireland*, 87–9.
6.   He was one of the O'Finn family, who were farmers and hostellers in west Bréifne. See O'Connell, *The diocese of Kilmore*, p. 340. The original Aed Finn was said to have given the land to St Caillín for this monastery at Fenagh and 'from him descended the sept of Aedh Find i.e. the third regal family of Connacht for ever.' See Hennessy & Kelly (eds), *The Book of Fenagh*, p. 121.
7.   *AFM*, 1149; Hennessy (ed.), *Chronicum Scotorum, a chronicle of Irish affairs*, p. 347.
8.   Gwynn, *The Irish church in the eleventh and twelfth centuries*, p. 256.
9.   Ó Corráin, *The Irish Church, reform and the English invasion*, p. 84.

Both she and her husband were present at the consecration of the Cistercian abbey of Mellifont in 1157 on which occasion, as we have already noted, she donated expensive gifts. Derbforgaill continued her contact with the Cistercians after the death of her husband Tighearnán in 1172 and in 1186, one year after the Cistercian bishop was appointed to Kilmore, she retired to Mellifont abbey where she remained until her death in 1193. As we have already noted, Eugenius Echtigern's clumsy attempt to expel the new Cistercian bishop and to subsume the diocese of Kells into his own diocese of Meath ended in failure.[10]

Henry II, the king of England, arrived in Ireland in October 1171 and left in April 1172. Tighearnán Ó Ruairc was just one of many Irish kings who, during that time, submitted to him, taking an oath of loyalty and giving him hostages.[11] When the Irish Church accepted the lordship of the English king it in effect accepted that the king had certain rights in the selection of bishops and also that the Crown could claim the revenues or temporalities of a vacant See for its own use.[12] Since medieval bishops were both pastors and secular landlords, both pope and king had a vested interest in their appointment and in 1215 King John and Pope Innocent III reached an agreement which stipulated that the electors of a bishop should first seek a licence from the king before they nominated a bishop. Furthermore, they should then apply for the king's assent before the metropolitan archbishop confirmed the appointment.[13] This resulted almost immediately in the appointment of English or Anglo-Irish bishops to dioceses in the ecclesiastical province of Dublin and in the diocese of Meath where English influence was also strong. It appears to have had little impact on the diocese of Tír Briúin, however, which was under Gaelic control and where the bishops were still selected from among the native clerical families of the diocese.

Seal of the Clergy

Following the Norman invasion in 1169 many Irish dioceses, both those under Norman and native Irish control, began to establish diocesan chapters - much like the English model of secular chapters attached to the diocesan cathedral.[14] One of the chapter's important functions was to nominate a bishop when the See became vacant. The diocese of Kilmore did not establish a cathedral chapter until 1455 and, in the

10. Ibid., pp 250–6.
11. Ó Corráin, *The Irish church, its reform and the English invasion*, pp 102–3.
12. Art Cosgrave, 'Irish Episcopal temporalities in the thirteenth century' in *Arch. Hib.* 32 (1974), p. 63.
13. A.F. O'Brien, 'Episcopal elections in Ireland *c*.1254–72' in *PRIA*, 73 (1973), p. 130.
14. K. Nicholls, 'Medieval Irish Cathedral Chapters' in *Arch. Hib.*, 31 (1973), p. 103.

Figure 4.1: Fourteenth-century seal of the clergy of Kilmore. (*Courtesy of the Trustees of the British Museum*).

absence of a chapter, the bishops of the diocese were usually nominated by the community of the clergy (*communitas cleri*) under the leadership of the archdeacon. The fourteenth-century circular-shaped seal of the clergy of Tír Briúin has survived and is held in the British Museum.[15] It depicts a mitred bishop kneeling beside the Virgin Mary who is seated on a gothic throne nursing the infant Jesus. It carries the inscription *S[igillum] commune cleri Tirbriunencis*[16] and was used by the clergy of the diocese to give the stamp of approval to their episcopal nominee - a nominee who would almost always be ratified by the archbishop of Armagh and accepted as a *fait accompli* by both the king and the papacy.[17]

15.   BM, Catalogue of seals, v, 712, no. 17, 379.
16.   Nicholls, 'Medieval Irish Cathedral Chapters', p. 103; *The Breifny Antiquarian Journal*, i, 1 (1920), p. 31; O'Connell, *The diocese of Kilmore*, p. lxvi.
17.   See R. Dudley Edwards, 'Ecclesiastical appointments in the province of Tuam, 1399–1477' in *Arch. Hib.*, 33 (1975), p. 91.

This common seal of the clergy of the diocese appears to have been a common seal of the priests and bishop of the diocese. In 1368 when Bishop Richard Ó Raghallaigh and 'the most important of his clergy' accepted the censure imposed by Archbishop Milo Sweteman on the bishop they promised to draw up letters to that effect which would be sealed with 'the common seal of the bishop and clergy' of the diocese (*sigillo episcopi et cleri communi*).[18]

The King and the Appointment of Bishops

In 1245 King Henry III gave an order to all bishops and archbishops 'that they were not to attempt anything against the king's crown and dignity on pain of the loss of the temporalities which they hold from the king'.[19] The fear of permanently losing the episcopal temporalities may have been the reason that in May 1250, following the resignation and then death of Bishop Congalach Mac Idneoil, a man named Patrick, who was a clerk of the diocese of Tír Briúin, applied to the king on behalf of the 'Dean and chapter' of the diocese for a licence to elect a new bishop.[20] The clergy selected Simon Ó Ruairc as their bishop and he obtained royal assent on 20 June 1251.[21] The clergy had elected one of their own - a member of the leading sept in west Bréifne - as their bishop and in doing so had observed, to the letter of the law, the orders of the king. This adherence to procedure was unusual in the province of Armagh at this time where in most episcopal elections the royal orders were either partially or completely ignored.[22] This was particularly true of the dioceses to the west and north in the province of Armagh. During a review of royal taxation in Ireland in 1285 it was reported that:

> [In certain] bishoprics in Ulster subject to Armagh [such] as Clogher, Derry, Raphoe [and] Thirburnensis [Kilmore] the K[ing] never had custody by the death of bishops as he has in other bishoprics in Armagh … nor was licence to elect demanded. But the archbishop of Armagh appropriates to himself vacancies … and appoints bishops therein against the kingly dignity to the great loss of the K[ing].[23]

18.   Smith, *The register of Milo Sweteman*, p. 71.
19.   *Cal. Pat. Rolls* 1232–47, p. 463; Cosgrave 'Irish Episcopal temporalities in the thirteenth century' p. 64.
20.   H.S. Sweetman (ed.), *Calendar of documents relating to Ireland, 1171–1251* (London, 1875), p. 454. This reference to the 'Dean and chapter' was a formula which the royal court used in granting licences to all dioceses and it does not imply that the diocese of Kilmore had a chapter at this time.
21.   James Ware, *The antiquities and history of Ireland* (London, 1705), p. 58.
22.   O'Brien, 'Episcopal elections in Ireland, *c*.1254–72', pp 134–6.
23.   Sweetman (ed.), *Calendar of documents relating to Ireland 1285–1292*, p. 9.

King Edward I was determined to change this situation despite stiff resistance from the archbishop of Armagh. In 1289 Nicholas Mac Máel Ísu, the archbishop of Armagh complained:

> That the justices of the Common Pleas, Dublin, had ad-judged to the K. by writ of *Quo warranto* the temporalities of 5 sees when vacant, namely, Derry, Dromore, Clogher, Raphoe and Kilmore, which temporalities the archbishop and his predecessors were always wont peaceably to take in vacancy. The state of the archbishop's church is thereby disparaged not only in its faculties but in its liberties.[24]

The archbishop was, in most instances, able to maintain his entitlements in those parts of the ecclesiastical province of Armagh which lay outside English control and in the *inter Anglicos* (among the English) territories he had to recognise the king's right to custody of the temporalities while the diocesan Sees were vacant.[25]

Simon Ó Ruairc, the 'bishop of Bréifne', died in 1285.[26] He was succeeded by Mauricius, a canon from the Augustinian abbey of Kells and the first of several Augustinians to be appointed bishop of the diocese.[27] 'Brother Thomas' who succeeded Mauricius as abbot of Kells, informed King Edward I that 'Brother Maurice, his late abbot [was] elected as Bishop of Tirburnensis' and the king duly sent the letters of licence to Thomas the abbot of Kells, allowing the consecration of Mauricius to proceed.[28] On 29 June 1287, the feast of Saints Peter and Paul, Bishop Maurice, together with the bishops of Dromore and Raphoe, consecrated Matthew MacCathassaidh bishop of Clogher in St Mary's church in Lisgoole.[29] Since we do not know the family name of Mauricius we cannot speculate about where he was from though we can say with some confidence that Maolpeadar Ó Duigenan, the 'archdeacon of Breffny from Kells to Drumcliff'[30] who died in 1296, was from west Bréifne or Muintir Eolais in present-day south Leitrim.[31]

24.   Ibid., p. 251.
25.   Cosgrave, 'Irish Episcopal temporalities', p. 66.
26.   *AFM,* 1285; *AC,* 1285.
27.   Sweetman (ed.), *Calendar of Documents relating to Ireland,* 1285–1292, p. 128.
28.   Ibid.
29.   K.W. Nicholls, 'The Register of Clogher' in *Clogher Record,* vii, 3(1971/72), p. 391.
30.   *Calendar of Documents relating to Ireland,* 1296.
31.   The learned family of Ó Duibhgeannáin had branches at Castlefore in south Leitrim and Kilronan in north Roscommon. See Bernadette Cunningham, 'The Ó Duibhgeannáin family of historians and the Annals of the Four Masters' in *Bréifne,* xi, 44 (2008), pp 557–72.

Matha MacDuibne, 'a man of great esteem in his country'[32] who was bishop from 1307 to 1314, was one of the MacGivney family from east Bréifne.[33] His appointment suggests a certain shift of power from west to east in the diocese and his episcopacy coincides with the strong leadership of Giolla Íosa Ó Raghallaigh.[34] However, the next two episcopal appointees were from west Bréifne. Patraic Ó Cridecáin (O'Cregan) who was bishop from 1320 to 1328 was one the clerical family from Drumlease where the Ó Ruaircs had a castle and Bishop Conchobhar MacConsnamha (Forde), who died in 1355, belonged to another clerical family from Muintir Cionnaith, a family with strong links to the parish of Innismagrath in west Bréifne.[35] Strangely, Simon Ó Ruairc was the only one of the dominant Ó Ruairc sept to be appointed bishop of the diocese although most of the bishops appointed between 1100 and 1350 were either from west Bréifne or, like the anonymous Cistercian, had the support of the Ó Ruaircs.

The Emergence of the Ó Raghallaighs

The death of Tighearnán Ó Ruairc in 1172 brought an end to the dominance of the Ó Ruaircs in east Bréifne. The kingdom of Meath was granted to Hugh de Lacy in that year and soon he controlled much of east Bréifne and c.1197, following the misbehaviour of Gilbert de Angulo in west Bréifne, King John granted all the land west of Lough Uachtair (*ultra lacus Therebrun*) to Walter de Lacy.[36] The dominance of the de Lacy family in Bréifne was not to last and their decline coincided with the improving fortunes of the Ó Raghallaighs of east Bréifne. Cathal Ó Raghallaigh, who founded the Premonstratensian priory at Lough Uachtair and was chief of the family from c.1226 until his death thirty years later, was particularly successful in expanding his influence not just in east Bréifne but in west Bréifne also. However, his defeat a the hands of the combined forces of Ó Ruairc and Ó Connor in the battle of Magh Sleacht at the foot of Sliabh-an-Iarainn in 1256 halted his rising power and established the era when neither the

32.   Ware, *The antiquities and history of Ireland*, p. 59.
33.   *AFM*, 1314. Seán Mac Duibhne, who died in 1343 was archdeacon of Drumlane. Another member of the McGivney family, Fear Sithe Mag Dhuibhne, was bishop of the diocese from 1455 to 1464. The townland of Greaghagibney [*Gréach Mhic Ghibhne*] is in the parish of Laragh.
34.   Ciaran Parker, 'The diocese of Tir Brun (Kilmore) in the middle ages' in *Bréifne*, viii, 33 (1997), p. 816.
35.   In *AFM sub anno* 1530 we read that 'O'Donnell entered Brefney and his forces burned the best wooden house which was in Ireland then [that is] the house of Mac Consnamha'.
36.   A.J. Otway-Ruthen, 'The partition of the de Verdon lands in Ireland in 1332' in *PRIA*, 66 (1967/68), p. 412; Colin T. Veach, 'A question of timing: Walter de Lacy's seisin of Meath 1189–94' in *PRIA*, 109C (2009), p. 176.

Ó Ruaircs or the Ó Raghallaighs would control all of Bréifne.[37] From 1256 onward there would be two independent kingdoms, that of east and west Bréifne, the former under the control of the Ó Raghallaighs, the latter controlled by the Ó Ruaircs. This division of the diocese into two independent kingdoms, separated by mountains and with no one sept strong enough to unite them, hindered the development of diocesan structures as envisaged by the twelfth-century reformers.

We have seen in chapter one how the creation of the Kilmore Romanesque doorway and the elaborate bishop's crosier *c*.1170 point to a concerted effort to establish a diocesan centre in the Lough Uachtair/ Kilmore area of the diocese at that time. The fact that the cathedral church was not formally established in the parish of Kilmore until almost 300 years later, may be due, at least in part, to the divisions between east and west Bréifne with the majority of the bishops of the diocese coming from Ó Ruairc country in west Bréifne even though from the late twelfth-century the preferred *cathedra* of the diocese, appears to have been at Kilmore in east Bréifne. In times of violence and uncertainty priests and bishops tended to reside close to their own sept where they felt safer and were assured of shelter and food. For these reasons the west Bréifne bishops may have been reluctant to establish their *cathedra* at Kilmore, in the heart of Ó Raghallaigh territory in east Bréifne. The setting up of the diocesan cathedral in the church of St Feidhlimidh in the parish of Kilmore in 1455 was very late - at least 200 years after most other cathedrals were established in the country. Crucially, the newly established cathedral was situated in east Bréifne close to the Ó Raghallaigh castles of Lough Uachtair and Tullachmongan.

Richard Ó Raghallaigh

The appointment of Richard Ó Raghallaigh as bishop of the diocese *c*.1356 was a turning point indicating a shift of power in the diocese from west to east Bréifne and an indication that the leading sept of east Bréifne was interested in ecclesiastical as well as secular power.[38] From this time onwards until early modern times the bishops of the diocese tended to be either from east Bréifne or, in just two instances, complete outsiders. Bishop Richard Ó Raghallaigh was a son of Máel Sechlainn Ó Raghallaigh and a grandson of Giolla Íosa Ruadh who died in the Franciscan friary in

---

37. *AC*, 1256. For accounts of the O'Reilly's fortunes at this time see Katherine Simms, 'The O'Reillys and the kingdom of east Bréifne' in *Bréifne*, v, 19 (1979), pp 305–17; Kieran Parker, 'The O'Reillys of east Bréifne *c*.1250 - *c*.1450' in *Bréifne*, viii, 2 (1991), pp 155–80.

38. Similar developments were taking place in the neighbouring dioceses of Ardagh and Raphoe at this time. See Parker, 'The diocese of Tir Brun (Kilmore) in the middle ages', p. 816.

Cavan in 1330.[39] Richard's sexual relationship with his first cousin Edina Ó Raghallaigh - who was 'wife of one Mcguyer' - led to ongoing conflict with Milo Sweteman, the archbishop of Armagh, and eventually to Richard's excommunication by the archbishop.

Archbishop Sweteman was born in Kilkenny of English settler stock and, being an outsider, resided not in Armagh *inter Hibernicos* but rather where he felt more secure in Dromiskin *inter Anglicos* in present-day County Louth.[40] The archbishop's background and outsider status meant that he was powerless to impose sanctions on Richard Ó Raghallaigh who lived in Gaelic-controlled east Bréifne. When Bishop Ó Raghallaigh ignored the excommunication order Archbishop Sweteman called him to a meeting on 20 June 1366 *'in ecclesia parochiali de Kylmaynan beg* [in the parish church of Kilmainhambeg]' to give reasons why the fruits of his bishopric should not be taken from him.[41] The meeting place at the church of Kilmainhambeg was just outside the diocese of Tír Briúin in present-day County Meath and was probably the chapel of the Knights Hospitaller foundation which was situated there and may have doubled as the parish church. The letter citing Richard to attend the meeting with the archbishop was sent by Peter Ó Cairrealláin, the chancellor of Armagh, to Cathal Ó Raghallaigh, asking him to deliver it to Bishop Richard, his own brother. The chancellor may have chosen this communication route because Cathal Ó Raghallaigh's wife, was his own foster sister.[42]

Philip Ó Raghallaigh, an uncle of Bishop Richard Ó Raghallaigh, was chief in east Bréifne at this time and he saw his nephew's indiscretions as an opportunity to seize the fruits of the bishopric.[43] Archbishop Milo Sweteman needed Philip, the secular power in east Bréifne, to carry out his sanctions against Richard and so he proposed a meeting between them somewhere 'beyond Kellmagnean Beg' for 26 July 1366.[44] The archbishop was obviously conscious of the power struggles between the different branches of the Ó Raghallaigh sept and he did not want the bishopric to become a pawn in that struggle and so he asked Philip to find a clerk, not a layman,

39.   Parker, 'The O'Reillys of east Bréifne *c.*1250-*c.*1450', Fig. I, p. 176.
40.   Brendan Smith, 'The adventures of Milo Sweteman archbishop of Armagh 1361–1380' in *History Ireland*, iv, 4 (Winter, 1996), p. 18.
41.   Smith, *The register of Milo Sweteman*, pp 73–4.
42.   Ibid., pp 74–5, 119. Peter Okerballan was later appointed dean of Derry diocese. See H.J. Lawlor, 'A calendar of the register of Archbishop Sweteman' in *PRIA*, xxix (1911–12), p. 251.
43.   Emmet O'Byrne has suggested that Edina or Eadaoin O'Raghallaigh, the cousin with whom Richard O'Raghallaigh had the relationship, was a daughter of Philip. This would give the chieftain another motive for moving against his nephew. See *DIB*, vii, pp 868–9; Simms, 'Gaelic lordships in Ulster in the later Middle Ages', i, pp 411–2; Adrian Empey, 'Irish clergy in the high and late Middle Ages' in T.G. Barnard & W.G. Neely (eds), *The clergy of the Church of Ireland, 1000–2000* (Dublin, 2006), p. 30.
44.   Smith, *The register of Milo Sweteman*, p. 55.

to whom the fruits of the bishopric could be given on a temporary basis. He promised that if Philip took an oath of obedience to the archbishop and helped the clerk to levy the fruits due to the bishop, he would pay him for his work and would not make any agreement with Bishop Richard without his consent. Obviously Cathal Ó Raghallaigh, the bishop's brother, wanted to exclude Philip and get the job of collecting the fruits of the bishopric himself. However, Archbishop Sweteman refused to allow him to do so because 'with the consent of Philip, king of Brefnia, clerks have been appointed to do so, and their custody has been refused to Philip and to all laymen'.[45]

The sanctions imposed by the archbishop had little effect. On the feast of St John the Baptist, 29 August 1366, Milo Sweteman wrote to Bishop Richard Ó Raghallaigh urging him to end his relationship with Edina Ó Raghallaigh or else incur the wrath of the pope.[46] Two days earlier, Sweteman had commissioned Peter Ó Cairreallán, his chancellor, to carry out a visitation of Tír Briúin. William Ó Farrelly, the coarb of St Maodhóg in Drumlane, was to assist him in this task. Clearly, the archbishop's sanctions had caused divisions in the diocese between those who continued to support the bishop and those who approved of the archbishop's sanctions. The bishop's support appears to have been strong in the deanery of Kilmore and less so in the deaneries of Drumlane and Dartry and when Archbishop Sweteman had proclaimed him excommunicated in Fore, Kells and Nobber he also pronounced all 'those obedient to him' to be similarly excommunicated.[47]

Peter Ó Cairreallán began the diocesan visitation and then asked William Ó Farrelly to complete the task. He was assisted by Adam MacTiarnan, the dean of Drumlane, which meant in effect,that the deanery of Drumlane, presumably with the backing of the Augustinians of Drumlane priory, was given the impossible task of disciplining not just the bishop of the diocese but also his supporters in their neighbouring deanery of Kilmore. Their work 'not having been finished in the case of the bishop and others in the deanery of Kilmore' the archbishop took matters into his own hands once more and ordered the bishop 'his official general the dean of Kilmore [Thomas O'Sheridan] and all the rectors etc of the deanery of Kilmore' to appear before him in the parish church of 'Kilmagnean beg' on 20 October 1366.[48]

---

45. Ibid., p. 119.
46. Ibid., pp 77–8.
47. Ibid., pp 76–7.
48. Ibid., pp 78–9.

The meeting on 20 October at Kilmainhambeg appears to have been inconclusive. One month later the archbishop cited Patrick MacBradaigh, apparently Bishop Richard's main supporter among the clergy of the diocese, to appear before him on 21 November 1366 in St Ronan's church in Dromiskin in present-day County Louth. He also ordered certain vicars, both inside and outside the diocese to proclaim Richard excommunicated. He then commanded 'all dignitaries, rectors etc in the deanery of Kilmore' to appear in the (parish) church of Kilmore on 1 December 1366. The archbishop, in excluding the bishop from this meeting, was trying to win over those from the deanery of Kilmore who continued to support him. There were also plans to hold similar meetings in the parish church of St Maodhóg in Drumlane deanery and at an unspecified venue in the deanery of Dartry. It is not clear if these meetings ever took place. What is clear is that despite confessions of his offences and promises of future good behaviour, Richard Ó Raghallaigh continued as before. In June 1367 Archhishop Sweteman, in a further attempt to resolve the problems in Kilmore, appointed Cornelius Olorkan, a canon of Armagh diocese and Nemias Macmolmartyn, vicar of Kilmore parish, to carry out a metropolitan visitation of the diocese.[49] Richard Ó Raghallaigh continued to resist the efforts of the ecclesiastical and civil powers to remove him and he wrote to Archbishop Sweteman in September 1367 seeking his help against Philip Ó Raghallaigh 'who had despoiled him and his clerks.' The archbishop had no sympathy for him because of Ó Raghallaigh's continued recalcitrance and his failure to pay the fines already imposed on him.[50] The relationship between Richard Ó Raghallaigh and Milo Sweteman had broken down completely, with the racial and cultural divide between the two merely exacerbating the problem.[51]

In January 1368 Archbishop Milo Sweteman announced that, 'owing to the demerits of the bishop', he was assuming jurisdiction of the diocese. Sweteman commissioned James Scotelare who was 'learned in law' to meet Bishop Richard at Rathdycke, near Moynalty on 15 January 1368 to impose further sanctions on him. There Scotelare imposed a penalty of £100 and forty marks on Richard Ó Raghallaigh. Then Ó Raghallaigh, having sworn that he would pay these fines and abide by the commands of the church, was given absolution by Thomas Ó Sheridan, the vicar-general of the diocese, and was duly restored as bishop. Following these preliminaries:

---

49. Lawlor, 'A calendar of the register of Archbishop Sweteman', pp 281, 286.
50. Ibid., pp 246–7.
51. For racial divisions among the Irish bishops see J.A. Watt, 'English law and the Irish church: the reign of Edward I' in J.A. Watt, J.B. Morrall & F.X. Martin (eds), *Medieval studies presented to Aubrey Gwynn* (Dublin, 1961), pp 135–7.

> The bishop and the most important of his clergy present, namely Master Thomas Ossiridean, his official general, Luke Mcgaurregan, Dionysiius Ossiridean, Luke Mcmonchan, Patrick Mcbraddy, and others swore that they would ensure that letters about the foregoing, to be drawn up by the primate in the name of the bishop and clergy, would be sealed with the common seal of the bishop and clergy and returned to the primate.[52]

This agreement, which was witnessed by William Ó Farrelly among others, resolved nothing. Ten months later, at a meeting in the parish church of Kilmainhambeg, Richard Ó Raghallaigh admitted to the archbishop that he had continued his relationship with his cousin Edina and had actively impeded the archbishop's commissaries.[53] This ongoing problem was only resolved by the death of Richard Ó Raghallaigh some months later. Both he and Hugh O'Neill, the bishop of Clogher, died in 1369. The Annals of the Four Masters referred to the bishop of Clogher as 'a pious and charitable prelate' and, charitably, refrained from making any judgment on Richard Ó Raghallaigh.[54] William Ó Farrelly, 'the archdeacon of Breifni … a felicitous sage' died in the same year, leaving a power vacuum in the diocese.[55]

The controversial episcopate of Richard Ó Raghallaigh gives us an insight into the persistent but mostly ineffective attempts by the archbishop of Armagh to resolve issues within the diocese of Tír Briúin and also an insight into the deanery and clerical divisions within the diocese. We also see that there were regular metropolitan visitations and that the bigger parish churches were used for meetings of the clergy and that important decisions were sometimes taken at the fringes of these meetings. We know that such a fringe meeting took place outside the parish church of Kilmainhamwood on 14 November 1368 when:

> the bishop [Ó Raghallaigh] and Patrick Macbradi, proctor of the whole clergy of Tirburnensis and many others of the clergy [who met] in the cemetery, towards the east part of the said church [and] conceded that the primate should

---

52.   Lawlor, 'A calendar of the register of Archbishop Sweteman', p. 71.
53.   This meeting took place on 14 November 1368. See Smith, *The register of Milo Sweteman*, p. 72.
54.   *AFM*, 1369; See also *AU*, 1369, *ALC*, 1369, *AC*, 1369.
55.   *AU*, 1369.

complete his visitation by Master Peter Okerbyllan, his commissary.[56]

The behaviour of Richard Ó Raghallaigh was not exceptional at this time[57] and the divisions among the various branches of the Ó Raghallaighs may explain the attention and notoriety his episcopacy attracted. Certainly Philip Ó Raghallaigh, chief of east Bréifne, contacted Archbishop Sweteman about the situation and saw an opportunity to enhance his own standing and seize the bishop's income. Philip seems to have failed on both accounts and in 1369, the year his nephew Richard Ó Raghallaigh died, Philip was captured by his own kinsmen and 'closely bound and fettered' was imprisoned in Clogh Uachtair castle. His arrest led to widespread violence in east Bréifne. Philip was rescued later in the year, not by any of his own sept, but by Philip Maguire, the lord of Fermanagh.[58]

Bishop Deposed

John Ó Raghallaigh 1, a son of Geoffrey Ó Raghallaigh, succeeded his cousin Richard as bishop of Tír Briúin *c*.1370.[59] He too had an unhappy relationship with the archbishop of Armagh. It appears that the trouble began in 1373 when John Ó Raghallaigh got involved in a dispute in the neighbouring diocese of Ardagh where there were three different claimants to the bishopric. Archbishop Sweteman felt that he had been deceived by Ó Raghallaigh about the situation in Ardagh and so censored the bishop and demanded an account of his behaviour.[60] Two years later John Croysse, the Benedictine prior of Fore, caused John to be cited to appear before the archbishop of Armagh at Dromiskin, presumably for appropriating the tithes of the diocese which were due to Fore. John Ó Raghallaigh protested that it was unsafe for him to travel to Dromiskin and wrote to the Roman curia to protest at the actions of the 'pretended prior of Fore'.[61] The archbishop then ordered him to appear at Atrium Dei (Ardee), a location nearer east Bréifne, but he again refused stating that it was not safe for him to do so as his proctors had been robbed in

56.   Smith, *The register of Milo Sweteman*, p. 73.
57.   For example the bishop of Down was dismissed in 1440 for his indiscretions. See W.G.H. Quigley & E.F.D. Roberts (eds), *Registrum Johannis Mey, the register of John Mey Archbishop of Armagh, 1443–1456* (Belfast, 1972), pp 47–9.
58.   *AFM*, 1369.
59.   He is usually referred to as John Ó Raghallaigh I to distinguish him from from a later bishop of the same name. See Parker, 'The diocese of Tir Brun (Kilmore) in the middle ages', p. 817.
60.   Lawlor, 'A calendar of the register of Archbishop Sweteman', pp 286–7.
61.   Smith, *The register of Milo Sweteman*, p. 142.

Atrium Dei *en route* to Dromiskin. John Ó Raghallaigh knew that the archbishop, being of English stock, was reluctant to travel into Gaelic territory even in his own archdiocese and so he proposed that they meet in 'the church of Armagh or in any place *inter Hibernicos* to which he [John Ó Raghallaigh] shall have safe access'.[62]

John Ó Raghallaigh also objected to the archbishop appointing Johanne Bette, the rector of Dromynge, as his commissary or intermediary claiming that he had provocatively and deliberately appointed someone who was inimical to him. Ó Raghallaigh felt secure in Gaelic-controlled Bréifne though his dogged and confrontational style led eventually to not only falling out with the archbishop of Armagh but also to his deposition by the pope, *c.*1387. However, unlike his predecessor, he seems to have had the support of the ruling Ó Raghallaighs and he managed to remain *in situ* despite the best efforts of pope and primate to remove him. In a final though not decisive move against John Ó Raghallaigh, the pope (Urban VI) appointed Thomas Rushook, an English Dominican, as bishop of Tír Briúin in 1389.

Thomas Rushook

Thomas Rushook had an extraordinary career.[63] He was prior of the Dominican convent in Hereford in 1372 and two years later was appointed provincial of the Order. King Richard II was only ten years old when in 1377, just one year after his father had died, he succeeded his grandfather Edward III. Shortly afterwards Thomas Rushook became the young king's confessor and mentor. Perhaps because of his royal court commitments, he was removed from his role as provincial of the Dominicans in 1379 by the Master-General of the Order, only to be restored to it by Pope Urban VI the following year.[64] The Dominicans or Black Friars established their first monastery in Dublin, where the Four Courts now stand, in 1224 and they were well established in Ireland by the time Thomas Rushook was appointed provincial. The Irish Dominicans were part of the English Dominican province and so Thomas Rushook was provincial of the Irish and English Dominicans although he appointed a vicar to help him oversee the Irish Dominicans.[65]

62.   Ibid.
63.   Chris Given-Wilson, *The Royal household and the King's affinity: service, politics and finance in England 1360–1413* (New Haven, 1986), pp 177–8.
64.   Walter Gumley, 'Provincial priors and vicars of the English Dominicans, 1221–1916' in *The English Historical review*, xxxiii, 130 (Apr. 1918), p. 246. It is possible that his demotion and re-instatement may have been due to the Great Western Schism and the fact that the Dominican Master General was a Frenchman.
65.   B. O'Sullivan, 'The Dominicans in medieval Dublin' in *Dublin historical record*, ix, 2 (June-Aug. 1947), p. 49; Benedict O'Sullivan, *Medieval Irish Dominican studies*, ed. by

The general chapter of the Dominican Order decreed in 1378 that Ireland should be established as an independent province. Before this decision could be enacted the Great Western Schism began with two rival popes - Urban VI based in Rome and Clement VII in Avignon – both claiming to be the legitimate pope. The Master General of the Dominican Order was a Frenchman and he backed the Avignon pope while Thomas Rushook and his fellow countrymen sided with Urban VI. Thomas Rushook, seeing the opportunity the schism offered, appealed to Rome against the decision to allow the Dominicans in Ireland to form an independent province. He won his appeal much to the disappointment of the Dublin Dominicans and in 1380 when John de Leycestre, his vicar in Ireland, tried to enter the Dominican monastery in Dublin he found the gates locked against him. Undeterred de Leycestre returned with armed men who forced their way into the monastery where a melee ensued before he and his followers were arrested by the lord mayor of Dublin.[66]

It would seem that Thomas Rushook was even more unpopular in England, where he continued to be part of the young king's inner circle, than he was in Ireland.[67] He resigned as provincial of his Order in 1382 on his appointment as archdeacon of St Asaph and he was made bishop of Llandaff in 1383 before being translated to Chichester in 1385. On 5 March 1388, Rushook was impeached for high treason by the parliament which resented the king's high-handed approach.[68] Rushook narrowly escaped execution and instead was exiled to Ireland where he was ordered to live in the city of Cork or within two miles of it.[69] On 8 July 1388, he was given royal protection and letters of assistance which stipulated that he must be at Bristol port by 1 August, that he could have 'forty marks for the first year, one bed, clothing, a book for saying his hours and two English servants' and that he must arrive in Cork before Michaelmas day (29 September).[70] Rushook's fall from grace was complete. His appointment as bishop of Tír Briúin in 1389 may have been an attempt by both pope and king to ensure that he would have a small income on which to survive.[71] The new bishop of

Hugh Fenning (Dublin, 2009), pp 194–8.

66.   Ibid., pp 50–1. Daphne D.C. Pochin Mould, *The Irish Dominicans* (Dublin, 1957), pp 59–60.

67.   Richard G. Davies, 'The episcopate and the political crisis in England of 1386–1388' in *Speculum*, li, 4 (Oct. 1976), pp 667, 672.

68.   *Rotuli Parliamentorum*, iii (London, 1832), pp 238–44; Given-Wilson, *The Royal household and the king's affinity: service, politics and finance in England, 1360–1413*, pp 175–88; Nigel Saul, *Richard II* (New Haven, 1997), pp 124–7.

69.   Costello, *De Annatis Hiberniae*, i, p. 255.

70.   Ibid.

71.   The king described the see of Tír Briúin as '*modicus*' in 1390. See Davies, 'The episcopate and the political crisis in England of 1386–1388', p. 674, n. 57.

Tír Briúin was granted an annual income of £40 by Richard II in 1390 following a petition from the bishop's 'poor friends'.[72] It is possible that he made the wise decision not to travel north from Cork to take possession of the remote diocese of Tír Briúin *inter Hibernicos*. Instead, he managed to return to England where he died in 1393 and was buried within the church of Saints Peter and Paul at Seal in Kent.[73]

John Ó Raghallaigh 1, despite having being deposed by Urban VI *c*.1387, appears to have remained in possession of the See of Tír Briúin and he was able to look to Clement VII in Avignon to give him legitimacy. For four years there were two bishops of the diocese, one who looked to Rome the other to Avignon, both dying in 1393. The annals make no reference to the death of Thomas Rushook but they do record *sub anno* 1393 that 'John, son of Geoffrey O'Reilly, bishop of Brefney died'.[74] He had remained the *de facto* bishop of the diocese until his death. The failure of the first attempt to impose an English bishop on the diocese did not prevent the appointment of John Stokes, an English Benedictine, to the diocese approximately thirty years later. He was appointed suffragan or assistant bishop in Lichfield in 1407 and Worcester in 1416 before being appointed bishop of Tír Briúin.[75] John Chourles, another English Benedictine monk, was appointed bishop of Dromore in 1410 and it seems that these appointments to Irish dioceses were not much more than honorary titles since it appears that both of them continued to spend most of their time in England carrying out their suffragan duties.[76] It was common practice for absentee bishops of Irish Sees to continue working as auxiliary bishops in England.[77] Besides, John Stokes was faced with the same difficulty as Thomas Rushook – the See that they were both appointed to was already occupied by a native of the diocese.

Nicholas MacBradaigh

Nicholas MacBradaigh, who was the bishop of Tír Briúin from 1395 to 1421, was the first of the MacBradaigh sept to hold that position.

---

72. Ibid.
73. James Ware wrote that he died 'tis thought of grief.' See Ware, *The Antiquities and history of Ireland*, p. 59. See also *Calendar of patent rolls of Richard II, iv, 1389–1392* (London, 1902), pp 228, 239.
74. *AFM*, 1393; *ALC*, 1393.
75. William Stubbs, *Registrum Sacrum Anglicanum, an attempt to exhibit the course of episcopal succession in England from the records and chronicles of the church* (Oxford, 1858), p. 205.
76. Ibid., p. 204; Gordon Beattie, *Gregory's Angels, a history of the abbeys, priories, parishes and schools of the monks and nuns following the rule of St Benedict* (Herefordshire, 1997), p. 47.
77. Michael Robson, 'Franciscan bishops of Irish dioceses active in medieval England' in *Coll. Hib.*, 38 (1997), pp 7–39. My thanks to Colmán Ó Clabaigh for this reference.

He was rector of Cúil Brighdín and Sendamair (Shantemon?), an area almost co-terminus with the parish of Castletara, before he was appointed bishop.[78] This rectory which was *sine cure* and the vicarage of the same name were held in successive generations by members of the MacBradaigh clerical family, though it is not certain that Nicholas ever held the vicarage. An entry in the *Miscellaneous Irish Annals* for the year 1396, which stated that 'Bishop Ruaidhri MacBradaigh, ie the Bishop of Bréifne came from Rome with bulls [of consecration]'[79] has caused some confusion by incorrectly naming him Ruaidhrí.[80] In other details the entry is correct as Nicholas got the approval of Boniface IX on 27 August 1395 and was consecrated in Rome before he returned to Ireland in 1396.[81] His kinsman Gilbert MacBradaigh, who was vicar of St Patrick's church in Drung and St Brighid's church in Laragh, was appointed bishop of Ardagh in the same year that Nicholas was approved for Kilmore.

Disputes

Following Gilbert's consecration the pope appointed Augustine MacBradaigh to the vacant vicarage of Drung and Laragh. Bishop Nicholas MacBradaigh contested the pope's right to do so and expelled Augustine from the vicarage.[82] In November 1398 the pope instructed the archbishop of Armagh to admonish Nicholas MacBradaigh 'and others concerned' in this expulsion and to order them to make satisfaction for the fruits they had received from the vicarage.[83] This dispute rumbled on for almost three decades and in September 1408 Augustine MacBradaigh lodged an appeal with Nicholas Fleming the archbishop of Armagh at a meeting in St John's church in Ardee against a previous ruling in favour of Bishop Nicholas MacBradaigh. The archbishop allowed the appeal and cited Bishop Nicholas, along with N. McBrady, Andrew McBrady, Patrick Magauran 'and all others who have an interest in the case' to appear before him in St Peter's church in Drogheda on 1 October 1408.[84] Augustine MacBradaigh was a wily opponent and, as we have already noted, he succeeded in holding onto the vicarage despite the best efforts of Bishop Nicholas and others to remove him.

78. *CPL*, v, p. 167.
79. Seamus Ó h-Innse (ed. & trans.), *Miscellaneous Irish Annals (AD 1114–1437), Fragment iii* (Dublin, 1947), p. 156.
80. This error was repeated by James Ware who referred to him as 'Roderick Brady'. See *The Antiquities and history of Ireland*, p. 59.
81. Costello, *De Annatis Hiberniae*, i, p. 255.
82. *CPL*, v, p. 168.
83. Ibid.
84. Lawlor, 'A calendar of the register of Archbishop Fleming', p. 120.

Figure 4.2: Grotesque head in St Patrick's church, Castletara.

There was also a protracted dispute between Bishop Nicholas MacBradaigh and some of the O'Sheridan priests in the diocese. Nicholas O'Sheridan had been appointed perpetual vicar of Kilmore by John Colton the archbishop of Armagh *c.*1394 when there was no bishop in the diocese. Bishop Nicholas refused to recognise the archbishop's right to make appointments when the See was void. He expelled Nicholas O'Sheridan from the vicarage and appointed Cormac Maconaind in his place. O'Sheridan appealed successfully to Rome and the pope ordered Bishop Nicholas to surrender the vicarage under pain of excommunication.[85] There was another particularly bitter dispute, beginning in the year 1412, between Patrick O'Sheridan, a clerk of the diocese, and Bishop MacBradaigh. Patrick O'Sheridan wrote to Rome making certain accusations against his bishop. Philip Nangle, the bishop of Clonmacnois, along with one or two others, was asked to adjudicate on the dispute. In evidence to the inquiry, Patrick O'Sheridan 'unjustly (as it is said) made diverse charges against him [Bishop MacBradaigh] and though frequently requested to recall them did not do so'.[86] We do

85.   Ibid., v, p. 399.
86.   Smith, *The register of Nicholas Fleming*, pp 234–6; H.J. Lawlor, 'A calendar of the register of Archbishop Fleming' in *PRIA*, xxx (1912–13), p. 158.

not know the precise nature of the charges Patrick O'Sheridan brought against Bishop MacBradaigh or how the dispute between them was resolved. The appointment of Donatus O'Gowan as bishop of the diocese on 13 August 1421 probably brought an end to that particular dispute if it had not been resolved before then.

It was during the episcopate of Nicholas MacBradaigh, in the early 1400s, that a concerted effort was made by some lay people and priests of the diocese to prevent tithes going to the Benedictine priory of Fore. Presumably they did so with the approval of their bishop. However, Archbishop Nicholas Fleming of Armagh sided with the priory of Fore in this dispute and his letter to bishop Nicholas in 1410 is unequivocal in declaring that 'under the provincial constitution of the church of Armagh' those who withheld the tithes 'have incurred the sentence of greater excommunication'.[87] The archbishop ordered Bishop Nicholas to admonish, those who were guilty and to get them to restore the tithes to the priory within twelve days. If those withholding the tithes continued to do so the bishop was to formally excommunicate them.

Bishop Nicholas MacBradaigh appears to have had a good relationship with the Augustinians in Drumlane. Some of his predecessors had taken the vicarage of St Maodhóg's (parish) church in Drumlane from the Augustinian canons, even though they claimed that right 'from ancient times'.[88] This resulted in the appointment of secular priests to the vicarage. When it became vacant during the episcopacy of Nicholas MacBradaigh he restored possession of it to the Augustinians who, thereafter, sometimes appointed their own canons and at other times secular priests to the vicarage. In almost every instance the vicars were members of the Ó Faircheallaigh family.[89] In 1401 Maurice Ó Faircheallaigh was removed from the vicarage of Drumlane and David Ó Faircheallaigh, who was not yet ordained, was installed in his place. The vicarage was valued at seven marks which was considered insufficient by David who appealed to Rome and was granted tithes from certain churches and townlands in the parishes of Kilsherdany, Laragh and Lavey.[90]

Crisis in the Diocese

When a general council to end the Great Western Schism was arranged for Pisa on 25 March 1409 by those 'desiring peace in the church', the

87. Ibid., p. 134.
88. *CPL*, vi, p. 159. As part of that right the vicars of Drumlane paid a yearly cess to the priory. See *CPL*, v, p. 452.
89. Ibid., p. 159.
90. Ibid., p. 450.

Figure 4.3: St Patrick's church, Moybolgue.

province of Armagh nominated Robert Montayne, bishop of Meath, and John Whythed, a theologian, to be their representatives at this council. These two proctors were approved at the end of January 1409 by Nicholas MacBradaigh along with the archbishop of Armagh and the bishops of Clogher and Ardagh.[91] At about the same time David Ó Faircheallaigh travelled to Italy to meet Gregory XII, one of the claimants to the papacy during the schism. Gregory XII, who was over eighty years old and based at Rimini, having being abandoned by most of the cardinals who had elected him, and believing that the See of Tír Briúin was vacant, duly appointed and consecrated David Ó Faircheallaigh as bishop of the diocese.

It appears that 'David Episcopus Triburnien' also met John XXIII, another claimant to the papacy[92], and on 26 March 1409 promised to pay him thirty-three florins for his 'very minute services'.[93] Having successfully been appointed bishop of the diocese and with the apparent backing of two of the claimants to the papacy, David O'Farrelly returned to the diocese in the late spring or early summer of 1409. Archbishop Fleming took immediate action to rectify the situation by calling a metropolitan visitation of the diocese for 9 July 1409 and then

91.   Smith, *The register of Nicholas Fleming*, pp 96–8.
92.   Baldassare Cossa, who took the name John XXIII, has been denied a place in the canonical lists of popes thus allowing Angelo Roncalli to adopt the same name when he became pope in 1958.
93.   Costello, *De Annatis Hiberniae*, i, p. 250.

instructed Bishop MacBradaigh 'to cite his clergy and to appear with them at St Patrick's church, Moybolge, on 18 July'. See Fig. 4.3. He specifically instructed him to cite 'David, claiming to be Bishop and Master Thomas [O'Sheridan], Archdeacon of Tír Briúin'.[94] Archbishop Fleming annulled David Ó Faircheallaigh's appointment and a few weeks later, in August 1409, Bishop Nicholas MacBradaigh, in a further sanction, removed the vicarage of Drumlane from Ó Faircheallaigh which he had held since 1401, and restored it to the Augustinians in Drumlane. David Ó Faircheallaigh travelled to Rome to appeal against the decisions of his archbishop and bishop and he died there in late 1410.[95]

Bishop Nicholas MacBradaigh died in 1421, having been an active bishop of the diocese for *circa* twenty-seven years. The many disputes he had throughout his episcopacy – disputes with the papacy, the archbishop of Armagh, the priory of Fore and individual diocesan priests - suggests a confrontational style. The reality was that he, and other late medieval bishops of the diocese, had limited powers and many frustrating restrictions on how they operated. The papacy insisted on its right to make appointments to certain vicarages and rectories and the many letters from people in the diocese to Rome throughout late medieval and early modern times encouraged the papal court's involvement in diocesan affairs. The archbishop of Armagh also retained the right to appoint clerics to vicarages when the See was vacant and also during metropolitan visitations of the diocese. The hands-on approach of the archbishop of Armagh in the affairs of the dioceses within his province and the regular visitations of the diocese of Tír Briúin either by the archbishop himself or by people delegated by him to do so, further restricted the role of the bishop.

The large area of the diocese which paid tithes to Fore and to Kells, both houses which were by this time located outside the diocese, was a considerable drain on an impoverished diocese. These religious houses also retained the right to make appointments to certain vicarages, further restricting the role of the bishop in the diocese. So the many disputes Bishop Nicholas MacBradaigh was involved in were not altogether due to his own personality but rather were attempts to lessen the power of ecclesiastics in Rome and Armagh to make appointments within the diocese and to stem the flow of tithes going to subsidise religious houses outside the diocese. Bishop MacBradaigh died in 1421 and the Annals of the Four Masters recorded that 'Nicholas MacBrady, Bishop of Bréifne, a man distinguished for wisdom, piety, continence and uprightness,

94.   Lawlor, 'A calendar of the register of Archbishop Fleming', pp 126–7.
95.   *CPL*, vi, pp 226–7.

died'.[96] The Annals of Ulster had a shorter entry stating that he was 'one eminent in piety and hospitality' and James Ware, writing in 1704, said that he was 'a man eminent for his charity to the poor'.[97]

Domhnall Ó Gabhann

The Great Western Schism which began in 1378 ended in 1417. The schism, where there were at first two and then three rival claimants to the papacy, had caused or at least allowed confusion and divisions to prevail even in the remote diocese of Tír Briúin in the north west of Ireland. During the schism there were three different periods when there were two rivals claiming to be bishop of the diocese. However, with the election of Pope Martin V in 1417 the schism came to an end at it was he who appointed 'Donatus Ogoband [O'Gowan]' bishop of the diocese on 13 August 1421:

> Pope Martin V, having heard that the bishoprick of Triburna was vacant by the demise … of Nicholas of good memory … after due deliberation made choice of Donatus Ogoband perpetual vicar of Villetempli [Ballintemple] who on trustworthy testimony had been recommended to him for his learning, blameless life and conversation, foresight and prudence in matters spiritual and temporal.[98]

It was almost a year later, on 10 June 1422, that the pope gave faculties to Domhnall Ó Gabhann to 'be consecrated by any Catholic bishop of his choice, assisted by two or three like bishops'. The consecrator was then to forward Bishop Donatus's oath of fealty to the pope 'without prejudice to the archbishop of Armagh'.[99] Then on 13 April 1423 Domhnall promised to pay thirty-three florins, the common service tax of his See, which was due to the papal courts.[100]

The episcopacy of Domhnall Ó Gabhann, which lasted twenty-three years, was less controversial than that of his predecessor even though he too had many disputes to deal with. The vicarage of Drung and Laragh continued to be troublesome even after the death of Augustine MacBradaigh in 1428. Cornelius Maconnayng, the vicar of these two churches, was silenced by Thomas O'Sheridan the archdeacon of the diocese in 1430 following complaints by Adam O'Fay of

96.   *AFM*, 1421; *AC*, 1421.
97.   Ware, *The Antiquities and history of Ireland*, p. 59.
98.   Costello, *De Annatis Hiberniae*, i, p. 256.
99.   *CPL*, vii, p. 202. See also pp 161, 201.
100.   Costello, *De Annatis Hiberniae*, i, p. 256.

Magherintemple. Cornelius then appealed to the pope against that sentence stating that his accuser 'was an abbreviator of papal letters'.[101] Two other priests, Philip MacBradaigh and David Omoghan, were in dispute over the vicarage of Kilsherdany and this dispute led to a series of letters being sent to and from Rome and the involvement of Archbishop John Swayne.[102] Patrick O'Sheridan lodged complaints against Patrick O'Farrelly the vicar of 'St Felim's parish church Kylmor' and managed to replace him in the vicarage. O'Farrelly appealed to Archbishop John Swayne who insisted that O'Farrelly's right to the vicarage be upheld pending an enquiry. O'Sheridan complained that 'Audoen [Eoghan] Orayly captain of his nation and Donald Orayly hindered him and did other things to prevent his peaceful possession of said vicarage'.[103] The O'Reillys, who were in dispute with Patrick O'Sheridan over certain lands in the parish of Kilmore, seized the opportunity to side with O'Farrelly. O'Sheridan prevailed in the dispute. Patrick O'Farrelly was later appointed vicar of Urney for a short period before joining the Augustinians in Drumlane.

The dispute over the tithes going from the diocese to the Benedictines in Fore continued to rumble on. In 1440 the prior of Fore complained to Archbishop John Mey that they had been prevented by the bishop of Kilmore (Domhnall Ó Gabhann), Owen O'Reilly and others from enjoying the fruits of certain churches in the diocese which were due to them. The archbishop first cited them to appear before him in St Peter's Church in Drogheda in September 1440 and later on mandated the bishops of Meath and Ardagh to deal with the dispute.[104] The bishop, together with Owen O'Reilly and other unnamed people, was, in November 1440, cited to appear before the archbishop's officials at Termonfechin and the all were warned that if they did not heed the citation, proceedings would be instituted for the deposition of the bishop.[105] The siting of the meeting at Termonfechin, which took its name from St Féichín of Fore, was ominous for the men from Bréifne. The bishop had to agree to continue to pay the tithes to Fore and Owen O'Reilly had, on his own behalf and on behalf of his kinsmen and subjects, to swear an oath of obedience to the archbishop of Armagh and he was told that if anything was 'done to the prejudice or loss of the church, two-fold restitution is to be made'.[106]

101.   *CPL*, viii, p. 374.
102.   Chart (ed.), *The register of John Swayne*, pp 75–6.
103.   Ibid., p. 80.
104.   Quigley & Roberts (eds), *Registrum Johannis Mey*, pp 63–4.
105.   Ibid., pp 14–16.
106.   Ibid., p. 46.

Coarbs and Erenaghs

Patrick O'Sheridan was not only a priest of the diocese he was also the erenagh of the church lands in the parish of Kilmore. Similarly Luke Magauran, the perpetual vicar of Killinagh, was 'principal erenach in that part'.[107] Bishop Ó Gabhann was unable, for a variety of reasons, to make appointments in several vicarages in his diocese. However, he seemed to have some involvement in the appointment of erenaghs and coarbs in the diocese. George Montgomery, the Church of Ireland bishop of Derry, Raphoe and Clogher from 1605–1610, was possibly the author of the early seventeenth-century report which described the role of the bishop in appointing an erenagh:

> When an Herenaghe died the successor was chosen after the manner of the countrye by the rest of the sept, who chose and presented one of themselves to the Bishoppe, who finding him capable of the place allowed and admitted him … and had for that allowance and confirmation a fine *pro introitu*. If the Bishoppe for just cause do refuse to admit the Herenaghe, the rest of the sept must choose and present an other, but not out[side] of the sept.[108]

The same report states that the erenaghs 'do for the most part of them speak Lattin, and they say that ancientlye they used to have primam tonsuram, yet nevertheless they affirme that they always used to marry'. The bishop carried out an annual visitation to see if the erenagh was carrying out the duties expected of him and he could remove the erenagh if he was found negligent.[109]

Bishop Domhnall Ó Gabhann, writing from the sleeping chamber of the Franciscan house of Cavan on 19 September 1438, fulfilled his role in the appointment of erenaghs following the death of Murianus O'Farrelly, 'the chief herenach of all the lands of the nation of Muntyr face allaich'.[110] In his letter the bishop granted 'the said office of coarb of St Medocius [Maodhóg] of Drumlechan … and the herenachy of said lands' to Nicholas O'Farrelly, a clerk of the diocese of Tír Briúin.[111] Bishop Domhnall also

107.   Ibid., p. 47.
108.   Bodleian Library, MS 612, f. 36; Quoted in Henry A. Jefferies, 'Erenaghs in pre-plantation Ulster: an early seventeenth-century account' in *Arch. Hib.* liii (1999), p. 17. See also 'A letter written in the year 1605 by Sir John Davis, Knt. Attorney General of Ireland to Robert Earl of Salisbury' in Charles Vallancey, *Collectanea De Rebus Hibernicis* (Dublin, 1786), i, pp 158–60.
109.   Ibid.
110.   Chart (ed.), *The register of John Swayne*, p. 180.
111.   Ibid.

appointed priests to vicarages in the diocese, though several of them, including Matthew O'Droma the vicar of Kinawley, felt so insecure in their vicarages, due to the manner of their appointments, that they wrote to Rome in order to have their appointments validated.[112] The bishop's role in making appointments was limited although Bishop Domhnall does not seem to have railed against these restrictions as much as his predecessor had done.

It is not known where exactly Bishop Domhnall Ó Gabhann or any of his predecessors resided. Since he and all his immediate predecessors were from prominent families in east Bréifne we can safely assume that they lived in east Bréifne near to their families and possibly in the parish of Kilmore. In 1441 it was suggested to the bishop of Killala that he write rather than travel to see Bishop Ó Gabhann 'it being dangerous and expensive to have access to him on account of the great distance to the place he commonly lives'.[113] We know for certain that he was in the sleeping chamber of the Franciscan friary in Cavan on 19 September 1438 and it is possible that he stayed there regularly.[114] There was still no cathedral or *cathedra* in the diocese though it would seem that his long episcopate and that of his predecessor, which together totalled fifty-two years, brought some stability to the diocese, which allowed his successor Andrew MacBradaigh to designate the parish church of Kilmore as the diocesan cathedral.

In late 1444 or early 1445, when he was 'in his seventieth year and more', Domhnall Ó Gabhann, wrote to Rome stating that he was burdened with age and an unspecified incurable disease and requesting that he be allowed to resign.[115] It appears that he also suggested that his successor would be Andrew MacBradaigh the 'archdeacon of Tír Briúin, who is an acolyte, is in his fiftieth year and more, is of noble race, and is very skilled in canon and civil law'. Pope Eugenius mandated the archbishop of Armagh to appoint Andrew MacBradaigh bishop of the diocese 'provided he find him fit, that he find no fraud or deception against the said Donatus, nor any simony between him and Andrew'.[116] Domhnall retired and, perhaps for that reason, there is no reference to his death in the annals, and according to his wishes, he was succeeded by Andrew MacBradaigh.

112.   *CPL*, ix, p. 441.
113.   Ibid., p. 178. In this year Bishop Domhnall Ó Gabhann and Bishop Piaras Maguire of Clogher were placed under excommunication by Archbishop John Prene because they supported Charles O'Mellan, the O'Neill backed contender for the position of dean of Armagh. See Lynch, 'The administration of John Bole' p. 54.
114.   Chart (ed.), *The register of John Swayne*, p. 180.
115.   *CPL*, viii, p. 250.
116.   Ibid.

Andrew MacBradaigh

It seems that Andrew MacBradaigh, who was born *c*.1394, had studied at Oxford. The rectory of Kedy, a much sought after benefice without cure and valued at eight marks, which he held from 1423 to 1436, helped to finance his education abroad. And although not yet ordained a priest, he was, by the late 1420s, the rural dean of Drumlane. Sometime before 1428, he, along with the archdeacon Thomas O'Sheridan and Bishop Domhnall Ó Gabhann, deprived Augustine MacBradaigh of the vicarage of Drung and Laragh.[117] It would appear that the bishop valued Andrew MacBradaigh's skills in canon law in such disputes and that he and Thomas O'Sheridan were part of the bishop's trusted inner circle. In 1436 Thomas O'Sheridan, in a surprise move, resigned from his position as archdeacon of Kilmore, which carried a benefice worth twelve marks, in favour of Andrew MacBradaigh who in turn gave O'Sheridan the rectory of Kedy.[118] It appears that by this time Andrew MacBradaigh had lost the rectory of Bali Mictonchabuil (Magherintemple), although he was still well subsidised by the three other benefices he held which were all *sine cure* and had a combined value of approximately twenty marks. He was still an acolyte in minor orders at the age of fifty when, on 9 March 1445, he was appointed bishop of Tír Briúin.[119] Since Eugene O'Reilly, 'who is by both parents of a stock of kings'[120] succeeded him as archdeacon of the diocese we can safely assume that the newly-appointed bishop had the backing of the ruling family in east Bréifne.[121]

The bishops in Ireland in the fifteenth century, including Andrew MacBradaigh, had to cope with the pope, the archbishop of Armagh and certain religious houses all claiming the right to make clerical appointments within their dioceses. The archbishop of Armagh insisted on his right to the temporalities of the diocese when the See was vacant and also on his right to make appointments to vacancies in Tír Briúin during the year in which his metropolitan visitation to the diocese was taking place. Exercising this latter right, Archbishop John Mey appointed Patrick Obiggegan, in July 1449, to the vicarage of the church of St Maolán in Annagh which had become vacant by the death of Nemeas O'Fay and he mandated the prior of Drumlane and Adam O'Fay to induct him or his proctor into the vicarage of Annagh.[122]

---

117. *CPL*, v, p. 168.
118. *CPL.*, viii, p. 605; Costello, *De Annatis Hiberniae*, i, p. 235.
119. Ibid. See also W.H. Grattan, 'The episcopal succession in the diocese of Kilmore, 1356–1560' in *The Breifny Antiquarian Society's Journal*, i, 1 (1920), p. 50.
120. *CPL.*, ix, p. 531.
121. Eugene O'Reilly was deposed as archdeacon of the diocese in 1474. See *CPL*, xiii, p. 372.
122. Quigley and Roberts (eds), *Registrum Johannis Mey*, p. 208.

Bishop Andrew MacBradaigh, being familiar with canon law, claimed that the archbishop could only make such appointments to vacancies which came about by deprivation and not by death and so he refused to recognise the appointment of Obiggegan.[123] Patrick Obiggegan may not have succeeded in taking possession of the vicarage at any time and his decision to retire from it in 1450 brought an end to this dispute.[124]

A Cathedral at Kilmore

Andrew MacBradaigh was bishop for ten years from 1445 to 1455 and it was during that time that the important decision was taken to establish a cathedral chapter in the diocese and to designate the church of St Feidhlimidh in the parish of Kilmore as the diocesan cathedral. This decision seems to have been taken in the first half of the year 1453. Andrew MacBradaigh:

> seeing that he was without a cathedral church and its canons, deputed and named, in an assembly of the whole clergy of the diocese and with their consent, the parish church of St Felimy, Cellmore to be the cathedral church.[125]

This collective decision was made at diocesan level before the bishop applied to Rome for approval. The death of Pope Nicholas V delayed proceedings and it was not until April 1455 that his successor, Calixtus III, gave formal approval to the setting up of the cathedral at Kilmore and a diocesan chapter consisting of thirteen canons.[126] From this time onwards the diocese would generally be called 'Kilmore' in most church documents, though occasionally the older Latinised title of *Tirburnenis* or variations of that spelling would be used.

The decision to establish the cathedral at St Feidhlimidh's church in the parish of Kilmore was merely confirming what had been the practice for some time. Three hundred years before this most of the diocesan Sees were established at earlier monastic sites which gave their names to the dioceses. The short-lived attempt to establish the Bréifne diocesan cathedral at Kells was followed *c.*1170 by an equally unsuccessful attempt to locate it at Kilmore with the creation of the wonderfully elaborate Kilmore Romanesque doorway and the 'MacBrady' crosier. The defeat of Tighearnán Ó Ruairc, the division of Bréifne into two separate kingdoms

---

123.   Ibid., pp 161–3.
124.   MacKiernan, *Diocese of Kilmore*, p. 147.
125.   *CPL*, xi, p. 240.
126.   Ibid; Costello, *De Annatis Hiberniae*, i, p. 252.

and the fact that the bishops of the diocese were almost exclusively from west Bréifne until the mid-fourteenth-century, had militated against establishing Kilmore as the diocesan cathedral. The regular violence between the various septs, the resultant instability and the impoverished state of the diocese prevented it from establishing a cathedral and chapter as most other dioceses had done in the late twelfth or early thirteenth centuries.[127] However, it is likely, especially from the mid-1300s when the bishops of the diocese were chosen from east Bréifne, that they resided in Kilmore parish and used St Feidhlimidh's church as their pro-cathedral. A papal document for the year 1446 refers to St Feidhlimidh's church of Kilmore 'at which the bishop of Triburnen [Andrew MacBradaigh] resides and holds his see'.[128] Presumably some of his predecessors did likewise.

Saint Mary's Augustinian priory in Drumlane could have been chosen as the diocesan See by the priests and bishops of the diocese in the early 1450s since it was the richest and most powerful ecclesiastical centre in the diocese at that time.[129] It had a larger church and greater income than any other religious house or parish in the diocese. It was located on the site of an early monastery with links to St Maodhóg and possessed the *Breac Maodhóg* and *Clog Maodhóg* and through these relics promoted devotion to the saint. By choosing Kilmore and not Drumlane as the diocesan See, the rather obscure St Feidhlimidh and not St Maodhóg became the patron saint of the diocese. In The Book of Fenagh 'Feidlim … and powerful, holy Mochaemhog' are listed among Saint Caillín's inner circle.[130] However, while Feidhlimidh remains a shadowy figure in the account of Caillín's Life, Maodhóg is a central character in it and it is in 'the house of faultless Mochoemog' that Caillín died and was buried in 'Relig-Mochaemhog' for a period of twelve years before his bones were brought back to Fenagh.[131] The cult of Maodhóg was promoted by the O'Rourkes and not by the O'Reillys and, with the establishment of the cathedral at Kilmore, devotion to Feidhlimidh increased. The Martyrology of Donegal recorded that Feidhlimidh of Cill-mór [Bishop and Patron] had his feast-day on 3 August and that it was marked by 'a holiday, fair, indulgence and octave'.[132]

Houses of Augustinian canons were located at many Irish Sees, including the neighbouring diocese of Clogher, and there seemed to have

127. Nicholls, 'Medieval Irish cathedral chapters', p. 103.
128. *CPL*, ix, p. 559.
129. See Nicholls, 'Medieval Irish cathedral chapters', p. 111; Parker, 'The diocese of Tir Brun (Kilmore) in the middle ages', p. 819.
130. Hennessy & Kelly (eds), *The Book of Fenagh*, p. 413.
131. Ibid., pp 111, 305.
132. Ó Cléirigh, *The Martyrology of Donegal*, p. 209.

been a good relationship between the Augustinian canons in Drumlane and the secular priests in the diocese, with diocesan priests regularly joining the Augustinians and the canons of Drumlane and Kells providing bishops for the diocese. Crucially Kilmore parish was situated in the heart of Ó Raghallaigh country near their fortresses at Lough Uachtair and Tullachmongan and they were not going to cede control of the cathedral to the O'Farrelly's, the coarbs of Drumlane or to the Magauran's of Tullyhaw who supplied Drumlane priory with clergy. Besides, Drumlane, more often than not, was under the control of the O'Rourkes. Andrew MacBradaigh died in May 1455. He was sixty-one years old. Chances are he had not received the letter from Rome recognising St Feidlhimidh's church as the diocesan cathedral before his death but, crucially, Rome had approved of the church of Kilmore becoming a diocesan cathedral.

Even though the decision was made to locate the cathedral of the diocese at Kilmore and not at Drumlane, the Augustinian order continued to have increasing influence and power in the diocese. The Augustinian canons, especially those based at Drumlane and Kells, wielded much greater power in the diocese than did the Franciscans of Cavan, the Premonstratensians of Lough Uachtair or the Benedictines of Fore. The Augustinians may have been better educated than the majority of the diocesan priests, some of whom belonged to clerical families with hereditary succession and most likely an apprenticeship approach to the education of clerics. A minority of diocesan priests were Oxford educated but this was expensive and led to unholy scrambling for the limited number of sinecure benefices that were available in the diocese to fund their education. It is not surprising then than that the Augustinians of Drumlane and Kells had a steady supply of clerical students from the diocese and also a steady flow of diocesan priests choosing to become canons regular in one or other of these religious houses. Besides, becoming an Augustinian did no harm at all to ones chances of promotion, as we shall see in the following chapter.

Chapter 5

The Augustinian era: 1455–1550

Bishop 'Mauricius' who was bishop of the diocese from 1286 until 1307 was the Augustinian abbot of Kells before being appointed bishop of Tír Briúin. It would be approximately 150 years later before another Augustinian, Thady Mag Duibhne, was appointed bishop of the diocese. Thady began an Augustinian dynasty of sorts because five of the seven bishops of the diocese between 1455 and 1550 were Augustinians. Two of them had been priors of Drumlane, two others had been abbots of Kells and one the prior of Tristernagh. Thady or Fear Sithe Mag Duibhne (Mac Givney), who succeeded MacBradaigh in 1455, was the first of this Augustinian line of bishops.

Thady MacGivney was already vicar of St Feidhlimidh's church in the parish of Kilmore in 1436 when he wrote to the papal courts asking them to confirm him in the position of vicar of St Brighid's church in the adjacent parish of Urney. To strengthen his case he stated that he had to 'keep great hospitality' and also that he 'by his grandmother on his father's side springs from a noble, even princely stock'.[1] He was granted the second vicarage thereby bringing his annual income from the two vicarages to sixteen marks.[2] Patrick O'Farrelly, the previous vicar in Urney, had joined the Augustinians in Drumlane and become prior there, although Cormac Magauran the son of Piaras Magauran, a previous prior, also claimed that position. In March 1445, following the death of Patrick O'Farrelly and the promotion of Cormac Magauran to the See of Ardagh, Thady MacGivney appealed to Rome to be allowed to be received as a canon in the priory of Drumlane, 'at present void'. His appeal was granted on condition that he would in due course resign as vicar of St Feidhlimidh's church in the parish of Kilmore.[3] Despite his appointment as bishop of Ardagh in 1444 Cormac Magauran continued to claim to be the prior of Drumlane, a lucrative benefice worth twenty marks at this time This claim was ended in March 1446 when Thady

1. *CPL*, viii, p. 599; Costello, *De Annatis Hiberniae*, i, p. 234.
2. *CPL*, viii, p. 599; *Costello, De Annatis Hiberniae*, i, p. 235.
3. *CPL*, ix, p. 493.

MacGivney was appointed prior of Drumlane by the pope and allowed to remain as vicar of Urney 'which church is not more than three miles of those parts from the said monastery, being nearer thereto than is St Fylemey's [church at Kilmore]'.[4]

Thady MacGivney, being the prior of Drumlane, held a prestigious position in the diocese and was obviously trusted by Bishop Andrew MacBradaigh who, when in failing health in 1454, nominated him as his proctor to settle certain disputes in the diocese.[5] Immediately following Bishop MacBradaigh's death in May 1455, Thady MacGivney travelled to Rome where he was appointed bishop of Kilmore and was consecrated there on 11 July 1455. Ten days later he paid the obligatory 33⅓ florins in tax to the papal courts.[6] When he returned to Ireland, Bishop Thady, taking a leaf out of Cormac Magauran's book, held onto his income as prior of Drumlane. Thady MacGivney was bishop of Kilmore for just one year when Peter Magauran, an Augustinian canon in Drumlane, wrote to Rome complaining:

> that the said bishop has for about a year unduly detained the said priory *in commendam* under pretext of certain papal letters which are surreptitious because he falsely stated therein that the fruits etc. of his episcopal *mensa* were so slender that he could not be maintained therefrom, whereas in fact they were then, as at present, so abundant that he could and can be decently maintained.[7]

Bishop Thady needed all the money he could get if for no other reason than the parish church of St Feidhlimidh, which had recently been designated the cathedral of the diocese, was not fit for purpose. Following his request to Rome he was, in 1461, given permission to grant indulgences to:

> penitents, who on the feast of St Feilimy the Confessor [3 August] and Whitsuntide visit and give alms for the completion and conservation of the church … which … bishop Thady [*Thyteus*] has at his own expense begun to build anew

4.   Ibid., p. 528. Robert Dudley Edwards interprets the bishop of Ardagh being deprived of the priory of Drumlane as a sign of a papal policy of church reform at work. See R.D. Edwards, 'Papal provision in fifteenth century Ireland' in *Medieval studies presented to Aubrey Gwynn*, p. 274.
5.   *CPL*, x, p. 729.
6.   Costello, *De Annatis Hiberniae*, i, pp 256-7.
7.   *CPL*, xi, p. 307.

Figure 5.1: Canons of the cathedral chapter *c*.1460.

Name	Year*	Other Positions Held
John Ogoband [Smith]	1457	Vicar of Kilsherdany (1446). Dean & vicar of Kilmore (1460)
Malachy Macbradayd [Brady]	1457	
Thomas Osyridean [Sheridan]	1458	
Maclochlaynd Yruayrc [O'Rourke]	1459	
Cornelius Maclaclaynd [McLoughlin]	1459	
Terence Oraghllg [O'Reilly]	1460	
Maurice Omolochary [Earley]	1460	Rector of Cineál Luacháin (1456)
Cormac Osiridean [Sheridan]	1460	Rector of Kilmore & Ballintemple (1471)
John Macmaelmartayn [Martin]	1460	Rector of Drumgoon (1455). Vicar of Annagelliff & rector of Kedy (1466)
John Omolmochory [Earley]	1460	Vicar of Drumreilly & Oughteragh (1453). Vicar of Carrigallen (1459)
Nemeas Odroma [Drumm]	1461	Vicar of Templeport & Tomregan (1453). Vicar of Urney (1455)
Terence Ooreguillyg [O'Reilly]	1461	
Donald Oflayn [Flynn]	1461	

* Year in which their names appear in papal documents.

and has for the most part finished, but for the completion of which the resources of the said bishop and church are insufficient.[8]

The second half of the fifteenth-century was a time of considerable church building in Ireland though the builders continued to use old techniques resulting in heavy buildings which lacked the elegance and aesthetic beauty of churches built in the Gothic perpendicular style

8.   Ibid., xii, p. 131.

popular in England at this time.[9] The surviving cathedral building at Kilmore, now used as a community centre, was built in this heavy style and has no architectural detail to match the finesse of the Romanesque twelfth-century doorway, which may have been incorporated into the cathedral that was built 'anew' at this time.[10]

The Diocesan Chapter

When Pope Calixtus III gave his approval of St Feidhlimidh's parish as the new diocesan cathedral in 1455 he also stipulated that there should be 'thirteen canonries for thirteen canons, who should in perpetuity be present [in the cathedral] at divine hours by day and by night'.[11] Bishop Thady MacGivney appointed the thirteen canons soon after permission to do so was granted and he selected canons from established clerical families throughout the diocese. See Fig. 5.1. Canons Cornelius Ó Ruairc who was vicar of Killasnett and William Ó Fergus from Rossinver, both a long distance away from Kilmore in the deanery of Dartry, could not possibly be present 'night and day' at the cathedral. Neither could Donald Ó Floinn from Carrigallen nor John and Maurice Ó Maolmochéirghe from Drumreilly be in the cathedral at all times for the divine office prayer. Canon Nemeas O'Droma, who was vicar of Templeport and Tomregan in 1453, moved much closer to the cathedral in 1455 when he was appointed vicar of Urney. Similarly Canon John Macmaelmartayn, who was rector of Drumgoon in 1455, later became vicar of Annagelliff, a vicarage within walking distance of the newly- established cathedral at Kilmore. Canon John O'Gowan, who was vicar of Kilsherdany, moved even nearer to the cathedral when he was appointed vicar of Kilmore parish. Bishop MacGivney had now a cathedral chapter to work with even if the chapter could not always be a choral chapter ever-present to chant the divine offices at the designated hours. There is no evidence that there were vicars choral in Kilmore, as was the case in some other dioceses in the country, where the cathedral choral duties were carried out by substitutes on behalf of the canons.[12] The canons appointed by Bishop MacGivney had great difficulty securing prebends for themselves and it would appear that while being appointed to the cathedral chapter brought increased status there was, at least initially, no corresponding increase in income.

9.   Corish, *The Irish Catholic experience*, p. 60.
10.   Donovan, *Archaeological inventory of County Cavan*, p. 201.
11.   *CPL*, xi, p. 240.
12.   Nicholls, 'Medieval Irish Cathedral chapters', p. 105.

Augustinian Cooperation

John Bole, who was the archbishop of Armagh during most of Thady MacGivney's episcopate, summoned MacGivney and all the other bishops of the province to a provincial council meeting to be held in St Peter's church, Drogheda on 9 June 1460. Of all the bishops summoned to the meeting, only Thady MacGivney of Kilmore and Cormac Magauran of Ardagh appeared. Both of them were natives of the diocese of Kilmore and had been priors in Drumlane before being appointed to their respective dioceses. It is not clear why these two Augustinian bishops travelled to Drogheda and all the other northern bishops did not, though the fact that the archbishop was himself an Augustinian may have been the deciding factor. The archbishop and two bishops waited in vain for a few days hoping that some of the other bishops would arrive and then decided to proceed with the business of the council. On 14 June 1460 Archbishop Bole, with the assent of the bishops of Kilmore and Ardagh, deposed Bartholomew O'Flanagan, the bishop of Derry, Laurence O'Gallchobhair II, the bishop of Raphoe along with the vicar-general of the diocese of Connor, 'because they have not attended the provincial nor replied to the summonses, nor sent an excuse or apology'.[13] Similarly, they condemned Hugh Omolon, the dean of Clonmacnois, who even though cited to attend and answer charges, had failed to do so. It was stated in a public reading of a letter on 30 June 1460 in the chancel of St Peter's church, Drogheda, and in the presence of the archbishop and 'Tytherus' bishop of Kilmore among others that Hugh Omolon 'does not well know concerning the faith of Holy Mother Church' and that he was to be excommunicated for two years.[14]

The Augustinians had considerable power both within the diocese of Kilmore and in wider ecclesiastical province of Armagh during the episcopate of Thady MacGivney. In contrast, the Premonstratensians whose priory at Lough Uachtair was approximately two miles away from the bishop's residence at Kilmore and who had experienced a resurgence in their fortunes throughout the 1400s, had little power in Kilmore and they provided no bishop for the diocese. Similarly the Franciscans who had their friary in Cavan town less than three miles away from the bishop's residence, wielded little or no power in the diocese even though they had gifted friars like William O'Reilly, who had studied in Oxford and was appointed the first Gaelic minister provincial of the Order in

---

13.   Lynch, 'The administration of John Bole, archbishop of Armagh, 1457-71', p. 149.
14.   Chart (ed.), *The register of John Swayne*, p. 204.

1445, a position he held despite many difficulties throughout all of Thady MacGivney's episcopate. It was not until 1580 that Richard Brady became the first Franciscan bishop of the diocese. The Annals of Ulster recorded *sub anno* 1464 that 'the bishop of the two Breifni, namely Fersithi [man of peace] Mag Uibne died this year on 27 November'. He was succeeded by another Augustinian, John Ó Raghallaigh, the abbot of St Mary's abbey in Kells.

John Ó Raghallaigh II

In 1445 John Ó Raghallaigh, an Augustinian canon of St Mary' abbey in Kells, received a dispensation from Rome as the son of an Augustinian abbot and then, some time later, was appointed abbot of Kells.[15] His father John Ó Raghallaigh 'the son of a prince' had also been appointed abbot there sometime between 1418 and 1420. John Ó Raghallaigh II was one of the ruling O'Reilly family of east Bréifne and on becoming bishop of Kilmore he was coming to live among his own kinsmen. It was Pope Paul II, having replaced the much more capable Pius II in 1464, who appointed John Ó Raghallaigh II the bishop of the diocese on 17 May 1465. The papal register describes the process:

> This [Kilmore] see being vacant by the demise of Thady ... Paul the second, he, after maturely considering with his brethren, the Cardinals, the matter of providing for the vacant church ... reflecting on the merits of John, abbot of Kells ... that he who in so praiseworthy a manner had presided over his monastery, would know how and be able ... to rule well and wisely the vacant church.[16]

Letters announcing this appointment were sent to the cathedral chapter, to the clergy and people of 'the city and diocese of the *ecclesie Kelmoren*', to the archbishop of Armagh and to King Edward IV.[17] John was to be consecrated by any Catholic bishop of his choice assisted by two or three other bishops after he had taken his oath of fealty to the pope in the presence of the consecrating bishop and the document was stamped and sealed before sending it to the pope. His consecration was delayed by at least eighteen months, apparently due to his failure to pay the papal tax of 33⅓ florins, and on 5 December 1466 John Macmaelmartayn the vicar of Annagelliff, in his role as proctor of John Ó Raghallaigh 'elect of Kilmore', promised to

15.   *CPL*, ix, p. 458.
16.   Quoted in Costello, *De Annatis Hiberniae*, i, p. 257. See also *CPL*, xii, pp 430-1.
17.   *CPL*, xii, p. 431.

pay one half of the tax within six months and the other half within one year.[18] John Ó Raghallaigh was later consecrated bishop, presumably in the first half of 1467. He became bishop at a turbulent time in both east and west Bréifne. In 1465, the year his appointment was announced, Domnall Ó Ruairc attacked MacConsnama in Inismagrath and MacConsnama 'and his son and many of his people were slain at Mass on Sunday'.[19] Three years later, 'the town of O'Reilly and the monastery of Cavan were burned by the English'.[20]

John Ó Raghallaigh II cooperated with the Augustinian archbishop of Armagh just as his predecessor had done. He was present at the provincial council meeting which was held *c.*1468 in Ardee to sit in judgment on William Sherwood, the powerful and controversial bishop of Meath. Bishop Sherwood sent two proctors to represent him at the meeting, claiming that he could not safely go to Ardee and asking that the council meeting be moved to Drogheda. Archbishop Bole and John O Raghallaigh II, together with the bishops of Derry, Raphoe, Ardagh[21] and Clonmacnois rejected Bishop Sherwood's excuse as frivolous, declared him stubbornly resistant to authority and excluded his proctors from the meeting because 'they had been appointed by one who is excommunicate'.[22]

Disputes

John Ó Raghallaigh also had disputes to deal with within his diocese. In 1466 Malachy O'Sheridan brought accusations against Fergal O'Sheridan, the Premonstratensian prior of Lough Uachtair, in a bid to replace him in the priory. John Ó Raghallaigh II, together with John O'Gowan and John Macmulmartyn, two of his canons, were delegated by Rome to decide on the issue. They upheld Malachy O'Sheridan's complaints and he was duly appointed prior.[23] Canon John O'Gowan, who was dean of Kilmore was himself involved in a bitter dispute in that same year with Odo MacKiernan, another priest of the diocese, over the vicarage of Killeshandra which apparently had been established as a prebend to provide an income for a canon in the cathedral chapter. John O'Gowan claimed that his prebend, which he held by apostolic authority, had been taken from him by Odo MacKiernan who, according to O'Gowan, the same prebend was claimed by MacKiernan 'by virtue of letters lately and

18.   Costello, *De Annatis Hiberniae*, i, p. 257.
19.   *AU*, 1465.
20 .   *AFM*, 1468.
21.   Cormac Magauran was still the bishop of Ardagh.
22.   Lynch, 'The administration of John Bole', p. 139. For William Sherwood see *DIB*, viii, pp 922-3.
23.   *CPl*, xii, p. 511.

Figure 5.2: St Mary's priory, Drumlane. (*Courtesy of Paddy Ronaghan*).

perhaps wickedly obtained from the archbishop's court'.[24] The archbishop mandated John Ó Raghallaigh II on 25 January 1471 to decide in favour of one or other of his priests, and then to 'restrain the wrongdoer with all canonical sanctions' and if necessary to get the secular powers to assist him. Bishop Ó Raghallaigh did as instructed, deciding in favour of John O'Gowan and, as instructed by the archbishop, enlisted the secular help of the O'Reillys to support him in his decision. Yet, less than two months later Archbishop John Bole intervened again, now telling him:

> to defend Odo Mcchernan, whom the archbishop had appointed to the perpetual vicarage of St Brigid, Kilseanrath, *jure devoluto*, and who has been disturbed in possession by John Ogoband who claims to be vicar, and is supported by Terence O Reilly, captain of his nation.[25]

In 1476 Thomas Ó Raghallaigh, a layman, appealed directly to the archbishop of Armagh, against a ruling in a matrimonial case which John Ó Raghallaigh II had ruled against him and in favour of Katherine

24.   Lynch, 'The administration of John Bole', p. 161.
25.   Ibid., p. 169.

Maguire of Clogher diocese. The ruling had been conveyed to him by 'Masters Galfridus Ogoun and Philip Oragilli' who were described as 'officials' of John Ó Raghallaigh II.[26] This case was still ongoing in October 1476, by which time Bishop Ó Raghallaigh II had already died.[27] He was succeeded by another Augustinian, Cormac MacSamradháin (Magauran), the prior of Drumlane.

Two Rival Bishops

As we have seen already, Cormac MacSamradháin came from a clerical family, his father being Cormac MacSamradháin the bishop of Ardagh and his grandfather Piaras a prior of Drumlane.[28] When he was appointed to the vicarage of Templeport in 1461 he applied for and received a papal dispensation 'as the son of an Augustinian canon, a priest noble and an unmarried woman'.[29] Six years later he became an Augustinian canon in Drumlane, by a special favour, being allowed 'to receive the habit and make his profession after and not before he has obtained possession of the priory'.[30] Having been prior of Drumlane for nine years he was appointed bishop of Kilmore by Sixtus IV on 4 November 1476.[31] His father, whose time as bishop of Ardagh was marked by controversy and repeated attempts to remove him, died that same year.[32] His son's episcopal career would prove to be more controversial still and soon after his appointment the papal courts turned against him.

Aubrey Gwynn has suggested that the Roman authorities turned against Cormac because he had concealed his illegitimacy from them but this can hardly be the case as we have seen that upon MacSamradháin's appointment to the vicarage of Templeport he had received a Roman dispensation 'as the son of a priest, OSA and an unmarried woman'.[33] It is possible, however, that the papacy learned soon after his appointment that he was the son of the troublesome bishop of Ardagh and that he had deliberately concealed this information prior to his appointment to Kilmore. It is also possible that from the beginning of his episcopacy he was guilty of behaviour unbecoming of a bishop at a time when, mainly

26.   Ibid., p. 145.
27.   Ibid.
28.   For his lineage see B.L., Egerton MS 1781, f. 128 and Gearóid Mac Niocaill (ed.), 'Dán do Chormac Mág Shamhradháin Easpag Ardachaidh 1444-1476' in *Seanchas Ard Mhacha*, iv, 1 (1960-61), p. 143.
29.   *CPL*, xii, p. 142.
30.   Ibid., xii, p. 564.
31.   Ibid., xiii, p. 277.
32.   *AFM*, 1476; *AC*, 1476.
33.   Aubrey Gwynn, *The medieval province of Armagh, 1470-1545* (Dundalk, 1945), p. 158; *CPL*, xiii, p. 277.

due to the Observant reforms, there was less tolerance of aberrant behaviour in the wider church.[34] Still another possibility is that he failed to meet the usual conditions of taking an oath of fealty to the pope or may not have paid the papal tax on time.[35] For whatever reasons, Pope Sixtus IV, ignoring all claims Cormac MacSamradráin had to the bishopric, took the extraordinary step of appointing a secular priest, Thomas MacBradaigh, to the See of Kilmore on 20 October 1480, 'the said church being vacant by the death of John [Ó Raghallaigh II]'.[36]

The papal letter of appointment, in describing Thomas MacBradaigh, seems to have been contrasting his qualities with those of Cormac MacSamradhráin. It stated that he was:

> Archdeacon of the said church of Kilmore, of noble race, born in legitimate wedlock and of legitimate age, and who on trustworthy evidence is recommended to him for his literary acquirements, integrity of life and conversation.[37]

The author of the letter of appointment, anticipating opposition, directed the 'chapter, clergy and people of the city and diocese [of Kilmore] to obey him as bishop'.[38] Thomas MacBradaigh had first come to the attention of the papal courts when he wrote to them in 1474, stating that Eugenius O'Reilly, who had been appointed archdeacon of the diocese in 1445, 'publicly keeps in his house a relation by kindred or affinity as his concubine, [and] has with his own hands killed a layman and has committed perjury and other crimes'.[39] Thomas MacBradaigh replaced the older man as archdeacon, a benefice worth twelve marks annually. When he was consecrated bishop in 1480 he was allowed to retain the position of archdeacon of Kilmore, in order to supplement his income.

The Great Western schism had ended in 1417 and cannot be blamed for the schism which began in the diocese of Kilmore in 1480 and lasted

---

34.   See F.X. Martin, 'The Irish Augustinian reform movement in the fifteenth century' in *Medieval studies presented to Aubrey Gwynn*, pp 230-64.

35.   Cormac's letter of appointment dated 6 November 1476 did state that if the proper procedures were not adhered to he would be suspended from the exercise of the pontifical office … and from the administration of his church'. See *CPL*, xiii, 1, p. 154. He was described as 'Cormarchus, Electus Kilmorensis' in a papal document dated 23 November 1483, which suggests that if he was consecrated bishop it was after this date. See Costello, *De Annatis Hiberniae*, i, p. 258.

36.   Ibid., p. 257; Richard Brady, 'Thomas MacBrady, Bishop of Kilmore (1480-1511)' in *Breifny Antiquarian and Historical Society Journal*, iii, I (1927), p. 104.

37.   Ibid.

38.   *CPL*, xiii, p. 85.

39.   Ibid., p. 372.

for more than thirty years. On 22 November 1487 Diarmaid Bacach Mac Parrthaláin, a scribe for the MacSamradháin sept of Tullyhaw, described the situation in the diocese:

> [agus] isin aimsir cétna dobí dá espoc a n-espoicdech Cille Móire.i. Cormac mac in espuic Mégsamhradháin [agus] Tomás mac Ainntriu Megbradaigh [agus] gach fer dibh gá rádha gurub é féin is espoc ann. [And at that time there were two bishops in the bishopric of Kilmore – that is to say, Cormac son of the bishop Magauran and Thomas, son of Andrew MacBrady, and each of them saying that he was the rightful bishop.][40]

The scribe gave a factual and accurate description of the crisis in the diocese, though the long poem praising Cormac MacSamradháin's father, the bishop of Ardagh, which was written by a member of the Mac Parrthaláin family *c.*1486, approximately ten years after his death, seems timed to boost the fortunes of the son rather than the posthumous reputation of the father.[41]

Before the Italian cleric Octavian del Palacio was appointed archbishop of Armagh in 1478 he had been papal nuncio in Ireland and in that capacity and while he was archbishop elect of Armagh he commissioned Cormac MacSamradháin, who was described as a cleric of the diocese, to act on his behalf in Kilmore. Cormac duly granted James Macculmarthayn the rectory of St Patrick's church in Drumgoon and was said to have 'sufficient power from Octavian for what he did'.[42] Later Thomas MacBradaigh appointed a namesake of his, a priest of the diocese, to the same rectory. The dispute over the rectory dragged on and the issue was finally resolved in 1491 when Pope Innocent VIII decided in favour of James Macculmarthayn. Octavian del Palacio was consecrated archbishop of Armagh in late 1479 or early 1480 and when he held his first provincial council meeting at Drogheda in July 1480 neither Cormac MacSamradháin nor Thomas MacBradaigh were present.[43] The archbishop did succeed in getting them to come together and reach agreement at the Augustinian house on Inismór Island in Lough

40.   B.L., Egerton MS 1781, f. 128v; See Flower, *Catalogue of Irish manuscripts in the British Library,* ii, p. 76.
41.   This poem is printed in Mac Niocaill, 'Dán do Chormac Mág Shamhradháin Easpag Ardachaidh 1444–1476', pp 142-6.
42.   *CPL*, xv, pp 409-11.
43.   Mario A. Sughi, 'The appointment of Octavian de Palatio as archbishop of Armagh, 1477-8' in *IHS*, xxxi, 122 (Nov. 1998), pp 145-64; Corish, *The Catholic community*, pp 8-9.

Gowna on 25 November 1482. Cormac MacSamradháin had already
built up support for himself in the deanery of Drumlane, where the
Magauran's were the chief clerical family, and in the deanery of Dartry in present-day north Leitrim where the O'Rourkes, natural allies of
the Magaurans, held sway. Cormac, who was described as the prior of
Drumlane, agreed to renounce all his emoluments from the rural deaneries of Drumlane and Dartry in return for a pension of fourteen marks
from Thomas MacBradaigh.[44] Cormac further promised to discontinue
his attempts to win papal approval for himself as bishop of the diocese.[45]

Despite the agreement reached on Inismór Island, Cormac Mac
Samradháin continued to claim that he was the rightful bishop of
Kilmore. The divisions, not just between the two rival claimants to the
bishopric but also those between their supporters, continued and in 1489
Archbishop Octavianus del Palacio appointed, John Payne the bishop
of Meath and William O'Farrell, the bishop of Ardagh, to negotiate a
settlement. They asked Bishop Edmund de Courci from Clogher to help
them in their task. It is not clear what the terms of this settlement were
though it appears that both claimants were recognised as bishops and
that the diocese was somehow divided between them. The divisions
that already existed in the diocese with the two separate kingdoms of
east and west Bréifne would lend itself to such a solution even though
Cormac MacSamradháin's main powerbase was in the deanery of
Drumlane, part of which was in east Bréifne.

The compromise reached had extraordinary and highly irregular
results with both Thomas MacBradaigh and Cormac MacSamradháin
being present at the provincial councils held in 1492 and 1495 and both
of them signing themselves as bishop of Kilmore.[46] At the provincial
council on the 6 July 1495 '*Thomas et Cormacus Kilmorensis, Episcopi
humiles ecclesiae*' were among the signatories of a letter condemning
attacks by unnamed people on the abbey of Mellifont.[47] The fact that
Cormac MacSamradháin was not present at the provincial council
meetings in 1504 and 1507 and that Thomas MacBradaigh was points
towards the latter being gradually accepted as the rightful bishop of the
diocese and the former receding into the background. At some stage,

44.   Mario A. Sughi (ed.), *Registrum Octaviani, the register of Octavian de Palatio Archbishop of
Armagh 1478-1513* (Dublin, 1999), ii, pp 473-4. This settlement was facilitated by Fergal
O'Raghallaigh, Layseach Offergall, Nicholas Magubin and many others.
45.   Gwynn, *The medieval province of Armagh*, p. 159.
46.   M.J. McEnery & Raymond Refaussé, *Christ Church Deeds* (Dublin, 2001), p. 102,
no. 362; Corish, *The Catholic experience*, p. 56.
47.   Fr Columcille, 'Seven documents from the old abbey of Mellifont' in *JCLAS*, xiii,
1 (1953), p. 55.

probably sometime between 1495 and 1507, a definitive judgment was given in favour of Thomas and against Cormac by the bishops of Meath and Ardagh who were acting with apostolic authority:

> The final and definitive finding … was in favour of said Thomas and against Cormac. They … adjudged the rule and administration and property of said church [Kilmore] to said Thomas and the proceedings regarding them of said Cormac they declared to be rash, unlawful and *de facto* presumptuous and imposed on him perpetual silence.[48]

Cormac MacSamradháin's son, Fergal, was ordained a priest *c.*1502 'notwithstanding a defect of birth as the son of a bishop and an unmarried woman' and in February 1503 he was appointed the perpetual vicar of Templeport, by papal authority.[49]

Assessment

Thomas MacBradaigh, despite having to cope with a rival claimant to the bishopric, was a reforming and active bishop for thirty-one years. He was bishop at a time when many parish churches, usually with cemeteries attached, were being built. It was during his episcopate, in 1502, that the Franciscan friary of Cavan adopted the Observant reforms and in 1508 that the Observant Franciscan friary was founded in Dromahair. He was, in his later years, accepted as 'bishop of the two Breffneys' and it was while he was in the Ó Ruairc stronghold of Dromahair - having gone there to there to consecrate the chapel in the Franciscan friary - that he died in 1511. Donatus Mooney, writing *c.*1617, stated that 'Thomas MacBrady, bishop of Kilmore, attended by a brilliant retinue of ecclesiastics and laics, consecrated the church and monastery under the invocation of St Francis'.[50] However, he makes no mention of the bishop dying there on the same occasion. His body was brought back to be buried in the Franciscan friary in Cavan. The *Annals of the Four Masters,* although adapting the usual formulaic style when recording the death of an ecclesiastic, is full of praise for Thomas MacBradaigh:

> Thomas, son of Andrew Mac Brady, bishop and archdeacon of the two Breffneys, for the space of thirty years, a prelate whom the English and Irish supported, a man distinguished

48.   Costello, *De Annatis Hiberniae*, i, p. 258.
49.   *CPL*, xvii, pp 574-5.
50.   Meehan, *The rise and fall of the Irish Franciscan monasteries*, p. 83.

Figure 5.3: East window of St Náile's church, Kinawley.

for wisdom and piety, a brilliant lamp which enlightened the laity and clergy by instruction and preaching, an affectionate shepherd of the church, after having ordained priests and ecclesiastics of all degrees, and having consecrated many churches and cemeteries, after having bestowed precious presents and food on the rich and poor, his spirit departed to heaven ... at Dromahaire having come to consecrate a church in Breffney, in the sixty-seventh year of his age.[51]

Others had a high opinion of him too. A papal document dated 3 June 1512 refers to him as 'Thomas of good memory'.[52] However, like his rival claimant to the See of Kilmore, he too had offspring. His son, Aedh, became a Franciscan friar and died at a relatively young age in 1490.[53] His daughter Siobhán, who married Thomas, son of Cathal Óg MacManus Maguire the chief compiler of the Annals of Ulster, died in 1515.[54]

A Lover of Peace and Tranquility

Pope Julius II appointed Diarmaid Ó Raghallaigh, the Augustinian abbot of Kells, bishop of Kilmore on 28 January 1512.[55] This prompt appointment, just six months after the death of Thomas MacBradaigh, was intended to prevent Cormac MacSamradháin reasserting his claim to the bishopric now that his long-time rival was dead. However, Cormac, despite his advanced years, continued to claim the position as his, leading Diarmaid Ó Raghallaigh to write to the papal courts *circa* Easter 1512 complaining that 'Cormac ... intruded himself into the rule and administration of this [Kilmore] church and continues to do so'.[56] This final attempt by Cormac to be accepted as the bishop of the diocese failed and his death in December 1512 brought the conflict to a close. The annalists who had given Thomas MacBradaigh a long and glowing obituary had much less to say about him. They wrote 'Cormac Mac Gauran, who was called bishop of Brefney, died before Christmas'.[57] With the deaths of these two men, the schism in the diocese, which had lasted for just over thirty years, came to an end.

Diarmaid Ó Raghallaigh, 'a learned man ... of a quiet temper'[58] was the fourth Augustinian priest and second prior of Kells to be appointed bishop

51.   *AFM*, 1511. See also Lynch, *De Praesulibus Hiberniae*, pp 251-2.
52.   Costello, *De Annatis Hiberniae*, i, p. 258; *CPL*, xix, p. 443.
53.   *AU*, 1490.
54.   Ibid., 1515; Corish, *The Irish Catholic experience*, p. 56.
55.   MacKiernan, *Diocese of Kilmore*, p. 13
56.   Costello, *De Annatis Hiberniae*, i, p. 258.
57.   *AFM*, 1511.
58.   Ware, *The antiquities and history of Ireland*, p. 60.

of Kilmore since 1455. During his episcopate the diocese, and particularly east Bréifne which was strategically situated between the English of the Pale and the Gaelic lordships of Ulster, was bedevilled by intermittent local wars.[59] The volatile and violent nature of life in east Bréifne in the early decades of the 1500s did not suit the quiet and retiring Diarmaid Ó Raghallaigh. Besides, there were ongoing wars of a different kind between certain diocesan clergy who continued to squabble over vicarages and other benefices and who were not shy about writing to Rome or to Armagh in order to denounce their opponents and to further their own case. Some of these disputes, such as the one over the vicarage of St Patrick's church in Lurgan in 1527, involved Diarmaid Ó Raghallaigh directly. Thomas O'Gowan, the vicar of Mullagh lodged a complaint with Archbishop George Cromer on behalf of 'Bernard', a cleric of Kilmore against Charles O Clerian, the vicar of Lurgan parish. He claimed that Diarmaid Ó Raghallaigh, who during his time as abbot of Kells, had, contrary to canon law, appointed Charles O'Clerian to the vicarage of Lurgan. The archbishop ordered O'Clerian to resign and appointed 'Bernard' in his place.[60]

It seems strange that the archbishop would decide against Diarmaid Ó Raghallaigh in a case like this but his decision was made easier by the bishop's absence from the diocese.[61] Bishop Ó Raghallaigh did not attend a provincial council meeting in Termonfechin on 17 August 1526 at which most of the other northern dioceses were represented and may have been living an isolated life in County Dublin by this time.[62] Sir James Ware explained his absence from the diocese:

> The times were very tumultuous in Ulster, and this prelate,
> being a lover of peace and tranquillity, withdrew to Swords
> in the County of Dublin, where for a long time he officiated
> as vicar and died in 1529.[63]

Diarmaid Ó Raghallaigh may have been based in Swords as early as 1523, because in that year he was described as 'a learned canonist'. In that year he and Walter Wellesley,[64] the prior of Connall, were asked to adjudicate in a dispute between Archbishop Hugh Inge and the dean

59.   See Parker, 'Cavan: a medieval border area', pp 48-9.
60.   L.P. Murray, 'Archbishop Cromer's register' in *JCLAS*, vii, 4 (Dec.1932), p. 344.
61.   Mervyn Archdall claimed that he was still the prior of Kells in 1523, though this may have been another person of the same name. See *Monasticon Hibernicum*, p. 546.
62.   Ibid., p. 343.
63.   Walter Harris (ed.), *The whole works of Sir James Ware concerning Ireland* (Dublin, 1739), pp 229-30.
64.   Wellesley was appointed bishop of Kildare in 1529. See Mary Ann Lyons, *Church and society in County Kildare, c.1470-1547* (Dublin, 2000), pp 100-3.

and chapter of Kildare over the archbishop's visiting rights during a vacancy in the See of Kildare.[65]

It is a sign of the changed times and the disturbed state of east Bréifne that an Ó Raghallaigh bishop would feel more secure in Swords than in the parish of Kilmore at the epicentre of the Ó Raghallaigh power base. Throughout the sixteenth-century a gradual Anglicisation of east Bréifne was taking place, largely due to a significant growth in trading between Cavan town and the Pale and the increased military and marital alliances between members of the Ó Raghallaigh and Anglo-Irish families from north Leinster.[66] The continuous interaction between Drumlane priory and its mother house in Kells and the strong links between clerical families such as the Earleys, Magaurans and Ó Raghallaighs and the Augustinians of Kells also contributed to this Anglicisation.[67] Besides, some of the Anglo-Norman families of north Leinster, particularly the Nugent family of Delvin, were extending their power base into east Bréifne and over such religious houses as Fore, Tristernagh and Multyfarnham.[68] So it is little surprise then that, in the absence of the bishop of the diocese, Edmund Nugent, the prior of Tristernagh, was asked on 8 March 1529 to resolve a dispute between Cognosius O'Gowan and Malachy O'Gowan over the vicarage of St Patrick's church in Kildrumferton.[69] Then on 3 September 1529 Edmund Nugent was commissioned by archbishop Cromer to carry out a metropolitan visitation of the diocese of Kilmore and one week later, following the death of Diarmaid Ó Raghallaigh, he was granted sub custody of diocese of Kilmore, *sede vacante*.[70]

Archbishop Cromer was busy dealing with disputes involving Kilmore clergy and laity during the vacancy in the diocesan See. The O'Reillys continued to carry out attacks where there were rich pickings in the counties of Meath and Louth and on 7 September 1529 Cathal O'Reilly, lord of east Bréifne, and 'other marauders' who had been excommunicated for raiding Archbishop Cromer's manor at Julianstown in County Meath the previous month,[71] were absolved by the primate 'from all censures, excommunications etc incurred by him on account of his invasion into

65. Harris (ed.), *The whole works of Sir James Ware*, p. 389.
66. Jonathan Cherry, 'The indigenous and colonial urbanization of Cavan town, *c*.1300–*c*.1641' in Brendan Scott (ed.), *Culture and society in early modern Bréifne/Cavan* (Dublin, 2009), pp 85-105; Ciaran Brady, 'The O'Reillys of east Bréifne and the problem of surrender and regrant' in *Bréifne*, vi, 23 (1985), pp 237-9.
67. Cunningham, 'The Anglicisation of east Bréifne' pp 57-8.
68. Lennon, 'The Nugent family and the diocese of Kilmore in the sixteenth and early seventeenth centuries', pp 361-2. For information on the early history of the Nugent family see Iske, *The green cockatrice* (Dublin, 1978).
69. Murray, 'Archbishop Cromer's register', viii, 4 (1936), p. 40.
70. Ibid., p. 38.
71. Jefferies, *Priests and prelates*, p. 117.

Julianston'. Cathal O'Reilly swore that he would 'make restitution to the injured tenants … and … obey the mandates of the church'.[72] His penance was severe. He was ordered:

(a)   To pay two cows towards the support of the cathedral of Armagh.
(b)   To make the pilgrimage either to the Purgatory of St Patrick or to the statue of Our Lady of Trim.
(c)   To give five denarii to the poor.
(d)   To recite the Office of the B.V.M. fifteen times during the Octave.
(e)   To protect the church and its tenants.

The priest Bernard McHugh was given the task of absolving all those who had aided and abetted O'Reilly.[73] This punishment did not act as a deterrent because five years later, on 20 March 1534, Odo O'Reilly, Cormac MacBrady and others were excommunicated for stealing eighty horses in the vicinity of Julianstown and in 1538 the O'Reillys went on a foray to Knockninny in Fermanagh and, among other depredations, burned the church of Kinawley.[74] It appears that there was a dispute over the church of Kinawley at this time. In April 1535 Pope Paul III had granted 'the parochial rectory of the church of Cillnail' to John Maguire, a cleric from Clogher diocese, provided that the bishop of Kilmore agreed to it.[75]

The archbishop also adjudicated on an internal dispute among the MacBradaigh sept. In November 1529 he denounced Maurice, Cornelius, Donatus and Patrick Rufus MacBrady who had seized 'the lands of Cassiltera which had been devised to the Church of St Patrick of the same place' and was, he said, the property of Bernard McBrady and his successors. The archbishop invoked the secular power of the O'Reillys to punish the offenders.[76] The secular power of 'Fergal O Rayle, captain of his nation' was also invoked by the archbishop in February 1530 to prevent Ludovicus Droma, a canon of the diocese, Eugene McBrady, a priest of the diocese and the guardian and friars of the monastery of Cavan, from interfering with the vicar of Annagelliff, until a resolution could be reached in a dispute over the vicarage.[77]

72.   Murray, 'Archbishop Cromer's register', viii, 4 (1936), p. 38.
73.   Ibid.
74.   Ibid., ix, 2 (1942), pp 116-27; *AU*, 1538.
75.   Vatican archives, *Dataria Apostolica, Minutae Brevium Lateranensium*, n. 3197. My thanks to Hugh Fenning who in 2004 found this and other miscellaneous documents relating to Kilmore in the Vatican archives.
76.   Ibid., viii, 4 (1936), p. 38.
77.   Murray, 'Archbishop Cromer's register', ix, 2 (1938), p. 127. Annagelliff vicarage and church struggled to survive because of its location, less than one mile distant from Cavan Franciscan friary. Besides, Annagelliff church had in 1590 only half a poll of termon land which was valued at a mere six pence per annum. The parishes of Urney and Annagelliff were united in the seventeenth-century. See O'Connell, *The diocese of Kilmore*, pp 293-4.

Edmund Nugent had in effect been carrying out the duties of a bishop in the diocese for at least a year before he was appointed bishop of Kilmore on 22 June 1530.[78] The disputes over the tithes going to religious houses outside the diocese rumbled on during his episcopacy and in March 1534 Archbishop Cromer, 'in order to make up for the neglect of his suffragan [Edmund Nugent]' wrote to the curate of Knockbride and to other curates in the diocese of Kilmore threatening them with excommunication because:

> the farmers and tenants who hold the lands of the vills of Bole Cleveloch [and] Balewelegan in the parish of Knockbride detain and usurp one third of the tithes and other fruits and emoluments within the parish which are due to the plaintiffs [in the abbey of Kells].[79]

The archbishop instructed the curates to warn all the tenants and farmers and all other clerks and laymen who detain the fruits to make restitution to the abbot and convent of Kells within three days.[80] Bishop Nugent may not have approved of the withholding of the tithes due to his fellow Augustinians in the abbey of Kells, but he was clearly being blamed by Archbishop Cromer for not taking action against those who were responsible for it.

Edmund Nugent was to be the last of the Augustinian-era bishops of the diocese. The appointment of a bishop from an Anglo-Irish family from outside of the diocese indicates an increase in the king's power in east Bréifne and a corresponding decline in the power of the west and east Bréifne clerical families from whose ranks virtually all of the bishops had been selected for the previous four hundred years. Yet, he could not have functioned as bishop of a diocese, virtually all of which was *inter Hibernicos*, without the support of the O'Reillys. He was faced with the difficult task of pleasing the royal administration in Dublin, his own Anglo-Norman relations and the Gaelic leaders in both east and west Bréifne.[81] Henry VIII's break with Rome, coming so soon after Nugent's appointment as bishop, forced him to decide between pope and king. He was allowed to remain as prior of Tristernagh after he was consecrated bishop in order to supplement his income and his support for the king became obvious

---

78. Vatican Library, MSS *Barberini Latini*, vol. 2867, ff. 77v-78r, 2868, f. 231r; Costello, *De Annatis Hiberniae*, i, p. 258.
79. A. Gwynn, 'Archbishop Cromer's register', x, 3 (1943), p. 174.
80. Ibid.
81. Lennon, 'The Nugent family and the diocese of Kilmore', p. 364.

on 30 November 1539 when he, in his position of 'commander or prior' of Tristernagh and 'with the consent of the convent' surrendered the priory to the officials of the king.[82] It is a tribute to his staying power that he was still functioning as bishop of the diocese eleven years later.[83] Nugent's death in 1550 brought an end to the era of Augustinian bishops of the diocese which had lasted ninety-five years. There had been a small number of bishops from a variety of religious orders in the adjacent dioceses during this period though none of these dioceses had a single religious order as dominant as the Augustinians were in Kilmore.[84] Throughout the period from 1455 to 1550 there had been an Augustinian bishop of the diocese although two of them, Cormac MacSamradháin and Edmund Nugent, had rival claimants to contend with. The Henrician reformation and the subsequent closing of the Augustinian houses in Drumlane, Kells and Tristernagh ensured that Edmund Nugent would be the last Augustinian bishop of Kilmore.

82.   James Morrin (ed.), *Calendar of the patent and close rolls of chancery of Ireland in the reigns of Henry VIII, Edward VI and Elizabeth*, i (Dublin, 1861), p. 57; Brendan Scott, 'Dissolution of religious houses in the Tudor diocese of Meath' in *Arch. Hib.*, lix (2005), p. 268.

83.   See Hans Claude Hamilton, *Calendar of the State papers relating to Ireland, 1509-1573* (London, 1860), p. 109; TNA, SP, 61/2/63.

84.   The diocese of Clonmacnois was somewhat similar to Kilmore having five Franciscan bishops between 1509 and 1568. My thanks to Colmán Ó Clabaigh for this observation.

Chapter 6

Kilmore on the eve of the Reformation

Historians have in the past been inclined to the view that the Church in Ireland and throughout Europe was in a deplorable state in the decades before the Henrician reformation. This view has been challenged in more recent years by Eamon Duffy, Henry Jefferies and others who claim that by looking closer at the state of the church in particular dioceses or parishes a more positive picture emerges.[1] In this chapter we will take an overview of the situation in the diocese of Kilmore between the years 1400 and 1534.

It is obvious from the preceding chapters that there were many problems in the diocese on the eve of the Tudor reformation. The elongated diocese which stretched from Kilmainhamwood in Meath to the Atlantic Ocean at Donegal was divided by mountains and lakes, rivers and woodlands. It was also divided into two separate lordships with the O'Rourkes dominant in west Bréifne and the O'Reillys in east Bréifne. These divisions, both natural and man-made, meant that the diocese was difficult to administer and it led to divisions among the clergy, many of whom identified more closely with their parishes and their septs than they did with their diocese. These divisions among the clergy were exacerbated by the scrambling for scarce benefices and the often scurrilous accusations which the clergy made against one another in order to persuade the papal courts to grant them a benefice. These vicious disputes among the clergy over rectories and vicarages mirrored the more violent disputes among their secular counterparts whenever there was a local leadership vacuum and these divisions militated against the diocese being able to take concerted action on any issue.

The twelfth-century Church reform had been effective in many ways but it clearly failed to put an end to clerical lineage families where ecclesiastical benefices were controlled by individual families and were

---

1. See Eamon Duffy, *The stripping of the altars: traditional religion in England, 1400–1580* (London, 1992) and *The voices of Morebath* (London, 2001). Henry A. Jefferies, 'The Armagh registers and the re-interpretation of Irish church history on the eve of the Reformations' in *Seanchas Ard Mhacha*, xviii, 1 (1999–2000), pp 81–99. The claim by Maurice Ó Maolmochéirghe in 1445/6 that 'divine worship has almost certainly ceased' in the deaneries of Drumlane and Darty seems like a desperate attempt by him to secure a benefice and therefore lacks credibility. See *CPL*, ix, p. 506.

handed on in lineal succession from father to son. These clerical families continued in the diocese and the fact that some priests did not abide by the rule of celibacy enshrined in canon law was used by some historians as sufficient evidence to conclude that the Church in medieval Ireland was indeed in need of reform. The papacy must accept some of the responsibility for this situation because during the pontificate of John XXII (1316–34) the granting of dispensations to the sons of priests in order to allow them to be ordained was revived - a policy that was continued by his successors and one that encouraged and perpetuated the clerical lineages.[2] Besides, there appears to have been a general acceptance among the laity of the practice of priests having children, some of whom would in turn become priests themselves.

Despite the fact that some priests did not adhere to the rule of celibacy it seems that generally the priests celebrated the sacraments and carried out their other pastoral duties quite well. However, there were a few exceptions. We have seen that in 1407, Nemeas O'Fay complained that no priest was willing to celebrate the divine office in Magherintemple chapel in the parish of Drung because there was no stipend for doing so and in 1447/48 Charles O'Flynn, a Kilmore priest, accused John Magillachuli, a priest of the diocese of Ardagh, of neglecting his church and duties of pastoral care and failing to administer the sacraments to a dying parishioner.[3] However, despite the large number and great variety of complaints forwarded to Rome, complaints about the clergy neglecting the pastoral care of their people were rare and there were no complaints at all about clergy being absent from their vicarages. So even though the clergy, in some instances, were not celibate, they appear to have been diligent in carrying out their pastoral duties.

The diocese was impoverished for much of the medieval period and the fact that most of the rectorial tithes went outside the diocese to the abbey of Kells and the priory of Fore merely added to the problem. These religious houses could appoint vicars to the parishes which were granted or impropriated to them and the archbishop of Armagh and the pope could, in certain circumstances, also make appointments within the diocese, thus significantly lessening the authority of the diocesan bishop. This dysfunctional system, where prior and pope, abbot and archbishop all claimed the right to make appointments, led to a glut of letters being sent from the diocese to Armagh and to Rome. It also led to innumerable disputes and furthered the divisions that already existed among the clergy of the diocese.

2.   Corish, *The Irish Catholic Experience*, p. 43.
3.   *CPL*, vi, p. 153; Ibid., x, pp 329–30.

Violence and Peacemakers

The regular outbreaks of local wars between and within the septs had a devastating effect on the Church in the diocese and the sanctuary of the parish church and religious house was often violated. At the beginning of the fifteenth-century the Franciscan friary in Cavan was burned and 'very many of the members of the house serving in its church were slain'.[4] The friary at Cavan was attacked again, this time by the English, in 1468.[5] Felim Ó Ruairc was killed 'within the precincts of Fenagh [abbey] by his own clan' in 1446.[6] In 1465 Domhnall Ó Ruairc attacked and killed MacConsnama and many others when they were at their most vulnerable while attending Sunday Mass in Inismagrath church.[7] In 1496, at his brother's first anniversary Mass, Donal Bearnach Magauran, the chief of Tullyhaw, 'was treacherously killed at the altar of Teampull-an-Phuirt, by Teige Mac Gauran' and it was said that 'the traces of the blows made at him are perceptible on the corners of the altar'.[8] In 1532 Eoghan O Rourke was killed by O'Mulvey and his kinsmen in the Franciscan friary at Creevelea.[9] The clergy, who were often the victims of violent attacks were, in some instances, the perpetrators of violence. Rory Magauran, the vicar of Templeport, wounded a clerk with an arrow *c.*1460 and in 1474 Eugene Ó Raghallaigh, the archdeacon of Kilmore, was accused of killing a layman with his own hands.[10] Yet, despite the volatility and violence of the time the clergy somehow managed to maintain the sacramental life of the Church and to meet the pastoral needs of the people.

The clergy, particularly the regular clergy attached to the monasteries, often acted as peacemakers between the warring septs in medieval Kilmore. In 1237 Cathal Ó Raghallaigh invited Clarus Mac Mailin, the abbot of Lough Cé Premonstratensian abbey, to set up a priory at Lough Uachtair, the epicentre of tensions between Norman and Gaelic forces in east Bréifne, knowing that he had successfully acted as peacemaker in Magh Luirg, another frontline of Norman and Gaelic strife.[11] In 1391 Tighearnán Mór Ó Ruairc and John Ó Raghallaigh chose Drumlane as their meeting place and presumably the Augustinian canons as their in-

---

4.   *CPL*, vi, p. 66.
5.   Ibid; *AU*, 1468.
6.   *AFM*, 1446.
7.   Ibid., 1465.
8.   Ibid., 1496.
9.   Ibid., 1532.
10. *CPL*, xii, p. 42; xiii, p. 372.
11. Clarus Mac Mailin and the Premonstratensians of Lough Cé were in regular communication and on good terms with the Normans in Connacht, probably due to their connection with their head abbey of Premontré in France. For his good relations with the Normans see *ALC*, 1235.

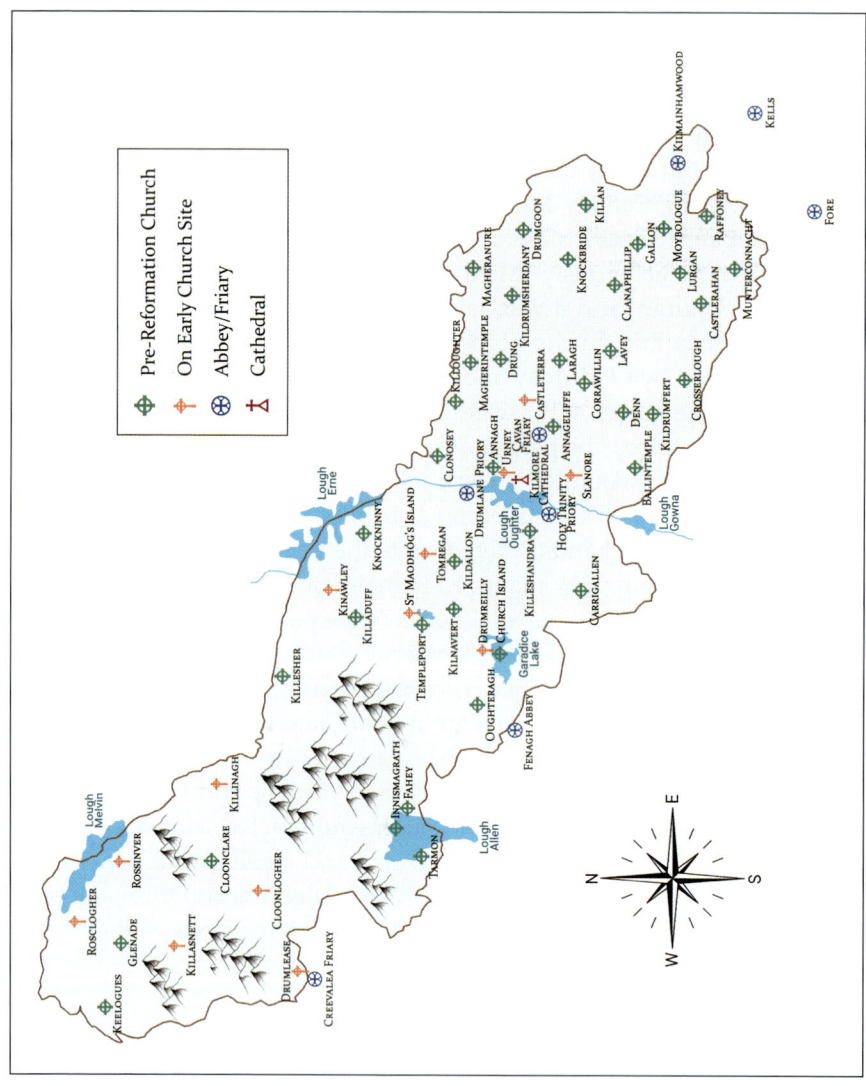

Figure 6.1: Pre-Reformation churches in Kilmore.

termediaries, when they wanted to establish peace between their warring septs.[12] The *Breac Maedhóg* reliquary, which was held at Drumlane, was greatly respected by both septs and it was regularly used for swearing oaths and making treaties and one of the Lives of Maodhóg stated that 'peace [was]not to be made in Uí Briúin without the coarb of Maedoc making it and drawing it up, otherwise they will be conspicuous for lack of peace'.[13] Fenagh abbey also fulfilled a peace-making role. The Book of Fenagh relates how St Caillín 'arrived in Ireland at the request of the Conmacni, to rescue them from the fratricide and breach of brotherhood they practiced'.[14] Individual clerics such as Tadhg Mag Duibhne, who was bishop of the diocese from 1455 to 1465, were noted peacemakers and he was given the title *Fear Sithe* (man of peace) Mag Duibhne.[15] And as late as 1600, even though they had already been ousted from their friary, the Franciscans in Cavan unsuccessfully tried to negotiate a peace settlement between the warring factions of the O'Reilly's.[16]

Church Building and Indulgences

One of the prevailing practises that Martin Luther railed against was the granting of indulgences for monetary gain and there are a number of instances of this happening in the diocese of Kilmore during the fifteenth-century. In 1405 the Franciscans in Cavan were given permission to grant indulgences to all who visited the friary on the feast of the Exaltation of the Cross and gave alms for the repair and conservation of the friary church.[17] In 1427/8, Pope Martin V allowed the Premonstratensians of Lough Uachtair to grant indulgences to all who 'devoutly visit [their] church on the feast of the Assumption and give helping hands towards its repair'.[18] Not to be outdone by the two other religious houses in the diocese, the Augustinians of Drumlane received permission in July 1431 to grant indulgences to all who visited their church on the feast of the Assumption and 'give alms for the building of

---

12.   *AU*, 1391.
13.   Plummer (ed.), *Bethada Náem nÉrenn*, ii, p. 196. The *Soiscél Molaisse* was used for a similar purpose. See Raghnall Ó Floinn, 'The Soiscél Molaisse' in Clogher Record, xii, 2 (1989), p. 51 and Griffin Murray, 'The Breac Maodhóg: a unique medieval Irish reliquary' in Cherry & Scott (eds), *Cavan history and society*, pp 109–10.
14.   Hennessy and Kelly (eds), *The Book of Fenagh*, p. 37. *The Book of Fenagh* was used to swear oaths on and to make peace, a practice continued into the nineteenth-century. See *The Book of Fenagh*, pp viii–ix.
15.   *AU*, 1464, n. 2.
16.   *CSPI, 1600, Mar.–Oct.,* p. 365.
17.   *CPL*, vi, p. 66.
18.   Costello, *De Annatis Hiberniae*, i, p. 247.

a cloister, refectory and several other necessary edifices'.[19] Five years later, in December 1436, the parish church of Drumlane received permission to give indulgences lasting three years to all who on the feasts of the Assumption and St Patrick visit and give alms 'for the repair of the parish church of St Modocius [Maodhóg] Druymleathan'.[20] The priory of Drumlane was not going to cede ground to the local parish church and so one month later - in January 1437 - it received permission to grant indulgences for five years to all who visited their church on the feasts of the Assumption and St Patrick and donated alms for the repair of their church.[21] Bishop Thady Mag Dhuibhne, having run out of funds while transforming St Feidhlimidh's parish church of Kilmore into a diocesan cathedral, applied for and got permission to grant indulgences for seven years to all who would visit the cathedral on the feast of St Feidhlimidh and give alms for the completion and conservation of the church.[22]

The papal documents confirm that the practise of granting indulgences to those who contributed to a particular church was used to raise funds, not just for the Vatican, but also for local churches in Ireland. Between the years 1405 and 1461 indulgences were granted on six occasions to churches within a ten mile radius of Cavan town. However, this practice of granting indulgences had ceased in the diocese three-quarters of a century before the Henrician Reformation began. The papal documents granting these indulgences indicates that the first half of the fifteenth-century was a time of considerable church-building in the diocese, a fact borne out by archaeological evidence from the ruined remains of pre-Reformation churches in the diocese. A recent survey of the ruined church on Church Island in Garadice Lake concluded that 'the west gable and central and western portions of the north and south walls appeared to date from the early thirteenth-century but the east gable and the eastern part of the north and south walls ... [were] of fifteenth-century date'.[23] Enough architectural fragments of the pre-Reformation church on St Maodhóg's Island in Templeport have survived to date them to 'the late fifteenth or early sixteenth-century'.[24] The ruins of the parish church

19.   *CPL*, viii, p. 384.
20.   Ibid., p. 589.
21.   Ibid., p. 592. Patrick O'Farrelly replaced Cormac Magauran as prior of Drumlane in 1436.
22.   *CPL*, xii, p. 131.
23.   The report compiled by Conleth Manning in March 2005 is published in Joseph E. Earley, 'Saving the medieval building on Church Island in Garadice Lake' in *Bréifne*, xi, 41 (2005), pp 85–8. More recent radiocarbon dating has confirmed the earlier findings. See Joseph E. Earley & Diarmuid Ó Seanacháin, 'The medieval island church in Lough Garadice' in *Bréifne*, xiii, 50 (2015), pp 456–7.
24.   O'Donovan, *Archaeological inventory of County Cavan*, p. 206; Oliver Davies, 'The churches of County Cavan' reprinted in *Bréifne*, xiii, 48 (2013), p. 140.

Figure 6.2: Cloonlogher pre-Reformation church, near Manorhamilton.

of St Brighid and St Laighne in the townland of Termon in Killinagh
parish have survived better than many other medieval churches in the
diocese yet, despite this, it is more problematic to date, having some
Romanesque features yet showing signs of having been re-worked in
the late medieval period.[25]

The two-light traceried and cusped window in the ruins of St Náile's
church in Kinawley has been dated to the mid-fifteenth-century, while the
carved bishop's head depicted on the hood moulding may represent a
new-found sense of diocesan identity following the establishment of the
Kilmore cathedral and chapter at this time.[26] See Fig. 5.3. The east window
of St Tighearnach's church in the townland of Killaghduff, a church which
may have been a chapel of ease in the parish of Kinawley, has survived,
and has been dated to the fifteenth-century.[27] The church of St Lasair in

25.   Rory Sherlock, 'The other Burren – archaeology and landscape in north-west Cavan' in
Cherry & Scott (eds), *Cavan history and society*, p. 74; Oliver Davies, 'Killinagh church and Crom
Cruaich', repr. in *Bréifne* xiii, 48 (2013), pp 149–53.
26.   Alistair Rowan, *The buildings of Ireland, north west Ulster* (Dublin, 1979), p. 337; Helen
Lanigan Wood, 'Ecclesiastical sites in County Fermanagh from the early Christian period until
the end of the medieval period' in Foley & McHugh, *An archaeological survey of County Fermanagh*,
i, 2, p. 659; William Roulston & Terence Reeves-Smyth, *Lakeland Heritage, antiquities of Fermanagh*
(Belfast, 2013), pp 49–50. St Náile's feast-day was celebrated on 27 January. See
Ó Cléirigh, *The Martyrology of Donegal*, p. 29 and Ó Riain, *A dictionary of Irish saints*, pp 509–10.
27.   The Baronial map for Tullyhaw shows a round tower adjacent to this church. See Davies,
'The churches of County Cavan', pp 133–4; O'Donovan, *The archaeological inventory of County
Cavan*, p. 200.

Killesher was a pre-Norman church and the fragment of a high cross from there, which is now in the museum in Enniskillen, has been dated to the '11th or early 12th century'.[28] However, the east window fragments with rounded heads and transom, which are to be found in the ruins of Killesher church, are dated to the sixteenth-century.[29]

A stone which 'may have formed part of a screen or more probably an altar front' was found at the old church of Rossinver and has been dated to the early sixteenth-century.[30] The ruins of the church in the townland of Kill and parish of Crosserlough can also be dated to this same period.[31] The grotesque head (See Fig.4.2.) and two stoups built into the present-day St Patrick's church at Castletara are late medieval as are the grotesque head and half-cusped ogee arch recorded by Oliver Davies at Clanaphilip church in 1948.[32] A similar, though somewhat damaged, grotesque head which Davies discovered built into a gate-post and which may have been part of the east window of Keelogues church in County Sligo would also appear to be of late medieval date.[33] The century before the Henrician Reformation was a time of fine stone work in the restoration of older churches and also the building of new ones such as the Franciscan friary church at Creevelea sometime after 1508. A similar pattern of church building and resto-ration in the fifteenth and early sixteenth-century has been noted in the rectory of Muintir Eolais in present-day south Leitrim.[34] The building of parish churches and new religious houses was often accompanied by the creation of adjacent walled cemeteries and the annalists recorded *sub anno* 1511 that bishop Thomas MacBradaigh died after 'having consecrated many churches and cemeteries' and it seemed fitting that his last official duty was consecrating the friary church at Dromahair.

The diocese was well provided with pre-Reformation churches and chapels. These churches were in almost every instance single-celled rectangular buildings. The *Breac Maodhóg* reliquary may be the best model we have of these medieval churches which had relatively low walls with

28.   Ann Hamlin, 'Two cross heads from County Fermanagh: Killesher and Galloon' in *UJA*, 43 (1980), p. 54.
29.   D.A. Chart (ed.), *A preliminary survey of the ancient monuments of Northern Ireland* (Belfast, 1940), p. 176. Foley & McHugh, *An archaeological survey of County Fermanagh*, i, 2, pp 769–71.
30.   Oliver Davies, 'Old churches in the parish of Rossinver, Co. Leitrim', repr. in *Bréifne*, xiii, 48 (2013), p. 155.
31.   O'Donovan, *Archaeological inventory of County Cavan*, p. 200.
32.   Davies, 'The churches of County Cavan', p. 116.
33.   Davies, 'Old churches in the parish of Rossinver', p. 156. This cemetery is in Ballintrillick, the only area of County Sligo which is still in the diocese of Kilmore.
34.   See Siobhán Scully, 'Medieval parish churches and parochial organisation in Muintir Eolais', unpublished MA thesis (NUIG, 1999), pp 46, 106–7, 127; eadem, 'Medieval parish churches in Muintir Eolais' in Brendan Scott & Liam Kelly (eds), *Leitrim history and society*, (forthcoming).

Figure 6.3: East window of Tarmon church looking on to Lough Allen.

high east and west gables and high-pitched roofs.[35] The twelve surviving pre-Reformation church ruins in east Bréifne average in size 15.46m x 6.7m. while the size of the seven surviving ruins in west Bréifne are slightly small-er averaging 15.1m. x 5.9m. The pre-Reformation churches in the diocese of Kilmore are more uniformly sized than those in the diocese of Kilfenora where the maximum length of the churches range from 5.24m to 38.35m[36] and they compare favourably in size with medieval parish churches in other parts of Ireland.[37] However, they are not as ambitious in size or design as some of the pre-Reformation churches in the wealthier and adjacent diocese of Meath.[38] Throughout Ireland the average size of medieval churches varied little with most of them ranging between 15m and 16m in length and between 6m and 7m in width.

There were more medieval churches in east than in west Bréifne and there were no churches in a large mountainous area separating the two which suggests that there may have been few people living in this area. See Figure 6.1. Many of the lakes, particularly the larger ones such as Lough Uachtair, Lough Melvin, Lough Allen and Garadice have churches on their lake islands and on their lake shores. Many of these lake-side churches, for example Tarmon in Innismagrath parish, tended to be on the west side of the lake with the east window looking on to the water. See Fig. 6.3. Unusually, Innismagrath parish church was located on an island on Lough Allen, though other churches such as the one on Church Island on Garadice Lake and on Inistemple on Lough Melvin were more suitable for hermitages, the islands being too small to support even a small community.[39] St Damhnad's church in the townland of Corrawillin in the parish of Lavey is the only surviving medieval church ruins which are aligned north to south. St Damhnad's church may have been an oratory or chapel of ease like the chapel of Saint Columba and Canice in Magherintemple in the parish of Drung.

Statues, Grotesque Heads and Sheela-Na-Gigs

The medieval churches in Kilmore and throughout Ireland were generally roofed with straw, rushes or shingles and there is no evidence in any of the surviving ruins in Kilmore of them having a paved floor.

35.   See Murray, 'The Breac Maodhóg: a unique medieval Irish reliquary', p. 97. Griffin Murray suggests that it may also have been modelled on a tomb.
36.   Sinéad Ní Ghabhláin, 'Church and community in medieval Ireland: the diocese of Kilfenora' in *JRSAI*, cxxv (1995), Table 1., p. 68.
37.   Scully, 'Medieval parish churches and parochial organisation in Muintir Eolais', Table 2, p. 86; Henry A. Jefferies, *The Irish church and the Tudor reformations* (Dublin, 2010), p. 19.
38.   Michael O'Neill, 'The medieval parish churches in County Meath' in *JRSAI*, cxxxii (2002), pp 1–53.
39.   Oliver Davies, 'Church architecture in Ulster' in *UJA*, vi (1943), p. 63.

These poor quality roofs had a short life-span, were vulnerable in storms and liable to leak. Besides, the churches were used at times to store agricultural produce, which meant that the churches were generally in a poor state. A Cashel provincial synod held in Limerick in 1453 directed that churches were to be kept clean and tidy and outlawed the keeping of animals or storing of corn in them.[40] That same synod decreed that every church should, at minimum, have a statue of the Virgin Mary and one of the patron saint of the church, together with a cross and tabernacle.[41] In the winter of 1588 the MacClancys, who were expecting an attack by the English, removed 'the ornaments and requisites for the church service and some relics' from Rosclogher church to their own island castle for safe-keeping.[42] When Msgr Dionisio Massari, dean of Fermo, visited the Holy Trinity island in Lough Uachtair in July 1646 he found scattered in the corner of the priory church 'many painted and guilt images of saints carved in wood … a crucifix, with statues of the Blessed Virgin and Child in her arms, of St Patrick, St Catherine, the Magdalen and three other saints'.[43] Chances are that the smaller parish churches and chapels were less well endowed with sacred images and statues.

The statues and other images in the churches were intended to help people to pray and to inspire them to imitate the lives of the saints depicted in them. The purpose of the grotesque heads and Sheela-na-gigs, which were built into the walls of some of the pre-Reformation churches, is less clear. It would seem, from the facial expressions, that both were meant to instil fear and deter people from certain actions and that the Sheel-na-gigs were to serve as a warning against the sins of lust, or perhaps were a residue of some pre-Christian fertility practice.[44] Several grotesque heads from the medieval churches of the diocese are still to be found and two Sheela-na-gigs, both of which are in Cavan County Museum, have survived. One of these was in Lavey church and another 'particularly terrifying' Sheela-na-gig was found 'in an old church near Cavan town'.[45] See Figure 6.4.

---

40.   TCD, MS 808 (5), 3, 69; cited in Jefferies, *The Irish church and the Tudor reformations*, p. 20.

41.   Ibid.

42.   Hugh Allingham & Robert Crawford (eds and trans.), *The Spanish Armada, Captain Cuellar's adventures in Connacht and Ulster A.D.1588* (London, 1897, repr. Sligo, 1988), p. 64.

43.   Msgr Massari, 'My Irish campaign' in *Catholic Bulletin*, ix (1919), p. 247.

44.   For this link to fertility rites see Shane Lehane, 'Sheelah: a forgotten vernacular deity' in *Intercom*, June 2017, pp 10–11.

45.   Eamonn P. Kelly, *Sheela-na-gigs, origins and functions* (Dublin, 1996), pp 16,33, 35; Starr Goode, *Sheela na gig, the dark goddess of sacred power*, (Rochester, 2016), p. 6; O'Donovan, *Archaeological inventory of County Cavan*, pp 194, 203.

Figure 6.4: Sheela-na-gig from an 'old church near Cavan town'. (*Courtesy of Cavan County Museum*).

Priest Residences

The vicars, or curates responsible for the pastoral care of parishioners, lived in the parishes and it appears that at least some of them resided in quarters attached to their parish church. The fifteenth-century cathedral at Kilmore had, at the west end, a semi-detached residence for a priest or bishop.[46] The priest's residence attached to Urney church was quite elaborate, the ground floor being divided into two chambers and a stone stairway leading to the upper floor.[47] The priest's accommodation at Relagh Beg church, which was attached to the transept, was also a two-storey building.[48] Oliver Davies suggests that one of the storeys may have been used as a school.[49] The priest's quarters at Fenagh church, near the parish of Oughteragh and in the diocese of Ardagh, was also a two-storey structure

46.   Rachel Moss (ed.), *Art and architecture of Ireland*, i, *Medieval c.400-c.1600* (Dublin, 2014), p. 352.
47.   Davies, 'The churches of County Cavan', pp 142–3; O'Donovan, *Archaeological inventory of County Cavan*, p. 211.
48.   Ibid., p. 208; *An introduction to the architectural heritage of County Cavan*, p. 14.
49.   Davies, 'The churches of County Cavan', p. 137.

Figure 6.5: Stone steps to priest's quarters at Urney church.

with the ground floor being barrel-vaulted and a stone stairway leading to the upper level.[50] The residence at Coolkill church, also in the parish of Fenagh, was at first floor level.[51] A small annex on the south wall and towards the west end of the medieval church in Carrickaboy townland in the parish of Denn may also have served as a priest's residence or possibly a sacristy. It appears that the priest's living accommodation at Rosclogher church was a wooden structure which was attached to the church.[52] There is not enough archaeological evidence to establish how wide-spread these church-attached priests' residences were in the diocese. However, this type of accommodation, where the priest's quarters were on a wooden or stone-vaulted first floor and were reached by internal or external stairs, was the most widespread type throughout the country.[53] Chances are that some of the priests lived in bell-towers attached to or near the church or else nearby in wooden houses.

Hospitals and Hospitality

These late-medieval churches were not just places of worship but were also centres where hospitality was provided for those in need. Providing hospitality was seen as a core Christian value in the middle-ages and the lives of the saints give many examples of great hospitality and people being fed miraculously. This account in *Beatha Lasrach* describes how the saint coped with some unwelcome guests:

> One day, as Lasair was in Cill Lasrach [Killesher][54] on the shore of Loch Mic nÉn (and at that time there was a scarcity of food and drink throughout Ireland) there came unto her nine enneads of poets and men of learning, and one man of them spoke in a weak and powerless voice, 'O Lasair,' said he, 'O woman-saint, noble and honoured, this poet-company has come seeking thee, for neither food nor drink has passed their lips for a long weary space of time ...' When Lasair heard these words ... she arose quickly and went to her own chapel and knelt down, and remained praying ardently and fervently to the Creator to

50.   Scully, 'Medieval parish churches and parochial organisation in Muintir Eolais', p. 149.
51.   Ibid.
52.   J.J. McDermott and Kieran O'Conor, 'Rosclogher castle: A Gaelic lordship centre on Lough Melvin, County Leitrim' in *Bréifne*, xiii, 50 (2015), p. 483.
53.   Helen Bermingham, 'Priest's residences in later medieval Ireland' in Fitzpatrick & Gillespie (eds), *The parish in medieval and early modern Ireland*, p. 170.
54.   Kay Muhr, 'The place-names of County Fermanagh' in Eileen M. Murphy & William J. Roulston (eds), *Fermanagh history and society* (Dublin, 2004), p. 587.

procure food for that hard insensate band that came unto her. Whereon Lasair beheld a nun approaching her in the cell under a full-mighty burden of food and drink. Then Lasair rendered thanks and gratitude to the Lord omnipotent, and thereafter bore the food unto those peevish and evil speaking folk; and they ate and drank their fill of food and drink.[55]

There are also examples in the lives of the saints of the punishments meted out to those who refused hospitality. In the Irish Life of St Náile when Dothearnóg refused to give the saint a drink of water he was banished from Kinawley for his inhospitality.[56] The Irish life of Maodhóg stated that his monastery at Drumlane would:

> Give refection to guests and destitute (travelling) companies and to strangers, to the weak and feeble and to all others who were in need, both in state and in church. He [Maodhóg] bequeathed to the place grace of clergy and coarbs, grace of prosperity and abundance, grace of welcome and entertainment forever.[57]

The dispensing of this hospitality did not always go smoothly. The late medieval Irish life of Maodhóg describes how Fergal Ó Ruairc, with a large company of men, arrived at Drumlane expecting the coarb, Concobhar Ó Faircheallaigh, to provide them with accommodation, food and drink. Having been treated hospitably for three days and three nights Ó Ruairc then demanded that the coarb keep his two hundred troops for a full year. The coarb refused and eventually Ó Ruairc and his men left and Maodhóg punished Ó Ruairc for abusing the hospitality of his house by destroying his wealth and fame.[58]

The erenaghs and coarbs continued that tradition of hospitality in medieval times by emulating the examples of hospitality and generosity they saw in the scriptures and in the lives of the saints. George Montgomery, who was Church of Ireland bishop of Derry, Raphoe and Clogher from 1605–1610, may be the author of the report which stated that 'the Herenagh was bound to keepe continuall residence and hospitallitie and to receive

55. Lucius Gwynn (ed. and trans.), 'Beatha Lasrach' in *Ériu*, v (1911), pp 84–5. See also, Seosamh Ó Dufaigh, 'Lasair of Aghavea' in *Clogher Record*, xviii, 2 (2004), pp 299–318.
56. *Life of Náile*, p. 132.
57. Plummer (ed.), *Bethada Náem nÉrenn*, ii, p. 201.
58. Ibid., i, pp 277–8, ii, pp 278–80; O'Sullivan, *Hospitality in medieval Ireland 900–1500*, p. 182.

pilgrims, strangers and travellars'.[59] In 1409 Nemeas O'Fay, a priest of the diocese of Kilmore, stated that he had 'decently repaired' the chapel at Magherintemple and 'in a house hard by keeps hospitality after the manner of the country'.[60] This practice of hospitality was widespread and the duty to care for the poor, the sick, the stranger, the old and the pilgrim was usually carried out not by the priest but by the lay erenagh or coarb who held the termon land attached to the church. Hospitality was also practised by local lords such as Gillaisa MacTiarnán, heir to the chieftaincy of Tullyuncho, who kept 'a general house of hospitality'[61] and Fergal Magauran of Tullyhaw, who died in 1393, was described as 'a man of unbounded hospitality to the clergy'.[62] Learned families such as the Ó Duigeannains of Castlefore in Leitrim kept houses of hospitality for scribes and scholars[63] and Bryan Ó Raghallaigh 'a patron of learned men and travellers', kept a similar *teach aoidh* in east Bréifne.[64] An inquisition taken at Cavan on 9 September 1590 found that there were forty-five 'hospitals' in County Cavan, each one with its own termon lands. The size and value of these termon lands varied considerably. Annagelliff had half a cartron of land valued at only 6*d* per annum while the half cartron of land attached to the Franciscan friary in Cavan was valued at 3*s* 4*d*. 'Dynn' parish church had eight cartrons of land valued at 8*s*. and Drumlane priory had a very large area of thirty-two cartrons valued annually at 32*s*.[65]

We have less information on the hospitals in west Bréifne although we know from papal documents that John Ó Maolmochéirghe was *rector Hospitalis Pauperam loci de Drumerbelaid* (Drumreilly)[66] in 1481 and that Bartholomew Ó Mithín, a priest of the diocese, was rector 'of the hospital of Ballagh [Meehan] called a coarbship in the diocese of Kilmore'.[67] Bartholomew Ó Fergus, also a priest of the diocese, was rector of the hospital of Rossinver in 1532.[68] This system of hospitality and pastoral care, which met the needs of the sick, the traveller and the poor, appears to have been under threat and struggling to survive in the decades before the Reformation. John Ó Maolmochéirghe, the rector of the hospital of Drumreilly, appealed for help to keep 'the poor hospital' going and was,

59.   Quoted in Jefferies, 'Erenaghs in pre-plantation Ulster: an early seventeenth-century account', p. 17.
60.   *CPL*, vi, p. 153.
61.   *AFM*, 1424.
62.   Ibid., 1393.
63.   Ibid., 1409.
64.   Ibid., 1481.
65.   For list of hospitals in County Cavan in 1590 see Archdall, *Monasticon Hibernicum*, pp 783–6.
66.   Costello, *De Annatis Hiberniae*, i, p. 239.
67.   Ibid., pp 240–1; See also Logan, 'Medieval hospital system in Bréifne', pp 55–6.
68.   Costello, *De Annatis Hiberniae*, i, p. 254.

in 1479, given the benefice of the rectory of Cinéal Luacháin to support it.[69] The hospital of Rossinver was in financial trouble by 1532 and the priest/coarb Bartholomew Ó Fergus was given the vicarage of Rossinver to supplement the income of the struggling hospital.[70] The hospital at Fenagh seemed to be faring better as Tadhg Ó Rodaighe, who was coarb there in 1516, was said to be:

> A man who observes the privileges and prohibitions of the place, in which he is, to wit that he should keep a house of general hospitality, and not deny the face of man, but be like an immoveable rock in humanity forever.[71]

It should not be forgotten that Maurice Ó Maoilchonaire, who wrote these lines in the Book of Fenagh, was in the pay of Tadhg Ó Rodaighe, and yet, despite the fact that he had a vested interest in praising his patron, it appears that there was at this time a functioning system of hospitality at Fenagh.[72]

Saints and Relics

We know who the patron saint was of thirty-four of the medieval churches in the diocese of Kilmore and of these seven had St Patrick and four had St Brighid as their sole patron. The parishes of Oughteragh and Laragh had Brighid as their sole patron while in Killinagh both Brighid and Laighne were patrons and in Kilsherdany parish Brighid was patron of the church along with Fincheall. The adjacent parishes of Drung and Castletara and the nearby parish of Drumgoon all had Patrick as the patron of their churches and all had holy wells dedicated to him. The church of Drumlease, an early Patrician site in west Bréifne, was also dedicated to St Patrick.[73] Other churches in west Bréifne were dedicated to less well-known local and regional saints such as Éimhearán in Drumreilly, Osnat in Killasnett, Curcach in Cloonlogher (See Fig. 6.2.)

---

69.   *CPL*, xiii, p. 650
70.   Costello, *De Annatis Hiberniae*, i, p. 254.
71.   Hennessy & Kelly, *The Book of Fenagh*, p. 311; Katharine Simms, 'Guesting and feasting in Gaelic Ireland', in *JRSAI*, cviii (1978), p. 71.
72.   Liam Kelly & Brendan Scott, 'Fenagh in 1516: the social and religious context for the Book of Fenagh' in Raymond Gillespie, Salvador Ryan & Brendan Scott (eds), *Making the Book of Fenagh, context and text* (Cavan, 2016), pp 32–4.
73.   See Colmán Etchingham & Catherine Swift, 'Early Irish church organisation: the case of Drumlease and the Book of Armagh' in *Bréifne*, ix, 37 (2001), pp 285–312.; Colmán Etchingham, *Church organisation in Ireland AD 650 to 1000* (Maynooth, 1999), pp 229–32. Tadhg Ó Rodaighe's late seventeenth-century report states that Drumlease church was dedicated to St 'Boey [Beoaid], though this may be an error. See John Logan, 'Tadgh O Roddy and two surveys of Co. Leitrim' in *Bréifne*, iv, 14 (1971), p. 331.

and Beoaidh in Ballinaglera.[74] Similarly, local saints like Lasair in Killesher, Náile in Kinawley and Ninnidh[75] in Knockninny were patrons of the medieval churches of Kilmore in present-day County Fermanagh. Other local saints were Bricín, who was patron of Tomregan parish church, Dallan of Kildallan and Maolán of Clonosey in the parish of Annagh. Killinkere parish church, while surrounded by churches dedicated either to Patrick or Brighid, had Uidhre and Ultan as joint patrons. Ultan, 'a poet as well as a true saint', was said to have been a companion of Maodhóg's and to have travelled to Rome with him.[76] The parish church of Kilmore was the only church in the diocese dedicated to St Feidhlimidh, which suggests that his cult was not widespread in the diocese before the church was chosen as the diocesan cathedral.

The cult of the saints was particularly important in the spirituality of the people of medieval Kilmore and the cult of St Maodhóg, the saint reputed to have been born on Port Island in Templeport, was widespread which suggests that he was the most popular of the local saints.[77] Needless to say, the parish church of Templeport was dedicated to Maodhóg, as were the parish churches of Drumlane and Rossinver. The O'Fergus family, the erenaghs of Rossinver, and the O'Farrellys, the coarbs of Drumlane, vied with one another for their particular church to be recognised as the pre-eminent centre of devotion to this popular local saint.[78] The second Irish Life of Maodhóg, which was written at Rossinver *c.*1536, increased Rossinver's status, claiming that the saint was buried there and that prayers offered to the saint from there were more effective than those offered elsewhere.[79] Despite Rossinver's

74.   My thanks to Pádraig Ó Riain for the information on Saint Éimhearán. 'Blessed Beo-Aedh' of Ardcarne is referred to in *The Book of Fenagh*. See Hennessy & Kelly (eds), *The Book of Fenagh*, pp 179, 185. Beoaidh's feast-day is on 8 March. See Ó Cléirigh, *The Martyrology of Donegal*, p. 71 and Ó Riain, *A dictionary of Irish saints*, p. 103; Michael Herity (ed.), *Ordnance survey letters, Londonderry, Fermanagh, Armagh-Monaghan, Louth, Cavan-Leitrim* (Dublin, 2012), p. 398.
75.   Ninnidh was based on Inishmacsaint (Inis Maighe Samh) on Lough Erne. See Ó Riain, *A dictionary of Irish saints*, p. 516; John J. Ó Ríordáin, *Early Irish saints* (Dublin, 2001), pp 53–7.
76.   Plummer (ed.), *Bethada Náem nÉrenn*, ii, pp 184, 244; Ó Riain, *A dictionary of Irish saints*, pp 580–2; Philip O'Connell, 'St Ultan' in *The Journal of the Breiffne Antiquarian Society*, iii, 2 (1929–30), pp 304–7.
77.   St Caillín of Fenagh predicted that 'It is through disrespect and irreverence for the saints that Ireland will be ruined.' See Hennessy & Kelly (eds), *The Book of Fenagh*, p. 289.
78.   Raymond Gillespie, 'The making of O'Rourke,1536' in Scott (ed.), *Culture and society in early modern Bréifne/Cavan*, pp 58–9. See also Gillespie, 'A sixteenth-century saint's life: the second Irish Life of St Maedoc' in *Bréifne*, x, 40 (2004), pp 147–54 and 'Saints and manuscripts in sixteenth-century Bréifne' in *Bréifne*, xi, 44 (2008), pp 533–57.
79.   Gillespie, 'Saints and manuscripts in sixteenth-century Bréifne', p. 544. The second Irish Life of Maodhóg was commissioned by the Ó Fergus family of Rossinver and compiled by Fionntan Ó Cuirnín.

claim to the high status *Breac Maodhóg* reliquary (the speckled shrine of Maodhóg) - so called because it contained a variety of relics of the saints Stephen, Laurence, Clement and Martin and the Virgin Mary - was held at Drumlane either by the O'Farrelly coarbal family or by the Magaurans who provided canons and priors to Drumlane in almost every generation.[80]

The *Breac Maodhóg*, which is 'arguably one of the most important reliquaries surviving from medieval Ireland'[81] (See Fig. 2.1.) is on permanent display in the National Museum in Dublin. Recent research by Griffin Murray, Raymond Gillespie, Marie Therese Flanagan and others has focussed attention on its significance.[82] The creation of the reliquary has been linked to the increased power of the Ó Ruaircs in the twelfth-century and the corresponding increase in the cult of St Maodhóg at that time.[83] It seems likely that the Ó Ruaircs were the patrons of this expensive reliquary which the twelfth-century poet Gilla Mo Duta Úa Caiside described as the pre-eminent relic of Maodhóg 'in which were gifts from Christ himself'.[84]

The *Breac Maodhóg* was also used in the coronation of the king of Bréifne and afterwards 'the king himself [was] to go on the morrow of his coronation to Drumlane or Rossinver with an offering'.[85] These two churches, along with the church of Ferns, were also to receive 'the dues of Maedóc' which were collected in Bréifne and in Leinster.[86] Templeport, the birthplace of the saint, had St Maodhóg as patron of the parish church and the Magauran family, the chieftains of Tullyhaw and coarbs of Templeport, had possession of the bell/relic of Maodhóg usually referred to as the *Clog Mogue*. Despite these significant links to the saint, Templeport struggled to compete with Rossinver, Drumlane and Ferns as a centre of devotion to him. However, the many members of the Magauran family who became Augustinian canons and priors in Drumlane helped to maintain their link with the saint and their presence in Drumlane is evidence that Maodhóg

---

80.   For the *Breac Maodhóg* see Murray, 'The Breac Maodhóg: a unique medieval Irish reliquary', pp 83–125; Flanagan, *The transformation of the Irish Church in the twelfth century*, p. 224.
81.   Murray, 'The Breac Maodhóg: a unique medieval Irish reliquary', p. 115.
82.   A panel depicting three ecclesiastics from the *Breac Maodhóg* adorns the front cover Marie Therese Flanagan's book *The Transformation of the Irish church in the twelfth century* and Seán Duffy's *Medieval Dublin, VII* (Dublin, 2006), and there are excellent images of the reliquary in Griffin Murray's 'The Breac Maodhóg: a unique medieval Irish reliquary' pp 90–8; Raghnall Ó Floinn, *Irish shrines and reliquaries of the middle ages* (Dublin, 1994), p. 32.
83.   Doherty, 'The transmission of the cult of St Máedhóg', p. 269; Murray 'The Breac Maodhóg: a unique medieval Irish reliquary', p. 114.
84.   Plummer (ed.), *Bethada Náem nÉrenn*, ii, p. 238.
85.   Ibid., p. 197.
86.   Ibid., p. 299.

Figure 6.6: St Caillín's shrine showing both long sides and the figure of the crucified Christ on the front. This shrine was gifted by the O'Rourkes to Fenagh abbey in 1536. (*Courtesy of the National Museum of Ireland*).

was held in high esteem among their sept in Tullyhaw. It is possible that other medieval churches in the diocese had St Maodhóg as patron since a report by Tadhg Ó Rodaighe on County Leitrim in 1683 states that Cloonclare, Cloonlogher, Killasnett and Killenummery all had Maodhóg as their patron saint.[87] Some of these churches had different patrons in the medieval times - which suggests either that Ó Rodaighe's report was inaccurate or that there was a seventeenth-century surge in devotion to the saint.

Literary Activity and Devotional Practices

The writing of the second Irish life of St Maodhóg at Rossinver in 1536 was not an isolated event but rather was part of an 'explosion of literary activity'[88] that took place in the late 1400s and early 1500s in the present-day counties of Cavan, Leitrim and Donegal. Much of this writing was devotional in nature and included new or re-worked lives

---

87.   Logan, 'Tadhg O Roddy and two surveys of Co. Leitrim', p. 331.
88.   Gillespie, 'Saints and manuscripts in sixteenth-century Bréifne', p. 533.

of the saints. The Egerton MS 1781 which is in the British Library was written by members of the Mac Parrthaláin scribal family between 1484 and 1487.[89] The Mac Parrthaláins were dependants of the Magauran sept of Tullyhaw and it is thought that part of the manuscript was written by Conall Bach Mac Parrthaláin at Ballycowan in Offaly and that the remainder of it was written by Diarmuid Bacach Mac Parrthaláin at Derrycassan Lake and on Port Island in the parish of Templeport. This manuscript, which was probably commissioned by the Magauran family whose fortunes were in decline at the time, ended up in the possession of the Ó Ruaircs who added their own notes to it in the sixteenth and early seventeenth centuries.[90] This MacParrthaláin manuscript has passages on the lives of such saints such as Alexius, Catherine of Alexandria, Margaret of Antioch, the patroness of childbirth, and a story of St Brendan meeting with Judas. It has many similarities to the *Liber Flavus Fergusiorum* which was compiled a generation earlier in Roscommon.[91] It includes a tract on the Eucharist, twelve articles of faith, guidelines for administering the sacrament of Extreme Unction and a list of sixteen conditions for making a good confession.

This late fifteenth-century manuscript, compiled by one of the learned families of the diocese, gives an insight into the devotional lives of people half a century before the Reformation of Henry VIII. There is considerable emphasis in the manuscript on the lives of the saints and stories about the cross and the passion of Jesus, though surprisingly little on the Virgin Mary. This deficit was rectified in another MacParrthaláin manuscript, the Rawlinson MS B.513, which was written about the same time as Egerton MS 1781, and is now in the Bodleian Library.[92] The Bodleian manuscript has a tract on a cleric who was devoted to the Virgin Mary and also a homily on Mary given by St Bernard. The story of Veronica and the death of Pontius Pilate are centred on two pieces of cloth – the towel that Veronica wiped the face of Jesus and the seamless garment that Jesus wore before his crucifixion which, according to the manuscript, had been made for him by his mother Mary.[93] This story

89.   Flower, *Catalogue of Irish manuscripts in the British Library*, ii, p. 526; Salvador Ryan, 'Wily women of God in Bréifne's late medieval and early modern devotional collections' in Scott (ed.), *Culture and society in early modern Bréifne/Cavan*, pp 31–2.

90.   Flower, *Catalogue of Irish manuscripts*, p. 526. Sebraid Ó Ruairc scribbled a note on the manuscript asking a blessing from whoever might read his entry. See Ryan, 'Wily women of God', p. 32.

91.   Ibid., Appendix I, p. 44.

92.   This manuscript was compiled by two scribes, one of whom was Conall Bacach Mac Parrthaláin. See Ryan, 'Wily women of God', p. 32.

93.   The relics, which reputedly were brought by St Caillín from Rome to Fenagh, were said to be wrapped in 'a cloth which pure Mary made, and which was round Christ when being fed.' See Hennessy & Kelly (eds.), *The Book of Fenagh*, p. 111.

and others portray Mary as the great intercessor for sinners and points to considerable devotion to her in medieval Kilmore.[94] Further evidence of this is found in the fourteenth-century seal of the clergy of Kilmore which depicts the Madonna seated on a throne with the child Jesus on her knee.[95] The first Irish life of Maodhóg tells of the saint saving a stag from baying dogs by placing his cloak over the horns of the animal while the second Irish life of the saint, written a generation after the Rawlinson manuscript, states that it was a rosary beads that was placed on the stags horns to save it from death.[96] This change suggests that the rosary was growing in popularity as a devotional prayer and in *A genealogical history of the O'Reillys*, we are told that Seaán Ó Raghallaigh, an aged man of fully eighty years, was killed '[agus] *é air a phaidrín*'.[97] The feast of the rosary was not instituted until 1573, though the practice of praying the rosary was there considerably earlier.[98]

Among the penances imposed by Archbishop Cromer on Cathal Ó Raghallaigh in 1529 for damaging church property were 'a pilgrimage to the statue of Our Lady of Trim' and reciting 'the office of the B.V.M. fifteen times'.[99] In the inscription on the shrine of St Caillín, which Brian Ó Ruairc gave to Fenagh abbey in 1536, he specifically asked for 'a Hail Mary'[100] for himself and his parents and in the poems dedicated to Tadhg Ó Rodaighe towards the end of the seventeenth-century are many references to Christ as the 'only son of Mary'.[101] Devotion to the Virgin Mary was widespread in medieval Bréifne though, interestingly, of all the churches in the diocese only the friary of Cavan and the priory of Drumlane were dedicated to her. The Premonstratensian priory on Lough Uachtair, while dedicated to the Holy Trinity, had devotion to Mary at the heart of its liturgy and prayer life and significantly, in 1428, indulgences were granted to all who visited the priory on the feast of the Assumption.[102]

94.   The *Annals of Ulster, sub anno* 1381 state that 'the image of Mary in Cell-mor in Tír Briúin spoke miraculously this year' – though it is possible that this was a reference to Tír Briúin na Sinna.
95.   O'Connell, *Diocese of Kilmore*, p. lxvi; Moss, *Art and architecture of Ireland*, i, p. 72.
96.   Gillespie, 'A sixteenth-century saint's life: The second Irish Life of St Maedoc', p. 150; For Scriptural references to cloths being used to effect miracles and healings see 2 Kings 2: 13 and Acts 19: 12.
97.   Carney (ed.), *A genealogical history*, p. 42.
98.   Clodagh Tait, 'Art and the cult of the Virgin Mary in Ireland, *c*.1500–1660' in Moss, Ó Clabaigh and Ryan (eds), *Art and devotion in medieval Ireland*, p. 172.
99.   Murray, 'Archbishop Cromer's register', viii, 4 (1936), p. 38.
100.   Paul Mullarkey, 'The shrine of St Caillín of Fenagh' in Gillespie, Ryan & Scott (eds), *Making the book of Fenagh*, p. 88.
101.   See, for example, *Laoi na mBuadh*, in TCD, MS 1391, 77; MacMuirí, *Tadhg Ó Rodaighe*, pp 339–40.
102.   Costello, *De Annatis Hiberniae*, i, p. 247; Clyne, 'Medieval Irish Premonstratensian monasteries' i, p. 32.

St Maodhóg's parish church in Drumlane and St Mary's priory in Drumlane were in 1436/7 allowed to grant indulgences to all who visited their churches on the feast of the Assumption though the choice of this feast day by both churches points more to a local turf war between priory and parish church rather than to devotion to the Virgin Mary.[103] The friars in Creevelea were also devoted to the Virgin Mary and the lily in a vase, the symbol of the Virgin's purity, which is carved on a mullion in the east window of Creevelea friary, suggests that there was there, at one time, a stained-glass window depicting the Annunciation.[104] In 1578 Friar Eoghan Ó Dubhthaigh, who was based in Cavan friary at different times, composed a long poem called *Léig dod chomórtas dúinn*, which, among other things, is a tribute to the Virgin Mary.[105]

Fenagh: Book and Shrine

The Book of Fenagh, which was commissioned by Tadhg Ó Rodaighe, coarb of St Caillín in Fenagh, was compiled by Muirgheas Ó Maoilchonaire, one of a well-known north Connacht learned family, in 1516.[106] The scribe states that it was Tadhg Ó Rodaighe who caused him to compile the book 'through the extent of his learning and through the excess of his devotion to Caillín'.[107] Tadhg Ó Rodaighe may also have had other motives for commissioning the book because even though it does contain a Life of St Caillín it is neither devotional nor liturgical in style. The book was compiled at a time of uncertainty and it seems intent on affirming the importance of Fenagh abbey and the rights and status of the Ó Rodaighe coarb family in a changing world.[108] The killing of Brian Mag Raghnaill by the sons of Maelsechlainn Mag Raghnaill at Leitrim castle in 1491

103.   *CPL*, viii, pp 589, 592.
104.   Moss, *Art and architecture of Ireland*, pp 71, 209; Raghnall Ó Floinn, 'Irish Franciscan church furnishings in the pre-Reformation period' in Raghnall Ó Floinn (ed.), *Franciscan faith: sacred art in Ireland AD 1600–1750* (Dublin, 2011), p. 8.
105.   Mícheal Mac Craith, 'Collegium S. Antonii Lovanii, quod Collegium est unicum remedium ad conservandam Provinciam' in Bhreathnach, MacMahon & McCafferty (eds), *The Irish Franciscans*, pp 248–9.
106.   For the *Book of Fenagh* see Gillespie, Ryan & Scott (eds), *Making the Book of Fenagh, text and context*. Bernadette Cunningham & Raymond Gillespie, 'Muirgheas Ó Maoilchonaire of Cluain Plocáin: an early sixteenth-century Connacht scribe at work' in *Studia Hibernica*, 35 (2008–9), pp 17–43; Bernadette Cunningham, 'Catholic intellectual culture in early modern Ireland' in Ó hAnnracháin & Armstrong, *Christianities in the early modern Celtic world*, p. 152; Gillespie, 'Traditional religion in sixteenth-century Gaelic Ireland', pp 39–40. The original manuscript is in the Royal Irish Academy, MS 23 P 26 (479).
107.   Hennessy & Kelly (eds), *The Book of Fenagh*, p. 311. For Saint Caillín see Pádraig Ó Riain, 'Caillín of Fenagh' in Gillespie, Ryan & Scott (eds), *Making the Book of Fenagh*, pp 45–60.
108.   The role of the coarb of Molaise of Devenish was also under threat at this time and it spurred Somhairle Séimh Ó Canann to compose a poem outlining the traditional coarbal privileges. See Tomás G. Ó Canann, 'A poem on the rights of the Coarb of Saint Molaise' in *Clogher Record*, xv, 1 (1994), p. 16.

triggered a sustained period of unrest in Muintir Eolais in which both Ó Ruairc and Ó Domhnaill got involved.[109] The setting up of the Franciscan friary in Creevelea, through the cooperation of both of these families, in 1508, merely added to the Ó Rodaighe family's alarm about what the future held for the church of Fenagh and for their role as hereditary coarbs there.

The newly-commissioned book, together with the *Clogh na Righ* relic, which they already held, and the Ó Ruairc gift of St Caillín's shrine to Fenagh in 1536 brought some reassurance to Ó Rodaighe and to Fenagh. The ornate St Caillín's shrine was a gift from Brian Ó Ruairc and it carries the inscription 'Pray for the man who covered the shrine of Caillín that is Brian son of Eoghan O'Ruairc, and for Margaret, daughter of O'Brien, and the year of our Lord was 1536. A Hail Mary'.[110] In giving the shrine to Fenagh, Brian Ó Ruairc was following the patronage example of his parents who founded Creevelea friary, and also a long Ó Ruairc family tradition of donating to churches and religious houses stretching back to the twelfth-century.[111] The fact that both Creevelea friary and Fenagh abbey were both located just outside the diocese of Kilmore in the diocese of Ardagh mattered little to their patrons who by 1536 were firmly in control of Fenagh in Muintir Eolais as well as Creevelea which was beside their power base in Dromahair. The compiling of *The Book of Fenagh* in 1516 and the creation of the shrine of St Caillín twenty years later involved considerable investment by the Ó Rodaighe and the Ó Ruairc families in the church of Fenagh on the eve of the Reformation.

Lives of Náile and Molaise

It appears that it was the Ó Mithín family of Ballaghameehan in west Bréifne, the coarbs of St Molaise, who commissioned the Irish life of St Molaise, c.1505–6.[112] The Life was written at Devenish where the cult of Molaise was strongest. However, there was considerable devotion to Molaise in Ballaghameehan where the Ó Mithín family were holders of the

---

109.   Cunningham & Gillespie, 'Muirgheas Ó Maoilchonaire of Cluain Plocáin', p. 36.

110.   See Mullarkey, 'The shrine of St Caillín of Fenagh', pp 85–122; Colum Hourihane, *Gothic art in Ireland 1169–1550* (Yale, 2003), pp 126–30; Raymond Gillespie, 'Relics, reliquaries and hagiography in south Ulster, 1450–1550' in Rachel Moss, Colmán Ó Clabaigh & Salvador Ryan (eds), *Art & devotion in late medieval Ireland*, (Dublin, 2006), pp 188–94; Raghnall Ó Floinn, 'Irish goldsmith's work of the later middle ages' in *Irish arts review yearbook*, xii (1996), pp 41, 44. St Caillín's shrine was damaged in the fire in St Mel's cathedral, Longford on Christmas day, 2009.

111.   For other motives for commissioning the shrine of St Caillín see Mullarkey, 'The shrine of St Caillín of Fenagh', pp 95–6.

112.   The manuscript for the Irish Life of Molaise is in the British Library, Additional MS 18, 205. For coarbs of Molaise, see Tomás G. Ó Canann, 'A poem on the rights of the coarb of Molaisse', p. 15; See also Gillespie, 'Saints and manuscripts in sixteenth-century Bréifne', pp 540–1; Ó Riain, *A dictionary of Irish saints*, pp 485–7; *AFM*, 1439.

Figure 6.7: Holy well at Killargue, County Leitrim.

important eleventh-century book shrine *Soiscéal Molaise* and where there was a holy well dedicated to the saint.[113] An Irish life of St Náile of Kinawley was also compiled in the 'early to mid-sixteenth-century'.[114] An early seventeenth-century copy, which was made by Brother Micheál Ó Cléirigh and other Franciscans at Drowes, has survived.[115] The Franciscans were not overly impressed with the Irish Life of Náile which they described as 'very late' and 'very poor'.[116] This Life of Náile describes how St Molaise, on nearing death, appointed Náile as his successor. Maodhóg and Náile then agreed to meet at Cluain Caem where Náile, despite being overcome by a great thirst, was refused a drink by Dothearnóg. Náile, then threw his staff and struck a large rock and 'a pure cold stream of blue water burst forth instantly'.[117] Náile banished Dothearnóg for his great act of inhospitality and predicted that in the new spring well 'fell diseases shall be healed by its water irresistibly'.[118] This story of the origins of St Náile's

113.   Ó Floinn, 'The Soiscél Molaisse', pp 51–63; Foley & McHugh, *An archaeological survey of County Fermanagh*, i, 2, pp 674–5.
114.   Ó Riain, *A dictionary of Irish saints*, p. 509. The anglicised 'Kinawley' is a poor translation of Cill Náile. See Nollaig Ó Muraíle, 'The Barony-names of Fermanagh and Monaghan' in *Clogher Record*, ii, 3 (1984), p. 389; Muhr, 'The place-names of County Fermanagh', pp 587–8.
115.   See Bibliotéque Royale, Brussels, MS 4190–4200, f. 129.
116.   Cited in Ó Riain, *A dictionary of Irish saints*, p. 509.
117.   http://www.ucc.ie/celt/online (accessed on 22 November 2014), Corpus of electronic texts edition, *Life of Náile*, p. 132.
118.   Ibid. A pattern was held each year at St Náile's well on the last Sunday of July. The waters of the well were said to cure warts and jaundice. See Gallogly, *The diocese of Kilmore*, p. 404.

holy well,[119] which is situated near the ruins of the medieval church of Ceall Náile, has scriptural echoes of both Moses striking the rock with a rod and water gushing out and Jesus telling his followers that anyone who gives a drink of cold water to one of his disciples will not lose his reward.[120]

This passage in the Irish Life of Náile is one of the better known origin-stories for holy wells which were so much part of the spirituality of people in medieval Ireland.[121] St Maodhóg's well in the townland of Kilnacross in Kildallan parish had a different type origin-story. It was said to be the place where Maodhóg baptised Aodh Finn the ancestor of all the Uí Briúin.[122] Other holy wells dedicated to saints were not spring wells but rather bullauns or pools of water in depressions on rock surfaces which were said to have curative powers. The rock indentation known as St Brighid's well in Greaghnafarna townland in Ballinaglera parish was said to have been caused by the saint's knee and its waters were used to relieve toothache.[123] The holy wells in the diocese were even more numerous than the parish churches and were, in many instances, located near them and shared the same patron saint. Patrick and Brighid, the two best known national saints, were patrons of the greatest number of holy wells and churches in the diocese. At Raffoney near Virginia the holy well is dedicated to Brighid and the well in the townland of Carrickatober near Crosskeys was dedicated to Patrick. The next most popular patron was Maodhóg with wells at Drumlane, Rossinver and Kildallan, although, surprisingly, the well at Bellaleenan in Templeport was dedicated to Patrick even though Maodhóg was said to have been born in Templeport and was the patron saint of the parish church there. The cult of St Éimheárán was a local one confined to Drumreilly, where he was patron of the parish church and a nearby holy well, and Fenagh where there was also holy well dedicated to him in the townland of Mullaghnameely.[124]

St Kilian's well is in the townland of Cloughballybeg in the parish of Mullagh and the 'pattern day' at this holy well was held on 8 July each year. The holy well in the townland and parish of Lavey is known as

119.   For a nineteenth-century description of St Náile's well see Angélique Day & Patrick McWilliams (eds), *Ordnance Survey memoirs of Ireland,* iv (Dublin, 1990), p. 112.
120.   Book of Numbers 20:11; Matthew 10:42.
121.   For a list of the known holy wells of the diocese of Kilmore see Daniel Gallogly, *The diocese of Kilmore 1800–1950* (Cavan, 1999), Appendix v, pp 402–5; O'Donovan, *Archaeological inventory of County Cavan*, pp 217–21; Moore, *Archaeological inventory of County Leitrim*, pp 187–91.
122.   Plummer (ed.), *Bethada Náem nÉrenn*, ii, p. 195.
123.   Gallogly, *The diocese of Kilmore 1800–1950*, p. 402.
124.   John O'Donovan states that St Éimheárán was the Mauranus mentioned in the *Tripartite Life of St Patrick*, who was appointed president of the church of Domhnach Mór. See Herity (ed.), *Ordnance Survey letters of Londonderry, Fermanagh, Armagh-Monaghan, Louth, Cavan-Leitrim*, pp 397–8.

Eas Damhnada called after Damhnad the patron saint of the local church.[125] The cult of St Beoaidh was not confined to one parish as he was patron of wells in both Innismagrath and Ballinaglera parishes.[126] The holy well in Killargue (See Fig. 6.7.) was dedicated to the Virgin Mary, though generally the holy wells, just like the parish churches in the diocese, were not dedicated to her. The *Tobar a'Bhainis* well in Doonmorgan townland in the parish of Drumlease may not have been a medieval holy well. Unusually, it did not have a patron saint but may have had links to fertility rites and was said to be a place where marriages took place during penal times.[127]

Water and stone were important elements in medieval piety in the diocese of Kilmore, a diocese which had a plentiful supply of both. Both elements are contained in the account of the baptism of Luan in the Irish Life of Náile:

> And he [Náile] laid hold of his hand-bell and filled it thrice
> from the fair water of the sunny lake and poured it on the
> head of the youth, greatly baptizing him; so that this bell
> of perfect form was the father and ever-illustrious font of
> baptism to Luan.[128]

Then Náile, having plunged Luan under the water of the lake, raised him onto the famous flagstone of Náile. This account is not just about the baptism of Luan but it is also about the anointing of the hand-bell and the flagstone as relics or tangible links to St Náile. St Caillín of Fenagh predicted that he would die 'at Mochaemhóg's famous *Lia* [flagstone]'.[129] W.M. Hennessy has suggested that this flagstone was located at Lemakevoge in County Tipperary.[130] However, there were several flagstones associated with the saint. St Maodhóg's first miracle was said to have enabled people to use the flagstone on which he was baptised to travel over water to and from Port Island in Templeport.[131] In the 1640s John Colgan listed a stone called *Leac Mhaedóc* in the townland of Killybeg in the diocese of Clogher.[132] Another stone was identified in the 1940s

125.   Ronan Foley, 'Therapeutic landscapes in Cavan' in Cherry and Scott (eds), *Cavan history and society*, p. 330.
126.   St Beoaidh is probably Beoaidh from Ardcarn. See Ó Riain, *A dictionary of Irish saints*, p. 103.
127.   Gallogly, *The diocese of Kilmore 1800–1950*, p. 403.
128.   *Life of Náile*, p. 137.
129.   Hennessy and Kelly (eds), *The Book of Fenagh*, p. 111.
130.   Ibid., p. 110, n. 2.
131.   Ó Cléirigh, *The Martyrology of Donegal*, p. 33.
132.   John Colgan, *Acta sanctorum* (Louvain, 1645), p. 233 cited in Gillespie, 'Saints and manuscripts in sixteenth-century Bréifne', p. 550.

by T.G.F. Paterson and Oliver Davies on St Maodhóg's Island in Templeport on which it was the custom to place a coffin three times before burial.[133] The earliest Ordnance Survey map records both a Tobarmogue (Maodhóg's well) and Leackmogue (Maodhóg's flagstone) in the townland of Derrintinny, which seem the most likely location for the medieval St Maodhóg's parish church of Drumlane.[134] Stones were used both to bless and curse. Saint Maodhóg's flagAstone in Templeport, or a portion of it, was used to bring curses on those responsible for evictions in the area and the large bullaun stone in the termon lands attached to Killinagh medieval church, which is known as St Brighid's stone, has rounded stones in each recession which were used as cursing stones.[135] A large stone, which was situated to the north of Magherintemple church, was said to give fertility and health to cattle which were herded past it on the first day of May.[136]

The Latin and later vernacular Lives of the saints advanced the standing of particular churches connected with those saints. They also spelled out the taxes due to the churches and the evils that would befall those who refused to pay. In the Irish Life of St Náile, the saint having banished Dothearnóg from Cluain Caem re-named it and predicted that his church there will match that of Bricín and Maodhóg:

> Cell Náile … shall be its name till doom shall come' … [and then Náile] remained behind ordering the fair church and levelling its cemetery and strengthening its oratories, and ennobling its altars, and making ready its monuments, and consolidating its crosses, and cleansing the side of its fountains, so that afterwards it was a church angelic.[137]

The remainder of the Irish life of Náile, much like the life of Caillín of Fenagh, is devoted to naming the respect and dues owed to his church

---

133.   T.G.F. Patterson & Oliver Davies, 'Ecclesiastical remains in Co. Cavan', repr. in *Bréifne*, xiii, 48 (2013), p. 147.

134.   This stone was referred to locally as *Glún Maodhóg*, the tradition being that the indentation on the stone was caused by the saint kneeling on it. See Gallogly, *The diocese of Kilmore 1800–1950*, p. 403. The nearby island of 'Innismuck', on Lough Innismuck, is thought to have originally been named Inis Maodhóg. William Petty's 'Down survey map' (*c*.1657) shows a church in the townland of Derrintinny. See www.downsurvey.tcd.ie (accessed 3 June 2017).

135.   O'Donovan, *Archaeological inventory of County Cavan*, pp 209, 215; Christine Zucchelli, *Sacred stones of Ireland* (Cork, 2016), pp 122, 124–5.

136.   My thanks to Oliver Patrick Mac Cathmhaoil, for giving me access to his unpublished paper on Magherintemple. See 'Survey of Magherintemple ecclesiastical enclosure, commonly known as Maghera fort and graveyard' (2001), p. 29.

137.   Patterson & Davies, 'Ecclesiastical remains in Co. Cavan', pp 135–6.

and the punishments which will follow for those who neglect to pay their dues.[138] Náile claims to have the backing of Maodhóg and Bricín in imposing sanctions on those who disrespect his church:

> Maedoc in his place laid a curse
> On every man of Bréifne who should do ill to me,
> To my bell or my church…
> Friendly Bricín promised me,
> And Maedoc of the great assemblies
> Destruction for the men of Bréifne of every territory
> For outraging my asylum.[139]

If, as it appears, this Irish Life of Náile was compiled *c.*1540, it was intended as a sharp rebuke for Ó Raghallaigh who, in 1538, had attacked Kinawley and burned the church there.[140] Even though these vernacular lives of the saints contained long passages taken from earlier Latin lives, they were nevertheless, a timely reminder to people of the status of patron saint, the church and the coarb and a reminder of the payments and respect that were due to both.

The abundance of writing which took place in the diocese of Kilmore and in territories adjacent to it in the late fifteenth and early sixteenth-century gives a good insight into the spirituality of the people in medieval times. The cult of the saints, together with objects and places associated with these saints, were important aspects of that spirituality. The patron saint, along with shrines, relics and places associated with that saint, gave both power and status to particular churches. It appears that there was some rivalry between the churches of Drumlane and Rossinver, Fenagh and Creevelea which spurred these churches to produce lives of the saints and other vernacular writings in the decades before the Henrician Reformation. The culture of Gaelic learning and writing survived longer among Gaelic learned and scribal families of the north-west than elsewhere. The Ó Cuirnín, Ó Maoilchonaire, Ó Duibhgeannáin, MacParrthalláin, Ó Rodaighe, Ó Droma and other learned and scribal families, with the backing of their patrons, produced an impressive collection of ecclesiastical literature on the eve of the Reformation which points towards a vibrant church rather than one in decline.

---

138.   Ó Riain, *A dictionary of Irish saints*, p. 510.
139.   *Life of Náile*, pp 147–8.
140.   Gillespie, 'Saints and manuscripts in sixteenth-century Bréifne', p. 547; *AU*, 1538.

Pilgrimages

Pilgrimages played an important part in the medieval spirituality of the people of the diocese. Some of the pilgrimages were local pilgrimages to a holy well, church or other place associated with a particular saint. Churches such as Rossinver, Drumlane, and Fenagh which possessed well-known relics, books, shrines, bells or crosiers could expect more visiting pilgrims than other churches which lacked such high-status sacred objects. Cavan friary, Drumlane and Lough Uachtair priories all had increased numbers of pilgrims visiting them after they were given permission to dispense indulgences. Other pilgrim sites were less local with people from the diocese going on pilgrimage to Lough Derg, to visit the statue of the Virgin Mary in Trim or the Cistercian monastery of Boyle.[141] In 1351 Aedh Ó Ruairc was captured by Mac Philipin Mac William Burke 'whilst coming from Cruach-Patraic' – an act which triggered general warfare in Connacht.[142]

Other pilgrimages involved travelling great distances to sacred sites throughout Europe. In 1231 Ualgarg Ó Ruairc, who was lord of Bréifne, died while on pilgrimage to the river Jordan.[143] Some of these arduous and costly pilgrimages were undertaken by ageing chieftains in atonement for all the death and destruction they had caused in their younger days.[144] The shrine of St James at Santiago de Compostella in northern Spain was also a popular place of pilgrimage and in 1428 Thomas Maguire died at Kinsale 'after cleansing of his sins in the city of St James'.[145] Some pilgrims never made it back to Ireland and a ship-load of pilgrims all drowned at sea while returning to Ireland from Compostella in 1507.[146] More people went on pilgrimage to Rome during Jubilee years such as 1450 when the *Porta Sancta* or holy door in Rome was opened and special indulgences were granted to all pilgrims who went there. In that year Andrew Ua Droma, son of Gilla-Crisd Ua Droma, 'a polished, conscientious man' died after

---

141.   This monastery was founded *c.*1162 and the church there, which was dedicated to the Virgin Mary, was consecrated in 1219. See Francis Beirne (ed.), *The Diocese of Elphin, people, places and pilgrimage* (Dublin, 2000), p. 31.

142.   *ALC*, 1351.

143.   *AFM*, 1231; *ALC*, 1231; *AC*, 1231.

144.   Ualgarg Ó Ruairc had, among other atrocities, killed 'a great number of [people in] Muinter-Eolais' in 1196. See *ALC*, 1196.

145.   *AU*, 1428.

146.   *AFM*, 1507. Scallop shells brought back by pilgrims from Compostela to Ireland in medieval times have been found during excavations at Mullingar, Tuam and Ardfert. See Roger Stalley, 'The Irish medieval pilgrimage to Santiago de Compostela' in *History Ireland*, 3 (Autumn 1998) 6, pp 3–11; idem, 'Sailing to Santiago: medieval pilgrimage to Santiago de Compostela and its artistic influences in Ireland' in John Bradley (ed.), *Settlement and society in medieval Ireland, studies presented to F.X. Martin*, (Kilkenny, 1988), pp 397–420.

coming from Rome 'in the fifty fifth year of his age'.[147] Thomas, the chief of the Maguire's, also went on pilgrimage to Rome that year and a week after he left home Donchadh Mag Uidhir, who had been fostered - presumably with the MacTighearnán's - in Tullyhunco, attacked his brother Cathal Mag Uidhir at Cnoc-Ninte (Hill of St Ninnidh) and took him and his spoil to Gortineddan in the parish of Tomregan where he killed him.[148] When Thomas Óg Mag Uidhir died in 1480 he was buried in the Franciscan friary in Cavan and the annalists recorded that he was 'a man that made churches and monasteries and Mass chalices and was [once] in Rome and twice in the city of St James on his pilgrimage'.[149] The medieval people of the diocese were a pilgrim and penitent people though these European pilgrimages were only for members of the stronger septs who could afford them. Others had to content themselves with visiting holy wells or lesser pilgrim sites within the diocese or elsewhere within easy reach.

Cathedral and Chapter

The twelfth-century attempt to establish Kells as the name of the diocese and location of the See was impractical and was abandoned after a relatively short time. The creation of the Kilmore Romanesque doorway and the elaborate crosier *c*.1170 points towards a concerted attempt to establish a new diocesan centre in the parish of Kilmore at that time. This second attempt to establish a diocesan centre also ended in failure because of the diminished power of the Ó Ruaircs and the resultant division of Bréifne into the two independent kingdoms of east and west, the former controlled by the Ó Raghallaighs and the latter by the Ó Ruaircs. This division of the diocese into two separate kingdoms and its elongated nature with a range of mountains dividing it in two meant that the diocese was a peculiarly difficult one to administer. The election of Richard Ó Raghallaigh as bishop of the diocese *c*.1356 marked the end of a 200 year period when the majority of the bishops of the diocese came from west Bréifne families and were consequently unlikely to reside comfortably at a diocesan See in Ó Raghallaigh-controlled east Bréifne. All of these difficulties resulted in the diocese of Tír Briúin limping along without a diocesan cathedral for three hundred years after the synod of Kells. This situation was rectified in 1455 when Bishop Andrew MacBradaigh, in a third attempt to establish a diocesan centre, nominated the church of

---

147. *AFM*, 1450.
148. Ibid.
149. *AU*, 1480; Michael J. Haren, 'The religious outlook of a Gaelic lord: and new light on Thomas Óg Maguire', in *IHS*, xxv, 98 (Nov., 1986), pp 195–7.

St Feidhlimidh in the parish of Kilmore as his diocesan cathedral and set up a diocesan chapter consisting of thirteen canons.

The impoverished newly-named diocese of Kilmore struggled to transform St Feidhlimidh's parish church into a cathedral and also to find prebend salaries for the thirteen new canons. However, despite these difficulties, largely through the efforts of Bishop Andrew MacBrady and his successor Tadhg Mac Dhuibhne, the diocese had by 1460 a modest cathedral and a functioning cathedral chapter. This mid fifteenth-century attempt to establish a diocesan See, the third such attempt, was successful and it is further evidence of a diocese not so much in decline but rather one that was, with renewed energy, giving itself a cathedral, a new name and an adequate administrative structure.

Franciscan Reforms

One anonymous Old English reformer gave, in 1515, a damning description of the clergy in Ireland:

> There is no archbishop nor bishop, abbot nor prior, parson
> nor vicar, nor any other person of the church, high or low,
> great or small, English or Irish, accustomed to preach the
> word of God, except the poor mendicant friars.[150]

It is obvious that the priests and bishops of the diocese had feet of clay and many of them were poorly educated and unable to preach effectively. When priests were being appointed to vicarages in the diocese during the 1400s they were required to be proficient in both reading and translating Latin and to be able to sing. There was no mention, however, of a prerequisite of having knowledge of the scriptures or being able to preach. A minority of the priests did go to Oxford and studied both canon and civil law there, though the above anonymous critic stated that they did so 'for covetousness of transitory lucre'.[151] Some of these canon lawyers succeeded not only in using their learning to get benefices for themselves but also supplemented their income by penning scurrilous letters to Rome on behalf of other less well educated clerics. So there was some truth in anonymous writer's description of the clergy in 1515 but it is fails to acknowledge that some clergy were well educated and gifted preachers. Thomas MacBradaigh, who was bishop of the diocese from 1480 to 1511, was one such man. He was praised by the annalists for being 'a man distinguished for wisdom

---

150.   TNA, SP, 60/1 no. 9, cited in Jefferies, 'The Armagh registers and the re-interpretation of Irish church history on the eve of the Reformation', p. 82.
151.   Ibid.

and piety, a brilliant lamp which enlightened the laity and clergy by instruction and preaching'.[152]

The Franciscan friars were noted for their pastoral work as preachers and confessors and even though many of them had no university training it appears that, judging by the library catalogue of the Youghal friary, they got a broad education at home.[153] Friar William O'Reilly, who was appointed the first Gaelic minister provincial of the Franciscans *c*.1445, probably studied with the Franciscans in Cavan before going to Oxford for further study. He was well educated being described as 'an inceptor and professor of theology'.[154] No significant archaeological elements of the medieval friary in Cavan have survived though the refectory pulpit in Creevelea and the depiction of St Francis preaching from a pulpit which is carved on one of the cloister pillars of the same friary is clear evidence of the importance the friars placed on spiritual reading and preaching.[155] This miniature carving at Creevelea of St Francis preaching from the pulpit shows a shrub growing out of the base of the pulpit on which are perched three birds listening intently to the words of the preacher, emphasising the close link between the world of nature and Franciscan spirituality.[156] The other stone carving at Creevelea which depicts Francis displaying the wounds of the crucified Christ gives a further insight into how the Franciscan friars promoted the cult of St Francis within their areas of influence. The knotted cincture, another Franciscan symbol, is to be found at the main entrance to the friary chapel at Creevelea and at several other locations throughout the site.

The founding of the Observant Franciscan friary of Creevelea in 1508 brought new life and vigour to the church in west Bréifne. Reforms were also taking place in Cavan friary at the beginning of the 1500s when in 1502 the friary there became a community of strict Observance.[157] The Franciscans, more than the other regular clergy in the diocese, had embarked on a path of reform in the decades before the Henrician Reformation and because of their education, the standard of their preaching, their ability to melt into the countryside when danger threatened and having a friary in both east and west Bréifne they were well positioned to play a leading role in the Counter-Reformation in the diocese.

The diocese still had many problems facing it on the eve of the Reformation. There were the clerical lineages, the pernicious letters being

152. *AFM*, 1511.
153. Ó Clabaigh, *The Franciscans in Ireland 1400–1534*, Appendix 1, pp 158–80.
154. Cited in Ó Clabaigh, *The Friars in Ireland 1224–1540*, p. 70.
155. Cochrane, *Creevelea abbey Co. Leitrim*, pp 11, 14.
156. Patrick Conlan, *Franciscan Ireland*, (Dublin, 1998), p. 28.
157. *AFM*, 1502.

sent to Rome and Armagh and the confusion caused by appointments to positions within the diocese being made by pope, primate, religious houses and bishop. These problems were systemic and hard to eradicate. The involvement of the archbishop of Armagh in diocesan affairs was, however, generally a positive one. The provincial synods and regular diocesan visitations meant that the archdiocese carried out its business in an efficient and effective way.[158] The archbishop adjudicated on local disputes, imposed sanctions and, during vacancies in the diocesan See and during metropolitan visitations, claimed the right to make certain appointments. The weakness in the system was that the archbishop of Armagh was unable to impose sanctions without the help of the secular authority in the diocese of Kilmore.

Nevertheless, when one considers all the church building, the establishment of the diocesan cathedral and chapter in 1455, the developments in the Franciscan friaries of Cavan and Creevelea, the explosion in devotional writing and vernacular lives of the saints and the work of individuals like Thomas MacBradaigh and William O'Reilly, it becomes clear that the church was vibrant and that reform was already well underway within the diocese in the decades before Henry VIII split with Rome.

158.   Henry A. Jefferies, 'The early Tudor reformations in the Irish Pale' in *The Journal of ecclesiastical history*, lii, 1 (Jan. 2001), p. 38.

Chapter 7

Tudor Reformation in Kilmore

The events of the year 1534, although a watershed year in relations between Henry VIII and Pope Clement VII, had little immediate impact on Ireland and even less on the diocese of Kilmore. Edmund Nugent, an outsider and member of an Anglo-Norman family from the borderland marches between the Pale and Gaelic Ireland, was already bishop of Kilmore for four years at this time. His appointment to diocese, which came after a long line of bishops selected from local Gaelic families within Bréifne, appears to have met with little or no opposition. Henry VIII, in a move designed to foster the Anglicisation of a Gaelic diocese, had recommended him for the bishopric and he was duly appointed bishop of Kilmore by the Pope Clement VII, on 22 June 1530.[1] Henry VIII, the king of many wives, was excommunicated by the same pope in July 1533 and, with the passing of the Act of Supremacy in November 1534, the breach with Rome was complete. This breakdown in the relationship between Edmund Nugent's two patrons meant that he was faced with a difficult dilemma. The fact that he survived as the *de facto* bishop of the diocese until his death in 1550 is a tribute to his ability to navigate the choppy waters of the Henrician reformation.

Edmund Nugent was, according to Aubrey Gwynn, 'soon to show himself a very tractable King's bishop'.[2] He, and many of the other Catholics from the English Pale, had less difficulty accepting royal supremacy than they had with accepting the later Protestant reforms of Edward VI.[3] Edward Nugent was a member of the House of Lords during the reformation parliament which met in Dublin at intervals between March 1536 and December 1537 and which

---

1.   Costello, *De Annatis Hiberniae*, i, p. 258.
2.   Gwynn, *The Medieval province of Armagh 1470–1545*, p. 162. See also Canice Mooney,
'The first impact of the Reformation' in Patrick J. Corish (ed.), *A history of Irish Catholicism*, iii,
2 (Dublin, 1967), p. 13.
3.   See Brendan Bradshaw, 'The Edwardian Reformation in Ireland, 1547–53' in *Arch. Hib.*, xxxiv
(1977), p. 96.

ratified the Reformation legislation.[4] This parliament introduced an act 'against the authority of the bishop of Rome'[5] and one to promote 'English order, habit and language'[6] and a further act providing for the suppression of thirteen monasteries within the Pale.[7] Despite the acquiescence of the bishop of the diocese to the passing of these acts it appears that the clergy of Kilmore still regarded the pope as head of the church and continued to turn to the papal courts and not the royal ones to resolve disputes. And so in July 1538 Andrew MacBradaigh, a canon of the diocese of Kilmore, wrote to Rome stating that there was no archdeacon in the diocese even though Patrick MacBrady, 'calling himself a clerk was in possession of it without any legitimate title'.[8] Pope Paul III mandated two Augustinians, the abbot of Kells and the prior of Drumlane, to investigate the situation and if they found the details supplied to Rome to be correct they were to appoint Andrew MacBradaigh - who was 'highly recommended to the Holy See by trustworthy witnesses' - the archdeacon of the diocese of Kilmore.[9]

Dissolution Of Kells and Fore

On 18 November 1539, just sixteen months after Richard Plunkett, the abbot of St Mary's Augustinian abbey in Kells, had carried out this task on behalf of the pope, he surrendered the abbey to the royal commissioners.[10] 'Richard Plonket, late abbot' was one of the jurors who met on 3 October 1540 and reported that 'the building which was the monastery church [is] now used as a granary' and that William Dormor, a farmer, occupied another portion of the abbey. A sale of the chattels of the abbey had raised £7 10s.while a church bell, which was owned by the parishioners, and another bell remained unsold.[11] On 10 July 1542 the abbey, together with attached lands and the right to the tithes of the rectories of Killann, Knockbride, Castlerahan, Templeport and Dartry in the diocese of Kilmore were granted to Gerald Fleming of Cabragh.[12] The dissolution of this twelfth-century Augustinian abbey in Kells, which was at the time of its foundation part of the diocese now called Kilmore, and which maintained

---

4. For an excellent treatment of the Nugent family's links to the diocese of Kilmore see Lennon, 'The Nugent family and the diocese of Kilmore in the sixteenth and early seventeenth century', pp 360–74.
5. Act 28 Henry VIII, *c.*13.
6. Act 28 Henry VIII, *c.*15.
7. Act 28 Henry VIII, *c.*16.
8. Costello, *De Annatis Hiberniae*, i, pp 254–5.
9. Ibid. The position of archdeacon of the diocese was a benefice worth twelve marks per year.
10.   White, *Extents of Irish monastic possessions, 1540–1541*, p. 264; Brendan Scott, 'Dissolution of religious houses in the Tudor diocese of Meath' in *Arch. Hib.*, lix (2005), p. 266.
11.   Ibid. pp 262–4.
12.   Archdall, *Monasticon Hibernicum*, p. 546.

links with the diocese until its dissolution, was the first real, although indirect, impact the Henrician reformation had on the diocese.

The Benedictine priory of Fore, like the abbey of Kells, was at its foundation within the diocese now called Kilmore. It was dissolved just nine days after the abbey of Kells when on 27 November 1539 the prior, William Nugent, surrendered it to his father, Richard Nugent, the baron of Delvin and was duly granted a substantial royal pension of £50.[13] Three days later, on 30 November 1539, Edmund Nugent, the bishop of Kilmore, who had been allowed to continue in his role as prior of the Augustinian priory of Tristernagh, surrendered the priory to the royal commissioners and received a sizeable pension of £26 13s. 4d. from the king.[14] He was allowed to keep the goods and chattels of the Tristernagh house, which otherwise would have been sold, because he was so much in debt to creditors for goods borrowed and bought for that house.[15] Further evidence of his allegiance to the crown is provided by his deposition on 24 October 1540 implicating certain individuals in the Geraldine rebellion of the mid-1530s.[16] Pope Paul III had by this time enough evidence to depose Edmund Nugent and on 5 November 1540, without making any reference to the existence of Nugent, he appointed John MacBrady, the parish priest Kildrumdferton, bishop of the diocese of Kilmore *'vacanti per obitum'* Diarmuid O'Reilly who had died eleven years earlier.[17]

Throughout the 1540s there were, once again, two individuals claiming to be bishop of the diocese - one approved of by the king, the other by the pope. Edmund Nugent had the advantage of being *in situ* for more than ten years when John MacBrady was appointed by the pope. Edmund Nugent was well connected in government circles and

---

13.   Morrin (ed.),*Calendar of patent and close rolls of Chancery of Ireland in the reigns of Henry VIII, Edward VI and Elizabeth*, i, pp 56, 108; Masterson, *Medieval Fore, County Westmeath*, pp 50–1; White, *Extents of Irish monastic possessions*, p. 274. This pension was one of the highest granted to any head of a religious house at this time. See Brendan Bradshaw, *The dissolution of the religious orders in Ireland under Henry VIII* (Cambridge, 1974), pp 132–3. An inquisition held at the monastery of Fore *c.*1540 found that the rectorial tithes from 'le Brewny' in the country of 'lez oreilles' were worth £5 6s.8d. 'when paid out of divers rectories'. See 'The Nugent papers', p. 128.

14.   Morrin (ed.), *Calendar of the patent and close rolls of chancery of Ireland in the reigns of Henry VIII, Edward VI and Elizabeth*, i, p. 64; *The Irish Fiants of the Tudor sovereigns*, i, p. 17; White, *Extents of Irish monastic possessions*, p. 280.

15.   See *Letters and papers, foreign and domestic of Henry VIII*, xvi, p. 373; Brendan Scott, *Religion and reformation in the Tudor diocese of Meath* (Dublin, 2006), p. 102; Lennon, 'The Nugent family and the diocese of Kilmore in the sixteenth and early seventeenth century', p. 365; White, *Extents of Irish monastic possessions*, p. 280.

16.   *Letters and papers of Henry VIII*, xvi, p. 137.

17.   Vatican Library, *Barberini Latini*, MS 2879, f. 188rv; W. Maziere Brady, *The episcopal succession in England, Scotland and Ireland 1400 to 1875*, i (Rome, 1876), p. 279. It is likely that John MacBrady studied at Oxford as he had a doctorate in canon law. See Costello, *De Annatis Hiberniae*, i, p. 258.

among the Anglo-Normans of the Pale. It also appears that he was accepted by the lords of east and west Bréifne as well as the laity and clergy of the diocese of Kilmore. John MacBrady had little option but to allow Edmund Nugent to hold on to the temporalities of the See while he retained his income as parish priest of Kildrumferton. Colm Lennon has suggested that the two bishops cooperated, with John MacBrady acting as a suffragan or assistant bishop to Edmund Nugent.[18] This viewpoint is supported by a letter dated 29 July 1544 which Archbishop George Dowdall sent to 'Bishop John [MacBrady], commissary or Vicar General of Edmond [Nugent] bishop of Kilmore', regarding a dispute over who was the rightful prior of Lough Uachtair Premonstratensian priory.[19]

William O Sheridan had written to Archbishop Dowdall complaining that he had been forcibly deprived of the Lough Uachtair priory by Thomas O Sheridan, a priest of the diocese. The archbishop's immediate response was to authorise the bishop of Kilmore to set up a commission to investigate the complaint. However, 'having heard the truth' from Thomas O'Sheridan, Dowdall revoked his earlier decision and approved the course of action Thomas had taken.[20] This nuanced and diplomatic letter from the archbishop to Bishop John MacBrady of Kilmore shows that he was aware of the irregular situation in the diocese and is evidence that both bishops cooperated in the administration of the diocese. It also suggests that John MacBrady may have been more involved in the administration of the diocese than was previously thought. This arrangement between the two bishops may have suited both since John MacBrady was permanently resident in the diocese and Edmund Nugent, apparently, spent much of his time living in the Pale.[21]

Surrender and Regrant

Following the arrival of Anthony St Leger as lord deputy in 1540 the government adopted a conciliatory policy of 'surrender and regrant' towards the Gaelic lords. During the early 1540s Bishop Nugent played an active role in helping Lord Deputy St Leger with this policy of assimilating the Gaelic lords into the English common law system.

18.   Lennon, 'The Nugent family and the diocese of Kilmore in the sixteenth and early seventeenth century', pp 365–6.
19.   Laurence P. Murray (ed.), 'A calendar of the register of Primate George Dowdall, commonly called the *Liber Niger* or *Black Book*' in *JCLAS*, vi, 3 (Dec. 1927), p. 151.
20.   Ibid.
21.   This peaceful co-existence of the two bishops in the diocese of Kilmore was in stark contrast to the situation in the neighbouring diocese of Clogher where there was, at this time, bitter feuding between rival claimants to the bishopric of the diocese. See Colm Lennon, 'Bishops in contention: secular and ecclesiastical politics in later sixteenth-century Clogher' in *Clogher Record*, xix, 1 (2006), pp 1–12.

Maol Mordha O'Reilly attended the St Leger parliament in June 1541. St Leger wrote to the king stating that:

> Orayly, being here at Your Graces Parliament and wearing thapparrell whiche Your Highnes sent unto hym of Your Graces gyfte, made humble suete unto us, to be petitioners for hym unto Your Majestie, that he mought have and holde hys lands upon Your Highnes to hym and to his heirs for ever … bycause he ys a man of great power, we thinke it convenient, that he have the honor of a vycount, and to be called the Vicount of Cavan.[22]

It is not clear what role, if any, Bishop Nugent played in O'Reilly's surrendering his land and it being re-granted back to him by the king, but it is clear that both he and O'Reilly were of one mind on this and other matters. Edmund Nugent was also involved in affairs outside the diocese, being a witness to the agreement drawn up between the lord deputy and Conn O'Neill on 21 June 1542.[23]

Brian Ballach Ó Ruairc, the lord of west Bréifne, was one of the last of the Gaelic lords to surrender his lands in order to have them re-granted by the king. He left the fastness of his Gaelic lordship in west Bréifne in early September 1542 and 'personally appeared before the Lord Deputy and Council at the castle of Meynoth [Maynooth] and voluntarily submitted to the King'.[24] The first two clauses of their agreement stated that Brian Ballach Ó Ruairc would acknowledge Henry VIII as his Lord and King and that he would renounce the usurped primacy of the Roman pontiff. The fourth clause of the agreement stipulated that the lord deputy 'shall present fitting priests to the ecclesiastical benefices in his country'- presumably priests who recognised the king as head of the church. The O'Rourkes and the O'Reillys were in dispute at this time over the Magauran territory of Tullyhaw and the MacKiernan territory of Tullyhunco. The agreement reached at Maynooth appointed Edward Staples, the bishop of Meath and Edmund Nugent of Kilmore, together with Thomas Cusack and another to be chosen by O'Reilly to arbitrate in this dispute. If they could not reach a settlement the final decision was to

---

22.   *SP, Henry VIII,* iii, p. 309 cited in Christopher Maginn, 'The limitations of Tudor Reform: the policy of 'Surrender and regrant' and the O'Rourkes' in *Bréifne,* xi, 43 (2007), p. 439; Ciaran Brady, 'The O'Reillys of east Bréifne and the problem of surrender and regrant', pp 239–40.
23.   J. Brewer & W. Bullen (eds), *Calendar of the Carew Manuscripts, 1515–1574* (London, 1868), pp 190–1.
24.   Ibid., p. 195.

Figure 7.1: Benedictine priory of Fore.

be made by the lord deputy and his council.[25] Brian Ballach O'Rourke, who was appointed 'Viscount of Dromaher' and a member of the Irish parliament, returned to west Bréifne where life continued much as before.[26]

Beyond the Pale

By the end of the year 1539 virtually all of the monasteries in the Pale and in Ormond had been dissolved.[27] Thomas Cusack, one of the royal commissioners, also claimed a small number of monasteries outside the pale including the Augustinian house on Inishmór island in Lough Gowna, which was apparently already derelict and in the possession of the ruling O'Farrell sept.[28] When Thomas Walshe, a king's commissioner, was tasked with surveying Inishmór and other monasteries in O'Farrell country he did so on 8 October 1540 from the safety of Tristernagh because he said the monasteries were 'among the Irish, for fear of whom it was not safe to approach thither for the purpose of making extents'.[29] The 1572 edition of Abraham Ortelius's map of Ireland has virtually no detail or place-names within the territories of O'Rourke and O'Reilly in Bréifne and

25.   Ibid.
26.   Maginn, 'The limitations of Tudor Reform', p. 445.
27.   Bradshaw, *The dissolution of the religious orders in Ireland under Henry VIII*, p. 121.
28.   Ibid., pp 116–7.
29.   White (ed.), *Extents of Irish monastic possessions*, p. 283.

has considerable detail elsewhere to the east and the south of Bréifne.[30] The diocese of Kilmore was largely *terra incognita* to the cartographer and to many in government circles and when the royal surveyors of monasteries met at Fore on 6 October 1540 they recorded that the priory had 'diverse other rectories, the names of which are not known in the Brenny in O Reli's district, where the king's writ does not run'.[31] West Bréifne was even further removed from the control of the king and as a result the friaries of Creevelea and Cavan and the priories of Lough Uachtair and Drumlane survived the Henrician reformation and remained intact until the reign of Elizabeth I.

In the early summer of 1538 rumours were spreading that Archbishop George Browne was intent on destroying all images particularly the shrine of the Holy Cross of Ballyboggan and the Virgin Mary's shrine in Trim, the latter which was a popular place of pilgrimage for people in east Bréifne.[32] The rumours were well founded and the Annals of Loch Cé recorded *sub anno* 1538 that:

> The very miraculous image of Mary which was in the town of Ath-truim, in which all the people of Eirinn believed … which healed the blind and deaf, and lame, and every other ailment, was burnt by Saxons; and the Bachall-Isa which was in the town of Ath-cliath working numerous prodigies and miracles … was burned … and there was not in Eirinn a holy cross or figure of Mary, or an illustrious image over which their [Saxon] power reached, that was not burned.[33]

The iconoclasts continued their work during the reign of Edward VI with the annalists recording *sub anno* 1552 that the monastery of Clonmacnois 'was plundered and devastated by the English of Athlone. They took the large bells out of the Cloicteach and left neither large nor small bell, image, altar, book, gem, nor even glass in a window of the walls of the church

---

30. Map titled *Eryn, Hiberniae Britannicae Insulae Nova Descriptio* (1572 edition).
31. White (ed.), *Extents of Irish monastic possessions*, p. 283; Rory Masterson, 'The dissolution of the monasteries and the parishes of the western liberty of Meath in the seventeenth century' in Salvador Ryan & Clodagh Tait (eds), *Religion and politics in urban Ireland, c.1500–c.1750: essays in honour of Colm Lennon* (Dublin, 2016), pp 138–9.
32. Bradshaw, *The dissolution of the religious orders*, p. 101; Colm Lennon, *Sixteenth century Ireland* (Dublin, 2005), p. 139.
33. These same events were mistakenly recorded in the *Annals of the Four Masters sub anno* 1537. It appears that the Trim statue of Mary may have been hidden rather than destroyed at this time. See Scott, *Religion and reformation in the Tudor diocese of Meath*, pp 43, 53.

that they did not carry away with them'.[34] The churches and monasteries of Kilmore, being outside the government's sphere of influence, survived the iconoclasm of the early Tudor reformations.

Archbishop George Browne[35] of Dublin and Edward Staples[36] the bishop of Meath, were to the forefront in promoting the Protestant Reformation in Ireland although their efforts at reform were half-hearted. And while Edmund Nugent 'took his line in ecclesiastical matters from the crown'[37] he did not disturb the peace in the diocese of Kilmore by attempting to enforce any liturgical or doctrinal changes. In 1543 Nugent was one of eight bishops, 'in whose fidelity we confide' who was chosen by the king to consecrate George Dowdall as archbishop of Armagh.[38] From the mid-1540s onwards he kept a low profile, possibly due to ill health or advancing age. It appears that he made no attempt to impose the Book of Common Prayer which was promulgated during the short reign of the child-monarch Edward VI (1547–53). Bishop Edmund Nugent died sometime before 28 October 1550. He had been bishop of the diocese during a difficult and divisive time and yet somehow managed to maintain good relations with all sides throughout his episcopate. His pragmatic approach meant that the diocese was protected from aggressive royal intervention and it ensured a smooth transition for John MacBrady who became the undisputed bishop of the diocese after his death.[39]

One Bishop

Lord Deputy Anthony St Leger and the Irish council wrote to the English Privy Council on 28 October 1550 stating that the bishopric of 'Brenny' was now vacant and recommending John Brady 'a man borne in those parts' who had been appointed previously to that position as a Catholic bishop by Rome. The letter outlined how John MacBrady had surrendered his bulls of appointment to the king and had allowed the late bishop quietly to enjoy the See. The letter also stated that John MacBrady was 'well frended', had the backing of the O'Reillys, would help to promote the peace of the area and was capable of setting forth

34.   *AFM*, 1552.
35.   James Murray, 'Ecclesiastical justice and the enforcement of the reformation: the case of Archbishop Browne and the clergy of Dublin' in A. Ford, J. McGuire & K. Milne (eds), *As by law established, the Church of Ireland since the reformation* (Dublin, 1995), pp 36–7.
36.   Scott, *Religion and reformation in the Tudor diocese of Meath*, pp 40–2.
37.   Lennon, 'The Nugent family and the diocese of Kilmore', p. 367.
38.   For the text of this mandate see Thomas Gogarty (ed.), 'Documents concerning Primate Dowdall' in *Arch. Hib.*, i (1912), pp 253–7.
39.   For an assessment of the episcopacy of Edmund Nugent see Lennon, 'The Nugent family and the diocese of Kilmore' pp 366–7.

'the king's most godly procedinge'.[40] Anthony St Leger had returned to Ireland as lord deputy just two months previously. His policy of favouring local candidates, who he hoped would prove to be enthusiastic reformers, was a source of tension between himself and some London officials.[41] The English Privy Council, nevertheless, accepted St Leger's recommendation and John MacBrady had his temporalites restored and was confirmed as the undisputed bishop of the diocese in January 1551.[42]

Three months later St Leger was recalled to London and replaced by Sir James Croft, a more forceful reformer. The archbishop of Armagh, George Dowdall, coming from Old English stock in County Louth, accepted royal supremacy at first and then proceeded to resist the efforts of James Croft to spread Protestantism in his diocese.[43] Faced with imprisonment he fled to the continent in the summer of 1551 and in his absence the title of 'primate of all Ireland' was given to George Browne, the archbishop of Dublin and the leading episcopal reformer in the country. Other bishops, including John MacBrady, avoided confrontation with the Edwardian reformers because their dioceses were outside the Pale and they could avoid facing the issue squarely by outwardly conforming yet quietly dissenting. Their lack of enthusiasm for, and their sullen opposition to, the Edwardian reforms blocked any progress James Croft and others hoped to make. Despite his best efforts, James Croft had to admit in March 1552 that 'the olde seremonies yet remayne in meny places'.[44]

John MacBrady was even less enthusiastic than Edward Staples, his fellow bishop in the neighbouring diocese of Meath, for the Edwardian reforms and thus avoided any controversy. He was in the happy and unusual position of having the support of both pope and king and the accession of Mary, the Catholic daughter of Catherine of Aragon and Henry VIII, to the throne in 1553, meant that he did not have to impose any of the contentious liturgical and doctrinal changes introduced during the reign of Edward VI. Sir Thomas Cusack reported to the Duke of Northumberland on 8 May 1552 that he met with 'O'Reilly [who] rules

---

40.   TNA, SP, 61/2/63; *CSPI, 1547–53*, p. 86; E.P. Shirley, *Original Letters and papers* (London, 1851), pp 43–4. O'Connell, *The diocese of Kilmore*, pp 384–5; Lennon, 'The Nugent family and the diocese of Kilmore', pp 366–7; Brady, *The episcopal succession*, pp 279–80.
41.   See Brendan Bradshaw, 'The Edwardian Reformation in Ireland, 1547–53' in *Arch. Hib.*, xxxiv (1977), p. 89.
42.   O'Connell, *The diocese of Kilmore*, p. 385.
43.   Henry A. Jefferies, 'Primate George Dowdall and the Marian Restoration' in *Seanchas Ard Mhacha*, xvii, 2(1998), p. 4.
44.   SP, 61/4 no. 28; Shirley, *Original letters*, p. 63; Bradshaw, 'The Edwardian Reformation in Ireland, 1547–53', p. 93.

the … territory of Bréifne. Together with his seven sons, he can call on 1,600 troops'. However, Cusack felt confident that 'under the influence of proper preaching and teaching, such men can be brought to do their duty to God and the king'.[45]

Queen Mary immediately set about reversing the reforms of Henry VIII and Edward VI and restoring the old religion. George Dowdall, now reconciled with Rome, returned as archbishop of Armagh and he, with the full backing of the queen and some support from the papal legate and aristocratic Englishman, Cardinal Reginald Pole, spearheaded the Marian restoration in Ireland.[46] One of Archbishop Dowdall's first actions on his return was to call a provincial council in St Peter's church in Drogheda in order to kick start the Marian restoration in the ecclesiastical province of Armagh.[47] Unfortunately no record of who attended this meeting has survived but it is likely that either John MacBrady himself or his representative was present. The archbishop of Armagh continued its long-standing practice of over-seeing the affairs of the diocese of Kilmore throughout the Tudor reformations and clergy of Kilmore continued to play an active role in affairs of the ecclesiastical province of Armagh. In 1540, Felimy Ó Maolmochéirghe, a 'canon of Kilmore Cathedral', was one of two people mandated by the archbishop of Armagh to resolve a dispute over the parochial church of Cloone in the diocese of Ardagh[48] and sixteen years later, in 1556, Eugenius O'Gowan, also a canon from Kilmore, assisted Archbishop Dowdall in resolving a dispute over an Augustinian abbey in the diocese of Clogher.[49] So the diocese continued to be involved in the affairs of the province of Armagh and we can safely conclude that it was represented at the provincial council meeting in Drogheda in 1553 and that decrees passed at it were applied, where necessary, in the diocese of Kilmore.

The sixth of the decrees which were passed at the Drogheda meeting in 1553 gets to the core of what this provincial gathering was about. It ordered both clerics and laity, under the pain of excommunication 'to restore all the ancient rites, practices, ceremonies, feasts, customs, sacraments and sacrifices' that had been abolished during the reign of Edward.[50] There were other decrees to appoint both diocesan and metropolitan inquisitors to seek out and prosecute heretics and another still designed to facilitate the burning of the new heretical books. Other decrees such as

45.   *CSPI, 1547–53*, pp 170–1.
46.   Jefferies, *The Irish church and the early Tudor reformations*, pp 108–20; idem, 'Why the Reformation failed in Ireland', p. 158.
47.   Murray, 'A calendar of the register of Primate George Dowdall', pp 154–5.
48.   Ibid., *JCLAS*, vi, 2 (1926), p. 94.
49.   Ibid., *JCLAS* (1927), p. 156.
50.   Ibid., p. 155.

those concerning clerical dress, the administration of the sacraments and the upkeep of ruined churches were not directly aimed at the Edwardian reformers. However, the decree to reconcile any clerics who, out of fear, had involuntarily 'celebrated Mass or administered Sacraments according to the heretical rite or had given it approval in their preaching'[51] was intended to rehabilitate priests who had adopted the Edwardian reforms. There was less sympathy for the clergy who had presumed to marry during the period of schism and in 1554 a royal commission was set up to remove bishops and priests who had got married. Among those removed were the bishops of Dublin, Meath, Kildare, Leighlin and Limerick.[52] John MacBrady was not among them and he remained as bishop of Kilmore throughout the reign of Mary. His episcopacy was uneventful and he 'of happy memory'[53] died in 1559, one year after Elizabeth I became queen of England. Archbishop Dowdall, Cardinal Pole and Queen Mary all had died the previous year. The attempts to restore the old religion, which had considerable success during the reign of Mary, came to an abrupt end.

Hugh O'Sheridan

Hugh O'Sheridan, a priest of the diocese of Raphoe, succeeded John MacBrady as bishop of Kilmore. He was appointed by Pope Pius IV, an uncle of the great reformer Charles Borromeo, on 7 February 1560.[54] Hugh O'Sheridan was a canon of the cathedral chapter in Raphoe and, by a special concession, was allowed to retain that position and presumably the income that went with it.[55] Like his immediate pre-decessors, Hugh O'Sheridan was permitted to keep an income from a previously held position, which suggests that the diocese was still impoverished with insufficient revenue to support a bishop.[56] The Kilmore O'Sheridan family was a strong clerical family providing priests for Lough Uachtair Premonstratensian priory and for the diocese of Kilmore for a period of more than 150 years before Hugh O'Sheridan was appointed bishop. However, there is no evidence to link Hugh O'Sheridan with the O'Sheridans of east Bréifne who resided a considerable distance away from the diocese of Raphoe. It was a new departure for the pope to appoint someone from another diocese in Ulster as bishop of Kilmore. It may well be that Rome was

51.   Ibid.
52.   Jefferies, *The Irish church and the early Tudor reformations*, p. 110.
53.   Brady, *The episcopal succession*, p. 280.
54.   Vatican Library, MSS, *Barberini Latini*, vol. 2882, ff. 14v-15r.
55.   Vatican archives, *Acta Camerarii*, ix, fol.10v; See 'Miscellanea Vaticano-Hibernica' in *Arch. Hib.*, v (1916), p. 168.
56.   An inquisition in 1609 discovered that the bishop of Kilmore's mensal or demesne lands amounted to 120 acres. The diocese of Clogher with 320 acres of mensal lands was the next low-est in Ulster. See Brewer & Bullen (eds), *Calendar of Carew Manuscripts*, v, p. 40.

appointing someone who, coming from a great distance away from the Pale, would, they hoped, not have had any baggage from or truck with the reforms introduced during the reign of Edward VI.

The Irish Reformation Parliament of Elizabeth I met in Christ Church cathedral in Dublin on 12 January 1560 and remained in session for the following three weeks.[57] It passed a series of nine acts, one of which acknowledged the queen as the supreme governor in all matters both temporal and ecclesiastical and it required all office-holders in church and state to take an oath recognising her supremacy. The Act of uniformity imposed a new vernacular liturgy on the Irish church though it did make the concession that priests who could not speak English could use a Latin version of the reformed liturgy prescribed by the act. In another concession the clergy were allowed to wear the traditional Mass vestments and to retain ornaments they had customarily used in the churches. These reforms were passed by the bishops sitting in the Irish House of Lords and were supported enthusiastically by Patrick Walsh the bishop of Waterford and Lismore, Archbishop Hugh Curwen of Dublin and Bishop Thomas O'Fihilly of Leighlin. Other bishops such as William Walshe of Meath and Thomas Leverous of Kildare vehemently opposed the new measures and refused to take the oath of supremacy. Both were deposed and the bishop of Meath was imprisoned a number of times for his continued opposition to the new measures.[58] Later, Hugh Lacey of Limerick was also deprived of his bishopric for opposing the new reforms.

Opposition among the bishops to the new reforms was limited. Steven Ellis has suggested that between six and eight bishops, not including the bishop of Kilmore, took the oath of supremacy.[59] Patrick Corish states that the other bishops who attended the parliament 'prudently made a hasty return to their sees'[60] and thus avoided having to choose between pope and queen. Hugh O'Sheridan, the bishop of Kilmore and the bishops of Clogher, Clonmacnois, Dromore, Derry, Raphoe, Killaloe and Kilfenora did not attend the parliament and did not take the oath of supremacy.[61] Hugh O'Sheridan was under no pressure to implement any of the Elizabethan reforms in Kilmore which was mostly under the control of the O'Rourkes and the O'Reillys. These reforms were carried out only where conditions were right, that is 'where the efforts of a favourably disposed bishop

57.   For information on this parliament see Henry Jefferies, 'The Irish parliament of 1560: the Anglican reforms authorised' in *IHS*, 26 (1988), pp 128–41.
58.   Scott, *Religion and reformation in the Tudor diocese of Meath*, pp 55–6.
59.   Steven G. Ellis, *Ireland in the age of the Tudors 1447–1603* (London, 1998), p. 229.
60.   Corish, *The Irish Catholic experience*, p. 83.
61.   Richard Nugent, the Baron of Delvin, was present at this parliament. For a list of the bishops present see, James Hardiman, *Tracts relating to Ireland* (Dublin, 1843), ii, pp 134–8; J.T. Ball, *The Reformed Church of Ireland: 1537–1886*, (London, 1886), pp 322–4.

were complemented by English royal authority'.[62] Such conditions did not prevail in Kilmore and, in stark contrast to the experience of William Walshe, the bishop in the neighbouring diocese of Meath, there was an air of normality in Kilmore during Hugh O'Sheridan's episcopacy. Thus we find Pope Pius V writing to O'Sheridan on 16 February 1571 granting him permission to give a marriage dispensation to the cousins John and Menninae O'Reilly in order to avoid scandal.[63]

Eight years later, on 15 March 1579, Pope Gregory XIII gave Hugh O'Sheridan permission to absolve Henry Sedgraff, a cleric from Meath diocese, from all censures and to promote him to higher orders, because there was no bishop in Meath since the death of Bishop Walshe in January 1577.[64] Philip O'Connell stated that O'Sheridan was in poor health for a considerable time before his death and since he died in 1579, it is not clear if he had been able to ordain Henry Sedgraff. Three years earlier Edmund Magauran, a 'scholar of Kilmore diocese' was apparently having difficulty getting the necessary dimissory letters[65] from Hugh O'Sheridan in order to be ordained and so Pope Gregory XIII gave him permission to be ordained 'at Rome to clerical and all holy orders'.[66] Remarkably, even though he was bishop of the diocese for nineteen years during the reign of Elizabeth, he, of all the bishops of Kilmore in the late medieval and early modern period, is the one we know least about. He was able to remain largely anonymous because the Tudor reformations did not impact to any great extent on the diocese of Kilmore until after his death.

Francisco de Cuellar

The last quarter century of the Tudor monarchy was a period of considerable violence and upheaval in the diocese of Kilmore. It was during this period that the O'Rourke and O'Reilly dynasties collapsed with east Bréifne being named County Cavan in 1579 and west Bréifne shired into County Leitrim in 1585. The death in 1583 of Aodh Conallach, the chief of the O'Reillys, sparked off a prolonged power struggle between different factions of the sept which hastened its decline.[67] Brian Na Murtha O'Rourke remained defiant in west Bréifne and when hundreds of shipwrecked survivors of the ill-fated Spanish Armada were washed up on the northwest coast of Ireland in the autumn of 1588 he gave shelter

---

62. Jefferies, *The Irish Church and the Tudor reformations*, p. 127.
63. Vatican archives, *Dataria Apostolica, Minutae Brevium Lateranesium*, n. 16305.
64. Ibid., n. 19632.
65. If a clerical student was being ordained away from his own diocese he needed a dimissory letter from his bishop granting him permission to do so.
66. Vatican archives, *Dataria Apostolica, Minutae Brevium Lateranesium*, n. 18789. Edmund Magauran would later become bishop of Ardagh and, later still, archbishop of Armagh.
67. Aodh Connallach and his wife Isabella Barnwell died about the same time. See *AFM*, 1583.

to any that came his way. Don Francisco de Cuellar, who had been captain of the *San Pedro* galleon, spent some months in O'Rourke and MacClancy country in north Leitrim, and his account of his time there, written in 1589 after he had safely reached Antwerp, gives an important insight into life in the most northerly part of the diocese of Kilmore towards the end of the sixteenth-century.

When Francisco de Cuellar was washed up on Streedagh strand on 25 September 1588 he decided his best chance of survival was to make for a nearby monastery[68] where he hoped to get food, shelter and some rest so that he might recover from his injuries. He wrote:

> I found it [the monastery] deserted and the church and images of the saints burned and completely ruined and twelve Spaniards hanging within the church by an act of the Lutheran English … All the monks had fled to the woods for fear of the enemies who … were accustomed to leaving neither place of worship nor hermitage standing; for they had demolished them all, and made them drinking places for cows and swine.[69]

The Franciscan friary of Creevelea, which lay about sixteen miles inland from Streedagh, was still intact at this time. However, there was a narrow corridor along the coast between the towns of Sligo and Ballyshannon which was controlled by the English and within which the full effects of the Tudor reformations were already felt. Francisco de Cuellar, having moved inland, modified his views somewhat about the effects of the reformation:

> Mass is said among them [the native Irish] and regulated according to the orders of the Church of Rome. The great majority of their churches, monasteries and hermitages have been demolished by the hands of the English who are in garrison and of those natives who have joined them, and are as bad as they.[70]

68.   Hugh Allingham has identified this monastery as the abbey of Staad which was founded by St Molaise and located near Streedagh strand. See Allingham, *Captain Cuellar's adventures in Connacht & Ulster A.D. 1588*, p. 11.
69.   Robert Crawford (trans.), *Captain Cuellar's narrative of the Spanish Armada* (London, 1897, repr. 1988), p. 53.
70.   Ibid., p. 62.

The Spanish soldier was intent on reaching the protection of Brian Na Murtha O'Rourke of whom he said 'although this man is a savage he is a very good Christian and an enemy of heretics, always carrying on war with them ... a very brave soldier and a great enemy of the queen of England and her affairs'.[71] The shipwrecked Spaniard described not only Brian Na Murtha O'Rourke but also all the native Irish in west Bréifne as 'savages' who 'were accustomed to live as the brute beasts among the mountains'. Having described the men 'who cover themselves with blankets and wear their hair down to their eyes' and the women, most of whom 'are very beautiful but badly dressed', he writes, in disbelief, that 'these people [dare to] call themselves Christians'.[72]

The people he met were superstitious. For amusement he began to examine their hands in order to tell their fortunes with the result that so many crowded around the exotic Spaniard that he begged Brian Na Murtha to allow him to leave the castle in order to escape from them. O'Rourke solved the problem by ordering everyone to leave de Cuellar alone. The people de Cuellar met valued relics greatly. Shortly after arriving at Streedagh he encountered a number of people including a girl 'of the age of twenty most beautiful in the extreme' who took the relics of the Holy Trinity which he had been wearing. She put the relics around her own neck indicating that she wished to keep them 'saying to me that she was a Christian: which she was in like manner as Mahomet'.[73] There were relics in some of the churches too. During his last weeks in north Leitrim de Cuellar stayed with Teige Óg MacClancy, lord of Dartry, at Rosclogher. While there, 'one Sunday after Mass', having heard of an impending attack by the English, the Irish removed 'the ornaments and requisites for the Church service and some relics' from Rosclogher church to the safekeeping of the island 'castle' on Lough Melvin.[74] See Figure 7.2. This removal of relics, images, chalices and other valuables from churches and monasteries and hiding them in safer locations was common-place, not just in Ireland but also in England, during the Tudor reformation.[75]

Francisco de Cuellar had difficulty communicating with the Gaelic-speaking people he met in the north-west of the diocese of Kilmore. However, some days after he landed, he was able to communicate with

71.   Ibid., pp 58, 60. Following the shipwreck word went out that the Spaniards would find refuge with O'Rourke. See *CSPI, 1588–92*, p. 63.
72.   Crawford, *Captain Cuellar's narrative*, pp 61–2.
73.   Ibid., p. 55.
74.   Ibid., p. 64; McDermott and O'Conor, 'Rosclogher castle: A Gaelic lordship', pp 478–9.
75.   Duffy, *The stripping of the altars*, p. 490.

Figure 7.2: Rosclogher church and island tower on Lough Melvin. (*Courtesy of the Royal Society of Antiquaries of Ireland*).

a young man who could speak Latin and 'the Latin-speaking man' gave him shelter in his hut, dressed his wounds and provided him with supper and a bed of straw to sleep on.[76] He also had other chance meetings which proved fortunate:

> I met by chance with a road, along which a clergyman in secular clothing was travelling (for priests go about thus in that kingdom, so that the English may not recognise them). He was sorry for me, and spoke to me in Latin, asking me to what nation I belonged and about the shipwrecks that had taken place. God gave me grace so that I was able to reply to everything he asked in the same Latin tongue; and so satisfied was he with me, that he gave me to eat of that which he carried with him.[77]

The same priest later rescued de Cuellar from a blacksmith who had enslaved him in order to work his bellows. He then made contact with Brian Na Murtha O'Rourke and made sure that the Spaniard reached him safely.

The Spanish soldier left north Leitrim 'one morning ten days after the Nativity' of 1588 and then travelled to the north of Donegal hoping to sail from there to Scotland before travelling on to Antwerp. While in Donegal he met 'Don Reimundo Termi' - Réamann Ó Gallachair the Catholic

76. Crawford, *Captain Cuellar's narrative* pp 55–6.
77. Ibid., p. 59.

Figure 7.3: The east wall of Rossinver church showing one section of the two-light lancet window. (*Courtesy of Colm Connaughton*).

bishop of Derry - who welcomed him, provided him with hospitality for six days and organised a boat to take him to Scotland. The Spaniard stated that 'this bishop was a very good Christian' and like the priest he had met earlier, 'went about in the garb of a savage for concealment'.[78] Francisco de Cuellar's description of such things as defaced images, closed churches and monasteries, the hiding of sacred objects and clergy going about in disguise is evidence that the Tudor reformations had already impacted on the extreme north-west of the diocese of Kilmore by the end of 1588. What seems likely is that the Tudor reformation had virtually no impact on the diocese at first, and then, with time, both the extreme north west of the diocese along the Atlantic coast and the south east of the diocese along the English Pale were the first areas of Kilmore to feel its effects. The hoard of ten coins which were found at Rossinver in 1949 and have been dated to the early 1540s, suggests that information about the Henrician reformation, or at least details of Henry's marital problems, had percolated through even to the remote northwest of the diocese at that time. Two of the coins in the hoard had the initials H A representing Henry VIII and Anne Boleyn; four had the initials H I representing Henry and Jane Seymour; a further two coins had the initials H R for *Henricus Rex*, 'Henry having decided after the Katherine Howard affair no longer to court ridicule by drawing attention to his matrimonial inconstancies'.[79] All the coins in the hoard bore, on the reverse side, the inscription *Dominus Hyberniae* or *Hyberniae Rex*.

Dissolution of Drumlane and Holy Trinity Priories

Early in the reign of Elizabeth I there were changes at the centre of the diocese too. On 9 January 1569, Turlough McCabe of Flinstown in Meath was granted 'the custody of the abbey of the Trinity Island and Churchton [Drumlane] situate within the Brenny'.[80] The lands of Trinity Island and Churchton were said to be 'waste and [to] yield no profit to her Majesty'.[81] However, on 26 September 1571, as part of a broader settlement, Henry Sidney the lord deputy of Ireland, granted Aodh Connallach O'Reilly, 'the chief of his nation':

---

78.   Ibid., p. 67. For Réamonn Ó Gallachair, see Ciarán Devlin, 'Some episcopal lives' in Henry A. Jefferies & Ciarán Devlin (eds), *History of the diocese of Derry from earliest times* (Dublin, 2000), pp 120–33; Brian Lacey, *Medieval and monastic Derry, sixth century to 1600* (Dublin, 2013), pp 136–7. The eighty-year old bishop was killed at Cumber on 7 March 1601.
79.   Michael Dolley, 'Medieval coin-hoards from the Ulster mearing' in *Clogher Record*, 7, 2 (1970), p. 217.
80.   *CSPI, 1509–73*, pp 399–400.
81.   TNA, SP 63/27/3; Bernadette Cunningham (ed.), *Calendar of State Papers, Ireland 1568–71* (Dublin, 2010), p. 125.

> The site of the monastery of the Holy Trinity of canons in the isle of Holye Trynytie in Loughoughter … [and] four parcels of land called Polle Drumore, Polle in Yllane and Dyrre, Pole Snavelogher, Drumore … and their tithes.[82]

He was also granted the much more valuable site of 'the monastery of the canons of the B.V.M. of Dromlahen' and a large area of eight polls of land which belonged to the priory together with the tithes of that land and the tithes of the rectories of Drumlane and Killeshandra.[83] This agreement between Aodh Connallach O'Reilly and the lord deputy tacitly accepted that the monastic lands belonged to the crown and therefore could be leased by the lord deputy to whoever he wished. The annual rent O'Reilly was to pay for the lands of Lough Uachtair priory was £2 16s. 8d. while his rent for the Drumlane priory lands was more than three times greater being set at £8 14s. 8d. Some of the O'Reilly's lived near the Lough Uachtair priory and the 'Annala as Bréifne' recorded that Cathal O' Reilly, the son of Aodh Connallach died 'ar Oileán na Tríonóide' in 1579.[84] Two years later, on 15 July 1582, the monastic lands of Drumlane and Lough Uachtair were taken from O'Reilly because he had failed to pay the rent for the previous seven years.[85] The Premonstratensian canons had managed to remain in the priory on Trinity Island while Aodh Ó Raghallaigh held the lease and the priory continued to contribute to the mother house in Lough Cé and the prior attended chapters held there into the last quarter of the sixteenth-century.[86] It appears that the Premonstratensians white canons vacated Holy Trinity Island on Lough Uachtair *c.*1582 – approximately 332 years after they had first arrived there.[87]

In September 1582 the Lough Uachtair priory lands were granted to 'Hugh Strobridge, gent' for a period of twenty-one years.[88] It is possible that Hugh Strowbridge was not able to collect any money due to him from these monastic lands and on 10 September 1586 Lucas Dillon, chief baron of the Irish exchequer and a native of Newtown near Trim in County

---

82.   *The Irish Fiants of the Tudor sovereigns*, no. 1681

83.   The agreement estimated that each poll of land consisted of thirty acres of arable land and twenty acres of pasture and mountain land. By this calculation Drumlane priory had approximately 400 acres of land.

84.   de hÓir, 'Annala as Bréifne', p. 74.

85.   R.J. Hunter, *The Ulster plantation in the counties of Armagh and Cavan, 1608–1641* (Belfast, 2012), p. 36.

86.   Clyne, 'Medieval Irish Premonstratensian monasteries', i, p. 104.

87.   Ibid., p. 112.

88.   *The Irish Fiants of the Tudor sovereigns*, no. 4025. Hugh Strowbridge was appointed clerk of first fruits and searcher of the towns of Youghal and Dungannon in 1597. See Hunter, *The Ulster plantation*, p. 36.

Meath, was granted both 'the site of the monastery of the Holy Trinity ... and the site of the monastery of B.V.M. Drumleaghan' along with their possessions for a period of sixty years at a rent of £31 19s. 8½d.[89] His lease of the monastic lands lasted until January 1604 when they were granted to William Taffe, a County Louth Catholic who, in his role as sheriff of Sligo, had made many enemies there because he illegally acquired land and brutally suppressed local uprisings.[90] Shortly after the plantation of Ulster the lands of Lough Uachtair and Drumlane were granted to James Dillon, a native of Westmeath who had a chequered career being, among other things, an MP for Westmeath, an officer in Owen Roe O'Neill's foreign army, a rebel in 1641 and governor of Jamestown in Leitrim.[91] The State Papers for the year 1606 lists Hugh Strowbridge as the owner of the Lough Uachtair and Drumlane monastic lands, though this would seem to be incorrect.[92] It is not clear who held these monastic lands during the first decade of the seventeenth-century because another report dated 1608 states that 'theis monastery lands [were] granted in fee farm to Lucas Dillan, Knight and now [are] in the tenure of his heir'.[93] What is clear is that the priories of Lough Uachtair and Drumlane and their lands were the earliest properties to be held by crown grant in County Cavan and that they were granted to a succession of men, mostly of Anglo-Norman stock, in the decades after the Augustinian and Premonstratensian canons had left.

The granting of the monastic lands to laymen in the period 1569–71 heralded the beginning of the end for the Premonstratensians in Lough Uachtair and the Augustinians in Drumlane. It would appear that both were small communities and that their best days were already past before their priories were leased to laymen. There is no evidence that the Premonstratensians in Lough Uachtair or the Augustinians in Drumlane, unlike the Franciscans in Creevelea and Cavan, had adopted any reforms before their priories were dissolved. Holy Trinity priory had it troubles in the early 1540s when William O'Sheridan was prior. He seems to have been unsuited to that role and he alleged that he was 'forcibly deprived

89.   *The Irish Fiants of the Tudor sovereigns*, no. 4923. For Dillon see *DIB*, iii, pp 304–7. John Watsone gave evidence on 11 Nov. 1642 that Luke Dillon of Trinity Island was with the rebels in the insurrection the previous year. See deposition of John Watsone (TCD, MS 833, f. 202r) and deposition of Ambrose Bedell (TCD, MS 833, f. 105r). Luke Dillon was described as a special friend of Bishop Bedell and was one of those who negotiated his release in January 1642. See E.S. Shuckburgh, *Two biographies of William Bedell* (Cambridge, 1902), p. 69.
90.   *DIB*, ix, pp 228–31.
91.   Ibid., iii, pp 290–1; Letter from John Davies to the Earl of Salisbury (1606) in Vallancey, *Collectanea de Rebus Hibernicis*, i, p. 174.
92.   *CSPI, 1606–08*, p. 60.
93.   Bodleian Library, Rawlinson MS A.237. See *Anal. Hib.*, iii (Sept. 1931), p. 205.

of it' by Thomas O'Sheridan, a priest of the diocese of Kilmore.[94] Thomas O'Sheridan had the backing of Archbishop Dowdall in this dispute and he may have taken up residence in the priory. However, from 1542 until 1568, Ruairi MacDermott, the abbot of Lough Cé, was also the prior of Lough Uachtair and chances are that he resided in the abbey and not the priory.[95] It is possible that Aodh Connallach O'Reilly allowed the white canons of Lough Uachtair and the canons regular of Drumlane to remain in their priories for a time after 1571, however, without their traditional income they could not survive indefinitely.[96] O'Reilly's possession of the priories was short-lived and from 1582 onwards both Lough Uachtair and Drumlane priories were occupied by Anglo-Norman families from the Pale.

Drumlane Augustinian priory had been in existence for over 400 years at this time and its closure marked the end of an era. It had been the richest and most important ecclesiastical centre in the diocese, providing many Augustinian priests and bishops throughout the fifteenth and sixteenth-centuries. The Premonstratensian priory on Lough Uachtair, which had lasted over 300 years, had been founded by the O'Reillys with the O'Sheridans later gaining control of it. There had been regular legal disputes between these two families over lands in the parish of Kilmore and the leasing of the priory to an O'Reilly in 1571 did not bode well for the O'Sheridans. The O'Sheridan clerical lineage, which had provided canons and priors for Lough Uachtair for generations, was now coming to an end. Similarly, the O'Farrelly erenaghs of Drumlane were unable to halt the changes that undermined their role. Their clerical lineage, together with that of the Magauran family of Tullyhaw, both of which had provided priors for Drumlane, would also soon come to an end. From 1571 onwards the two best and most ornate churches in the diocese, both centrally located, would be in lay hands and as a result the cult of Saint Maodhóg, which had long been promoted at Drumlane, began to decline. The Franciscans managed to hold on to their friary in Cavan for approximately twenty years after their neighbouring religious houses in Drumlane and Lough Uachtair had been closed and even when they were removed from their friary they, like Franciscans elsewhere, proved, as we shall see later, to be resilient and well equipped to adapt and survive.

94.   Murray, 'A calendar of the register of Primate George Dowdall', p. 151.
95.   *ALC*, 1568; Backmund, *Monasticon Premonstratense*, ii, p. 143.
96.   Ibid., pp 142–3.

Chapter 8

Franciscans: 1534–1620

The Franciscan Order in England was vehemently opposed to the reforms of Henry VIII and as early as 1534 Francis Faber, who was the Franciscan minister provincial of England, visited the Irish houses to inform them of developments across the Irish Sea and to whip up opposition to the Henrician reforms. Cavan and Creevelea friaries, being relatively secure *inter Hibernicos* in territories still controlled by O'Reilly and O'Rourke, did not pass into lay hands until approximately twenty years after the priories of Lough Uachtair and Drumlane had done so. Besides, the friary in Multyfarnham – largely due to the protection of the Nugents of Delvin - continued to function and it provided a refuge for Richard Brady, the Franciscan bishop of the diocese. These three Franciscan houses were to play a key role in opposing the Tudor reforms in the diocese of Kilmore in the last quarter of the sixteenth-century.

St Mary's Friary, Cavan

Cavan friary survived the dissolution of monasteries which took place during the reign of Henry VIII as well as subsequent reforms of Edward VI and, largely due to the protection of the O'Reillys, survived until the last decade of the sixteenth-century. The 1502 Observant reform was largely imposed on the Franciscans in Cavan and, it would appear, was not universally accepted by the friars.[1] Nevertheless, the adopting of the Observant rule gave new life and vigour to the friary and from the mid-1550s onwards it acted as a headquarters and place of refuge for the Franciscans in Ireland. Patrick Ó Maoláin, who was minister provincial for three years, died in 'conventu de Cavan' in 1556.[2] The following year the provincial chapter was held in Cavan friary, most likely because it was considered a safe location.[3] In 1558 the friary was involved in the civic affairs of Cavan town when 'Conascius McCuart at this time guardian

---

1. The change from Conventual friars to friars of strict Observance in Cavan and elsewhere was a process that took time and experienced setbacks. See Ó Clabaigh, *The Franciscans in Ireland, 1400–1534*, pp 65–6.
2. Jennings, 'Brussels MS 3947', p. 107.
3. *Brevis synopsis*, ii, p. 155; Gwynn & Hadcock, *Medieval religious houses*, p. 245.

of Cavan and Friar Niellan Flanus and some other friars and laymen' facilitated and witnessed a legal contract between Myles O'Reilly, chief of his nation, and Bernard McBrady, a merchant, 'for the paving of one street in the town of Cavan'.[4] The contract was made official when it was stamped with the seal of the convent of Cavan.[5]

It would appear that Cavan friary had a successful *studia* where the liberal arts and theology were taught at this time because from 1573 to 1583 three Cavan Franciscans were successive minister provincials of the order in Ireland. Richard Brady was minister provincial from 1573 until he was appointed bishop of Ardagh in 1576. John O'Gowan (Smith), who was said to be gentle and pious, succeeded Richard Brady in 1577 and Eoghan Ó Dubhthaigh, the famous preacher, replaced him as minister provincial and held that position from 1580 to 1583.[6] Then in 1590, after a seven year gap, another Cavan Franciscan, Cormac O'Gowan, was appointed minister provincial of the order. He was arrested in Multyfarnham friary c.1607 by Sir Dudley Loftus, a son of Adam Loftus the archbishop of Dublin, and was imprisoned for seven years.[7] All these leadership roles given to Franciscans from St Mary's friary in Cavan suggests that it was a relatively safe location, a thriving *studia* and one of the foremost friaries in Ireland which continued to function decades after many other Franciscan houses had been dissolved.[8] The Franciscans managed to remain in Cavan friary after 1571 when their two neighbouring religious houses at Lough Uachtair and Drumlane passed into lay hands. However, tragedy struck in 1576 when 'the great monastery of Cavan, and the entire of Cavan itself, from the great castle downwards to the river were burned'.[9] The fire was caused by Mary Nugent, the second wife of Aodh Connallach O'Reilly, who, being of unsound mind, set fire to the house of someone she disliked, the fire spread rapidly devouring the friary and the whole town.[10]

Following the deaths in 1583 of Aodh Connallach O'Reilly and his third wife Isabell Barnwell, (both were both buried in Cavan friary), much of the county descended into chaos as the various claimants to the lordship battled it out among themselves. Despite the fire of 1576

4. Gearóid Mac Niocaill, 'Cairt Ó Mhaolmhordha Ó Raghallaigh, 1558' in *Bréifne*, i, 2 (1959), p. 136.
5. Ibid; Cherry, 'The indigenous and colonial urbanization of Cavan town, c.1300-c.1641', pp 88–9.
6. *Brevis synopsis*, ii, p. 170.
7. Jennings, 'Brussels MS 3947', p. 100.
8. For Donagh Mooney's view on the significance of Cavan friary at this time see Jennings, 'Brussels MS 3947', p. 49; Terence O'Donnell, *Franciscan abbey of Multyfarnham* (Multyfarnham, 1951), p. 23.
9. *AFM*, 1576; MacKiernan, *St Mary's abbey*, p. 10.
10. de hÓir, 'Annala as Bréifne', pp 73–4. This account dates the fire to 7 May 1575.

and the local wars, a detailed map of 'The Tovne of the Cavan' which was drawn *c.*1591 shows the chapel of Cavan friary to be a substantial roofed building with a tower or belfry at its centre and a cross mounted on both gable ends.[11] (See Fig. 8.1). The Nine Years War, beginning in 1594, brought further instability and destruction to the town and the friary. On 20 April 1594 Captain John Dowdall, who was waging war against Maguire of Fermanagh, wrote from Cavan friary, which he was then using as a military barracks, and noted that he had 'laid down directions for two spurs for the better defence of the abbey of Cavan'.[12] Their attempts to improve the defences of the friary must have been effective because when Hugh Maguire and Bryan MacMahon attacked the English in Cavan in 1595 it was reported that they:

> Did not leave a hut in which two or three persons might
> be protected, in the entire of Cavan, that they did not com-
> pletely burn, except the monastery of Cavan, in which the
> English were at that time.[13]

Five years earlier, an inquisition taken at Cavan on 19 September 1590, found that 'the site and precinct of the Monastery of Cavan containing half a pull, worth per annum 3*s.* 4*d.*' belong and 'ought to pertain to our said lady the Queen'.[14] The friary and attached lands were found to 'have been long concealed' and they were granted, along with many other properties in Leitrim and Longford, to Edmund Barrett on 1 July 1591.[15] In March 1605 the monastery and its lands were acquired by Theobald Bourke[16] and about six years later they were held by Sir Thomas Ashe.[17]

11.   This map is in the National Archives in London. See TNA MPFi/81, 'Fermanagh and Cavan.' See also Annaleigh Margey, 'Surveying and mapping plantation in Cavan *c.*1580–1622' in Scott (ed.), *Culture and society in early modern Bréifne/Cavan*, pp 106–7.
12.   *CSPI, 1592–1596*, p. 236; MacKiernan, *St Mary's abbey*, pp 10–11.
13.   *AFM*, 1595. Another report stated that 'Cavan is burned all but two castles of the Bradyes which still remain'. See *CSPI, 1592–96*, p. 299.
14.   Meehan, 'Termon or hospital land in Cavan', p. 219.
15.   *The Irish Fiants of the Tudor sovereigns*, no. 5504; Morrin (ed.), *Calendar of the patent and close rolls of chancery of Ireland in the reigns of Henry VIII, Edward VI and Elizabeth*, i, p. 456. R.J. Hunter has suggested that Barrett may have been sheriff of Cavan at this time. See, Hunter, *The Ulster plantation*, p. 36; Ciaran Brady, 'The end of the O'Reilly lordship, 1584–1610' in David Edwards (ed.), *Regions and rulers in Ireland 1100–1650* (Dublin, 2004), p. 183; *CSPI, 1592–96*, p. 530.
16.   *Calendar of the patent rolls of Ireland during the reign of James I*, (Dublin, 1827), pp 53–5.
17.   TCD, MS 570, f. 312; *Calendar of patent rolls of James I*, p. 199. Thomas Ashe was a soldier who married into a Meath family. See Ciaran Brady, 'The end of the O'Reilly lordship, 1584–1610', p. 194. Ashe was described in 1622 as a 'servitor and very aged' who had received a pension of £73 from Lord Mountjoy in 1602 'in consideration of service done and to be done.' He bought 500 acres at Murmod and also held 750 acres at Dromsheel with his brother John. See Victor Treadwell (ed.), *The Irish Commission of 1622* (Dublin, 2006), pp 445, 513–4.

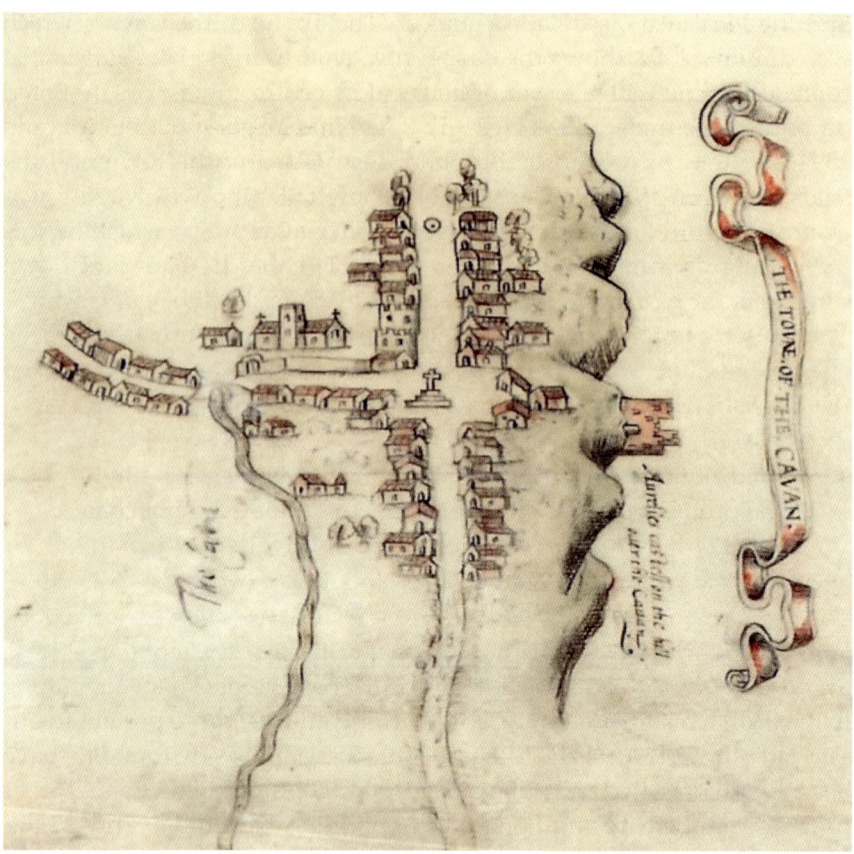

Figure 8.1: Detail of *c*.1591 map of Cavan town showing the Franciscan friary
and the market cross. (*Courtesy of the National Archives, Kew*).

The Franciscans, having moved from their friary in Cavan, lived in
thatched cabins nearby. Oliver Davies has suggested that they may have
lived in the nearby townland of Keadew where 'there is a small pool
known as the 'Friar's Well' in a secluded hollow near an old road'.[18] It
is possible that after the ending of the Nine Years War in 1603, when the
friary was no longer being used as a military garrison, that the friars
returned to it. This was happening not just with the Franciscans but
with several of the religious orders throughout the country – so much
so that in 1611 it was proposed to introduce an act 'That all friars and
monks and nuns shall be expelled out of their dissolved houses, where

18.   Davies, 'The churches of County Cavan', p. 143.

for the most part, they still keep and hover'.[19] It was also proposed that those who had been granted the properties and allowed the religious orders to return to them should forfeit their estate and endure fines and imprisonment.

The Cavan friars were no longer in St Mary's friary in 1611. Francis O'Mahony, writing in 1629, stated that the friary was burned in 1608, and that later the remaining walls were levelled.[20] Donagh Mooney, wrote *c*.1617, that the walls of Cavan friary, which had been a fine building, were razed to the ground and that friars no longer lived there.[21] This destruction of the friary in 1608 looks like a last and desperate attempt to remove Franciscans from the friary which had been a base for the Order for approximately 300 years. On 8 January 1610 the lord deputy and plantation Commissioners gave orders for:

> Sir Thomas Ashe to be dealte w[i]thall, that the Abbey of ye Cavan maie be Converted to a p[ar]ishe Church and free schoole, towards w[hi]ch he shalbe allowed twenty pounds.[22]

The free school was to be allocated 375 acres of land with a further 100 acres belonging to 'the Castle of the Cavan' being given to it and the 'stone of the Castle to be Carried to the Abby for to builde the school withal'.[23] It is not clear when this plan to build a school on the friary grounds was carried out, however, it is certain that a Church of Ireland school was established there.[24] In 1611 it was proposed under an 'Act for the re-edifying and repairing of cathedral and parochial churches' that Kilmore cathedral be established 'at the Cavan in the priory there'.[25] The proposals that the friary be used as a parish church and cathedral of the diocese would suggest that the friary chapel, or at least its walls, had survived the destruction carried out in 1608. The friary chapel became the Protestant church for the parish of Urney and remained so for more

---

19.   *CSPI, 1611–14*, p. 189.
20.   *Brevis synopsis*, ii, p. 155.
21.   Jennings, 'Brussels MS 3947', p. 50; MacKiernan, *St Mary's Abbey*, p. 11.
22.   TCD, MS 747. See T.W. Moody, 'Ulster Plantation papers 1608–13' in *Anal. Hib.*, 8 (1938), pp 242–3.
23.   Ibid.
24.   David J.W. McCready, 'Cavan Royal school' in *Bréifne*, xi, 43 (2007), p. 462. An article by J.E. O'Reilly titled 'Notes on Cavan Abbey' which was printed in *The Anglo Celt* dated 31 March 1848 stated that 'The Abbey stood where the old [Protestant] Church lately was; the late Mr W. Stuart remembered having been at school in an apartment which was a vestige of it. No trace of the ruins remain at the present time'.
25.   *CSPI, 1611–14*, pp 188–9.

than 200 years until the new parish church was opened on 12 November 1815.[26] Cavan friary continued to be the preferred burial place for the O'Reillys for some time after the Franciscans had moved from there. In 1638 Philip O'Reilly of Drumloman specified in his will that he be buried in the abbey of Cavan '(soe that it be allowed by his Ma[jes]ti[e]s lawes) otherwise at [my] parish church of Killedromfearta'.[27] And even though Archbishop Hugh O'Reilly died at Holy Trinity priory on Lough Uachtair in 1653 he too was buried at the Franciscan friary.

Despite finally losing their friary in 1608 the Franciscans maintained a presence in County Cavan for at least 200 years more. The collapse of the power of the O'Reillys deprived them of protection and patronage and yet they managed, in 1616, to build an alternative friary for themselves, possibly in Keadew townland near to Cavan town, when John Jeffery, a noted preacher, was guardian.[28] Msgr Massari, who visited the friary and stayed in it in June 1646, stated that it was situated in a wood and had a church, refectory, cells and other apartments and was 'a marvellous structure in the Ulster fashion' being made of wood and roofed with sods.[29] Later, *c.*1650, they had, for safety reasons, to abandon this location and live in more remote parts of the county and they had a base in Croaghan in Castlerahan parish by the end of 1651.[30] Their mobility and their intimate knowledge of the landscape, which they had acquired through their questing tours, helped them to cope with the changed world they were living in and they settled, among other places, in the townlands of Carricknamaddoo in Killinkere parish and Gallonnabraher[31] in Lurgan parish.[32]

26.   J.B. Leslie, revised and edited by D.W.T. Crooks, *Clergy of Kilmore, Elphin and Ardagh, biographical succession lists* (Belfast, 2008), p. 127. Philip O'Connell states that the last Protestant service was held in the old friary church on Christmas Day 1815. See O'Connell, *The diocese of Kilmore*, p. 335 and MacKiernan, *St Mary's abbey*, p. 11.

27.   NAI, RC 5/25, p. 276. See Clodagh Tait, 'The wills of the Irish Catholic community, *c.*1550-*c.*1660' in Robert Armstrong & Tadhg Ó hAnnracháin (eds), *Community in early modern Ireland* (Dublin, 2006), p. 191.

28.   *Brevis synopsis*, p. 155; Brian Mac Cuarta, 'Catholic revival in Kilmore diocese, 1603–41' in Scott (ed.), *Culture and society in early modern Bréifne/Cavan*, p. 154. John Jeffrey, a native of Meath diocese, entered Louvain Franciscan college in 1607. See Brendan Jennings & Cathaldus Giblin (eds), *Louvain papers 1606–1827* (Dublin, 1968), pp 11, 13, 57.

29.   'My Irish campaign' in *The Catholic bulletin and book review*, viii (1918), pp 248–9.

30.   R. O'Ferrall and R. O'Connell, *Commentarius Rinuccinianus de sedis … per annos 1645–9*, ed. by S. Kavanagh, 6 vols (Dublin, 1932–49), iv, p. 658; Benignus Millett, *The Irish Franciscans 1651–1665* (Rome, 1964), p. 89.

31.   Other placenames in the diocese with references to *bráthair* (brother) include Cornabraher in the parish of Kilsherdany and Cornabroher in Aughnasheelin in County Leitrim.

32.   The name of the townland and the 'Friar's well' and 'Friar's orchard' in the same townland point towards a Franciscan presence. See Davies, 'The churches of County Cavan', p. 136.

Eoghan Ó Dubhthaigh, OFM

The Franciscan friars, unlike the diocesan priests, had a reputation for being good preachers and they railed against the Tudor reforms at every opportunity. Friar Eoghan Ó Dubhthaigh, who was based in the friary in Cavan and was minister provincial from 1580 to 1583, was one of the most effective of these preachers in the Tudor period.[33] A report on the state of the church in Ireland in the year 1580, which may have been drawn up by Dermot O'Hurley, stated that 'Friar Eugene Odouhius, Provincial of the Franciscans in Ireland, [has] no English, but goes about all Ireland preaching like an apostle'.[34] Fortunately, Donagh (Donatus) Mooney has given a detailed description of his unusual, though effective style of preaching:

> [Eoghan Ó Dubhthaigh] was a most renowned preacher, and not less distinguished for his austere and saintly life. His fame extended to the most remote parts of the kingdom, and is yet on the tongues of all ... He always travelled barefooted, rejecting even the slight protection which sandals would have afforded him. He preached with such wonderful force and unction that he never seemed tedious to his hearers, although he spoke at great length, sometimes for three hours together. While delivering his discourses he never looked in the faces of his audience, not even opened his eyes. He rebuked the evildoer with great severity, and his words were seldom without effect. Yet in his sermons he was mild and gentle, rarely giving offence to individuals. When he met seculars in society (which, indeed, was very seldom) he conversed in an agreeable and pleasant manner. He had such intimate knowledge of the writings of St Augustine, especially on his smaller works on devout subjects, that his whole doctrine seemed sometimes founded upon the doctrine and made up of the sayings of the great saint, as if he had consulted no other author.[35]

33. Mooney, 'Some Cavan Franciscans of the past', p. 20; Benignus Millett, 'The Irish Franciscans and education in late medieval times and the early Counter-Reformation, 1230–1630' in *Seanchas Ard Mhacha*, 18, 2(2001), pp 1–30.
34. Myles V. Ronan, *The Reformation in Ireland under Elizabeth 1558–1580* (London, 1930), Appendix i, p. 641.
35. St Augustine was held in high esteem by the Franciscans at this time. Another Franciscan, Florence Conroy, 'was particularly expert in the teaching of St Augustine and had read his works seven times.' See Brendan Jennings, 'Micheál Ó Cléirigh, chief of the Four Masters, and his associates' in Nollaig Ó Muraíle (ed.), *Micheál Ó Cléirigh, his associates and St Anthony's College, Louvain* (Dublin, 2008), p. 27.

At the conclusion of each sermon, even of the longest, he was in the habit of reciting elegant verses in the Irish language, which contained the pith of what he had said. These verses were so fruitful of good that they appear to have been inspired less by the spirit of poetry than by the unction of the Holy Ghost.[36]

His long poem *Léig dod chomórtas dúinn*, which he composed in 1578, is a poem in praise of the Virgin Mary and also a very pointed denunciation of the Franciscan Miler Magrath and two other Catholic priests who had abandoned their faith in order to become bishops in the Church of Ireland.[37] Both in his counter-reformation poetry and preaching Eoghan Ó Dubhthaigh drew clear distinctions between the Catholic Irish and the Protestant English - leading Marc Caball to conclude:

> His portrayal of Protestantism as an alien and intrusive English imposition is in implicit contrast to the 'nativeness' of Catholicism. Such cultivation of popular perception of reformation as the religious arm of hegemonic colonialism was to become a serious obstacle to the advancement of Protestant evangelisation in Ireland.[38]

Not all the friars were gifted preachers like Eoghan Ó Dubhthaigh though his preaching and the continued presence of the friars who hovered near Creevelea and Cavan helped to build up resistance to the Tudor reforms in the diocese of Kilmore in the decades before the collapse of the Ó Ruairc and Ó Raghallaigh septs in west and east Bréifne.

Conn O'Rourke and Patrick O'Healy

Despite his high profile and fierce opposition to the Tudor reforms, Eoghan Ó Dubhthaigh survived and died of natural causes c.1600.[39] Other Franciscan friars such as Conn O'Rourke and Patrick O'Healy were

36. Jennings (ed.), 'Brussels MS 3947', pp 49–50 and translated in *The Franciscan tertiary*, v (1894), pp 196–7.
37. Mac Craith, 'Collegium S. Antonii Lovanii, quod Collegium est unicum remedium ad conservandam Provinciam', pp 248–9.
38. Marc Caball, *Poets and politics: continuity and reaction in Irish poetry, 1558–1625* (Cork, 1998), p. 60. See also Mícheál Mac Craith, 'Creideamh agus athartha: idé-eolaíocht pholaitíochta agus aos léinn na Gaeilge i dtús an seachtú haois déag' in M. Ní Dhonnachadha (ed.), *Nua-léamha: gnéith de chultúr, stair agus polaitíocht na hÉireann, c.1600-c.1900* (Dublin, 1996), pp 7–19.
39. Tomás Ó Cléirigh, *Aodh Mac Aingil agus an scoil Nua-Ghaeilge i Lobháin* (Dublin, 1985), p. 100.

not so lucky. Conn O'Rourke, who was born *c.*1549, entered the friary of Creevelea which his father, Brian Ballach O'Rourke, had helped to rebuild after the fire of 1536. Conn, who was a grandson of Margaret and Eoghan Ó Ruairc, the founders of the friary, was ordained and afterwards went to Paris for further studies arriving there towards the end of 1576 or at the beginning of the following year.[40] Patrick O'Healy may also have been attached to Creevelea friary, although this is less certain. In a letter dated 24 June 1575 he is called *'fray Patricio Oheli de Petra'*[41] and the friary in Creevelea was referred to by commentators as *conventus de Petra Patritii* – a possible reference to *Carraig Phádraig* the Irish name for the rock on which the friary is built.[42] He may have belonged to the Ó hÉilidhe sept which was based in County Sligo at the foot of the Curlew Mountains on the western shore of Lough Arrow, not too distant from Creevelea.[43] However, the evidence is not conclusive that he had been attached to Creevelea friary and yet, when he decided to return to Ireland from France sometime before 18 July 1579, Conn O'Rourke, who had studied at Creevelea, was either chosen or volunteered to travel back to Ireland with him as a *socius* or travelling companion.[44]

Patrick O'Healy had left Ireland for the continent in 1562 and studied at Alcalá de Henares in Spain. After his ordination he travelled to Rome where, on 4 July 1576, he was appointed bishop of Mayo. O'Healy travelled extensively throughout Europe and was in contact with the pope and Philip II of Spain regarding the plight of Catholics in Ireland. He was also in contact with James Fitzmaurice who was trying to whip-up support in Catholic Spain for an armed intervention in Ireland.[45] However, O'Healy had distanced himself from any involvement in the proposed armed intervention several months before he returned to Ireland. He sailed from Brittany, most likely in early July 1579, accompanied by Conn O'Rourke who is referred to as 'a certain student

40.   TNA, SP,63/58/2 1.
41.   Cited in Millett, 'Patrick O'Healy and Conn O'Rourke', p. 32.
42.   Jennings, 'Brussels MS 3947', p. 48. Another, though less likely, possibility is that he was attached to 'Conventus de Carrig' in Carrick-on-Suir. See Jennings, p. 80.
43.   Myles Ronan states that he was 'a native of Dromohair'. See Ronan, *The Reformation in Ireland under Elizabeth 1558–1580*, p. 507.
44.   Millet, 'Patrick O'Healy and Conn O'Rourke', p. 43. Patrick O'Healy taught Franciscan students in Paris for a number of months before he returned to Ireland. Canice Mooney, *Irish Franciscans and France* (Dublin, 1964), p. 22.
45.   Ibid., pp 32–3. See letter in J. Hagan, 'Miscellanea Vaticano-Hibernica 1420–1631' in *Arch. Hib.*, iv (1915), p. 219. This is a letter of recommendation for the bishop of Mayo because of 'his efforts to restore the faith by means of the conquest of Ireland'.

of noble birth'.[46] A few days after they arrived in Smerwick Harbour, disguised as sailors, the friars were arrested and imprisoned in Limerick. Lord Justice William Drury, the lord president of Munster, condemned them to death on charges of treason after only the semblance of a trial. O'Healy and O'Rourke were both hanged at Kilmallock *c.*13 August 1579 and their bodies were hanged on gibbets for approximately a week before they were buried by John Fitzgerald of Desmond.[47] The *Annals of Loch Cé* recorded:

> The Bishop O'hElidhe, ie the paragon of learning and piety of the whole world, and the son of O'Ruairc, ie Connbrathar, the son of Brian, son of Eoghan O'Ruairc, came from the east, after their education and tour. The Justiciary of Eirinn apprehended them; and they were both hanged, to the profanation of God and men. And that was a pitiful deed, ie to put an honourable, most pious bishop and a friar minor of noble blood, to death in an unbecoming manner.[48]

The public and ignominious hanging of the Franciscan bishop and the Franciscan son of Brian Ballach O'Rourke at Kilmallock in August 1579 was a warning to all clergy, both secular and regular, of the dangers of adhering to the old religion.[49] Four years later, on 16 July 1583, Patrick McGowan, possibly a priest of the diocese of Kilmore who had returned from the continent, was proclaimed a traitor and placed on a wanted list:

> This wicked practiser of sedition … with his bulls, masses and other popish trumperies [will] bringe the people to error, and to mislike of her majestie and the state here …

46.   Mooney, *Irish Franciscans and France*, p. 38.
47.   There is a field behind the church in Kilmallock called Crocta (hanged) in which a monument was erected in 1988 to Patrick O'Healy and Conn O'Rourke. William Drury died a short time after they were hanged. See Clodagh Tait, 'The just vengeance of God: reporting the violent deaths of persecutors in early modern Ireland', in David Edwards, Padraig Lenihan & Clodagh Tait (eds), *Age of atrocity, violence and political conflict in early modern Ireland* (Dublin, 2007), pp 130–6; Benignus Millet, 'A report from the president of Munster, Sir William Drury, 24 March 1577' in *Coll. Hib.*, 46/47 (2004/2005), pp 7–15.
48.   *ALC*, 1579.
49.   Patrick O'Healy and 'Conrad' O'Rourke were beatified by John Paul II on 22 September 1992. Their feast day, along with fifteen other 'Irish martyrs' from the period 1579–1654, is celebrated on 20 June each year. See Patrick J. Corish, 'The Irish martyrs and Irish history' in *Arch. Hib.*, xlvii (1993), pp 89–93; Millett, 'The Irish Franciscans and education in late medieval times', p. 18; idem, 'The beatified martyrs of Ireland: Bishop Patrick O'Healy, OFM and Conn O'Rourke, OFM' in *Irish Theol. Quart.*, lxiv (1999), pp 55–61; idem, 'Patrick O'Healy, OFM and Conn O'Rourke, OFM: two Irish martyrs' in *Bréifne*, xii, 46 (2011), pp 237–45.

Figure 8.2: Richard Verstegen's (*c.*1560–1640) depiction of the torture of clerics in Ireland including, in the background, the hanging of Conn O'Rourke and Patrick O'Healy.

> And if anie person or persons shall take or apprehend …
> and bringe him to us the Lds Justices either alive or dead,
> he shall have given to him in reward from her majestie the
> sum of one hundred markes sterling.[50]

Two Bishops: Richard Brady and John Garvey

On the 12 March 1580, just nine months after the hangings at Kilmallock, Richard Brady, another Franciscan, was appointed bishop of Kilmore.[51] He had been made bishop of Ardagh on 23 January 1576 and four years later returned as bishop to his native diocese. We know considerably more about Richard Brady than we do about his predecessor, Hugh O'Sheridan, because he lived in more turbulent times

---

50. John J. Meagher, 'Proclamation against Patrick MacGowan, priest, 16 July 1583' in *Coll. Hib.*, 25 (1983), pp 22–3.
51. Gregory XIII to Richard Brady, 12 March 1580 in P.F Moran (ed.), *Spicilegium Ossoriense.*, i (Dublin, 1874), pp 71–2; P.F. Moran, *History of the Catholic Archbishops of Dublin* (Dublin, 1864), i, p. 180; W.H. Grattan Flood, 'The episcopal succession in the diocese of Kilmore, 1560–1910', in *Breifny Antiquarian and Historical Society Journal*, iii, 1 (1927), p. 88; James J. McNamee, *History of the diocese of Ardagh* (Dublin, 1954), pp 276–9; John Monahan, *Records relating to the dioceses of Ardagh and Clonmacnoise* (Dublin, 1886), pp 363–5.

and because of the writings of his fellow Franciscan, Donagh Mooney. Even though Mooney was considerably younger than Richard Brady, he obviously knew him well. They stayed together for a time in the Franciscan friary in Multyfarnham and also were in prison together in Ballymore castle.[52] Richard Brady was one of the MacBradaigh sept from Cúil Brighdín (Castletara).[53] He was the eldest son of Cathal Maol MacBradaigh and descended from Fearghall an Cóitín, so-called 'on account of the beautifully brilliant adorned long scarlet coat he wore'.[54] Ignatius Fennessy calculated that Richard Brady was born c.1530[55] and we know that he was 'very aged' in 1606, the year before he died.[56] We depend on Donagh Mooney for information on his early life:

> [He] sprang from the noble house of his name, which for many an age ruled with princely sway in Breffny-O'Reilly. At a very early period of his life he distinguished himself as a jurist, for indeed he was profoundly versed in the canon and civil law … he renounced the world and took our poor habit in the convent of Cavan. His piety, learning and prudence were the theme of every tongue.[57]

Mooney's account and his claim that Richard Brady 'never left Ireland' raises questions both about where he received his qualifications in canon and civil law and where he was ordained.[58] It is possible that he studied in Spain and may even have been ordained there before he returned to Ireland.[59] Richard Brady was obviously held in high esteem within the order and was appointed minister provincial of the Franciscans in Ireland in 1573, a position he apparently held until Pope Gregory III appointed him bishop of Ardagh on 23 January 1576.[60] He was bishop of Ardagh for just four years when, on 9 March 1580, he was translated to Kilmore.[61]

---

52.   Jennings, 'Brussels MS 3947', pp 93–6; Canice Mooney, 'Some Cavan Franciscans of the past', pp 19–20.
53.   Ibid., p. 23.
54.   Seán Ó'Raghallaigh MacBradaigh, 'Teallach Cearbhuill: the genealogy of Macbradaigh of Cúil Brighde in Cavan' in *Bréifne*, v, 17 (1976), p. 155.
55.   Ignatius Fennessy, 'Richard Brady, OFM, Bishop of Kilmore 1580–1607' in *Bréifne*, ix, 36 (2000), p. 228.
56.   *CSPI, 1603–06*, p. 18.
57.   Jennings, 'Brussels MS 3947', pp 97–8; Meehan, *The rise and fall of the Irish Franciscan monasteries*, p. 49.
58.   Ibid.
59.   Fennessy, 'Richard Brady, OFM', pp 228–9.
60.   Vatican archives, *Acta Camerarii*, ix, f. 193.
61.   Ibid., f. 286v; Moran, *History of the Catholic archbishops of Dublin*, i, p. 180.

Less than five months earlier, on 26 October 1579, Pope Gregory III had asked him to intervene in a dispute in the parish of Templeport where the local priest, Fergal Magauran, claimed the church or chapel of Kilnavart (*ecclesiae seu capellae de Cillfert*) had been usurped by nobles and the vacancy left by the death of Bishop 'Odo (Hugh O'Sheridan) of happy memory' had left him without the support of a bishop.[62] Richard Brady's successor in Ardagh was Edmund Magauran, a native of Tullyhaw barony in west Cavan, who was appointed to Ardagh on 11 September 1581.[63] It appears that he continued to receive the rectorial tithes from Kinawley and Knockninny after being appointed to Ardagh and Pope Sixtus V intervened on his behalf when an attempt was made to wrest them from him in 1586.[64]

Richard Brady's unambiguous opposition to the Elizabethan reforms quickly earned him powerful enemies. William Drury, the Lord Justice who had Conn O'Rourke and Patrick O'Healy hanged, wrote from Trim on 14 January 1579/80 that there was 'a popish Bishop ordered in Cavan in O'Reilly's country of whom he wishes to make an example'.[65] On 25 October 1584, John Perrot, just months after he had returned to Ireland as the newly appointed lord deputy, wrote 'a lettre to the Lords of the Council' stating that:

> There is a see called Kilmorensis diocess, the jurisdiction whereof is over the Cavan, Oreilighe's country, and other parts adjoining. It was never bestowed upon any Englishman or Irish by the Queen's Majesty or any of her progenitors within memory. Of late there is a lewde friar come from Rome, a delegate of the pope's that hath usurped it, dispensing abroad seditious bulls and such like trash. I have disseised him of the place and hope to catch him to answer [for] his lewdness, or at least to bring him to submission.[66]

John Perrot had learned of the existence of Richard Brady but seemed to have little firm information about him, not knowing either his name or his whereabouts.[67] The Franciscan friary in Multyfarnham was one of the few dissolved monasteries in Ireland that managed to hold onto

62. Vatican archives, *Dataria Apostolica, Minutae Brevium Lateranensium*, n. 20099.
63. Ibid., *Acta Camerarii*, ix, f. 152v; *DIB,*, vi, pp 234–5; Daniel McCarthy (ed.), *Collections on Irish church history: from the MSS of the late V. Rev. Laurence Renehan* (Dublin, 1861), pp 18–20.
64. Vatican archives, *Dataria Apostolica, Minutae Brevium Lateranensium*, n. 24308.
65. *CSPI*, 1574–85, p. 157.
66. 'The Perrot papers' in *Anal. Hib.*, xii (1943), p. 11.
67. One report even described Richard Brady as a 'Polish bishop'; see *CSPI, 1588–92*, p. 393.

its property and to continue functioning until the end of the sixteenth-century. This was due in no small part to the patronage and protection of the Nugent family, particularly Christopher Nugent who was baron of Delvin from 1565 until his death in prison in 1602.[68] Bishop Brady used the Multyfarnham friary as his main base during his time as bishop of Kilmore. It was said that:

> He dwelt constantly in Multifernan, and never left it except
> on the business of his diocese, when he always preferred
> such accommodation as he could find in some house of our
> order to the comforts and hospitality which he might have
> received from the Catholic nobility and gentry.[69]

Richard Brady was a reluctant bishop and remained a Franciscan at heart, continuing to wear the Franciscan habit and to observe the strict rules of the Observants. It is a sign of the changed times that it was not the ruling O'Reillys or the O'Rourkes who gave him protection but rather his own Franciscan Order and the Nugents of Delvin, who lived in the Pale.

Having tried to dispossess Richard Brady of the diocese of Kilmore in October 1584 John Perrot then asked the Lords of the Council to allow him to install John Garvey, who was archdeacon of Meath and dean of Christ's Church, as the bishop of the diocese with royal approval. He explained his motives in making this request: 'I judge it would be an increase of her majesty's authority amongst those barbarous people to have a bishop placed there and he a man of account and credit with them … for surely I hope he shall do good in it'.[70] John Garvey, although Irish born was said to be 'englissh harted'.[71] He had consented to become the bishop of Kilmore despite there being little prospect of him receiving a decent income. 'He is content to accept it not for profit or ambition (for he refused better things) but for a desire to do good'.[72]

---

68.   For an account of the role of the Nugents in protecting the friary see Lennon, 'The Nugent family and the diocese of Kilmore', pp 370–3; Meehan, *The rise and fall of the Irish Franciscan monasteries*, p. 42.
69.   Jennings, 'Brussels MS 3947', p. 98; Meehan, *The rise and fall of the Irish Franciscan monasteries*, p. 50.
70.   'The Perrot papers', p. 11; Richard Mant, *The Church of Ireland from the Reformation to the Revolution* (London, 1840), p. 311.
71.   Quoted in Scott, *The Tudor diocese of Meath*, p. 57. Garvey had previously been suggested as a possible bishop of Ardagh. See Ronan, *The Reformation in Ireland under Elizabeth 1558–1580*, pp 400–1.
72.   Ibid. John Perrot's claim 'that he refused better things' is misleading. Despite having been recommended for the archdiocese of Armagh (in 1567 and 1584), as well as the dioceses of Ardagh (1572) and Kildare (1583), Garvey was passed over each time. See *DIB*, iv, p. 34.

It was agreed that if appointed bishop he would 'hold the rest of his livings in commendam'.[73] John Perrot's request was granted and John Garvey was duly consecrated bishop of Kilmore on 25 April 1585.[74] He had been heavily involved in civil administration and had sat on several royal commissions before being appointed to Kilmore and he continued working for the government after becoming bishop of the diocese. Just five months after he was consecrated bishop, on 27 September 1585, he along with Sir John Perrott and Lysagh O'Ferrall, the royally approved bishop of Ardagh,[75] negotiated a settlement with Brian Na Murtha O'Rourke and a host of other lesser chieftains from west Bréifne on behalf of 'Elizabeth by the grace of God queen of England, France and Ireland [and] defender of the faith'.[76] Garvey also continued in his role as a member of the Irish Privy Council and on 28 January 1586 he was one of the signatories on a report to the English Privy Council on the state of the realm.[77]

It appears that John Garvey lived in Meath, possibly in Kells, and spent more time on government business in Dublin than he did in Kilmore. In the spring of 1586, less than a year after being appointed to Kilmore, John Perrot was arguing the case for him to be appointed bishop of Ossory. He argued that John Garvey 'doth well deserve to be preferred from this small see [Kilmore], worth but thirty pounds a year, to another that is somewhat better'.[78] Adam Loftus, the archbishop of Dublin, had his own candidate for Ossory and did not want Garvey to get it. His damning description of Garvey ensured that he would not be appointed to Ossory. He wrote that John Garvey was 'now very aged … no preacher, and scarcely well thought of for religion, as one just suspected to incline to papistry, if he had any religion at all'.[79] Needless to say Garvey was not appointed to Ossory and on 20 January 1588/9 he sent a letter to Lord Burghley, the queen's chief advisor, and another to Francis Walsyngham, her chief secretary, outlining how he had 'thirty years daily service done to her Majesty amongst the Irish borderers' and requesting that he be appointed archbishop of Armagh.[80] Sir Nicholas White, the Master of the Rolls,

73. 'The Perrot papers', p. 11.
74. *DIB*, iv, p. 34; Leslie, *Clergy of Kilmore, Elphin and Ardagh*, pp 494–5.
75. See Leslie, *Clergy of Kilmore*, p. 743.
76. Martin Freeman (ed.), *The Compossicion booke of Conought* (Dublin, 1936), p. 150.
77. *CSPI, 1586–88*, pp 10–13.
78. Cited in Brian McCabe, 'An Elizabethan prelate: John Garvey (1527–1596)' in *Bréifne*, vii, 26 (1998), p. 599.
79. TNA, SP, 63/12/1 (1586–8), p. 35; Alan Ford, *The Protestant Reformation in Ireland 1590–1641* (Dublin, 1997), p. 33.
80. *CSPI, 1588–92*, p. 109.

also wrote to Burghley recommending John Garvey for Armagh stating that 'he is an ancient grave councillor, a great housekeeper and expert in the language of the country'.[81] White elaborated by saying that Garvey, 'by his own good example of life and conversation ... doth edify more than many that be apter in the pulpit'.[82] The letters had the desired effect and the queen appointed him to Armagh on 24 March 1589.

Sir Richard Bingham had also sent a letter to the queen recommending 'old Mr Garvey' for Armagh.[83] Bingham's begrudging endorsement of Garvey may have stemmed from their disagreements over the causes of and solutions to the widespread disturbances in Connacht at this time. John Garvey had been appointed one of the commissioners who were given the task of trying to restore peace in Connacht and he continued in this role for some months after he was nominated for Armagh. In his report to Burghley on 10 May 1589 Garvey blamed the behaviour of Richard Bingham, and those under his control, for the disturbed state of the province stating that:

> It was the cruel and hard parts of sheriffs, sub-sheriff, bailiff errants, kearnty, and the daily extortion of soldiers ... exacting meat and money that provoked them [the rebels] thus to fall from their loyalty.[84]

And having failed to negotiate a peace he complained that after they left the province Bingham proclaimed all the rebels 'and now doth prosecute them with fire and sword both by sea and land'. It appears that John Garvey took exception to the way the people of his native province were being mistreated by the war-mongering Bingham.[85]

John Garvey was in Drogheda in the archdiocese of Armagh on 10 May 1589 when he wrote to Walsingham explaining that he had been so busy with government business that he had not yet had a free day for his consecration as archbishop of Armagh. It appears that he was consecrated shortly after that date and he held that position until his death in 1595. His time as bishop of Kilmore was short and he had

81. Ibid., p. 118.
82. TNA, SP, 63/141/4 (1588–92), p. 118.
83. Ibid., p. 110.
84. Ibid., p. 167.
85. He was born in Murrisk in Mayo c.1515. See *DIB*, iv, p. 34.

made little impact on the diocese during his tenure there.[86] However, he may have been the one who began the process of appointing Protestant clergy in the diocese because in 1590 'Cornelius Jordan, son of the dean, from *Ecclesia Magna* [Kilmore]' was given a royal pardon.[87] Meanwhile, Richard Brady, to the great annoyance of the government, continued to carry out his episcopal duties from his base in Multyfarnham friary. By August 1590 both he and the Nugents were being spied on by Walter Farranan who reported back to the Dublin government. His main claim was that Richard Brady 'the supposed bishop of Kilmore' was the medium between the disaffected in Ireland and the Prince of Parma. Farranan outlined how Richard Brady could be arrested but he thought it would be unwise to do so 'as others might be frightened into flight'.[88]

On 13 May 1591, Lord Deputy William Fitzwilliam, the archbishop of Dublin Adam Loftus and Thomas Jones, the bishop of Meath, reported that:

> They have used all the means which they could devise for the apprehension of [Richard Brady] … who according to Walter Farranan's detections was the carrier of letters to the Duke of Parma. The matter is in the hands of one who hopes daily to succeed, though the bishop is most secretly harboured by the Nugents, especially by the Baron himself. All secrecy is used, and the Nugents themselves live in great security.[89]

The previous September, the same three gentlemen had expressed the view that the baron of Delvin and other members of the Nugent family were not to be trusted and the archbishop complained that Edward Nugent, a lawyer, had the audacity to go into the lower house of parliament in Dublin and give 'a premeditate speech in defence of the mass and Romish religion'.[90]

After John Garvey was translated to Armagh in 1589 there was no royally-approved bishop of Kilmore until Robert Draper's appointment in 1604. However, the See was during this time in commission to

---

86. Alan Ford states that John Garvey 'never resided as a bishop, or exercised any jurisdiction within Kilmore'. See Ford, 'The Reformation in Kilmore' in Gillespie (ed.), *Cavan: essays on the history of an Irish County*, p. 76.
87. *The Irish Fiants of the Tudor sovereigns*, iii (1590) no. 5466.
88. *CSPI, 1588–92*, p. 361.
89. Ibid., p. 393.
90. Ibid., p. 365.

Edward Edgeworth, a canon of Christ Church and St Patrick's church, and it appears that he held that commission until a few months before he was appointed bishop of Down and Connor in 1593.[91] Richard Brady continued to be the *de facto* bishop of the diocese. It was reported in 1592 that:

> In O'Reilly his country being but XXX myles or thereabouts from Dublin, is Richard Braday, Buishopp of Kilmore, and although there is a kinde of custodian granted to a Preist there, in her Majesty's name, yet he [Brady] is in possession, using all manner of jurisdiction therein, although the country is governed by English laws and officers.[92]

Miler Magrath, the archbishop of Cashel, was granted Kilmore by patent on 19 December 1592 though it appears that he, just like John Garvey and Edward Edgeworth before him, made no impact on the diocese.[93]

Thomas Jones, the Protestant bishop of Meath, wrote to Adam Loftus the archbishop of Dublin and Lord Chancellor 'almost at the setting of the sun' on 1 September 1596 saying that he had met 'one Caddell, a merchant, newly come from the Brenny [Bréifne]' who told him that four ships had arrived in Donegal from Spain. On board one of the ships was 'a messenger of a friar who arrived in the company of the said Spaniards and was sent with a letter and a little book from that friar to Bishop Bradie who haunts the Brenny'.[94] The government continued to receive regular reports on Richard Brady and yet, because of his intimate knowledge of the diocese, the support of the Brady sept, the Franciscan Order and the Nugents of Delvin, he managed to remain at large and to carry out at least some episcopal duties in the diocese. Cardinal William Allen, at this time based in the English College in Rome, wrote towards the end of 1593 to the three Ulster bishops - 'Raymond of Derry, Richard of Kilmore and Cornelius of Down' - giving them faculties:

> To absolve penitents from all their sins no matter how enormous ... and to preach, administer the sacraments of the Church and perform universally, even in profane places, all functions profitable to the welfare of souls ... In particular, we authorise you to celebrate Mass in fit and

91. Leslie, *Clergy of Kilmore, Elphin and Ardagh*, p. 6.
92. Bodleian Library, Rawlinson MS C.98, f. 20; Brady, *The episcopal succession*, p. 281.
93. Leslie, *Clergy of Kilmore, Elphin and Ardagh*, p. 6.
94. *CSPI, 1596–7*, p. 98.

convenient places even before daylight on portable altars and to bless vestments etc., having regard to decency and such propriety as circumstances in those places will admit of.[95]

These senior Ulster bishops were being granted special faculties to help them cope with the extraordinary circumstances of their time.

Edmund Magauran

Edmund Magauran, the Kilmore-born bishop of Ardagh, was appointed archbishop of Armagh on 4 July 1587.[96] He was in Rome at that time and later travelled extensively throughout Europe visiting Lisbon, Brussels and Madrid in order to outline the increasingly difficult situation Catholics were experiencing in Ireland and to plead for Spanish military assistance to relieve them.[97] He was at Lisbon on 26 May 1592 when John Howlin, a Jesuit priest, wrote to Thomas Strong bishop of Ossory who was in Santiago de Compostela stating that:

> The Lord Primat is here [at Lisbon] and sought to goe to his contry, but seeing Oroke [Brian na Múrtha] which was his chiefe frend, is executed in London and that there be sherifes in all his contry appointed by the Lord Deputy, his mother and sisters sported and leaft beare naked ... I see not howe his Lordship may goe into Ireland.[98]

Despite hearing this distressing news from home Edmund Magauran, having met King Philip of Spain in September 1592, returned to Ireland before the end of that year. He based himself mostly in Maguire country in Fermanagh though it seems he also stayed in Cavan town with Walter Brady who, in 1600, was accused of having received into his house some years earlier 'the traitorous Primate Magawran'.[99] While in Ulster

95. Ciarán Devlin, 'Some Episcopal lives' in Jefferies & Devlin (eds), *History of the diocese of Derry*, p. 127.
96. Vatican archives, *Acta Camerarii*, x, f. 65v; McNamee, *History of the diocese of Ardagh*, pp 280–3; Magauran was appointed to Armagh which was vacant 'per obitum Riccardi [Creagh]' who died in the Tower of London *c*.1586. For Richard Creagh see *DIB*, ii, pp 982–4.
97. Micheline Kerney Walsh, 'Archbishop Magauran and his return to Ireland, October 1592' in *Seanchas Ard Mhacha*, xiv, 1 (1990), pp 68–70. For his Spanish passport see Brendan Jennings, 'Miscellaneous documents I, 1588–1634' in *Arch. Hib.* xii (1946), p. 71.
98. British Library, Lansdowne 71, no.49, ff. 100–100v; Kerney Walsh 'Archbishop Magauran', p. 70. When Edmund Magauran was bishop of Ardagh he was 'maintained by O'Rourk'. See *CSPI*, 1586–88, p. 7.
99. *CSPI, 1600, Mar.-Oct.,* p. 420.

Edmund Magauran continued to communicate with his fellow bishops and some northern princes in a bid to secure military aid from Spain.

Richard Brady, the Franciscan bishop of Kilmore, was also involved in the attempts to persuade King Philip of Spain to send military aid to the besieged Catholics in Ireland. On 3 July 1593 Sir George Bingham wrote to his brother Sir Richard that:

> James O Crean came lately out of the north [Donegal] …
> where, as he saith, he saw seven bishops. Some of them
> he named unto me, other some he could not name. But the
> chiefest among them was the Bishop M'Gawran who the
> Pope hath made Lord Primate of all Ireland. They were in
> great council for two or three days together and have made
> some great despatch … to the Pope and the King of Spain.[100]

Presumably the meeting O Crean was referring to was the one which took place in Enniskillen, at the end of which, on 8 May 1593, Richard Brady, Edmund Magauran, together with five other northern bishops and the Gaelic chieftains Hugh Maguire and Brian Óg O'Rourke, signed a letter addressed to King Philip of Spain.[101] They described in the letter how the Queen of England's forces were attacking them with increasing fury because of the support the princes of the north gave to the shipwrecked survivors of the Spanish Armada in 1588 and they pleaded with the king to send a military force of 8,000 to 10,000 men to reach them by 8 September or shortly afterwards. Six weeks after the signing of this letter, on 23 June 1593, Edmund Magauran was killed in a skirmish between Hugh Maguire and Sir Richard Bingham near Tulsk in County Roscommon. Some of the annalists explaining his death said that Primate Magauran 'accidentally happened to have been along with Maguire'[102] however, two weeks earlier Richard Bingham had reported that:

> McGawran which termith himself the prymate … is still
> with McGwire and always at hand with the tratoures to set
> them forward to every rebellious accion, riding on his cheif
> horse with his staff and shirt of mail.[103]

100.   *CSPI, 1592–96*, pp 71–2.
101.   See reproduction of letter in Kerney Walsh, 'Archbishop Magauran and his return to Ireland', p. 75; Frederick M. Jones, 'The Counter-Reformation' in Corish (ed.), *A history of Irish Catholicism*, iii (1967), p. 43.
102.   *AFM*, 1593.
103.   *CSPI, 1591–96*, p. 103.

Edmund Magauran's death was lamented among the Irishry 'as if it were their utter overthrow'.[104]

Persecution of Franciscans

Richard Brady had his troubles too. From his base at the Franciscan friary in Multyfarnham he wrote to the Vatican in 1600 requesting that he be allowed to resign due to his ill-health and advanced age.[105] However, he was not to enjoy a peaceful retirement. Sir Francis Shane, writing in February 1601, stated that 'the chiefest organ alienating the subjects hearts from her Majesty are the friars of Multyfarnham, and wandering priests wherewith the country swarmeth'.[106] Nine months later, on 1 October 1601, Shane attacked the friary with a party of soldiers and arrested Richard Brady together with John McGrath, the minister provincial of the order, Bernard Moriarty the dean of Ardagh, Nehemiah Gray the guardian of the friary and several others. The prisoners were taken under escort to the castle of Ballymore. Some of the troops remained two days at the friary and then, having looted all the valuables, set it on fire.[107] Francis Shane's attack on the friary at Multyfarnham was an attack not just on the Franciscans but also on the Nugent family with whom he had disputes over the ownership of land.[108]

The twenty-four year old Donagh Mooney, who was nearing the end of his novitiate year in Multyfarnham, was present for this attack and, even though he could have escaped, he had himself arrested so that he could make his profession in the presence of the minister provincial and Bishop Richard Brady in their prison at Ballymore.[109] Recalling his

104.   Ibid., p. 110; Moran, *History of the Catholic archbishops*, p. 290. Some historians had diffi-culty accepting that Edmund Magauran had died during the course of a skirmish even though he may not have been an active combatant. For example M.J. Brenan, in *An ecclesiastical history of Ireland* (Dublin, 1814), p. 430, refers to *Analecta sacra de processu martyriali* (1619) and writes that Edmund Magauran was mortally wounded 'while engaged in receiving the confession of a dying man ... and died near Armagh.' Laurence Renehan, in a more plausible explanation, states that Archbishop Magauran was killed 'a short distance from the engagement admin-istering the last sacraments and hearing the confessions of some of the mortally wounded soldiers'. McCarthy (ed.), *Collections of Irish church history*, i, p. 19.
105.   Vatican archive, Fondo Borghese, 124C, f. 78rv. See Dominic Conway, 'Guide to documents of Irish and British interest in Fondo Borghese, series ii – iv' in *Arch. Hib.*, xxiv (1961), p. 81.
106.   *CSPI, 1600–01*, p. 197. For Francis Shane see Joseph Mannion, 'Sir Francis Shane, 1540–1614' in Christopher Maginn & Gerald Power (eds), *Frontiers, states and identity in early modern Ireland and beyond: essays in honour of Steven G. Ellis* (Dublin, 2016), pp 164–87.
107.   Jennings, 'Brussels MS 3947', pp 93–5; Williams (ed.), *The 'Annals of Multyfarnham': Roscommon and Connacht provenance*, pp 35–9. Thomas Jones, the Protestant bishop of Meath, claimed that it was by his procurement that 'the warrant was sent to Sir Francis Shane to ap-prehend the friars of Multyfarnham and burn their friary'. See *CSPI, 1601–3*, pp 136–7.
108.   Mannion, 'Sir Francis Shane, 1540–1614', pp 168, 181.
109.   Terence O Donnell, 'Father Donagh Mooney, OFM: the Franciscan convent of Donegal' in O'Donnell (ed.), *Father John Colgan OFM 1592–1658* (Dublin, 1959), p. 131.

profession in such unusual circumstances, Mooney wrote sixteen years later that 'God knows what joy filled my heart at that hour. I cannot find words to express it, nor can I recall it without experiencing that fullness of joy again'.[110] Bishop Brady, who was an old man, was released from Ballymore and was allowed to stay with a Catholic gentleman from the area on the condition that he presented himself to the Dublin authorities when the winter was over. He did so and was duly arrested again and kept in prison until the summer of 1602 when he was released after some friends paid a heavy fine. It is unlikely that he was able to attend the provincial chapter of the Franciscan Order which was held in a secret place in woods near Leitrim village on 2 August 1602 because it was unsafe to hold it in Creevelea friary. This was the first, though not the last, provincial chapter to be held outside the walls of a friary.[111]

The friars resolved to rebuild the friary at Multyfarnham as best they could and Richard Brady, now infirm and unable to walk or stand, spent all of his time there. He was present in July 1604 when the friary was once more attacked and burned, this time by Sir Francis Rochfort.[112] Rochfort arrested several of the friars intending to take them to Dublin. The bishop, being too feeble to travel, was divested of his habit, thrown into nettles, abandoned and left to die.[113] Unlike some of his contemporary bishops, however, Richard Brady survived all attacks - largely due to the support of the Nugent family and his own Franciscan Order. Brady's feeble state during his last years meant that he posed no threat and this may have saved him from a violent death. Despite his advanced years and ill health, however, he continued to carry out some episcopal duties. On 11 August 1606, Teig O'Corkran, the secretary to Maguire of Fermanagh who had conformed and received a benefice from Miler Magrath, the former Franciscan who became the Protestant archbishop of Cashel, gave evidence that 'lately [on the insistence of Maguire] he went to Multifernan to the supposed Bishop Bradie, by whom he confesseth he was reconciled and received absolution'.[114]

Donagh Mooney was somewhat in awe of Richard Brady, his fellow Franciscan, and ten years after the bishop's death he wrote:

> I had frequent opportunities of witnessing the austerities
> he practised … Even when broken down by old age and

110. Jennings, 'Brussels MS 3947', p. 95.
111. Ibid., p. 108; O Donnell, 'Father Donagh Mooney', p. 132; Brian Mac Cuarta, *Catholic revival in the north of Ireland 1603–41* (Dublin, 2007), p. 19.
112. Mooney, 'Some Cavan Franciscans of the past', p. 19.
113. Jennings, 'Brussels MS 3947', p. 97.
114. *CSPI*, 1603–06, p. 566; Mac Cuarta, 'Catholic revival in Kilmore diocese, 1603–41', p. 150.

infirmities he could never be induced to wear a coarse linen shirt, and despite all remonstrances of our friars he rejected any little luxuries we could procure for him … saying that he had chosen a life of mortification and would die as he had lived.[115]

Richard Brady resigned as bishop of Kilmore early in 1607 and died in September of that year.[116] Remarkably, he had survived as bishop of the diocese for more than twenty-seven years in a time of upheaval and persecution. He was buried in the cloister of Multyfarnham friary.

Creevelea Franciscan Friary 1550–1603

The Observant friary at Creevelea was the last Franciscan house to be established in Ireland before the Tudor reformations began and, because of its location in the fastness of O'Rourke's territory in west Bréifne, it survived later than many other religious houses in the country. The fire of 1536, which destroyed 'many valuable books' and 'a goodly portion of the edifice'[117] happened in the dead of night when the friars were asleep and two friars, Eremon O'Donnell and Maol-Sheachlainn Magauran, lost their lives.[118] Brian Ballach O'Rourke set about rebuilding the friary, but owing to the many wars he was involved in was never able to fully repair it. In his settlement with the English lord deputy at Maynooth Castle in September 1542, Brian Ballach agreed to acknowledge Henry VIII as his lord and king and to renounce the primacy of the Roman pontiff.[119] This agreement did not bode well for the Franciscans of Creevelea whose friary was adjacent to O'Rourke's castle at Dromahair. However, Brian Ballach and his son, Brian na Murtha O'Rourke, who succeeded him, continued to support and give protection to the friary and so the Franciscans were able to remain in undisturbed possession of their house in Creevelea. A report on 'Connaught and Thomond' drawn up in March 1572 confirms that Creevelea was at that time still occupied by the friars.[120]

The hanging of Connbrathar O'Rourke and Patrick O'Healy at Kilmallock in August 1579 was a reminder to the friars in Creevelea that they were living in dangerous times. When Brian na Murtha O'Rourke gave shelter to the soldiers from the shipwrecked Spanish Armada in

115. Jennings, 'Brussels MS 3947', p. 98.
116. O'Connell, *The diocese of Kilmore*, p. 392.
117. Meehan, *The rise and fall of Irish Franciscan monasteries*, p. 83.
118. *AU, ALC, AFM*, 1536; Canice Mooney, 'Some Leitrim Franciscans of the past' in *Bréifne*, I, 4 (1961), p. 329.
119. Brewer & Bullen (eds), *Calendar of Carew MSS*, 1515–74, p. 195.
120. Ibid., 1601–03, p. 474.

the autumn and winter of 1588-89 his actions were seen as traitorous
and resulted in regular attacks from Sir Richard Bingham. These attacks
weakened O'Rourke and following Bingham's decisive victory over
him in March 1590, Brian was left with no option but to flee.[121] His fall
from power, along with his subsequent arrest and hanging at Tyburn
on 3 November 1591, put Leitrim in the hands of the Binghams, leaving
the friars of Creevelea without patron or protector.[122] Donagh Mooney,
writing *c*.1617, described how the friars of Creevelea had:

> Continued to live there, labouring, praying and educating
> the youth of the district, till they were expelled from their
> venerable abode by Sir Richard Bingham, who, on more
> than one occasion, turned the monastery and church into
> quarters for his soldiers, pillaged the place, and burnt the
> richly-carved panels of the choir for fuel.[123]

The Oxford-educated Brian Óg O'Rourke, who succeeded his father as
lord of west Bréifne, had only a small band of followers at first and so
was unable to provide much protection to the friary of Creevelea and
in February 1591 Richard Bingham reported 'that the young traitor
O'Rourke lieth on the borders of Maguire country [Fermanagh]'.[124] By
1593 O'Rourke, following a dispute with Richard Bingham over unpaid
taxes, was ready to go on the offensive once more and, having teamed up
with Donough Óg Maguire, they attacked George Bingham's stronghold
in Ballymote, devastating the town and all the villages around it.
O'Rourke then 'returned to his country with preys and much booty'.[125]
A dispute ensued between Maguire and O'Rourke over the division of
the spoils and it was only settled by the intervention of Primate Edmund
Magauran, who, as we have seen, had strong links and long-standing
friendships with both families.[126]

Brian Óg Ó Ruairc was one of the signatories on the letter sent by
Edmund Magauran to King Philip of Spain pleading for military assistance in early May 1593.[127] Although they got little military help from

121.   Dan Gallogly, 'Brian Oge O'Rourke and the Nine Years war' in *Bréifne*, ii, 6 (1963), p. 171.
122.   *AFM*, 1590; Dan Gallogly, 'Brian of the Ramparts O'Rourke (1566–1591)' in *Bréifne*, ii,
5 (1962), p. 78.
123.   Meehan, *The rise and fall of the Irish Franciscan monasteries*, p. 84.
124.   *CSPI, 1588–92*, p. 386.
125.   *AFM*, 1593.
126.   Gallogly, 'Brian Oge O'Rourke and the Nine Years war', p. 177; *CSPI, 1592–96*, pp, 103, 105.
127.   Kerney Walsh, 'Archbishop Magauran and his return to Ireland', p. 75.

Figure 8.3: Chapel and east window of Creevelea Franciscan friary.

Spain they got plenty of encouragement from the king. In February 1596 King Philip wrote:

> To the noble and greatly beloved O'Rourke … seeing it is so notable a work to fight for the Catholic Faith, whereas the enemies thereof endeavour so mightily to tread the same under foot, I may not doubt, but that you who hitherto (as we hear), in the defence of God's cause have so well laboured, will now with might and main give yourself to the same course; for mine own part I would be a director unto you, that you prosecute the same hereafter, lest the obdurate enemies of true religion, damnify it at all, but rather they be repulsed. The which if you perform you shall do me a most grateful work, and always find the same favour wherewith I accustom to grace and true defenders of the Catholic Religion.[128]

At the same time, Cornelius O'Mulrian, the bishop of Killaloe, wrote to Ó Ruairc from Lisbon complimenting him on 'having dealt valiantly in these wars and obtained victory against the enemies of the Catholic Faith'. He exhorted him to 'obey the Earl of Tirone in everything' and to get some learned man of Irish birth to write to the pope asking him to separate Ireland for ever from under English domination and to appoint the earl of Tyrone king of Ireland.[129]

Brian Óg Ó Ruairc, who succeeded his father as lord of west Bréifne, having weighed up his options, threw in his lot with O'Neill, O'Donnell and Maguire and took an active part in the Nine Years War. His many absences from Dromahair during that protracted war left the Franciscans in Creevelea open to attack and *c.*1598 they were driven out by the English who destroyed part of the friary and occupied the rest of it.[130] The Franciscans, more than the other religious orders, had learned how to adapt and survive, following the dissolution of their friaries. They usually built temporary shelters in the locality and then, if the opportunity presented itself, moved back into friaries once more. This appears to have happened in Creevelea because Donagh Mooney, who had already first-hand experience of attacks on the friaries of Donegal and Multyfarnham, went to Creevelea *c.*1601 and was ordained and said

128.   *CSPI, 1588–92*, p. 452.
129.   Ibid., pp 465–6.
130.   *Brevis synopsis*, ii, p. 161; Gwynn and Hadcock, *Medieval religious houses*, p. 248; Jennings, 'Brussels MS 3947', p. 49; Mooney, 'Some Leitrim Franciscans', p. 330.

his first Mass there.[131] They would not be left undisturbed for long and on 2 August 1602 the Franciscan provincial chapter was held in woods near Leitrim village as it was deemed unsafe to hold it in Creevelea friary.[132]

Brian Óg O'Rourke, although still in rebellion after the 1603 treaty of Mellifont, was becoming more isolated. The government sided with his half-brother Teige, whom they regarded as the only legitimate son of Sir Bryan, in an attempt to get rid of Brian Óg and to establish its grip on County Leitrim. With enemies both within the county and outside it, Brian Óg O'Rourke had no option but to flee and he died of fever in Galway on 28 January 1604. He was buried at Rosserilly Franciscan friary in Galway.[133] Less than two weeks after his death, on 10 February 1604, King James granted Teige O'Rourke:

> The castles, Lordships or Manors of Dromahair, Leatrym and Newton … situate in O'Rourke country … reserving to the Crown all spiritual livings, monasteries, advowsons[134] and other spiritual hereditaments.[135]

Teige did not enjoy his new-found status for long. He died in 1605 and was buried 'with due honours in the monastery of St Francis at Carrick-patrick [Creevelea]'.[136]

An inquisition taken on 24 September 1603 found that the last warden of Creevelea friary was 'seized of a carucate of land' and the rectories of Killen, Dronlies, Kilruffmena, Killifargan, Clenlogher and Ballinchineachain, which were valued at 40s. and the site of the friary valued at another 5s.[137] The friary in Creevelea, unlike the one in Cavan, had a considerable income from rectories in north Leitrim and Sligo, although from c.1598 onwards that income was no longer available to them. On 16 July 1614, King James granted 'the site and circuit of the late monastery of Crelew [Creevelea] … and plowland there-to belonging' to Sir John Davies, his attorney general in Ireland, for

131. Jennings, 'Brussels MS 3947', p. 49.
132. Ibid., p. 108; O Donnell, 'Father Donagh Mooney', p. 132; Brian Mac Cuarta, *Catholic revival in the north of Ireland 1603–41* (Dublin, 2007), p. 19.
133. Gallogly, 'Brian Oge O'Rourke', p. 203; Mooney, 'Some Leitrim Franciscans', p. 330; *AFM*, 1604.
134. Advowson refers to the hereditary right of a patron, often a layman, to make appointments to a particular church or parish.
135. *Calendar of Irish patent rolls of James I*, p. 9.
136. *AFM*, 1605.
137. *Monasticon Hibernicum*, pp 408, 808.

an annual rent of 4s.[138] Davies had little interest in the property and, sixteen months later, on 27 November 1615, he sold it to:

> Walter Harrison, gent, in consideration for a certain sum of money, the scite, circuit and precinct of the late monastery of De Crelew alias Creeveleagh with one carucat of land … to hold forever in free and common soccage.[139]

Two years earlier, Lieutenant Harrison had been granted 'the fort of Dunbrandon situate on a little island … in the river Bunned, with all its lands assigned and adjoining thereto'[140] – a fort which was located approximately one mile down-river from Creevelea friary.[141] Harrison was allowed to hold a market each Thursday and a fair from 18 to 20 October each year at 'Crynileigh'. Later Walter Harrison and his son of the same name were granted a licence to keep taverns and sell wine in the barony of Dromahair.[142] Having bought the friary Walter Harrison lost little time in trying to recoup his money. Donagh Mooney described how the friary, which was 'a handsome structure in a delightful location', had been completely burned by the heretics and that it was (*circa* 1617) occupied by an 'English heretic whose name is Harizon' who thatched the church with straw, lived in the convent and charged the people a fee for the privilege of burying their dead in the adjacent cemetery.[143]

Donagh Mooney was provincial of the Franciscan Order in Ireland from 1615 to 1618, and during that time the Franciscans experienced the beginnings of a revival.[144] They were learning to adapt to the loss of their friaries and to build alternative accommodation. In the year 1618, having helplessly watched Walter Harrison become the owner[145] of Creevelea friary, the friars, with the help and encouragement of their then minister

---

138.   *Calendar of Irish patent rolls of James I*, p. 257. Davies had travelled to south Ulster in 1606 and later drafted a long report on the situation in Fermanagh, Cavan and Monaghan. *DIB*, iii, pp 70–4.

139.   *Calendar of Irish patent rolls of James I*, p. 389. Walter Harrison was listed as just one of four undertakers who were resident in the county in 1622. He was resident in the county before the 1620 plantation of Leitrim. See Treadwell (ed.), *The Irish Commission of 1622*, p. 675. Harrison was convicted of treason *c*.1638. See *CSPI, 1633–47*, p. 200.

140.   *Calendar of Irish patent rolls of James I*, p. 238; Dominic Rooney, *The life and times of Sir Frederick Hamilton 1590–1647* (Dublin, 2013), p. 29; Brian Mac Cuarta, 'Leitrim plantation papers 1620–22' in *Bréifne*, ix, 35 (1999), pp 126, 130–1. Gerard MacAtasney, *The plantation of County Leitrim: 1585–1670* (Carrick-on-Shannon, 2013), p. 61.

141.   The earliest Ordnance survey map shows 'Harrison's castle' at this site.

142.   *Calendar of Irish patent rolls of James I*, p. 292.

143.   Jennings, 'Brussels MS 3947', p. 49; Mooney, 'Some Leitrim Franciscans', p. 330.

144.   Canice Mooney, 'St Anthony's College, Louvain' in Ó Muraíle (ed.), *Mícheál Ó Cléirigh, his associates*, p. 206.

145.   Harrison was regranted the 'abby as [well as] temporall lands' under the terms of the 1620 plantation of Leitrim. See MacCuarta, 'Leitrim plantation papers 1620–22', p. 126.

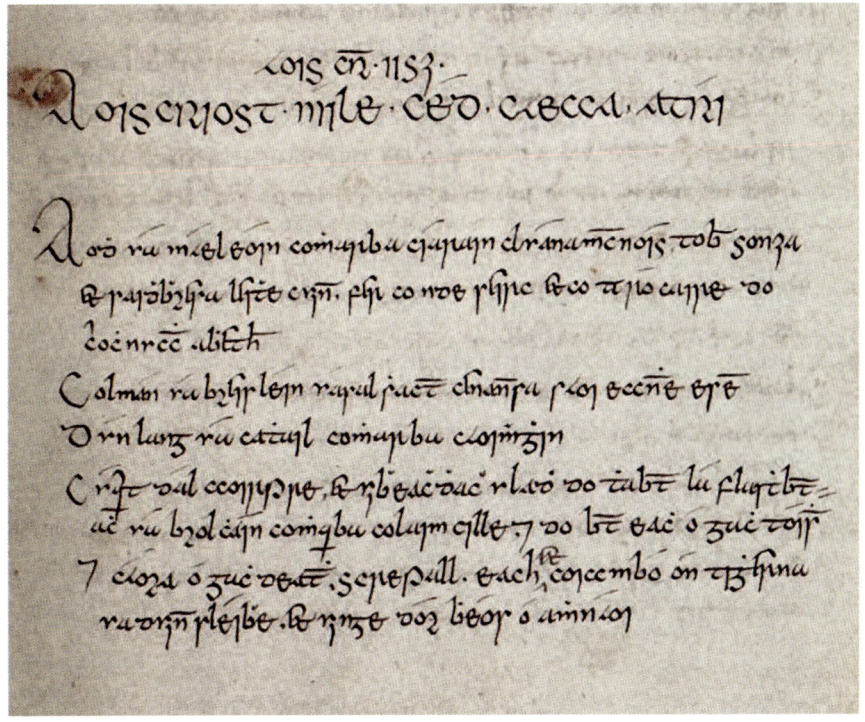

Figure 8.4: Manuscript page (*s.a.* 1153) of the Annals of the Four Masters which was written at Bundrowes in the 1630s. (*Courtesy of the Royal Irish Academy, MS.C iii 3, f.502r*).

provincial Eugene Field, built another house for themselves in the locality and Patrick Davitt became their superior.[146] This new accommodation was most likely a thatched cabin, somewhat similar to the wooden house which was roofed with sods in Cavan[147] or the thatched cabins of the friars near Multyfarnham later in the century.[148] However, it was not difficult to house the Creevelea friars at this time because the community, being a small one, had not sufficient numbers to grant it voting rights at the Franciscan provincial chapter in 1612.[149]

The Franciscans who were driven out of Donegal friary re-settled much nearer to Creevelea at Bundrowes, on the border between Donegal and Leitrim. There Brother Micheál Ó Cléirigh, together with

146.   Jennings, 'Brussels MS 3947', p. 110; *Brevis synopsis*, p. 161; Mooney, 'Some Leitrim Franciscans', p. 330.
147.   Massari, 'My Irish campaign', pp 248–9.
148.   Raymond Gillespie, 'The Irish Franciscans 1600–1700' in Bhreathnach, MacMahon & McCafferty, *The Irish Franciscans 1534–1990*, p. 59.
149.   Jennings, 'Mícheál Ó Cléirigh chief of the Four Masters', p. 41.

Cú Choigcriche Ó Cléirigh, Fearfeasa Ó Maoil Chonaire and Cú Choigcriche Ó Duibhgheannáin, who was from Castlefore in south Leitrim,[150] compiled what has become known as the 'Annals of the Four Masters' between the years 1632 and 1636. Despite all of his travels around the country collecting and transcribing materials, Brother Mícheál Ó Cléirigh does not seem to have stayed with the friars in Creevelea.[151] Perhaps the friary there, which had been in existence for just over one hundred years, had no manuscripts of note to match those in the older friaries elsewhere in the country.

When Oliver Lambert, the governor of Connacht, attacked Donegal friary in 1602 'he seized the entire … sacred furniture which he desecrated by turning the chalices into drinking cups and ripped up the brocaded vestments for the vilest uses'.[152] Presumably, the friars of Creevelea had a similar experience when their friary was attacked, burned and then a section of it occupied by the military. Perhaps for this reason and also to mark the setting up their new residence in the locality Mary O'Donnell, sister of Red Hugh O'Donnell and wife of Tadhg O'Rourke, son of Brian Na Murtha O'Rourke, donated a chalice (See Fig. 8.5.) to the friars of Creevelea in 1619 which carried the inscription:

Maria Ní Domnaill filia Hugonis Magoni Pro AiA Thaddei Ruairc Sui Mariti me fieri fecit Monasterio Chrivelelhae 1619.[153]

The O'Donnell, Maguire and O'Rourke families, despite their weakened circumstances, continued to support the Franciscans as best they could and in 1633 Mary Maguire, wife of Brian Oge O'Rourke, donated a chalice to the Donegal Franciscans for their new settlement at Bundrowes.[154]

150.   For Ó Duibhgheannáin see Bernadette Cunningham, 'The Ó Duibhgheannáin family of historians and the Annals of the Four Masters', *Bréifne*, pp 557–72; eadem, *The Annals of the Four Masters, Irish history, kingship and society in early the early seventeenth century* (Dublin, 2010), pp 49–54; eadem, 'Scribes and scholars associated with the Book of Fenagh' in Gillespie, Ryan & Scott (eds), *Making the Book of Fenagh*, pp 125–142.
151.   Ó Muraíle, *Micheál Ó Cléirigh, his associates and St Anthony's College*, pp 1, 16–17.
152.   Meehan, *The rise and fall of the Irish Franciscan monasteries*, p. 16.
153.   This chalice is in St Aidan's Church in Butlersbridge, Co. Cavan. See *IER*, xix (1922), i, pp 656–7; O'Connell, *The diocese of Kilmore*, pp 140–1; Mooney, 'Some Leitrim Franciscans', p. 320. This was Mary O'Donnell's third marriage. See Jerrold Casway, 'The last Lords of Leitrim: The sons of Sir Teigue O'Rourke' in *Bréifne*, vii, 26 (1988), pp 561–2, 574.
154.   Malgorzata Krasnodebska-D'Aughton, 'Franciscan chalices, 1600–50' in Bhreathnach, MacMahon & McCafferty (eds), *The Irish Franciscans 1534–1990*, pp 298, 301; Mac Cuarta, *Catholic revival in the north of Ireland*, p. 128; for a good photograph of and some information on this chalice see Michael Kenny, 'Irish secular silver, 1600–1750' in Ó Floinn (ed.), *Franciscan faith: sacred art in Ireland*, pp 45–8; P. Ó Gallachair, 'A missing Maguire chalice' in *Clogher Record*, i, 3 (1955), n.p.

Figure 8.5: The O'Rourke chalice which was donated to the Creevelea Franciscans in 1619 showing some of the detail on the base of the chalice.

It is not known where exactly the Donegal friars settled along the Drowes
River, however, according to a local tradition the friars came by sea 'in
small boats' arriving at *Locán na tSáile* near Tullaghan where they stayed
for a time before moving inland along the banks of the river Drowes and
settling in a townland now called Rossfriar, just south of the river and
near the Lough Melvin shore.[155]

Walter Harrison did not retain Creevelea friary for very long. In
1622 he was granted forty-six acres in lieu of 'abbey lands he formerly
held'.[156] The friary continued in lay ownership and changed hands
regularly. On 1 April 1658, 'the Abbie of Crulea together with all
the quarters and cartrons thereunto belonging' was leased by Owen
Wynne from a Welshman named Hugh Pennant for a period of
twenty-one years, during which Wynne promised not to 'committ any

155.   www.duchas.ie (accessed 16 January 2017), County Leitrim schools folklore collection, vol. 0190, pp 57–60. There is a church site and a 'friar's garden' on Inniskeen Island, a
small island near the north shore of Lough Melvin. However, it would appear that this was a
pre-Reformation ecclesiastical site. See Moore, *Archaeological inventory of County Leitrim*, p. 180.
156.   He already had 1,870 acres in the county. See Treadwell (ed.), *The Irish Commission of
1622*, pp 673, 675–6.

wilful waste upon the same'.[157] The Franciscans 'continued to live in thatched cabins in the neighbourhood' of the friary and if an opportunity arose they returned to it briefly only to be expelled once more.[158] At some stage, either Harrison or the friars, during one of their brief interludes back in the friary, adapted the tower so that it could be used for living rooms and bedrooms. It would appear that the friars lived in the tower for a time because on the first floor a 'curious drop or well, 8ft in depth and 3ft 6ins in breath' was made and floored over creating a 'secret hiding place' for the friars to hide their valuables whenever an attack was imminent.[159] The Franciscans, despite being ousted from their friary, maintained a presence in the locality though when the persecution became more severe they removed themselves further inland to New Creevelea near Drumkeerin and then to Sliabh-an-Iarainn mountain in the present-day parish of Ballinaglera. From their hiding place the friars continued to travel throughout much of north Leitrim preaching and questing for alms. They also continued to receive novices from County Leitrim families and from 1607 onwards, with the founding of St Anthony's College in Louvain and later other Franciscan colleges in continental Europe, some of these Franciscans, such as Brian MacEgan who entered Louvain on 1 February 1615 and later returned to become guardian of Creevelea,[160] were receiving a Tridentine education before returning to Ireland to play an important role in the revival of the Church in the first half of the seventeenth-century.[161]

157.   Clwyd Record Office, Harwarden, DINA/580; Benignus Millet, 'Lease of the friary of Creevelea (Dromahair) in County Leitrim to Owen Wynne, 1 April 1658' in *Coll. Hib.* 41 (1999), pp 7–9.
158.   Meehan, *The rise and fall of the Irish Franciscan monasteries*, p. 86.
159.   Quoted in Mooney, 'Franciscan architecture in pre-Reformation Ireland', p. 172. A similar hiding place was created in Donegal friary. See George T. Stokes (ed.), *Pococke's tour in Ireland in 1752* (Dublin, 1891), pp 69–70.
160.   Millett, *The Irish Franciscans 1651–1665*, pp 49–50; C. Mooney, 'The Franciscan friary of Jamestown' in *Ardagh & Clonmacnois Antiquarian Society Journal*, ii, 11 (1946), pp 6–7; Ignatius Fennessy, 'Two letters from Boetius (Augustine) MacEgan OFM, on the death of Archbishop Florence Conroy, OFM, 1629' in *Coll. Hib.*, 43 (2001), pp 9–10. Patrick Brady, another Franciscan from Kilmore, had entered Louvain Franciscan College in 1614. See Jennings & Giblin (eds), *Louvain papers*, p. 55. Another Kilmore student, 'Eugenius Relly', aged eighteen, was a student in Louvain in 1625. Moran, *History of the Catholic archbishops of Dublin*, i, p. 302.
161.   Canice Mooney referred to the period 1615–50 as 'the golden age of the Irish Franciscans.' See Cunningham, *The Annals of the Four Masters, Irish history, kingship and society in early the early seventeenth century*, p. 17.

Chapter 9

Plantations and Catholic Revival: 1603–1628

The death of Elizabeth I and the accession of James I to the throne on 24 March 1603 were followed, less than a week later, by the submission of Hugh O'Neill to Mountjoy at Mellifont. The Nine Years War, the seven year civil war among the different factions of the O'Reillys, the wars in west Bréifne with the English and between the brothers Brian Óg and Tadhg O'Rourke - all had resulted in widespread destruction, starvation and death in the diocese of Kilmore. The Flight of the Earls (1607) was followed by the Plantation of Ulster (1610) and the Plantation of Leitrim (1620) - all traumatic events for the native Irish of the diocese of Kilmore and the wider province of Ulster. Many Catholics lost their lands and their churches during these years and Lochlainn Ó Dálaigh, a Gaelic poet from east Bréifne, captured the turmoil and upheaval of the period in his poem '*Cá háit ar ghabh na Gaeil*?' (Where have the Gaels gone?).[1] He bemoans the fact that the Irish have been uprooted and replaced by English and Scottish settlers who are now using the churches and fencing-in the land:

> Comhthionól tuata I dteach naomh,
> Seirbhhís Dé faoi dhíon fionnchraobh,
> Cuilt cléire ina gcuilce tána,
> Sliabh ina ghortaibh gabhála.

> [A boorish crowd in the house of God,
> While God's service is held beneath boughs,

---

1.   B. Ó Doibhlín, *Manuail de Litríocht na Gaeilge*, ii (Dublin, 2006), pp 245–7. Little is known about Lochlainn Ó Dálaigh except that he flourished as a poet in the 1590s and early 1600s. See Darren McGettigan, 'Lochlainn Ó Dálaigh', in *DIB*, vii, p. 335; Diarmaid Ó Doibhlín, 'The Plantation of Ulster: aspects of Gaelic letters' in Éamonn Ó Ciardha and Micheal Ó Siochrú (eds), *The plantation of Ulster, ideology and practice* (Manchester, 2012), pp 202–3. The Ó Dálaigh family provided bardic poets for the O'Reillys of east Bréifne. This poem is undated and it was first published in 1631 in the 'Book of O'Conor Don'. See Raymond Gillespie, 'The Gaelic Irish and the Ulster plantation' in Brendan Scott & John Dooher (eds), *Plantation, aspects of seventeenth-century Ulster society* (Belfast, 2013), pp 14–15.

The clerical robes are bedding for cattle,
The mountain fenced into fields.]

The power of the O'Rourkes and the O'Reillys, the two main patrons
of the church in Kilmore, had collapsed and the Catholic community in
the diocese would now have to learn to survive in very changed times.

There had been no Church of Ireland bishop of Kilmore since John
Garvey was translated to Armagh in 1590. James Ware, the Anglo-Irish
historian who was born in 1594, says that this long vacancy was 'occa-
sioned by the confusion of the times', though it seems more likely that
it was a tacit acceptance that anyone appointed to the diocese would be
a bishop there in name only.[2] Nevertheless, there were attempts to fill
the vacancy. In 1593 John Garvey recommended William Hughes for
Kilmore and three years later Walter Chatfyld applied for the vacant
bishopric - though nothing came from either of these moves.[3] It was not
until March 1603/04 that Robert Draper, the rector of Trim who was
described as 'an ancient master of arts, a learned preacher and a good
keeper of hospitality', was appointed bishop of Kilmore and Ardagh.[4]
Among the reasons given for his appointment was that 'he was well
acquainted with the conditions and dispositions of that people and was
able to instruct them in the Irish tongue and thereby likely to do more
good among them'.[5] Because the bishop of Kilmore's income was regarded as inadequate Draper was allowed to retain the rectory of Trim,
a benefice worth about £150 per annum.[6]

Robert Draper

The appointment of Robert Draper as the bishop of Kilmore in 1604
was the first serious move by the Established Church to evangelise the
native population of the diocese. He could speak their language and,
unlike his predecessors Edmund Nugent and John Garvey, he resided
in the diocese. He was one of six bishops appointed by James I to Ulster
dioceses between the years 1603 and 1607 and as he took office he set
about claiming the cathedral, churches, cemeteries, income and administrative systems previously held by the Catholic Church in Kilmore.[7]
Draper would soon discover, however, that the churches were virtually all in ruins and that clerical incomes were miserable in the extreme.

---

2.   Harris (ed.), *The whole works of Sir James Ware*, p. 231.
3.   *CSPI, 1592–6*, pp 127, 541.
4.   *CSPI, 1603–06*, pp 86, 114,172.
5.   *Calendar of Irish patent rolls of James I*, p. 5; Mant, *History of the Church of Ireland*, p. 357.
6.   *CSPI, 1603–06*, p. 172.
7.   Ford, 'The Reformation in Kilmore', p. 77.

However, conditions were more favourable for him than they had been for his predecessors with the changed landscape in the diocese following the collapse of the powerful septs at the end of the Nine Years war. Besides, there was no resident Catholic bishop to compete with since Richard Brady, now old and decrepit, was based a considerable distance away with the Franciscan community in Multyfarnham and, after his death in 1607 no Catholic bishop was appointed to Kilmore until 1625. This lack of leadership and the absence of seminary-trained priests, left the Catholic clergy of the diocese rudderless, and by 1607 a number of them had already been absorbed into the Established Church.[8]

The newly-appointed Bishop Draper had the law on his side and in July 1605 a proclamation was issued stating that 'titulary bishops, Jesuits, seminaries, friars and Romish priests be banished from the realm, except they that will reform themselves'.[9] This enactment, together with the bishop's presence in Cavan and the work of the assize courts from 1606 onwards in administering the oath of supremacy, meant that there was considerable pressure on the native clergy to conform to the Church of Ireland.[10] Besides, the benefices of the Established Church appealed to the native, impoverished clergy, some of whom had families to support. Robert Draper may have had no option but to attempt to work with the native clergy and persuade them to conform because of the reluctance of English clergy to take up appointments in a Gaelic-speaking and impoverished diocese. This problem persisted and by 1612, the year Draper died, only two English clergymen, both Cambridge graduates, had taken up positions in the diocese.[11]

Robert Draper appears to have had more success in temporal matters than he had in evangelising the natives of the diocese. And even though some of the native clergy conformed and continued to hold office, seventeen parishes in the diocese remained without a Protestant pastor throughout his episcopate.[12] This may have suited him as the bishop received the income from these vacant parishes. Sir John Davies,

---

8. Mac Cuarta, 'Catholic revival in Kilmore diocese', p. 148.
9. *CSPI, 1603–06*, p. 134.
10. It is possible that the pressure on the native clergy to conform was greater in County Cavan than in the other parts of the diocese of Kilmore since in 1617 and again in 1622 all of the native Irish who became Church of Ireland clergy appear to be from Cavan.
11. They were Nathaniel Hollington, vicar of Drumlane and John Bockock (Bostock), vicar of Drumlease, See NLI, MS 2865, p. 151; Hunter, *The Ulster plantation in Armagh and Cavan*, p. 297; Leslie, *Clergy of Kilmore*, pp 360, 546. See also Ford, 'The Reformation in Kilmore' p. 81. He states that Hollington was ordained by Thomas Moigne in 1616 and was not appointed to Drumlane until 1618.
12. Mac Cuarta, *Catholic revival in the north of Ireland*, p. 42.

who accompanied Chichester on a tour of the 'unreformed counties'[13] of Cavan, Monaghan and Fermanagh in the months of July and August 1606, was scathing in his criticism of Draper, who holds 'the best parsonage in this kingdom [Trim]' and is 'a man of this country birth, worth nigh £400 a year'. He outlined how Robert Draper:

> doth now live in these parts [Cavan] … but there is no divine service or sermon to be heard within either of his dioceses [Kilmore and Ardagh].[14] His lordship might have saved us this labour of enquiry touching matters ecclesiastical, if he had been as careful to see the churches repaired and supplied with good incumbents, as he is diligent in visiting his barbarous clergy, to make benefit out of their insufficiency, according to the parable … that an Irish priest is better than a milch cow.[15]

John Davies may have been unfair to Robert Draper since he faced many obstacles on becoming bishop, not least being the number and quality of the clergy at his disposal.[16] Davies 'saw many of them in the camp' when he visited Cavan and described them as being 'poor, ragged, ignorant creatures'[17] and it appears that Draper relied almost entirely on these 'barbarous' priests he had inherited from the Catholic Church.[18] It was during the episcopacy of Draper that the greatest number of native priests conformed, at least outwardly, to the Protestant faith, though it appears that they made little attempt to convert their kin groups and continued to celebrate the traditional liturgies much as they had always done. The Kilmore rectories which were formerly held by the priory of Fore were now held by the Nugents of Delvin; those held in the past by the abbey of Kells were in the hands of the Flemings of Cabragh and those previously held by the Premonstratensians of Lough Uachtair were now held by the Dillon family. These Old-English Catholic

13.   Henry Morley (ed.), *Ireland under Elizabeth and James the First* (London, 1890), p. 361.

14.   Sir Arthur Chichester agreed with Davies on this point. He wrote 'the care of the church hath been neglected, whereby God's service hath been omitted.' See *CSPI, 1603–06*, p. 563.

15.   Sir John Davies to the Earl of Salisbury, in Vallancey, *Collectanea De rebus Hibernicis*, p. 175; Sir John Davies, *Historical tracts* (Dublin, 1787), p. 267.

16.   Others, such as Sir Robert Jacob, the Solicitor General for Ireland, were also critical of the bishops of the Established Church at this time. Writing from Cavan on 28 February 1614, Jacob proposed that the king should write 'a sharp letter to the bishops, reprehending them for their negligence and corruption in keeping the profits of Church livings in their hands and not providing competent ministers'. Francis Bickley (ed.), *Report on the manuscripts of the late Reginald Hastings*, iv (London, 1947), p. 15. My thanks to Brendan Scott for this reference.

17.   Vallancey, *Collectanea De rebus Hibernicis*, p. 175.

18.   Ford, 'The Reformation in Kilmore', p. 78.

families from the Pale exerted considerable influence in the diocese and discouraged any radical liturgical changes in the parishes where their influence was strongest. During the episcopate of Robert Draper there was what Brian Mac Cuarta has called 'a period of denominational flux, as parish clergy drifted into a nominal conformity to the Established Church'.[19] However, some of those who conformed did so on a more permanent basis because, while there was probably a greater number of native Protestant clergy during the episcopate of Robert Draper, there were still six native Irish men holding positions in the Established Church in the diocese in 1622[20] and five in 1626.[21]

In late 1608 King James I ordered that 'there shall be one Free School at least appointed in every county [of Ulster] for the education of Youth in learning and religion'.[22] It was not until three years later, on 5 October 1611, that John Robinson, on the recommendation of Robert Draper, was appointed 'schoolmaster and teacher' in Cavan Royal School, 'during his good behaviour'.[23] The original idea was to build a new school on the site of the Franciscan friary in Cavan with stones taken from Tullachmongan castle.[24] The Royal School, which started small and was slow to get off the ground, had four schoolmasters, John Robinson, Alexander Julius, John Stern and Nicholas Higginson, in the first thirteen years of its existence.[25] Robert Draper, who died within a year of the first schoolmaster being appointed, is best remembered for being the first Church of Ireland bishop to reside in the diocese and for being the one who was instrumental in setting up Cavan Royal School.

Thomas Moigne

Robert Draper died in August 1612 and by the end of that month Sir Thomas Lake, the Secretary of State to King James, had already received a letter recommending 'Mr Moine, Dean of St Patrick's, for the bishopric of Cullemor, now void and worth £300 per annum'.[26] Thomas Moigne, a Cambridge graduate, was born in Lincolnshire and had been archdeacon of Meath before being appointed Dean of St Patrick's in 1608, a benefice

19. Mac Cuarta, 'Catholic revival in Kilmore', p. 147.
20. TCD, MS 550, pp 142–53 cited in Mac Cuarta, *Catholic revival in the north of Ireland*, p. 49.
21. James Morrin (ed.), *Calendar of the patent and close rolls of Chancery in Ireland in the reign of Charles I* (Dublin, 1863), pp 185–8.
22. Brewer & Bullen (eds), *Calendar of Carew MSS*, v, p. 21; Jonathan Bardon, 'The plantation and the Royal Schools, Ulster before 1608' in *The 1608 Royal Schools celebrate 400 years of history* (Armagh, 2007), p. 11.
23. McCready, 'Cavan Royal School', p. 461; idem, in *The 1608 Royal schools celebrate*, p. 85.
24. TCD, MS 747; Moody, 'Ulster Plantation papers 1608–13', pp 242–3.
25. *Calendar of Irish patent rolls of James I*, p. 579; Michael Quane, 'Cavan Royal School' in *JRSAI*, c, 1 (1970), pp 44–5.
26. *CSPI, 1611–14*, p. 282.

he resigned in 1625.[27] He was consecrated bishop of Kilmore in Drogheda on or before 12 January 1613. The appointment of an Englishman to Kilmore who, unlike his predecessor was unskilled in the Irish language, seems an acknowledgement that his two predecessors, both of whom were Irish speaking, were ineffective and that the role of the Established Church in the diocese was to minister to the recently settled colonists rather to evangelise the native Irish.[28] The newly appointed bishop's approach to recruiting clergy differed greatly to that of Robert Draper who had focussed mainly on enlisting the native Irish. Thomas Moigne, on the other hand, in the wake of the Ulster plantation and the later (1620) Leitrim plantation, set about providing English and Scottish clergy to ecclesiastical positions in the diocese of Kilmore.

It is estimated that Thomas Moigne appointed thirty English or Scottish clergymen to positions in the diocese between 1613 and 1628.[29] The earliest of these appointments were to parishes such as Drumlane, Castletara, Annagh and Kildallan, all of which were relatively near to the bishop's residence at Kilmore. The Leitrim appointments generally came from 1620 onwards, following the plantation of that county. Fifteen of the new clergymen had been to university, five of whom were fellow students of Thomas Moigne in Cambridge.[30] He obviously persuaded some of his college friends to follow him to the rural diocese of Kilmore in the north-west of Ireland.

Thomas Moigne's friendship with James Ussher, who was on the staff of Trinity College in Dublin at this time, also proved useful. Bishop Moigne helped finance some of the students in Trinity College by granting them benefices without cure which became available in either Kilmore or Ardagh diocese. It would appear that John Patrick, a student, was granted the rectory of Killinagh in 1613.[31] Thomas Moigne also noticed that the rectorial tithes of Muintir Eolais, in the diocese of Ardagh, which were worth £12 or 20 marks per annum and had 'fallen in lapse ... [and] hath for a long tyme bene usurped and intruded upon by some of the Renoldes in the County of Letryme' and he felt that this benefice, which was without cure, was 'of that nature that anie scholler

27.   Leslie, *Clergy of Kilmore*, p. 692; Harris (ed.), *The whole works of Sir James Ware*, p. 231.
28.   Similarly in the south-east of Ireland the clergy of the Church of Ireland adopted a policy at this time of ministering only to those who were already members of the Established Church. See Áine Hensey, 'A comparative study of the lives of Church of Ireland and Roman Catholic clergy in the south-eastern dioceses of Ireland from 1550 to 1650', unpublished PhD thesis (NUIM, 2012), p. 319.
29.   Ford, 'The Reformation on Kilmore', p. 81.
30.   Ibid., pp 81–3; Brian Mac Cuarta, 'The plantation of Leitrim, 1620–41' in *IHS*, 32, no. 127 (2001), pp 297–320.
31.   Leslie, *Clergy of Kilmore*, p. 782.

is capable of it'.[32] He wrote to his 'very good frend' James Ussher, sometime after 1613 when the latter was vice chancellor of Trinity College, asking him to have a 'good worde' with the lord deputy in order that John Patrick might receive the benefice.[33] John Patrick graduated with an MA, was ordained and later ministered in the parishes of Ballintemple, Mullagh, Killinkere and Templeport.[34] John Hill, who lived in the townland of Togher in the parish of Kilmore was dean of Kilmore (deanery) and vicar of the parishes of Kilmore and Ballintemple in 1619, also had been a student in Trinity College.[35] During the episcopate of Robert Draper, a 'poor scholar from Cavan' called Charles Brady was subsidized by the state in Trinity College.[36] However, there is no record of him ever serving in the diocese and it would appear that the relatively new Trinity College was already failing to meet one of its main aims – that of providing native Irish clergy for the Established Church.

Not all of the newly-appointed ministers came from Cambridge or Trinity. Some of them arrived along with the settlers from England or Scotland. In 1611 it was reported that Sir Alexander Hamilton, who had received grants of land in the Killeshandra area of Cavan, had brought a minister over with him 'who was not yet allowed by the bishop'.[37] Thomas Moigne does not seem to have recruited any new native Irish clergy, although a group of six native Church of Ireland clergy who were serving in the diocese in 1617 were still there in 1622.[38] Of the six native Irish Kilmore clergy listed in 1622, only Nicholas O'Gowan junior, who was vicar of Kilsherdany, had attended university. He had graduated from Trinity College with a BA in 1602 and he was

32.   Thomas Moyne to James Ussher in Elizabethanne Boran (ed.), *The correspondence of James Ussher*, i (Dublin, 2015), p. 20.
33.   This letter has been incorrectly dated to 23 July 1607. It is clear from the content of the letter that it was written after Thomas Moigne's consecration and James Ussher's marriage in 1613.
34.   Leslie, *Clergy of Kilmore*, p. 782.
35.   Ibid., p. 540.
36.   H.F. Berry (ed.), 'Probable early students of Trinity College, Dublin (being wards of the crown) 1599–1616' in *Hermathena*, xvi (1911), pp 25–7; cited in Ford, 'The Reformation in Kilmore', p. 77.
37.   M. Perceval-Maxwell, *Scottish migration to Ulster* (London, 1973), p. 325; William Roulston, 'The Scots in plantation Cavan, 1610–42' in Scott (ed.), *Culture and society in early modern Bréifne/Cavan*, p. 122; Ford, 'The Reformation in Kilmore', p. 81. The bishop and Hamilton were in dispute at this time over 'a polle of land called Annagh' and this may, at least in part, explain why the minister had not been granted a parish. See *CSPI, 1611–14*, p. 216. William Roulston has suggested that the minister referred to here was Adam Watson who became the vicar of Killeshandra. See Roulston, 'The Scots in plantation Cavan', p. 139.
38.   These native conforming clergy, a third of the total Chuch of Ireland clergy in the diocese, comprised of four rectors and two curates.

the only one of the six to be listed as a preacher in 1622.[39] However, he did not remain in the diocese, choosing instead to end his days as 'Nicholas Smith', the vicar of Rathoath in the more Anglicised diocese of Meath.[40] There were other problems too apart from the native Irish clergy's inability to preach. Hugh McComyn or McConnyne, a native Irish priest who converted to Protestantism, was rector of Drumgoon in 1612.[41] He lived in 'a poor Irish house' and had, by 1622, been suspended for certain un-named misdemeanours, possibly for celebrating the liturgies in the old Catholic style.[42] However, the suspension was a temporary one because he was once more rector and vicar of Drumgoon in 1626.[43]

The native conforming clergy who could speak Irish were largely uneducated and were either unable or unwilling to preach and evangelise. The English and Scottish preachers were willing to do both but could not speak the language of the vast majority of the people living in the diocese. William Andrews, the vicar of Annagh parish who lived in Belturbet, had an MA and was a preacher, but was unable to communicate with his Irish-speaking parishioners and so 'he alloweth £10 per annum to an Irish curate to read divine service in the Irish tongue'.[44] The Irish curate he employed may have been Thomas Brady, the vicar of Lavey who was said to be 'a minister of the country birth'. He was a busy man because he also served as curate in Templeport and Killinagh parishes. Similarly, John Hill, the rector in Ballintemple, employed Philip O'Siredor (O'Sheridan) as a curate for an annual fee of £6 6s. 8d. The English-speaking clergy were more effective in the more Anglicised south-eastern part of the diocese and in 1618 the surveyor Nicholas Pynnar reported that Captain Culme had already built eight timber houses in Virginia 'and put into them English Tenants;

---

39.   The six native clergy listed by Bishop Thomas Moigne in 1622 were Hugh McConnyne, Phillip O'Siredor (Ballintemple), Nicholas Smith (Kildromfertan), Shane O'Gowan (Castlerahan), Nicholas Smith junior (Kilsherdany) and Thomas Brady (Lavey). The same six men were on a 1615 list. See TCD, MS 550, pp 144–51; Ford, *The Protestant Reformation in Ireland 1590–1641*, p. 143. For a list of the Church of Ireland clergy who served in Kilmore between 1603 and 1641 see appendix to Ford, 'The Reformation in Kilmore', pp 96–8.
40.   Ibid., p. 83.
41.   NLI, MS 2685, p. 114; Hunter, *The Ulster plantation in Armagh and Cavan*, p. 297.
42.   TCD, MS 550; Thomas Moigne, *A True copy of all the rents, procurations, tithes and pensions as belong to the two united bishoprics of Kilmore and Ardagh* (1622), n. 3; Brendan Scott, 'The 1622 Royal visitation of the Church of Ireland in Ulster' in Scott & Dooher (eds), *Plantation, aspects of seventeenth-century Ulster society*, p. 60.
43.   Morrin (ed.), *Calendar of the patent and close rolls of Chancery in Ireland in the reign of Charles I*, p. 186.
44.   TCD, MSS 550, 2629; Hunter, *The Ulster plantation in Armagh and Cavan*, p. 297.

of which town there is a Minister [George Creighton], which keepeth School and is a very good Preacher'.[45]

Churches, Houses and Glebe Lands

By the early 1600s the Church of Ireland bishop was the legal owner of the churches, chapels and termon lands of the diocese although, it would appear, that securing possession of them happened gradually over a period of several decades. As a result of this change of ownership, the erenagh and coarb families who had, for centuries, taken care of the church lands and who had kept houses of hospitality, were now redundant. Fearghal Muimhneach Ó Duibhgeannáin, one of the learned and scribal family with branches in Castlefore in Leitrim and Kilronan in Roscommon, addressed his poem *Maith, trá do thoigheacht, a Thaidhg* to Tadhg Ó Rodaighe, one of the coarb family of St Caillín from Fenagh, urging him to defend the erenaghs of Connacht and to reverse their serfdom.[46] Ó Rodaighe travelled to London in 1688 in a futile legal attempt to reverse the dispossession of the coarbs and erenaghs.[47] In effect, the battle for the possession of the churches and church lands had been lost decades earlier.

The churches of the diocese of Kilmore which belonged to the church 'as by law established' in the early 1600s were virtually all roofless and those 'presented to be in reparation are covered only with thatch'.[48] Josias Bodley's *c.*1609 maps of the Cavan baronies, although they are incomplete and omit several churches, show most of those depicted to be unroofed. The baronial map of Tullyhaw shows both Templeport parish church and Kilnavart chapel to be roofless while the church on St Maodhóg's island in the same parish has a roof. Besides being in a poor physical condition, many of the churches were in remote rural areas and not in the recently-established towns and villages preferred by the settlers.[49] The church in Annagh parish was said to be in a ruinous state in 1622 and since William Andrews, the rector of Annagh and archdeacon of the diocese, was living in Belturbet, the parish church at Annagh was deemed to be 'unfit to be repaired by reason of its remoteness from Belterbett'.[50] The commissioners reported

---

45. Pynnar's Survey of Ulster in Walter Harris (ed.), *Hibernica: or Some Antient Piecese relating to Ireland* (Dublin, 1757), p. 76.
46. TCD, MS 1419, 303r; Mac Muirí, *Tadhg Ó Rodaighe*, pp 356–66; RIA, B iv I, 125r.
47. Mac Muirí, *Tadhg Ó Rodaighe*, p. 10.
48. Davies to Salisbury, in Morley, *Ireland under Elizabeth and James*, p. 377.
49. Sir Robert Jacob, writing from Cavan on 28 February 1614, proposed 'to compel the Irishry to live together in towns and villages … and not to suffer them to live dispersed in woods and other uncouth places'. See Bickley, *Report on the manuscripts of the late Reginald Hastings*, iv, p. 16.
50. TCD, MS 550, n. 1.

in 1622 that 'there is a great store of protestants in and about the town [of Belturbet] and there should be a church builded there, but as yet no course taken for it'.[51] The church at Castletara was described as 'ruinous and remote from Bellahayes'. The church of Urney was ruinous and it was said that 'a church to be built at the Cavon is the fittest place'. Similarly the ruined church in Lurgan was in the wrong place for the settlers and the recommendation was that a new one be built in the recently established town of Virginia.[52] Besides, the glebe lands, if such existed, were often a considerable distance away from the church. Sir Arthur Chichester, the lord deputy, reported in 1608 that:

> The churches in … Cavan, Fermanagh, Donegall and indeed all Ulster are so defaced, and the glebe and bishop's lands so obscured that all is confused and out of order, as if it were in a wilderness, where neither Christianity nor religion was ever heard of.[53]

The instructions given to the commissioners for settling differences between grantees in Ulster in June 1612 acknowledged that 'much of the land designed for gleb is not soe contiguous unto the churches as weare to be wished' and advised them to find 'other lande lyeinge more convenient to the said Churches or Chappells'.[54] However, the problem persisted and Thomas Moigne, in his 1622 report, complained that 'in the county of Letrym the glebes for the most part are laid out in the most unprofitable places and remotest from the church'.[55] In Killargue parish the vicar, William Holliwell, was bound under the terms of the Leitrim plantation to build a house. However, the glebe land which was in another parish had been given to Collo McMurrey and so the vicar 'cannot peaceably enjoy it'. In both Urney and Lavey parishes the glebe lands were ten miles distant from the parish church.[56] Bishop Mogine stated that in the parish of 'Dyime [Denn]' where Robert Whiskins was

---

51.   Treadwell (ed.), *The Irish Commission of 1622*, p. 518.
52.   There was a considerable delay in building the church in Virginia: R.J. Hunter, 'An Ulster plantation town – Virginia' in *Bréifne*, iv, 13 (1970), pp 50–1.
53.   *CSPI*, 1608–10, p. 64.
54.   Moody, 'Ulster plantation papers 1608–13', p. 263.
55.   TCD, MS 550, no.5.
56.   Ibid., 5, 7, 17, 30. The glebe lands in County Cavan in 1622 ranged in size from 60 to 220 acres. Kinawley in County Fermanagh had 240 acres of glebe land and Killesher had 120 acres: Treadwell (ed.), *The Irish Commission*, pp 641–2. County Leitrim was poorly provided with glebe lands. In 1620 there were no glebe lands in the barony of Rosclogher and only twenty acres in Carrigallen barony. Dromahair had 405 acres of glebe lands, the largest of any barony in the county. See NLI, Ms 8014, vi.

vicar 'the church is ruinous' and the 'glebe not convenient'.[57] Alexander Clogie, chaplain to and biographer of William Bedell, wrote that 'the county town of Cavan had [glebe] lands in two parishes many miles distant from the church, but none within the parish'.[58] The glebe lands continued to be a problem and in 1626, in a bid to resolve the situation, twenty-seven grants of glebe lands were granted to the Protestant clergy of the diocese.[59]

The clergy of the Established Church were expected to repair the existing churches or build new ones and also to build 'parsonage houses' on the lands granted to them. Thomas Moigne reported in 1622 that even though most of the churches in the diocese were in ruins and the glebe houses were either non-existent or of very poor standard, some small progress had been made. He had given leadership in this matter because with the help of £175 from recusant[60] fines he reported that:

> The cathedral church [is] newly built and repaired ... A fair stone house built at Kilmore by the now bishop, the which, together with the building of other out houses and of seats in the chancel and body of the church of Kilmore had cost £600.[61]

Despite these renovations, William Bedell, who succeeded Thomas Moigne in 1629, was not impressed with the 'newly built and repaired' cathedral at Kilmore. He described the church as being 'without bell or steeple, font or chalice'.[62] Nearby, in the same parish of Kilmore, Thomas Robinson, the dean of Kilmore who died in 1619, had built 'a sufficient dwelling house with convenient houses of office'.[63] In the adjacent parish of Killeshandra the vicar, Adam Watson, had 'a sufficient house' and the church was newly repaired. In Knockninny, where there was a village of forty mud-walled and timber houses inhabited by newly arrived British settlers, Lord Balfour had 'a church ready for the roof, 66 foot long and 30 foot broad, all the windows of freestone and a chancel to it, 23 feet long and 19 foot broad' and a free

57.   TCD, MS 550.
58.   Shuckburgh, *Two biographies of William Bedell*, p. 103.
59.   Morrin (ed.), *Calendar of the patent and close rolls of Chancery in Ireland in the reign of Charles I*, pp 185–8.
60.   The Roman Catholics who refused to attend Church of Ireland services were known as 'recusants' and they were regularly fined for non-attendance at Protestant services.
61.   TCD, MS 550.
62.   Bedell to Laud, 1 April 1630, in Mant, *History of the Church of Ireland*, p. 436.
63.   TCD, MS 550.

school with 'shingles ready to be put on it'.[64] He had received recusant fines from Fermanagh and Cavan to help build the church and school. In the north-Leitrim parish of Killasnett, where James Metcalf was vicar, the church was 'in repair' and a house was being built and in his other vicarage of Rossinver, the church was also in reasonable repair.[65] In Castlerahan, where Nicholas Smith, junior, a native Irishman, was vicar, there was a house built on the glebe land.[66]

The lack of glebe houses, the poor state of the churches, the small clerical incomes and the complete absence or else the small number of Protestant laity in some parishes resulted in many of the English and Scottish clergymen being non-resident and pluralists, receiving revenues from several parishes without having to provide any services or pastoral care in return. To remedy this situation, the 1620 royal instructions for the plantation of Leitrim included a clause 'for the building of sevrall howses for the ministers in the severall parishes whereby all pretences of non residence may be taken away'.[67] However, the problem of pluralism persisted throughout the diocese and it was not until William Bedell became bishop that any serious attempt was made to resolve it.

Reformation Makes Little Progress

Alan Ford has written that 'in many cases the main interest which pluralist British ministers had in their native Irish parishes was to ensure that they secured their income from tithes and dues'.[68] The traditional Gaelic way to pay tithes was to donate farm produce and following the plantations of Cavan and Leitrim this changed to the English way of tithing which involved the handing over of money. The result was, as Ford has pointed out, 'a repeated temptation, to which many ministers succumbed, to exact both English and Irish tithes at unacceptably high level'.[69] In many instances it was not the ministers themselves who collected the tithes but rather the tithe proctors appointed to work on their behalf. Faithful Teate, who was rector of Castletara, Drung and Laragh[70] appointed Hugh Brady from Cullentra as his proctor and the minister claimed that as a result Brady was 'raised by him from poverty to a rich estate'.[71] Felix Crane who was granted the vicarages of Rossinver

64.   Treadwell (ed.), *The Irish Commission of 1622*, pp 523–4.
65.   TCD, MS 550.
66.   Ibid., no. 9.
67.   Mac Cuarta (ed.), 'Leitrim Plantation papers 1620–22', p. 122.
68.   Ford, 'The reformation in Kilmore', p. 85.
69.   Ibid.
70.   Leslie, *Clergy of Kilmore*, p. 876.
71.   TCD, MS 833, f. 61r; Clarke (ed.), *1641 Depositions*, ii, p. 184. Hugh Brady joined the rebels in 1641.

and Killasnett by Bishop Moigne[72] had charged exorbitant fees for baptisms and had two bailiffs working for him collecting recusancy fines in a previously held benefice in Clogher diocese.[73] William Bedell, son of the bishop of the same name, described how one parishioner in the diocese of Kilmore who had failed to pay 3*d*. for tithe turf ended up having to pay £5.[74] Such instances as these, together with the over-zealous approach of the diocesan chancellor Alan Cooke in imposing recusant fines, resulted in deep-rooted animosity towards the Established Church.[75]

On 26 March 1625 the ageing Bishop Thomas Moigne, in a congratulatory letter to James Ussher who had been nominated archbishop of Armagh two months earlier, complained that the growth of the Church of Ireland, 'notwithstanding all his majesty's endowments and directions, receives every day more impediments than ever'.[76] He instanced how certain benefits were being taken away from his clergy and stated that 'the more is taken away from the king's clergy, the more accrues to the Pope's'. He could not hide his disappointment that, despite all his efforts on behalf of the state church since arriving in the diocese thirteen years earlier, little growth had occurred and the tide seemed to be turning in favour of the Catholics once more. James Ussher, along with Thomas Moigne and ten other bishops, signed a letter of protest on 26 November 1626, against 'the abomination of Popery' and the new freedoms being granted to Catholics. The letter stated that:

> The religion of the Papists is superstitious and idolatrous; their faith and doctrine erroneous and heretical; their church, in respect of both, apostastical. To give them therefore, a toleration, or to consent that they may freely exercise their religion, and profess their faith and doctrine is a grievous sin.[77]

---

72. Leslie, *Clergy of Kilmore*, p. 423.
73. Ford, 'The reformation in Kilmore', p. 87; NLI, MS 8014/X.
74. Shuckburgh, *Two biographies of William Bedell*, p. 123.
75. Alan Cooke was sovereign of Cavan town in 1633 and MP for County Cavan the following year. See Cherry, 'The indigenous and colonial urbanization of Cavan town', p. 102.
76. Moigne to Ussher in Mant, *History of the Church of Ireland*, p. 419. Two and a half weeks earlier, on 8 March 1625, Thomas Moigne and the bishops of Clogher, Raphoe, Dromore and Derry had written to the King begging relief for their clergy who were being deprived of 'a great part of their maintenance'. *CSPI, 1615–25*, p. 568.
77. Mant, *History of the Church of Ireland*, p. 423. John Hill, the dean of Kilmore who lived in the townland of Togher, had written a month earlier to James Ussher urging him not to yield to 'Tolleration or Libertye to poperie'. See Boran (ed.), *The Correspondence of James Ussher*, i, p. 378.

Figure 9.1: Ecclesiastical figure on a MacGargan gravestone in Moybolgue cemetery.

However, by this time the battle for the hearts and minds of the native Irish in the diocese had already been lost[78] and the new, more tolerant approach of both James I and Charles I towards Catholics, irritated the Established Church and afforded the Catholics in the diocese an opportunity to re-organize after decades of upheaval, confusion and chaos.

Catholic Revival

The death of Richard Brady, the Franciscan bishop of the diocese, took place in September 1607, the same month that the Ulster chieftains took flight from Lough Swilly in Donegal. It was a time of great change and upheaval, although the death of the bishop had a minimum impact on the diocese since he had been old and invalided and was based in Multyfarnham from approximately 1600 onwards. And even though he had been assaulted, arrested and imprisoned a number of times he had died peacefully in his bed, unlike the violent deaths experienced by his fellow bishops Patrick O'Healy, Edmund Magauran and Réamonn Ó Gallachair. At the time of Richard Brady's death the Catholic Church in the diocese of Kilmore and throughout Ulster was weakened and in disarray. And yet, during the 1610s, largely due to the leadership of the vice-primate, David Rothe, and the preaching of Franciscan, Louvain-trained roving missionaries, Catholicism in Kilmore and in Ulster generally experienced a remarkable revival.[79] This reform continued throughout the 1620s and 1630s and it got new impetus in Kilmore with the appointment of Bishop Hugh O'Reilly in 1625 and Bishop Eugene MacSweeney in 1628.

From the early 1590s onwards, due to the difficult situation prevailing in Ireland, the Vatican policy was to appoint vicars-apostolic rather than bishops to vacant dioceses.[80] James Plunkett, the vicar-apostolic for Meath diocese, held a similar position in the diocese of Kilmore for a period *c.*1613.[81] He was said to be 'ellected of Kilmore' and to live by 'private tyethes and his function'.[82] Plunkett obviously had considerable contact with some Kilmore priests because when he was being processed by Rome as a candidate for the bishopric of Kildare in 1623 two

78.   There is general acceptance among historians that the Reformation failed in Ireland, though there is much less consensus about when this failure occurred. For a recent (2016) treatment of the topic see Henry A. Jefferies, 'Why the Reformation failed in Ireland', pp 151–70.
79.   Brian Mac Cuarta, 'The Catholic Church in Ulster under the plantation, 1609–42' in Ó Ciardha & Ó Siochrú (eds), *The plantation of Ulster, ideology and practice*, p. 124.
80.   Corish, The *Catholic Community*, p. 19; idem, *The Irish Catholic experience*, p. 100; Mac Cuarta, *Catholic revival in the north of Ireland*, p. 76.
81.   O'Connell, *The diocese of Kilmore*, pp 395–6; Mac Cuarta, 'Catholic revival in Kilmore', p. 151.
82.   TCD, MS 567, f. 36r; Brian Mac Cuarta, 'Irish Government lists of Catholic personnel, *c.*1613' in *Arch. Hib.*, lxvii (2015), p. 82.

Figure 9.2: Canon Hugh Brady, a native of Castletara, who was rector of Louvain University in the 1660s. (*Courtesy of the National Gallery of Ireland.*)

Kilmore priests, Thady Lynch and Donald Gavan, were among the witnesses testifying in his favour.[83] Donald Gavan, who was sub deacon of the diocese of Kilmore and about thirty-five years old, said that he had known Plunkett in the diocese of Meath and in the houses of the nobility there for the previous ten years and that he saw him celebrate Mass and heard him preach in a field to a great number of Catholics who had gathered there to hear him. Thady Lynch, who was about thirty years old, said that he knew Robert Plunkett and Elizabeth Nugent, the parents of James Plunkett, that they were 'very generous, noble and catholic parents' and he added that, at James Plunkett's direction, he had carried out pastoral work in the diocese of Meath in 1622.[84]

83.   APF, *Processus Datariae*, vol. ii, ff. 146v-149r, 149r-151v; The Franciscan Fathers (eds), *Father Luke Wadding commemorative volume* (Dublin, 1957), pp 528–9.
84.   Ibid.

Lynch states that Plunkett was vicar-apostolic[85] in Meath, though neither he nor Donald Gavan make any reference to him being vicar-apostolic or vicar-general in Kilmore.[86] Instead, the picture which emerges from the evidence of Thady Lynch and Donald Gavan is that they, and perhaps other priests from Kilmore, benefitted from the protection and hospitality of some of the Old English Catholic families of Meath and that James Plunkett was their mentor while they were there.

Sometime about the year 1616, in a move which may have been initiated by the remnants of a cathedral chapter, Maurice Gargan was appointed vicar-general of the diocese.[87] The MacGargans or Gargans had been chieftains of the barony of Clankee and owned considerable territory around Moybolgue. They were also a clerical family, supplying many priests to the parishes of Moybolgue/Kilmainhamwood and Mullagh in the diocese of Kilmore.[88] A horizontal gravestone in Moybolgue cemetery depicts a cleric wearing vestments, cross, cincture, head-dress (not a mitre) and shoes, with his right arm raised in blessing and left hand clutching a chalice. According to local tradition a Bishop Gargan is buried there. However, it seems more likely that it is the burial place of a parish priest of Moybolgue/Kilmainhamwood and it is possible that it is the burial place of Maurice Gargan, who was vicar general of Kilmore at a time when the diocese was without a Catholic bishop.[89] See Figure 9.1.

Maurice Gargan may not have been the only 'arch-priest' in the diocese *c*.1620 because when Thomas Moigne gave his detailed report

---

85.   A vicar-apostolic is someone appointed by Rome to administer a diocese when it becomes vacant.

86.   James Plunkett was living with his cousin Count Plunkett and he was described as an 'archpriest' and living near Ross on the Westmeath/Longford border *c*.1613. See 'A Note on divers priestes and fryers who are for the most part in and near the borders of Westmeath' in www.ucc.ie/celt/published/T100077.html (accessed 15 February 2015), p. 15; Mac Cuarta, 'Irish Government lists of Catholic personnel, *c*.1613', p. 95.

87.   TCD, MS 550, pp 142–3.w

88.   Patrick MacGargan was parish priest of Kilmainhamwood and Moybolgue in 1542 and he was succeeded by Philip Roe MacGargan. Four members of the Gargan family were parish priests in Mullagh in the 1600s. See MacKiernan, *Diocese of Kilmore*, pp 99, 127. Philip Gargan was secretary to Archbishop Hugh O'Reilly in 1634. See Moran (ed.), *Spic. Ossor.*, i, pp 197; Harold O'Sullivan, 'The Franciscans in Dundalk' in *Seanchas Ard Mhacha*, iv (1960–1), p. 46. In 1664 Donagh Gergan, dean of the [Kilmore] cathedral for about 36 years, 'an exemplary and zealous man, but otherwise of mediocre gifts' was listed among possible candidates for a bishopric. See, APF, *Fondo di Vienna*, ff. 192r-195v; Benignus Millett, 'Calendar of Irish material in vols 12 and 13 (ff. 1–200) of *Fondo di Vienna* in Propaganda archives' in *Coll. Hib.*, xxiv (1982), p. 76. John Gargan spent five years in France where he studied philosophy and rhetoric in Angers before entering the Irish College in Rome in 1697. See oath of John Gargan in *Collegium Hibernorum De Urbe, an early manuscript account of the Irish College, Rome 1628–1678* (Rome, 2003), p. 219; Matteo Binasco and Vera Orschel, 'Prosopography of Irish students admitted to the Irish College, Rome, 1628–1798' in *Arch. Hib.* lxvi (2013), p. 48.

89.   See Philip O'Connell, 'Moybolge and its ancient church' in *Breffny Antiquarian journal*, ii, 2 (1924), p. 218.

on the situation in the dioceses of Kilmore and Ardagh in 1622 he stated that 'jurisdiction is likewise exercised by Murto McGearga, Brian McIcorbe, John Óge McIngawna, Sorne McOliff, Ffiall O'Mulconra and others, being vicar-generals and commissaries established by the pope's authority'.[90] It appears that Maurice Gargan did not study on the continent and may have been taught by the Franciscans in Cavan or Dundalk, and being resident in the diocese, was well positioned to give leadership and to promote the Counter-Reformation in Kilmore. Maurice Gargan was vicar-general at a time when greater tolerance was being shown to Catholics, with the result that he was able to invite roving bands of Jesuit and Franciscan missionaries into the diocese and then give them his full support when they arrived.

During the period 1607 to 1625, when there was no Catholic bishop of Kilmore, the ecclesiastical landscape of the diocese changed considerably with the arrival of plantation settlers first in Cavan and later in Leitrim. Besides, there was then, for the first time, a resident Protestant bishop in the diocese and from 1612 onwards Church of Ireland clergy were being appointed to the parishes. The Catholic priests who had previously served in the parishes were being displaced and dispossessed, losing the tithes they had been receiving and the churches they had been using to the clergy of the Established Church. Besides, the diocese had virtually no resident Old English Catholic families such as those in the south and the east of the country who were supporting impoverished priests and sponsoring young men in the newly established seminaries on the continent. Nevertheless, a small number of men from the diocese such as Bernard O Gowan did study on the continent in the early 1600s. He studied the humanities for two years in Paris and three in Aix, before going on to study philosophy in Bordeaux and then, at the age of twenty-five, entered the seminary of Salamanca on 22 February 1607.[91] However, he was one of a very small number of Kilmore men who went to continental seminaries at this time and there is no record of him returning to Ireland or ever ministering in the diocese of Kilmore.

Hugh Brady was another continentally-trained Kilmore priest who did not return to Ireland. He was born in Castletara parish (*ex oppido Bellehais, in comitatu Cavaniensi Hibernus*) c.1600 and enrolled in the university of Louvain in 1620. He was registered as a pauper and his progress was slow, only qualifying with a bachelor of law in 1635.[92] Two years later, on 2 September 1637, having received a scholarship

90.   TCD, MS 550, pp 142–3, 206.
91.   Denis J. O'Doherty, 'Students of the Irish College Salamanca (1595–1619)' in *Arch. Hib.*, ii (1913), p. 21.
92.   Anon., 'Very Rev, Hugh Canon Brady' in *Breifny Antiquarian Journal*, i, 3 (1922), pp 336–7.

from the archbishop of Malines, he entered the Irish Pastoral College[93] in Louvain and persisted, against the wishes of the archbishop and the college, in doing further studies in law rather than in theology. Besides, he did not observe good discipline, failing to take the oath to return to the Irish mission and developing the reputation of being a heavy drinker. However, he rallied, persisted in his studies, became a doctor of law and was ordained a priest by the bishop of Antwerp on 23 February 1641. After ordination he taught law in the University of Louvain and was later rector of the university for two short periods - from February to August 1661 and from August 1663 to February 1664. (See Fig. 9.2). He was also president of the College of St Anne from 1643 until 1669. He was described as 'one of the most brilliant professors of law' in Louvain and was a vigorous opponent of Jansenism.[94] He died in Louvain on 14 October 1669.[95] Cornelius Macgraurike, another Kilmore priest, is also on the Antwerp ordination-register for 1641, though there is no evidence that he returned to Ireland.[96] Others such as Malachy Tiernan, the son of Magonus and Catherine Tiernan and a native of Kilmore diocese who was ordained in Rome in 1630 *ad titulum missionis in Hibernia*, may have returned to work in the diocese.[97] However, the problems persisted for the impoverished diocese of Kilmore. It had only a scattering of students in continental seminaries in the early decades of the 1600s and at least some of these were either unwilling or unable to return to work in the diocese after ordination.[98]

Franciscan Missions in 1614 and 1623

The Franciscan friars were much better equipped than the diocesan priests to cope with the changed world of the early 1600s. They had the benefit of the Observant reform within their Order and, with the backing of a growing network of seminaries on the continent and a printing press in Louvain, they promoted the Counter Reformation in Kilmore and throughout the country. Tyrlogh M'Crodyn, a Franciscan friar, was busy preaching to large crowds of laity and clergy in Ulster in the autumn of 1613. He deprived some priests of their benefices,

93.   The Irish Pastoral College was established in 1623. Mary Ann Lyons, 'St Anthony's College, Louvain' in Raymond Gillespie & Ruairi Ó hUiginn (eds), *Irish Europe 1600–1650* (Dublin,
2013), p. 23.
94.   Éamonn Ó Ciardha, 'Hugh Brady' in *DIB*, i, p. 767.
95.   For Hugh Brady, see Jeroen Nilis, 'Irish students at Leuven University, 1548–1797' in *Arch.
Hib*. lx (2006–07), pp 51–2; MacKiernan, *Diocese of Kilmore*, p. 152; APF, Acta 14, ff. 50, 51.
96.   Jeroen Nilis, 'The Irish College Antwerp' in *Clogher Record*, xv, 3 (1996), p. 50.
97.   Hugh Fenning, 'Irishmen ordained at Rome, 1572–1697' in *Arch. Hib*., lix (2005), p. 13.
98.   For an explanation as to why continentally-trained priests did not return to Ireland see L.W.B.
Brockliss, 'The Irish colleges on the Continent and the creation of an educated clergy' in Thomas
O'Connor & Mary Ann Lyons (eds), *The Ulster Earls and Baroque Europe* (Dublin, 2010), p. 163.

'some for keeping women, others for presuming to exercise the function of priest, who had not been properly called, and for having more benefice than one'.[99] The provincial synod, which was presided over by David Rothe and held at Drogheda in 1614, drew up regulations for promoting the Counter-Reformation in the province of Ulster and the Franciscans were to play an important role in trying to impose these regulations in the diocese of Kilmore.[100] The Franciscans had managed to maintain a presence near to Cavan town and in 1616 John Jeffery, was their guardian.[101] He was a noted preacher and, no doubt, he and the other Franciscans based in Cavan, continued their preaching and questing rounds within a wide radius of Cavan town and when doing so urged their listeners to adhere to their traditional beliefs and to have no truck with the Established Church. However, it was probably the missions given by roving bands of Louvain-trained friars that had the greatest impact in the diocese at this time. This band of approximately seven friars went on a Lenten tour of south Ulster in 1614 and, along with some diocesan priests, held several missions in County Cavan in the second half of February of that year.[102] Sir Robert Jacob, writing from Cavan on 28 February 1614, stated that:

> This last week there were six or seven Popish priests in this county of Cavan, who brought with them from beyond the seas a cross which they say is of that very cross whereupon Christ was crucified. There came flocking unto them 3 or 4,000 people at a time and some gave sixpence, some more, some less; but hearing of our coming in the circuit they are gone away and mean to go their circuit before us, possessing the people that Tyrone [O,Neill] will be here this summer with all the power the Pope and the King of Spain can make, and encouraging them to persevere in their religion and, when the forces shall be landed to adventure their lives for their religion and to rebel against his Majesty. But we have done our best endeavours to stop their proceedings, by sending directions

---

99.   *CSPI*, 1611–1614, p. 430.
100.   Alison Forrestal, *Catholic Synods in Ireland, 1600–1690* (Dublin, 1998), pp 36, 195; Corish, *The Irish Catholic experience*, p. 101.
101.   *Brevis synopsis*, p. 155; Mac Cuarta, 'Catholic revival in Kilmore diocese', p. 154; Jennings, *Wadding papers 1614–38*, pp 61–2.
102.   Mac Cuarta, 'Catholic revival in Kilmore', pp 154–5.

privately to all the Sheriffs in Ulster for apprehending of them, and it is very likely we shall take them.[103]

Despite the warrants for their arrests the friars managed to evade the sheriffs. Nine years later, at the beginning of October 1623, another roving band of Franciscan friars visited Cavan:

> There was an assembly of twelve friars in their robes at the shire town of the Cavan, and to attend them at least 2,000 people assembled together to the terror of the poor English that dwelt in those parts.[104]

Captain Arthur Forbes, from Newtown Forbes, reported that up to three thousand 'from divers corners and divers countries of the Kingdom' had gathered in Cavan to hear the Franciscans where they had 'their solemn masses and public preachings, things heretofore never heard of'.[105] He had heard rumours that they also planned to visit his parish church in County Longford and he added 'if they did … if God would give him grace he should make the antiphonie of their mass be sung with [the] sound of musket'.[106] It would appear that some of the diocesan priests also attended this 'mission' in Cavan as another account reported that 'a great multitude of people with priests and friars' attended it.[107] The number of people, both laity and clergy, stated to have gathered in Cavan may have been exaggerated. Nevertheless, the large assemblies and fact that the friars wore their robes in public are an indication of the increased tolerance experienced by Catholics from 1620 onwards and are also a sign that the Counter- Reformation revival was making progress in the diocese. By this time the Lough Derg pilgrimage site was also undergoing a revival and no doubt pilgrims from the diocese of Kilmore were among the increasing numbers going there.[108]

103.   Bickley (ed.), *Report on the manuscripts of the late Reginald Hastings*, iv, pp 14–15. In the same letter Robert Jacob recommended that the king take 'a severe course' against all 'priests and the relievers of them.' Ibid., p. 15; Raymond Gillespie, 'Popular and unpopular religion: a view from early modern Ireland' in J.S. Donnelly and Kerry Miller (eds), *Irish popular culture 1650–1850* (Dublin, 1999), p. 40.
104.   *CSPI, 1615–25*, p. 432.
105.   Ibid., p. 433. For Sir Hugh Culme's report on these events see TNA, SP 63/237, f. 124.
106.   *CSPI, 1615–25*, p. 433.
107.   Ibid., p. 432.
108.   Bernadette Cunningham & Raymond Gillespie, 'The Lough Derg pilgrimage in the age of the Counter-Reformation' in *Éire-Ireland*, 39: 3 & 4 (2004), 167–79, cited in Mac Cuarta, 'Catholic revival in Kilmore', p. 156.

Jesuit Missions in 1616 and 1621

The Society of Jesus, which was formally approved in 1540 and had Ignatius of Loyola as its first superior general, was to the forefront in promoting the Counter-Reformation throughout Europe. Less than two years after the Society was approved by Pope Paul III, two Jesuits were sent on a mission to Ireland with instructions, to admonish the clergy of all ranks and to urge them to live better lives.[109] This mission, which was confined to the north of Ulster and only lasted five weeks, had a limited impact. However, through the leadership of David Wolfe[110] - a Limerick diocesan priest who became a Jesuit in 1554 and papal commissary to Ireland in 1560 - the Jesuit role in promoting Tridentine discipline in Ireland became more prominent. Although the young men from Ireland who joined the Jesuits tended to come from Old English families from the south and east of the country and the Society had little affinity with the diocese of Kilmore yet, possibly at the request of Maurice Gargan, the Jesuits ventured on a mission into the counties of Longford and Leitrim in 1616. This initiative was intended to support the claims of native landowners who feared that they would lose their lands in the plantation of Leitrim which was still in the planning stage. They had hoped to return to the same counties in 1617 but decided not to - calculating that it was too dangerous both for themselves and their hosts.[111]

The situation was more relaxed in the autumn of 1621 when two Jesuit preachers moved into the south-east of County Cavan from neighbouring Meath and began a missionary tour among the well-disposed Old English recusant families.[112] The weather was bad and the harvest late when they moved north into the baronies of Clankee and Tullygarvey where the English and Scottish landowners and their tenants were firmly established. This roving mission, which lasted three weeks, made a big impact with people travelling great distances and bringing their sick to meet the Jesuits. The Jesuit preachers were assisted by between six and ten local priests who helped with confessions in the morning, noon and evening. This was followed by Mass at which many people received Communion. The reputation of the missionaries soared when an invalided man's condition improved after confession and Holy Communion and was able to walk the next day with the aid of a stick.

---

109. Fergus O'Donoghue, 'The Jesuits come to Ireland' in *Studies*, lxxx, 317 (Spring, 1991), pp 16–17.
110. *DIB*, ix, pp 1016–8.
111. IJA, Jesuit annual letter 1617; Mac Cuarta, 'Catholic revival in Kilmore', p. 156.
112. For what follows see Mac Cuarta, 'Catholic revival in Kilmore', pp 152, 156–7.

This Jesuit mission was aimed at the native Irish lay-people who, because of the turbulent times they were living in, had neglected to attend the sacraments as required by the Council of Trent.

The Jesuit mission was also aimed at the diocesan clergy who, for the most part, lacked seminary training and were generally pre-Tridentine in their thinking. Some of them, belonging to clerical lineage families, were the sons of priests and had children themselves. This clash between the strict clerical discipline required by the Counter-Reformation Church and the lax older ways of some of the clergy came to a head during the Jesuit mission of 1621 when it was discovered that one of the local priests assisting the missionaries had been living with a women for two years. The missionaries admonished the cleric, and he, following public penance, promised to dismiss her and live a celibate life. However, the woman continued to live nearby and serve as his housekeeper, and it took a further intervention by the missionaries, who had the backing of the vicar-general of the diocese, to separate them.[113] Before the missionaries left Cavan they met with Maurice Gargan, the vicar-general of the diocese, and some of the other priests, to impress on them the need for clerical reform and the importance of regular attendance of the laity at the sacraments.[114]

For a period during the early 1600s the lines between the Established Church and the Roman Catholic Church in the diocese were somewhat blurred. This blurring of lines was obvious when some of the native Irish who became Protestant clergymen continued to celebrate the liturgies in the traditional way or with the minimum of changes and in doing so hindered rather than helped the spread of the state church. Besides, some of the lay people of the diocese who remained Catholic at heart attended Protestant services in order to avoid having to pay the recusant fines. During the late 1610s and early 1620s, largely due to the efforts of Maurice Gargan and the missions carried out by roving bands of Franciscans and Jesuits, these lines became clearly drawn once more. There were increasing worries among the settlers that the native Irish were becoming more confident in their Catholicism and in March 1624, 'Benedick Cotnam of Derevoney in the parish of Dromlayn [Drumlane]' gave evidence that the Irish in Leitrim were saying that the Catholic earl of Westmeath (Richard Nugent) should

113.   The Franciscan missionaries were also challenging the clergy throughout Ulster to live celibate lives. See Mac Cuarta, 'The Catholic Church in Ulster under the plantation', p. 125.
114.   Jesuit annual letter, Ireland, 1621–2, Archivium Romanum Societatis Iesu, Rome, Anglia vol. 41, ff. 148r-v, cited in Mac Cuarta, 'Catholic revival in Kilmore', p. 152. See forthcoming publication, Vera Moynes (ed.), *Irish Jesuit annual letters 1604–1674* (Dublin, 2017). My thanks to Brian Mac Cuarta for this information.

Figure 9.3: Chalice of Bishop Hugh O'Reilly (1628) showing some of the detail on the base of the chalice.

be king of Ireland.[115] Sir Charles Coote, the president of Connacht, was so concerned about this situation that he took statements from Geoffrey Burnbury and James Nangle at Jamestown in County Leitrim on 2 April 1625. Both men gave evidence that the 'priests in the latter end of their mass did usually pray for … Philippum Regem nostris' - the Catholic king of Spain.[116]

The Counter-Reformation in the diocese was further boosted by continentally-trained priests, though there is no evidence that either Thady Lynch or Donald Gavan who were in Rome in 1623, ever returned to minister in the diocese. However, Thomas MacKiernan, who had studied in the Irish college in Seville, returned to Ireland and became dean of Kilmore in 1624.[117] And even though there was still only a trickle of seminary-trained priests returning to the diocese the very fact that such appointments were being made is sign that the revival of Catholicism in the diocese was already underway. The appointment of a Catholic bishop to the diocese in 1625, after an eighteen-year gap, is further proof of that revival.

Hugh O'Reilly

From about 1620 onwards Roman policy was changing, preferring to appoint bishops rather than vicars-apostolic to the Irish dioceses. This policy continued and the appointments to vacant Sees were speeded up following the establishment of the Congregation of Propaganda Fide in Rome in 1622. The diocese of Kilmore had lacked leadership for quarter of a century before Hugh O'Reilly was nominated bishop at a consistory meeting in Rome on 21 May 1625. Three other bishops, Boetius Egan (Elphin), Edmund Dungan (Down and Connor) and John O'Cullenan (Raphoe) were also nominated on the same day.[118] The appointments took effect three weeks later on 9 June 1625, however, it was not until late July the following year that Hugh O'Reilly, Edmund Dungan and Boetius Egan were ordained bishops in St Peter's church, Drogheda, by Thomas Fleming, the archbishop of Dublin.[119] Hugh O'Reilly had been

---

115.   *CSPI, 1615–25*, p. 477.
116.   *CSPI, 1625–32*, pp 14–15. Charles Coote was a much feared man. See, Tait, 'The just vengeance of God', pp 141–4; Raymond Gillespie, *Devoted people: belief and religion in early modern Ireland* (Manchester, 1997), pp 1, 88; *DIB*, ii, pp 827–8; Victor Treadwell, *Buckingham and Ireland 1616–1628*, (Dublin, 1998), pp 200–02.
117.   MacKiernan, *Diocese of Kilmore*, p. 152; Mac Cuarta, 'Catholic revival in Kilmore', p. 153; this is probably the same Thomas MacKiernan who in 1640, became the Franciscan guardian of Dundalk friary. See O'Sullivan, 'The Franciscans in Dundalk', pp 58–9.
118.   APF, *Acta Consistorialia*, vol. 2889, f. 14r.
119.   Brady, *The Episcopal succession*, p. 282. For Hugh O'Reilly see Séamus P. Ó Mórdha, 'Hugh O'Reilly (1581?-1653): A reforming primate' in *Bréifne*, iv, 13 (1970), pp 1–42; idem, 'Hugh O'Reilly (1581?-1653): A reforming primate' in *Bréifne*, iv, 15 (1972), pp 345–69; O'Connell, *The diocese of Kilmore*, pp 405–21; McCarthy, *Collections on Irish church history*, pp 27–9, 33–48; Lynch, *De Praesulibus*, pp 142–4; *DIB*, vii, pp 854–5.

carrying out administrative work in the diocese before his appointment and was, it appears, vicar-apostolic of Kilmore for a time before being appointed bishop although there is no Vatican record of his appointment to that position.[120] Either before he was appointed bishop or else in the period after his appointment and before consecration, he had a bronze seal made which carried the O'Reilly arms surmounted by a coronet and 'HVGO . RELLIVS . KILMOREN . VIC . APOST' inscribed around the verge of the seal.[121] On 27 July 1626, the *episcopus electus Kilmorensis* and other northern clergy signed a testimonial letter refuting certain allegations that had been made against the archbishop of Dublin.[122] Chances are that they were all gathered at Drogheda for Hugh O'Reilly's consecration and that of Edmund Dungan and Boetius Egan.

Hugh O'Reilly was born *c.*1581 to Maelmórdha and Mór O'Reilly in the townland of Aghaweeley Lower in the parish of Ballintemple.[123] He was educated in the diocese of Kilmore, most likely by the Cavan-based Franciscans even though by that time they had lost their friary in Cavan town.[124] The Franciscan Observants, who were to the fore-front in promoting the Counter-Reformation, appear to have had a lasting influence on him.[125] He was ordained in Ireland before travelling to Rouen to study philosophy and later to Paris and Rome to study theology. Hugh MacCaughwell, a native of Down and the definitor general of the Franciscan Order, stated in 1625 that Hugh O'Reilly was 'not a doctor in theology … but he has sufficient knowledge to teach others'.[126] It seems likely that O'Reilly taught in the Franciscan *friary* in Cavan as a young priest. The Franciscan Bonaventure Magennis, a native of County Down and later to

120.   Lynch, *De Praesulibus Hiberniae*, i, p. 143; Ó Mórdha, 'Hugh O'Reilly a reforming primate', p. 16.
121.   This seal was found in the parish of Kilmore *c.*1860. See *The Journal of the Kilkenny and South-East of Ireland archaeological society*, iii, 2 (1861), p. 377; *The Irish Examiner*, 23 November 1863.
122.   Jennings, *Wadding papers*, pp 143–4; Moran, *History of the Catholic archbishops of Dublin*, pp 340–1.
123.   MacKiernan, *Diocese of Kilmore*, p. 14. His family lands in Ballintemple were confiscated during the plantation of the county and the family was granted poorer land in the barony of Tullyhaw. See *Calendar of Irish patent rolls of James I*, p. 145.
124.   Moran (ed.), *Spic. Ossor.*, i, p. 171.
125.   Hugh O'Reilly's respect for the Franciscans was obvious throughout his life. In 1631, as archbishop of Armagh, he wrote to Rome stating that the Order of Canons Regular of St Augustine was almost dead throughout Ireland and asked that Franciscans 'the most numerous among our regulars and best suited to rough places' be given spiritual charge of St Patrick's Purgatory on Lough Derg. See John Ryan, 'St Patrick's Purgatory', in *Studies*, xxi, 83 (Sept.1932), p. 458; Historical Manuscripts Commission, Franciscan MSS, p. 37.
126.   APF, *Processus Datariae*, vol. iv, ff. 299r-304r; *Father Luke Wadding commemorative volume*, p. 538. Hugh MacCaughwell was consecrated archbishop of Armagh in Rome on 7 June 1626 and died there on 22 September of that year as he was preparing to return to Ireland. He is buried in St Isidore's in Rome. McCarthy, *Collections on Irish church history*, pp 24–5.

become the bishop of Down and Connor, gave evidence in 1628 that 'when he was at home in Kilmore, he studied under O'Reilly ... [who] taught him *litteras humaniores*' and he added 'he is held to be a good theologian and canonist'.[127] Hugh O'Reilly's first language was Irish and he had fluent Latin, although his English was weak.[128] Decades later Archbishop Oliver Plunkett stated that Hugh O'Reilly was 'a man well versed in canon law'.[129] He was a reforming bishop and a good administrator who knew his diocese and resided in it. He spoke the language of the people and had the support of his kinship group, living close to them in the parish of Kilmore for the remainder of his life.[130]

When Bishop Hugh O'Reilly returned to live in the diocese of Kilmore in July 1626 there was, for the first time, a resident Catholic and Protestant bishop in the diocese. They were both living within a few miles of each other in the parish of Kilmore, with the now elderly Thomas Moigne occupying the bishop's house and cathedral and receiving the bishop's revenues raised in the diocese. On becoming bishop, Hugh O'Reilly discovered that there was 'much confusion and deviation from ecclesiastical discipline [*pleraque confusa et a disciplina Ecclesiastica deviantia repperi*]' in the diocese.[131] In order to tackle the indiscipline he ordained 'none save suitable subjects to the priesthood' that is only 'those suitable or useful or highly necessary to the country'. He ordered his clergy 'to wear becoming dress and to refrain absolutely from improper conversation and illicit acts' and any priests found to be conducting themselves otherwise, he deprived of all benefices, sometimes even banishing them from the diocese.[132]

Throughout Ulster there were attempts in the 1620s to improve public liturgies and to erect purpose-built Mass-houses.[133] Hugh O'Reilly was unhappy that the 'Holy Sacrifice of the Mass was being celebrated either in the open air or in [other] unsuitable places' and he ordered that *domos*

---

127. APF, *Processus Datariae*, vol. vii, ff. 211r-214r; *Father Luke Wadding commemorative volume*, p. 545. Bonaventure Magennis's grandmother was Annabella O'Reilly and it appears that he stayed with his relations in Bréifne and was educated by the Cavan Franciscans; Ó Mórdha, 'Hugh O'Reilly (1581?-1653): A reforming primate', p. 13; Ó Cléirigh, *Aodh Mac Aingil agus an Scoil Nua-Ghaeilge i Lobháin*, p. 66.
128. Ó Mórdha, 'Hugh O'Reilly (1581?-1653): A reforming primate ', p. 13.
129. Oliver Plunkett, *Jus Primatiale, The ancient right and preheminency of the see of Armagh* (London, 1672), pp 30–1.
130. It is possible that Hugh O'Reilly lived on Trinity island under the protection of Maol Mórdha Mac Phillip O'Reilly. It was there that he died *c*.1653. Carney (ed.), *A genealogical history of the O'Reillys*, p. 108; TCD MS 833, f. 106r.
131. J. Hagan (ed.), 'Relationes Status' in *Arch.Hib.* v (1916), pp 80–1 with a translation in O'Connell, *The diocese of Kilmore*, pp 406–9.
132. Ibid.
133. Mac Cuarta, *Catholic revival in the north of Ireland*, pp 115–6.

ecclesiasticos, Mass houses or neat oratories be erected in every parish.[134] Besides, he wanted every parish priest to buy and maintain either a gold or silver chalice and also to have clean altar cloths and vestments for the celebration of the sacraments. Hugh O'Reilly gave good example by commissioning a hexagonal-based silver chalice in the early months of 1628, a short time before he was appointed archbishop of Armagh. (See Fig. 9.3). The inscription on the chalice, which reads *Hugo Relly Killmorensis ep[iscopu]s in honorem pretiosi sanguinis Xti me fieri facit 1628*, tells us that his motivation in ordering the chalice for himself, and pre-scribing other priests to do the same, was to give due honour to the precious blood of Christ.[135] He also stipulated that the blessed oils be re-newed each Holy Thursday and that all the sacraments be administered with proper decorum. In the absence of a diocesan bishop, the sacrament of confirmation had been neglected for many years and he described how he had administered confirmation in the diocese to 'fifteen hundred people [both adults and children] a day throughout a period of three entire weeks'.[136]

He had some success with his reforms and had an adequate supply of both priests and chapels because William Bedell, having been the Church of Ireland bishop of the diocese for approximately six months, wrote on 1 April 1630, that 'every parish hath its priests; and some two or three a-piece, and so their mass-houses also; and in some places mass is said in the churches'.[137] Obviously the seizing of the parish churches by the Estab-lished Church was a gradual process because in a letter to James Ussher, written on 18 September 1630, William Bedell described how he had asked 'to be excused from going in person to take possession of the Mass-houses', perhaps because he found the process distasteful.[138] There is no evidence, archaeological or otherwise, that the native Irish began the wide-spread building of stone chapels during the episcopate of Hugh O'Reilly. What seems more likely is that they continued to use the chapels of ease and the small oratories on the lake islands for the celebration of the sacraments.[139] In some parishes, where there was neither a Protestant population nor a resident Church of Ireland minister, they continued to use the parish

134. O'Connell, *The diocese of Kilmore*, pp 406–9.
135. This chalice has survived and is held in Cavan cathedral. See J.J. O'Reilly, *The history of Bréifne O'Reilly* (New York, 1975), p. 141.
136. Hagan (ed.), 'Relationes Status', p. 81.
137. Bedell to Laud, 1 April 1630, in Mant, *History of the Church of Ireland*, p. 436.
138. Boran (ed.), *The correspondence of James Ussher*, ii, p. 37.
139. It is possible that the parish church of Drung, a substantial stone-walled church measur-ing 20m x 8m, may have been built at this time. See Davies, 'The churches of County Cavan', p. 113. The ruins of Callowhill church near Derrylin may also date from the early seventeenth-century. Foley & McHugh, *An archaeological survey of County Fermanagh*, i, 2, p. 699.

church as before. Bishop Bedell's evidence that there were Mass houses in every parish would point towards simple wooden structures being erected in the parishes where the Catholic community had neither church nor chapel.[140] Some accommodation was reached at local level which allowed both Catholics and Protestants to be buried in the cemeteries adjoining the parish churches.

One of the greatest obstacles to the reform of the Catholic Church at this time was the fact that the majority of the diocesan priests were poorly educated and had not had the benefit of seminary training. By the time that Hugh O'Reilly was translated to Armagh considerable progress had been made in providing educational facilities within the diocese. It was reported *c.*1630 that there was a school in the diocese of Kilmore:

> Which is nothing else but a seminary and nursery of priests, the school-master being an Irishman, conformable for fashion, and teaches above 100 scholars, the most part of them are come to perfect mans age who he instructs in logic and philosophy (which is a great hinderance to God's glory and to Trinity College Dublin) and not one of them go to [the Established] church.[141]

This junior seminary type school and the education provided by the Franciscans in Leitrim and Cavan helped prepare young men for their further education in the continental seminaries.

Another issue Hugh O'Reilly needed to tackle was the lax approach to marriage in the diocese. Clandestine marriages and divorces - from which 'very many scandals and disorders were arising'- were commonplace. In order to resolve this unsatisfactory situation the bishop insisted on marriage banns being announced before weddings took place and he ordered an end to all divorces. He also claimed to have settled lawsuits and quarrels of the nobles, clergy and people 'to the great benefit, peace and quietness of the country'.[142] His reform policies were clearly based on the decrees of the Council of Trent which emphasised the importance of having a good bishop resident and active in the diocese, a good priest resident and active in the parish and the Eucharist and other sacraments being celebrated in a suitable place and in an appropriate way in each

140.   Some of these may have been a simple scathlán where the altar alone was covered.
141.   TCD, MS 1188, f. 12v; Aidan Clarke, *The Old English in Ireland*, 1625–42 (Dublin, 2000), pp 121–2.
142.   Hagan (ed.), *'Relationes Status'*, p. 81.

parish. Hugh O'Reilly was bishop of Kilmore for only three years when, on 21 August 1628, he was appointed archbishop of Armagh.[143] However, in those few years he had done much to restore discipline and morale among the Catholics of the diocese and established a network of priests and Mass-houses to meet their pastoral needs.

'Matthew O'Queely',[144] who was a priest of the diocese of Killaloe and one of the witnesses recommending Hugh O'Reilly for Armagh, stated that he had known O'Reilly for the past ten years in Ireland and that they had been students together in Paris where O'Reilly studied theology while he himself was studying philosophy. Queely described how 'O'Reilly has held ordinations in Kilmore diocese and administered confirmation, and has said Mass in private houses and sometimes in the woods' and went on to say that he considers O'Reilly to be a 'learned, prudent and zealous bishop, and worthy to be transferred to Armagh'.[145] In 1626, the then 'earl' of Tyrone wrote to Propaganda Fide urging the cardinals to appoint a native of Ulster to the vacant See of Armagh. Hugh O'Reilly was his second choice for the position, his first being the Franciscan, Robert Chamberlain. In recommending O'Reilly he stated that he was 'of ripe age, good life, well versed in both civil and canon law and theology and acceptable to the clergy, nobles and people of Armagh'.[146] Following his translation to Armagh, Hugh O'Reilly was replaced in Kilmore by Eugene MacSweeney, a priest of the diocese of Raphoe who had studied along with him in Paris. By this time the Catholic revival was well underway in the diocese and in the country. On 20 December 1629, Sir Thomas Dutton summarised the situation when he wrote to the king stating that 'except for the northern settlements, the whole of Ireland is now more addicted to Popery than it was in the time of Queen Elizabeth'.[147]

The years 1628 and 1629 were transitional years for the diocese of Kilmore. On 1 January 1629, only a few months after Hugh O'Reilly was appointed archbishop of Armagh and Eugene Mac Sweeney was nominated as his successor in Kilmore, Thomas Moigne, the Church of Ireland bishop of the diocese, died of apoplexy while on a visit to Dublin. He was buried there two days later, in St Patrick's Church.[148]

---

143. Vatican Library, MSS, *Barberini Latini*, 2933, ff. lvi(v)-lvii(r).
144. Malachy O'Queally later became archbishop of Tuam.
145. APF, *Processus Datariae*, vii, ff. 214r-216v; *Father Luke Wadding commemorative volume*, p. 546.
146. *Report on Franciscan manuscripts preserved at the convent, Merchant's Quay* (Dublin, 1906), pp 96–7.
147. *CSPI, 1625–32*, p. 498.
148. Harris (ed.), *The whole works of Sir James Ware*, p. 231.

By the time of his death there were two parallel networks of clergy in the diocese, one with the backing of the law and the other with the overwhelming support of the native Irish. A diocese which had struggled throughout the medieval period to support one set of clergy was now being asked to support two. The last years of Moigne's episcopacy had seen a strong Catholic revival and also growing animosity among the native Irish towards the Established Church which seemed more intent on emptying their purses than winning their hearts. The Church of Ireland ministers, many of whom were pluralists, collected the tithes from people who got no benefit in return and the persistence of the chancellor in collecting recusant fines merely exacerbated the problem. By the end of the 1620s the Protestant Reformation had already failed in the diocese and in the country. Robert Draper and Thomas Moigne had both resided in Kilmore and made honest attempts to establish the state church on a solid footing in the diocese. The former had focussed on establishing a network of native Irish clergy while the latter appointed mostly English ones. Neither strategy had much success. Thomas Moigne's successor, William Bedell, would bring a different attitude and adopt a novel approach.

Chapter 10

Reforms and Resistance: 1629–1641

On 16 April 1629 King Charles I wrote to the lord deputy of Ireland ordering him to 'appoint William Bedle, B.D., Provost of Trinity College near Dublin, to the vacant bishoprics of Kilmore and Ardagh'.[1] William Bedell was formally appointed on 20 May 1629 although it was not until 13 September that he was consecrated bishop. This new post meant that he left Dublin, where he had been living for the previous two years, and went to live in the rural parish of Kilmore just west of Cavan town. This move was a cultural shock for the Essex-born, erudite clergyman who had ministered in England for brief periods before and after his three-year (1607-10) sojourn in Venice where he had served as chaplain to the king's ambassador, Sir Henry Wotton.[2]

During his two year stint as Provost of Trinity College Bedell demonstrated his willingness to challenge the status quo and his conviction that familiarity with the Gaelic tongue was essential for all students wishing to become Church of Ireland clergymen. Both these characteristics would prove useful to him in Kilmore, however, neither his learning nor varied experiences would appear, at least at first, to prepare him adequately for being bishop of a rural diocese where the great majority of people were culturally different, being both Catholic and Gaelic speaking. Nevertheless, Bedell's linguistic skills, his efforts to learn and promote the use of the Gaelic tongue, his pastoral empathy towards all, his reforming zeal, his willingness to take legal action against perceived injustices and his respect for the native Irish, were

1. *CSPI, 1625–32*, p. 447.
2. It was said that the English ambassador's house in Venice was often thronged with 'nobles and others' who went to hear Bedell preaching there. See *Calendar of State Papers and manuscripts relating to English affairs existing in the archives and collections of Venice*, xi, 1607–1610, p. 7. Marc Caball and John McCafferty argue that Bedell's short time in Venice was the most important and formative period of his life. See Marc Caball, 'Solid divine and worthy scholar: William Bedell, Venice and Gaelic culture' in James Kelly & Ciarán Mac Murchaid (eds), *Irish and English: essays on the Irish linguistic and cultural frontier, 1600–1900* (Dublin, 2012), pp 43–57 and John McCafferty, 'Venice in Cavan: the career of William Bedell, 1572–1642' in Scott (ed.), *Culture and society in early modern Bréifne/Cavan*, pp 173–87.

qualities that stood him in good stead during his episcopacy and which would, with time, establish him as the best-remembered bishop of the diocese.

William Bedell's son-in-law, Alexander Clogie, described the rural landscape into which the bishop arrived in 1629:

> Kilmore itself was but a meer countrey village, of good large bounds, but so thinly inhabited that no where in the whole parish any street or part of a street was to be found … The bishop's house join'd close to the church, being built upon one of the highest hills in the country, not near any neighbour of any quality by a mile.[3]

Although unaccustomed to rural living, the bishop insisted on travelling 'to the remotest parts' of his diocese though these journeys were 'sometimes dangerous by reason of the mountains and boggy waies and loughs and rivers not passable but by boat, besides the intemperate rains that fell almost all summer long in those northern parts'.[4] William Bedell was a tall man who had 'great strength and health of body' which helped him cope with the difficult terrain.[5] However, he had come to live in a rural world unlike anything he had experienced before, and it would soon become clear to him that the challenges posed by the rural landscape would be the least of his concerns.

Approximately six months after he was consecrated bishop, William Bedell described how he had during that time 'been about my dioceses' of Kilmore and Ardagh and 'out of my knowledge and view' came to the conclusion that both dioceses were 'very miserable indeed'.[6] He elaborated on this in a letter sent to William Laud, the archbishop of Canterbury, on 1 April 1630:

> The Cathedral Church of Ardagh … together with the Bishop's House there, [is] down to the ground. The Church here [Kilmore], built, but without Bell or Steeple, Font or Chalice. The Parish Churches all in a manner ruined and unroofed and unrepaired.[7]

---

3. Shuckburgh, *Two biographies of William Bedell*, p. 57.
4. Ibid., pp 33–4.
5. For a description of Bedell's physique see Gilbert Burnet, *The life of William Bedell, DD, bishop of Kilmore in Ireland* (London, 1685), pp 219–21.
6. William Bedell to William Laud, 1 April 1630, quoted in Burnet, *The life of William Bedell*, p. 45; Brendan Scott, *Cavan, 1609–1653, Plantation, war and religion* (Dublin, 2007), p. 24.
7. Ibid.

He discovered that Hugh O'Reilly, 'the Popish Bishop of this Diocese is lately chosen Primate'.[8] Bedell decided that he would write to O'Reilly who 'lives in my parish, within two miles of my house'[9] and 'offer some intercourse'.[10] He also learned that Eugene MacSweeney, the recently-appointed Catholic bishop of Kilmore, 'lives in another part of my diocese further off'. Both Catholic bishops had their vicar-generals and officials who were so confident that they excommunicated anyone who had recourse to the courts of the Established Church. Such an affront, Bedell wrote, 'hath been offered myself by the Popish Primate's Vicar General; for which I have begun a process against him'.[11] There were also many Catholic priests, both secular and regular in the diocese. Bedell wrote that there was:

> A Popish Clergy more numerous by far than we, and in full exercise of all Jurisdiction Ecclesiastical … Every parish hath its priest; and some two or three a piece and so their Mass-Houses also. In some places Mass is said in the Churches. Fryers there are in diverse places who go about, though not in their Habit.[12]

It was obvious to Bishop Bedell that the efforts to convert the native Irish in Kilmore to Protestantism had failed. 'The people' he wrote to Laud, 'saving a few British Planters here and there (which are not the tenth part of the remnant) [are] obstinate Recusants'. And he blamed this, at least in part, on the fact that he had only seven or eight ministers 'of good sufficiency' in Kilmore. Besides, they had 'not the tongue of the people, nor can [they] perform any Divine Offices, or converse with them' and 'many of them [hold] two or three, four or more vicarages apiece'.[13] He also observed that 'Popery hath possessed not only the ancient inhabitants, but also our English which planted here at first, almost universally'.[14] His empathy for and what Marc Caball calls his 'pastoral sensitivity'[15] towards the native Irish of the diocese was

---

8.   Bedell to Samuel Ward, 6 Oct. 1629, printed in Shuckburgh, *Two biographies of William Bedell*, p. 299.
9.   Burnet, *The life of William Bedell*, p. 45.
10.   Shuckburgh, *Two biographies of William Bedell*, p. 300.
11.   This may be a reference to the vicar-general of Ardagh. See Bedell's letter to Ussher dated 15 February 1630 in Boran (ed.), *The correspondence of James Ussher*, ii, pp 493–4.
12.   Burnet, *The life of William Bedell*, p. 45. It would appear that Bedell overstated both the number of priests and chapels in the diocese.
13.   Ibid., pp 46–7.
14.   Shuckburgh, *Two biographies*, p. 300.
15.   Marc Caball, 'A star of the first magnitude: William Bedell (1571–1642)' in Cherry & Scott (eds), *Cavan history and society*, p. 187.

Figure 10.1: St Feidhlimidh's medieval cathedral of Kilmore, now a parish hall, with its western tower.

obvious from the outset. He saw them as a hungry, impoverished, over-taxed and much oppressed people. In his letter to William Laud he listed some of the causes of their plight:

> Paying double tithes to their own clergy[16] and to ours, from the dearth of Corn and the death of their Cattle these last years, with the Contributions to their Souldiers and their Agents; and which they forget not to reckon among other causes, the oppression of the Court Ecclesiastical, which ... I cannot excuse, and do seek to reform.[17]

Ten months into his episcopacy, and having familiarised himself with his diocese, Bishop Bedell was aware of the hunger, poverty and other problems facing him in Kilmore. However, he was determined to be a reforming bishop and to tackle injustices wherever he saw them.

16.   Bedell was particularly critical of the Franciscan friars in Kilmore who 'by their importunate begging impoverish the people'. He had also been critical of the Franciscans during his time in Venice.

17.   Burnet, *The life of William Bedell*, p. 46. In a letter to Samuel Ward, which was written on 24 May 1629, Bedell gives more graphic detail about the famine afflicting the poor people of his diocese. He wrote 'Many are dead, the residue have no bread; horse and dog's flesh is eaten'. See Shuckburgh, *Two biographies of William Bedell*, p. 297. See also Lord Falkland's letter to Viscount Conway on 15 May 1628, TNA, vol. ccxlvi, no.58.

Eugene MacSweeney

Eugene MacSweeney was appointed Catholic bishop of Kilmore on 18 September 1628 although his consecration did not take place until early in 1630, several months after William Bedell had arrived in the diocese.[18] MacSweeney was an outsider, being born in the diocese of Raphoe *c.*1591 and ordained for that diocese *c.*1618. He belonged to the MacSweeney family from Fanad who had been gallowglasses to the O'Donnells and during the plantation of Ulster had been granted two thousand acres in the barony of Kilmacrennan. His connection to the O'Donnells is clear from the letter the 'earl' of Tyrconnell sent to Rome on 18 October 1628 expressing his thanks for the appointment *'subditi me eximy dni Swin*i' to the See of Kilmore.[19] MacSweeney may have studied in Armagh[20] before going to Paris where he studied philosophy and theology and then entered the University of Rheims where he obtained a doctorate in theology 'with great distinction'.[21] There are indications that upon his return to Ireland MacSweeney may have stayed with the O'Connors of Sligo or perhaps been based in the parish of Drumcliff for a short time before being appointed vicar-apostolic of Derry diocese on 10 September 1626.[22] Then two years later, following the translation of Hugh O'Reilly to Armagh, he was appointment bishop of Kilmore. At a great meeting of the priests of Derry diocese, which was held in November 1629, Eugene MacSweeney 'gave up his place' as vicar-apostolic of the diocese to Terence O'Kelly before moving to Kilmore.[23] Hugh O'Reilly and Eugene MacSweeney had been together in Paris and it would appear that O'Reilly, anxious that his successor

18.   Vatican Library, MSS *Barberini Latini*, 2869, f. 9v and 2933, f. cxlviii(r).

19.   Cited in Donal F. Cregan, 'The social and cultural background of a Counter-Reformation episcopate, 1618–60' in Art Cosgrave & Donal McCartney (eds), *Studies in Irish history presented to R. Dudley Edwards* (Dublin, 1979), p. 94; SCAR, Codex 1.D.io.

20.   Edmund Codan, who gave a testimony recommending MacSweeney for Kilmore, stated that 'he knew him in the town of Armagh and afterwards in Paris where both of them studied together.' See *Father Luke Wadding commemorative volume*, p. 548.

21.   Robert Chamberlin, OFM, refers to him in Spanish as 'Doctor Suyneo' in a letter to Luke Wadding on 4 August 1628 printed in Jennings, *Wadding papers*, p. 264. For information on the early life of Eugene MacSweeney see APF, *Processus Datariae*, vii, ff. 223r-233v; *Father Luke Wadding commemorative volume*, pp 546–8; Jennings, *Wadding papers*, pp 189–90, 221; Lynch, *De Praesulibus Hiberniae*, i, p. 254.

22.   Charles Coote reported in May 1624 that one 'Donell MacSwiney is head of the Connaught priests as their Vicar-General, and a very dangerous man'. See Mary Hickson, *Ireland in the seventeenth century or the Irish massacres of 1641–2*, i (London, 1884), p. 88. Following the violent death of Bishop Reamonn Ó Gallachair in 1600 a series of vicars-apostolic administered the diocese until 1720. See Philip Donnelly, 'Church policy in the diocese of Derry after the Reformation' in *Clogher Record*, xix, 2/3 (2007/08), p. 283; Jefferies and Devlin, *History of the diocese of Derry*, pp 133–9; Ciarán J. Devlin, *The making of medieval Derry* (Dublin, 2013), pp 347–8; Lynch, *De Praesulibus Hiberniae*, i, p. 254; MacKiernan, *Diocese of Kilmore*, p. 14.

23.   *CSPI, 1625–32*, p. 512.

would continue the reforms he had begun in Kilmore, had a say in the appointment of this learned outsider.

The decision by O'Reilly and MacSweeney, about the year 1629, to ask Patrick Cahill, a Meath man and parish priest of St Michael's parish in Dublin, to commission a Dublin silversmith to make two episcopal seals, one to be used by the archbishop of Armagh and the other by the bishop of Kilmore, had unforeseen consequences. The authorities heard about it and Cahill was arrested, charged with 'illegal assumption of ecclesiastical titles' and imprisoned in Dublin castle. He later escaped only to discover that he had been deprived of his parish by Archbishop Thomas Fleming on the technicality that he had been appointed by the vicar-general and not the archbishop of the diocese.[24] There were accusations that Fleming, a Franciscan, gave preferential treatment to other Franciscans and Patrick Cahill may have been a victim of the growing tensions between the regular and secular clergy in the country at this time.[25] To complicate the issue Hugh O'Reilly was friendly with both Fleming and Cahill. Patrick Cahill gathered testimonial letters from Hugh O'Reilly, Eugene MacSweeney and others before going to Rome to argue his case. Both O'Reilly and MacSweeney signed another testimonial letter for Cahill, dated 26 November 1630, which they forwarded directly to Rome.[26] Cahill successfully argued his case and was restored to St Michael's parish. The Cahill affair did not seem to sour relations between the archbishop of Dublin and the two Kilmore-based bishops. Hugh O'Reilly and Thomas Fleming continued to cooperate on other matters and it was Archbishop Fleming who officiated at the consecration of Eugene MacSweeney as bishop of Kilmore. He was assisted at the consecration, which was delayed because of 'great difficulties' until the early months of 1630, by Thomas Dease, bishop of Meath and John Cullenan, bishop of Raphoe.[27]

By Easter-time in 1630 there were three bishops in Kilmore. William Bedell was living beside, and in possession of, the diocesan cathedral in the parish of Kilmore. Hugh O'Reilly, now archbishop of Armagh, was living less than two miles away from him in the same parish. Eugene MacSweeney, possibly deciding that the parish of Kilmore was already rather crowded with bishops, opted to live 'further off' and 'in another

24. *Wadding papers*, p. 469.
25. Ó Mórdha, 'Hugh O'Reilly (1581?-1653): A reforming primate', pp 33–4; W.D. O'Connell, 'The Cahill Propositions, 1629' in *IER*, 5, lxii, pp 118–23; Renehan, *Collections on Irish church history*, ii, p. 33; Moran, *History of the Catholic archbishops of Dublin*, i, pp 341–2.
26. Jennings, *Wadding Papers*, pp 442–3.
27. 'Miscellanea Vaticano-Hibernica' in *Arch. Hib.*, v. (1916), p. 83.

part' of the diocese.[28] He lived the last decades of his life in County Leitrim and it is possible that he also spent some of the early years of his episcopacy in that county, which had the advantage of being somewhat nearer, though still a considerable distance away from, his relations in Donegal. John Lynch, the archdeacon of Tuam, writing just three years after MacSweeney's death in 1669, stated that the bishop was based in Glenade in north-Leitrim during the Cromwellian wars[29] – placing him in the county at least a decade before he is known to have sought refuge on Sliabh-an-Iarainn mountain, where he spent the last years of his life.

Eugene MacSweeney quickly realised that his new diocese was an impoverished one and that his own income was inadequate and so set about redressing the problem. On 10 October 1630 he assisted Thomas Walsh, the archbishop of Cashel, in consecrating Malachy O'Queally archbishop of Tuam in a private chapel in Galway.[30] While there he talked to both archbishops about the dire financial situation in Kilmore and persuaded them to write to Luke Wadding in Rome urging him to use his influence to have the vacant diocese of Ardagh joined to that of Kilmore. Malachy O'Queally, writing on behalf of 'my brother and dearr frreind Mr Owen Swyny' suggested that Primate Hugh O'Reilly was also in favour of such a move and would, in due course, be writing to Rome outlining why the two dioceses should be amalgamated.[31] Nothing came of this. In that same year Eugene MacSweeney wrote to Propaganda Fide requesting that the tithes of the many parishes in Kilmore which had for centuries been going to the monasteries of Kells and Fore and now being received respectively by the commendatory abbots Rev. Terence Brady and Rev. William Dease, be given instead to the diocese of Kilmore.[32] Archbishop Hugh O'Reilly was asked to give his views on this request and he wrote a long letter '*ex loco mansionis meae*' on 2 December 1630 outlining how the diocese of Kilmore was the poorest in the province of Armagh. He stated that this poverty was due, firstly, to the fact that most of the church lands in the diocese were

28.   Burnet, *The life of William Bedell*, p. 46.
29.   Lynch, *De Praesulibus Hiberniae*, i, p. 255.
30.   Moran, *History of the Catholic archbishops of Dublin*, p. 347.
31.   MacSweeney and O'Queally studied together in Paris and O'Queally gave one of the testimonies recommending MacSweeney for Kilmore. APF, *Processus Datariae*, vol. vii, ff. 230v-233r; *Wadding papers*, pp 419–20; *Report on the Franciscan manuscripts preserved at Merchants Quay*, p. 30. Walsh's letter was dated 12 October and O'Queally's 13 October 1630. A letter from the 'clergy and laity of Ardagh' had requested the previous year that Francis Ferrall, OFM, be appointed to the diocese. Benignus Millett, 'Catalogue of Irish material in fourteen volumes of the *Scritture originali riferite nelle congregazioni generali*' in *Coll. Hib.*, x (1967), p. 11; APF, SOCG, MS 14, 16rv, 18rv.
32.   Millet, 'Catalogue of Irish material', p. 37; APF, SOCG, MS 100, 317rv.

occupied by vassals who largely ignored the bishop and, secondly, to money being given to the monasteries of Kells and Fore which ought to go to the sustenance of the bishop and clergy of Kilmore.[33] Despite the backing of the archbishop, this MacSweeney initiative also failed.[34]

Undeterred by these setbacks Eugene MacSweeney worked for reform within the diocese and cooperated with his friends Malachy O'Queally and Hugh O'Reilly and others on church affairs outside the diocese. The tensions between the regular and secular clergy in Ireland had been building for some time when, on 10 May 1631, Propaganda Fide established a commission, consisting of the archbishops of Dublin and Tuam and the bishops of Kildare and Kilmore to investigate the truth or otherwise of certain allegations which had been made against the regulars. The Franciscan Archbishop Thomas Fleming and Bishop MacSweeney replied on 4 September 1631 stating that they examined the relevant witnesses and found no truth in the allegations.[35] A few days later Malachy O'Queally and Roche MacGeoghegan, the Dominican bishop of Kildare, wrote to Rome in a similar vein.[36] Further evidence of Eugene MacSweeney's good relationship with the regular clergy was his letter to Rome dated 10 September 1631, less than a week after his earlier letter, which he co-wrote with Bonaventure Magennis, the Franciscan bishop of Down and Connor, recommending Thaddeus Clery, a Derry diocesan priest, for the bishopric of that diocese.[37]

The provincial synods which were held at intervals in the ecclesiastical province of Armagh were an important element in the Catholic revival in the north of Ireland between 1603 and 1641. Armagh had held provincial synods in 1614, 1618 and 1626 and Hugh O'Reilly continued that trend by applying to Rome for permission to hold such a synod in 1632. Permission was duly granted[38] and the synod, which was held in the diocese of Ardagh, lasted from 10 to 14 July of that year. Archbishop O'Reilly, in his opening address, stated that one of the purposes of the synod was 'the repair of ruined churches', though it is not clear whether he was referring specifically to church buildings or to

33.   Moran (ed.), *Spic. Ossor.*, i, pp 171–2; Brady, *The episcopal succession*, i, pp 282–3.
34.   James Kelly, 'The Catholic church in Kilmore, 1580–1880' in Gillespie (ed.), *Cavan, essays on the history of an Irish county*, p. 117.
35.   Jennings, *Wadding papers*, pp 571–3.
36.   Moran, *History of the Catholic archbishops of Dublin*, p. 379.
37.   APF, SOCG, 14, ff. 53rv, 55r-56v & 137, ff. 328r-329v; Millett, 'Scritture originali riferite nelle congregazioni generali', p. 15.
38.   APF, SOCG, 294, ff. 228r-235r; Millett, 'Scritture originali riferite nelle congregazioni generali', pp 23. For synods held in Ireland between 1600 and 1640 see Forrestal, *Catholic synods in Ireland*, p. 195.

the church generally.[39] Other bishops present at the synod were Eugene MacSweeney of Kilmore, Thomas Dease of Meath, John O'Cullenan of Raphoe and Bonaventure Magennis of Down and Connor together with the vicars-apostolic of Ardagh, Dromore and Derry and the vicar-generals of Clonmacnois and Clogher.[40]

All the northern dioceses were represented at the synod and the five bishops present who spear-headed the Church reform in the north of the country in the 1630s had all studied in France where they had been taught the necessity of church reform along Tridentine lines. Hugh O'Reilly had taught Bonaventure Magennis in Cavan before they both went to study in Paris.[41] While there, both of them became acquainted with Eugene MacSweeney who was also studying in Paris and Thomas Dease who had studied in Douai and Paris before becoming rector of the Irish College in Paris.[42] John O'Cullenan, who had been fostered by the O'Donnells, had also studied in Paris before receiving a doctorate in Rheims, though it is not clear if he met his fellow northern bishops while in France.[43] The French-connected bishops present at the synod felt that it was important that appointments be made to the vacant Sees in the northern province and, midway through their sessions, they wrote to Pope Urban VIII, requesting him to appoint Francis MacDonnell to the diocese of Clogher, a diocese which had been vacant since Eoghan Matthews was translated to Dublin in 1611.[44] This request was not granted and Clogher remained without a bishop for a further eleven years until 1643 when Eimhear MacMahon, who had been recommended for Clogher by Thomas Fleming the archbishop of Dublin in 1627, was appointed bishop of the diocese after having spent a short period as bishop of Down and Connor.[45]

Before Eugene MacSweeney left Paris to become the vicar-apostolic of Derry diocese he wrote to Rome on 17 December 1626 saying that he was 'about to revisit my country … there to labour to the best of my

39.   Moran, *History of the Catholic archbishops of Dublin*, p. 399.
40.   Ibid.; APF, SOCG, 294, ff. 227r-236v; Millett, '*Scritture originali riferite nelle congregazioni generali*', pp 23–4. It is not clear who represented Clogher at the synod since it appears that Heber MacMahon, who had been appointed vicar-apostolic of the diocese, was still in Louvain at this time.
41.   APF, *Processus Datariae*, vol. vii, ff. 214r-216v.
42.   Cregan, 'Counter-Reformation episcopate', pp 95, 112–13; Mac Cuarta, *Catholic revival in the north of Ireland*, p. 34.
43.   Ibid., p. 82; Cregan, 'Counter-Reformation episcopate', p. 112.
44.   *Wadding papers*, pp 623–4.
45.   For Eimhear MacMahon see Seamus P. Ó Mórdha, 'Heber MacMahon, soldier-bishop of the Confederation of Kilkenny' in *Clogher Record, iii, Clogher Record album: a diocesan history* (1975), pp 41–62; Benignus Millet, 'Heber Mac Mahon, bishop of Clogher (d.1650)', in *Clogher Record*, xvi, 1 (1997), pp 136–44.

energy in clearing the Lord's vineyard of tares of heresy and schism'.[46] He continued that pro-active approach after he arrived in the diocese of Kilmore. However, his letter to Urban VIII, dated 17 June 1633, asking him to ratify certain appointments he had made to benefices within the diocese of Kilmore suggests that he was having difficulties establishing himself as bishop and his *relatio status* report to Rome the following year bears this out. He did not travel to Rome in 1634 to deliver his *relatio* in person because of the great distance and dangers by land and sea nor did he send any of the clergy from his chapter or diocese for similar reasons and also because of 'lack of money'.[47] Instead, he nominated Edmund O'Dwyer, who was based in Rome, to be his procurator and to personally deliver his *relatio status* to the pope. In his report Eugene MacSweeney outlined how he had, as required by the decrees of the Council of Trent, 'resided continually in my diocese' and 'applied myself ... to the discipline and reformation of the clergy and laity'. He described how he had:

> Confirmed innumerable multitudes both in my own and the neighbouring dioceses ... ordained many priests, reconciled sixty heretics or thereabouts to the Catholic Church and frequently arranged for missions for reconciling sinners in my diocese ... I preached the word of God to the people as often as my health or the pressure of business permitted. I made visitation of my diocese annually and twice a year as often as deemed necessary. I used assemble my clergy and in those assemblies drew up many salutary statutes for the reformation of both clergy and laity.[48]

The fact that he was an outsider in the diocese who was living a considerable distance from his kinsfolk and without wealthy Catholic families to support him meant that he lacked both moral and financial support. Besides, his determined attempts to reform both clergy and laity met with strong resistance and created many enemies for himself - so much so that he felt unsafe in the diocese. He described in his *relatio status* how he was being persecuted because of the reforms he was trying to introduce:

---

46.   *Wadding papers*, pp 189–90; O'Connell, *The diocese of Kilmore*, p. 422.
47.   J. Hagan, 'Miscellanea Vaticano-Hibernica' in *Arch. Hib.* vi (1917), p. 82; O'Connell, *The diocese of Kilmore*, p. 425.
48.   Hagan, 'Miscellanea Vaticano-Hibernica', p. 83; O'Connell, *The diocese of Kilmore*, p. 426.

I have suffered various persecutions and molestations, both from certain obstinate clerics and from laymen, so much so that, at times, I have been compelled not alone to go into hiding but even to withdraw from my diocese[49] … Frequently summoned and cited by my persecutors to appear before secular tribunals I have always refused, in order to defend, as far as possible, ecclesiastical immunity. As a result of this I am now in evident danger for having treated such summonses with contempt. I may incur being exiled by the edict of secular judges.[50]

Four years after arriving in Kilmore, Eugene MacSweeney believed that his situation in the diocese was intolerable. He felt that he was surrounded by opponents on all sides and was at risk of imprisonment or exile. And even though at the end of his report he expressed the hope that 'better times [will] arrive', the picture he painted was a bleak one. He was aware that the situation in Derry diocese, where he had been vicar-apostolic and where there was 'an exceptionally benevolent climate for Catholic clergy'[51] from the early 1620s onwards, would be much preferable to his predicament in Kilmore. It was no great surprise then that on 2 March 1634 he wrote to Rome, and after complaining about the obstinate and incorrigible clergy, the difficult laity and other dangers he had to contend with in Kilmore, he asked to be transferred to the diocese of Derry where he thought he could live more peaceably in a diocese 'which is close to where I was born'.[52] Hugh O'Reilly, who could survive more easily in Kilmore because he had remained among his kinsfolk, favoured MacSweeney's transfer to Derry.[53] The bishop of Raphoe, John O'Cullenan, was equally unhappy in his diocese and in 1636 he too requested that he be transferred to Derry. This request was followed by the suggestion that Eugene MacSweeney could then replace him in Raphoe.[54] Rome ignored all these requests and Eugene MacSweeney would remain as bishop of Kilmore until 1669, thirty-five years after he first requested to leave it.

49. He gave his address as '*in loco refugii nostri*' and expressed the fear that his *relatio status* might be intercepted.
50. Ibid.
51. Mac Cuarta, *Catholic revival in the north of Ireland*, pp 107–8; Moran (ed.), *Spic. Ossor.*, i, p. 208.
52. Ibid., i, p. 192; Scott, *Cavan, 1609–1653*, p. 21.
53. APF, SOCG, 140, ff. 159rv, 160rv, 168rv; Millet, '*Scritture originali riferite nelle congregazioni generali*' in *Coll. Hib.*, 13 (1970), p. 36.
54. Ibid., p. 38; APF, SOCG, 140, ff. 183rv, 188rv.

This request by the bishop of Kilmore to be translated to Derry resulted, in 1636, in a brief report on both dioceses being sent to Rome.[55] In this report the diocese of Kilmore was described as being mostly wooded and mountainous though with some fertile parts too. There was, it reported, no city in it and the town of Cavan, which previously held a Franciscan convent, had now only a few friars living in private houses. There were twenty-eight priests caring for the people of the forty parishes in the diocese and there were throughout much of the diocese English and Scottish 'heretics' living among the Catholics. The cathedral church was occupied by the 'pseudo-bishop' and the diocesan chapter had died out, though a dean and archdeacon re-mained.[56] This report, although designed to show how the diocese of Kilmore compared unfavourably with Derry, does show that there were, when the Franciscan priests are taken into account, at least thirty and perhaps more priests working in the diocese.[57] So by 1636, largely due to the efforts of Hugh O'Reilly and Eugene MacSweeney, considerable reforms had been made and a network of priests was in place to admin-ister the sacraments and meet the pastoral needs of the people.

Hugh O'Reilly called another provincial synod in May 1637. Among those present were the bishops of Kilmore, Meath and Down and Connor. A notable absentee was John O'Cullenan, the bishop of Raphoe, who the previous year had complained to Rome that Hugh O'Reilly had undermined his authority by admitting appeals from some Raphoe priests he had disciplined because of their scandalous living.[58] The dioceses of Clogher, Clonmacnois, Derry, Ardagh and Dromore were still without bishops and by 1637 it was clear that Rome was in no hurry to fill these vacancies. Those present at the synod resolved that the diocese of Clogher should be administered by Armagh, Clonmacnois by Meath, Derry by Raphoe, Ardagh by Kilmore and Dromore by Down and Connor. This resolution was approved by Propaganda Fide in March 1638.[59] The synod also censored a number of people and some of those disciplined informed

55.   APF, SOCG, 140, f. 159rv. Both reports are printed (in Latin) in Moran (ed.), *Spic. Ossor.*, i, p. 208. The Kilmore report is also in O'Connell, *The diocese of Kilmore*, p. 428.

56.   Terence O'Gowan, the parish priest of Laragh and Drung, was archdeacon of Kilmore and Donagh Gargan, the parish priest of Mullagh, was dean of Kilmore in 1630. DDA, Emilio Ranuzzi, *Sfoglio dei volume per obitum dell archivio segreto Vaticano per le diocese d'Irlanda*, ii, 1630, nos 16 & 19; MacKiernan, *Diocese of Kilmore*, pp 151–2.

57.   It is likely that there were Franciscans priests with links to Creevelea friary based in north Leitrim at this time.

58.   APF, SOCG, 140, ff. 169rv, 181rv; Millet, '*Scritture originali riferite nelle congregazioni generali*' in *Coll. Hib.*, 13 (1970), p. 37.

59.   Moran, *History of the Catholic archbishops of Dublin*, p. 406; Edward Rogan, *Synods and catechesis in Ireland, c.445–1962* (Rome, 1987), p. 34; Forrestal, *Catholic synods in Ireland*, p. 195.

the government about the synod and accused the primate of plotting against the state. As a result Hugh O'Reilly was arrested and imprisoned in Dublin castle for a period of six weeks. In a letter to Dr Edmund O'Dwyer in Rome, dated 24 October 1637, Hugh O'Reilly stated that his health had not recovered from his spell in the damp dungeons of Dublin castle.[60]

During the late 1630s tensions were rising between the Dominicans and the Franciscans over questing rights in the ecclesiastical province of Armagh. The Franciscans, unlike the Dominicans, had a long established presence in the province and they resented the attempts by the Dominicans to expand their sphere of influence in Ulster. Both Hugh O'Reilly and Eugene MacSweeney had an affinity with the Franciscans and sided with them. In 1639 the Dominicans complained to Rome that their questing(begging) and preaching rights in Ulster had been severely restricted by O'Reilly and MacSweeney who then proceeded to give the Franciscans the freedom to preach and quest at will.[61] There were tensions too between the regular and diocesan clergy over questing rights and these tensions would rumble on for decades more.

William Bedell's Synod

The Church of Ireland bishop of the diocese also got into trouble for calling a synod at this time. William Bedell decided to hold a diocesan synod at the cathedral church of Kilmore in mid-September 1638 'for the better ordering of his clergy'[62] and had twenty-two reforming articles passed at this synod before it wound up on 19 September. He hoped that such synods would become an annual event with the first two articles resolving that a diocesan synod be held each September and that in the event of the bishop being absent the archdeacon of the diocese would preside at it.[63] The Catholic Church had a long tradition of holding synods at diocesan, provincial and even national level to help bring about reform. However, no such tradition existed in the Church of Ireland and William Bedell's synod was looked on by some of his co-religionists as being highly irregular. The lord lieutenant was informed and it was argued that the bishop should have, under the English Act for Submission of the Clergy, sought royal approval before proceeding with the synod

---

60. Moran, *History of the Catholic archbishops of Dublin*, pp 401-2.
61. APF, SOCG, 400, ff. 127r, 140v, 144r, 156v; Thomas S. Flynn, *The Irish Dominicans 1536–1641* (Dublin, 1993), p. 237.
62. Shuckburgh, *Two biographies of William Bedell*, p. 110; Burnet, *The life of William Bedell*, pp 79–80.
63. For the articles passed at the synod see Shuckburgh, *Two biographies*, pp 110–13.

and was therefore guilty the crime of praemunire.[64] James Ussher, the archbishop of Armagh, did not approve of this synod but felt powerless to do anything about it. Instead, on 30 November 1639, he wrote to William Laud, the archbishop of Canterbury:

> Your grace hath heard I know long since of the Canons made in my Lord of Kilmore's Diocesan Synod. I could wish, that your grace (as of yourself) would friendly advise him to forbear the Execution of them: as far as they are singular, and different from the Canons of the Nationall Synod confirmed by his Majesties supreme Authority ...
> I beleeve that he will rather forgo his Bishoprick, than acknowledge that he hath done amiss in his proceedings.[65]

Bedell's diocesan synod faced much criticism and he was forced to abandon his plan to hold synods each September. His enemies, among them the diocesan chancellor Alan Cooke, continued to stir up the controversy though in the end William Bedell escaped without sanction.

Kilmore and Ardagh

Eugene MacSweeney, who had failed in his attempt to have the diocese of Ardagh annexed to Kilmore in 1630, nevertheless seems to have been granted some jurisdiction in that diocese following the resolutions of the 1637 provincial synod and the subsequent approval of them by the Vatican. It is not clear, however, how much he involved himself in Ardagh although, in the eyes of the Vatican, the borders between the two dioceses had become somewhat blurred at this time. During the last decades of the 1500s and the early decades of the 1600s the Vatican continued to make appointments to certain benefices in Irish dioceses vacant *per obitum* which, for a variety of reasons, had devolved to it. In 1595 it appointed Donald O'Gowan, a priest of Kilmore diocese, to the parish of Granard in Ardagh diocese and twenty-eight years later appointed him prior of Inishmore, a priory which was in the diocese of Ardagh.[66] Similarly, the Vatican appointed a Kilmore priest, Patrick Trenoir, to the Ardagh parish of Killenummery and Killery in 1633.[67] Giving some jurisdiction in Ardagh to the Catholic bishop of Kilmore and the blurring of the edges between the two Catholic dioceses was in

---

64.   Ford, 'The Reformation in Kilmore', p. 92.
65.   Boran (ed.), *The correspondence of James Ussher*, ii, pp 808–9.
66.   Ranuzzi, *Sfoglio dei volume per obitum*, i, 1595, no.4 & 1623, no.7.
67.   Ibid., ii, 1633, no.52.

sharp contrast to developments in the Church of Ireland when in 1633 William Bedell, in an effort to give good example to his pluralist clergy, resigned the See of Ardagh in favour of John Richardson, the archdeacon of Derry.[68]

Opposition to Reforms

Many of the Church of Ireland clergy in Kilmore held more than one benefice, arguing that the income from one was insufficient to maintain them. William Bedell, however, wanted them to hold just one benefice, to reside in that parish and to provide for the pastoral needs of the people there. Despite his wishes, the state continued to make pluralist appointments in his diocese with Edward Stanhope being appointed vicar of 'Kilgaughorke [Kiltoghert] in the diocese of Ardagh and Drumreilly in the diocese of Kilmore' in June 1634 and, two months later, William Hamond being appointed to the vicarages of Oughteragh in Leitrim and Shrule in County Longford.[69] The government appointment of Randall Ince to the vicarage of Kinawley which had become 'void by lapse' in May 1634, although not a pluralist appointment, does seems to have displeased Bishop Bedell and soon afterwards his nephew, William Bedell, was the vicar there.[70] Clearly some parishes in the diocese, particularly those with few Protestants residing in them, were unable to provide an adequate income for a clergyman. Nevertheless, the picture which emerges from the 1641 depositions, even allowing for exaggerated claims, is that some of the Protestant clergy in Kilmore were quite wealthy, owning large tracts of land, great herds of cattle, several horses and considerable supplies of grain together with many household valuables. Faithful Teate, who had Hugh Brady as his tithe-proctor, owned property in the vicinity of Ballyhaise worth £1,500 and in 1641 he held corn and cattle valued at about £2,800.[71] At the beginning of the rebellion, fearing that he would be attacked, he put £300 'in gold and some silver' into his pockets, before riding at speed towards Dublin only to be waylaid and robbed by the rebels 'in a little wood betwixt Virginia and Lough rammer'.[72] Alexander Comyn, the vicar of Killann and Knockbride, was less well-off, having in 1641 horses

68.   Shuckburgh, *Two biographies of William Bedell*, p. 102; Leslie, *Clergy of Kilmore, Elphin and Ardagh*, pp 807–8.

69.   Mark Empey (ed.), *Early Stuart Irish warrants, 1623–1639, The Falkland and Wentworth administrations* (Dublin, 2015), pp 131, 163. My thanks to Brendan Scott for this reference.

70.   Ibid., p. 117. It appears that James Slacke was also vicar in Kinawley for a short period in 1634: Leslie, *Clergy of Kilmore*, p. 97.

71.   *DIB*, ix, p. 284.

72.   TCD, MS 833, f. 61r; Raymond Gillespie, 'The Church of Ireland clergy, *c.* 1640: representation and reality' in Barnard & Neely (eds), *The Clergy of the Church of Ireland*, p. 73.

worth £40, sheep valued at £33 and 'kowes' worth £54. He also had an income from money-lending having £323 owed to him at the time of the rebellion.[73] The property of Walter Frasor, the vicar of Carrigallen in County Leitrim, was valued at a modest £190 in 1641, which would seem to indicate that the clergy working in parishes with considerably more natives than newcomers had the lowest incomes.[74]

On 15 February 1630, having spent less than a year in the diocese, William Bedell wrote to Archbishop James Ussher stating that 'since it has pleased God to call me to this place … I have met with many impediments and discouragements, and chiefly from my own profession in religion'.[75] His main headache during his early months in Kilmore was not one of his own profession but rather Alan Cooke, the lay chancellor he had inherited from his predecessor, who had done considerable damage to the reputation of the Protestant Church by the widespread imposition of unjust fineson Catholics. Bedell wrote to the bishop of London on 7 August 1630 stating that:

> The greatest impediment to the work of God amongst us is the abuse of ecclesiastical jurisdiction. There is no use in our living and preaching well if the ecclesiastical courts are allowed to prey on the people. The worst offender in this respect was one Alan Cooke, Chancellor to my predecessor.[76]

Bedell declared that he 'could not be quiet' nor could he 'without pity hear the complaints' of those unjustly treated by Cooke's ecclesiastical courts.[77] He, ill-advisedly, declared at a meeting of the diocesan chapter that the chancellor's patent of appointment was null and void and then proceeded to take over the running of the ecclesiastical courts

---

73.   TCD, MS 832, f. 205r. Protestant clergymen in Fermanagh were also money lenders where they were said to have suffered 'as much for their money-lending activities as for their protestant faith' during the rebellion. See Charlene McCoy & Micheál Ó Siochrú, 'County Fermanagh and the 1641 Depositions' in *Arch. Hib.*, lxi (2008), pp 68–9.

74.   TCD, MS 831, f. 35r. The Protestant clergy of Leitrim and Longford sent a petition to the king *c*.1630 outlining how the rectories in both those counties had been impropriated and so they could only collect their vicarage tithes and not 'their milches and other predial [rectorial] tithes.' *CSPI, 1647–60*, pp 353–4.

75.   Boran (ed.), *The Correspondence of James Ussher*, ii, p. 489. If we compare this statement with Eugene MacSweeney's claim that 'I have suffered various persecutions and molestations, both from certain obstinate clerics and from laymen' it becomes clear that both reforming bishops were struggling to establish themselves in the diocese and that their main opposition came from within their respective churches.

76.   *CSPI, 1625–33*, pp 564–5.

77.   Ibid., p. 490.

himself. This action, which softened the approach of the ecclesiastical courts and won him friends among the native Irish, resulted in protracted legal battles with Alan Cooke and a sharp exchange of letters between himself and his metropolitan, James Ussher.[78] Bedell refused to appoint Nicholas Bernard, who had been Ussher's chaplain and secretary, to the vicarage of Kildromfertan on the grounds that he was already the dean of Kilmore, vicar of Ballintemple and rector of Keady and could not speak Irish. This refusal added further to the tension between the two prelates. Despite Bedell's best efforts, Nicholas Bernard, with the support of James Ussher, secured the vicarage of Kildromfertan and continued to undermine Bedell's authority in the diocese.[79]

Laurence Robinson, another pluralist who was chancellor of Armagh and rector of Urney, Annagelliff and Kilsherdany, also proved to be a thorn in Bedell's side. In a letter to James Ussher, written from Farnham on 18 January 1630, he described how at a meeting of the Protestant clergy in the church of Kilmore, William Bedell had 'shewed much grief' because of 'diverse scandalous reports rais'd of him'.[80] Among the accusations made against William Bedell were:

> That he was a Papist, an Arminian, an Equivocatur, Politician, and traveller into Italy; that he bow'd his knee at the name of Jesus, pull'd down the late bishop's seat, because it was too near the altar, preached in his surplice …[81]

And while Robinson did report that Bedell had, at their clerical gathering, denied some of the accusations made against him 'and others he show'd reasons for' and he 'gave us all good satisfaction' nevertheless, he continued to raise doubts about Bedell's orthodoxy. Robinson informed Ussher that Bedell had given a Catholic-style absolution to an Irish recusant. Bedell, in a letter to Samuel Ward dated 14 November 1630, defended himself against the charge of 'leaning to popery' by writing:

---

78.   Ussher reprimanded Bedell saying that 'To pronounce in a judicial manner of the validity or invalidity of a Patent, is no office of the Ecclesiastical, but of the Civil Magistrate'. Boran (ed.), *The Correspondence of James Ussher*, ii, p. 496.

79.   Nicholas Bernard preached the sermon at James Ussher's funeral in London in 1656 and his biography, *The life and predicions of the Rev. James Ussher* (London, 1656), is an extended version of that sermon. *DIB*, i, pp 494–9; Leslie, *Clergy of Kilmore, Elphin and Ardagh*, p. 349.

80.   Boran (ed.), *The correspondence of James Ussher*, ii, p. 485.

81.   Ibid.

> My words … were that if at the saying the name of the
> Father and of the Sonne etc. any of the people did Crosse
> themselves, the Minister should tell them it was not amisse
> if they did so, provided they put no confidence in the signe,
> but in him that died on the Crosse.[82]

In this, and so many other letters, Bedell, because he was different, was forced to explain and defend himself, though in most instances he was more than capable of doing so.

William Bedell, in his impatience to bring about reform, was in the habit of taking rash actions that would later bring trouble on his head. His decision in 1633 to put his name to 'The humble petition of the Protestant inhabitants, both clergy and laity, within the County of Cavan, to the Right Honourable the Lords Justices and Council'[83] asking that the burden of the army levy be removed and his decision to put aside the 12*d* recusancy fines for non-attendance at church on a Sunday brought a particularly stern rebuff from William Laud, the archbishop of Canterbury. In a letter dated 14 October 1633, Laud told Bedell that news of these things 'is come to his Majesty's ears, and he doth not take it well'.[84] The lord deputy, Thomas Wentworth, was none too pleased either and in a long letter to Wentworth William Bedell explained that he wanted to lessen the taxes and fines on the people because they were in the process of raising money for the 're-edifying of the Churches in the diocese of Kilmore'. He described how he had 'personally surveyed the Decays [ruined churches]' and had to lay a charge of £1,199 for the improvement of the churches in County Cavan alone, the work on which was supposed to be completed by 20 May 1634.[85]

Repairing Churches

The amount levied for each church in County Cavan gives a good indication of the condition of the particular churches. (See Fig. 10.2). The cathedral church at Kilmore and the nearby parish church of Killeshandra were in the very good condition, requiring only levies of £15 and £20 respectively for repairs. Both these churches had also received positive reports in Thomas Moigne's report of 1622. Urney and Killinagh churches, both of which were described as ruinous in 1622, now only required £22 and £30 respectively for repair work while the churches in Denn (£60) and Lavey (£70) were obviously in much worse

82.   Shuckburgh, *Two biographies,* p. 317; Phil Kilroy, 'Bishops and ministers in Ulster during the primacy of Ussher, 1625–1656' in *Seanchas Ard Mhacha,* viii, 2 (1977), p. 294.
83.   William Knowler (ed.), *The Earl of Strafforde's letters and dispatches* (London, 1739), i, pp 150–1.
84.   Ibid., p. 125.
85.   Ibid., pp 147,149.

condition. Drumlane parish must have needed a new parish church or else it was planned to repair the large Augustinian priory for a parish church, considering the huge levy of £300 required for the work in that parish. Excluding Drumlane church the average levy for the repair of the other twenty-three Cavan churches in the diocese of Kilmore was £39, presumably enough to re-roof the churches and carry out other basic repairs to doors and windows. Less is known about the repair or building of churches at this time in the parts of Leitrim, Fermanagh and Meath which are in the diocese of Kilmore, though it is known that a new parish church was built in Manorhamilton c.1638.[86] Bedell's son reported that before 'the bishop's death all the churches were repair'd and fit for the people to meet in for God's service', before adding ruefully 'had the people been as willing to meet in them'.[87] This building and repairing of the churches during the 1630s may well be one of Bedell's most successful ventures in the diocese of Kilmore.

Bedell and the Native Irish Clergy

William Bedell's idealism, combined with his single-mindedness and unbending determination to bring about reform, meant that his episcopacy was never going to be a comfortable one either for himself or for those around him. He was determined that he and his clergy would not only minister to the Protestants living in the diocese, most of whom had settled there during the plantations of Cavan and Leitrim, but also that they would reach out to the native Irish and, as far as possible, that they would do so through the medium of Irish. Each Sunday William Bedell watched on as Owen O'Sheridan, a deacon, read in Irish from the Book of Common Prayer in the church of Kilmore 'for the benefit of those he had brought from popery, but understood not the English tongue'.[88] In 1631 Bedell published a short, single-sheet catechism, with parallel English and Irish texts, to help the native Irish better understand the principal doctrines of the Established Church. This catechism, *The A.B.C. or the Christian Institution of a Christian*, contained the creed, the Lord's Prayer, the commandments and a few short scriptural texts from Galatians and the Book of Job. (See Fig. 10.3). William Bedell had copies of the catechism distributed throughout the diocese.[89] More significantly,

---

86.   Rooney, *The life and times of Sir Frederick Hamilton*, pp 90, 143; Moore, *Archaeological inventory of County Leitrim*, p. 183. This church was abandoned in 1783.
87.   Shuckburgh, *Two biographies of William Bedell*, p. 55.
88.   Ibid., pp 133–4.
89.   Burnet, *The Life of William Bedell*, p. 117. John McCafferty has suggested that this catechism might be a student's translation of an earlier catechism by James Ussher. See John McCafferty, 'Venice in Cavan: the career of William Bedell, 1572–1642', p. 186.

Figure 10.2: The sums of money imposed upon the several parishes of the County of Cavan for the re-edifying of the churches before the 20th May 1634.*

Kilmore	£15	Knockbride	£40
Ballintemple	£40	Kilcan [Killann]	£35
Hannagh	£30	Lurgan	£36
Urney	£22	Castle-rahen	£40
Killeserdinne	£60	Mointerconaght	-
Castleterra	£60	Kildromfarten	£35
Drong and Lerra	£40	Drumlahen	£300
Dromgoone	£40	Templeport	£40
Lawy [Lavey]	£70	Killinagh	£30
Moybolge	£30	Killishandra	£20
Mullagh	£30	Kildallen	£36
Dynne	£60	Tomregan	£40
Anaghcliff [Annagelliffe]	£50		

* This list was compiled by Bishop Bedell and it was published in William Knowler, *The Earl of Strafforde's letters and dispatches*, I (London, 1739), P.150.

he commissioned two native Irishmen, Muircheartach Ó Cionga (Murtagh King) and Séamus de Nógla (James Nangle) to translate the Old Testament into Irish.[90] Both these men became Protestants and Bedell ordained Muircheartach Ó Cionga before appointing him vicar of Templep`ort in 1632.[91]

Muircheartach Ó Cionga, who belonged to a well-known learned family from the midlands, had, according to Bedell's son, converted to Protestantism under his father's influence *c.*1628.[92] In that year, Bedell in his capacity as provost of Trinity College in Dublin, employed Ó Cionga to read for an hour each day an Irish translation of the Book of Common Prayer to the students in order 'to frame them to the right pronunciation

90.   Ibid., p. 55.
91.   Leslie, *Clergy of Kilmore*, p. 588.
92.   Shuckburgh, *Two biographies*, p. 55. It is likely that his conversion was required before he could be employed in Trinity College. However, Alexander Clogie claims that Ó Cionga converted to Protestantism during the reign of King James (1603–25); Shuckburg, *Two biographies*, p. 132.

and exercise of the language'.[93] Bedell obviously knew the importance of employing the Irish learned elite in converting the native Irish to Protestantism and he persuaded Ó Cionga to follow him to Kilmore.[94] Ó Cionga's appointment to Templeport, a parish not too far distant from Bedell's house in Kilmore, was intended to give him an income while he and Séamus de Nógla worked on the translation of the Old Testament into Irish. This appointment, and the appointment of other native Irishmen to benefices in the diocese, irked some of Bedell's English and Scottish clergy. There were numerous complaints against Ó Cionga, a list of which was compiled in 1638 and has survived in the State Papers.[95] Ó Cionga got caught up in a vicious dispute between William Bayly and William Bedell.[96] Bayly had been granted the vicarage of Denn and other benefices by John Greenham, a brother-in-law of Thomas Moigne, the late bishop of Kilmore, despite Bedell's insistence that his clergy reside in their parish and hold only one benefice. Bedell suspended Bayly who then appealed unsuccessfully to the lord deputy. Having failed to recover the vicarage of Denn, Bayly set out to defame Ó Cionga and thereby succeeded in replacing him in the vicarage of Templeport.[97]

The list of accusations levelled against Muircheartach Ó Cionga in 1638/9 provide an insight into how the native Irish Church of Ireland clergy were never fully accepted by either natives or newcomers and how, at least some of them, tried to bridge the gap between Church and Mass house.[98] Among the charges levelled against Ó Cionga were that he was ignorant of the word of God, that he never preached and that he cannot 'distinctly and intelligently read divine service' - presumably in the English tongue since he was a gifted Irish scholar. It was also said that 'while his Curate was officiating in his church he came to the Church dore and went not in thither, but went to the Mass house in tyme of Mass' and that he also 'suffers his wife and children to go to Mass'.[99] It was also alleged that when giving communion to a parishioner he 'used not the words appointed by the Book of Common

93.   Boran (ed.), *The Correspondence of James Ussher*, ii, p. 440; Terence McCaughey, *Dr Bedell and Mr King: the making of the Irish bible* (Dublin, 2001), p. 32.

94.   Caball, 'Solid divine and worthy scholar', pp 54–5.

95.   TNA, SP 63/256/126; *CSPI, 1633–47*, p. 206. For Ó Cionga and the accusations against him see Brendan Scott, 'Accusations against Murtagh King, 1638' in *Arch. Hib.*, lxv (2012), pp 76–81.

96.   Scott, *Cavan, 1609–1653*, p. 26.

97.   Leslie, *Clergy of Kilmore*, p. 337.

98.   The full text of the accusations against Ó Cionga are given in Scott, 'Accusations against Murtagh King, 1638', pp 80–1.

99.   William Bedell reported in September 1630 that of the thirty-two ministers and curates in the diocese of Kilmore and Ardagh there were three clergymen 'whose wives come not to church.' Burnet, *Life of William Bedell*, p. 59.

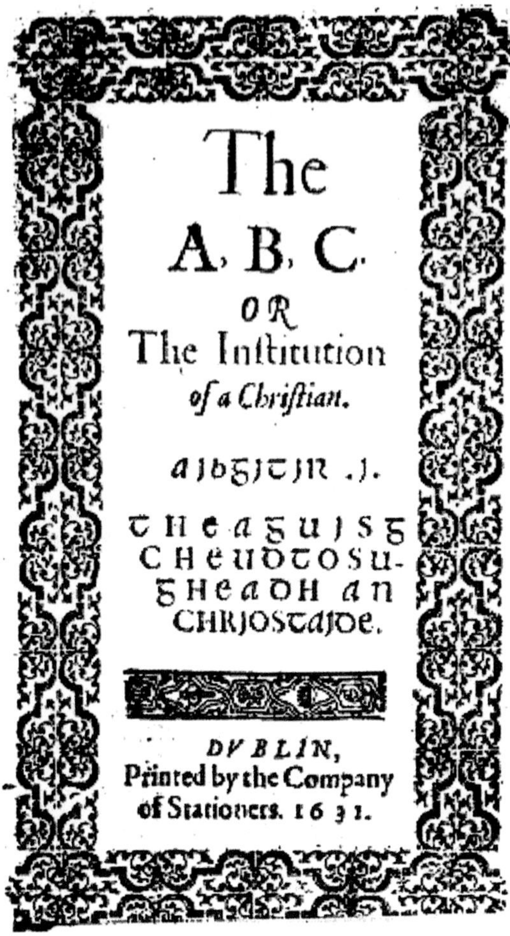
The
A. B. C.
OR
The Inſtitution
of a Chriſtian.

Aibgitir .i.

Theaguisg
Cheudtosu-
gheadh an
Chriostaidhe.

DVBLIN,
Printed by the Company
of Stationers. 1631.

Figure 10.3: Title page of William Bedell's catechism.

Prayer, but bade him. Eat this according to our Saviour's meaning'. The final accusation against him - 'that hee was conformable against his conscience' - was probably true.

Among Bedell's near neighbours in Kilmore were the Sheridans, a clerical family with long links to the Holy Trinity priory on Lough Uachtair and the diocese of Kilmore. Denis Sheridan was in contact with Bedell during his first months in Kilmore and he, along with other members of the Sheridan family, became firm friends and remained loyal supporters of Bedell throughout his time in the diocese. It appears that Denis Sheridan had been baptised a Catholic before being educated and brought up in the Protestant faith in the house

Figure 10.4: William Bedell, bishop of Kilmore 1629–1642. (*Courtesy of Bishop Ferran Glenfield*).

of John Hill, the dean of Kilmore, who lived nearby in the townland of Togher.[100] William Bedell ordained him deacon in 1634 and duly appointed him vicar of the parish of Killesher.[101] Denis Sheridan may not have been the first member of the family to become a clergyman in the Established Church as, it seems likely that 'Phillip O'Siredor' who was Church of Ireland curate in Ballintemple in 1622, was one of the O'Sheridan family.[102]

William Bedell wrote a long letter to Cornelius O'Sheridan in 1636 in an attempt to persuade him of the merits of Protestantism.[103] His efforts were successful and Bedell appointed him as a schoolmaster in the diocese, though he reverted to Catholicism after the 1641 rebellion.[104] Another member of the family, Owen O'Sheridan, was made deacon by Bedell and it was he who read from an Irish translation of the Book of

100.   *DIB*, viii, p. 918.
101.   Leslie, *Clergy of Kilmore*, p. 835. He was also appointed vicar of Drung and Laragh in 1645.
102.   TCD, MS 550.
103.   Shuckburgh, *Two biographies of William Bedell*, pp 127–9.
104.   TCD, MS 832, f. 148 & 833, f. 131r; Ford, 'The Reformation in Kilmore', p. 90.

Common Prayer each Sunday at one o'clock in the church at Kilmore. Denis Sheridan continued to support Bedell throughout the traumatic events of the 1641 rebellion and it was at his house that the bishop died on 7 February 1642.[105] His sons William, Patrick, Thomas and James all were graduates of Trinity College and his eldest son, William, who was born in Togher *c*.1634 would, in 1682 become the Protestant bishop of Kilmore and Patrick, another son, was bishop of Cloyne from 1679-82 though it appears he never resided there because of his wife's unwillingness to move to Munster.[106]

Gilbert Burnet, Bedell's biographer, had a low opinion of the Catholic clergy of Kilmore stating that they were 'a strange sort of people, that knew generally nothing but the reading [of] their offices, which [was] not so much as understood by many of them: and they taught the people nothing but the saying of their *Paters* and *Aves* in Latin'.[107] However, Bedell was not so dismissive of them. He had a considerable amount of contact with the priests and regularly lodged with them during his travels around the diocese.[108] He knew that a clergyman who could speak Irish would be much more successful in converting the native Irish than those who did not and so he used every available opportunity to persuade some of the 'learnedst priests and friars, that were bred in the seminaries beyond the seas, to forsake popery and be converted' to Protestantism.[109] Bedell was prejudiced against the Franciscan friars since his time in Venice and in a letter to the lord deputy in December 1633 claimed that they had become insolent in setting up new houses in Ireland and that people flock in great numbers to hear them preaching 'superstitious and detestable doctrines, such as their own priests are asham'd of'.[110] Bedell contacted the Franciscans in Cavan town in order to convince them of the errors of their ways and we know that Daniel O'Creane, a 'learned friar' who had earlier converted to Protestantism and held a benefice in the diocese of Raphoe, visited Bedell shortly after he arrived in Kilmore in the autumn of 1629.[111] Two years later Bedell appointed him vicar of the parish of Killinkere where, according to Alexander Clogie, 'there not

105.   Ford, 'The Reformation in Kilmore', p. 90; *DIB*, i, p. 412.
106.   *DIB*, viii, pp 918–9; Leslie, *Clergy of Kilmore*, p. 835. For the Sheridan dynasty see Don Sheridan, 'The Sheridan family, a study in the interplay between fact and romantic myth' in *Bréifne*, xi, 43 (2007), pp 473–505; Diarmuid Breathnach, 'Sirideánaigh éirimlúla Chábháin' in the *Irish Press*, 28 November 1961; Schlegel, 'The Sheridans untangled', pp 816–33.
107.   Burnet, *The Life of William Bedell*, pp 114–5.
108.   Shuckburgh, *Two Biographies of William Bedell*, p. 34.
109.   Ibid., p. 126.
110.   Ibid., p. 97.
111.   O'Creane may have been sent to Bedell by James Ussher. See Boran (ed.), *The Correspondence of James Ussher*, ii, p. 493. Though see also p. 536 which states that Denis Sheridan had previously heard him 'preach as a friar in that very place'.

being one Protestant in all the parish he did much good and did turn many away from iniquity'.[112] Daniel O'Creane was taken prisoner by the rebels during the rebellion, though he too, like Denis Sheridan, remained steadfast in the Protestant faith.[113]

During Bedell's time in Kilmore, thirty-eight clergy were appointed to parishes in the diocese for the first time. Nine, or just less than one quarter of these, were native Irish and all except one were appointed between 1631 and 1635.[114] It is possible that Hugh Swiney, who was installed as vicar of Drung on 25 March 1635 was a brother of Eugene MacSweeney, the Catholic bishop of Kilmore.[115] Alexander Clogie states that William Bedell had 'long entertained in his house and at his table' the brother of Eugene Mac Sweeney and 'had converted him from the error of his way, from Jesuitism to Christianity and preferred [him] to a way of livelihood'.[116] However, it is possible that this appointment was short-lived as no other record of him has survived. Bernard Reynolds was ordained by William Bedell on 10 June 1634 and one week later was installed as vicar of Drumreilly in south Leitrim.[117] Cormac O'Hogley was appointed vicar of Cloonlogher in north Leitrim in 1635.[118] It seems likely that both these Leitrim appointments were short-lived also. Manus McAuley, who was a scholar in Trinity College in 1635, was appointed rector and vicar of Bailieborough on 6 February 1641.[119] The 1641 rebellion, and not their unsuitability for the role, may explain why at least some of these vicars disappeared so soon after their first appointment.

William Bedell's policy of appointing Irishmen to parishes where most of the people were Irish speaking was not always successful. William, the bishop's eldest son who was appointed vicar of Kinawley in 1634, described in his biography how these Irishmen, 'some of which were such as had been popish, and some priests and friars, who either by some injury or disgrace from those of their own religion, or through poverty and desire of preferment' had converted to Protestantism and had been appointed by Bedell to parishes in the diocese.[120] When Hugh O'Reilly was appointed bishop of Kilmore in 1625 he found 'much confusion and deviation from ecclesiastical discipline' among the priests of the diocese and began to discipline and suspend priests as he saw fit.[121] This reforming

112.   Ibid., p. 129; Ford, 'The Reformation in Kilmore', p. 90.
113.   Dep. of George Creighton, TCD, MS 833, f. 231v.
114.   Ford, 'The Reformation in Kilmore', pp 94, 97.
115.   Leslie, *Clergy of Kilmore*, p. 870.
116.   Shuckburgh, *Two Biographies of William Bedell*, pp 180–1.
117.   Leslie, *Clergy of Kilmore*, p. 806.
118.   Ibid., p. 757.
119.   Ibid., p. 620.
120.   Ibid., p. 42.
121.   J. Hagan (ed.), 'Relationes Status', pp 80–1; O'Connell, *The diocese of Kilmore*, p. 407.

policy was continued by Eugene MacSweeney who complained to Rome in 1634 about the opposition he was experiencing from obstinate clerics. It seems likely that some of the priests who had been suspended by O'Reilly or MacSweeney, particularly those who flouted the Church's celibacy rules or had a fondness for alcohol, may have contacted Bedell who 'meerly out of his zeal for the conversion of the Irish' gave them appointments in the diocese. However, his son and biographer reported that:

> Some of these men proved scandalous, returning again to their vomit; not by revolting to popery, but by breaking out into dissoluteness of life, to the great dishonour of God, disgrace to the ministry and grief of the bishop.[122]

These failures fuelled the criticisms of Bedell's English and Scottish clergy who felt that his policy of appointing Irish speaking men to positions in the diocese was wrong, that it deprived themselves of further income and that the conversion of the Irish should be accompanied by a process of Anglicisation, a process that would be helped by exposing them to liturgies delivered in the English tongue.

The bishops of Kilmore, Eugene MacSweeney and William Bedell, were outsiders who struggled to establish themselves in the diocese. Both these reformers experienced considerable opposition from within their own clergy and laity, with Bedell, the more radical reformer, experiencing the greater criticism. Their efforts at reform took its toll on both men. The ongoing dispute with William Bayly and the arrest and imprisonment of his friend, Muircheartach Ó Cionga[123] left Bedell despondent and his failure to hold a synod as planned in September 1639 seemed like an admission of defeat. By July 1640 Bedell was 'clearly depressed'[124] and MacSweeney was becoming increasingly dependent on alcohol. Of the three prelates resident in the diocese, Hugh O'Reilly, the Catholic archbishop of Armagh, seemed to be coping best. He too was a reformer and experienced opposition and, for a short period, imprisonment. Unlike the others, however, he had the advantage of living among his own kinsfolk in the parish of Kilmore. As the new year of 1641 began none of the three prelates could have imagined the upheaval and chaos that would ensue before the end of the year.

122.   Shuckburgh, *Two Biographies of William Bedell*, pp 42–3.
123.   Scott, 'Accusations against Murtagh King, 1638', pp 77–8.
124.   McCafferty, 'The career of William Bedell', p. 187.

Chapter 11

Rebellion and Chaos: 1641–1642

Early on the morning of 23 October 1641 rumours began circulating in Belturbet and Cavan town that there was a general uprising in Ulster which had spread into the neighbouring counties of Fermanagh and Monaghan and would, most likely, soon engulf County Cavan. Stephen Ellis, the sovereign of Cavan town, who was then living in the 'Abby of Cavan' heard about the uprising from a terrified Edward Aldriche who had been chased by the Monaghan rebels as far as Ballyhaise and who predicted that 'the tymes wer likely to be very dangerous'.[1] His prediction proved correct and the diocese of Kilmore became one of the most turbulent areas in the country in the ensuing rebellion.[2] On the 24 October the towns of Belturbet, Butlersbridge, Cavan and Virginia were relieved of their arms by rebels - led mostly by members of the O'Reilly sept who claimed to have the king's broad seal for what they were doing. Within a week the settlers were being attacked, robbed of their clothes and other belongings before being driven away to seek refuge where they could. Some headed for Drogheda and Dublin while others stayed within the county seeking refuge either in the castle of Sir James Craig at Croaghan in the parish of Tomregan or that of Sir Francis Hamilton at Keelagh only about one mile away in the nearby parish of Killeshandra.[3] Others sheltered, not behind the strong walls of castles but rather behind the good reputation of some Church of Ireland clergymen such as Bishop Bedell and Denis Sheridan at Kilmore and George Creighton in the newly established town of Virginia.[4]

Francis Hamilton, James Craig and George Creighton were all Scotsmen and since the Scottish Presbyterian Covenanters were also at

1. Dep. of Stephen and Judeth Allen, TCD, MS 832, f. 175v.
2. William J. Smyth, 'A Cultural geography of the 1641 rising/rebellion' in Micheál Ó Siochrú & Jane Ohlmeyer (eds), *Ireland: 1641 contexts and reactions* (Manchester, 2013), pp 76–7.
3. Alexander Clogie, *Memoir of the life and episcopate of Dr William Bedell*, ed. by W.W. Wilkins (London, 1862), p. 214; William Roulston, 'The Scots in plantation Cavan, 1610–42', p. 143.
4. For the rebellion in Cavan see Scott, *Cavan, 1609–1653*, pp 29–44; Roulston, 'The Scots in plantation Cavan, 1610–42', pp 121–46.

war with England, the Scottish settlers in the diocese of Kilmore were, at first, treated more leniently than their English neighbours.[5] One of the O'Rourke rebels told John Browne of Cloone in County Leitrim that 'they had a warrant from the King to take all the Englishmen's goodes but not to take away any man's lyffe or meddle with Scottishmen'.[6] The rebellion had spilled over into County Leitrim on 24 October when, following the burning of the ironworks in Garrison in County Fermanagh, 'seven or eight score men, women and children, most of them English belonging to those Iron workes' fled to Sir Frederick Hamilton's castle in Manorhamilton for safety.[7] The following day Charles Magawran and William Greham from Tullyhaw in Cavan led a group of rebels into Ballinamore where they were joined by Leitrim rebels including Brian, Phelim and Teige Oge O'Rourke from Oughteragh and Farrell and Geffrey McRannell from the parish of Drumreilly.[8] By 1 November, Sir Richard Blake wrote from Galway that 'the suddenness of this Northern gust, and the news from our near neighbour the county of Leitrim had much astonished and frighted'.[9] The rebels continued to rob and drive out the English settlers in Leitrim, as they had done elsewhere, and when Elizabeth Vawse, wife of the vicar of Carrigallen, asked the rebels why they were robbing them 'they asked againe whoe sent you over, and being answered that God and the King did it, they the said Rebells sayd Lett your King fetch you out againe'.[10]

The English war with the Scottish Covenanters, the quartering of a large army in Ulster, the bad harvests of 1640 and 1641 and the loss of land to the settlers in the Ulster plantations have all been given as explanations for the unexpected rebellion in the autumn of 1641. In Leitrim there were local issues too. Brian MacEgan, the Franciscan guardian of Creevelea, stated that the two main grievances the rebels had were 'the blood that the Binghams had formerly spilt in the province of Connagt and the monies and fines that had been leavied and taken up from the Recusants'.[11] Despite the best efforts of William Bedell to soften the approach of the ecclesiastical courts there were still lingering resentments towards

5. Raymond Gillespie, 'Destabilizing Ulster, 1641–2' in Brian Mac Cuarta (ed.), *Ulster 1641: aspects of the Rising'* (Belfast, 1993), p. 111.
6. Dep. of John Browne, TCD, MS 831, f. 025r.
7. 'A true Relation of the manner of our Collonell Sir Frederick Hamilton's return …' in *Another tract of Severall Letters from Ireland …* (London, 1643), p. 18.
8. Dep. of Elizabeth Kiddier, TCD, MS 831, f. 32r and Nicholas Ward, MS 831, f. 18r. For an account of the rebellion in Leitrim see Domhnall Mac an Ghallóglaigh, '1641 Rebellion in Leitrim' in *Bréifne*, ii, 8 (1966), pp 441–54. Brendan Scott, 'Reporting the 1641 rising in Cavan and Leitrim' in Scott (ed.), *Culture and society in early modern Bréifne/Cavan*, pp 200–14.
9. Ulick John de Burgh, *The Memoirs and letters of Ulick, Marquis of Clanricarde* (London, 1757), p. 7.
10. Dep. of Elizabeth Vawse, TCD, MS 831, f. 19r.
11. Dep. of William Browne, TCD, MS 831, f. 67v.

the Established Church because of the tithes and fines it imposed on the native Irish and among the first to be robbed and driven out by the rebels in Cavan and Leitrim were the Church of Ireland clergymen. However, unlike in north Armagh and east Tyrone where several Protestant clergymen were killed or badly injured, those in Kilmore diocese were treated with more leniency.[12]

Attacks on Protestant Clergymen

Faithful Teate from Ballyhaise was one of the first Church of Ireland clergymen to flee from Cavan.[13] Not waiting for the rebels to arrive, he reached Virginia about midnight on 23 October only to be robbed and beaten by the rebels there and then left to walk seven miles 'without boots and onely with a cap of blood on his heade'. His wife and five young children later fled towards Dublin 'it being then both frost and snowe' they had their clothes stolen at Stradone and were attacked several more times before they reached Dublin. Faithful Teate reported that 'since my comming to towne [Dublin] two of my foresaid children are dead: myself, my wife and the rest of my children and most of my servants have been extreamly sick and near to death, through ill usage'.[14] The treatment that he and his family received from the rebels may help to explain the extreme anti-Catholic tenor of his sermon at the funeral of Sir Charles Coote in May 1642.[15] William Aldrich, the rector of Drumgoon and later an assistant to Henry Jones in collecting the depositions, accompanied Faithful Teate on his flight from Ballyhaise to Dublin. Earlier he, together with his wife Frances and his uncle Edward Aldrich, the sheriff for Monaghan, were 'most furiously pursued by the rebells of County Monaghan for the space of nyne miles' between Clones and Ballyhaise.[16]

Henry Jones, the nephew of Archbishop James Ussher who was vicar and dean of Kilmore, was living with his family in a castle in Ballinagh when the rebellion broke out. See Fig. 11.1. He remained there undisturbed until 29 October 1641 when Mulmore MacEdmund O'Reilly, the sheriff

12.   For a list of some of the clergymen killed in Armagh and Tyrone see Brian Mac Cuarta 'Religious violence against settlers in south Ulster, 1641–2' in Edwards, Lenihan & Tait (eds), *Age of Atrocity*, pp 158–9.
13.   For Faithful Teate see Terry Clavin, 'Faithful Teate' in *DIB*, ix, pp 283–5. His son of the same name was a Puritan minister and poet.
14.   Dep. of Faithful Teate, TCD, MS 833, f. 61r.
15.   *The Souldiers commission, charge … in a sermon preached in Christ-Church Dublin, May 14, 1642 … by Faithfull Teate DD.* (Dublin, 1658); Raymond Gillespie, 'The Church of Ireland clergy, c.1640: representation and reality', in Barnard & Neely (eds), *The clergy of the Church of Ireland*, p. 64; Kevin Forkan, 'Inventing an Irish Protestant icon: The strange death of Sir Charles Coote, 1642' in Edwards, Lenihan & Tait (eds), *Age of Atrocity*, pp 213–4.
16.   Dep. of William Aldrich, TCD, MS 832, f. 173r. William Aldrich was granted the rectory of Drumgoon on 4 February 1634: Empey (ed.), *Early Stuart Irish warrants, 1623–1639*, p. 87.

Figure 11.1: Henry Jones, Dean of Kilmore, headed the Depositions commission
after the 1641 rebellion. (*Courtesy of Representative Church Body Library*).

of the county, at the head of 3,000 rebels seized the castle and placed a
garrison in it before taking Henry Jones and his family prisoners and
committing them to the care of his uncle Philip MacMulmore O'Reilly
who lived about a mile away at Lismore.[17] On 6 November Jones was
sent by the O'Reillys to Dublin to deliver a 'Humble Remonstrace' to
the government while his family was held hostage in order to guarantee his return. This remonstrance, which was signed by nine leading
members of the O'Reillys, declared that 'we harbour not the least thought
of disloyalty towards his Majesty ... we must have freedom of conscience

17.   Relation of Henry Jones in John T. Gilbert, *A contemporary history of affairs in Ireland from
1641–1652*, ii, 2 (Dublin, 1880), p. 480.

and honest government'.[18] When Henry Jones arrived back in Cavan on 12 November with the government's ambiguous reply the situation had become more volatile.[19] Jones, who was held 'not altogether against my will' soon made his escape to Dublin. He had remained in Cavan for approximately six weeks after the rebellion began and had been treated well because he had proved useful to the rebels. On 23 December 1641 he was commissioned to head up a group of eight clergymen who were tasked with taking depositions from those dispossessed by the rebels.[20] In March 1642 he went to London where he appealed in person to the House of Commons for relief for his fellow ministers and for urgent action to protect the colony. His appeal, which was promptly printed, described the Irish rebellion as:

> A most bloudy and Antichristian combination and plot hatched, by well-nigh the whole Romish sect, by way of combination from parts forraign, with those at home, against this our Church and State; thereby intending the utter extirpation of the reformed Religion and the professors of it.[21]

He returned to Dublin where he continued to work on the depositions. He was appointed bishop of Clogher in 1645, vice-chancellor of Trinity College in Dublin in 1646 and bishop of Meath in 1661. Jones was a great admirer of William Bedell and managed to salvage his translation of the Old Testament. However, he showed little of Bedell's tolerance, being strongly opposed to all who differed to him in religion.[22]

George Gonne, the vicar of Fenagh and Kiltubrid who lived in Drumrane in the parish of Oughteragh, was 'robbed and despoiled' by the rebels on his glebe lands on both 25 and 26 October 1641.[23] Having been threatened by Cahir MacShane Oge O'Rourke that he would have his head cut off if he 'would not joine with them in going to Masse' he took flight, leaving his wife Martha and their two children in Longford castle while he continued on to Dublin.[24] Walter Fraser, the vicar of

18.   'Copy of the remonstrance of the Gentry and commonalty of the Co. Cavan' in *CSPI, 1633–47*, pp 347–8.

19.   Aidan Clarke, 'The '1641 massacres' in Ó Siochrú & Ohlmeyer (eds), *Ireland: 1641*, p. 39.

20.   Idem, 'The 1641 depositions' in *Treasures of the Library, Trinity College Dublin* (Dublin, 1986), pp 111–22.

21.   Henry Jones, *A Remonstrance of divers remarkable passages concerning the church and kingdome of Ireland* (London, 1642), p. 1; Aidan Clarke, 'The 1641 rebellion and anti-popery in Ireland' in Mac Cuarta (ed.), *Ulster 1641*, pp 149–50.

22.   Aidan Clarke, 'Henry Jones (1605–82)' in *DIB*, iv, p. 1025.

23.   For Drumrane see Dan Gallogly, *Sliabh an Iarainn slopes* (Monaghan, 1991), p. 234.

24.   Dep. of George Gonne, TCD, MS 831, ff. 34r, 34v.

Carrigallen, was robbed on 24 October and then sought refuge in Sir James Craig's castle at Croaghan in County Cavan, where it appears he died along with James Craig and many others of an infectious disease caused by overcrowding and malnutrition. Croaghan castle was a place of refuge for many other clergy and when the besieging rebels allowed the occupants of the castle to leave and head towards Drogheda on 15 June 1642 there were ten ministers in their midst, including Thomas Price, the archdeacon of Kilmore, who later became bishop of Kildare (1661-67) and archbishop of Cashel (1667-85).[25] Henry Jones reported in the summer of 1642 that 'From Drogheda, the said ten ministers, and above 1,000 poore besides the poor souldiers repaired to Dublin where now they are expecting conveniency of passage to England, if they may not be relieved there'.[26]

William Liston and Thomas Fullerton, 'two godly ministers', were not so lucky. They were part of a group of 120 English and Scottish settlers who were led by Sir Robert Hannay and had been sheltering in Belleek Castle in County Mayo when they negotiated a deal with the rebels allowing them to travel through Sligo and Leitrim and on to Ballyshannon where they hoped to take a boat to Scotland.[27] They were attacked at several points along the way before twenty-one of the group, including Hannay and the two ministers, were arrested and then handed over by the O'Connors of Sligo to Colonel Owen O'Rourke in Dromahair. O'Rourke hoped to exchange them for his brother Con O'Rourke and some other prisoners who were being held in Manorhamilton Castle by Frederick Hamilton. Those held captive by O'Rourke wrote a letter, which was signed by Hannah, Liston, Fullerton and two others, to Frederick Hamilton pleading that he release the prisoners he held in order to save their lives.[28] Hamilton not only refused to exchange prisoners but in the presence of the messenger hanged Con O'Rourke - an action which resulted in the revenge killing on 24 January 1642 of ten or eleven of the prisoners held by O'Rourke, including Robert Hannay and the two clergymen William Liston and Thomas Fullerton.[29]

25.   'Relation by Henry Jones, D.D., of proceedings in Cavan 1641–2' in Gilbert, *A contemporary history of affairs in Ireland from 1641–1652*, p. 496; Leslie, *Clergy of Kilmore*, pp 797–8.
26.   'Relation by Henry Jones,' p. 497.
27.   Rooney, *The life and times of Sir Frederick Hamilton*, pp 129–30.
28.   Frederick Hamilton, *The information of Sir Frederick Hamilton, Knight and Colonel, given to the Committees of both Kingdoms …* (London, 1645), pp 19–20.
29.   Ibid.; Edmund Borlase, *The history of the Irish rebellion* (Dublin, 1743), p. 401. Frederick Hamilton claimed that Patrick Drumond, who was killed by the rebels at this time, was also a clergyman, however, this does not seem to be the case. See *Another extract of severall letters*, p. 46; Dep. of John Layng, TCD, MS 831, f.84r; Dep. of Andrew Adaire, TCD, MS 831, f. 97r.

Sir William Cole, a military man who had been granted extensive lands around Enniskillen in the plantation of Fermanagh, blamed Frederick Hamilton's 'ill disposition' for the deaths of the two clergymen and some other prisoners held by O'Rourke.[30] This ill disposition was again evident on 17 March 1642 when Hamilton toyed with the rebels daring them to rescue a prisoner he held in the castle 'who was to be hanged in honour of St Patrick'.[31] The rebels watched the hanging from a distance, unaware that it was an effigy and not a prisoner that was suspended from the castle walls. Hamilton had his entertainment and his clerk boasted how 'our hang-man sitting on the gallows called to them if they had charity in them to send the poor prisoner a priest, they imagining that sack to be a man, fell on their knees in our view praying for the prisoner's soule'.[32] Two months later, on 18 May, he set out with a party of soldiers 'intending towards the Fryers of Crewly [Creevelea]'. However, he found the 'house uncovered and the Fryers fled'.[33] Hamilton had more success against the Dominican friary in Sligo, when during his attack on that town in July 1642:

> He crost a Foard which brought him close to the Friery where the foote met and fired their brave masse house and Fryery, where it is said, we burnt many good things which people had given in keeping for safety to the Fryars, and all their superstitious trumperies belonging to the Masse. It was thought some of the Fryers themselves were likewise burnt, two of them running out were killed in their habits. As we finished this worke … [we gave] God the praise for our successe.[34]

The Franciscan friars of Creevelea had, like the Dominican friary in Sligo, been entrusted with valuables for safekeeping at the beginning of the rebellion. They had returned to their friary when the 1641 rebellion started, possibly occupying the tower or erecting a temporary dwelling within the shelter of the friary walls, and a few days after the rebellion began, William Parke, who lived in the castle at Dromahair, moved most of the goods he had within the castle and 'delivered them a keeping, to

30. *The Answere and vindication of Sir William Cole …* (London, 1645), p. 16; For William Cole see R.J. Hunter, 'Sir William Cole, the town of Enniskillen and plantation County Fermanagh' in E.M. Murphy and W.J. Roulston (eds), *Fermanagh history and society* (Dublin, 2004), pp 105–45.
31. *Another extract of severall letters*, pp 24–5.
32. Ibid; Scott, 'Reporting the 1641 rising in Cavan and Leitrim', p. 203.
33. *Another extract of severall letters*, pp 24–5, 27.
34. 'A true relation of the manner of our Collonel', pp 30–1.

the Friers then dwelling at Crimley, not a half mile from the said Castle of Dromahear'.[35] The O'Rourkes and other rebels from Leitrim and Sligo had set up camp near Creevelea friary and obviously controlled the property previously held by the friars as Lucas Taffe, one of their leaders, warned his men on 31 March 1642 'to guard the Baggage left at Crewly … and not to spoile any thing belonging to the Abby, as they shall answer it at their peril'.[36]

In 1636 Sir Frederick Hamilton bullied Matthew Moore, who had been the vicar of Cloonclare for the previous eleven years, into resigning his post. William Bedell, who had his own brush with Hamilton, appointed John Cunningham, an 'able' man in his place. John Cunningham had married the daughter of Dr Craig, a physician of Bedell's acquaintance during his time in Venice, and fortunately the new vicar related more easily to Frederick Hamilton than his predecessor had done.[37] When the rebellion began John Cunningham not only joined Hamilton in the castle but also fought under his command against the rebels.[38] However, on Holy Saturday in 1643 he was 'deadly shot with a musket bullet in the body' in one of the many skirmishes between Hamilton's forces and the rebels and he died two days later.[39] It would appear that two other clergymen, John Long and Alex Mountgumery, also stayed in the castle at Manorhamilton at this time as they and John Cunningham signed a letter dated 14 January 1643 verifying the accuracy of statements which Frederick Hamilton had collected to use in evidence against Robert Parke of Newtown.[40] Robert Parke was imprisoned by Hamilton for disobedience and on suspicion of being too friendly with the rebels. Among the charges levelled against Parke was that he 'kept diverse Irish servants' but that none of them went to church.[41]

John Cunningham was the only Protestant clergyman who had been ministering in the diocese to be killed by the rebels since William Liston and Thomas Fullerton, the two who were executed in retaliation by the O'Rourkes, had come from Mayo. The English-born Protestant clergy in the diocese were targeted by the rebels in the early days of the 1641 rebellion. They and their families were robbed and driven out, with some

35.   *The Information of Sir Frederick Hamilton*, p. 69.
36.   *Another extract of severall letters*, pp 47–8.
37.   Shuckburg, *Two biographies*, pp 106–7.
38.   Rooney, *The Life and times of Sir Frederick Hamilton*, p. 98.
39.   'A true relation of the manner of our Collonell', p. 46.
40.   *The Information of Sir Frederick Hamilton*, pp 87–8. For Robert Parke see Claire Foley & Colm Donnelly, *Parke's Castle, Co. Leitrim: archaeology, history and architecture* (Dublin, 2012), pp 11–16.
41.   *The Information of Sir Frederick Hamilton*, p. 70.

Figure 11.2: The Bedell stained glass window in Emmanuel College, Cambridge, showing Clogh Uachtair castle over the bishop's right and a Venetian building over his left shoulder. (*Courtesy of Emmanuel College, Cambridge*).

of them being beaten and wounded, before they escaped to Dublin or to one or other of the relatively few safe houses or castles within the diocese. It appears that none of the English-born clergy were left undisturbed in the diocese in the early weeks of the rebellion except William Bedell, whose dealings with the native Irish in the previous twelve years had established his reputation as someone who respected the Irish and their language and was fair-handed in his dealings with them. He was assured by the rebels that 'he should be the last Englishman that should be put out of Ireland' and they allowed him to remain in his house adjoining the church at Kilmore.[42] He was joined there by his son William who was vicar in Kinawley, his son-in-law, Alexander Clogie, the vicar of Urney and John Hodson the rector of Annagh who would, in 1667, be appointed the bishop of Elphin.[43]

Soon many more terrified settlers arrived to stay at his dwelling-house and out-houses at Kilmore including Abigail Moigne, widow of the previous bishop of the diocese, who 'came thither in the habit of the poorest beggar'.[44] The tolerance shown to the Scottish-born clergy in the early weeks of the rebellion did not last long. George Hamilton was celebrating divine service in the house of Alex Anderson in the townland of Corraneary in Knockbride when they were disturbed by rebels. The intruders told all present 'that they were at the divils service and it was a good deed to burne the house over their heads'.[45] The rebels threatened them with death and told them that afterwards they would not allow them to be buried in the church or churchyard because they were not Christians. After this George Hamilton 'dared not come into the country being threatened with death'.[46]

The rebels left William Bedell largely unmolested in his house for almost two months after the rebellion broke out. However, his cattle were stolen and the settlers sheltering in the vicinity of his house were harassed and had their meagre belongings taken from them. In the early weeks of December 1641 the Cavan rebels were focussing their attacks on James Craig's castle at Croaghan and Francis Hamilton's at Keelagh and when the Scottish settlers managed to capture 'four principal leaders of the O'Rourkes' the rebels imprisoned William Bedell, his two sons William and Ambrose, his son-in-law Alexander Clogie and some others in Clogh Uachtair castle on 18 December in order to exchange them for the high-profile prisoners held by Craig and Hamilton. This

42.   Shuckburg, *Two biographies*, p. 176.
43.   Ibid.; In 1660 it was reported that John Hodson 'was a great sufferer by the rebellion and was necessitated for many years to absent himself in England and is not returned.' Leslie, *Kilmore Clergy*, p. 543.
44.   Shuckburg, *Two biographies*, p. 176.
45.   Dep. of William Murdoghe, TCD, MS 833, f. 175r.
46.   Ibid., f. 174v.

exchange did not happen until 7 January and on his release William Bedell went to stay at the home of Denis Sheridan, one his Irish clergy who lived nearby in Drumcor. William Bedell died one month later, on 7 February 1642.[47] Bishop Bedell had stipulated in his will that he be buried 'without any funeral pomp in the church-yard of Kilmore … in the same grave or hard by the corps of my dear wife Leah and my son John … with this inscription: GULIELMI QUONDAM KILMORENSIS EPISCOPI DEPOSITUM'.[48] He was buried alongside his wife and son, despite the initial objections of Eugene MacSweeney, though the inscription on his grave-stone was not quite what he had asked for.[49] His wishes to have a funeral without pomp were ignored by the native Irish. Large numbers of them gathered at the house of Denis Sheridan where he had died, and, with various members of the Sheridan sept acting as bearers, they followed his remains to Kilmore. As they neared the church they were met by a party of musketeers under the control of Edmund Mac Mulmore O'Reilly, which, to the beat of a drum, provided a guard of honour and escorted the coffin to the church where the sheriff, Mulmore O'Reilly:

> Told the bishop's sons that they might use what prayers, or what form of burial, they pleased; none should interrupt them. And when all was done, he commanded the musquetteers to give a volley of shot, and so the company departed.[50]

William Bedell, the clergyman and son of Bishop Bedell and Alexander Clogie his son-in-law remained on at Denis Sheridan's house until 17 June where they 'were marvellously sanctuaryed in the midst of their enemyes'.[51] On that date they joined approximately 1,200 settlers who had abandoned Croaghan and Keelagh castles having been promised a safe passage to Drogheda by the rebels. These two clergymen, both of whom would later write biographies of Bishop Bedell, were numbered among the ten Protestant clergymen who travelled with this group to the east coast of Ireland and from there on to England.[52]

47. Dep. of Arthur Culme, TCD, MS 833, f. 129r.
48. Shuckburg, *Two biographies*, p. 74.
49. The inscription reads GULIELMI BIDELI/ QUONDEM KILMORENS/IS EPISCOPI/ DEPOSITUM. Mant, *History of the Church of Ireland*, p. 567.
50. Shuckburg, *Two biographies*, p. 75.
51. Ibid., p. 210.
52. Ibid., pp 210–13; Henry Jones, *A remonstrance of the beginnings and proceedings of the rebellion in the County of Cavan* … (London, 1642), p. 39; Dep. of Richard Castledine, TCD, MS 833, f. 115v. See also article by T.J. Barron, 'The exodus of Protestant settlers from County Cavan in 1642' in *The Heart of Bréifne*, iii (1980).

Richard Parsons, the vicar of Drung and Laragh, remained in County Cavan and claimed that he was on the run for a year and a half and that 'hee lay out in boggs, mountains and fields in frost snow and rain to hide himself from danger'.[53] His wife was Irish which may have been a help. However, Thomas Crant of Cavan gave a different version of events, stating that Parsons went to Eugene MacSweeney, the Catholic bishop of the diocese, and 'recanted his Protestant Profession and ther did swere to continue in the Romish Catholick religion dureinge his life'.[54] Thomas Brady, the vicar of Lavey, also remained in the area. He not only reverted to Catholicism but was said to have been 'a notorious Rebell and a theife' who 'robbed and pilledged the Englishe more than any other Rebell'.[55] Denis Sheridan, one of the Sheridan sept from the parish of Kilmore, was allowed to remain in his house and also to give shelter to some of his Protestant neighbours 'on account of the Family he was of'.[56] Several of the Sheridan family, including 'John Sheriden brother to Mr Sheriden the minister' were listed among the rebels of County Cavan, and his relationship with these rebels may also have acted in his favour.[57] Daniel O'Creane, the former Franciscan and vicar of Killinkere, did not escape so lightly. He had boldly asserted in the presence of Thomas MacKiernan, the Franciscan guardian of Dundalk friary, that:

> The Friers had preached in his parrish that the Irishe should not leave with any English Protestant the worth of 2*d* of any goods … [and he] did likewise complaine before diverse of the Irish that to his knowledge the Preists and fryers had undone O'Neile and O'Donald and now that they had raised up that mischeeffe [the rebellion] that would go neere to undoe the whole Kingdome.[58]

His boldness almost cost him his life and only the pleas of George Creighton prevented the rebels from taking him away. Instead he was placed under house arrest in Virginia, first with Philip MacHugh O'Reilly's mother and later with Creighton himself. George Creighton managed to

53. TCD, MS 833, f. 275r.
54. Ibid., f. 213r.
55. Dep. of Symon Wesnam, TCD, MS 833, f. 205r, f. 1v, f. 8r.
56. Ware, *The whole works of Sir James Ware*, p. 240; James O'Gallagher with his wife and children fled from Dresternan in Fermanagh to Sheridan's house for shelter where they 'amongst a great number of other English were harboured'. TCD, MS 835, f. 243r.
57. TCD, MS 832, f. 42r.
58. Dep. of George Creighton, TCD, MS 833, f.231r.

remain in Virginia until the 15 September 1642.[59] Creighton was tolerated by the rebels at first because he was Scottish and they 'were their kinred and had not oppressed them in government'.[60] Later he proved useful to the locals by persuading Christopher Plunket the Earl of Fingal[61] to allow them hold a market[62] in Virginia every Thursday and by somehow curing an outbreak of red water in the cows of Meath. In general the Irish born Church of Ireland clergy tended to stay in the diocese largely undisturbed while the English and later the Scottish clergy were regularly robbed and driven away. By the summer of 1642 virtually all of the non-native clergy, with the exception of George Creighton in Virginia and those remaining in the castle at Manorhamilton, had left the diocese and the country.

Church Property Destroyed

The killing by the rebels of approximately thirty-six settlers who were thrown into the river in Belturbet at the end of January 1642 was widely reported and was said to have resulted in ghostly appearances, un-earthly noises and an absence of fish from the river for a long time afterwards.[63] Sometime before these events the rebels had forced their way into the church in Belturbet where 'they did in most scornful and malicious manner … thrust their pikes into and through the Kinges armes and then pulled them down and trode them under their feet'.[64] John Anderson, a merchant from Belturbet, reported in July 1642 that the rebels 'burnt the bible and other Church bookes which they found in the Church of Belturbett and knoweth that the Rebells have burned the seates in the said Church and much defaced and blackened the said Church with fyer'.[65] At Easter time the following year, the church 'which was a goodly faire building' was completely burned along with 'the most part of the towne' by the soldiers of Philip Roe O'Reilly.[66] Bibles were

---

59.   Ibid., f. 237v.
60.   Ibid., f. 229r; Gillespie, 'The Church of Ireland clergy *c.*1640', p. 71.
61.   *DIB*, viii, pp 155–6.
62.   A licence had been given when the town was established to hold a market every Thursday in Virginia and a fair once a year on St Peter's day (probably 29 June, the feast of Saints Peter and Paul): *Calendar of Irish patent rolls of James I*, p. 236.
63.   Scott, *Cavan, 1609–1653*, pp 35–7; idem, 'Reporting the 1641 rising in Cavan and Leitrim' in Scott, *Culture and Society*, p. 206; Gillespie, 'Destabilising Ulster, 1641–2', pp 118–9.
64.   Dep. of Elizabeth Poke, TCD, MS 833, f. 256r. This broken stone tablet bearing the king's arms may be the one which has survived and was, in 2016, unveiled in Belturbet library. See photograph in Micheál Ó Droma & Marcella Loughman, 'Archaeological investigations at the Town Hall, Belturbet, County Cavan' in *Bréifne*, xiii, 50 (2015), p. 556. A new 'Kings Arms' was commissioned by Belturbet corporation in 1722. See Cavan County Library Archive, BC2, M3571, pp 278, 297.
65.   TCD, MS 833, f. 99r.
66.   Dep. of Awdrey Carington, TCD, MS 833, f. 282r.

targeted by the rebels from the beginning of the rebellion. On 24 October 1641 they took the bible belonging to Edward Slacke from the parish of Kinawley 'opend it, and laying the open side in a puddle of water lept and stampt upon it, saying a plague on this booke [which] hath bred all the quarrel'.[67] It was further reported that 'all the protestant bookes as bybles and the rest, that were not of the Romish stampe and party were burned in great heapes at the highe Crosse of Belturbett'.[68] The market cross was a pivotal point in Cavan town too and it was from there that Donell Bradie, a sergeant of Cavan, having proclaimed a market in the town, then 'prayed God keip Collonell Rellie and not (according to the old forme) of god save the king'.[69] Neither of these market crosses have survived, although the cross which was erected in Tullaghan village on Leitrim's Atlantic coast in 1778, may well be a market cross from this period.[70] See Figure 11.3.

Parish Churches in Catholic Hands

The burning of the church in Belturbet was an exceptional event and was not copied in other parishes in the diocese. The reason for this may be that the Belturbet church was regarded as a 'Protestant' church since it had been built by the settlers and had not, like most other churches in the diocese, previously been in Catholic hands. However, the contents of several other churches were confiscated. William Jamesone, from the parish of Drumgoon, stated that the 'Preist Mackbride … broke all the seats in the Church and took them home to his howse'- presumably for fire stuff.[71] Henry McCabe, a rebel from Cavan town forcibly entered Annagelliff church and, using stones, broke open a strong trunk from which he took a gown, surplice, table and pulpit cloths and the liturgical books belonging to the church.[72] Rather than destroying buildings, the Catholic priests tended to re-occupy the churches they felt were rightfully theirs, some of them having been taken over by the Established Church less than a decade earlier during the episcopate of William Bedell. Richard Harrison,

---

67.   TCD, MS 835, f. 170r.
68.   Dep. of Richard Parson, TCD, MS 833, f. 279r. Some of the rebels told Jonathan White from Kilmore parish that Mulmore O'Reilly, the high sheriff of the county, had told them to 'burne my books and papers whatsoever'. This may have been a way of destroying all records relating to rents, loans and other debts. Mac Cuarta, 'Religious violence against settlers', p. 172.
69.   Dep. of William Sharpe, TCD, MS 833, f. 184v; Dep. of John Watsone, TCD, MS 833, f. 202r. John Walter, 'Performative violence and the politics of violence in the 1641 depositions' in Ó Siochrú & Ohlmeyer (eds), *Ireland: 1641 contexts and reactions*, pp 141–2. The Cavan town market cross is clearly shown on the *c*.1591 map of Cavan town. See Fig. 8.1.
70.   According to local tradition this cross was found nearby on the Atlantic shoreline. See Moore, *Archaeological inventory of County Leitrim*, p. 186.
71.   TCD, MS 833, f. 160r.
72.   Dep. of Jenett Kearnes, TCD, MS 833, f. 254r.

Figure 11.3: Cross at Tullaghan, County Leitrim.

Figure 11.4: Clogh Uachtair castle where Bishop Bedell was imprisoned.

who had detailed knowledge about County Cavan, complained in 1644 that they had to watch the priests 'setting up their Idolatrous Masses in all our Churches, whereof they have taken possession and banished our best Divines'.[73] Turlogh O'Gowan, the parish priest of Laragh, having demanded and received the key of the church of Laragh from George Cooke's brother, declared that 'the papists would have their churches, lands and goods to themselves from the English and be noe more slaves' to them.[74] Thomas Crant, a gentleman from Cavan town, reported that on the Sunday before Christmas 1641 'the Romish Bishop McSwane [MacSweeney] came to the Church of Kilmore and ther did Consecrate it anew, and sett upp an Alter ther and soe said Mass'.[75]

Four days earlier, on 18 December 1641, Edmund Mac Mulmore O'Reilly had imprisoned William Bedell and his sons in Clogh Uachtair

73.   Richard Harrison, *Irelands misery since the late cessation: sent in a letter from a gentleman in Dublin, to his brother in law, now residing in London, sometime living in the county of Cavan …* (London, 1644), p. 2.

74.   Dep. of George Cooke, TCD, MS 832, f. 207v. For 'Terence' O'Gowan, parish priest of Laragh see MacKiernan, *Diocese of Kilmore*, p. 117. This policy of Catholics taking over the churches was confirmed at the provincial synod of Kells in March 1642 which stated that 'In churches where Mass was not hitherto celebrated, Parish Priests are authorised to officiate with portable altars, as they have hitherto done on hills, in woods and in private houses'. John T. Gilbert (ed.), *History of the Irish Confederation and the war in Ireland, 1641–1643* (Dublin, 1882), i, p. 291.

75.   TCD, MS 832, f. 216r; Jones, *A remonstrance of the divers remarkable passages concerning the Church and Kingdome of Ireland*, p. 36.

castle and then installed both himself and Eugene MacSweeney in the bishop's house at Kilmore.[76] Before these arrests MacSweeney had suggested to Bedell that he would join him in the bishop's house in order to protect him from attack. Bedell, in a well-crafted letter written in Latin, politely declined the offer saying that there were 'many things that hinder me from making use of the favour you now offer me' and mentioned the great number of people he was harbouring and the sickness that was afflicting them. However, the biggest obstacle he saw was 'the difference of our way of worship' explaining that they read the scriptures and sang the psalms in the vulgar tongue each day and he told MacSweeney that 'these things would offend your company if not yourself'.[77] MacSweeney did not push the matter any further until Bedell had been arrested and then he 'came by the direction or consent' of Edmund Mac Mulmore O'Reilly 'into the said howse and there liveth'.[78] The rebels also seized the house of Alexander Comyn, the vicar of Killann and Knockbride, who then 'did leave Cormah Roe Mc clearie, the popishe Preist of the parishe of Kilkan [Killann] dwelling in the said house and plowing the land' belonging to Comyn.[79] When the settlers had been driven out of Cavan town the Franciscans did not seize the opportunity to move back into their friary, where Stephen Ellis the sovereign of the town had been living. Instead, it appears that they remained in their Irish style houses and occupied the house of Thomas Crant, who also lived in the town, for use as a school. Crant reported that following the seizure of his house by the rebels 'ther are now placed [in it] a Colladge of friars, and they and others [have] possessed my Corne'.[80]

With the rebels in control of virtually all of Kilmore diocese, the clergy, both secular and regular, seized the opportunity and took control of the churches and some of the houses previously held by the clergy of the Established Church. There was still no church in the recently established

76. 'Proceedings in Cavan, 1642' in Gilbert, *A contemporary history*, ii, 2, p. 787; Shuckburgh, *Two biographies*, p. 69.
77. Ibid., p. 181; Burnet, *The life of William Bedell*, pp 188–90. J.T. Ball, in his history *The Reformed Church of Ireland, 1537–1886*, (London, 1886), p. 137 states that it was 'due very much to the example and precept' of MacSweeney that Bedell was treated so well in the early weeks of the rebellion. Bedell's son and son-in-law, however, judged MacSweeney much more harshly - both depicting him as an uncouth drunkard. Bishop Bedell seemed to have had considerably more respect for MacSweeney addressing him in his final letter as *Reverendo in Christo fratri Eugenio Gulielmus Kilmor* and while regretting greatly the loss of his own library to the rebels he got 'some little satisfaction … thinking that it should come into the hands of scholars; for [Edmund] O'Reilly told him, such things should be left to the bishop [MacSweeney]'. See Shuckburgh, *Two biographies*, p. 66.
78. Dep. of Ambrose Bedell, TCD, MS 833, f. 105v.
79. Dep. of Alexander Comyn, TCD, MS 833, f. 205r. A number of the MacClery family were parish priests of Killann: MacKiernan, *Diocese of Kilmore*, p. 81.
80. Dep. of Thomas Crant, TCD, MS 833, f. 219v.

town of Virginia[81] although Owen Ó Loinsigh, the parish priest of Lurgan, informed George Creighton, the Protestant vicar of that parish, that by law he had the right to take possession of all his goods. When the rebels had taken over the town a priest, probably Ó Loinsigh, came and celebrated Mass for them in Thomas Lock's stable. This was the first time Mass was celebrated in the town since it was established thirty years earlier and the parish priest, 'a proud yong Rogue' according to Creighton, did not like the Old English Catholics of the Pale who were now living in Virginia and he would not allow any of their priests or friars to celebrate Mass in his parish.[82] The rebel leaders installed the Catholic priests in the properties they had seized and, it seems, also helped them to recover tithes which had not been collected by the Church of Ireland ministers. Teig O'Connor, the colonel of the rebels in County Sligo, commanded all the inhabitants of Calry, a parish in County Sligo adjacent to the diocese of Kilmore:

> To pay or cause to be payed unto father Connor O'Hary pastour of the said parish, all such tithes and other duties as he can find out were unpayed to the former Minister of the said parish, and in failing hereof I promise to assist him as best I can.[83]

The rebels seemed as intent on recovering the churches and their revenues as they were on recovering the lands lost in the plantations.

Catholic Priests and the Rebellion

The depositions, virtually all of which were given by Protestant settlers who had been dispossessed during the rebellion, generally paint the Catholic clergy in an unfavourable light. George Creighton, a Puritan 'who was euer an enemy to drunckards', ridiculed Eugene MacSweeney who 'was drincking and exceeding merry' in an alehouse in Virginia and who, 'having drunck very much' almost fell off his horse as he left the town.[84] William Reynolds, the yeoman from Curragarrah (Killygarry) who complained that 'the very boyes and children of the rebels' did throw stones at him and pursue and showte after him' as he passed through the streets of Cavan, said that there was a 'cruell and most deboist … Irish Monck who lived about the Cavan and would ordinarily

---

81. Hunter, 'An Ulster Plantation town – Virginia', p. 50.
82. Dep. of George Creighton, TCD, MS 833, f. 236v.
83. 'Paper found in a priest's pocket, being killed and stript' in *Another extract of severall letters from Ireland*, p. 51.
84. Dep. of George Creighton, TCD, MS 833, ff. 237r, 233r, 233v.

bee drunck and sweare and prophane gods name extreamely'.[85] Other priests such as Laghlin boy O'Farrell (Kildallan), Owen O'Reilly (Drumgoon), Shane McBrian from Kilsallagh (Templeport), Ternan Mc Treor[86] (Oughteragh), Adam O Fay (Carrigallen or Drumreilly?), Charles O'Fay (Carrigallen), Thomas Mac Murtagh Brady (Annagh), Cormac Roe Mac Cleary (Killann) and Turloch O Gowan (Laragh) were all listed in the depositions as either being with the rebels or having some links with them. Henry Jones gave evidence that a friar, Fr O'Rourke, was killed when he, 'in the habit of his order did lead the company of rebels' in an attack on Francis Hamilton's castle at Keelagh.[87] Walter Fraser stated that he was 'credibly informed and partly knoweth' that Bishop Eugene MacSweeney and others were 'acters and carriers of armes against his Majesty and loyall subjects'.[88]

The role of the Catholic clergy in the 1641 rebellion is exaggerated in the depositions collected by Henry Jones and others. Robert Maxwell, the rector of Tynan in County Armagh, gave his deposition on 22 August 1642, just seven months before he was consecrated Church of Ireland bishop of Kilmore. In his deposition he claimed that in the twelve months before the rebellion 'he observed frequent and extraordinary meetings of preists and friars almost everywhere', who 'under cover of visitacions' were planning the rebellion. He added that Sir Felim O'Neill introduced him to a friar, saying 'this is the friar that said Masse at Finglasse upon Sunday morning, and in the afternoon did beat Sir Charles Coote at Swords' and that the friar said that he hoped to say Mass in Christchurch in Dublin within eight weeks.[89]

It seems certain that there were Catholic priests accompanying the rebels at various times throughout the rebellion though their precise role among the rebels is less clear. The priest who celebrated Mass for the rebels in Thomas Lock's stable in Virginia would seem to have been acting in the role of a chaplain and the Armagh provincial synod, which was held in Kells on 22 March 1642 as an emergency response to the chaos which

---

85. TCD, MS 833, ff. 258v, 259r. The monk referred to here may be Redmond ffitz Simmondes, a Cistercian monk who complained to Arthur Culme of Clogh Uachtair about Henry VIII, Calvin and Luther saying they 'had sett all Christendome on fire'. See Dep. of Arthur Culme, TCD, MS 833, f. 130r. See also Dep. of John Whitman, TCD, MS 833, f. 274r. It is possible that this is the 'Fr Edmundus Fitz-Simon' who attended the provincial synod in Kells in March 1642. See Moran (ed.), *Spic. Ossor.*, ii, pp 6, 8.

86. Ternan Travers was educated in Salamanca. See MacKiernan, *Diocese of Kilmore*, p. 153.

87. 'Relation by Henry Jones', p. 488. Richard Harrison named this friar as 'Anthony O'Lork' and states that he was killed at the battle of Clodeum Mill in the County of Cavan'. Harrison, *Irelands misery since the late cessation*, p. 4.

88. TCD, MS 831, f. 35r.

89. TCD, MS 809, ff. 5r, 6r.

had gripped the province since the previous autumn, emphasised the importance of this chaplaincy role.[90] This synod decreed that every legion of rebel soldiers should have two chaplains and a special preacher who would administer the sacraments to the soldiers and give them instructions as to how they were to behave.[91] This chaplaincy role was spelled out in a Catholic Confederation document in December 1642 which was signed by Hugh O'Reilly and 'Philp Rely'[92] among others, appointing Thomas Preston in charge of the rebel army in Leinster. It stated that there must 'sufficient preachers and confessors in the armie, as in all Catholicke armies; that the armie frequent the sacraments once a month and before battaile'.[93] The presence of chaplains, the celebration of Mass and other religious ceremonies and the use of religious objects to protect or to bring success in battle was commonplace in the early months of the rebellion.[94]

It appears likely that at least some of the priests present with the rebels both before and after this synod took place were there as chaplains and not as combatants.[95] It also would seem that the accounts in the depositions and elsewhere which state that it was the priests, Jesuits and friars who planned the rebellion and were leaders in it were wide of the mark and these accounts neglect to point out that some of the priests actually sided with the settlers and protected them from the rebels. Ellenor Reynolds of Lissanover in the parish of Templeport gave evidence that 'the Masse priest of the parish'[96] prevented the rebels from murdering her husband and father by threatening to place a curse on them if they did so. The priest also concealed in his house two trunks 'full of fine linen wearing apparel and plate and other goods and writings of great concernment' belonging to the Reynolds family in a failed attempt to safeguard them from the rebels.[97] Similarly, George Creighton was saved by friars from imprisonment on two different occasions. The friar Laughton O'Reilly came to his rescue in an alehouse in Virginia when Eugene MacSweeney threatened to commit the Scottish minister to Cavan jail because he refused to go to Mass, and on another occasion he was saved from imprisonment by a friar named Gregory.[98] William Bickerdick from Kinawley described how the rebels had killed

90. Moran (ed.), *Spic. Ossor.*, ii, pp 2–8; Rogan, *Synods and catechesis in Ireland*, p. 35.
91. Moran (ed.), *Spic. Ossor.*, ii, p. 8, no.12; Patrick J. Corish, 'The origins of Catholic Nationalism' in *A History of Irish Catholicism*, 3, (Dublin, 1968), pp 31–2.
92. Presumably this is the leader of the rebel army in Cavan.
93. Gilbert (ed.), *History of the Irish Confederation*, i, p. 94.
94. Gillespie, 'Destabilizing Ulster', pp 116–7.
95. Canice Mooney, 'The Irish sword and the Franciscan cowl' in *The Irish Sword*, i, 2 (1950–51), p. 84.
96. Possibly a reference to Fr Shane MacBrian who lived in the townland of Kilsallagh.
97. TCD, MS 832, f. 167v.
98. See Dep. of George Creighton, TCD, MS 833, f. 233v; MS 832, f. 153r.

Richard Sullyard despite the fact that a 'Romish preest' had him in his arms trying to protect him.[99]

Coercion and Conversion

The rebels were intent on driving out the Protestant settlers, destroying their bibles and other symbols of their religion and attempting, by force if necessary, to convert them to Catholicism. William Jameson, from the townland of Cran in the parish of Drumgoon, stated that the rebels from the parishes of Kill and Knockbride did several times 'hang up this deponent to confesse mony and go to Masse'.[100] John Hickman from Tuncker in the parish of Annagh and his brother-in-law Donnel O Lery 'a mere Irishman and yet a protestant' - both of whom had recovered and buried the bodies of six people drowned by the rebels in Belturbet – were threatened with death if they did not go to Mass and later the rebels offered O'Lery to have all his stolen property returned to him if he would 'forsake his religion and go to Masse'.[101] Arthur Culme, the caretaker of Clogh Uachtair castle, reported that 'severall preistes and fryarrs repayred to mee perswadeing mee to goe to masse and that I should have my goodes and lands, and bee preferred and bee made … a fellow of the nobles' if he became a Catholic. He named the monk Redmond Ffitz Simmondes as one of those most prominent in trying to persuade him to change his religion.[102] John Anderson claimed that it was 'ffzsimons a Monck' who committed him to Cavan jail and told the jailer to keep him there because he would not go to Mass.[103]

Eugene MacSweeney boasted that he had convinced 3,000 Protestants to become Catholics, threatening those who refused to do so with imprisonment in Ballinacargy or Clogh Uachtair castles or in Cavan jail. However, it would seem that some Protestants, including three Englishmen and their wives, voluntarily came to him asking to be admitted to the Catholic Church.[104] It appears that considerable number of Protestants, both settlers and native Irish, did become Catholics in the wake of the rebellion. William Hoe of Drumlane parish said that Philip O Cur, Shane McCurr and Turloagh mcCaddow 'lost ther religion being Protestants and fell to papistry'.[105] Richard Ashe, from Lisnamaine in Drumlane parish, was chancellor in William Bedell's ecclesiastical court before he became a Catholic and Cornelius or Cochonaght O'Sheridan, the school-teacher

99.   Ibid., MS 835, f. 76r.
100. Ibid., MS 833, f. 160r.
101. Dep. of John Hickman, TCD, MS 833, f. 156r.
102. Dep. of Arthur Culme, TCD, MS 833, f. 130r; Manning, *Clogh Oughter Castle*, pp 19–20.
103. Dep. of John Anderson, TCD, MS 833, f. 99.
104. Dep. of Thomas Crant, TCD, MS 832, f. 213r.
105. Ibid., MS 833, f. 11r.

Bedell persuaded to become a Protestant in 1636, returned to Mass in the wake of the rebellion.[106]

The rebellion which began on 23 October 1641 and the breakdown in law and order which followed in its wake changed radically the ecclesiastical landscape of the diocese of Kilmore. By the summer of 1642 Frederick Hamilton's castle in Manorhamilton was the only stronghold in the diocese not in rebel hands and the only Protestant clergy remaining in Kilmore were either sheltered with him in Manorhamilton or were native Irish men such as Denis Sheridan who could remain because of his strong family support in the parish of Kilmore. Most of the parish churches, which had been ceded to the Established Church in the previous half century, were reclaimed by Catholics though the situation in the diocese was far from normal. Catholic Church leaders were concerned with the continuing lawlessness in the country and were trying to work out how best to establish an alternative government, one that would grab the reins of the runaway horse that the rebellion had become. The primate Hugh O'Reilly would play a central role in doing this, although he would have to move southwards, at least for a time, from his base in Kilmore to Kilkenny, leaving Eugene MacSweeney the only bishop residing in Kilmore.

---

106.   Shuckburgh, *Two biographies of William Bedell*, pp 127–9; TCD, MS 831 f. 39v; 832, f. 48; 833, f. 131r; Ford, 'The Reformation in Kilmore', p. 90.

Chapter 12

Aftermath of the Rebellion: 1642–1669

The Armagh provincial synod, which met in Kells in the third week of March 1642, was Archbishop Hugh O'Reilly's first attempt to establish some order after the chaos of the previous five months. He presided over the synod, which was also attended by Eugene MacSweeney in his capacity as bishop of Kilmore and procurator of Raphoe.[1] All of the northern dioceses were represented. Eimhear MacMahon, the bishop-elect of Down and Connor, Patrick Hanratty, the vicar-apostolic of Dromore, Terence O'Kelly, the vicar-apostolic of Derry, Cornelius Gaffney the vicar-general of Ardagh, William Coghlan the vicar-general of Clonmacnois, George Plunkett the archdeacon of Meath and the Cistercian abbot of Bective, Fr 'Edmundus Fitz-Simon', were all present. The secretary at the synod was James Gowan (Smith), the Louvain-trained Kilmore priest who was ordained in 1635 and had been acting as secretary to Hugh O'Reilly since he returned to Ireland c.1640.[2] With O'Reilly, MacSweeney and Govan present as influential players at the synod, the decrees it promulgated can be taken to reflect the views of the leading Catholic clergy living in the diocese of Kilmore.

Thomas Dease, the bishop of Meath, was absent from this synod even though it was being held in his own diocese.[3] He was closely related to the Nugents of Delvin and had connections with other old Anglo-Norman families of the Pale and was firmly opposed to the 1641 rising from the outset. His absence posed a problem for the synod, despite the fact that his diocese was represented by George Plunkett, the archdeacon of Meath. The synod complained that 'at this juncture, when unanimity is essential', the bishop of Meath was 'unconformable'. He was ordered to revoke all his words and deeds in opposition to the

---

1.   Moran (ed.), *Spic. Ossor.*, ii, p. 8; Kelly, 'The Catholic church in Kilmore', p. 118; C.P. Meehan, *The Confederation of Kilkenny* (Dublin, 1846), p. 20.

2.   Moran (ed.), *Spic. Ossor.*, ii, p. 8, no. 13; MacKiernan, *Diocese of Kilmore*, p. 153; APF, SC, *Irlanda*, 351r-377v; Fondo di Vienna, 13, f. 142; *IER*, lxxvi, p. 234; *Coll. Hib.*, xxiv (1982), p. 67; Nilis, 'Irish students at Leuven university', pp 66–7.

3.   'Aphorismical discovery' in Gilbert, *A contemporary history of affairs in Ireland*, i, pp 34–6. For Dease see A. Cogan, *The diocese of Meath, ancient and modern* (Dublin, 1867), ii, pp 22–50; *DIB*, iii, pp 114–5.

war and sign the decrees of the synod. If he did not do this within a period of three weeks he would be suspended.[4] The fault lines between the Anglo-Norman and Gaelic Catholics, which became more obvious as the 1640s progressed, were already beginning to show at the synod of Kells.

Thirteen propositions were passed at the Kells synod - one of which declared the war to be a just one since it was being waged against those who plotted the destruction of Catholicism. However, one of the main aims of the synod was to try to impose discipline on rebels whose behaviour at the beginning of the rising had been relatively orderly but which had quickly degenerated into wanton acts of robbery and violence. Coming less than two months after the horrific drownings of the settlers at Belturbet, the synod unequivocally decreed that all who carried out murders, mutilations or were guilty of stealing, serious striking or extortion would be excommunicated.[5] Another decree recommends a similar punishment for all usurpers of Catholic or Protestant lands and also their patrons and assistants and all who aid the Puritans or other enemies of the king.[6] Because of the chaotic situation the synod recommended that a country-wide council consisting of clergy and laity 'with authority to rule and govern' be set up.[7] This provincial synod of Kells was followed by a national synod in Kilkenny from 10 to 13 May which drafted an oath of association for all Catholics, calling for unity and an end to distinctions between Old Irish and Old English Catholics. A number of lay leaders were invited to join them in June although it was not until October that the first meeting of the General Assembly of what became known as the Confederation of Kilkenny took place. This exclusively Catholic body was to meet nine times over the next seven years and in effect it tried to provide a parallel and alternative administration to the one based in Dublin.[8]

Archbishop Hugh O'Reilly showed leadership in calling the synod Kells and the subsequent synod in Kilkenny which led to the establishment of the Confederation of Catholics in that city. He spent most of the second half of 1642 and virtually all of 1643 in Kilkenny working with other clergy and lay leaders - drafting documents, negotiating between different factions, trying to impose discipline on the rebel soldiers and writing letters to the pope and Catholic kings and

---

4.   Moran (ed.), *Spic. Ossor.*, ii, p. 6, no. 6; Cogan, *The diocese of Meath*, ii, p. 39; Gilbert (ed.), *History of the Irish Confederation and the war in Ireland, 1641–1643*, i, p. 291; *DIB*, iii, pp 114–5.
5.   Moran (ed.), *Spic. Ossor.*, ii, p. 3, no. 2; Forrestal, *Catholic synods*, pp 103, 123; Rogan, *Synods and catechesis in Ireland*, p. 35.
6.   Moran (ed.), *Spic. Ossor.*, ii, pp 3–5.
7.   Gilbert (ed.), *History of the Irish Confederation*, i, p. 291.
8.   Patrick J. Corish, 'The rising of 1641 and the confederacy, 1641–5' in Moody, Martin & Byrne (eds), *A new history of Ireland*, iii, pp 298–300.

emperors around Europe explaining their cause and pleading for help. As a Catholic bishop, Eugene MacSweeney was automatically a member of the Catholic Confederation although he seems to have had little involvement with the day to day workings of it. Other bishops such as Eimhear MacMahon (Down and Connor and later Clogher), John Bourke (Clonfert) and Thomas Fleming, the archbishop of Dublin, were part of the inner circle of the Supreme Council and worked closely with the primate. Christopher Plunkett, the earl of Fingal who had taken refuge in Virginia shortly after the rebellion began, was one of the lay people representing the Old English, while Philip MacHugh O'Reilly, a fluent Irish speaker and MP for Cavan, represented the Old Irish viewpoint in Kilkenny.[9] Among the confederate representatives from Leitrim were Hugh and Owen O'Rourke from Dromahair, Charles Reynolds from Jamestown and Tadhg O'Rodaigh, one of the Fenagh coarb family and keepers of *The Book of Fenagh*.[10] Philip MacHugh O'Reilly was a kinsman of Primate Hugh O'Reilly's and was a signatory to several Confederate supreme council documents, including one which was written in Kilkenny on 7 December 1642 and addressed to Luke Wadding, the Catholic Confederation's representative in Rome.[11]

Throughout the 1640s Hugh O'Reilly was busy travelling between Cavan and Kilkenny for meetings of the general assemblies of the Confederation[12] and presiding over national synods in Waterford (1643), Kilkenny (1643), Kilkenny (1646), Galway (1648), Clonmacnois (1649), Jamestown (1650) and Clogh Uachtair (1651). He was a firm supporter of Owen Roe O'Neill, the general who had learned his soldiering skills on the continent and returned to Ireland in July 1642 before taking charge of the Ulster rebel army.[13] For much of the next seven years O'Neill's main camp was in County Cavan only a short distance away from Hugh O'Reilly's base in the parish of Kilmore. O'Reilly's efforts to establish more permanent links between the Confederation and Rome resulted in two high ranking clerics, Pier Francesco Scarampi and Charles Francis Invernizi, arriving in Ireland in August 1643. Invernizi, in his report to

9.   Donald F. Cregan, 'The Confederation of Kilkenny: its organisation, personnel and history' (unpublished PhD thesis, UCD, 1947), pp 114–5; Gilbert, *History of the Irish Confederation*, ii, pp 117–8; Joseph Cope, 'The experience of survival during the 1641 Irish rebellion' in *The Historical Journal*, xxxxvi, 2 (2003), p. 308.

10.   Donal F. Cregan, 'The Confederate Catholics of Ireland: the personnel of the Confederation, 1642–9' in *IHS*, xxix, 116 (1995), p. 495. For a list of representatives at the Confederation of Kilkenny see Gilbert, *History of the Irish Confederation*, ii, pp 212–8.

11.   Ibid., pp 116–7.

12.   These eight general assemblies took place in Kilkenny between the following dates: 24 Oct. – 21 Nov. 1642, 20 May – 19 June 1643, 7 Nov.-1 Dec. 1643, 20 July-31 Aug. 1644, 15 May-31 Aug. 1645, 7 Feb. – 4 Mar. 1646, 10 Jan. – 4 Apr. 1647 and 12 Nov. – 24 Dec. 1647.

13.   Scott, *Cavan, 1609–1653*, p. 45.

Rome later that year, described Hugh O'Reilly as being pious and gentle and, while admitting that he did not know Eugene MacSweeney, he was less complimentary towards him.[14] Two years later, on 12 November 1645, Archbishop Giovanni Rinuccini arrived in Kilkenny as the papal envoy to the confederates. He came 'to restore and re-establish the public exercise of the Catholic religion in the island of Ireland' but due to his intransigence and lack of understanding of the complexities of the situation in Ireland he proved to be a divisive figure. However, Hugh O'Reilly and most of the Old Irish Catholics who wished for a reversal of the plantations and the restoration of the Catholic religion, supported him to the end.[15]

Summer 1646: Massari in Cavan

In late June 1646 Archbishop Rinuccini sent Msgr Dionisio Massari to Cavan to consult with Owen Roe O'Neill and give him money to finance his army. While there he met with and formed a very favourable impression of Hugh O'Reilly:

> He is a man of noble birth, great influence, prudence, learn-ing, goodness, noble heart, is worthy of the highest esteem, and is most devoted to the Holy Apostolic See and to the Su-preme Pontiff. I detained him for dinner, and after a stay of many hours with me, he returned to his temporary residence not far away, leaving me with a high idea and extraordinary impression of his worth, wisdom and learning.[16]

Massari had arrived in Cavan on 28 June 1646 and appears to have remained there for approximately one week. He was based in Clogh Uachtair castle and from there visited both the Franciscans in Cavan and the ruins of the Premonstratensian priory on Holy Trinity island.[17] He stayed for a few days with the Cavan Franciscans in the Irish-style accommodation they had built for themselves near the town having been ousted from their friary in Cavan. Massari described their accommodation:

> It was situated within a wood and was a marvellous struc-ture in the Ulster fashion, the church, cells, refectory and all the other apartments being of wood, roofed with sods.

14. J. Hagan, 'Miscellanea Vaticano-Hibernica' in *Arch. Hib.*, vi (1917), pp 116–7. He is described in 'Aphorismical discovery' as 'a godly and upright prelate'. See Gilbert, *A contemporary history*, i, 1, p. 35.
15. Corish, *The Catholic community*, p. 45.
16. Massari, 'My Irish campaign', p. 247.
17. Scott, *Cavan, 1609–1653*, p. 45.

> I was accommodated in a room well plastered with mud on the outside, and full within of branches of odoriferous shrubs and rushes, with a good bed in the Ulster fashion. I took a hearty supper, slept soundly and tranquilly, and enjoyed the pleasant company of these holy religious.[18]

Msgr Massari's also visited 'the ancient church of a ruined monastery' on Holy Trinity Island in Lough Uachtair from where the Premonstratensian canons had departed three quarters of a century earlier.[19] He stated that:

> He found in a corner many painted and gilt images of saints carved in wood. These were now lying exposed to wind and rain, having been overturned by the heretics who dominated the district … There was a crucifix, with statues of the Blessed Virgin and Child in her arms, of St Patrick, St Catherine, the Magdalen and three other saints.

The Italian was so overcome with emotion on seeing 'the ruin and outrage done to the sacred images' that with tears he kissed them and, with the help of the islanders who had gathered to see him, raised the statues up and 'placed them in more becoming places, pouring out our prayers before them'.[20] He devoutly drank water from a holy well nearby, with all the islanders following his example.[21] Before he departed Msgr Massari distributed hundreds of blessed medals to the islanders, who were well pleased with them.

In December 1645, just one month after Rinuccini arrived in Kilkenny, the first volume of Fr John Colgan's *Acta Sanctorum Hiberniae* was published in Louvain. About five years earlier John Colgan, Bernard Conny and others wrote from Louvain stating how they 'have of late erected a new Irish printe, whence we hope will come manifold fruites, redounding to the great good and glorie of our church and catholike countrymen' and describing how they were 'by continuall labour diviseing how to restore the neglected honor of our sainctes, church and country' but were being hampered by lack of funds.[22] Hugh O'Reilly encouraged John Colgan and others who were helping to gather information on the lives of the saints

18.   Massari, 'My Irish campaign', pp 248–9.
19.   Massari mistakenly thought that it was either the Cistercian or Augustinian Order that had been based in the priory on Holy Trinity Island.
20.   Massari, 'My Irish campaign', p. 247.
21.   There were two holy wells nearby, one on Eonish dedicated to St Patrick and one in Kilmore Upper dedicated to St Feidhlimidh.
22.   *Fourth report of the Royal Commission of historical manuscripts* (London, 1874), i, p. 604.

and it appears that he spoke at the chapter of the Franciscan province in Multyfarnham on 27 August 1641, where it was decided that each Franciscan convent would contribute to the cost of publishing Colgan's work.[23] However, this initiative must not have been very successful because Hugh O'Reilly seems to have paid the full cost of publishing the first volume himself with the result that Colgan dedicated the book to him and thanked him for his great encouragement and liberal munificence.[24] Despite being preoccupied with affairs in Ireland, O'Reilly took time to promote the work of the Franciscans based in Louvain.

Divisions within Catholicism

Msgr Riniccuni's arrival in Kilkenny was greeted with great fanfare though it soon became apparent that he would be a divisive figure. His insistence on settling for nothing less than the Catholic Church being established as the state religion, to the exclusion of the Protestant king who would have no authority over it, alienated quite a few of the Old English Catholic clergy and laity. They, being more pragmatic, were prepared to remain loyal to the throne provided Catholicism was tolerated to such an extent that they could celebrate the sacraments privately much as they had done for the previous few decades.[25] Hugh O'Reilly continued to support Rinuccini, though the relationship between them was not always an easy one. In his first letter to the nuncio after his arrival in Ireland, O'Reilly asked:

> That no one be admitted for promotion to the vacant sees in the province of Armagh who is from an outside province or dioceses since in each diocese there are available a goodly number of men both of the secular and regular clergy who are suitable for and capable of undertaking such a task.[26]

Rinuccini ignored Hugh O'Reilly's advice and, despite further objections from some clergy and laity of Armagh province, appointed Patrick Plunkett to Ardagh and Oliver Darcy to Dromore in January 1646, both

---

23.   Harrison, *Ireland's misery since the late cessation*, pp 5–6. The copy of Hugh O'Reilly's address was found on Friar Anthony O'Rourke's body after he was killed in battle near Keelagh castle some months later. Harrison seems to err in stating that it was an address to the Catholic bishops gathered in Granard on that day.
24.   Brendan Jennings, 'Fr John Colgan's Acta Sanctorum' in Ó Muraíle, *Mícheál Ó Cléirigh, his associates and St Anthony's College, Louvain*, pp 118–9; Bernadette Cunningham, 'John Colgan as historian' in Raymond Gillespie & Ruairí Ó hUiginn (eds), *Irish Europe 1600–1650, writing and learning* (Dublin, 2013), p. 124; Jennings & Giblin (eds), *Louvain papers*, p. 143.
25.   Raymond Gillespie, *Seventeenth century Ireland* (Dublin, 2006), p. 170.
26.   *Comm. Rinucc.*, ii, p. 31;

being outsiders, the former a Cistercian and the latter a Dominican.[27] In the early autumn of 1646, following Rinuccini's decision to replace the supreme council which had agreed a peace deal with Ormond, the archbishop of Armagh's influence on national events appears to have waned. By May 1648 the split within Catholicism in Ireland was clear to all. Riniccuni's response was to excommunicate all those who disagreed with him and as Patrick Corish has put it Riniccuni 'sailed from Galway on 23 February 1649, leaving half the Irish Catholics excommunicated'.[28] Eimhear MacMahon, now bishop of Clogher, was gradually assuming the leadership role among the Irish bishops supporting Rinuccini. However, following Rinuccini's departure, Hugh O'Reilly began to find his voice again and a letter written to the pope on 18 May 1649 *'ex campo nostro apud Cavan'* explaining the complex divisions among the Catholics in 'this miserable kingdom of Ireland' was signed by Hugh O'Reilly, Eugene MacSweeney, John Cullinan bishop of Raphoe, Owen Roe O'Neill and Philip MacHugh O'Reilly.[29]

Prominent Franciscans

Thomas MacKiernan, a native of the diocese of Kilmore, was elected provincial of the Franciscans in Ireland at the provincial chapter held in Ross, County Galway in September 1647. One of his first acts was to censure Francis Magruairk, a fellow Franciscan and native of Kilmore, who had been very critical of the Irish Franciscans in Ulster.[30] However, Magruairk would prove himself to be an able and formidable opponent for MacKiernan and he was adept at using his connections, both in Kilmore and in Rome, to further his cause. Anthony Burke, another Franciscan who was critical of the Franciscans in Ulster, was called to account at an unauthorised intermediate congregation of the Franciscans which was held in Cavan at the beginning of February 1649. When asked if he had stated that the Ulster Franciscans were incapable of being reformed he replied in the negative and only admitted to saying that they wander through the hills with cattle and have no fixed abode.[31] Before leaving Cavan Burke was forced to sign a document withdrawing the statements he had previously made about the provincial and the Ulster Franciscans. The 'middle' or intermediate chapter of the Franciscans was held in Cavan on 4 February 1648 and the previous year Cavan friary had

27.   Ibid., pp 183–5; Ó Mórdha, 'Hugh O'Reilly – a reforming Primate', pp 28–9.
28.   Corish, *The Irish Catholic experience*, p. 110.
29.   Moran (ed.), *Spic. Ossor.*, ii, pp 32–3.
30.   Canice Mooney, 'Father Francis Magruairk, OFM' in *Seanchas Ard Mhacha*, ii, 2 (1957), p. 232.
31.   Ibid., p. 235.

been designated as a novitiate suitable for the study of philosophy.[32] These activities in Cavan friary coincided with Thomas MacKiernan's term as minister provincial of the order. However, they also confirm that the Cavan friary - which Msgr Massari described two years earlier as 'a marvellous structure in the Ulster fashion' - was large enough to host meetings of the provincial chapter and also to accommodate novices studying philosophy. The Leitrim-based Franciscans were also flourishing at this time. Jamestown Franciscan friary, which was established *c*.1643, may have been the community of Pól Ó Colla, the Franciscan scribe who, while based in the parish of Kiltubrid, made a copy of Keating's *Foras Feasa ar Éirinn* in 1644.[33] It appears that there was also an attempt by the Franciscans to move back into Creevelea friary at this time.[34] In April 1649 Thomas MacKiernan appointed Bonaventure Meehan, a native of Ballaghameehan, professor of moral theology and sacred scripture at St Anthony's College in Louvain.[35]

Philip O'Reilly, another influential Franciscan at this time, was born in County Cavan *c*.1600, presumably joined the Franciscans in St Mary's friary in Cavan and was ordained a priest sometime before 15 August 1629.[36] He arrived in Louvain on 23 August 1629 and it appears that he taught both there and in Prague for a number of years. He was back in Ireland in 1648 and, like his kinsman Primate Hugh O'Reilly, was a firm supporter of Archbishop Rinuccini.[37] Philip was appointed guardian of the Irish Franciscan house in Prague at the chapter meeting in Kilconnell, County Galway on 17 August 1650, a position he held until early 1654.[38] In 1650, shortly after becoming guardian in Prague, he translated *Introduction á la vie devote* by St Francis de Sales into Irish, calling his translation *De theacht isteach ar an mbeathaid chrábhaidh*.[39] Another Cavan Franciscan

32.   Cathaldus Giblin (ed.), *Liber Lovaniensis, a collection of Irish Franciscan documents 1629–1717* (Dublin, 1956), p. xx; Jennings & Giblin (eds), *Louvain papers*, p. 159.
33.   My thanks to Bernadette Cunningham for this information on Pól Ó Colla. Another member of the Ó Colla family – 'Bernard Ycolla' - was vicar of Kiltubrid and died *c*.1425. See *CPL, Lateran Regesta*, cclii, p. 398; Paris, Bib. Nat. Fonds Celtique MS 66 (NLI, microfilm P463) cited in Bernadette Cunningham, *The world of Geoffrey Keating, history, myth and religion in seventeenth-century Ireland* (Dublin, 2000), pp 11, 177. Another copy of *Foras feasa* had been completed in Muintir Eolais six years earlier by Flaithrí Ó Duibhgeannáin, one of the scribal family from Castlefore in County Leitrim. His copy was completed on 17 October 1638. See BL, Egerton MS 107 and Cunningham, *The world of Geoffrey Keating*, p. 174.
34.   Meehan, *The rise and fall of the Irish Franciscan monasteries*, p. 86.
35.   Ibid., pp 207–8; Jennings & Giblin, *Louvain papers*, pp 162–3.
36.   Giblin, *Liber Lovaniensis*, p. 7.
37.   Anselm Faulkner, 'Philip O'Reilly, O.F.M. (*c*.1600–1660)' in *Bréifne*, v, 19 (1979), p. 321.
38.   He had to deal with dissension and disputes while guardian in Prague. See Jan Parez & Hedvika Kucharová, *The Irish Franciscans in Prague 1629–1786* (Prague, 2015), pp 68–71, 192.
39.   Faulkner, 'Philip O'Reilly, O.F.M.', pp 320, 327.

friar of the same name, possibly a nephew, was the author of *Tractatus de sacramentis* which was published in 1678.[40]

Oliver Cromwell

The arrival of Oliver Cromwell in Dublin on 15 August 1649 and the death of Owen Roe O'Neill less than three months later at Clogh Uachtair on 6 November changed the religious, political and military landscape in Ireland.[41] Hugh O'Reilly was present at the national synod of bishops which was held in Clonmacnois from 4 to 13 December 1649, though it may have been Anthony MacGeoghegan, the newly elected Franciscan bishop of Clonmacnois, or Eimhear MacMahon who called the synod and cajoled the bishops into signing a statement of unity in which they declared that all the 'divisions and jealousies … are now forgotten and forgiven among us on all sides' and promising that they would work together in the cause of their religion and their king.[42] This declaration, which was to be published in every parish, papered over the divisions still existing among the hierarchy, athough they managed to agree on decrees which stated that Cromwell was not to be trusted and urged the faithful to support the war in a gesture of loyalty to both the king and to James Butler, the earl of Ormond.[43] This war-time synod tried to impose some social order and it declared 'excommunicated those Highway Robbers commonly called Idle Boys that take away the Goods of honest men or force men to pay them'.[44] Most of the dioceses of Ireland were represented at this synod by either a bishop or senior clergyman though Hugh O'Reilly and Thomas MacKiernan, the provincial of the Franciscans, were the only Kilmore representatives present, Eugene MacSweeney being a notable absentee.

Oliver Cromwell responded to the decrees passed at Clonmacnois in *A declaration of the lord lieutenant of Ireland for the undeceiving of deluded and seduced people* and he berated the bishops for the manner in which they taught their flocks:

> You either teach them not at all, or else you do it … by
> sending a company of silly ignorant priests who can but

40.   Ibid., p. 321; Parez & Kucharová, *The Irish Franciscans in Prague*, pp 75, 192.
41.   Hugh O'Reilly, Eugene MacSweeney and Philip MacHugh O'Reilly were present when he died. Scott, *Cavan, 1609–1653*, p. 46.
42.   Ibid., pp 40–1; *Comm. Rinucc.*, iv, pp 318–40; Monahan, *Records relating to the dioceses of Ardagh and Clonmacnoise*, pp 101–6.
43.   Corish, 'The Cromwellian conquest, 1649–53' in *A new history of Ireland*, iii, pp 343–4.
44.   Moran (ed.), *Spic. Ossor.*, ii, p. 42; Forrestal, *Catholic synods*, pp 103–4; Rogan, *Synods and catechesis*, p. 37.

say the mass, and scarcely that intelligibly; or with such stuff as these your senseless Declarations and edicts.[45]

Shortly after this response, written from Cork in January 1650, Cromwell resumed his ruthless and effective military campaign in Ireland following a winter break and when he returned to England at the end of May he appointed his son-in-law, Henry Ireton, in his place giving him instructions to bring his campaign in Ireland to a successful conclusion. Given what was happening militarily in the country, Cromwell was correct in calling the Clonmacnois declarations and edicts 'senseless'. Yet the bishops persisted in their approach and called another national synod which began on 6 August 1650 and was held in the recently established Franciscan friary at Jamestown in County Leitrim.[46]

Synods at Jamestown and Lough Uachtair

Hugh O'Reilly called the Jamestown national synod and this time Eugene MacSweeney was present. The Kilmore-born Franciscan priest, Brian MacEgan, who had been guardian of Creevelea and the first guardian of Jamestown friary, was also present at the meeting as procurator for the minister provincial of his order.[47] Eimhear MacMahon, the bishop of Clogher who had given leadership at the previous synod, was absent from this one. He had been elected to succeed Owen Roe O'Neill as head of the Ulster forces at a Provincial Council meeting in Belturbet in March 1650. This series of meetings, which was plagued by regional, cultural and familial divisions, began on 18 March and was chaired by Eugene MacSweeney.[48] Francis Magruairk, who had spent most of the previous two years in Rome, returned to Ireland in time for the Belturbet meeting with instructions from the pope for Irish Catholics to heal their differences

45.   Oliver Cromwell, *The letters and speeches of Oliver Cromwell with elucidations by Thomas Carlyle* (London, 1904), ii, p. 14.
46.   The Jamestown friary was established *c*.1643. See Canice Mooney, 'The Franciscan friary of Jamestown' in *The Journal of Ardagh and Clonmacnois antiquarian society*, ii, 11 (1946), pp 3–25; Liam Kelly, 'Franciscans in County Leitrim 1508-*c*.1800' in Scott & Kelly (eds), *Leitrim history and society* (forthcoming); Rolf Loeber, 'A gate to Connacht: the building of the fortified town of Jamestown, County Leitrim, in the era of plantation' in *The Irish Sword*, xv, 60 (Summer, 1983), pp 149–52; James Butler, 'Why Jamestown was fortified' in *Journal of Ardagh & Clonmacnoise Antiquarian Soc.*, i, 5 (1935), pp 75–80.
47.   Thomas de Burgo, *Hibernia Dominicana* (Kilkenny, 1762), p. 692; Francis Grose, *The antiquities of Ireland*, i (London, 1791), p. 22; Mooney, 'The Franciscan friary of Jamestown', pp 6–7. This Leitrim-born Franciscan was ordained in Louvain on 20 May 1617. Millet, *The Irish Franciscans 1651–1665*, pp 49–50; Ignatius Fennessy, 'Two letters from Boetius (Augustine) MacEgan, OFM, on the death of Florence Conry, OFM, 1619' in *Coll. Hib.* 43 (2001), pp 7–10.
48.   Jerrold Casway, 'The Belturbet Council and election of March 1650' in *Clogher Record*, xii, 2 (1986), p. 166.

Figure 12.1: Church at Jamestown, the likely venue for the 1650 synod.

and unite against 'the common menace to their homes and altars'.[49] MacMahon, who was an astute politician and friend of Owen Roe O'Neill, was elected as a compromise candidate. He reluctantly accepted the role even though he had no military skills. The Ulster army needed new recruits and firm leadership and soon Magruairk set about raising new recruits in Cavan. However, Sir Charles Coote defeated Eimhear MacMahon's forces at Scarrifhollis in Donegal on 21 June 1650 and shortly afterwards the bishop was arrested near Enniskillen and hanged.[50]

The synod of Jamestown was mostly concerned with Ormond, the king's representative in Ireland who had by this time lost the support of many of the churchmen previously on his side. After six days of discussion the synod released a statement which accused Ormond of misappropriating money raised by Catholics and of 'revelling in pleasures and merriment, remote from the foe, while other parts of the kingdom were bleeding under the sword of the enemy'.[51] Having listed a series of accusations against Ormond the synod concluded that Catholics could no

49.   Mooney, 'Father Francis Magruairk', p. 238.
50.   Corish, 'The Cromwellian conquest' pp 346–7.
51.   Cogan, *The diocese of Meath*, ii, p. 69. For Jamestown synod see also Gilbert, *A contemporary history*, ii, p. 100; *Comm. Rinucc.*, iv, pp 417–25; M.J. Masterson, 'The Jamestown declaration with notes and addenda' in *Journal of Ardagh and Clonmacnoise Antiquarian Society*, i, 5 (1935), pp 1–16; Monahan, *Records relating to the dioceses of Ardagh and Clonmacnoise*, pp 140–7; Kelly, 'The Catholic church in Kilmore', p. 118.

longer accept him as their leader and those present then moved to have all who supported him excommunicated. This excommunication was made public on 15 September 1650, further negotiations with Ormond having failed.[52] In the spring of 1651 Hugh O'Reilly decided to send Francis Magruairk, 'a prudent man' with a message to Rome explaining the divisions among Irish Catholics between those who supported the nuncio and those who did not, and also outlining his own loyalty to the Rinuccini. Eugene MacSweeney also delegated Magruairk to bring a letter to Rome explaining how he had absented himself from various clerical gatherings lest his presence would be seen to support their stance against the nuncio.[53] It was clear that both O'Reilly and MacSweeney backed Rinuccini and placed considerable trust in Magruairk. MacSweeney wrote:

> I have thought it good to communicate all my private views and opinions on the matter to Father Francis Magruairk of the Order of Friars Minor, so that he can convey them to your lord eminences and propose means by which the honour of the Roman see and the authority of the apostolic nuncio and loyal prelates of this kingdom shall be preserved untarnished in such a great flood of misfortunes. I most humbly beseech your lord eminences to deign to place your confidence in him.[54]

There was an air of desperation about the synodal discussions in Jamestown because, in the background, the Cromwellian forces were progressing rapidly with the conquest of the country. The venues chosen for the national synods of Clonmacnois and Jamestown and the provincial synod which Hugh O'Reilly convened at Lough Uachtair on 29 July 1651 were all within the ever-decreasing area not-controlled by the Cromwellian army. Besides, these local venues suited Hugh O'Reilly, who by this time was in his seventies, in failing health and unable to travel far from his base at Lough Uachtair. There were thirty-two clergymen present at the 'Clochuachtir' synod which was presided over by Hugh O'Reilly. However, Eugene MacSweeney and Anthony MacGeoghegan, the only other bishops present, and Fr Nicholas Bern, the procurator of the bishop of Down, assisted the feeble Hugh O'Reilly in chairing the various sessions of the synod.[55] The diocese of Kilmore was well represented at Lough

52.   Corish, 'The Cromwellian conquest', pp 348–9.
53.   *Comm. Rinucc.,* iv, pp 556–7.
54.   Ibid.
55.   Moran (ed.), *Spic. Ossor.,* ii, p. 93.

Uachtair by Ferdinand Farrelly,[56] the prior of Drumlane, Thomas Brady, the archdeacon of Kilmore, Donagh Geargan,[57] the dean of Kilmore, Bryan Reilly the pastor of Kilmore parish in which the synod was being held and James Gowan, Hugh O'Reilly's secretary.[58] The others present were representatives of the various dioceses or religious orders in the province of Armagh. The Franciscans, with whom Hugh O'Reilly had strong links throughout his life, were particularly well represented by, among others, Henry Mellan, Thomas MacKiernan the ex-minister provincial, Anthony Govan, the guardian of Cavan and Anthony Heslin, the 'Guardianus de Muntereolais' (Jamestown).

This synod, which was probably held on Holy Trinity Island to accommodate the ageing Hugh O'Reilly who was living there, lasted for four days. It passed twelve decrees which were signed by all present. The synod attempted to impose discipline on the soldiers of the northern army as it appears that indiscipline, low morale and absenteeism had set in following the deaths of Owen Roe O'Neill and Eimhear MacMahon. All Catholic army officers of either horse or foot that absented themselves from the field without permission were to be excluded from assisting at Mass.[59] More senior officers who were absent without permission were to be excommunicated. As in other synods there was a decree excommunicating robbers and thieves of all kinds. No one was to act as a tithe-proctor for 'heretics' but rather they were to make contributions to the continuing war effort. Those present at the synod declared that the Irish nation should not be blamed for the expulsion of the papal nuncio and there were also directions that the decrees passed at the synod be published in the province by both secular and regular clergy every month at Masses in the churches, chapels, oratories and convents.[60] This was to be Hugh O'Reilly's last synod. He spent his last days on Holy Trinity Island and died there less than two years later *circa* February 1653.[61]

Holy Trinity Island, Hugh O'Reilly's place of refuge, was one of the last places in Ireland to succumb to Cromwell's New Model Army. It was captured just weeks after the archbishop's death and immediately before

56.   Ferdinand Farrelly was also the perpetual vicar of Drumlane. MacKiernan, *Diocese of Kilmore*, p. 152.

57.   *Comm. Rinucc.*, iv, p. 582; MacKiernan, *Diocese of Kilmore*, p. 151.

58.   For list of those present see Moran (ed.), *Spic. Ossor.*, ii, pp 95–6.

59.   Gilbert, *A contemporary history*, ii, p. 182.

60.   Ibid., pp 93–6; Rogan, *Synods and catechesis*, p. 37; Forrestal, *Catholic synods in Ireland*, pp 87–8; O'Connell, *The diocese of Kilmore*, p. 418.

61.   Several dates have been given for his death. See Renehan, *Collections*, pp 47–8; O'Connell, *The diocese of Kilmore*, pp 419–20, MacKiernan, *Diocese of Kilmore*, p. 14. Bishop MacKiernan's date of February 1653 seems the most likely.

Clogh Uachtair castle surrendered. Colonel John Jones wrote to Major Thomas Scott on 1 March 1653 stating that:

> This day we have intelligence from Colonell Barrow that Trinity Island, in the county of Cavan … and some other island thereabouts, are delivered up unto him, and that he is now before Cloughwater Castle … and hopes in a short time that it will be rendered or quitted. This is their most confideing garrison in Ulster. God hath brought them very low both in spirit and number in the north.[62]

The strong walls of Clogh Uachtair castle were pummelled with cannon ball by the Puritan army and on 27 April 1653 Philip MacHugh O'Reilly, after a long siege, surrendered the castle to Colonel Theophilus Jones - a brother of Henry Jones, the former vicar and dean of Kilmore and now the bishop of Clogher.[63] With the capitulation of Clogh Uachtair Castle, the Cromwellian conquest of Ireland was complete.

Persecution of Priests

On 6 January 1653, the Commissioners of the English Parliament for Irish affairs published an edict banishing 'Jesuits, seminary priests and persons in Popish orders' from Ireland, giving them twenty days to leave.[64] It had already been clear that in the interregnum between the execution of Charles I in January 1649 and the return of Charles II to London in May 1660 the Cromwellian government was not going to tolerate priests or popery in Ireland. During the Cromwellian conquest of Ireland a considerable number of priests had been killed and so the edict of January 1653 was seen as a more humane method to rid the country of Catholic priests. The settlement terms resolved on 27 April 1653 between Colonel Jones and Philip MacHugh O'Reilly on the surrender of Clogh Uachtair castle reflected this new approach with the fifth clause of the settlement stating that:

> Priests or any other in Popish orders [are] to goe away within one month: Provided during their stay they exercise not their function, and had no hand in murthers, massacres and robberies.[65]

---

62. Gilbert, *A contemporary history*, iii, no. 2, p. 371; Manning, *Clogh Oughter castle*, p. 30.
63. Ibid., p. 31.
64. Benignus Millet, 'Survival and Reorganization 1650–95', in *A History of Irish Catholicism*, iii, p. 4.
65. Gilbert, *A contemporary history*, iii, 2, p. 374.

A somewhat similar clause had been inserted in the settlement reached a month earlier on 19 March 1653 when the walled town of Jamestown in Leitrim capitulated to the Cromwellian forces. The agreement drawn up between Donogh O Harte and Major Robert Ormsby for the surrender of 'the Castle or holt of Newtowne' in Dromahair on 3 June 1652 made no reference to the fate of Catholic clergy as it pre-dated the edict of 6 January 1653.[66]

The exodus of priests from the country to continental Europe was well underway by the time these strongholds in Leitrim and Cavan had fallen to the Cromwellian forces. It is estimated that at least 1,000 priests left the country between 1650 and 1654. Some of those who dared re-main were arrested and deported to Europe or to the 'tobacco islands' of the Barbados.[67] Others were interned on Arran Mór or Innisbofin islands until after the Restoration.[68] Adam Fay, who was ordained c.1628 and had been parish priest in Carrigallen, was said in 1664 to have 'suffered much, including long imprisonment, for his zealous ministry'.[69] James Gowan, the secretary to Archbishop Hugh O'Reilly, was deported to Spain where he stayed for some time before travelling to Belgium and then returning to Ireland in 1661 when persecution had eased.[70]

Belturbet became a holding centre for priests, not just from Kilmore diocese but also from the neighbouring diocese of Clogher, who were arrested and were awaiting deportation. It was ordered on 8 January 1654:

> That Donnogh O'Corran [a] priest now prisoner at Belturbet be forthw'th sent up in safe custody to ye city of Dublin, and bee delivered to Marshall Peak. And ye Governor of Belturbet is to take care that he bee sent with a sufficient Convey from garrison to garrisons and delivered as aforesaid.[71]

---

66.   Ibid., pp 322, 373. The Jamestown agreement stipulated that the names of the priests be given.
67.   Priests who were under forty, and therefore fit to work in the plantations, were more likely to the transported to Barbados. Those over forty were deported to 'France, Portugal or other neighbouring kingdoms in amity with this Commonwealth'. Seán O'Callaghan, *To Hell or Barbados* (Dingle, 2000), p. 62; Liam Swords, *A people's church, the diocese of Achonry from the sixth to the seventeenth century*, (Dublin, 2013), p. 188.
68.   Millet, 'Survival and reorganization', pp 5–7.
69.   Ibid., xii, f. 192r. He may have been a native of the Magherintemple area of the parish of Drung.
70.   APF, *Fondo di Vienna*, xii, f. 142r; Millet, 'Calendar of Irish materials' in *Coll. Hib.*, xxiv (1982), p. 67.
71.   'Commonwealth records', in *Arch. Hib.* vii (1918–21), p. 20.

The risk of attempts being made to free the priests from the military was very real. Captain Sharples, writing from Belturbet on 19 October 1660, described how a small group of military went from there to Killevan in County Monaghan and 'happened on the place where they were all met at mass and seeing the priest in vestments seized upon him … The priest was rescued by the multitude, their arms taken from the soldiers and they ill-treated and beaten with stones and clubs'.[72] A number of the people who attacked the soldiers were later arrested and held in prison pending trial.[73]

On 27 October 1656 James Gerrard 'receiver of ye Revenue for ye precinct of Belturbett' was given the sum of £21 7s. 6d. to be given as a reward for the capture of four priests and also to cover the cost of their deportation. The going rate for the capture of a priest was £5 and Gerrard was instructed to pay £5 each to Cormick McDonnell, Turlogh O Keenan, Donogh McCaffrey and Sergeant Nashil Marsh for the capture of Philip O'Shee and Denis O'Corkan, both priests who were both arrested on 6 May, and two other priests, Owen O'Connelly and Turlogh McCoskey, who were captured five weeks later on 14 June 1656. The remaining £1 7s. 6d. that Gerrard received was for costs incurred in escorting 'Several Popish and others in Popish Orders in restraint att Belturbett … to Carrickfergus att ye rate of Six pence each perdiem'.[74] The names of the arrested priests suggest that they were from the diocese of Clogher.

The regular priests were also targeted at this time. On 1 November 1658 Lieutenant Edward Wood arrested Thomas McKernan, Terlagh O'Gowan, Hugh McGeon, Terlagh [Fitz[Simons and Owen O'Rely who 'on examination confest themselves to be both Papists, Priests and friers'. He brought them before William St George, a Justice of the Peace in County Cavan, and was paid £25 for 'Good Service p[er]formed by him'.[75] All were sentenced to terms of imprisonment, with Thomas MacKiernan and Terlagh O'Gowan being sent to prison in Galway city

72. William P. Burke, *The Irish priests in the Penal times, 1660–1760* (Shannon, 1969), pp 5–6.
73. *CSPI, 1660–62*, p. 61.
74. 'Commonwealth records' in *Arch. Hib.* vii (1918–21), pp 25–6. Carrickfergus was a holding centre for priests awaiting transportation to Barbados. Corish 'The Cromwellian regime, 1650–60' p. 383; Peter Berresford Ellis, *Hell or Connaught, the Cromwellian colonisation of Ireland, 1652–1660* (Belfast, 1975), p. 167.
75. 'Commonwealth records', in *Arch. Hib.* vi (1917), p. 179; John P. Prendergast, *The Cromwellian settlement of Ireland* (Dublin, 1922), pp 320–1; Myles O'Reilly, *Memorials of those who suffered for the Catholic faith in Ireland in the sixteenth, seventeenth and eighteenth centuries* (London, 1868), p. 344; Oliver P. Rafferty, *Catholicism in Ulster 1603–1983* (South Carolina, 1994), p. 44.

while the others may have been sent to Inisboffin.[76] Thomas McKiernan[77] was the former minister provincial of the Franciscans who had been in Virginia during the 1641 rebellion and was later a firm supporter of Rinuccini. The four others arrested with MacKiernan were almost certainly Franciscans who were attached to Cavan friary and had, for safety reasons, re-located elsewhere – perhaps to Carricknamadoo in the parish of Killinkere or to Croaghan in Castlerahan parish.[78] Terlagh O'Gowan may be the 'Terentius Gauan' who was appointed guardian of Cavan friary at a provincial chapter held in County Longford the previous month.[79] Edmund O'Reilly,[80] the Dublin-born priest who had replaced Hugh O'Reilly as archbishop of Armagh, wrote to Propaganda Fide in December 1658 stating that the persecution of priests was still severe and he added:

> … however, things are improving every day, although recently Fathers Thomas MacKiernan and Francis O Farrell, ex-provincials of the Friars Minor, were captured and imprisoned with four other Franciscans who were living together in the woods and mountains.[81]

Thomas MacKiernan was still in Galway jail on 18 June 1659 when he wrote to the internuncio in Flanders stating that all the Franciscan prisoners were in great distress and pleading with him to send financial aid to the missionaries who, not having received the annual contribution from the congregation, were having to take greater risks as they went about questing for alms.[82] The prison regime took its toll on Hugh McKeon, one of those arrested in Cavan in November 1658. Anthony Doherty, the minister provincial reported on 18 July 1663 that, 'because of the ill-treatment he received in prison, Hugh McKeon died after his release' and he included McKeon in his list of martyrs who had died for his faith.[83]

76.   Giblin (ed.), *Liber Lovaniensis*, pp 39–40.
77.   Bhreathnach, MacMahon & McCafferty (eds), *The Irish Franciscans*, pp 58, 61, 335; TCD, MS 833, f.231r.
78.   Burke, *The Irish priests*, pp 3–4.
79.   Giblin (ed.), *Liber Lovaniensis*, p. 54; Millet, *The Irish Franciscans*, p. 283.
80.   For Edmund O'Reilly see Tomás Ó Fiaich, 'Edmund O'Reilly, Archbishop of Armagh, 1657–1669' in *Father Luke Wadding commemorative volume*, pp 171–228.
81.   APF, *Fondo di Vienna,* vol. 13, f. 386r; Benignus Millet, 'Calendar of volume 13 of the *Fondo di Vienna*', in *Coll. Hib.*, xxv (1983), p. 60.
82.   APF, *Fondo di Vienna* 14, f. 316r.
83.   Quoted in Millet, *The Irish Franciscans*, p. 287.

Thomas MacKiernan and Terlogh O'Gowan survived their terms in prison and five years later, on 28 June 1663, both of them attended a meeting of Franciscans in Ballybay.[84] Thomas MacKiernan, Anthony Gowan, the guardian of Cavan friary[85] and Thomas Brady, the archdeacon of Kilmore, were among a group of priests who were imprisoned for a time in July 1664 before being released on bail.[86] However, with Charles II now firmly established on the throne, there was an easing of the policy of imprisoning and deporting priests from the country. A report drawn up *c.*1664 listed some priests who had managed to stay in the country during the persecution and who were held in high esteem. Among them were the Kilmore priests Donagh Gargan aged seventy, James Gowan aged fifty-five, Adam Fey 'who has had the care of souls for the past thirty-six years', Malachy Farrelly who 'has had the care of souls for the past forty years' and sixty year old Edmund Gargan.[87]

It is hard to be precise about the number of Kilmore priests who were imprisoned and deported at this time. What is clear is that most of the work of the reforming bishops Hugh O'Reilly and Eugene Mac Sweeney, who tried valiantly to establish a Tridentine model of church in Kilmore, was undone at this time. The parish system collapsed and the Church went underground with any priests who remained in the diocese going *incognito* and the sacraments being celebrated under cover of darkness and in out-of-the way places. A report on Kilmore in 1636 stated that there were twenty-eight priests in the diocese and twenty-six years later Edmund O'Reilly reported that this number had been reduced to sixteen.[88] If these figures are accurate then the persecution of the 1650s may not have been as devastating as folk tradition would have us believe and indeed the large number of Mass rocks scattered throughout the diocese, which point towards a clandestine church, also suggests the presence of a sizeable number of priests.[89] The Mass rock called *Carraig Scaoilte* in Lurgan parish, with a rocky eminence nearby called *Carraig an Amhairc*, (the look-out rock), tells of a Church learning to survive despite the prevailing persecution. The tradition in Inismagrath parish that

84.   Burke, *The Irish priests*, pp 3–4.
85.   This may be the 'Anthonius Gavanus' who, writing from Louvain, gave a character reference for Brother Charles Reilly, a native of Kilmore, in 1633. See Jennings & Giblin (eds), *Louvain papers*, pp 100–01.
86.   O'Connell, *The diocese of Kilmore*, p. 325.
87.   APF, *SOCG*, 1, ff. 423r-436v, 437r-454v.
88.   Ó Fiaich, 'Edmund O'Reilly', p. 192. The number had increased to seventeen two years later. See B. Millet, 'Archbishop Edmund O'Reilly's report' in *Coll. Hib.*, ii (1959), p. 108.
89.   For Mass rocks in Kilmore see Appendix IV in Gallogly, *The diocese of Kilmore 1800–1950*, pp 399–401. For Mass rocks in Leitrim see also Moore, *Archaeological inventory of County Leitrim*, pp 196–9.

a portable wooden altar was used for Mass in the townland of Tawnacorry and that a *seal foscaid* or *scalán* - a wickerwork and thatched shelter - was used to cover the Mass altar in the townland of Drummonds, suggests an inventiveness that helped laity and priests cope and survive.[90] The *dúróg* or *diúróg* which was introduced to the parish of Ballinaglera was further evidence of this inventiveness:

> It was an oval-shaped wicker basket about 18 inches long and a foot wide with an opening at one end. In it were placed some consecrated clay, a wooden cross, holy water and some straw or tow for use at a burial. There was one in each townland. Whenever a priest could not be available for a funeral, these items were used by a layman who presided at the burial ceremony and recited the *De Profundis*.[91]

In the townland of Carntulla, situated in Ballinaglera parish on the western slopes of Sliabh-an-Iarainn mountain, is *Cloch an t-Sagart* and in the adjacent townland of Sranagarvanagh is *Cloch na h-Altóra* – both rocks associated with the friars who ministered in the area.[92] (See Fig. 12.2). Similarly, in the parish of Killinkere in County Cavan there is a tradition that Mass was celebrated on *Carraig na mBráthair* and *Carraig an Altóir* in the townland of Carricknamadoo.[93] The hidden glen called Glananehrin[94] in the townland of Cormaddyfuff, which is now in the parish of Castlerahan, takes its name from *Gleann an Aifhrinn* (the Mass glen), and place-names such as these are the best evidence of a clandestine church during the worst of the penal persecutions.

The persecution of Catholic clergy in Ireland in the 1650s discouraged Irish priests on the continent from returning home, although it is possible that people like James Mochory (Ó Maolmochéirghe), a native of Leitrim who was ordained in Lisbon on 4 March 1651, never intended returning home.[95] Apparently he had been learning Latin in Leitrim in the 1640s before abandoning his studies due the disturbed state of the

90. Gallogly, *The diocese of Kilmore 1800–1950*, p. 400.
91. Eileen Clancy & Patrick J. Forde, *Ballinaglera and Inishmagrath, the history and tradition of two Leitrim parishes* (Leitrim, 2003), p. 41.
92. See www.duchas.ie, (accessed 1 November 2015), County Leitrim schools folklore collection, vol. 0206, p. 287.
93. Gallogly, *The diocese of Kilmore 1800–1950*, p. 400; O'Connell, 'Mass rocks and churches' in *JBAHS*, iii, 2 (1929–30), p. 319.
94. Philip O'Connell, 'Ecclesiastical history of Lurgan parish' in *Breifny antiquarian journal*, ii, 2 (1923), p. 34.
95. Hugh Fenning, 'Irishmen ordained at Lisbon 1587–1615, 1641–60' in *Coll. Hib.*, 31/32 (1989), pp 106, 110, 113–4.

Figure 12.2: 'Cloch na h-Altóra' Mass rock in the townland of Sranagarvanagh
(Ballinaglera), overlooking Lough Allen.

county. Following the death of his father in 1648 he went to Waterford
where he survived by begging along the quays. Possibly in an attempt
to get to the continent to continue his studies, he enlisted in the Spanish
army and sailed to Ayamonte in Andalusia before marching to Badajoz
on the Spanish-Portugese border where he deserted in July 1649.[96] His
maternal uncle, Patrick Chacrano, a medical doctor in Lisbon, may have
helped him gain entry to the Jesuit college of St Anthony in Lisbon, where
he was ordained two years later. To celebrate the ordination his uncle
hosted a dinner to which he invited some of the Irish Dominican community and other Irish exiles living in the city. However, James Mochory
soon fell out with his uncle and, without a living in Lisbon, went to Évora. There he managed to get an Irish scholarship in the Jesuit college
where his first cousin, Arthur Chacrano, was already a student. Because
of an inappropriate relationship with a local woman James Mochory was
forced to flee from Évora and using the identity of William O'Connor, a
recently deceased Irish student, he fled to the Spanish capital, Madrid.[97]

Having arrived in Madrid, James Mochory got temporary lodgings in
the General Hospital and John Martin, the rector of the Irish college in the

96.   My thanks to Thomas O'Connor for this information on James Mochory's exploits in Spain
and Portugal. See Thomas O'Connor, *Irish voices from the Spanish Inquisition, migrants, converts
and brokers in early modern Iberia*, (London, 2016), pp 78–81.
97.   AHN, INQ 129, exp.6 (Madrid, 1652).

city, allowed 'William O'Connor' to celebrate public Masses in the college chapel. James Mochory begged Barnaby Kiernan, chaplain to the marquis of Leganes, for alms and Kiernan was taken in by him at first. Later, with the help of Lieutenant Cornelius Doody, who had been Mochory's superior officer in the Spanish army, Barnaby Kiernan discovered Mochory's true identity.[98] Barnaby Kiernan denounced James Mochory to the Holy Office and Mochory was duly arrested and interrogated by the Madrid tribunal of the Spanish Inquisition. During his trial, on the night of the 6-7 May 1652, in a desperate attempt to escape, he burrowed through the mud wall of his cell and, while still shackled, injured himself jumping into the street below, before being re-arrested. He was fortunate that Nicholas de León (Lyons), a Dominican who had known James Mochory in Lisbon, was in Madrid and he gave evidence to the Inquisition stating that although the prisoner was not William O'Connor he was, in fact, an ordained priest. This evidence helped Mochory's case and his sentence was a relatively light one: he was banned from Madrid for eight years and had his ordination certificate revoked indefinitely. The extraordinary life of James Mochory suggests that for unemployed Irish priests on the continent life could be precarious and fraught with danger, although Mochory had been, for the most part, responsible for his own downfall. Andrew Magaghran, a Kilmore man who was ordained in Lisbon on the same day as James Mochory, had a less eventful life. He returned to Ireland and was listed as the ninety-year old prior and parish priest of Drumlane, living in the townland of Derrintinny, when the 1704 list of priests was taken.[99]

Eugene MacSweeney: His Last Years

Bishop Eugene MacSweeney remained in Ireland throughout the Cromwellian period, surviving by hiding away in the mountainous areas of Leitrim and because he was growing old and incapacitated he was not seen as a threat by the government. During the worst period of persecution, in the early to mid-1650s, he hid in the mountains near Glenade in north Leitrim in *baronia de Rosclochair, sive Dartria Macglanc qua infra comitatus Letrimensis*.[100] On 9 April 1656 MacSweeney wrote 'from his hut in the woods' outlining how the priests 'have to roam through the wilderness and mountains and live in woods and caves, hungry, thirsty, cold and badly clothed to assist their scattered flocks … the clergy and people are in dire need'.[101] He later moved 'to a dwelling house … on the mountain of Slewnerin

98.   O'Connor, *Irish voices from the Spanish Inquisition*, p. 80.
99.   *A list of the names of the popish parish priests throughout the several counties in the Kingdom of Ireland …* (Dublin, 1705), p. 5.
100.   Lynch, *De Praesulibus Hiberniae*, i, p. 255.
101.   APF, *Fondo di Vienna*, vol.15, ff. 29rv – 31rv; *Coll. Hib.*, xxxiii (1991), p. 59.

Figure 12.3: 'Mass rock in the townland of Tawly, near Leitrim's Atlantic coast, with an incised cross and the inscription 'IHS' on it.

[Sliabh-an-Iarainn]'[102] in County Leitrim where he was to remain for the rest of his life and from this location he wrote his letters *ex loco refugii nostri*. From the middle of the year 1654 until the autumn of 1659 Eugene MacSweeney was the only bishop in the country. Of the other bishops, three had been killed, another had died in jail, others died of natural causes and the remainder were living in exile in Catholic Europe.

Despite his isolation and increasing incapacity Eugene MacSweeney pleaded with Rome in 1656 that, because of the extraordinary situation in the country, he be given special faculties which would be valid not just for this own diocese but for the entire province of Armagh and also would allow him to minister to the faithful who had been driven by the Cromwellian forces into Connacht.[103] His request was granted and his faculties allowed him to appoint both secular and regular clergy, which helped facilitate the roving missionary work by various religious orders since the parish system had collapsed.[104] By isolating himself on Sliabh-an-Iarainn mountain Eugene MacSweeney was making it difficult not only for government forces but even his own clerical students to find him. In 1658 Malachy O'Rourke, a Kilmore student studying on the continent, wrote to Propaganda Fide stating that he cannot contact his bishop and asking them for dimissory letters which would allow him to proceed to ordination.[105] John Heslenan, the Franciscan guardian of St Isidore's College in Rome, and probably, like O'Rourke, a native of County Leitrim, gave the clerical student a testimonial letter stating that he was 'of legitimate birth, virtuous life and requisite learning' and recommended that he be ordained.[106] Armed with this letter and a similar one from some Irish bishops based on the continent, O'Rourke proceeded to ordination and later, on his return to Ireland, was appointed parish priest of Carrigallen.[107]

When writing to Propaganda Fide in 1656, Eugene MacSweeney was bold enough to ask that any bishops appointed to the province of Armagh be compelled to reside in the province since 'titular prelates living overseas are of no use to this poor, forsaken kingdom'.[108] The

102.   Burke, *The Irish priests*, p. 3.
103.   APF, *Fondo di Vienna*, vol.15, ff. 29rv – 31rv; *Coll. Hib.*, xxxiii (1991), pp 59–60. It is possible that MacSweeney's abode on Sliabh-an-Iarainn was in the northern end of the parish of Kiltubrid in the diocese of Ardagh and county of Leitrim which would bring him into contact with people who had their lands seized and were driven into Connacht.
104.   Millet, 'Survival and reorganization', p. 11. Eugene MacSweeney, in his role as 'bishop of Kilmore and vice-primate' had appointed Thady O'Beirne vicar-general of Down and Connor in October 1654: APF, *Fondo di Vienna*, vol.15, f. 246r.
105.   APF, *Fondo di Vienna*, vol. 12, f. 57r-58v; *Coll. Hib.*, xxiv (1982), p. 56.
106.   Ibid., ff. 60r-61v. For John Heslenan see Mooney, 'The Franciscan friary of Jamestown', pp 9–10; Gregory Cleary, *Father Luke Wadding and St Isidore's College, Rome* (Rome, 1925), pp 113–4.
107.   MacKiernan, *Diocese of Kilmore*, p. 154.
108.   APF, *Fondo di Vienna*, vol. 15, f. 31rv.

pope appointed Edmund O'Reilly to be the new archbishop of Armagh on 15 March 1657, although it was not until October 1659 that he arrived in Ireland. Anthony MacGeoghegan, the bishop of Clonmacnois who had been out of the country since the end of 1652, had returned to Ireland - as bishop of Meath - a few months before O'Reilly. By Christmas 1659 there were three bishops in the country and Eugene MacSweeney would, at least for a time, cooperate with the other two in trying to reorganise church structures in the country after the devastation of the Cromwellian era.

Eugene MacSweeney was not present at the Armagh provincial synod which began on 8 October 1660, even though it was held in Clonelly in County Longford, a townland adjacent to the parish of Carrigallen in his diocese of Kilmore. This synod, which lasted for a week, was the first real attempt at Church reorganisation in the province after the devastation of the 1650s and the nineteen statutes passed at it are remarkable for their normality in a far from normal time. The statutes are mostly relating to Church discipline, dealing with such issues as the obligation to preach on Sundays and feast days, the condemnation of some superstitions, the method of publishing marriage banns and the prohibiting of wandering missioners who were without the necessary approval from their superiors or from the bishop of the diocese.[109] The thirteenth statute, which declared that the decrees of the Council of Trent be adopted in the diocese of Meath, Clonmacnois and County Louth with the same reverence as has been shown for eighty years in the other portions of the province would seem like a swipe at the Old English Catholics of the province and a sign that the wounds and divisions from the Confederation days were still not healed.

All the dioceses and religious orders of the Armagh province were represented at the Clonelly synod with Thomas Brady, the archdeacon of Kilmore, representing Eugene MacSweeney. Two months later, the bishop of Kilmore was the first signatory to a letter from 'the bishop and clergy of the province of Armagh' which was sent to Rome in support the beleaguered archbishop of Armagh.[110] Other clerics from Leitrim and Cavan who signed this letter were Bernard MacEgan, now minister provincial of the Franciscans, Anthony Gowan, the guardian of Cavan friary, Bonaventure Heslenan the guardian of Jamestown friary, Thomas Brady, the archdeacon of Kilmore and Donagh Geargan the deacon of the diocese.[111] In January 1661 Anthony MacGeoghegan, Edmund O'Reilly

---

109.   For the statutes of this synod see Monahan, *Records relating to the dioceses of Ardagh and Clonmacnoise*, pp 27 – 31 and for a summarized English translation see 'Synod of Clonelly' in *JACAS*, i, 6 (1937), pp 85–6.

110.   APF, *Fondo di Vienna*, vol.13, f. 436rv. See also ff. 438r-439v.

111.   Monahan, *Records relating to the dioceses of Ardagh and Clonmacnoise*, pp 33–4.

and Eugene MacSweeney were among the signatories to a procuration authorising Peter Walsh, a Franciscan now moving in government circles in London, to congratulate Charles II on his recent crowning and to plead for toleration for Catholics in Ireland.[112] Walsh, a close ally of Ormond's, supported a Remonstrance drawn by Irish Catholic landowners in the winter of that year which pledged loyalty to the king and which also significantly curtailed the role of the pope in church affairs. This was a step too far for MacSweeney and for many others in Ireland and, with Archbishop O'Reilly no longer in the country, the opposition to the Remonstrance was led by Anthony MacGeoghegan, Eugene MacSweeney and others such as Thomas MacKiernan, the former provincial of the Franciscans and a native of the diocese of Kilmore.[113]

In 1663 the primate Edmund O'Reilly wrote to Pope Alexander VII stating that Eugene MacSweeney was 'an octogenarian who has been bed-ridden for ten years'.[114] His description of both MacSweeney's age and condition[115] were exaggerated, although MacSweeney did admit, in a letter written on 22 February 1665 to Patrick Daly the vicar-general of Armagh, that he was suffering from a desperate illness (*quia nimia infirmitate impeditus*) which curtailed his movement.[116] The 1704 survey of popish priests in Ireland lists seven Kilmore priests still living, who were ordained in the 1660s. Three of these, Patrick Brady (1661), Murtagh Gargan (1661) and Daniel Reilly (1663) were ordained in County Offaly by Anthony MacGeoghegan, the bishop of Meath. Three others, Bryan Brady (1666), John Brady (1666) and Loughlin MacGloune (1667) were ordained in Dublin by Patrick Plunkett, the bishop of Ardagh.[117] Bishop MacSweeney did ordain Patrick Brady[118] in County Leitrim in 1667 though the fact that the six others were ordained by other bishops suggests that Kilmore clerical students in the 1660s found it more convenient to get another bishop to ordain them and that for the last decade of his life Eugene MacSweeney, despite being involved in some national issues in the early 1660s, was barely functioning as bishop of the diocese. He was not mobile but, with

112.   Anne Creighton, 'The Remonstrance of December 1661 and Catholic politics in Restoration Ireland' in *IHS*, xxxiv, 133 (May, 2004), p. 23.

113.   Ibid., p. 33.

114.   APF, *Fondo di Vienna*, 13, f. 442rv.

115.   Ibid. MacSweeney had been active for most of the 1650s and since it would appear that he was born *c*.1591 and ordained *c*.1618 he was still in his early seventies in 1663.

116.   Peter Walsh, *The history and vindication of the loyal formulary or Irish Remonstrance…* (London, 1674), p. 607.

117.   *A list of the names of the popish parish priests throughout the several counties in the Kingdom of Ireland*, pp 5–6.

118.   Patrick Brady, who was parish priest of Kildallan and Tomregan in 1704, had studied in Louvain University and was ordained in 1667 and not 1676 as printed in *A list of names of Popish priests*. See *Arch. Hib.*, lx (2006–7), p. 113; *Coll. Hib.*, xxvii (1985–6), p. 65.

the help of John Reilly, his secretary or clerk, he was still able to write letters and thereby exert some influence on church affairs.[119]

Eugene MacSweeney and Archbishop Hugh O'Reilly had lived in the diocese of Kilmore for twenty-four years and had no public disputes during that turbulent period. Edmund O'Reilly, who was appointed archbishop of Armagh in May 1658, was in Ireland for an eighteen-month period between October 1659 and April 1661 and during that time he received cooperation and active support from the ageing MacSweeney. However, as the 1660s progressed the relationship between the two men broke down completely. This breakdown may have been partly due to O'Reilly's confrontational style but was, without doubt, also due to MacSweeney's intransigence, his poor health and alcoholism. From 1665 onwards, Eugene MacSweeney opposed O'Reilly's attempts to remove the vicar-apostolic of Derry diocese and also his plan to appoint a vicar-general in the diocese of Kilmore.

Archbishop O'Reilly tried a number of times to remove Terence O'Kelly, the vicar-apostolic of Derry diocese who had replaced Eugene MacSweeney in that position in 1629, and who, according to O'Reilly, was related to MacSweeney.[120] Edmund O'Reilly wrote to Propaganda Fide in October 1665 stating that Terence O'Kelly 'had been living openly in concubinage for more than twenty years ... to the great scandal of Catholics' and he recommended that O'Kelly be removed and replaced by Patrick Daly, the vicar-general of Armagh diocese.[121] Edmund O'Reilly, in an attempt to dislodge O'Kelly, appointed two vicars to begin a canonical process against him. However, Eugene MacSweeney stated that the primate, since he was no longer resident in the country, had no jurisdiction in the case and so MacSweeney continued to exercise the special missionary faculties which had been granted to him approximately ten years earlier. He dismissed the two vicars and even threatened them with excommunication.[122] This opposition frustrated Edmund O'Reilly's attempts to remove O'Kelly and the exasperated O'Reilly reported to Rome in 1665 that

119.   Burke, *The Irish priests*, p. 2; Ó Fiaich, 'Edmund O'Reilly', p. 205.
120.   John Hanly states that O'Kelly was a nephew of Eugene MacSweeney. See John J. Hanly, 'Saint Oliver Plunkett 1625–1681' in Hughes & Nolan (eds), *Armagh history and society*, p. 434. For Terence O'Kelly see Edward Daly & Kieran Devlin, *The clergy of the diocese of Derry, an index* (Dublin, 2009), p. 11; Devlin, *The making of medieval Derry*, pp 351–4; Jefferies & Devlin, *History of the diocese of Derry*, pp 133–9; Thomas O'Connor, 'The Irish College, Rome in the age of religious renewal' in *Collegium Hibernorum De Urbe*, pp 31, 113.
121.   APF, *Fondo di Vienna*, 13, f. 498r.
122.   Ibid., vol. 13, f. 508r. Terence O'Kelly was a controversial character even during his student years in Rome and he was eventually deposed by Archbishop Oliver Plunkett at the synod of Clones in 1670. See Patrick J. Corish, 'The beginnings of the Irish College, Rome' in Dáire Keogh & Albert McDonnell (eds), *The Irish College, Rome and its world* (Dublin, 2008), p. 9.

MacSweeney 'cannot stand up' and 'the only part of him that is alive is his tongue'.[123]

Two years earlier, on 22 August 1663, Edmund O'Reilly reported to Rome that 'the bishop of Kilmore is in his diocese but because he is infirm and unable to function he must be given a priest as his vicar'.[124] Archbishop O'Reilly recommended that either 'Bernard Geaghran, STL of Paris, or James Gowan, STL of Louvain, both being natives of the diocese' be appointed vicar-general in Kilmore.[125] Edmund O'Reilly also recommended James Gowan, who had been secretary to Hugh O'Reilly, and 'Thomas Fitzsimon, STD of Louvain who is in Ireland and is a good and learned man' to be appointed bishop of Dromore or Raphoe. He also suggested that Brian O'Reilly 'a theologian and an undoubtedly good man, who belongs to Kilmore diocese' be appointed bishop of Raphoe.[126] There were obviously a number of capable and well-educated priests in the diocese but, despite this, MacSweeney was not willing to allow the primate to appoint a vicar-general. In October 1665 Edmund O'Reilly reported to Rome that:

> In Kilmore diocese the old bishop is still alive; he is very old and confined to bed; he subsists on drinks of whiskey or brandy; he neither conducts visitations nor makes corrections; he does not wish to nominate a vicar general or to accept one nominated by another; he lives like an anchorite on his mountain; his entire pastoral care consists in purchasing whiskey from the parish priests of his diocese.[127]

Oliver Plunkett, soon to be archbishop of Armagh, reported *c*.1668 to Propaganda Fide, in more measured tones, that Eugene MacSweeney 'was in residence in Kilmore, but was incapable not only of administering the diocese but even of saying the office for many years now'.[128]

On 25 June 1666 the primate, Edmund O'Reilly, in an ill-advised bid to resolve the situation, appointed Thomas Fitzsimons, a Cavan-born and

123. APF, *Fondo di Vienn*a, 13, f. 489r; *SOCG*, 1, ff. 318r-319v; *Coll. Hib.*, 6 & 7 (1963–4), pp 99–100.
124. APF, *Fondo di Vienna*, 13, ff. 454r-461v; *Coll. Hib.*, xxvi (1984), p. 25.
125. Geaghran was described as 'a learned and upright man'. See APF, *Fondo di Vienna*, 13, f.4 99v.
126. Ibid., ff. 482r-483v.
127. Ibid., 13, f. 498rv.
128. John Hanly (ed.), *The letters of Saint Oliver Plunkett 1625–1681* (Dublin, 1979), pp 22–3.

Louvain-trained priest, as vicar-general of Kilmore.[129] Patrick Plunkett later claimed that Fitzsimons was appointed with the consent of the clergy of Kilmore even though Fitzsimons himself, in evidence to Propaganda Fide, stated that he had been appointed by Edmund O'Reilly 'at a clergy assembly in Dublin'.[130] Clearly this appointment had not the support of all the Kilmore clergy and it proved to be divisive in the diocese with the supporters of MacSweeney and Fitzsimons quarrelling to such an extent that it caused scandal 'even at the altar'.[131] It may have been at this stage that MacSweeney casually appointed (*ad nutum*) Bernard Geaghran, the parish priest of Urney, as his vicar-general.[132] This unseemly quarrel in Kilmore was not exceptional at this time. There were similar disputes in several other Irish dioceses - the almost inevitable result of a lack of leadership and the collapse of diocesan structures during the Cromwellian period. Patrick Plunkett, who had been appointed bishop of Meath in January 1669, wrote to Rome on 31 August 1668 informing them that:

> The Bishop of Kilmore, being continually infirm in body and sometimes too in mind, is not able to repress the dissensions which have arisen in the diocese. The only remedy would be to give him a coadjutor.[133]

This seems like an early admission that the appointment of Thomas Fitzsimons as vicar-general was not going to resolve the problems in Kilmore. However, no coadjutor was appointed and the dispute rumbled on.

Owengalles Provincial Council

The death of Archbishop Edmund O'Reilly in France on 8 March 1669 meant that Eugene MacSweeney was once more the senior bishop in Armagh province and either he, or others on his behalf, seized the opportunity and called a provincial council which was held in the townland of Owengalles, near Bawnboy in County Cavan in the last

---

129.   For Thomas Fitzsimons see Francis J. MacKiernan, 'Thomas Fitzsimons (1614–80)', in *Bréifne*, ix, 37, pp 313–42; Carney (ed.), *A genealogical history of the O'Reillys written in the eighteenth century by Eóghan Ó Raghallaigh and incorporating portion of the earlier work of Dr Thomas Fitzsimons*; Pádraig Ó Suilleabháin, 'Thomas Fitzsimons and the Primer of the Blessed Virgin Mary' in *Bréifne*, iv, 13 (1970), pp 92–3.

130.   APF, *SOCG*, 467, f. 235; MacKiernan, 'Thomas Fitzsimons', pp 316, 327.

131.   APF, SC, *Irlanda* 2, f. 102r cited in Millet, 'Survival and reorganisation', p. 41.

132.   Geaghran was born in 1616 and was described by Oliver Plunkett in 1676 as a man who holds 'a licentiate from the Sorbonne and is a man of saintly life. He was in other circumstances vicar general'. Hanly (ed.), *The letters of Saint Oliver Plunkett*, pp 477–8.

133.   Patrick F. Moran, *Memoirs of the Most Rev. Oliver Plunkett* (Dublin, 1861), p. 3.

week of May 1669.[134] Malachy Corcoran, a Franciscan friar, acted as secretary for this council although the names of the others who attended it have not survived. On 25 May, this provincial council deposed and excommunicated Thomas Fitzsimons because of his 'contumacy and disobedience' and later Eugene MacSweeney signed a document confirming the excommunication by depriving him of all ecclesiastical jurisdiction because of his 'contumacy, calumnies, detraction and dissensions'.[135] Some years later, when he was defending charges brought against him by Oliver Plunkett, Fitzsimons admitted 'I was excommunicated once by virtue of a censure unjustly opposed by the late bishop of Kilmore in that farce of a council in Owengalles, at the insistence of those who are opposed to me today'.[136] Patrick Plunkett, the bishop of Meath, was delegated by Rome to investigate and resolve the crisis in Kilmore.[137] However, before he could carry out his investigation Eugene MacSweeney died, offering Rome fresh hope of a resolution to the problems in Kilmore. Bishop MacSweeney died on 18 October 1669 and was, with the permission of Robert Maxwell, the Church of Ireland bishop of the diocese, buried in the old cathedral of Kilmore.[138] He had been bishop of Kilmore for forty years, spanning periods of great violence, upheaval and persecution, and, despite all his reforming work in the early decades of his episcopacy, at the time of his death the diocese was in disarray.

134.   Lynch, *De Praesulibus Hiberniae*, i, p. 256.
135.   Hanly (ed.), *The letters of Saint Oliver Plunkett*, p. 484; Moran, *Memoirs*, p. 204.
136.   APF, SOCG 467, f. 231; MacKiernan, 'Thomas Fitzsimons', p. 317;
137.   Moran, *Memoirs*, p. 204.
138.   O'Connell, *The diocese of Kilmore*, p. 435.

Chapter 13

Disputes and Persecutions: 1669–1690

The death of Eugene MacSweeney in October 1669 marked the beginning of a period of fifty-nine years when the diocese of Kilmore would be without a Catholic bishop. During this period the diocese was administered by a number of different vicars general, vicars capitular and apostolic administrators - a situation which resulted in continued instability and divisions among the diocesan clergy. Just one week after the death of MacSweeney, the bishop of Meath, Patrick Plunkett, gathered the Kilmore clergy together and following their discussions it was said that the older and wiser heads (*maior et senior pars*) were supporters of Thomas Fitzsimons.[1] Then, on 25 October 1669, Patrick Plunkett declared Fitzsimons to be the lawful vicar-general of the diocese and granted a general absolution to all those who had incurred ecclesiastical censures during earlier disputes in the diocese. Oliver Plunkett, the new archbishop of Armagh, arrived in Ireland on 7 March 1670 and within days ratified the decisions taken by his cousin, the bishop of Meath.[2]

Oliver Plunkett

Archbishop Oliver Plunkett, in what may have been his first report to Propaganda following his arrival in Ireland, thanked God that the bishop of Meath 'has settled all the controversies which existed in the province with the result that peace reigns among the secular clergy'.[3] The new archbishop was naively optimistic and eighteen months later, on 10 October 1670, he wrote to Rome stating that:

> I found the diocese of Kilmore torn apart by factions, one adhering to Thomas Fitzsimons and the other to Bernard Geaghran, because of the late Bishop of Kilmore.[4]

1. APF, SOCG, 467, f. 227; Moran, *Memoirs*, p. 204.
2. Ibid.
3. Hanly (ed.), *The letters of Saint Oliver Plunkett*, p. 65.
4. Ibid., p. 137.

Archbishop Plunkett initially blamed Eugene MacSweeney and not Thomas Fitzsimons for the troubles in Kilmore, a view he reversed five years later. In the early 1670s, however, he held Fitzsimons in very high esteem and gave him his full support in any actions he took against his adversaries in Kilmore. He even recommended Fitzsimons, 'a very learned and eloquent man', for a number of different bishoprics. On 16 July 1672 he wrote to secretary Baldeschi in Propaganda Fide begging him to give consideration to the merits of:

> Father Thomas Fitzsimons, vicar general of Kilmore, a learned, exemplary and prudent man, with a view to promoting him to the episcopate or making him vicar apostolic in the same diocese, since he is already in possession of the government of that diocese. He is the most capable man in the province of Ulster and is worthy of every promotion.[5]

Despite these glowing recommendations Fitzsimons remained as vicar-general of Kilmore and with time it was becoming increasingly clear that prudence was not one of his virtues. He persisted in treating some of the Kilmore priests harshly and unreasonably and in doing so perpetuated existing divisions and created more enemies for himself in the diocese.

The relationship between Thomas Fitzsimons and Oliver Plunkett deteriorated dramatically in the first half of 1675 following an appeal by three Kilmore parish priests to the primate claiming that they had been unjustly suspended by Fitzsimons.[6] Thomas Fitzsimons claimed that he had cited the three un-named priests in the presence of other priests on 25 April 1675 for failing to preach on Sundays and feast days as required by various provincial synods. When they refused to respond to his citation he duly suspended them.[7] Archbishop Plunkett upheld the appeal of the three priests and re-instated them on 12 May 1675. Fitzsimons stated that the three priests were 'disobedient, contumacious and guilty of notorious crimes' and he refused to accept the primate's ruling.[8] Oliver Plunkett deposed Fitzsimons in October 1675 and restored Bernard Geaghran, 'who is 60 years of old, holds a licentiate

5.   Ibid., pp 311–2.
6.   For the details of the protracted dispute between Thomas Fitzsimons and Oliver Plunkett see MacKiernan, 'Thomas Fitzsimons (1614–80)', pp 322–34.
7.   APF, *SOCG*, 467, f. 230.
8.   Ibid., f. 218.

Figure 13.1:   1704 list of Kilmore priests ordained by Archbishop Oliver Plunkett.

Priest	Age	Parish	Year Ordained	Place of Ordination
Hugh Clery	66	Killinkere	1670	Ardpatrick
Terence Smith	58	Kildrumferton	1671	Ardpatrick
Bryan Riley	65	Kilsherdany	1671	Rosslough
Edmund Smith	57	Lurgan/ Castlerahan	1671	Ardpatrick
Edmund Deane	52	Templeport	1672	Dundalk
Hugh Brady	53	Cavan	1673	Dundalk
Bryan Donoghue	52	Drumreilly	1674	Louth
Miles Reilly	52	Carrigallen	1674	Louth
Philip Tully	50	Kilmore	1676	Ardpatrick
Edmund Magaghran	52	Drumlane	1677	Louth
Connor Reilly	50	Annagh	1678	Cavan

Source: *A list of the names of the popish parish priests throughout the several counties…* (Dublin, 1705).

from the Sorbonne' and is 'a man of saintly life', as vicar-general in his stead.[9] During the early months of 1676, however, Bernard Geaghran was feeling unwell and so Archbishop Plunkett appointed Brian Brady, the parish priest of Laragh, as his assistant, 'because the diocese of Kilmore is about fifty miles long and the good, elderly Geaghran was not able to do everything' on his own.[10] Oliver Plunkett described Brian Brady as a man 'who is thirty eight years old and has been vicar forane for these past twelve years. He is a man of good judgement'.[11]

Archbishop Plunkett ordained at least eleven Kilmore priests between the years 1670 and 1678. Connor Reilly, who later became the parish priest of Annagh, was the only one of these to be ordained in County Cavan. The others travelled to various locations in County Louth to be ordained by him. (See Fig. 13.1). As the dispute escalated between Thomas Fitzsimons and Oliver Plunkett the former accused Archbishop Plunkett of ordaining too many priests and of filling 'the ranks of the clergy with ignorant priests so that he may get money for

9.   Hanly (ed.), *The letters of Saint Oliver Plunkett*, p. 478.
10.   Ibid.
11.   Ibid; MacKiernan, *Diocese of Kilmore*, p. 156;

ordaining them'.[12] Oliver Plunkett did ordain quite a few priests in Armagh province during the 1670s, however, this criticism seems unfair since most dioceses in the province had no bishop and the pattern of ordinations in Kilmore in the 1670s was somewhat similar to what it had been a decade earlier. It appears that Hugh Brady[13] who was ordained by Oliver Plunkett in 1673 had been a student in Louvain University in the 1660s, although it is not known what training the other ten priests listed in Fig.13.1. had undergone. However, it is clear that a sizeable minority of Kilmore priests were being trained on the continent at this time. James Fitzsimons and Patrick Kiernan were ordained in Rome in 1670 and James Magauran was ordained in Lisbon in 1651. Most likely they had studied in these cities before their ordinations.[14] Fergus Laurence Lee, a native of Edgeworthstown, did his studies in the Irish College in Paris before being ordained for Kilmore in 1670[15] and James Kiernan entered the seminary in Santiago de Compostela c.1673.[16]

The majority of the Kilmore priests wanted an end to the ongoing dispute in the diocese and, in a bid to resolve the situation, Bernard Brady, the vicar-general, and seventeen other diocesan priests wrote c.1677 to Pope Innocent XI asking him to appoint John Brady, minister provincial of the Franciscan Order in Ireland, to the See of Kilmore. He was, they said, 'a man of mature age and strong faith which has been tested by fire, of exemplary life and habits, a son of the diocese, and born of a noble family'.[17] At first Oliver Plunkett had a very high opinion of John Brady stating in March 1671 that he was 'as regards birth, learning and prudence' one of the most outstanding friars in the province of Armagh.[18] However, following Oliver Plunkett's decision in October of that same year to grant the Dominicans questing rights in the province, despite strong Franciscan protestations, the relationship between Oliver

12.   APF, *SOCG*, 467, f. 233v. The archbishop of Dublin, Peter Talbot, also felt that Oliver Plunkett was ordaining too many priests. See Tomás Ó Fiaich, *Oliver Plunkett, Ireland's new saint* (Dublin, 1975), p. 56.
13.   *Arch. Hib.*, lx (2006–07), p. 116.
14.   *A list of the names of the popish parish priests throughout the several counties …* (Dublin, 1705), pp 5–6; *Arch. Hib.*, lix (2005), p. 26. The names of the Kilmore priests ordained by 'Blessed Oliver Plunkett' were published in the *Anglo Celt*, 21 August 1937.
15.   Daly and Devlin (eds), *The clergy of the diocese of Derry*, p. 12. He was appointed bishop of Derry in 1694.
16.   Patricia O'Connell, *The Irish College at Santiago de Compostela 1605–1769* (Dublin, 2007), p. 102.
17.   Brendan Jennings, 'Miscellaneous documents III', in *Arch. Hib.*, xv (1950), p. 65. The other Kilmore priests who signed this petition were Andrew Geaghran (Drumlane), Bernard Reilly, Nicholas Brady, John Geaghran (Drumgoon), Patrick Brady (Drung), John Gavan (Killeshandra), Patrick Drom, Terence Gavan, Patrick Droma, Junior, Peter Droma, Cormac Cornyne, Hugh Brady, Eugene Reilly, Patrick Brady, Constantine Gavan, Patrick Brady (Lurgan) and John Brady (Castletara).
18.   Hanly, *The Letters of Saint Oliver Plunkett*, nos 75, 97.

Plunkett and John Brady began to deteriorate rapidly. Archbishop Plunkett also met resistance from John Brady and other Franciscans in Armagh province when he tried to impose stricter discipline and reduce the number of Franciscans being ordained. He wrote on 20 December 1672 that:

> This John Brady seemed to be a very different kind of man when I first came into this country, but to tell you the truth I find him to be factious, insolent and proud, a man who under the cloak of privileges wishes to do whatever he pleases.[19]

John Brady had been a lector in Rome and in Prague and was a definitor and guardian of Drogheda friary when Oliver Plunkett was appointed to Armagh.[20] He was obviously held in high esteem within his own Order because on 23 August, 1675, at a chapter held under the cover of a fair day in Athlone in order to avoid the attention of the authorities, he was elected minister provincial of the Order in Ireland. Without the support of the archbishop of Armagh it was unlikely that the pope would appoint him bishop of Kilmore. Instead, he was appointed guardian of Cavan friary in 1684 and master of novices there three years later.[21] The initiative of the priests in writing to the pope *c.*1677 recommending him for the diocese came to naught and the divisions within the diocese and the dispute between Thomas Fitzsimons and Oliver Plunkett continued unabated.

Thomas Fitzsimons would soon become involved in another dispute, this time in the neighbouring diocese of Clogher where the Franciscan bishop, Patrick Tyrrell, accused him of stirring up the priests against him.[22] It was becoming clear to Oliver Plunkett that the now deceased Eugene MacSweeney may not have been totally to blame in his dispute with Fitzsimons and in 1676 Archbishop Plunkett referred to MacSweeney as 'a learned and venerable prelate for the most part infirm of body' and went on to describe how Fitzsimons had the audacity to excommunicate his own bishop during their dispute in the 1660s.[23] Plunkett accused Fitzsimons of being a drunkard

19.   Ibid., no. 134.
20.   Parez & Kucharová, *The Irish Franciscans in Prague*, pp 76, 179.
21.   Ibid., p. 179; Mooney, 'Some Cavan Franciscans', p. 20.
22.   APF, *SOCG*, 467, ff. 200rv, 202rv; MacKiernan, 'Thomas Fitzsimons', pp 329–34; Moran, *Memoirs*, pp 204–8. Patrick Tyrrell, a Franciscan and a Palesman, was seen as an outsider and met with considerable opposition when he was appointed to Clogher. See Tomás Ó Fiaich, 'The appointment of Bishop Tyrrell and its consequences' in *Clogher Record*, i, 3 (1955), pp 1–14.
23.   Hanly (ed.), *The Letters of Saint Oliver Plunkett*, no. 181.

and said that he had suffered an illness (dysentery) 'after which he was never again sound of mind'.[24] Thomas Fitzsimons appealed to Rome to lift the sanctions Archbishop Plunkett had placed on him and to restore him as vicar-general of the diocese. Propaganda Fide made its decision, in favour of Oliver Plunkett, on 1 February 1678 and then proceeded to appoint Patrick Tyrrell, the bishop of Clogher, apostolic administrator of the diocese of Kilmore. Thomas Fitzsimons died in Flanders in 1680. This well-educated and capable man, who at first had received such glowing recommendations from Oliver Plunkett and others, not only failed to resolve the divisions in the diocese but actually made them worse. Things improved considerably with the appointment of Patrick Tyrrell as apostolic administrator. By then, the diocese was ready for 'a new beginning'.[25]

Robert Maxwell: Bishop and Landowner

Robert Maxwell, who was consecrated Church of Ireland bishop of Kilmore on 24 March 1643, was quite unlike his predecessor William Bedell. His deposition relating his experiences during the 1641 Rising, in which he claimed that 154,000 were killed by the Irish in the first months of the rebellion, has been described as 'long and rambling … a good deal of which is mis-remembered and in some places invented'.[26] He was consecrated in St Patrick's Cathedral in Dublin and was one of just eight Church of Ireland bishops to survive the Commonwealth.[27] Chances are that he did not move to Cavan until a decade later since the parish of Kilmore, where the bishop's residence was, and the nearby Clogh Uachtair castle were not captured by the Cromwellian forces until the Spring of 1653.[28]

Archbishop Hugh O'Reilly had died a few weeks before the Cromwellians captured Trinity Island, where he had spent the last years of his life, and Bishop MacSweeney, now old and decrepit and living on Sliabh-an-Iarainn mountain, posed no threat. From mid-1653 onwards it would appear that Robert Maxwell was the only active bishop in Kilmore diocese. In 1647, by which time the English parliament had defeated Charles I, the Protestant episcopacy was abolished in Ireland and the Book of Common Prayer proscribed.[29] During the period 1653 to 1658, five Commonwealth ministers were appointed in Kilmore. John Read

24. Ibid., p. 478.
25. MacKiernan, 'Thomas Fitzsimons', p. 235.
26. Gillespie, 'The Church of Ireland clergy', p. 69.
27. Margaret MacCurtain, *Tudor and Stuart Ireland* (Dublin, 1972), p. 166.
28. Gilbert, *A contemporary history*, iii, no.2, p. 371; Manning, *Clogh Oughter castle*, p. 30.
29. T.C. Barnard, 'Almoners of Providence: the clergy 1647 to c.1780' in Barnard and Neely (eds), *The clergy of the Church of Ireland*, p. 78.

was appointed to Annagh in 1653 and was replaced by Eber Birch, another Commonwealth minister two years later.[30] Robert Wasse was appointed to Cloonclare in 1657 with an income of £100 per annum and he appears to have remained in the diocese longer than some of the other Commonwealth ministers.[31] Patrick Maxwell was sent to Lurgan parish approximately six months after his ordination and 'in consideration of his poverty, the great charges of transportation of his family and the small rent reserved upon the tithes of the parish', he was given a once off payment of £20 in January 1659.[32] Jonathan Edwards was the Commonwealth minister in Drumgoon from September 1657, receiving an income of £120. With the death of Oliver Cromwell in 1658 the ecclesiastical landscape changed considerably and Jonathan Edwards was replaced by Alexander Martin in 1660.[33]

In 1661 the diocese of Ardagh was annexed once more to that of Kilmore, the combined dioceses giving Bishop Maxwell the considerable annual income of £1,200.[34] He was obviously a wealthy man because in 1661 he donated £200 to Trinity College in Dublin and three years later he was able to buy Dromellan castle and 7,000 acres of land from his near neighbour, Sir Thomas Waldron, who was forced to sell because of gambling debts he had incurred.[35] These lands were created into 'the manor of Farnam, in which the Bishop and his heirs may make freeholders' thus creating the Farnham estate, which would later become the largest estate in County Cavan, incorporating more than 30,000 acres.[36] His wealth continued to grow and in January 1667, following rumours of a secret society being formed in the county, he sent £3,500 under armed guard to Dublin – almost twelve times the amount Faithful Teate had fled with at the beginning of the 1641 uprising.[37] Sir George Rawson was unimpressed with Robert Maxwell's actions stating that the bishop of Down, who had armed twenty of his tenants

30.   Leslie, *Clergy of Kilmore*, pp 16, 353, 803.
31.   Ibid., p. 900.
32.   Ibid., p. 680; J.D. Seymour, 'Notes relating to Commonwealth Ministers of the Gospel, extracted from the Commonwealth records in the Public Records Office', pp 62, 127.
33.   Leslie, *Clergy of Kilmore*, pp 53, 463.
34.   *CSPI, 1666–9*, p. 675.
35.   *CSPI, 1663–5*, pp 433–5.
36.   Ibid.; Farnham papers, NLI, D.20433 & 20438. For the Maxwell family see Jonathan Cherry, 'The Maxwell family of Farnham, County Cavan: an introduction' in *Bréifne*, xi, 42 (2006), pp 125–47; idem, 'The united dioceses of Kilmore, Elphin and Ardagh' in Claude Costecalde and Brian Walker (eds), *The Church of Ireland, an illustrated history* (Dublin, 2013), p. 235; Brendan Scott, *Farnham images from the Maxwell estate, County Cavan* (Dublin, 2010); Lyn Franks, 'The Maxwell family, barons and sometimes earls of Farnham, County Cavan – a genealogy' in *Bréifne* xiv, 52 (2017), pp 91–106.
37.   *CSPI, 1666–69*, pp xxxii, 274.

with muskets, had proved 'a stouter soldier'.[38] However, the memories of what had happened in 1641 were still fresh in the mind and the Robert Maxwell's fears were not without foundation. Bands of Tory rebels, native Irish whose lands had been confiscated, were active in Leitrim, Fermanagh and Cavan in the 1660s and when the 'King's good subjects and some of the army' pursued the tories in 1666, they 'fled to the mountains and there stand upon their keeping and … cannot be brought to justice'.[39] These raparees continued to be active in the 1670s although there was little sympathy for them among the Catholic clergy gathered at the provincial synod of Ardpatrick, which was convened by Oliver Plunkett and held in August 1678. Their first statute of the Ardpatrick synod decreed:

> That the clergy should warn the faithful against aiding or countenancing the bodies of lawless bandits, who were called Tories … and that they should likewise make known to their flocks what dishonour the deeds of these wicked men brought upon their religion and country.[40]

The treatment meted out to the Kilmore Church of Ireland clergymen during the rebellion and the loss of their favoured position during the interregnum took its toll on them. It appears that none of the clergy who had been driven out by the rebels in the early 1640s opted to return to the diocese after Charles II was crowned king on 23 April 1661 and the presence of these pockets of tory rebels throughout the diocese may also have been a deterring factor in their deciding not to return to Kilmore. Denis Sheridan, the native Irish clergyman who had sheltered William Bedell in the weeks before his death, was an exception. He remained in the diocese throughout his life. The Act of Uniformity which was passed in 1662 in effect restored the Established Church to the position it held before the rebellion and it soon became clear that the Church of Ireland was establishing itself once more in the diocese and was in no mood to tolerate Catholics or Protestant dissenters such as the Presbyterians or the Religious Society of Friends, better known as the Quakers.

Quakers: Progress and Persecutions

Following a series of religious experiences and insights between the years 1643 and 1645 George Fox (1624–91), a layman from the north of

38.   Ibid.
39.   Ibid., p. 137.
40.   Moran, *Memoirs*, p. 131; Hanly (ed.), *The letters of Oliver Plunkett*, pp 516–20.

England, rejected the trappings of formal religion and instead chose to be guided by the inner light of Christ and by the Scriptures.[41] His friends and followers - called Quakers because they trembled ecstatically with religious fervour – refused to take oaths, pay tithes, give undue deference to people or attend Anglican services. They prospered under the freedom of conscience advocated by the Puritan government and some were given lands in Ireland following the Cromwellian conquest of the country. Colonel Nicholas Kempson, who had been granted large tracts of land in the Killeshandra area of County Cavan, was well disposed to the Quakers and so leased parcels of land to William Edmundson, a prominent Quaker, and several other 'Families of Friends' in the county in 1655.[42] Among these early Quaker settlers in Cavan were Richard and Anthony Jackson, John Thompson, Richard Fayle, William Moon and John, a brother of William Edmundson.[43] (See Fig. 13.2). William Edmundson, 'the principal figure in the propagation of Quakerism in Ireland' had some success in evangelising other settler families in the County Cavan.[44] He reported that 'now Truth was much spread, and Meetings settled in several places, many being convinced and brought to the knowledge of God were added to Friends'.[45] Quaker meetings 'for the worship of God' were held in Belturbet and Cavan although from the beginning the Friends were persecuted because they would not conform by attending the state religious services, paying tithes or taking off their hats when hauled before the courts.[46]

Richard West, the Provost of Belturbet, came with some 'rude people' and broke up a meeting of the Quakers which was being held in that town *c*.1656 and he held all the Friends in prison overnight, the women being 'mightily pinched with cold, it being frost and snow'.[47] All were released the next morning except their leader, William Edmundson, who was placed in the stocks in Belturbet's market place. Robert Wardell, a young boy and son of the master of the military store in the town, was also put in the stocks alongside Edmundson for daring to tell the Provost that he had set a better man than he (West) in the stocks. The townspeople were unhappy with the

41.   For George Fox see Rufus Jones (ed.), *George Fox – an autobiography* (London, 1908); John Nickalls (ed.), *The journal of George Fox* (Cambridge, 1952).

42.   William Edmundson, *A Journal of the life, travels, sufferings and labour of love in the work of ministry of … William Edmundson* (London, 2nd ed., 1774), pp 28–9.

43.   Thomas Wight & John Rutty, *A history of the rise and progress of the people called Quakers in Ireland from the year 1653 to 1700* (London, 1800), p. 99.

44.   Lawrence W. White & Jessica March, 'William Edmundson (1627–1712)' in *DIB*, 3, p. 581.

45.   Edmundson, *A Journal of the life*, p. 29.

46.   *An abstract of the sufferings of the people call'd Quakers … from the year 1660 to the year 1666*, iii (London, 1738), p. 307.

47.   Edmundson, *A Journal of the life*, pp 31–2.

Figure 13.2: Willian Edmundson (1627–1712), the Quaker leader, was imprisoned in Belturbet and Cavan town.

actions of Richard West and both Wardell and Edmundson were released, the latter insisting that the Provost personally release them from the stocks. Robert Wardell afterwards became a Quaker and 'a serviceable man for truth and a preacher of it'.[48] The 'towne and coporation' of Belturbet made it clear that only members of the Established Church would be tolerated there. It was recorded in the Belturbet Corporation Book, dated 3 October 1660 that:

> It is this day ordained by the Provost, burgesses and com-
> monality of this corporation that all papists whatsoever
> that doth live and inhabit within this Corporation ... shall
> remove themselves and familys by [date illegible] Day of
> December next upon paine of twenty shill sterling each one
> that remain.[49]

Two months later Richard Fayle, John Lunn and several other Quakers were arrested in Belturbet for 'upon the Lord's Day coming within this Corporation' and 'thinking by their hereticall opinions and teachings'

48.   Ibid., p. 32.
49.   Archive of Cavan County Library, BC2, M3571.

to draw people away from the 'true worshipping of God'. The Provost, Burgesses and Commons of Belturbet decided that:

> If any Quaker, Anabaptist or Papists shall at any time hold … any such unlawfull meetings or assemblies within this Corporation … they shall (ipso facto) be formally punished according to law.[50]

The Quakers were also being persecuted elsewhere in the county. William Edmundson was imprisoned for fourteen weeks 'in a nasty dungeon amid thieves and robbers' in Cavan jail.[51] While in prison Edmundson struggled to cope with the smell of excrement and the choking smoke from the fire which the prisoners lit in order to keep warm. He wrote:

> In the day the prisoners would beg turf and at night, when the door was closed shut, they would kindle a fire which filled the dungeon with thick smoke, there being little air; this annoyed me very much, but they could endure it, being used to the like in their cabins.[52]

He described how he had fainted from 'the noisome smell and smoke' and how people who came to the grate to see him 'could not endure the smell, but many times went away with tears'.[53] Following his release from prison he, and several other Quaker families, had their land leases terminated and they opted to move to Rossennallis in County Laois.[54] Despite this exodus from the county, Quaker meetings continued in Belturbet and Cavan town. Later new Quaker groupings were set up in Ballyhaise and Cootehill and Edmundson returned regularly to support them.[55] In 1661 he, together with Thomas Lunn, Richard Faile, William Parker, Thomas Hutchinson and others, 'having been at a Meeting near Cavan to worship God, were much abused … by George Spicer, Sub-Sheriff, attended by a company of rude men, who beat and cut and abused' them before committing them to Cavan jail.[56] Richard Faile suffered considerably for refusing to conform

---

50. Ibid., 4 December 1660.
51. Edmundson, *A Journal of the life*, p. 37; Patrick Cassidy, 'The Quakers of County Cavan 1655–1900' in *Bréifne*, xii, 45 (2009–10), pp 14–15.
52. Edmundson, *A Journal of the life*, p. 37.
53. Ibid., p. 38.
54. Wight & Rutty, *A history*, p. 107.
55. Patrick Cassidy, 'Non-conformist religious denominations in County Cavan in the 17th and 18th centuries' in Cherry and Scott (eds), *Cavan history and society*, pp 200–6.
56. *A compendious view of some extraordinary sufferings of the people called Quakers … in the Kingdom of Ireland from the year 1655 …* (Dublin, 1751), pp 56–7.

to the Established Church. In 1660 and again in 1661, he was hauled before Cavan's town court by John Walwood, the vicar of Urney, Kilmore, Annagelliff and Denn, for refusing to pay tithes. Faile had goods to the value of £6 10s. seized from him in lieu of the tithes and previously two of his horses were seized, apparently as a fine for refusing to take off his hat at the Cavan assizes.[57] In 1670 he was committed to Cavan prison once more and was left there for eighteen weeks for failing to attend services in his parish church.[58] Other Quakers in the county were also victims of wanton violence:

> Thomas Lunn, being at his honest labour near his own house, was taken thence by two Troopers, belonging to Major Moor, and dragged between their horses about two miles, and cruelly used and beaten, to the astonishment of the beholders, for no other cause, but being called a Quaker.[59]

The sporadic persecution of the Quakers in County Cavan continued through the remainder of the seventeenth-century and into the early decades of the eighteenth-century. Their numbers in County Cavan began to decline as they emigrated to Pennsylvania or moved elsewhere to escape harassment. The Toleration Act of 1689, designed to give freedom of worship to dissenters, brought some relief. The battle of Cavan on 11 February 1690 – part of the broader Williamite wars which resulted in the town being burned - was devastating for the pacifist Quakers as well as the other residents of the town, and even though their members survived the carnage, they ceased holding meetings there.[60] The small Quaker group which met at Mullalougher near Ballyhaise thrived in the early decades of the 1700s and survived until 1755. The Belturbet Quaker meeting, which endured much harassment, dispersed c.1718.[61] The persecution of Quakers in the county eased during the early decades of the 1700s - principally because the more numerous Presbyterians were then seen as a greater threat. There was also an increase in sympathy for the mistreated pacifists. When two Quakers, James Simpson and Joshua Deale, were 'through the severity of Hugh Reilly, a popish tithe-taker'[62] imprisoned in Cavan jail in

---

57.   *An abstract of the sufferings*, pp 306–7, 314.
58.   *A compendious view*, p. 109.
59.   Ibid., p. 118.
60.   Wight & Rutty, *A history*, pp 145–6. For the battle of Cavan see Brendan Scott 'Accounts of the Battle of Cavan town, 1690' in Brendan Scott (ed.), *Cavan Town, 1610–2010 – a brief history* (Cavan, 2010), pp 19–27.
61.   Richard West and Matthew French, both Provosts of Belturbet, were active against the Quakers.
62.   Hugh Reilly was tithe proctor for Wettenhall Sneyd, the vicar of Kilsherdany. Wight & Rutty, *A history*, p. 346.

the 1730s, they were, through the kindness of the jailer, allowed to return home to their families.[63] Conditions were more conducive for the Quakers in Cootehill than elsewhere in Cavan and despite fines for non-payment of tithes and other persecutions, they, with the support of the Coote family, prospered and Quakerism survived in the town until 1900.[64]

Presbyterianism: Growth and Conflict

In the plantation of Cavan the baronies of Clankee and Tullyuncho, the former centred on Bailieborough and the latter on Killeshandra, were allocated to Scottish settlers. And even though some of the Scotsmen who were granted lands in Cavan did not reside there, Eugene MacSweeney, in his report to Rome in 1636, stated that there were Scottish as well as English 'heretics' living among the Catholics of the diocese.[65] Among those who migrated from Scotland to Kilmore in the early decades of the 1600s were at least thirteen Protestant ministers, though this was a smaller number than in other northern dioceses and none of the bishops of Kilmore from this period were of Scottish background.[66] The stand-off in 1611 between Bishop Robert Draper and the minister which Alexander Hamilton had brought with him from Scotland - presumably for the parish of Killeshandra - was an early sign of the uneasy relationship that would exist between some Scottish ministers and Protestant bishops of the diocese. William Bayly's protracted dispute with William Bedell is the best known of these disputes and even George Creighton, the capable Scottish minister involved in the setting up of the town of Virginia, preached against his bishop, William Bedell.[67] However, as Robert Armstrong has pointed out, the Scottish ministers who came to Ulster at this time were able, for the most part, to 'fit themselves quite comfortably within the Church of Ireland' even though they were reformers at heart who wanted to nudge that church in the direction of Puritanism.[68]

The rebellion which started in the autumn of 1641 targeted the English settlers and the rebels resolved 'not at all to touch or meddle with the Scots inhabiting amongst them' but rather to 'call them brothers'.[69]

63. *A collection of the Epistles and works of Benjamin Holme* (London, 1753), p. 77.
64. Patrick Cassidy, 'The Quakers of Cootehill', in *Bréifne*, x, 38 (2002), p. 571.
65. APF, *SOCG*, 140, f. 159rv.
66. Ford, 'The Reformation in Kilmore', p. 98; Roulston, 'The Scots in Plantation Cavan', p. 138.
67. Scott, *Cavan, 1609–1653*, p. 27.
68. Robert Armstrong, 'Cavan and the Presbyterian frontier in the early eighteenth century' in Cherry & Scott (eds), *Cavan history and society*, p. 220. It will be obvious that my treatment of Presbyterianism at this time depends considerably on the research of Robert Armstrong.
69. TCD, MS 833, f. 276r.

This goodwill towards the Scottish settlers did not last and the surrender of the castles of Keelagh and Croaghan in June 1642 and the subsequent forced march to Drogheda of approximately 1,200 - mostly Scottish – settlers and their ministers who had sought sanctuary there did not augur well for the future of Presbyterianism in the diocese. Yet, it was in that same year that the first two Presbyterian congregations were formally established in Ulster, one on the Antrim/Down border and the other in the Laggan area incorporating parts of Donegal, Derry and Tyrone.

Presbyterianism would make no progress at this time in the diocese of Kilmore since it remained in Confederate hands throughout the remainder of the 1640s and into the early years of the following decade. And even though there was greater toleration of non-conformists during the Cromwellian era the clampdown by the newly restored Church of Ireland bishops and the state in the 1660s ensured that Presbyterianism made little progress in the province and was therefore late coming to Cavan.[70] The Williamite wars undid any progress the Presbyterians made in Ulster in the more lenient 1670s and Samuel Kelso, who was minister for the Killeshandra Presbyterian congregation before 1689, fled to Scotland and died in Galloway in 1695.[71] It was not until the 1690s, with the ending of the wars between William and James, that Presbyterianism, buoyed by the arrival of a large number of Scottish migrants, began to put down firm roots in the province and by 1702 the Killeshandra congregation had a Presbyterian minister once more.[72]

William Sheridan, the eldest son of Denis Sheridan the native Irish clergyman in whose house William Bedell died, followed his father's footsteps into ministry. He took a Doctorate of Divinity degree in Trinity College and was consecrated bishop of Kilmore and Ardagh in Dublin's Christchurch on 19 February 1682. When Sheridan refused to take the oath of allegiance to William and Mary he was deprived as a non-juror

---

70.   S.J. Connolly, *Religion, law and power, the making of Protestant Ireland 1660–1760* (Oxford, 1992), p. 26. For the growth of Presbyterianism in Ulster at this time see Raymond Gillespie, 'The Presbyterian revolution in Ulster, 1660–1690' in William J. Shiels & Diana Wood (eds), *The Churches, Ireland and the Irish* (Oxford, 1989), pp 159–70.

71.   Kathleen M. Middleton, 'Religious revolution and social crisis in southwest Scotland and Ulster, 1687–1714' (unpublished PhD thesis), TCD, 2010, pp 288, 292 – cited in Armstrong, 'Cavan and the Presbyterian frontier', p. 223.

72.   Armstrong, 'Cavan and the Presbyterian frontier', p. 223; Patrick Cassidy, 'The origins and growth of the Presbyterian Church in County Cavan' in *Bréifne*, xii, 47 (2012), p. 510.

in 1692.[73] He was succeeded as bishop of Kilmore and Ardagh by William Smyth, who was translated from Raphoe in 1693. One of the issues William Smyth faced during his time in Kilmore was the increasing tensions between his own Church of Ireland members and the newly arrived Scottish Presbyterian settlers. On 18 November 1695, Brockhill Newburgh and eighteen other Cavan gentlemen wrote to Bishop Smyth warning him that there were people trying to promote disunity among Protestants and that there was a move afoot to get 'a dissenting Minister to settle in this Countrey'. They feared that such a move would seduce 'some of the meaner sort of inhabitants' to abandon the Anglican Church and they suggested that the bishop should inform the government so that it might take action to 'prevent this mischief'.[74] William Hansard, a Church of Ireland clergyman who held rectories as far apart as Fenagh and Kiltubrid in Leitrim and Castlerahan in Cavan, reported to William Smyth, when requested to do so, that he had heard a Presbyterian gentleman named Kennedy say that he hoped to see the day when there would be no more bishops.[75]

There were more bishops. William Smyth died on 24 February 1699[76] and less than two months later Edward Wettenhall, who had been bishop of Cork and Ross, was appointed to Kilmore and Ardagh, a position he held until his death on 12 November 1713.[77] The tensions between the Presbyterians and Church of Ireland members continued during his episcopacy as the Presbyterians settlers increased in numbers and tried to appoint clergymen and establish meeting houses for themselves. Hugh MacMahon, the Catholic archbishop of Armagh and the apostolic administrator of the diocese of Kilmore, was also unhappy with the influx of Presbyterian settlers. He complained that 'from the neighbouring country of Scotland, Calvinists are coming over here daily in large groups of families, occupying the towns and village, seizing the farms in the richer

---

73.   Leslie, *Clergy of Kilmore*, p. 835; Harris (ed.), *The whole works of Sir James Ware*, pp 243–4; *DIB*, viii, pp 918–9. William Sheridan was not the only Protestant with Jacobite sympathies. In 1696 Robert Saunderson, who would later become MP for Cavan, was expelled from parliament for refusing to subscribe to an association defending King William. See Eamonn Ó Ciardha, *Ireland and the Jacobite cause, 1685–1766* (Dublin, 2002), p. 108. Thomas Otway, the Church of Ireland bishop of Ossory, declined for a time to pray for William and Mary before eventually taking the oath of abjuration. See Ian McBride, 'Catholic politics in the penal era' in John Bergin, Eoin Magennis, Lesa Ní Mhunghaile & Patrick Walsh (eds), *New perspectives on the penal laws* (Dublin, 2011), pp 119–20.
74.   NLI, Smythe of Barbavilla papers, MS 41, 575/15. My thanks to Brendan Twomey for this reference.
75.   Armstrong, 'Cavan and the Presbyterian frontier', p. 224.
76.   He was buried in St Peter's Church in Dublin.
77.   For Edward Wettenhall see *DIB*, ix, pp 862–4.

parts of this country and expelling the natives'.[78] MacMahon described how Kilmore had an advantage over Clogher because it was a greater distance away from Scotland and therefore less likely to be trampled underfoot by the Scottish settlers.[79] Scottish settlers continued to move southwards in Ulster and into County Cavan and by 1707 there were moves afoot to set up a Presbyterian meeting house in Bailieborough.[80] However, it was in Belturbet that the best known 'frontier showdown'[81] between Presbyterians and the Established Church and state authorities took place.

The Belturbet Affair

The Presbyterians had already a meeting house near Belturbet for some time before the 'Belturbet affair' took place in December 1712. The fledgling congregation there was supported and advised by the Synod of Ulster and, more locally, by the Monaghan presbytery. When the Belturbet members expressed a wish to have their own permanent minister they were advised 'to fix their eye upon some young man in order to your settlement'. They chose Robert Thompson, a recent graduate from the University of Glasgow.[82] Bishop Edward Wettenhall and John Richardson, the local rector, were both absent from the diocese at this critical time. However, Jeremiah Marsh, the Church of Ireland dean of Kilmore who was anxious to curtail 'these pernicious designs and practices' actively opposed the Presbyterians, claiming that there were no Presbyterians of any note in Belturbet except William Hansard, an apothecary, and Cummin, a 'small merchant'.[83] The presbytery of Monaghan convened in Belturbet on 9 December 1712 to appoint Robert Thompson as a trainee minister and to establish a meeting house in the town and the following day a number of them, including approximately ten ministers, were duly arrested and charged with unlawful assembly and 'for endeavouring to disturb the peace and union of the Corporation of Belturbet who were generally church men and where no Dissenting preacher had hitherto been settled'.[84] They were listed to appear before Cavan spring assizes. However, it soon became clear that a case of this magnitude would have

78.   Moran (ed.), *Spic. Ossor.*, ii, p. 471; P.J. Flanagan, 'The diocese of Clogher in 1714', in *Clogher Record*, i, 2 (1954), p. 40.
79.   Moran (ed.), *Spic. Ossor.*, ii, p. 481; Kathleen Middleton, 'John Richardson at Belturbet: demographic change and evangelistic opportunity in South Ulster, 1690–1727' in *Eighteenth century Ireland/Iris an dá chultúr*, xxviii (Dublin, 2013), p. 57.
80.   Leslie McKeague, *First Bailieborough Presbyterian Church* (Bailieborough, 2014), pp 17–18.
81.   Middleton, 'John Richardson at Belturbet', p. 55.
82.   Armstrong, 'Cavan and the Presbyterian frontier', p. 225.
83.   Jeremiah Marsh to Matthew Handcock, 17 Dec. 1712 cited in Armstrong, 'Cavan and the Presbyterian frontier', p. 237; Middleton, 'John Richardson at Belturbet', p. 55.
84.   Marsh to Matthew Handcock, 17 Dec. 1712.

to be transferred to Dublin, or even to London where the defendants felt they might have a better chance of getting justice.[85]

The arrests in Belturbet caused a furore. Leading Presbyterians protested at the arrests and lobbied the authorities in both Dublin and London to have the charges dropped. The Lord Chancellor, Constantine Phipps, sided with the magistrates. He stated that the local magistrates in Cavan:

> Oppose them [the Presbyterians], alleging that the town [Belturbet] always enjoyed peace and unity, and there was an entire uniformity in the inhabitants of the old established religion, and that their permitting a Dissenting congregation to be settled there would introduce schism, and divide the town into factions and parties.[86]

However, following a meeting of a delegation of the Presbyterian ministers with the Lord Chancellor on 23 April 1713, he recommended that the charges be dropped. In return, the ministers had to give assurances that they would not set up a meeting house in Belturbet, that they would move their existing meeting house a greater distance away from the town and that they would be of good behaviour in the future. The charges were duly dropped and while Robert Thompson was ordained on 23 August 1713 and remained in Belturbet until 1725, the Belturbet congregation remained small and after Thompson's departure had no permanent minister again until 1854. David Symes was ordained in Bailieborough on 25 March 1714 and remained as minister in Corglass meeting house for ten years. He was replaced by William Wilson in 1726.[87] Despite a legal system that was loaded against it and ongoing, though more low key local opposition, Presbyterianism blossomed in Killeshandra, Bailieborough and Cootehill during the early decades of the 1700s and the Toleration Act of 1719 brought some relief to them.[88]

Popish Plot

The popish plot fabricated by Titus Oates in the late summer and early autumn of 1678 falsely claimed that there was a plot to kill Charles II and replace him with James, his younger Catholic brother, and this

---

85.   Eoin Magennis, 'Belturbet, Cahans and two Presbyterian revolutions in South Ulster, 1660–1770' in *Seanchas Ard Mhacha*, xxi/xxii (2007–08), p. 139.
86.   Phipps to Earl of Oxford, 26 December 1712, *HMC Portland MSS,* v (1899), p. 254.
87.   McKeague, *First Bailieborough Presbyterian Church*, pp 19–21.
88.   Moody, Martin & Byrne (eds), *A new history of Ireland*, viii, p. 262. For a brief description of the Presbyterian congregations in Cavan see Appendix I in Armstrong, 'Cavan and the Presbyterian frontier', pp 232–6.

plot triggered a three-year period of intense persecution of Catholics. Patrick Tyrrell, the bishop of Clogher who had been appointed vicar-apostolic of Kilmore just six months before the plot was hatched, was imprisoned and then escaped with the help of sympathetic prison guards. He was re-arrested on 21 October 1680 and, on the evidence of John MacMoyer who also gave evidence against Oliver Plunkett, was charged with high treason.[89] Edmund O'Reilly, the parish priest of Crosserlough and Tyrrell's vicar-general in Kilmore diocese, was also imprisoned at this time. Letters continued to be exchanged between the two men despite the fact that O'Reilly was lodged in Cavan jail and, unsurprisingly, some of them fell into the hands of the Dublin authorities. On 28 June 1681, the Irish Privy Council wrote to Humphrey Perrott, the High Sheriff of Cavan, stating that it had decided that:

> The letters directed to Edmund Rely, prisoner in the gaole of Cavan, from Patrick Tyrrell be returned to you and that you examine Rely whether he doth know the said Tyrrell and of what calling or profession he is and if a clergyman whether he bee a Bishopp and of what place he bears his title and whether the titular Bishopp of Clogher be called Tyrrell. You are likewise to examine the said Rely concerning the great pacquett of letters said to be conveyed out of the Gaole.[90]

Both Patrick Tyrrell and Edmund O'Reilly were released from prison.[91] However, Charles Meehan, a Franciscan priest and native of the diocese of Kilmore, was not so lucky.

Charles Meehan, OFM

Charles Meehan was born *c.*1645 in the parish of Ballaghameehan in north-Leitrim. He joined the Franciscan Order and studied in Louvain where he was ordained in 1671.[92] Meehan was back in Ireland the following year and was given faculties to hear confessions at the provincial chapter which was held in Elphin on 21 November 1672.[93] His stay in Ireland was short,

---

89.   Moran, *Memoirs*, p. 298; *DIB*, ix, p. 547.
90.   Burke, *The Irish priests*, p. 80.
91.   It is possible that this was the same 'Edmond Reilly, archdeacon of Kilmore' who was in Paris in 1708. See Liam Swords, 'Patrick O Donnelly, 1649–1719, bishop of Dromore' in *Seanchas Ard Mhacha*, 15, 2(1993), p. 88.
92.   Patrick F. Meehan, *Blessed Charles Meehan, OFM, 1645–1679* (Portlaoise, *c.*1990), p. 9.
93.   Giblin (ed.), *Liber Lovaniensis*, p. 131.

however, and he returned to Louvain in November 1674. From there Meehan was sent onwards to Hammelburg in Bavaria to study philosophy. Two years later he began to teach in St Isidore's College in Rome. In the early summer of 1678 Charles Meehan was asked to return to Ireland to work among his compatriots. However, the ship that he was travelling on was caught in a storm off the coast of England and, while Meehan managed to get ashore with some of his belongings, he was arrested in June 1678 when making his way through north-Wales to the coast, where he had hoped to get a boat to Ireland. He was released through the intervention of a Catholic earl only to be re-arrested and imprisoned.[94] On 6 July 1678 Sir John Williamson wrote to Sir Job Charleston stating that there was:

> An Irishman apprehended at Denbigh on suspicion of being a Popish priest. I have had some of the books and papers seized on him put into my hands by Sir John Salusbury … the town of Denbigh would be glad he were sent to the county gaol.[95]

A month later, on 8 August, John Salusbury wrote to Williamson stating that the prisoner was still being held in Denbigh 'to the great charge of the poor inhabitants of the town' and asking him to order Charles Meehan to be sent to the county gaol and to send back 'such books and papers found with him as you deem requisite to accuse him of the crime he is suspected of'.[96] When he received no reply, an exasperated Salusbury wrote to Williamson again on 10 September, stating that the assizes were due to commence shortly and looking for directions or else 'we shall not know what to allege against or prosecute him for'.[97] This last letter had the desired effect and four days later Williamson wrote to Salusbury, returning the books and papers which had been found on the prisoner, directing that the prisoner be moved to the county jail and giving clear instructions that the prisoner 'be brought to his trial according to law'.[98]

Charles Meehan's trial was not held during the autumn assizes and his case and that of William Llyod, another imprisoned priest,

---

94.   See letters in Kaspar Liebler, *Annales Conventus SS. Auxiliariorum extra muros Hammelburgenses OFM Recollectorum* (Hammelburg, 1648–80), *ad an.* 1674, pp 180–1, *ad an.* 1676, p. 195, *ad an.* 1679, p. 221 which are published in Canice Mooney, 'Further light on Father Charles Meehan, OFM' in *Coll. Hib.*, 6 & 7 (1963–64), pp 227–29.
95.   *Calendar of State Papers, Domestic Series*, 1678, p. 279.
96.   Ibid., pp 348–9.
97.   Ibid., p. 400.
98.   Ibid., p. 405.

were discussed in the House of Commons on 16 November 1678. The members of parliament, in an address to the king, noted that 'Charles Mehaine hath continued in custody in the borough of Denbigh since June last upon violent suspicion of being a Popish Priest' and as the king's good 'Protestant subjects, [who were] filled with present fear of Popery' they urged the king to 'have the laws speedily and effectually executed upon Popish priests'.[99] The Titus Oates popish plot did not surface until two or three months after the arrest of Meehan, but the delay in bringing his case to trial meant that it was held when anti-Catholic sentiment was at fever pitch. His trial took place in Ruthin on 28 April 1679. Thomas Roberts gave evidence that Meehan had complained that he was abused and severely dealt with by William Shaw his jailer, who was a glover in Denbigh.[100] Shaw also gave evidence stating that 'Charles Mihan … hath several times confessed … that he was a priest of the Romish religion, and wished to be a good priest and would die on it'.[101] Charles Meehan was convicted of treason and sentenced to be hanged, drawn and quartered - a sentence which was carried out at Ruthin on 12 August 1679.[102] A contemporary account of his last words has survived:

> Now God Almighty is pleased I should suffer Martyrdom, his Holy Name be praised, since I dye for my Religion. But you have no right to put me to death in this country, though I confessed myself to be a priest, for you seized me as I was going to my native country, Ireland, being driven at sea on this coast, for I never used my function in England before I was taken, however God forgive you; for I do and shall always pray for you, especially for those who were so good to me in my distress, I pray God bless our King and defend him from his enemies, and convert him to the Holy Catholick Faith, Amen.[103]

99.   H.C., 1678, viii, pp 828–9.
100.   PRO, Wales, 4/31, Mem.33 cited in J.M. Cronin, 'The other Irish martyr of the Titus Oates plot' in *Blessed Oliver Plunkett: historical studies* (Dublin, 1937), pp 139–40.
101.   PRO, Wales, 4/31, Mem.34.
102.   Meehan, *Blessed Charles Meehan*, p. 11.
103.   BM, 'An account of the words spoken by Mr Charles Mahony, an Irish priest of the Holy Order of St Francis, who was executed in his habit at Ruthin in North Wales, August, 12. 1679' in *Last speeches of three priests that were executed for religion, Anno Domini 1679* (London, 1679), p. 2. The same source states that Meehan's 'age was under forty, he was tryed and condemned at Denby, confessing himself to be a priest.'

His prayer for the conversion of the king was answered when Charles II professed himself a Catholic before his death in 1685. Charles Meehan was declared venerable by Pope Leo XIII on 4 December 1886 and was beatified by Pope John Paul II on 22 November 1987. His feast day is celebrated along with the English and Welsh martyrs on 4 May each year.[104] Two years after Meehan's death, on 11 July 1681, Archbishop Oliver Plunkett, was similarly executed at Tyburn on 11 July 1681 on a trumped-up charge of treason. He was the last high-profile victim of the Titus Oates plot although at the time of his death Oates had been discredited and the persecution was already easing.

104.   There is a plaque in memory of Charles Meehan in the Catholic church in Ruthin. For Charles Meehan see Cronin, 'The other Irish martyr of the Titus Oates plot', pp 133–53; Canice Mooney, 'The Ven. Charles Meehan, OFM' in *Franciscan College Annual*, 1952, pp 91–3; idem, 'Some Leitrim Franciscans of the past', pp 337–8.

Chapter 14

The Penal Laws: 1690–1728

The death of Thomas Fitzsimons in 1680 and the acceptance of Patrick Tyrrell, the bishop of Clogher, as administrator of the diocese eased the divisions among the Kilmore clergy. The accession of the Catholic king, James II, to the throne in 1685 meant there was an air of optimism when Patrick Tyrrell called a synod at Cavan on 7 June 1687 to draw up statutes for the diocese. The statutes drawn up in Cavan borrowed from the provincial synod of Ardpatrick (1678), the synod of Meath diocese (1686)[1] and previous synods which were held in Kilmore during the episcopacy of Eugene MacSweeney. This Cavan synod was yet another attempt to establish Tridentine norms and discipline in the diocese.[2]

The synod's first eight statutes, under the heading *De vita et honestate Clericorum*, were intended to impose stricter discipline on the clergy. All parish priests were to have a fixed residence, were forbidden to frequent taverns and were to avoid any situation that might endanger their vows of celibacy. They were to wear clerical clothes and be properly vested when celebrating the sacraments. Priests were obliged to preach on Sundays and feast days and, if they were unable to do so, substitute preachers were to be provided. Clerical conferences were to be held each month (except during the winter months of November, December and January) and priests were instructed to leave their books and sacred vessels to the parish or to the diocese when they died. There were also regulations for the keeping of parish registers for baptisms, confirmations and deaths. Drinking and other abuses at wakes were to be curtailed and keeners (*clamores et vociferationes foeminarum*) were to be banned from funerals. Patrick Corish has suggested that 'the sharp tone' of the marriage legislation in the Cavan synod and in the 1670 Armagh provincial synod points towards the persistence of 'gross sexual habits' among

---

1. For Meath diocesan statutes see Patrick Fagan, *The diocese of Meath in the eighteenth century* (Dublin, 2001), pp 48–59.
2. Forrestal, *Catholic synods*, p. 77.

the laity in Ulster.[3] The Meath diocesan synod of the previous year had stipulated that:

> No parish priest in future shall celebrate Mass on Sundays or feastdays in the open air, and those who decline to build houses or chapels in which the divine mysteries can be celebrated, shall go without Mass on feastdays and Sundays until they construct a large house or chapel.[4]

The fact that no such statute was enacted at the Kilmore synod of 1687 seems like a tacit acceptance that, perhaps due to poverty and persecution, conditions were not right for the building of chapels and Mass houses in the diocese at this time.

War and Persecution

The forty-six statutes which were agreed in Cavan were passed in the expectation that the Catholic Church would soon emerge from the shadows of persecution and would be able to celebrate the sacraments freely and publicly once more. It was a false hope. In 1688 James II fled to France and on 13 February 1689 William of Orange and his wife Mary became joint monarchs of England and Ireland. The war between William and James, which brought devastation, not just to Cavan town but also to the surrounding countryside in the early months of 1690, was followed by the enactment of a series 'penal laws' which drove Catholicism underground once more and rendered obsolete the statutes passed at the synod of Cavan.[5] When Patrick Tyrrell was transferred from Clogher to Meath diocese in early 1689 he ceased to be apostolic administrator of Kilmore and Hugh O'Reilly, a diocesan priest, was appointed vicar capitular instead.[6] In poem XXVII of the *Poems on the O'Reillys* he is described as 'ceann cléire Cille Móire' and is praised as 'Fear fíorchumhdaigh gach rúine, sgrudaightheoir na scrioptúire, gairmeadh dochtúir dhe, is dleacht ní fortúin é acht aiceacht. [A man who is a true keeper of every secret, a scriptural scholar, it is proper that he be called a doctor; it is not [a matter of] chance but [of] learning]'.[7]

3.   Corish, *The Catholic community*, p. 69. The Latin text of the statutes of this synod are published in *Spicilegium Ossoriense*, iii, pp 109–15. For summary in English see MacKiernan, 'The diocese of Kilmore (1678–1728)', pp 518–9.
4.   Fagan, *The diocese of Meath in the eighteenth century*, p. 51.
5.   Richard Doherty, *The Williamite war in Ireland 1688–1691* (Dublin, 1998), p. 103; Scott, 'Accounts of the battle of Cavan', pp 19–27.
6.   Moran (ed.), *Spic. Ossor.*, ii, p. 481. When a diocese became vacant by the death, resignation or transfer of a bishop, the diocesan chapter elected a vicar capitular to administer the diocese until another bishop was appointed.
7.   James Carney (ed.), *Poems on the O'Reillys* (Dublin, 1950), p. 138.

The banishment act of 1697 required all Catholic bishops, vicars general, deans and regular clergy to leave Ireland by 1 May 1698 though it appears that Hugh O'Reilly managed to remain in the country until his death sometime before 1704.[8] Bryan Brady, the parish priest of Laragh, who was living in the townland of Lissatavin, became vicar-general in his place.[9] The registration act of March 1704 required all parish priests to register at the next quarter sessions and forty-one Kilmore priests did so on 10 July 1704 – two at Enniskillen, eleven at Carrick-on-Shannon and twenty-eight in Cavan town.[10] Bryan Brady was registered as parish priest of Laragh even though, as vicar-general, he was in the country illegally under the banishment act of 1697. However, his sureties were William Tate and George Cottnam, both Protestant landowners in his parish, who helped his cause and ensured that he could remain in the country until his death in 1710. 'Patrick Currin', the registered parish priest of Drumlease in 1704 who was ordained in 1683 by Bishop Tadhg Keogh of Clonfert, was probably the noted Gaelic poet, an tAthair Pádraic Ó Cuirnín, one of the learned Ó Cuirnín family who were the historians for the O'Rourkes.[11] The fact that the Gaelic scholar and antiquarian, Tadhg Ó Rodaighe from Fenagh, went surety for him in 1704 would seem to support this viewpoint. Pádraic Ó Cuirnín dedicated poems to several of his contemporaries, including Tadhg Ó Rodaighe, Tadhg Ó Ruairc the bishop of Killala, Hugh O'Donnell of Larkfield and Charles O'Conor, the noted antiquarian from Ballinagare.[12]

Registered and Unregistered Priests

Unusually, two priests, Andrew Magaghran and Edmund Magaghran, registered for the parish of Drumlane, though the fact that Andrew was ninety years old may explain the government allowing this exception or perhaps, as Philip O'Connell has suggested, the parish was divided into upper and lower Drumlane thus allowing both priests to be registered for the parish.[13] Bryan Donogher, who lived in the townland of Clogher in Lower Drumreilly, was not attached to any parish.[14] He was still there in July 1714 by which time the authorities had learned that he was 'a registered popish priest but not for any parish' who 'goes by the name

8. Burke, *The Irish priests*, p. 118.
9. MacKiernan, 'The diocese of Kilmore (1678–1728)', p. 522.
10. *A list of the names of the popish parish priests*, pp 5–6, 25, 42–3; O'Connell, *The diocese of Kilmore*, pp 464–73.
11. Cuthbert Mhág Craith, *Dán na mBráthar Mionúr, nótaí* (Baile Átha Cliath, 1980), pp 215–7; Proinnsíos Ó Duigneáin, *Dromahaire, story and pictures* (Manorhamilton, 1990), pp 72–3.
12. Seosamh Mac Muirí, *Tadhg Ó Rodaighe, an scolaidhe treitheach* (Baile Átha Cliath, 2014), pp 280–303.
13. O'Connell, *The diocese of Kilmore*, p. 465.
14. Clogher townland is in Coraleehan church area with Aughawillan being the other church in Lower Drumreilly.

of Dr Donagher [and is] deemed to be a moderator over the popish clergy in the diocese of Killmore and Ardagh'.[15] Philip Fay was not registered to any parish either. He was attached to Magherintemple church in the parish of Drung and was continuing a link between the Fay family and this chapel of ease stretching back to medieval times.[16] Similar links going back in some instances to the 1400s between clerical families and particular parishes are obvious from the 1704 list of clergy with John Gargan in Moybolgue and Kilmainhamwood, Hugh Clery in Killann, John Brady in Castletara, Thomas O'Droim in Kinawley and Myles Parlane in Innismagrath. This 1704 list does not take account of the Franciscan priests who were furtively ministering in the diocese and who, under the terms of the 1697 banishment act, were supposed to have left the country. The names and whereabouts of some of the Franciscans in County Leitrim were disclosed at a special court sessions held in Carrick-on-Shannon on 27 July 1714:

> Oughy Duigenan a ffranciscan ffryer in the in the parishes of Ffenagh and Killtubret and … Owen O'Rorke alias Donell alias Robin the Juggler a ffranciscan ffryer in the parish of Oughteragh and Drumreilly … and Cormac Shanley a ffranciscan ffryer of the parish of Oughteragh.[17]

The authorities do not seem to have learned the names or whereabouts of the Franciscans in north Leitrim though they had information on the priests in the Kilmore parishes in County Fermanagh. Mervyn Archdale reported from Enniskillen on 23 June 1714 that:

> Doctor McKue priest of Killasher, registered but not taken the oaths … Hugh McHue a frier, curate and assistant to Doctor McKue aforesaid in Killaster parish not registered nor taken the Oaths. John Drum priest in Kinaulty, Registered but not taken Oaths. [Philip] Shenan[18] a frier in the said parish not registered nor taken the Oaths. Roger Maguire,

---

15.   Burke, *The Irish priests,* p. 443. He was appointed vicar-apostolic of Ardagh diocese on 20 August 1699 and remained in charge of the diocese until 1718. He may have been parish priest of Fenagh for a time. See James Kelly, 'The Catholic Church in the diocese of Ardagh, 1650–1870' in Raymond Gillespie & Gerard Moran (eds), *Longford, essays in county history* (Dublin, 1991), pp 71–3.
16.   Philip Fay was still in Magherintemple in 1723. See 'Kilmore Clergy list of 1723' in *Bréifne,* iii, 11 (1968), p. 411.
17.   Burke, *The Irish priests,* p. 443.
18.   Philip Shenan was the guardian of Lisgoole several times in the early decades of the 1700s. See Giblin (ed.), *Liber Lovaniensis,* pp 297, 314, 328.

a fugitive priest not registered in said parish. Bryan Ban Cassidy alias Treassy a friar officiating in Killastre, priest not registered nor taken the oaths.[19]

Priests and bishops adopted various disguises and there is a tradition in the Kiltyclogher area that Patrick Donnelly (1649–1716), the bishop of Dromore who posed as a travelling musician and was better known as 'bold Felim Brady, the Bard of Armagh' had, on one occasion, confirmed seven or eight thousand people near a Mass rock on Thor Caorach mountain, near Kiltyclogher.[20] Chances are that there were approximately fifty priests, between secular and regular, resident in the diocese of Kilmore in the early 1700s. The parish priests were generally registered and they were assisted by others, mostly Franciscans, who were not registered. All tended to remain close to their native parishes and their families and so were better able to avoid capture if the magistrates decided to move against them.

Most of the diocesan clergy had cooperated and registered under the terms of the 1704 act, however, they did not cooperate with the 1709 act requiring priests to take an` oath of abjuration declaring that the Stuarts now in exile 'hath not any right or title whatsoever to the crown of these realms'.[21] With the passing of the 1709 act the authorities had an impressive array of penal laws at their disposal which, if applied uniformly and to the letter of the law, would have devastated the Catholic Church in Ireland. This did not happen. The penal laws were more concerned with separating Catholics from their land than they were with separating them from their religion and while the laws relating to property were generally enforced, those relating to religion were applied sporadically and unevenly - usually at the whim of local magistrates.[22] There were instances, however, in which the laws against Catholic clergy were enforced. In 1704 Philip Brady, a Franciscan friar, was brought from Cavan to Dublin to be transported.[23] Three years later another un-named Kilmore cleric, who had been imprisoned for a time, was released.[24] In 1710 James Brady, one of the newly-appointed vicar-generals of the diocese, went into hiding 'because

---

19.   Burke, *The Irish priests*, pp 279–80.
20.   TSC, Corracloona N.S., vol. 0193, p. 323.
21.   Burke, *The Irish priests*, pp 184–5.
22.   Corish, *The Irish Catholic experience*, p. 123.
23.   Mooney, 'Some Cavan Franciscans', p. 24.
24.   Vatican Archive, *Nunziatura di Fiandra*, ix, vol. 150, 53r. The report says that it was the 'bishop of Kilmore' who was imprisoned. Kilmore had no bishop at this time. It may have been Bryan Brady, the vicar-general of the diocese, who was imprisoned.

of a procedure against him'.[25] The *Dublin Gazette* dated 16 February 1712 reported that:

> A letter bearing date 14th day of January last, sign'd J.M. and directed to Father Murphy at his lodging in Cavan, was lately dropped at the Four Courts in Dublin and the said letter … [contained] an account of wicked and treasonable practices and designs against her majesty's person and government.

A reward of £200 was offered for information causing those involved in this incident to 'be apprehended and convicted'.[26] It was reported from Youghal on 26 June 1713 that Cornelius Reynolds, a native of Jamestown in County of Leitrim who had been ordained in Spain in the early 1680s and had remained there ever since, was arrested aboard a boat recently arrived in the harbour. It was said that the priest was now old and wished to return to Jamestown to live out his remaining days with his two poor sisters. He was found to have a trunk on board containing 'books, papers, vestments, pieces of new silk and calicoe'.[27]

The Situation in Leitrim

Gilbert Ormsby, one of the magistrates for County Leitrim, was more zealous than most in pursuing the priests. He was convinced that the priests were in league with the Jacobites in France and were leaders in a plot to carry out another rebellion. In a letter to the Dublin authorities on 23 February 1712, he wondered if 'it may not be proper immediately to seize and commit all priests' and two weeks later he suggested that they should 'prohibit publick masses' and that they had sufficient reason 'to ridd the nation of [priests] that dangerous sett of men'.[28] Instructions were sent back stating that all the priests should be arrested, though Cunningham, the high sheriff of the county, reported on 7 March 1712 that 'warrants have been issued but I cannot find that any of the priests are yet taken'. Five days later Gilbert Ormsby, having described Catholicism as a 'scurvy religion' went on to say that:

25. APF, CP, 34a, ff. 454–5.
26. King to Dopping, TCD, MS 750/11/1, f. 301. John Brady, *Catholics and Catholicism in the eighteenth century press* (Maynooth, 1965), p. 17. Ó Ciardha, *Ireland and the Jacobite cause*, p. 129.
27. Burke, *The Irish priests*, p. 173.
28. Ibid., p. 440. Gilbert Ormsby was also actively pursuing the priests in County Roscommon. See Beirne (ed.), *The diocese of Elphin, people, places and pilgrimages*, pp 93–4.

> All our unhappiness and misfortunes proceed from the Priests … Nor do I believe we shall ever be safe or quiet till a wolf's head and a priest's be the same rate. Such a time I remember and then there was not a quieter populace in the world.[29]

On 20 March 1712 a proclamation was issued in County Leitrim ordering all the priests to surrender themselves within a week. It had no effect. The magistrates, writing from Carrick-on-Shannon on 11 November 1712 reported that:

> We summoned all the popish Clergymen that are registered for and reside in this County to appear and take the Oath, but not one priest appeared at the Quarter Sessions. We adjourned the Sessions and issued out fresh summons … but believe it will be to little purpose, the Clergy having generally withdrawn themselves from their usual place of abode and either quit the County or at least abscond so that they cannot be brought to justice.[30]

The actions of the magistrates merely drove the clergy underground once more. Not much had changed two years later when Thomas Crofton, the Mohill-based high sheriff of the county, wrote:

> I do not find one of the priests are taken, I know indeed it is very difficult, the much greater part of the county being papists, to take any of the priests or other ecclesiastical persons and the few protestants in it are afraid of meddling with them.[31]

It appears, particularly from the strong folk tradition in the parish of Ballinaglera, that some of the Protestant landowners in the county were not only inactive in pursuing the priests but were actively involved in protecting them from the military and the magistrates.[32] A similar

29. Burke, *The Irish priests*, p. 440.
30. Ibid., p. 442.
31. Ibid., p. 443.
32. See www.duchas.ie, (accessed 1 November 2015), County Leitrim schools folklore collection, vol. 0206, pp 113–5, 117–8, 284; Dr Logan, 'Leitrim priests in penal times' in *Ardagh and Clonmacnois Antiquarian Society Journal*, ii, 11 (1946), pp 64–5; Eileen Clancy & Patrick J. Forde, *Ballinaglera parish, Co. Leitrim, aspects of its history and traditions* (Dublin, 1980), pp 31–5; Peter Clancy, *Historical notices of the parish of Inishmagrath* (Ballinaglera, 1956), pp 49–50.

situation prevailed in County Cavan where in 1704 at least seventeen of the people providing sureties for the priests of the county were Protestant gentlemen and two of them, William Tate of Laragh and George Humphreys of Castletara, gave sureties for more than one priest.[33] The Catholic population and some of the Protestant landholders in the diocese supported the Catholic clergy and protected them from over-zealous magistrates and military.

The situation in Leitrim seems to have been replicated elsewhere in the diocese as the magistrates tried, with varying degrees of determination, to impose the oath of abjuration as required by the act of 1709. The detailed report on the province of Ulster, which Hugh MacMahon, the archbishop of Armagh and apostolic administrator of Kilmore sent to Rome in 1714, confirms that the situation throughout Ulster was largely similar to that in Leitrim. He described how, since the introduction of the 1709 legislation 'the open practice of religion either ceased entirely or was considerably curtailed' and 'when there is even a slight breathing space the exercise of religion is carried on mostly at night and hurriedly'.[34] As a further precaution he and other priests in the province celebrated Mass with their faces veiled lest they be recognized by spies or 'priest-hunters'. The main effect of the 1708 legislation requiring all Catholics to take the oath of abjuration was to drive Catholicism underground and, according to Hugh MacMahon, 'no one in the diocese of Clogher – lay or cleric – has taken the oath, and in the whole province of Ulster, no more than one or two'.[35] At a quarter sessions held in Cavan on 26 April 1715 it was reported that sixteen registered priests in the county 'have neglected to come in to take the Oath of Abjuration notwithstanding [that] summons and warrants have been often granted against them'. The court recommended that orders be issued to 'bring in the severall registered priests … to appear either at the next Assizes or next General Sessions of the Peace'.[36] However, there does not seem to have been the political will to have these priests arrested for their failure to take the oath of abjuration.

Kilmore Priests in Paris: The Early 1700s

While priests in the diocese were experiencing persecution in the early 1700s other Kilmore priests, such as John Farrelly, were flourishing on the continent. He was ordained by Tadhg Keogh, the bishop of Clonfert, on 24 September 1682 before going to Paris where he began his philosophy

---

33.   *A list of the names of the popish parish priests*, pp 5–6; O'Connell, *The diocese of Kilmore*, p. 477.
34.   P.J. Flanagan, 'The diocese of Clogher in 1714', in *Clogher Record*, i, 3 (1955), p. 129.
35.   *A list of the names of the popish parish priests*, p. 41.
36.   Burke, *The Irish priests*, p. 285.

studies in the Collége de Montaigu in September 1683.[37] He was to spend the next fifteen years studying in Paris, becoming a 'Doctor of the Sorbonne' in 1698. He was a resident of Collége de Plessis in 1710 when he was elected as the Ulster provisor or superior of the students from the province of Ulster in the Collége des Lombards. In 1728 he was appointed principal of the college with the provisors from the three other provinces being subject to him.[38] Priscilla O'Connor has described Farrelly as 'one of the most socially distinguished clerics to hold the office of provisor in the college' –because of his network of contacts in Paris and further afield.[39] He was tutor to the children of the Duke of Berwick, a natural son of James II, and he acted as attorney for Irishmen in the Jacobite regiments in France and for prominent clergy and laity based in Paris and in Ireland.

Several other members of the extended Farrelly family, including priests, medical doctors and soldiers, were living in Paris at this time and in 1716 John Farrelly appointed Daniel Farrelly, a Kilmore priest, to the positon of steward or bursar in the Collége des Lombards and in 1727 he appointed another Kilmore priest, Bernard Reilly, to that same position.[40] In his will, dated 27 April 1735, John Farrelly left a burse worth 200 *livres* per year for the education of a relative from Kilmore bearing the Farrelly name. The bishop of Kilmore or, in his absence, his vicar-general, was given the right to decide who would get the burse and if a suitable candidate could not be found in Kilmore another student was to be selected, preferably from the neighbouring dioceses of Ardagh or Meath.[41] John Farrelly died, in his eightieth year, on 7 June 1736 and was buried in the chapel vault of the Collége des Lombards.[42]

Paris was a place of learning and refuge for Kilmore priests in the early 1700s and during John Farrelly's fifty-three year stay in that city approximately twenty-five other Kilmore clerics studied in the University of Paris.[43] Considering the conditions back in Ireland it is not surprising that many of them remained in France after they

37.   For John Farrelly, see Liam Swords, 'Fr John Farrelly, Doctor of the Sorbonne (1657–1736)' in *Bréifne*, ix, 35(1998), pp 911–21; Priscilla O'Connor, 'Irish clerics and Jacobites in early eighteenth-century Paris, 1700–30' in Thomas O'Connor (ed.), *The Irish in Europe, 1580–1815*, (Dublin, 2001), pp 179–81; L.W.B. Brockliss & Patrick Ferté, 'Prosopography of Irish clerics in the Universities of Paris and Toulouse' in *Arch. Hib.*, lviii (2004), p. 25; MacKiernan, *Diocese of Kilmore*, p. 161. Terence Smith, another Kilmore priest, was superior of the Irish priests in Collége de Montaigu for a period in the 1690s. See Swords, 'Fr John Farrelly', p. 913.
38.   Ibid., p. 917.
39.   O'Connor, 'Irish clerics and Jacobites', p. 179.
40.   Brockliss & Ferté, 'Prosopography of Irish clerics', pp 25, 161; Swords, 'Fr John Farrelly', p. 916.
41.   Ibid., p. 920.
42.   The inscription on his tombstone reads: *Hic jacet/M.Joannes Farley/S.Fac. par Dr hujusce collegii/Per plures annos/Provisor et primaries/Indefessus Obiit die/ Jun. 7 anno 1736/Requiescat in Pace.*
43.   Brockliss & Ferté, 'Prosopography of Irish clerics', pp 24–8.

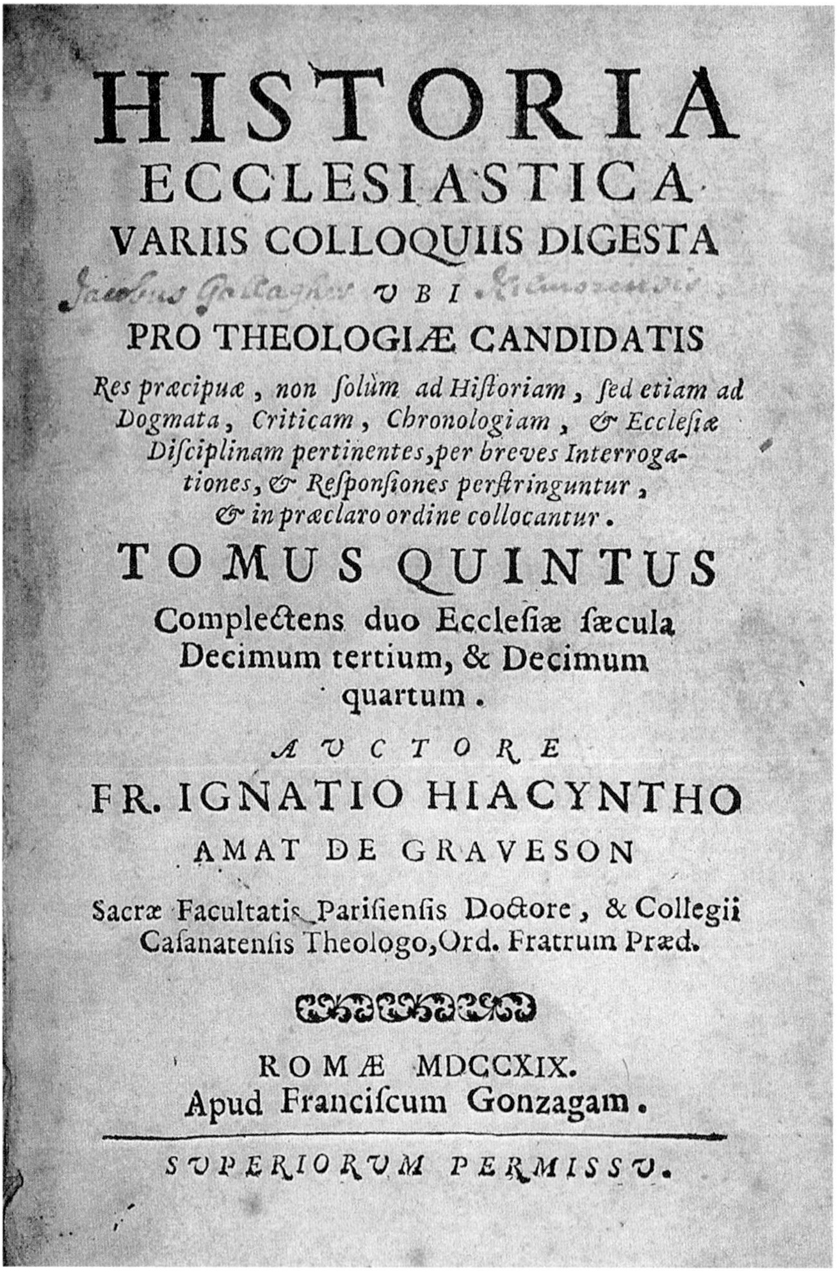

HISTORIA
ECCLESIASTICA
VARIIS COLLOQUIIS DIGESTA
UBI
PRO THEOLOGIÆ CANDIDATIS
Res præcipuæ, non solùm ad Historiam, sed etiam ad Dogmata, Criticam, Chronologiam, & Ecclesiæ Disciplinam pertinentes, per breves Interrogationes, & Responsiones perstringuntur, & in præclaro ordine collocantur.
TOMUS QUINTUS
Complectens duo Ecclesiæ sæcula Decimum tertium, & Decimum quartum.
AUCTORE
FR. IGNATIO HIACYNTHO
AMAT DE GRAVESON
Sacræ Facultatis Parisiensis Doctore, & Collegii Casanatensis Theologo, Ord. Fratrum Præd.

ROMÆ MDCCXIX.
Apud Franciscum Gonzagam.

SUPERIORUM PERMISSU.

Figure 14.1: Ecclesiastical history book from the student days of Bishop James Gallagher. The handwriting 'Jacobus Gallagher Kilmorensis' is probably his own. (*Courtesy Cavan County Library*).

had completed their studies. However, some of them such as James Gallagher and James Matthew Brady, did return home, the former to become bishop of Raphoe (and later Kildare and Leighlin) and the latter to become bishop of Ardagh. Valentine Tully, who was studying in Paris *c*.1708–11, did return to work in the diocese in the early decades of the 1700s and was parish priest of Drung at the time of his death in 1751.[44] Similarly, Michael O'Reilly, having obtained a doctorate in canon and civil law in Paris, returned to the diocese and was appointed parish priest of Urney and vicar-general of Kilmore sometime before 1723.[45] However, it would appear that the majority of the diocesan priests who studied in Paris in the early decades of the 1700s opted to remain in France after their studies were completed.

John Richardson: Rector of Annagh

John Richardson, the Gaelic speaking and evangelising Church of Ireland rector of Annagh, described the impact of the legislation requiring Catholics to take the oath of abjuration. He wrote that:

> In the beginning of 1710, when most of the Popish Priests in Ireland, had by declining the Oath of Abjuration, render'd themselves liable to great penalites if they exercised their function; they forbore, for the greatest part, to perform any religious Offices, so that for some time their people went to no Publick Worship.[46]

John Richardson felt that the weakening of the Catholic Church, due to the cumulative effect of the penal laws and the uncertainty caused by the influx of Scottish settlers, presented an opportunity to convert the native Irish to Protestantism.[47] This could only be achieved, he insisted, through 'mild and gentle means' and through relating to the Irish in their native tongue.[48] He had the support of his bishop, Edward Wettenhall,

44.   Ibid., p.164; MacKiernan, *Diocese of Kilmore*, p. 163

45.   Francis J. MacKiernan, 'The O'Reillys and MacQuaids of Lisdoagh' in *Bréifne*, viii, 2(1991), pp 184–5.

46.   John Richardson, *A short history of the attempts that have been made to convert the Popish natives of Ireland to the Established Religion with a proposal for their conversion* (London, 1712), p. 44. The Catholic Church ceased to function in Dublin city 'in the summer of 1710 when the oath crisis was at its height.' See James Kelly, 'The impact of the penal laws' in James Kelly & Dáire Keogh (eds), *History of the Catholic diocese of Dublin* (Dublin, 2000), pp 149, 179.

47.   Middleton, 'John Richardson at Belturbet', pp 38, 49, 58. See also Toby Barnard, 'Revd John Richardson (*c*.1669–1747): County Cavan rector and Irish-language enthusiast' in Cherry & Scott (eds), *Cavan, history and society*, pp 241–9.

48.   Ibid., p. 11.

at first, though that relationship soured towards the end of Wettenhall's episcopacy.[49] Richardson went to London in 1711 to present a petition to the Duke of Ormond advocating the publication of prayer books, catechisms and sermons in Irish.[50] He spent a considerable time there getting his writings published and Wettenhall blamed Richardson's absence for the debacle surrounding the arrest of the Presbyterians in what became known as 'the Belturbet affair'.[51]

Philip (an ministéir) MacBradaigh, a priest of the diocese of Kilmore who conformed to the Established Church in 1682, was rector of Innismagrath when he translated into Irish one of the sermons John Richardson included in his 1711 publication *Seanmóra ar na Priomh Phoncibh na Chreideamh.*[52] Hugh MacMahon reported in his 1714 *relatio* that he had met Philip MacBradaigh who told him that since he had married a few times and had a large family he would need financial support from MacMahon if he were to revert to being a Catholic.[53] He remained rector of Innismagrath until 1719 - probably the year of his death. He has been described as 'a figure of folklore, a sort of local Dean Swift' and 'many tales were told of his amusing adventures and biting repartee'.[54] Fourteen years later it was reported that there was no Church of Ireland clergyman resident in Innismagrath and that the parish had 'no church in repair'.[55]

John Richardson, like Bedell before him, met considerable opposition from his fellow churchmen in his attempts to convert the Irish to Protestantism through the medium of their native tongue. As early as 1711 a committee of seven bishops met in the house of Narcissus Marsh, the archbishop of Armagh, and voted against Richardson's Irish language missionary programme and in favour of a policy of Anglicization.[56] However, following the appointment of the Englishman, Timothy Goodwyn,[57] as bishop of Kilmore in 1714, John Richardson seemed energized once more. Richardson's sermon on the occasion of the consecration of St James's Church in Cootehill on 25 July 1715 was published the following year and begins with an address to Bishop

49.   Edward Wettenhall died on 12 November 1713.
50.   Vincent Morley, *DIB*, vii, p. 484. He was introduced to Ormond by Jonathan Swift.
51.   Middleton, 'John Richardson', p. 56.
52.   Vincent Morley, *DIB*, v, pp 728–9.
53.   Moran (ed.), *Spic. Ossor.*, i, pp 481–2.
54.   Seamus P. Ó Mórdha, 'Some aspects of the literary tradition of the Bréifne-Fermanagh area' in *Bréifne*, vi, 21 (1982), pp 49–50.
55.   PRONI, DIO/4/24/2/23.
56.   Jeremiah Falvey, 'The Church of Ireland episcopate in the eighteenth century: an overview' in *Eighteenth century Ireland*, viii (1993), p. 105.
57.   Jonathan Swift had recommended Dr Pratt, the Provost of Trinity College, for Kilmore. See his 'Prefermts of Ireland' in Huntington Library, HM 27943; George P. Mayhew, 'Jonathan Swift's Prefermts of Ireland, 1713–1714' in *Huntington Library Quarterly*, xxx, 4 (Aug. 1967), p. 298. He also recommended that Jeremiah Marsh, the Dean of Kilmore, be appointed to Ardagh.

Goodwyn in which he welcomes him to Kilmore and expresses the wish that his presence in the diocese will put an end 'to all our divisions and distinctions'.[58] Three months later when Richardson preached in Belturbet on 'the occasion of Captain Bryan Reily's renunciation of the Errors of the Church of Rome' he criticized the Catholic Church for emphasizing 'the vertue of Relicks, consecrated Beads, Agnus Dei's and the like; and pilgrimages to places of pretended Sanctity'.[59] He was especially critical of pilgrimages to St Patrick's purgatory on Lough Derg, which continued throughout the worst years of persecution.[60] Bishop Hugh MacMahon, writing in 1714, described how thousands of people went there on nine-day pilgrimages and how Masses were celebrated continuously, mostly by Franciscan priests, from dawn to midday each day during the three-month pilgrim season. He added:

> An extraordinary feature of the pilgrimage is that none of the Protestants in the locality ever interfere with the pilgrims, although people are forbidden by law of Parliament to make it. When I visited there, disguised as a Dublin merchant – for prelates and non-registered priests usually find it necessary to adopt some disguise – the minister of the district received me hospitably. The result is that while in the rest of the country the practice of religion has practically ceased as a result of persecution, here, as in another world, religion is practised freely and openly.[61]

Many people from Kilmore made the pilgrimage to Lough Derg and several elaborately-carved 'penal crosses' - made from yew tree and bearing dates from the early 1700s - were brought home by pilgrims and some have survived in the diocese. See Figure 14.2.

58.   John Richardson, *A Sermon preached at the Consecration of St James's Church at Coot-Hill: July the 25th 1715 by John Richardson, rector of the parish of Annah…* (Dublin, 1716), p. vii. See also *Acts and statutes made in a Parliament begun at Dublin the twenty first day of September, Anno Dom. 1703. In the Second year of the reign of our Most Gracious sovereign Lady Queen Anne …* (Dublin, 1710), pp 74–5. The Benedictine priest and scholar Bernard de Montafaucon, in his preface to his *Sancti Patris Joannis Chrisostomi opera omnia* which was published in Paris in 1718, thanks 'the genial and learned Timothy Godwin, bishop of Kilmore' who secured the help of John Potter, the erudite bishop of Oxford and was 'tireless in his attention to my needs.' See Thomas Halton, 'Timothy Godwin, Bishop of Kilmore' in *Bréifne*, iii, 11 (1968), p. 390.
59.   John Richardson, *The true interest of the Irish Nation: in a sermon preached in the Church of Belturbet on Sunday 23rd of October, 1715, on the occasion of Captain Bryan Reily's Renunciation of the errors of the Church of Rome* (Dublin, 1716), p. 41. The sermon was published in both English and Irish.
60.   See John Richardson, *The great Folly, superstition and idolatry of pilgrimages in Ireland, especially of that to St Patrick's purgatory …* (Dublin, 1727).
61.   Flanagan, 'The diocese of Clogher in 1714', p. 129.

Figure 14.2:   Front and back of Penal cross dated 1712. (*Courtesy of Michael Deane*).

In the absence of Catholic chapels and Mass houses during the penal era the holy wells dotted around the diocese took on a greater significance and were revered as sacred sites and places of healing - much as they had been in medieval times. In 1727, John Richardson published a letter he received from Patrick Bredin 'a very grave and religious man', describing how a great crowd of men, women and children gathered each year on mid-summer's eve at St Brighid's well near Urney church and moved about a mound of stones on their knees to kiss a stone which they said represented St Brighid. Patrick Bredin attempted to stop the 'abominable idolatry' by 'drawing away most of the water and removing the heaps of stones'[62] and yet he feared that all his efforts 'will not hinder their coming'.[63] Both diocesan and provincial Catholic synods tried to regulate these pilgrimages which were peddling a pre-Tridentine religion and the bishops were anxious not so much to stop them but rather to eradicate the abuses associated with them.[64]

The waters of 'Lough Lhieghs' - a small lake about two miles east of Bailieborough - were said to have curative powers and in the mid-1730s 'tents were erected for the conveniency of those who resort to it, who are seldom less than two or three hundred a day'. Josiah Hort, the Church of Ireland bishop of Kilmore, was concerned about these developments and asked the Rev. William Henry to investigate the phenomenon and draw up a report. William Henry interviewed many people, including Rev. James Cottingham, the 'Minister of Baylyborough', who described a lady from Mullingar whose face was covered with 'red fiery carbuncles', and after bathing in the water each day for three weeks, 'the rawness of her flesh was removed, the carbuncles on her face withered and dropt off by degrees, and a fair new skin appeared'.[65] William Henry's report detailed instances of people being cured of such diverse ailments as rheumatism and headaches, falling sickness and the pox and his sources of information were local people, both Protestant and Catholic. He found, that there was no religious dimension to these cures and expressed surprise at this, noting that:

> Since the Irish have provided Patron Saints for every Tree
> that has any kind of Virtues, but have forgot hitherto to

62. A similar heap of stones, apparently brought there by pilgrims, is to be found at St Molaise's holy well at Ballaghameehan. See 'The schools' (folklore) collection', vol.189, p.161.
63. Richardson, *The Great Folly*, pp 68–70.
64. Corish, *The Catholic community*, p. 37.
65. *An account of Lough Lheichs, Anglice. The Lake of cures in the County of Cavan, in a letter to the Right Reverend Josiah Hort, Lord bishop of Kilmore and Ardagh by the Reverend William Henry* (Dublin, 1736), pp 7–8.

sanctify this Lough, tho' the surprizing cures performed at it, might bring greater honour to the imaginary Patron Saint, and more profit to the Priests than most of the wells in the Kingdom.[66]

John Richardson's grand programme to convert the Irish to Protestantism through the medium of Irish, never got off the ground, despite his best efforts. In June 1730 Hugh Boulter, the archbishop of Armagh, wrote to John Carteret, the lord lieutenant of Ireland, explaining that many years ago John Richardson was:

> Concerned in a design to translate the Bible and Book of Common Prayer into Irish, in order the better to bring about the conversion of the natives; but he met at that time with great opposition, not to say oppression here, instead of either thanks or assistance; and suffered the loss of several hundred pounds expended in printing.[67]

Boulter requested that Richardson be appointed dean of Kilmacduagh, a benefice worth about £130 per annum, in order to support the ageing cleric. The archbishop's request was granted and John Richardson spent his remaining years in Belturbet, being cared for by one of his daughters until his death in 1747.[68]

Leadership Issues: 1710–1728

The persecution of Catholics in the early decades of the 1700s was severe and it brought the public celebration of the Catholic faith to a virtual standstill. However, the Catholic clergy of the diocese were less likely to be imprisoned or killed in those decades than their counterparts were in the Puritan-led persecution of the 1650s or the Titus Oates period of intense persecution from 1678 to 1681. The penal legislation ensured that there would be no resident Catholic bishop in the diocese and would, instead, be administered by a variety of vicars, either from within the diocese or from the neighbouring diocese of Clogher. This lack of strong leadership resulted in confusion and perpetuated the on-going divisions among the clergy. In August 1710, following the death of Bryan Brady the vicar-general, a number of

---

66. Ibid., pp 6–7.
67. *Letters written by His Excellency Hugh Boulter, D.D. Lord Primate of All Ireland to Several Ministers of State* … (Oxford, 1770), ii, p. 29; Connolly, *Religion, law and power*, pp 299–300. A new volume of the Boulter letters has been published recently. See Kenneth Milne & Paddy McNally (eds), *The Boulter letters* (Dublin, 2016).
68. Morley, *DIB*, viii, p. 484.

priests of the diocese proposed that both Bryan O'Reilly and James Brady both be appointed vicars general.[69] Since there was no surviving member of the diocesan chapter, the duty of appointing a vicar capitular rested with the archbishop of Armagh and since that position was vacant the Armagh chapter, in an ill-advised move, met and appointed John Verdon, the parish priest of St Peter's in Drogheda, as vicar capitular of Kilmore. He accepted both James Brady and Bryan O'Reilly as his vicars general in the diocese and then proceeded to appoint another one. The bishop of Dromore, who was already in dispute with John Verdon, appointed Patrick Dowdall as vicar capitular in Armagh and he in turn nominated another vicar capitular for Kilmore, leading to utter confusion within the diocese.[70]

The divisions in Kilmore were exacerbated by similar divisions in other northern dioceses and by 1710 the diocese was in a chaotic state having four contending vicars and nobody quite sure who was in charge. Besides, Michael Smith, who had studied in the Sorbonne and was resident in Paris, applied to Propaganda Fide several times to be appointed either vicar-apostolic or bishop of his native diocese of Kilmore. Despite a testimonial stating that he was 'a priest of remarkable qualities' his requests were repeatedly ignored.[71] This confusion about the leadership in Kilmore coincided with one of the worst periods of persecution in the diocese and prompted some of the leading clergy and laity to write, on 13 August 1710, to Bishop Hugh MacMahon of Clogher asking him to petition Rome that he be appointed vicar-apostolic of Kilmore diocese – just as his predecessor Patrick Tyrrell had been.[72] They complimented the bishop on the peaceful state of the diocese of Clogher and said that his appointment as administrator of Kilmore would ease divisions and prevent violence. The letter was signed by the vicar-general, Bernard Reilly, and sixteen others and, while none of the signatories were from Leitrim, the letter claimed to represent the views of those in more distant parts of the diocese who were prevented from gathering because of the distance and uncertainties of the time.[73] The letter had the desired effect and Hugh MacMahon was appointed vicar-apostolic of Kilmore on 22 August 1711, a position he held until 1728.

69.   APF, *CP*, 34a, ff. 256.
70.   Ibid., f. 456.
71.   APF, *SOCG*, 544, ff. 3rv, 4v. For Michael Smith see, Francis J. MacKiernan, 'Father Michael Smith, candidate for the bishopric of Kilmore' in *Bréifne*, i, 4 (1961), pp 387–93; idem, 'Diocese of Kilmore (1678–1728)', pp 522–4.
72.   Hugh MacMahon's mother was Eileen O'Reilly, a daughter of Philip MacHugh O'Reilly. Laurence J. Flynn, 'Hugh MacMahon Bishop of Clogher 1707–15 and Archbishop of Armagh 1715–37' in *Seanchas Ard Mhacha*, vii, 1 (1973), p. 109.
73.   APF, *CP*, 34a, f. 456; *Bréifne*, iv, 14 (1971), pp 216–7; MacKiernan, 'The diocese of Kilmore (1678–1728)', p. 525.

Hugh MacMahon was appointed archbishop of Armagh in August 1715 and within days of his translation from Clogher three Kilmore priests, Thomas Clery (Killann), Edmund Deane (Templeport) and Myles MacParlan (Innismagrath) and two laymen, Myles O'Reilly and Patrick Brady, wrote to John O'Coigligh in Rome asking his assistance in getting Michael Smith appointed bishop of Kilmore.[74] The campaign in favour of Michael Smith continued, and six weeks later, on 27 September 1715, twenty-seven parish priests of the diocese of Kilmore met in the valley of Sliabh Glah (*in valle Montis Clehensis*) in Lavey parish and, after celebrating Mass of the Holy Spirit, wrote to Pope Clement XI asking him to appoint Michael Smith bishop of Kilmore. They reminded the pope that this was their fourth time to make such a petition, though they did admit that it was possible that the previous three petitions got no further than Louvain.[75] Clearly they felt that Hugh MacMahon could no longer administer the diocese after his translation to Armagh and they may also have been unhappy with him for appointing the young parish priest of Cavan, Michael O'Reilly, as his vicar-general about this time.[76] They explained how they wanted to have their own bishop to resolve the frequent disputes and other problems that arose in the diocese. They stated that all the canons of the cathedral chapter had died, that 'we alone are left, old men, no longer able to work in the vineyard' and that it was too dangerous for young men to go carrying dimissory letter to bishops in other dioceses in order to be ordained.[77] Hugh MacMahon wrote to Rome stating that Michael Smith was unduly ambitious and that he had Jansenist leanings and it is likely that it was this letter, more than anything else, which sealed Smith's fate.[78] Smith was not appointed bishop, although he did return to Ireland and is buried in Lavey old cemetery. His gravestone inscription reads:

> Here lyeth the body of Father Michael Smith doctor Sorbonne
> who died June 3, 1723, aged 63 years.
> Repaired by Thomas Smith, Pottle.

74.   APF, *SOCG*, 544, ff. 3rv, 4v.
75.   APF, *SC, Irlanda*, 7, ff. 492–3; Owen F. Traynor, 'More Kilmore clergy lists' in *Bréifne*, iv, 14 (1971), pp 220–1. This document may not be reliable, and may even have been a forgery, as most of the 'signatures' appear to have been written by the same hand. See Traynor, 'More Kilmore clergy lists' pp 201–2, n. 5; MacKiernan, 'Diocese of Kilmore (1678–1728)', p. 527. See also BM, Add. MS 20311, n. 793, p. 519.
76.   Thomas O'Connor, 'Michael O'Reilly', *DIB*, vii, p. 863; MacKiernan, *Diocese of Kilmore*, p. 161. Hugh MacMahon had been appointed vicar-apostolic of Kilmore 'while he would remain bishop of Clogher'. See APF, *SC*, viii, f. 481.
77.   Owen F. Traynor, 'More Kilmore clergy lists' in *Bréifne*, iv, 14 (1971), pp 220–1; MacKiernan, 'The diocese of Kilmore (1678–1728)', pp 527–8. See also APF, *SC, Irlanda*, vii, f. 506.
78.   APF, *SC, Irlanda*, vii, ff. 521–2; Flynn, 'Hugh MacMahon', p. 144.

Decline in Number of Priests

The greatest impact of the penal legislation of the late 1600s and early 1700s on the diocesan clergy was not to banish, imprison or kill them, but rather to impoverish them, reduce their numbers, curtail their celebration of the sacraments and prevent them giving effective leadership in the diocese. The reduction in the number of priests was obvious. Edward Wettenhall, the Church of Ireland bishop who had been translated from Cork and Ross to Kilmore in 1699, wrote, together with several other 'gentlemen and clergymen', to the Duke of Ormond in 1710 about the impact of the penal laws. The letter stated:

> Several laws have been lately made in Ireland, to discourage and weaken Popery in that Kingdom and one Statute particularly hath been enacted to prevent the Succession of the Popish Clergy, by virtue whereof, the number of Popish Priests is already sensibly decreased in it; and it is probable, that in some counties, the whole succession may be extinct within a few years.[79]

Bishop Wettenhall's observation about the declining number of priests was accurate although his prediction about their extinction was not. The Registration Act, which appeared to give legal status to the parish priests, was intended to reduce their numbers and eventually lead to their extinction. The hope was that as the registered priests died out the laws already in place would prevent others taking their place.[80] The twenty-seven priests who gathered in Lavey in 1715 to petition the pope to appoint Michael Smith bishop of the diocese explained in their letter that the diocese was suffering from a great scarcity of priests and that they themselves were ageing and unable to look after the pastoral needs of the diocese.[81] James Kelly has calculated that there was a reduction of about one-third (from c.40 to c.27) in the number of Kilmore diocesan priests between the years 1704 and 1723.[82] And, while it is more difficult to measure, it seems likely that the number of Franciscan friars in the diocese also decreased for a time after the banishment act of 1697. Those who remained in the diocese ceased any semblance of community living and spread themselves thinly, for their own safety, near to their extended families in parishes throughout the diocese. Gradually these scat-

---

79. Richardson, *A short history*, pp 47–8; idem, *A proposal for the conversion of the Popish natives of Ireland to the Establish'd Religion* (London, 1712), p. lxxv.
80. Maureen Wall, *The Penal Laws, 1691–1760* (Dundalk, 1976), p. 16.
81. APF, SC, *Irlanda*, 7, ff. 492–3.
82. Kelly, 'The Catholic Church in Kilmore', pp 124–5.

tered friars were absorbed into the diocesan structures, serving as curates and parish priests. The friars were targeted more than the registered parish priests in the early decades of the 1700s and the folk-tradition about priests in penal times seems strongest in the parishes of Killinkere in Cavan and Ballinaglera Leitrim, the parishes where the Franciscans from Cavan and Creevelea friaries regularly sought refuge during the worst years of the persecution.

Mass Rocks

The early decades of the 1700s is the period most associated with Mass rocks, portable altars and sacraments being celebrated in private houses and under the cover of darkness. Dan Gallogly, in his book *The diocese of Kilmore 1800–1950*, has identified seventy-five Mass rocks in twenty-seven Kilmore parishes and some other Mass rocks have been located since his book was published in 1999.[83] These Mass rocks which are distributed throughout the diocese, suggests that there were priests available to celebrate Mass and congregations willing to risk attending them despite the difficulties and dangers they encountered. Hugh MacMahon, the administrator of the diocese of Kilmore, explained in 1714 that people continued to go to Mass and developed hand-signals to tell others when and where it was taking place.[84] However, the folk-tradition that Mass was always celebrated in remote locations and unknown to the authorities seems to be wide of the mark. Nicholas Brown, an evangelising Church of Ireland clergyman in the diocese of Clogher who was 'a perfect master of the [Irish] language' met with Catholics *c.*1702 by:

> Attending them at the places, where they usually assembled to hear Mass. He ordered matters so as to be with them just when Mass was ended and before the congregation was dispersed and then read … prayers to them in their own language.[85]

The twenty-seven Kilmore priests who met in September 1715 to petition the pope to appoint Michael Smith bishop of the diocese were able to celebrate Mass and hold their meeting under the noses of the authorities in the parish of Lavey and only about five miles distant from Cavan town. The Mass rocks were created as a response to real and immediate persecution and many of them were hidden away in remote locations. However, the fact that others were 'openly underground'

83. Gallogly, *The diocese of Kilmore 1800–1950*, pp 399–401.
84. Flanagan, 'The diocese of Clogher in 1714', p. 42.
85. Richardson, *A short history of the attempts*, p. 30.

points towards a certain leniency by the magistrates and sporadic rather than constant persecution. Dr Richard Pococke, the travel writer who would later become Church of Ireland bishop of Ossory (1756–65) and Meath (1765), described how in 1752 he was able to see people attending Mass at a Mass rock in County Donegal from a considerable distance away:

> Several hundred people spread all over that plain spot and the priest celebrating Mass under the rock, on an altar made of loose stones, and tho' it was a half mile distant, I observed his Pontifical vestment with a black cross on it; for in all this country for sixty miles west and south as far as Connaught, they celebrate in the open air, in the fields or on the mountains; the Papists being so few and poor, that they will not be at the expence of a public building.[86]

The survival of some Mass rocks throughout much of the 1700s and even, in some instances, into the 1800s is due more to poverty than persecution and often the location and times of these open-air Masses was a well-known secret.[87]

The penal laws were much more effective in reducing Catholics to penury than they were at suppressing their faith. These laws were designed to exclude Catholics from the professions, from parliament and from the ownership of property and they largely succeeded in doing so.[88] The Catholic share of Irish land, which was 59% in 1641 had fallen to 22% in 1688, 14% in 1703 and, due to the effects of the penal laws, was a mere 5% by the 1770s.[89] The Catholic diocese of Kilmore, which had been poor throughout the late medieval and early modern times, was further impoverished when Catholic landholders were dispossessed and their reduced state meant that there was neither an income for priests nor money for building and maintaining churches.[90] Hugh MacMahon

86.   See Stokes (ed.), *Pococke's tour in Ireland in 1752*, p. 60.
87.   For an example of the survival of Mass rocks into the 1800s see Alexander Ayton's photograph entitled 'Mass in the mountains of Donegal' which was taken in 1867 and reproduced in W.A. Maguire, *A century in focus, photography and photographers in the north of Ireland 1839–1939* (Belfast, 2000), p. 31.
88.   Wall, *The Penal laws*, p. 7.
89.   Corish, *The Catholic community*, p. 74.
90.   The dispossession of Catholic lands was particularly acute in the diocese of Kilmore and in 1688 less than 4% of the land in Leitrim and Fermanagh and less than 9% of land in Cavan was held by Catholics. See J.W. Simms, 'The restoration, 1660–85' in Moody, Martin & Byrne (eds), *A new history of Ireland*, iii, p. 428. Marianne Elliott states that 'The Catholics of Ulster and adjacent north Connacht were generally the poorest in the country'. See *The Catholics of Ulster* (London, 2000), pp 121–2.

reported in 1714 that 'since the people of Ulster are living in dire poverty, the remuneration of their pastors is necessarily small and altogether
insufficient'.[91] When the clergy, nobility and people of Kilmore wrote to
Pope Clement XI in 1716 to ask him to appoint Michael Smith as their
bishop, they explained that one of the reasons they wanted him to do so
was the extreme poverty of the clergy.[92]

The 1731 'Report on the state of Popery in Ireland' outlines the
scarcity of Mass houses throughout the dioceses of Ulster and north
Connacht and describes how 'Mass is said in most places *sub dio*
[under the sky] or under some sort of shed, built up occasionally to
shelter ye priest from ye weather … [or in] cabins when ye weather
is extremely bad' and 'upon mountains or in private houses'.[93] The
absence of chapels and Mass houses was greatest in dioceses such as
Kilmore in the north and north-west of the country where church
organisation was weakest and poverty greatest.[94] William Smyth has
described the places for Sunday Mass in Ulster and North Connacht at
this time as being 'mobile in character and unprotected'.[95] Patrick Corish
has suggested that the lack of Mass houses in Ulster, where the Protestant
population was greatest, may be due, at least in part, to 'landlord
hostility'.[96] There were isolated attempts to build Mass houses during
the penal era and it appears that the chapel in Annagelliff Lane in Cavan
parish was built in the first decade of the eighteenth-century.[97] Bishop
Josiah Hort's report in 1731 confirms that while attempts were being
made to build a small number of chapels, in general, Mass was celebrated
in 'huts' or in the open air:

> The Lord Bishop of Kilmore and Ardagh [Josiah Hort]
> observes that there is in his diocese three Mass-houses
> building and one intended to be built at Rossenver, towards
> which they offered at Mass to contribute five pounds, and
> that there is one being enlarged. That there are thirty eight

91.   Flanagan, 'The diocese of Clogher in 1714', p. 127.
92.   MacKiernan, 'Diocese of Kilmore (1678–1728)', p. 528.
93.   'Report on the State of Popery in Ireland, 1731' in *Arch. Hib.*, i (1912), pp 17–18. See William
J. Smyth, *Map-making, landscapes and memory* (Cork, 2006), pp 371–3; Elliott, *The Catholics of
Ulster*, p. 201.
94.   Smyth, *Map-making, landscapes and memory*, pp 371–3; Elliott, *The Catholics of Ulster*, p. 200;
Ciarán Mac Murchaidh, 'My Repeated Troubles' in Bergin, Magennis, Ní Mhunghaile & Walsh
(eds), *New perspectives on the Penal Laws*, p. 154.
95.   Smyth, *Map-making, landscapes and memory*, p. 372.
96.   Corish, *The Irish Catholic experience*, p. 130.
97.   APF, *SC, Irlanda*, xiv, f. 238.

huts used as Mass-houses, and many moveable altars and in some parishes Mass is said in the fields.[98]

There were isolated attempts to build more substantial churches although the walls of Kilbride church, which were built in the parish of Innismagrath in 1735 when the penal laws were more relaxed and while Myles MacPartlan was parish priest, were never given a roof.[99] From the 1740s onwards some more 'huts' or Mass-houses with wattled/mud walls and thatched roofs were built although it was not until the last decades of the eighteenth-century, with the further relaxation of the penal laws, that the more substantial barn churches were built.[100]

Strong Catholic Families

The diocese of Kilmore, unlike its neighbouring diocese of Meath, had few strong Catholic landowners to cushion the church from the worst excesses of the Protestant reformation. The Catholics that remained were dispossessed by the penal laws, further impoverishing them and their Church. A branch of the Maguire family, which was based in Knockninny in County Fermanagh, was an exception to the rule and by leasing large tracts of land became upwardly mobile in the late 1600s and early 1700s. Their patronage of Callowhill Chapel was a demonstration of their new-found wealth and the improved chapel provided a fitting burial place for the Maguire family.[101] John Dolan's *History of Fermanagh*, which was written in the years 1718–19, states that:

> The chapel of Callihill was dedicated to St Ronan by Connor Modera Maguire who brought a Bishop to consecrate therein in order to be a place of burial for himself and his family; and his son Bryan Maguire erected a stately tomb over his body with his achievements and ensigne armorial engraved thereon.[102]

98.   Quoted in Gallogly, *The diocese of Kilmore, 1800–1950*, p. 365.
99.   Clancy & Forde, *Ballinaglera and Inishmagrath, the history and tradition of two Leitrim parishes*, pp 290–1. Myles MacPartlan also commissioned a chalice which bears the inscription *Milesius McParlan Kilbride presbyter me fieri fecit A.D. 1718*.
100.   The barn church has been defined as 'a type of church typical of the late 18th and early 19th century, usually of rubble stone rendered, with a roof of moderate pitch, sometimes planned in form of a T. most commonly Catholic or Presbyterian'. See John Bradley, 'The Irish Barn Church' in *Seanchas Ard Mhacha*, 21/22 (2007–08), p. 236. See Fig. 17.2.
101.   See Bernadette Cunningham & Raymond Gillespie, 'The purposes of patronage: Brian Maguire of Knockninny and his manuscripts' in *Clogher Record*, xiii, 1 (1988), pp 38–49.
102.   Padraig Ó Maolagáin, 'An Early History of Fermanagh' in *Clogher Record*, ii, 2 (1958), p. 291. For the tomb inscription see Angelique Day & Patrick McWilliams (eds), *Ordnance survey memoirs of Ireland, parishes of Fermanagh 1834–5* (Belfast, 1990), p. 116.

Brian Maguire, most likely a son of Connor Modartha Maguire, gathered and published Irish historical, devotional and literary manuscripts in the 1710s and 1720s and the largest of the manuscripts, which is 890 pages long, has become known as the *Book of Knockninny*.[103] The earliest of Brian Maguire's surviving manuscripts, which was transcribed by Séamus (Bacach) Mág Uidhir[104] in 1712, includes lives of Saint Brighid and Saint Patrick and descriptions of the Lough Derg pilgrim site.[105] There is also a version of the Life of the local Saint Maodhóg in a manuscript transcribed by John Magauran.[106] Other Maguire manuscripts from this period have devotional prayers, psalms and catechisms in the Tridentine tradition although, as Bernadette Cunningham and Raymond Gillespie have pointed out, the popular religion at lower social levels in Fermanagh at this time had many elements of earlier religious practices.[107] They also identified a Franciscan influence in these manuscripts and it is possible that Philip Shenan, the guardian of Lisgoole, Bryan Bán Cassidy and Hugh McHugh, all friars hiding out in the vicinity of Knockninny at this time, or Doctor Owen McHugh[108] the registered parish priest of Killesher in 1704, may have acted as advisors to Brian Maguire.[109] By spending considerable sums of money on Callowhill Chapel and on the historical, devotional and literary manuscripts, the Maguire's of Knockninny were demonstrating both their wealth and their commitment to their church. The high-point of Maguire's patronage of Gaelic culture seems to have been the great 'gathering of books' or 'congress of Gaelic learning' which was held in Knockninny in 1718.[110]

Brian Maguire had used the Maguire name to boost his status in County Fermanagh and similarly Hugh O'Donnell of Larkfield in County Leitrim, who was also a patron of Gaelic literature, benefitted from his family name and was even described as 'Iarla' Ó Domhnaill in two poems written in his honour.[111] Despite the legal obstacles facing Catholics, Hugh O'Donnell managed to become wealthy through leasing

103.   RIA, MS C. vi, 1; Cunningham & Gillespie, 'The purpose of patronage', pp 39, 44.
104.   For Séamus Mág Uidhir see Nollaig Ó Muraíle, 'Séamus Mág Uidhir, a scribe of Bréifne, and his work' in *Bréifne*, xi, 42 (2006), pp 207–26. The scribe worked in a number of different locations including the townlands of Stranamart and Doobally in west Cavan.
105.   RIA, MS 23A. 15, ff. 275–354.
106.   TCD, MS 1297.
107.   Cunningham & Gillespie, 'The purpose of patronage', p. 47.
108.   MacKiernan, *Diocese of Kilmore*, p. 158.
109.   The different branches of the Maguire family had long-standing links with the Franciscans and many of their members joined the order. See Noel Maguire, 'Inscriptions in Kinawley cemetery' in *Clogher Record*, i, 4 (1956), p. 163.
110.   Ó Muraíle, 'Séamus Mág Uidhir, a scribe of Bréifne, and his work', p. 212.
111.   Proinnsíos Ó Duigneáin, 'Hugh O'Donnell of Larkfield – patron of Gaelic literature (1691–1754)' in *Bréifne*, vi, 24 (1986), p. 391.

land from the Lane-Fox estate and because of his new-found wealth was seen as a leading Catholic layman in the diocese. Richard Pococke met with O'Donnell during his tour around Ireland in 1752.[112] He wrote about him:

> They say he is the head of that family descended from the Earl of Tyrconel and tho' he has only leases, yet he is the head of the Roman Catholick's in this country, and has a great interest, is a sensible man, and well vested in in the Irish History, both written and traditional.[113]

Brian Maguire and Hugh O'Donnell had much in common. They both exploited the family name and demonstrated their new-found wealth through the patronage of Gaelic literature and their local parish. Both employed Séamus Mág Uidhir as their scribe and were seen as leading Catholic laymen in a diocese where most of the Catholics were impoverished and in no position to give leadership in or patronage to their Church.

'The Charles Borromeo of Ireland'

Philip Tully, the parish priest of Kilmore who was based in the townland of Bleancup in that parish, got caught up in the dispute over the rival claims of Dublin and Armagh to the primatial See in Ireland. It appears that the archbishop of Armagh gave a ruling against him and, by subsequently contacting the archbishop of Dublin, Philip Tully appeared to be undermining the authority of Armagh. Certainly most of his fellow-priests in Kilmore did not approve of his actions and in July 1723 a letter was drawn up and signed by twenty-three priests of the diocese denying that there was any truth in the allegations made by Philip Tully, their fellow priest, against Hugh MacMahon, the archbishop of Armagh and vicar-apostolic of Kilmore.[114] The first signatory was Michael Reilly, Hugh MacMahon's vicar-general in Kilmore, and when Hugh MacMahon published his *Jus Primatiale Armacanum* in 1728, a defence of the primacy of Armagh, it included a letter of approval from 'Michael Reily, Juris utriusq. Doctor,

---

112.   For Richard Pococke see Rachel Finnegan, 'Fraternising with Papists: an Anglican clergyman abroad' in Brendan Leahy & Salvador Ryan (eds), *Treasures of Irish Christianity*, iii (Dublin, 2015), pp 83–5; eadem, 'A voyage to see scenes of Our Saviour's life and passion: Richard Pococke's eastern journey (1737–41), pp 86–8; eadem, *Letters from abroad: the grand tour correspondence of Richard Pococke and Jeremiah Milles* (Kilkenny, 2013).
113.   Stokes (ed.), *Pococke's tour in Ireland in 1752*, p. 71.
114.   SCAR, codex 1, vol. i, f. 168rv; The Latin text of this letter is given in Owen F. Traynor, 'Kilmore clergy list of 1723' in *Bréifne*, iii, 11 (1968), pp 411–2.

et Vs. Gs. Ks'. (Michael Reily, Doctor of Law and vicar-general of Kilmore).[115] It also included a sworn statement from Philip Tully saying that he had not appealed to the archbishop of Dublin against a decision of the primatial see of Armagh.[116] His defence was that he had contacted the archbishop of Dublin, not to reverse Armagh's decision, but rather to retrieve some documents relating to the case and with the publication of *Jus Primatiale Armacanum* the dispute came to an end.[117]

Michael O'Reilly had the backing of the majority of the priests in the diocese and it appears that despite the sporadic persecutions he, in his role as vicar-general, managed to restore some discipline and bring about some reforms in the diocese. He was convinced of the importance of preaching and catechising and had the reputation of being a strict disciplinarian.[118] It was generally held that he wrote his much-used dual language catechism sometime after 1739, the year he was appointed bishop of Derry, with the result that his catechism became known as the 'Derry catechism'.[119] However, it is now clear that he wrote his catechism much earlier and that he was already using it in his Cavan parish and possibly elsewhere in Kilmore diocese by 1727. In that year John Richardson published *The great folly, superstition and idolatry of pilgrimages in Ireland* and in it praised O'Reilly's catechism:

> One thing very remarkable hath occurred of late, much to the Commendation of the Popish Priest of Cavan: In a Catechism, which (as I am told) he composed and distributed, not long since, among his people and others: He gives up the worshipping of Saints in these Words, which to do him justice, I shall insert here as they are therein expressed by himself, by way of question and answer ... Q. Is it lawful to worship the Mother Mary or the Saints? A. It is not lawful, because this is an honour due to God alone. Q. Doth this Commandment forbid us to give Honour to the Saints? A. it doth not, because we do not give the same Honour to them, as to God; for we honour them only as friends and as faithful servants of God.[120]

---

115.   See under 'Approbatio Doctorum' in *Jus Primatiale Armacanum*.
116.   See under 'Memorandum' in *Jus Primatiale Armacanum*.
117.   Flynn, 'Hugh MacMahon', p. 172.
118.   Michael Tynan, *Catholic instruction in Ireland 1720–1950* (Dublin, 1985), p. 25.
119.   See Diarmaid Ó Doibhlin, 'Penal days' in Jefferies & Devlin (eds), *History of the diocese of Derry*, pp 172–3; Donnelly, 'Church policy in the diocese of Derry after the Reformation', p. 284.
120.   Richardson, *The Great Folly*, pp 116–7; Tynan, *Catholic instruction in Ireland*, pp 19–23.

No doubt John Richardson admired, not just the content of Michael O'Reilly's catechism, but also his use of both the Irish and English language to communicate his message.

Twenty-one years later, on 6 December 1748, when the staff of the Irish College in Paris were recommending Michael O'Reilly to the pretender James III for the vacant See of Armagh they wrote that 'Hugh MacMahon made him Vicar General of Kilmore; which diocese from being the seat of the greatest abuses, he, in a very short space of time, brought to be the best regulated in the whole kingdom' and then goes on to describe him as 'the Charles Borromeo of Ireland'.[121] They may have overstated their case and yet it seems clear that Michael O'Reilly was using an early draft of his catechism and had begun some reforms before he left Kilmore in 1730. His catechism, which he titled *An teagasg Criostuidhe, agus na gnáth-úrnaighthe*, was written in phonetic Irish and English and would continue to be used, with only slight modifications, into the twentieth-century. Thomas Magauran, a Franciscan priest from the diocese of Kilmore, was also busy providing spiritual reading for native Irish speakers in the early 1700s. He had been guardian of St Isidore's in Rome for a time before leaving there in 1685. He was guardian of Cavan friary in 1697 and again in 1708 and in between these two terms as guardian of Cavan he translated Angleo Elli's *Specchio spirituale del principio e fine della vita humana* from Italian into Irish. His translation, which he called *Sgáthán Spioradálta*, was published about the year 1704. He died in 1715.[122]

Following the uncovering of the plot by Francis Atterbury, the Bishop of Rochester, to unseat George I and install James III, the Stuart 'Old Pretender' living in France in his stead, the Irish House of Commons drew up the heads of a new bill in 1723 entitled 'A Bill for explaining and amending the Acts to prevent the Growth of Popery and for strengthening the Protestant Interest in Ireland'.[123] There was a feeling abroad that priests were now more visible and were increasing in number and that a new and severe bill was needed to address the situation. The new bill stated that any regular or unregistered priest or others exercising ecclesiastical jurisdiction found in Ireland after 25 March 1724 would be guilty of high treason and therefore liable to be hanged. Josiah Hort, the Church of Ireland bishop of Ferns and later

121.   Patrick Fagan, *Ireland in the Stuart Papers, 1743–65* (Dublin, 1995), pp 97–8; MacKiernan, 'Diocese of Kilmore (1678–1728)', pp 531–2; Hugh Fenning, *The undoing of the Friars of Ireland* (Louvain, 1972), pp 157–8.
122.   Anselm Faulkner, 'Thomas Magauran O.F.M. (*c*.1640–1715)' in *Bréifne*, iv, 13 (1970), pp 87–91.
123.   Burke, *The Irish priests*, pp 455–60.

to become the bishop of Kilmore, was generally in favour of the bill though he expressed some slight reservations about it stating that if the bill became law 'the coup de grace will be given to Popery' in Ireland.[124] Timothy Goodwyn, the bishop of Kilmore, was completely opposed to the bill stating that it was 'a cruel one' and added 'I could never have come into it'.[125] By the mid-1720s, Protestant clergy and laity alike had come to realise that the penal laws were not suppressing Catholicism and that instead, as Hugh MacMahon had explained in 1714, 'the greater the severity of the persecution, the greater the fervour of the people'.[126] Michael O'Reilly's use of his new catechism in the diocese of Kilmore from 1727 until he was transferred in 1730 to Drogheda to be parish priest there and vicar-general of Armagh, was an indication that, despite the penal laws, fresh attempts were being made to rebuild the Catholicism in Kilmore along the lines envisioned by the Council of Trent.

124.   Connolly, *Religion, law and power*, p. 284.
125.   Ibid.
126.   Flanagan, 'The diocese of Clogher in 1714', p. 42.

Chapter 15

Dominican Bishops: 1728–1753

There were, at most, just three bishops in Ireland at the beginning of the 1700s and Patrick Donnelly of Dromore was the only one in the northern half of the country. Despite periods of intense persecution in the early 1700s, the Vatican changed its policy and from 1707 began appointing bishops to Irish dioceses once more. In that year five Irish dioceses were filled and, over the next forty years, twenty-one more appointments were made. However, it was not until 1728, after a period of fifty-nine years without a Catholic bishop, that an appointment was made to Kilmore.[1] To the consternation of many within the diocese, however, Pope Benedict XIII appointed Michael MacDonogh, a twenty-nine year old Dominican from County Derry, as bishop of the diocese and consecrated him in the Vatican on 12 December 1728.[2]

Michael MacDonogh had been ordained a priest in 1723 by Vincenzo Maria Orsini, the Dominican bishop of Beneventum, who a year later would become Pope Benedict XIII. The pope knew and admired the capable young Irishman who was teaching in the college of SS. Sixtus and Clement in Rome. While in Rome, MacDonogh acted as the Roman agent for the English Dominicans and for the provincial of the Irish Dominicans. He, and Bonaventure O'Gallagher a Franciscan friar, also claimed to be the Roman agents for all the religious of Ireland.[3] The English Dominican, Thomas Rushook, had been bishop of Kilmore from 1389 until 1393 without ever setting foot in the diocese. Apart from that appointment, the Dominicans had virtually no connection with Kilmore although members of the O'Rourke family of west Bréifne tended to be buried at the Holy Cross Dominican priory in Sligo until the Franciscans

1. For episcopal appointments at this time see Maureen Wall, *Catholic Ireland in the eighteenth century* (Dublin, 1989), pp 29–30.
2. Hugh Fenning, 'Michael MacDonogh, O.P., Bishop of Kilmore 1728–46' in *IER*, cvi, 3 (Sept.1966), pp 138–53; De Burgo, *Hibernia Dominicana*, pp 421, 504–5; Seán P. Donlan, 'Michael MacDonagh', *DIB*, v, pp 920–1. Fenning states elsewhere that Michael MacDonogh may have been only twenty-seven years old when he was made bishop of Kilmore. Hugh Fenning, *The Irish Dominican Province, 1698–1797* (Dublin, 1990), p. 131. It will be clear from this chapter that I am greatly indebted to the research and writing of Hugh Fenning, O.P.
3. APF, *SOCG* 98, ff. 526r-527v and 662, f. 323.

friary was established in Creevelea in 1508.[4] Besides, there were several well-educated Kilmore priests in the early 1700s who could have been appointed bishop of their native diocese at this time. Thaddeus O'Rourke, a Franciscan priest and direct descendant of the O'Rourke sept from west Bréifne, had been appointed bishop of Killala in 1707, a position he held until his death in 1736.[5] James Gallagher, another north-Leitrim man, was appointed bishop of Raphoe in 1725. His book, a collection of sixteen sermons which was published in 1736 in both the Irish and English language, proved to be immensely popular and was still being used into the twentieth-century.[6] Because of persecution he had to flee from Raphoe in 1734 and, three years later, he was appointed bishop of Kildare and Leighlin, a position he held until his death in 1751.

Michael O'Reilly, who had been an effective and reforming vicar-general of the diocese since 1713, was the most obvious local candidate for the bishopric of Kilmore. He had the support of the archbishop of Armagh and the majority of the priests of the diocese and his innovative dual-language catechism was already being put to good use in Cavan. Michael MacDonogh remained in Rome for at least eighteen months after he was appointed bishop of Kilmore. By the time he had returned to Ireland, in the summer of 1730, Hugh MacMahon had rescued Michael O'Reilly from the diocese and appointed him parish priest of Drogheda and his vicar- general in Armagh. Michael O'Reilly would later say that MacDonogh's appointment to Kilmore in 1728 was 'the amazement of Ulster'.[7] In 1739 O'Reilly was appointed bishop of Derry and ten years later archbishop of Armagh. He died in 1758.[8]

4.   For some O'Rourke burials in the Dominican priory in Sligo see *AFM*, 1386, 1402, 1418. In contrast to Kilmore, the neighbouring diocese of Ardagh had a long connection with the Dominicans who established a convent in Longford in 1400. See J.J. McNamee, 'Ardacha Dominicana' in *Journal of Ardagh & Clonmacnois antiquarian society*, 12 (1951), pp 5–27.
5.   Thaddeus O'Rourke lived with his relative the Catholic lawyer Terence MacDonagh and later with his other relatives, the O'Conor family of Ballinagare. He taught the young Charles O'Conor and travelled about using the pseudonyms of Fielding or Fitzgerald. See Diarmaid Ó Catháin 'Some account of Charles O'Conor and literacy in Irish in his time' in Luke Gibbons & Kieran O'Conor (eds), *Charles O'Conor of Ballinagare, life and works* (Dublin, 2015), pp 31–2; Nollaig Ó Muraíle, 'Keeping the embers alive: Charles O'Conor and Irish manuscripts – his own and others' in Gibbons & O'Conor (eds), *Charles O'Conor of Ballinagare*, p. 192; Charles O'Conor, 'Charles O'Conor of Belangare' in *Studies*, xxiii, 89 (Mar.1934), pp 125–40.
6.   Ciaran MacMurcaidh, 'Dr James Gallagher, alumnus Kilmorensis: bishop of Raphoe (1725–37) and Kildare and Leighlin (1737–51)' in *Bréifne*, x, 40 (2004), pp 219–37; idem, 'Text and translation of James Gallagher's 'A sermon on the assumption of Our Blessed Virgin Mary' (1736)' in *Arch. Hib.*, lxii (2009), pp 154–82; Eoghan Ó Raghallaigh, 'James Gallagher' in *DIB*, iv, p. 10.
7.   APF, *SC Irlanda* 9, ff. 543–6.
8.   Hugh Fenning, *The undoing of the Friars of Ireland*, pp 156–67; Thomas O'Connor, 'Michael O'Reilly' in *DIB*, vii, p. 863; Daly & Devlin, *The clergy of the diocese of Derry*, p. 12; Ó Doibhlin, 'Penal days' in Jefferies & Devlin (eds), *History of the diocese of Derry*, pp 172–3; Tynan, *Catholic instruction in Ireland*, pp 22–36.

When Michael MacDonogh returned to Ireland he resided with the Dominican nuns in Channel Row (now North Brunswick Street) in Dublin and visited his diocese each summer.[9] Bishop MacDonogh was not about to abandon his Dominican Order. Instead, as Hugh Fenning remarked, 'he remained what he had been in Rome – a crusader for the rights of regular clergy and for the order of St Dominic in particular'.[10] Surprisingly, given his new appointment, he continued to be quite critical of diocesan priests stating that 'the secular clergy of this kingdom would crush as much as can lye in their power the Regulars and will hinder them of their rights'.[11]

A Dominican 'Convent' in Kilmore

In 1734 Michael MacDonogh wrote to the general of the Dominican Order outlining his plans to establish a Dominican house in County Cavan. Perhaps in an attempt to strengthen his argument for doing so, he claimed that the Dominicans had established a priory in Cavan in the fourteenth-century which had subsequently been given to the Franciscans.[12] He was proposing that the Dominican priory of Cavan would be permanently situated in Drumlane parish which was capable of supporting a community of four and so would not be a burden on the people of the diocese. During his first visitation of the diocese Bishop MacDonogh explained his plans to both the secular priests and the Franciscans and even though the Franciscans opposed the plan MacDonogh still felt that he would be able to proceed with it.[13] It is possible that Michael MacDonogh's efforts to establish a Dominican priory in Cavan were intended to provide both a residence and support system for himself in the diocese.

Michael MacDonogh tried valiantly to establish the Dominican priory in Kilmore diocese on a sound footing although he met with considerable opposition, not least from Bernard MacMahon who had been appointed archbishop of Armagh in 1737. Stephen MacEgan, the Dominican bishop of Meath, had similar plans to establish a link between the parish and priory of Mullingar thwarted by MacMahon. He wrote on 30 November 1738 to Edmund Burke in Rome:

9.   Fenning, 'Michael MacDonogh', p. 142.
10. Ibid., p. 143.
11. *AGOP*, iv, 214, ff. 113–4.
12. Thomas de Burgo also claimed that the Dominicans had a priory in Cavan from 1300, that *c*.1393 they were expelled and the Franciscans installed in their place. See de Burgo, *Hibernia Dominicana*, p. 286. Benedict O'Sullivan states that 'Cavan was certainly a Franciscan house and no notice need be taken of the assertion that it was originally Dominican and afterwards passed to the Friars Minor'. See O'Sullivan, *Medieval Irish Dominican studies*, p. 88.
13. Fenning, 'Michael MacDonogh', pp 144–5.

I shall for the future be more careful in depending on him [MacMahon]. He has used Mr MacDonogh worse [than me], and I believe he intirely defeated his project about the house of Cavan, which he doubtless represented to be a new Erection, tho' to my knowledge there have been Priors nominated there since my comeing to Ireland [1708]. Yet Mr Primat labours to defeat him.[14]

This statement by Stephen MacEgan suggests that there was a Dominican presence in County Cavan for at least two decades before Michael MacDonogh was appointed bishop of the diocese. It is possible that Andrew and Edmund Magaghran, the two priests listed for Drumlane parish in 1704, were both Dominicans, and in that list Andrew Magaghran is described as parish priest and prior of Drumlane.[15] It would appear that he was the Dominican prior of Drumlane and that he had no association with the former Augustinian priory of Drumlane. The engraving of the 'Priory of Drumlane, Co. Cavan' by J. Newton, which was carried out in July 1794 and published by N. Hooper, shows the priory to be roofed.[16] (See Fig. 15.1). It was at this time being used by Drumlane Church of Ireland community and in 1938, Joan Wilson, a pupil of Fairgreen National School, wrote: 'In my great grandfather's time it was the Church of Ireland parish church and he was present at the last service held there … the roof was made of shingles'.[17] Drumlane's Church of Ireland parish church, which is dedicated to St Columba, was built *c.*1820[18] and the priory of Drumlane then ceased to be used as a church.

There was, it appears, a small, loose and informal cluster of Dominicans either based in Drumlane or nominally attached to it in the early 1700s and, at the Dominican provincial chapter, which was held in Dublin in August 1720, it was proposed that a superior be appointed to 'the destitute [Dominican] convent of Cavan'.[19] Following MacDonogh's

14.   SCAR, Codex iv, doc. 23 quoted in Fenning, 'Michael MacDonogh', p. 145.
15.   Andrew Magaghran, a native of Kilmore diocese who was ordained in Lisbon on 4 March 1651 and in a petition from the Kilmore clergy to Pope Innocent XI *c.*1678 he described himself as 'Prior de Drumlahan'. See *Arch. Hib.*, xv (1950), p. 65; Fenning, 'Irishmen ordained at Lisbon', p. 110. According to the 1704 list of priests Andrew Magaghran lived in the townland of Derrintinny and Edmund in Tirliffin. See *A list of the names of the popish parish priests*, p. 5. These Magaghran priests may have been natives of Corcanadas in Drumlane parish and a Patrick Magaghran from Crossdoney went surety for both of them in 1704. In 1715 Edmund Magaghran was described as 'pastor ecclesiae S. Madochi.' See *Bréifne*, iv, 14(1971), p. 221.
16.   Grose, *The antiquities of Ireland*, ii, p. 64.
17.   www.duchas.ie (accessed 7 July 2017), Schools folklore collection, vol. 0972, p. 369.
18.   Two different dates, 1819 and 1821, have given for the building of this church. Perhaps building started at the earlier date and was completed by the later one. See Lewis, *Topographical dictionary of Ireland*, p. 94 and Leslie, *Clergy of Kilmore, Elphin and Ardagh*, p. 57.
19.   Fenning, *The Irish Dominican province*, p. 86.

Figure 15.1: The 1794 engraving of Drumlane priory by J. Newton which was published by N. Hooper.

appointment to Kilmore in 1728 the number of Dominicans working in the diocese began to increase and by 1734 he had two 'outsider' Dominicans, Dominic Ó Brolacháin, who was known as 'the Friar Bán', and Bernard MacHenry helping him in the diocese.[20] Bernard MacHenry, a native of Antrim, had studied and taught in Louvain. He was provincial of the Dominicans in Ireland from 1734 to 1738 and again from 1749 to 1753. MacHenry was parish priest of Drumlane between 1738 and 1749 and his residence, 'near Belturbet' in the parish of Drumlane, was regularly referred to as the Dominican 'convent of Cavan'.[21] Dominic Ó Brolacháin was from Derry diocese.[22]

Bishop MacDonogh stated that since coming to Ireland he had received several young men into the Order and by the end of 1735 he had five Dominicans attached to the Drumlane house. We know the names of the five Dominicans who were attached to 'Conventus Cavaniensis B. Mariae Virginis' four years later from the papers found on Michael MacDonogh when he was arrested on 6 June 1739. Those listed in the seized papers were Richard Nugent, Patrick Sheridan,[23]

20.   *AGOP*, iv, 214, ff. 98–9.

21.   Fenning, *The Irish Dominican Province, 1698–1797*, pp 145–50, 170, 216, 631; L.P. Murray, 'Father Brian MacHenry, O.P., Drogheda' in *JCLAS*, vi, 4 (1928), pp 250–2. MacHenry signed a document in 1747 as parish priest of Drumlane. See ASV, *Fondo Missioni*, 117.

22.   Daly & Devlin, *The clergy of the diocese of Derry*, p. 142.

23.   Patrick Sheridan, 'a professor of theology and pastor of Oughteraghy' was said to have preached for ten years in the vicinity of the Dominican convent of Cavan. Fenning, *The Irish Dominican province*, p. 609.

Thomas Fitzsimons, Patrick Becan[24] and Dominic Keernan.[25] Judging by their names it would appear that most if not all of these men were from the diocese of Kilmore. Bishop MacDonogh's policy of recruiting young men from the diocese into the Dominican Order was meeting with considerable success and in 1743 Edmund O'Reilly, a recently-ordained Dominican from Cavan who had studied in Louvain University, was granted faculties to preach and hear confessions in the diocese of Malines.[26]

Despite the growing number of Dominican priests from and within the diocese, Michael MacDonogh struggled to get official recognition for his Dominican 'convent of Cavan'. While in Rome in 1740 he made one final and ultimately unsuccessful attempt to get papal recognition for the Dominican priory in Drumlane arguing that 'it would give the Dominicans a refuge under the title of secular priests'.[27] Hugh Fenning estimates that the Dominican priory in Kilmore was in existence for 'at most twenty years' although there were Dominican priests working in the diocese for considerably longer than that.

Bishop MacDonogh's Travels

Michael MacDonogh travelled long distances on horseback, not just between Dublin and Kilmore but throughout much of Ulster.[28] However, his trip to Derry in October 1737 to install his cousin John Ó Brolacháin, the parish priest of Coleraine, as dean of the diocese was an ill-advised intrusion into the affairs of his native diocese. Despite his poor health, Neal Conway, the bishop of Derry, protested to Rome about the intrusion and stated that Michael MacDonogh should not be appointed archbishop of Armagh, a position MacDonogh had looked for some months earlier.[29] There already had been complaints

24.   Patrick Backahan (Buchannnan) was a native of Gowna. MacKiernan, *Diocese of Kilmore*, p. 167.
25.   Dominic MacKiernan was a student at Holy Cross College in Louvain in 1738 and two years later was studying in Corpo Santo in Lisbon. See AGOP, iv, 217, p. 54 and Fenning, *The Irish Dominican province*, p. 198. This list was compiled by Bernard MacHenry *c*.1735. Fenning, *The Irish Dominican Province*, p. 198; idem, *The Fottrell papers, 1721–39* (Belfast, 1980), p. 77; idem, 'Some problems of the Irish mission, 1733–1774, Documents from Roman archives' in *Coll. Hib.*, 8 (1965), pp 93–4.
26.   Nilis, 'Irish students at Leuven University', pp 194–5; Brendan Jennings, 'Irish preachers and confessors in the archdiocese of Malines', *Arch. Hib.*, xxiii (1960), pp 162–3.
27.   Fenning, 'Michael MacDonogh', p. 145.
28.   He was equipped for travelling. In his will, which was written on 12 September 1746, he left his two year old filly to Patrick Masterson, the parish priest of Urney and Annagelliff. He bequeathed his two saddles, portmanteau, boots, whip and spurs to Mary Doyle, the Dominican prioress of the convent in Channel Row where he resided in Dublin.
29.   APF, SC *Irlanda* 9, ff. 543–6, 596–7; AGOP, iv, 217, f. 16.

to Rome about MacDonogh not residing in his diocese[30] which further damaged his chances of promotion to Armagh.[31] In May 1739 Bishop MacDonogh set out with John Fottrell, the Dominican Provincial, on his visitation of the Dominican houses in Ulster and both of them were arrested at Toomebridge in County Antrim on 6 June 1739 and subsequently thrown into prison. With insider help they managed to escape although all Michael MacDonogh's belongings, including his pectoral cross, episcopal ring and a large number of documents had been taken from him.[32] MacDonogh fled to Dublin and, with a reward of £200 for his arrest, he had no option but to leave the country. He travelled incognito through London on to Brussels and reached Rome towards the end of 1739, remaining there for the next twelve months.

While in Rome Bishop MacDonogh met the newly-elected Pope Benedict XIV and impressed on him the risks posed by the Charter Schools in Ireland.[33] In 1741 he sent a detailed report to Propaganda Fide outlining the problems these proselytising schools were causing and suggesting some actions which could be taken to counteract them.[34] There were already 'Charity schools' in the diocese.[35] Belturbet had a Charity school as early as 1714 with £7 being given by the 'Lord of the Mannor and £3 by the Minister', for the teaching of poor children there.[36] In 1730 there was a Charity School in Cavan town, which was supported by the minister of the parish and it had fourteen boys in attendance. A nearby Charity School at Kilmore, where twelve boys were 'taught, clothed and apprenticed'[37] was supported by the Protestant bishop and dean of the diocese. There was a Charity School in Dromahair which had fourteen boys on the rolls[38] and another in Cloonclare where the minister 'keeps four poor boys at school and cloths and intends to put them out to apprentices'.[39] These Charity Schools were well scattered, had few on

30. APF, *SOCG* 698, ff. 279–80v; *Arch. Hib.*, xxviii (1966), p. 73.
31. Ibid.
32. Fenning, 'Michael MacDonogh', p. 147. His papers which were seized are to be found in PRONI, D. 1449 and have been published in Fenning, *The Fottrell papers 1721–39*.
33. Fenning, 'Michael MacDonogh', pp 148–9. The Charter Schools took their name from the charter of George II (6 February 1734) by which the Incorporated Society in Dublin for promoting English Protestant Schools in Ireland was established. The schools were principally for 'the children of Popish and other poor natives'. See S.J. Connolly (ed.), *Oxford companion to Irish history*, (Oxford, 1998), p. 90.
34. SCAR, Codex ii, 60; 'Report of Bishop McDonagh, 1741' in *Bréifne*, ii, 8 (1966), pp 438–40.
35. The Charity Schools were usually small schools established by individual landlords or clergymen and some of them prepared children for working in linen production.
36. *An account of the Charity Schools in Great Britain and Ireland* (London, 1714), p. 77.
37. Kilmore visitation Report, 1733. See PRONI, DIO/4/24/2/1.
38. *An account of the Charity Schools in Ireland* (Dublin, 1730), pp 4, 13. See also Philip O'Connell, *The schools and scholars of Bréifne* (Dublin, 1942), pp 227–8.
39. PRONI, DIO/4/24/2/1.

the rolls and had little impact on the diocese.[40] However, the Charter Schools, which were to be established country-wide from 1733 onwards 'to teach the children of the papists the English tongue, and the principles of the Christian religion'[41] were seen by the Catholic hierarchy to pose a much greater threat. Joseph Story, the Church of Ireland bishop of Kilmore, had high hopes for the Charter Schools in 1746 when he stated that 'The Government have (*sic*) shewn their great regard and desire for the Conversion of Papists by the very useful foundation of Charter Schools, which begins to make a considerable progress, and will in time produce excellent results'.[42] Bishop Story's hopes and Bishop MacDonogh's fears were without foundation and in 1750 MacDonogh's successor, Laurence Richardson, reported that no Charter school had been established in the diocese of Kilmore.[43]

By the beginning of 1741 Michael MacDonogh had left Rome and was taking a circuitous route through France back to Ireland. In Flanders he met with Michael O'Gara the archbishop of Tuam, Patrick MacDonagh the bishop of Killaloe and Bishop James Gallagher, the Kilmore native who four years earlier had been transferred from Raphoe to Kildare and Leighlin. They penned a long letter to the pope describing the miserable state of Catholics in Ireland, outlining how the well-off Catholics were deserting their faith in order to hold on to their land and the poor Catholics who remained were unable to support the large number of regular and secular priests in the country. They recommended that all bishops and archbishops in the country ordain priests only as they were needed for pastoral work. They also recommended that the number of regular clergy, who have increased 'beyond all bounds' be reduced and that the superiors of religious communities order 'their subjects to teach and instruct the people in the towns and villages in which they are accustomed to quest for alms'.[44] Michael MacDonogh, perhaps under pressure from the other three bishops, seemed to have changed sides in the ongoing tensions between regular and secular clergy in Ireland.

---

40.   Part of the motivation for setting up the Charter Schools may have been to prevent children becoming Presbyterians. See David Hayton, 'Did Protestantism fail in early eighteenth-century Ireland? Charity schools and the enterprise of religious and social reformation, *c*.1690–1730' in Ford, McGuire & Milne (eds), *As by law established*, p. 180.
41.   *Letters written by his excellency Hugh Boulter*, i (London, 1769), p. 9.
42.   Joseph Story, *The Bishop of Kilmore's charge to the Clergy of his Diocese at his ordinary visitation held at Cavan June 26, 1746*, (Dublin, 1747), pp 18–19.
43.   *Relatio*, 9 June 1750. Hagan, 'Miscellanea Vaticano-Hibernica', pp 132–3; O'Connell, *The diocese of Kilmore*, pp 495–6.
44.   Vatican Archive, *Nunziatura di Fiandra*, 6, ff. 267v-269r; *Coll. Hib.*, 10 (1967), pp 89–91.

Back in Ireland

The magistrates had found nothing objectionable in the MacDonogh papers seized at Toomebridge in 1739 and so he was left undisturbed for a time after he returned to Ireland. In 1739 he had made some progress at re-establishing the diocesan chapter in Kilmore - which would consist of a dean, archdeacon, theologian, treasurer and cantor - and in February 1742 he appointed Eugene Farrelly, the parish priest of Annagh, the dean on the chapter.[45] It would appear that deans were appointed in each deanery because two years later, it was reported that 'Owen McPharlon otherwise Bartley'[46] - the parish priest of Innismagrath - was a 'titular Deane of the diocese of Kilmore' and John O'Reilly, the parish priest of Crosserlough who lived at Drumkilly, was said to be 'the Popish Deane of Killmore' and Hugh Duggan the vicar-general.[47]

The Catholic clergy experienced a period of intense persecution in the early months of 1744 because, given the renewed war in Europe, the government feared that there would be a French-Jacobite invasion of Ireland.[48] The lord lieutenant of Ireland issued a proclamation ordering all the existing laws to be applied rigidly against bishops, friars and all other Catholics exercising ecclesiastical jurisdiction. Monasteries and friaries were to be closed and sheriffs and others in authority were ordered to draw up reports giving 'the name and place of abode of all persons being, or suspected of being popish archbishops, bishops, vicar generals, deans, Jesuits, monks and friars'.[49] John Jones, the sovereign of Belturbet reported on 14 March 1744 that 'The Popish Bishop of Killmore, known by the name of Clarke, lives in Dublin'.[50] He listed five friars based in east Cavan and named John Reilly as the dean and Hugh Duggan as the vicar-general of the diocese. A report drawn up in Sligo on 9 March 1744 stated that John McKeown was the guardian of Creevelea Franciscan friary and that James McKeown, Patrick Early, Edmund O'Hara and Phelim McMorrey were also attached to that

---

45.   SCAR, Codex I, i, ff. 182–3.

46.   Burke, *The Irish Priests*, p. 444. Michael MacDonogh refers to him as 'Eugene Bartly' in his will. See William Carrigan, 'Catholic episcopal wills' in *Arch. Hib.*, i (1912), p. 183. It is said that a medical doctor named MacPartlan changed his name to the more Anglicised 'Bartley' in order to be appointed a dispensary doctor in the parish of Innismagrath. See Clancy & Forde, *Ballinaglera and Innishmagrath*, p. 282.

47.   Burke, *The Irish priests*, pp 291, 437, 444.

48.   Ó Ciardha, *Ireland and the Jacobite cause*, p. 307.

49.   Quoted in Gerard O'Brien (ed.), *Catholic Ireland in the eighteenth century, collected essays of Maureen Wall* (Dublin, 1989), p. 56.

50.   Burke, *The Irish priests*, pp 290–1.

friary.[51] Arthur Ellis, the high sheriff of Leitrim, compiled his list on 26 March 1744 and named 'Michael McDonagh otherwise Clarke, of Abbey street in the Citty of Dublin' as the 'Titular Pope of the diocese of Kilmore' and he thought that 'James Martin near Temp[le]port' was a vicar-general in Kilmore.[52] It was a particularly difficult period for Michael MacDonogh since the authorities had accurate information about him. He was accused of treason and had to move house twelve times in two months in order to avoid arrest.[53] In late September, when the persecution had eased, he wrote to the Dominican minster-general describing 'the storms and tempests in which we have nearly been lost' and he added that the storms were now 'only beginning to subside'.[54]

Sickness and Death

Michael MacDonogh, although still in his early forties in 1742, was in a frail state of health. It was reported in May 1742 that Dr MacDonogh who was unwell 'is getting better of a severe defluxion'[55] and the strain of being on the run in the early months of 1744 took a further toll on his health. The income of the Catholic bishop of Kilmore was paltry and was said to be 'much less than [that of] many chapels' in Dublin.[56] Michael MacDonogh was, at times, so poor that he had scarcely enough to eat, further aggravating his health problems.[57] On 8 September 1746 Archbishop Bernard MacMahon wrote that the bishop of Kilmore 'is much indisposed with the Rheumatism this long while past and is ordered by his Physicians to go to some hot Country for a time in order to recover his health'.[58] Four days later, 'being sick and weake of body' he made his will. He had only £7 15s to divide between his parents and seven siblings and he bequeathed his 'Pontificals now at Cavan to my successor in Kilmore' and some books, his horse, and vestments were left to Patrick Masterson, the parish priest of Cavan.[59] MacDonogh's riding gear, books and episcopal trappings were left to various members of the Dominican Order. He appointed Stephen MacEgan, the Dominican bishop of Meath and the two Kilmore priests, Patrick Masterson and Eugene Bartly, as his executors and he stipulated that he be buried in

51.   Ibid., p. 438.
52.   Ibid., p. 444.
53.   Fenning, *The Irish Dominican province*, p. 188.
54.   SCAR, Codex ii, 3, ff. 712v–713.
55.   Ibid., iv, doc. 88; *Coll. Hib.*, 8 (1965), p. 77.
56.   Thomas Brennan to Michael Fitzgerald (10 Jan. 1747), AICR, Liber xxvi, ff. 149–50.
57.   Vatican Archive, *Nunziatura di Fiandra*, 135 D, f. 203.
58.   SCAR, Codex i, 1, ff. 136–7; Fenning, 'Michael MacDonogh', p. 152.
59.   Patrick Masterson studied in Salamanca and was parish priest of Cavan parish from 1742 to 1782. See MacKiernan, *Diocese of Kilmore*, p. 164.

'Munterconnachty' – the last parish in Kilmore diocese on the road to Dublin.[60] He sailed to Portugal and died at the young age of forty-eight in the Dominican convent of *Corpo Santo* in Lisbon on 26 November 1746. The inscription on his headstone stated that he was 'a man of prudence, zeal for the faith and religion' and that he died 'after various persecutions by heretics'.[61]

Assessment

It is difficult to assess what impact Michael MacDonogh had on Kilmore during the eighteen years of his episcopacy. The fact that he remained in Rome for eighteen months after his appointment to Kilmore and that he resided in Dublin when he returned to Ireland, suggests that he may have ruled with a light hand and spent considerably more time outside the diocese than he did in it. However, these were difficult times for bishops in the country and among the special faculties Pope Clement XII granted him in 1731 were those:

> Of celebrating Mass in any decent place, even in the open air or underground … on a portable altar, even though it be broken or damaged, or lack the relics of the saints … Of secretly carrying the Most Holy Sacrament to the sick without candles, and of reserving it without candles … Of wearing secular clothes if he could not otherwise reach the places committed to his care or remain in them … Of reciting the Rosary or other prayers if he cannot carry a breviary with him.[62]

These were faculties for abnormal times. His arrest in 1739, his use of the pseudonym 'Clarke' and his time on the run for most of the first half of 1744 attest to the need for these special faculties. The lack of a bishop's residence and the poverty of the Catholics in Kilmore where 'none of them own even a little land' and where they and their priests 'are compelled to live in low and wretched dwellings' and where 'the visitor or traveller finds it difficult to obtain a suitable place for a night's

---

60.   Carrigan, 'Irish episcopal wills', pp 182–4.
61.   The inscription on his headstone reads: *Hic jacet/Illustrissimus ac Reverendissimus Dominus/ Fr.Michael MacDonogh, Hibernus/ Episcopus Kilmorensis, Solio Pontificio Assistens/ E Sacra Praedicatorum Familia Assumptus/Vir Prudentia, Fidei Zelo, ac Religionis Amore Praeclarus/ Post varias Haereticorum Persecutiones/Diuturna Infirmitate Consumptus/Obit Ullyssipone 6 Kal. Decembris Anno 1746/ Aetatis 48.* See de Burgo, *Hibernia Dominicana*, p. 421; O'Connell, *The diocese of Kilmore*, p. 489.
62.   Fenning, *The Fottrell papers*, p. 125.

rest or refreshment'[63] left it even more difficult for MacDonogh, a Dominican outsider, to function in the diocese. Despite these difficulties he insisted that on each Sunday the people in every parish be taught the norms of the Roman catechism and that the rules of the Council of Trent regarding matrimony be enforced. Bishop MacDonogh also wanted the clergy of each deanery to hold monthly conferences. He established throughout the diocese the Confraternity of the Most Holy Name of Jesus to counteract blasphemy, perjury and unlawful oaths and he managed to curtail the practice of 'providing alcoholic drink, as for a feast, at funerals'.[64] It would appear that when the nuncio Crivelli praised MacDonogh in 1741 for 'the exemplary zeal with which he pre-sided over his diocese'[65] he may not have been too wide off the mark.

Six weeks after Michael MacDonogh's death Thomas Brennan, a Jesuit priest who would later become rector of the Irish College in Rome, wrote that the bishop's death 'was very much regretted by all who had the pleasure of his acquaintance, and particularly by my [Jesuit] Brothers and me'.[66] Patrick Masterson, a priest of the diocese and one of the executor's of MacDonogh's will, stated in 1755 that the late bishop had shown him 'extraordinary marks of friendship' though not all the priests of the diocese held Bishop MacDonogh in high esteem.[67] Daniel O'Reilly, a native of the parish of Lurgan and president of the Irish College in Antwerp, wrote from there on 3 February 1747, stating that the Kilmore priests 'had reasons to complain grievously of their late bishop for his public partiality to the friars of his own order'.[68] Hugh Fenning's agrees with that viewpoint stating that MacDonogh embarrassed his former Dominican comrades by granting them excessive favours.[69] However, these criticisms must be tempered by an understanding of the extraordinary difficulties Michael MacDonogh faced during his tenure as bishop of Kilmore.

The Established Church

When Timothy Goodwyn, the Church of Ireland bishop of Kilmore and Ardagh, was translated to Cashel in 1727 he was replaced by Josiah Hort,

63. Hagan, 'Miscellanea Vaticano-Hibernica', pp 132–3; O'Connell, *The diocese of Kilmore*, pp 495–6.
64. Ibid.
65. Vatican Archive, *Nunziatura di Fiandra*, 135 D. f. 203.
66. AICR, Liber, xxvi, ff. 149–50; Hugh Fenning, 'Letters from a Jesuit in Dublin on the Confraternity of the Holy Name, 1747–1748' in *Arch. Hib.*, xxix (1970), p. 138.
67. *IER*, xi (Oct. 1874), p. 102.
68. Fagan, *Ireland in the Stuart Papers 1743–65*, p. 55. Daniel O'Reilly was appointed bishop of Clogher in 1747. MacKiernan, *Diocese of Kilmore*, p. 162. He died aged seventy-nine-on 24 March 1778 and is buried in Lurgan cemetery. See O'Connell, 'Ecclesiastical history of Lurgan parish' p. 31.
69. Fenning, 'Michael MacDonogh', p. 143.

another Englishman who had been bishop of Ferns since 1721. (See Fig. 15.2). Hugh Boulter, the archbishop of Armagh, was concerned that there were only nine English bishops on the Irish bench and so he had recommended that an Englishman be appointed to Kilmore, a position which he estimated to be worth about £2,000 per annum.[70] During the 1729 visitation of his diocese Bishop Hort gave some practical advice to his clergy about preaching which he said 'should be done in the plainest and easiest manner, laying aside the Metaphysical niceties, and the jargon of the schools'.[71] He explained that public prayers should be 'prayed and not read' and that by using 'a certain propriety of accent, cadence and gesture' they will succeed in drawing out the 'attention and affection of the congregation'.[72] He recognised that the Penal Laws had proved ineffective and he urged his clergy to catechise in order to make converts of people 'whether Protestant dissenters or Papists' explaining that:

> The way of persuasion and reasoning is the only way of doing this effectually. Coercive laws may restrain and disable those who hold Principles that are destructive to the Church and to the State, but they can never convince nor convert any body; they may bind men's hands and tongues but they can never reach their hearts.[73]

He confronted the problem of absenteeism by reminding the clergy of their 'indispensible duty of residence' in their parishes and he hoped that they would build 'convenient houses where they are wanting on your Glebes, so that your residence may be rendered more easy, comfortable and useful'.[74] In some parishes the glebe lands were quite a distance from the church and this discouraged the building of houses on them. The Board of First Fruits, which provided grants for the building and repairing of glebe houses, had been established in 1712. However, the uptake on these grants was slow throughout the country leading

---

70. *Letters written by his excellency Hugh Boulter, D.D. Lord Primate of all Ireland*, i (Oxford, 1769), p. 142. When the diocese of Killala became vacant in 1734 Archbishop Boulter stated that it would be 'very dangerous to let the majority of natives who are already twelve on the bench, grow greater' and so he recommended that 'some prudent English divine of good character' be appointed to that diocese. See *Letters written by his excellency* ii (London, 1770), p. 128.

71. Josiah Hort, *Instructions given by the Lord Bishop of Kilmore and Ardagh to his clergy at his visitations, Anno 1729* (Dublin, 1730), p. 4.

72. Ibid., p. 7.

73. Ibid., p. 10.

74. Ibid., pp 14, 16.

Figure 15.2: Josiah Hort, Church of Ireland bishop of Kilmore (1727–1741). (*Courtesy of Representative Church Body Library*).

Bishop Nicolson of Derry to complain in 1720 about the clergymen who choose to 'live in a cabine on a lay-farm sooner than on any inheritance in his church'.[75]

75.   Quoted in William Roulston, 'Accommodating clergymen: Church of Ireland ministers and their houses in the north of Ireland, *c*.1600–1870' in Barnard & Neely (eds), *The clergy of the Church of Ireland*, p. 110.

The report titled *A state of the diocess of Killmore as it appears in ye Triennial visitation in 1733*[76] states that no parish had received a grant for the building of a glebe house before 1733 and there were only three glebe houses in the diocese by 1741.[77] Denn parish was the first to get a grant from the Board of First Fruits, receiving it in 1740.[78] Some of the clergymen's houses were in good repair. The dean's house in Kilmore parish, which had been built after 1700, was in good repair and was valued at £373 5*s*. 10*d*. The vicar of Drung and Laragh had an even better house, it being valued between £700 and £800.[79] The 'parsonage house' in Belturbet, which was situated on the north side of the town, was a substantial building and had been fortified by Colonel William Wolseley of the'Inniskilleners' during the Williamite wars.[80] The bishop's house at Kilmore was 'long, lofty and capacious, about one hundred feet in length and forty in width'.[81]

Several of the rectors and vicars were absentees. John Singleton, the rector of Drumgoon, resided in Dunleer in County Louth and Michael Leigh, the curate he employed who 'lives very near ye parish' though not in it, had a salary of £40 per annum. Patrick Moore, the rector of Kildrumferton, lived in his former parish of Clonbroney in County Longford and employed Richard Knight as his curate to care for the parishioners. And even though the glebe lands in Kildrumferton amounted to 300 acres, they were said to be too distant from the church and so no manse house had been built. The parish of Innismagrath in north Leitrim was particularly badly served having neither a resident vicar nor curate and the parish had 'no church

---

76.   For report see PRONI, DIO/4/24/1–28. My thanks to Desmond McCabe for this source. For analysis of the report see William Roulston 'The 1733 visitation of Kilmore: a window on an early eighteenth-century Church of Ireland diocese' in *Bréifne*, xi, 42 (2006), pp 282–92.
77.   Roulston, 'The 1733 visitation of Kilmore: a window on an early eighteenth Church of Ireland diocese', p. 289; idem, 'Accommodating clergymen', p. 114.
78.   PRONI, DIO/4/11/2. Denn received another grant of £618 in 1817 for the building of a glebe house. See Lewis, *Topographical dictionary of Ireland*, p. 92.
79.   PRONI, DIO/24/2/1 and 10.
80.   Charles S. King, *Henry's Upper Lough Erne in 1739* (Dublin, 1892), p. 19. William Henry, who wrote this account, was rector in Killesher from 1731 to 1740. Lord Galmoy and his Jacobite forces hanged Captain Woolston Dixie, a son of Edward Dixie the vicar of Denn, in 1689 and in a further act of outrage were said to have kicked his head 'about Belturbet market place in a grisly game of football'. See Doherty, *The Williamite war in Ireland*, p. 75; John Oldmixon, *Memoirs of Ireland from the Restoration to the present times* (London, 1716), pp 92–3.
81.   King, *Henry's Upper Lough Erne in 1739*, p. 8. A report approximately one hundred years later stated that 'The parish church of Kilmore is very small and ancient, it joins the bishop's palace which is a large house encompassed with a fine demesne'. See John C. Erck, *An account of the ecclesiastical establishment subsisting in Ireland as also an ecclesiastical register of the names of the dignitaries and parochial clergy* … (Dublin, 1830), p. 47.

in repair'.[82] Luke Sterling, the rector of Lurgan parish, resided in Oldcastle and employed his son Edward Sterling as curate and, despite there being 600 acres of glebe land in the parish, there was no manse house and the curate lived in a small house of little value. The vicar of Kilsherdany lived a considerable distance away in Ballintemple and his curate resided in a 'farm house' which had stone walls and a thatched roof and was situated on glebe lands about a mile from Kilsherdany church.[83]

The early decades of the 1700s saw a considerable number of Church of Ireland churches being built or repaired in Kilmore and in the other northern dioceses. In 1733 twenty-two of the thirty benefices in Kilmore had a church and churches were in the process of being built in both Lavey and Killinkere. The church in Lurgan parish was the only one in the diocese to be slated although the church on the Franciscan site in Cavan was said to be in 'pretty good order'.[84] Killeshandra church had a shingle roof and was the only church in the diocese which had a ceiling. The aisles of this church were flagged and the enclosed area around the communion table had a marble floor. The good condition of this church may be explained by the fact that there were '80 church families' in the parish and the rector, William Ennery, resided in the town.

The church in Belturbet was in 'very good order' and William Henry, the rector in Killesher, informs us that Belturbet church was 'a large church, which is generally crowded, all the inhabitants within the corporation being Protestants'.[85] Ten churches were roofed with shingles while the churches in Denn, Killann, Knockbride and perhaps some others were covered with thatch. The cathedral church at Kilmore was said to be in 'good order' and a report six years later stated that it had been 'much adorned by the present Bishop [Josiah Hort], who has sashed it, flagged it, pewed and painted it'.[86] In Killinagh the church was in ruins and services were held in a little house and while Killinkere church was being built, services were held in a 'bad chapel'.[87] Despite the fact that Dominick Bulteel, the vicar of Oughteragh, lived beside the town and that there were sixty Protestant families in the parish, the church in Ballinamore was in poor condition. It had a shingle roof in bad repair and no ceiling, the aisles were not flagged and the 'ordinary communion table' was not railed in. The parish had four hundred acres of glebe land

82.   PRONI, DIO/4/24/2/23.
83.   PRONI, DIO/4/24/2/6.
84.   Roulston, 'The 1733 visitation of Kilmore', p. 33.
85.   King, *Henry's Upper Lough Erne*, p. 19.
86.   Ibid., p. 10.
87.   PRONI, DIO/4/24/2/22.

only two miles distant from the church although there was no manse house on it.

There were particular difficulties in some parishes in the diocese where the Church of Ireland population was small although not all of the difficulties were in the northern, more sparsely populated part of the diocese. The parish of Denn, not far distant from Cavan town and described in the 1733 visitation report as a 'stripe of 6 or 7 miles in length and no part of it a mile broad' had only five or six Protestant families living in it.[88] Denn parish church in the townland of Carrickaboy was in a poor state, being thatched and without any seating inside, though it did have rails separating the communion table from the rest of the church.

In his 1729 instructions to his clergy Josiah Hort urged them to visit all the families in their parishes 'in a constant and settled course'.[89] However, the general absence of glebe houses and the absence of several ministers from their parishes militated against the missionary outreach which Bishop Hort wanted his clergy to adopt. The ministers were often distant physically and culturally from their parishioners and, even though they usually employed curates, the gap between clergy and laity remained. Towards the end of the 1730s the Church of Ireland parishioners of Killinagh complained that even though they were numerous, consisting of twenty-six families and 122 souls, they were being neglected so badly by their clergy that there was a danger that some of them would defect to the Roman Catholic church.[90] A similar fear was expressed by Bishop Hort in 1729 when he stated that 'the emissaries of the Church of Rome are busy 'trying to 'instill their pernicious errors into weak and incautious minds' and he urged his clergy to be diligent 'in order to prevent this growing mischief'.[91]

A Missionary Church

Bishop's Hort's fears were not without foundation. In 1746 Joseph Story, who had succeeded Josiah Hort as bishop of the diocese in 1741, expressed his surprise when addressing his clergy in Cavan that 'During above 150 years since the Reformation an absurd Religion should rather gain than lose ground: And that we should hear of more perverted to Popery than recovered from it, though

---

88. Virtually all of the Protestants living in Denn were named Heaslip. See Liam Kelly, 'The parish of Denn in the early 1800s' in *Bréifne*, xii, 46 (2011), p. 275.
89. *Instructions given by the Lord Bishop*, p. 11.
90. Wynne papers, PRONI, MIC/666/D/3/1–11.
91. *Instructions given by the Lord Bishop*, pp 12–13. Bishop Hort was quite outspoken at times in his criticism of Catholic priests and Catholicism in general. For examples, see *Sixteen sermons by Josiah, Lord bishop of Kilmore and Ardagh* (Dublin, 1738), p. 147 and *Sermons on Practical subjects inscribed to the clergy of Kilmore and Ardagh* (Dublin, 1737), p. 139.

we have both Reason and Revelation strongly on our side'.[92]
He then reminded the clergy of 'the strict obligations we all lye
under to exert our utmost endeavours, our power and ability in
reclaiming these deluded people'.[93] He told his hearers that all souls
in their parishes are committed to their care 'whether they be Infidels,
Jews, Turks, Papists or Protestants' and that they must cease calling the
parishes where there 'are no churches built and few or no Protestants'
by the name of 'noncures'.[94] He, like his predecessor, recommended
that the clergy adopt a missionary approach. He told them:

> Make yourselves well acquainted with every one of your
> parishioners, with their way and manner of living, their
> tempers and inclinations, vices and virtues … This in a
> short time may be accomplished so as to be both a diver-
> sion and to contribute to your health by riding or walking
> among them in good weather, by chatting to them at their
> labour, by entering into their houses and cabins.[95]

Bishop Story reminded his clergy that the language barrier was not so
great as it had been in the past since the Irish 'almost all understand your
language and can answer you in the same' and so 'you have little or no
occasion for an interpreter'. By the 1740s it was clear that Catholicism had
survived the Penal Laws and would not be crushed by coercive means.
Bishop Story had a grudging admiration for the Catholic priests who were
prepared to 'compass sea and land to make proselytes' and were willing
'to endure all manner of toils and hazards to propagate their errors'. He
told his clergy 'such difficulties are not required of us but it is expected
that we should shew the same zeal within the verge of our cures'.[96]

Laurence Richardson: 1747–53

On 3 January 1747, approximately five weeks after the death of Bishop
Michael MacDonogh in Lisbon, the archbishop of Armagh, Bernard
MacMahon, named Eugene Bartley vicar capitular of Kilmore so that
he might administer the diocese until a new bishop was appointed.[97]

92.   Story, *The Bishop of Kilmore's Charge to the clergy of his diocese, at his ordinary visitation, held at Cavan June 26, 1746*, pp 3–4.
93.   Ibid., p. 4.
94.   Ibid., p. 7.
95.   Ibid., p. 11.
96.   Ibid., p. 19.
97.   Hugh Fenning, 'Documents of Irish interest in the *Fondo Missioni* of the Vatican archives' in *Arch. Hib.*, xxxxix (1995), p. 9.

Eugene Bartley, more commonly known as Owen MacPartlan, had graduated with a doctorate from Seville and was one of the executors of Bishop MacDonogh's will.[98] He had been curate in Templeport before being appointed parish priest of Innismagrath in 1737.[99] By 12 January 1747 'the chapter and clergy' of diocese met and they recommended three people for the vacant See of Kilmore - Eugene Bartley, John Reilly, a canon lawyer and parish priest of Crosserlough and Charles Magauran, who had a doctorate in theology and was parish priest of Killinagh.[100] The document was signed by twenty-four priests, approximately two-thirds of the priests of the diocese, and was sent to James III in Rome who had the right of nominating a successor.[101] This letter to Rome was followed by another dated 1 February 1747, recommending Eugene Bartley for Kilmore. It was signed by John Linegar, the archbishop of Dublin and ten of his canons and by Stephen MacEgan, the Dominican bishop of Meath, Patrick French the Franciscan bishop of Elphin and the former Dominican provincial John Fottrell.[102] Eugene Bartley also had the support of the Dublin-based Jesuit, Thomas Brennan, who wrote on his behalf to Michael Fitzgerald, the Jesuit rector of the Irish College in Rome, pleading with him to 'use all your endeavours to obtain that seat [Kilmore]' for Bartley.[103] In his letter, dated 10 January 1747, Brennan stated that Eugene Bartley:

> Is a person of middle age, a notorious friend of ours, our student, very learned, intimate with the greatest nobility and gentry in the Kingdom, a man of parts: in a word, en-dowed with all the qualifications suitable for that dignity. Moreover, as he commonly acted as vicar to the Gentle-man deceased [Michael MacDonogh], so he is thoroughly acquainted with that critical diocesss.[104]

Despite all the support for Eugene Bartley nothing came of it. The real power broker in Rome for Irish affairs at this time was the Dominican priest, Patrick Brullaughan and on 6 February 1747, possibly before the letter with the signatures of the bishops of Dublin, Meath and Elphin

---

98.   *Arch. Hib.* xxix (1970), p. 138.
99.   MacKiernan, *Diocese of Kilmore*, p. 161.
100.   Fenning, 'Documents of Irish interest in the *Fondo Missioni*', p. 9.
101.   The document was signed by Patrick Masterson, a close friend of the late bishop, and by priests from every deanery in the diocese. See *Arch. Hib.*, xlix (1995), p. 9.
102.   Fenning, 'Documents of Irish interest in the *Fondo Missioni*', p. 9.
103.   AICR, Liber xxvi, f. 150.
104.   Ibid.; Fenning, 'Letters from a Jesuit in Dublin', pp 138, 146.

reached there, Laurence Richardson, a Dublin born Dominican, was appointed bishop of Kilmore.[105] Writing in 1968, Hugh Fenning commented:

> Thus, for the second time in succession, the bishopric of Kilmore was bestowed by royal patronage on a member of regular clergy who had never lived or worked in the diocese. Dr MacDonogh had at least belonged to the ecclesiastical province of Armagh, but Dr Richardson was a Dubliner born and bred.[106]

Laurence Richardson was born *c.*1701 and took the Dominican habit in Dublin *c.*1718. Shortly afterwards he went to study in Holy Cross College in Louvain and while still a student there was appointed *lector artium*, helping the teaching staff of the college. He and some others in Holy Cross College soon became involved in political wrangling within the Dominican Order. This caused Stephen MacEgan, the Dominican provincial and later Bishop of Meath, to write:

> I do not wonder at their attempting such things, since the aforesaid *lector* Laurence Richardson, not yet a priest, wrote recently to a certain religious living here [Dublin] asking him whom he wished to see prior of Louvain; that it was in his power to put in anyone he wanted … The man has ability, but he is full of pride and ambition … These are childish but very dangerous things.[107]

Because he was thirteen months under-age, Laurence Richardson had to get a dispensation to be ordained a priest by the archbishop of Malines on 23 December 1724. For the next five years he remained on the continent teaching - mostly in Louvain – before returning to Ireland in the summer of 1729. Back in Ireland he became prior of the Dublin Dominican house and was promoted rapidly within the Order, being named a Master of

---

105.   Brady, *The episcopal succession*, i, p. 285.
106.   Hugh Fenning, 'Laurence Richardson, O.P., Bishop of Kilmore, 1747–53' in *IER*, cix (Mar.1968), p. 146. Hugh Fenning, in this article on Richardson, states that we have to jettison earlier (presumably Philip O'Connell's) impressions of Laurence Richardson which depicted him as a 'placid, other worldly pastor'. He was, according to Fenning, 'a politician born, a formidable controversialist, and one of Dublin's most prolific Catholic writers between 1730 and 1750.' See Fenning, 'Laurence Richardson', p. 137 and O'Connell, *The diocese of Kilmore*, pp 492–502.
107.   AGOP, xiii, 157. Translated in Fenning, 'Laurence Richardson', p. 138.

Sacred Theology in 1734. Despite, or perhaps because of his promotion within the Order he continued, to involve himself in ecclesiastical politics, controversies and writing.[108]

Resentments

Laurence Richardson was consecrated bishop of Kilmore on 1 May 1747 by John Linegar, the archbishop of Dublin who was assisted by Stephen MacEgan, the bishop of Meath who, twenty-three years earlier, had described Richardson as 'full of pride and ambition'. Archbishop Linegar was also assisted at the consecration by James Gallagher, a native of Kilmore who was at this time bishop of Kildare and Leighlin. Significantly, the consecration took place in the Dominican convent in Channel Row in Dublin, where, like his predecessor, Laurence Richardson would continue to reside during his time as bishop of the diocese. Bishop Richardson's presence in Dublin soon irritated some of the Dublin clergy, both diocesan and religious, who began to lodge complaints about the bishop spending too much time in the capital city and not enough in his rural diocese. The Jesuit, Thomas Brennan, was very critical of him in his letter to Michael Fitzgerald in Rome:

> Many are scandalised greatly that Mr Richardson does not reside in his own diocese and attend to his own sheep which stand in great need of instruction. On the other hand there is no need at all for his presence here. Never was a city better provided with learned and zealous instructors than Dublin is at present. Besides, Mr Richardson takes great airs upon himself in many respects.[109]

The opposition to Richardson's presence in Dublin may have been due to the suspicion that he wished to succeed John Linegar as archbishop of Dublin.[110] The complaints persisted and in May 1750 Laurence Richardson wrote to Cardinal Corsini in Rome stating that he was one of ten Irish bishops 'prevented' from residing in their dioceses and he questioned the motives of those who made complaints against him and not against the other absentee bishops. He described how the diocese of Kilmore consisted of lakes and barren mountains,

---

108. Among Laurence Richardson's writings were *An essay on the Rosary of the B.V.M.* (1736), *The impossibility of salvation outside the Roman Catholic Church* (1742), *The manner of hearing Mass with prayers before Confession and Communion* (1746), *An appendix to the manner of hearing Mass* (1748) and *A letter to the R.C. clergy of the diocese of K[ilmore]* (1749).

109. Fenning, 'Letters from a Jesuit in Dublin', pp 147–8.

110. Fenning, 'Laurence Richardson', p. 147.

explaining that the people were poor and that there were not three houses in the diocese which could offer him a bed. Despite these difficulties he told the cardinal that he had visited the diocese twice or three times a year and that he had spent May, June, July and September of 1749 holding conferences with his clergy. As an indication of the progress that had been made he claimed, with unwarranted optimism, that the abuses of drunkenness at wakes and the failures to teach the catechism and to keep parochial records had all been remedied. It is a sign of the pressure he was under that he asked the two bishops who had taken part in his consecration to add their signatures to his letter.[111]

The *relatio status*, dated 9 June 1750, which Laurence Richardson submitted to Rome, was similar in many respects to the letter he had sent to Cardinal Corsini five weeks earlier.[112] The main tenor of his report was that the diocese was so poor that it could not provide a suitable residence for a bishop and that, despite this poverty and his absence, the Church affairs in the diocese were functioning normally and that reforms had already taken place there. He claimed that the Confraternity of the Most Holy Name of Jesus had been established throughout the diocese by his predecessor and that the practice of 'profane oaths has been thereby greatly diminished'. He further claimed that the 'ancient custom of this diocese' - whereby the clergy of each deanery meet monthly in conference to discuss theological and pastoral issues, continues.[113]

Patrick Corish questions the veracity of this report and states that Laurence Richardson was 'deceiving himself' in the many claims he made about the healthy state of the diocese.[114] James Kelly holds a similar view, dismissing the claims of the 'unreliable Richardson'.[115] However, despite decades of penal law persecution, by mid-century the

111.   APF, *CP* 110, ff. 176–7. For absentee bishops at this time see Liam Swords, *The diocese of Achonry 1689–1818, a hidden church* (Dublin, 1997), p. 302. Patricia Lysaght, 'Hospitality at wakes and funerals in Ireland from the seventeenth to the nineteenth century' in *Folklore*, 114 (2003), p. 209. Laurence Richardson and Lord Trimleston had, in 1748, given a judgment against Bishop MacEgan of Meath in a dispute over the right of patronage in the parish of Kildalkey. See Cogan, *The diocese of Meath*, iii, p. 670; Fagan, *The diocese of Meath*, p. 118.
112.   *Arch. Hib.*, v (1917), 132–3 and translation in O'Connell, *The diocese of Kilmore*, pp 495–7. For other versions of this document see APF, *SC Irlanda* 10, ff. 306–7 and ff. 314r-5v. See also Hugh Fenning, 'A guide to Eighteenth-century reports on Irish dioceses in the archives of Propaganda Fide' in *Coll. Hib.*, 11 (1968), p. 27.
113.   O'Connell, *The diocese of Kilmore*, pp 496–7.
114.   Corish, *The Catholic community*, p. 97.
115.   Kelly, 'The Catholic Church in Kilmore, 1580–1880', p. 126. Cathal Ó Háinle also suggests that Dr Richardson's claims should be taken '*cum grano salis* [with a grain of salt]'. See Cathal Ó Háinle, 'Registers of a midland parish 1791–1810: Ballinahown, County Offaly and County Westmeath' in *Arch. Hib.*, lxv (2012), p. 222.

diocese may have been in a healthier state than previously thought. The reforms of the vicar-general Michael O'Reilly, who introduced his cate-chism in the diocese in the late 1720s and who proved a strict disciplinarian wherever he went, may well have been continued by Michael MacDonogh as Laurence Richardson claimed. Richardson's report to Rome dated 4 October 1750 confirms that there were pastors in every parish and that a sizeable minority of them had theological qualifications acquired on the continent.[116] The diocese was provided with deans and a vicar-general. It had a cathedral chapter of sorts and the 'ancient custom' of deanery con-ferences may not have been a figment of Bishop Richardson's imagination.

In Laurence Richardson's booklet *A letter to the R.C. clergy of the diocese of K[ilmore] impowering them to erect the Confraternity or Sodality of the Most Holy Name of Jesus, against the hateful vice of cursing and swearing* which was published in 1749 he describes how those joining the sodality must kneel before a priest and say 'I … firmly purpose and resolve with the help of God to avoid profane cursing and swearing in my self and according to my ability to hinder it in others'. Then, towards the end of his booklet he states that 'every one of our parish priests is … required, without delay, to erect in his parish chapel or chapels … the sodality thus explained'.[117] This booklet (See Fig. 15.3.) provides evidence that he was engaging with his clergy and was making an honest attempt to bring about some reform in the diocese. One year after this booklet was published he claimed that sodalities had been erected throughout the whole diocese.[118] Laurence Richardson's book *The manner of hearing* Mass, which was first published in 1746, contained explanations of each part of the Mass, prayers for before and after Communion and Confession, sections on the seven penitential psalms and love of one's enemies. Chances are that it was more beneficial to the priests than the laity of the diocese. It obviously continued to be used and in demand after he was appointed bishop of Kilmore as it was reprint-ed, with new additions, in 1754, one year after his death.[119] However, his claims about drunkenness at wakes being 'wholly abolished' and the use of profane oaths being 'greatly diminished' demonstrates either a naivety on the part of the bishop or else his desperation to convince Rome that all was well in the diocese and that he was able to administer it adequately from his base in Dublin.

116. O'Connell, *The diocese of Kilmore*, pp 496–7.
117. Laurence Richardson, *A Letter to the R.C. Clergy of the Diocess of K...* (Dublin, 1749), p. 4.
118. Hagan, 'Miscellanea Vaticano-Hibernica', p. 133.
119. The 'Office for the Dead in both Latin and English' was included in the 1754 reprint which suggests that it was intended as a manual for priests.

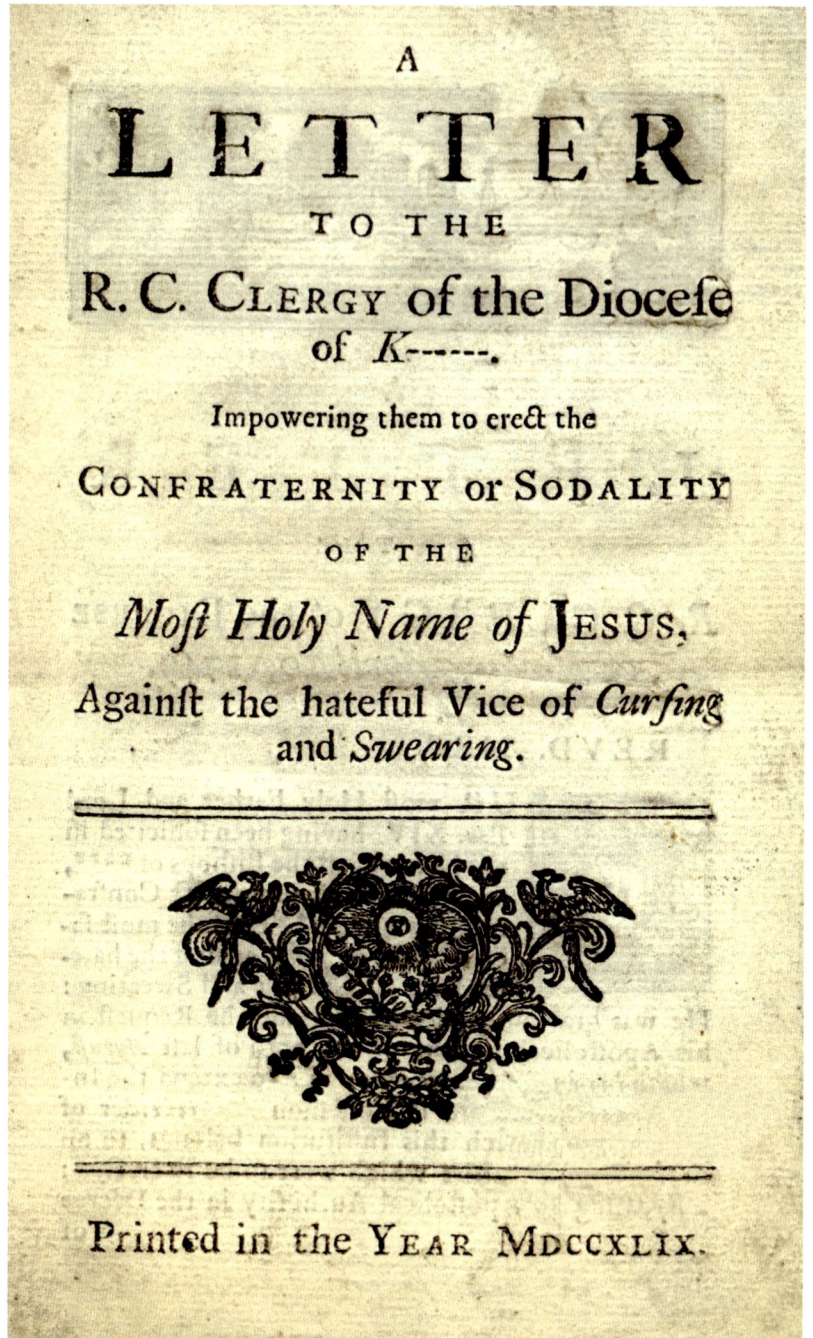

A
LETTER
TO THE
R. C. CLERGY of the Diocese
of *K*------.

Impowering them to erect the

CONFRATERNITY or SODALITY

OF THE

Most Holy Name of JESUS,

Againft the hateful Vice of *Curfing*
and *Swearing*.

Printed in the YEAR MDCCXLIX.

Figure 15.3: Title page of Bishop Laurence Richardson's 1749 *Letter to the R.C. Clergy of the diocese of K[ilmore].*

Secular and Regular Priests

Some of the Irish bishops were wont to ordain any young man with a smattering of Latin with the result that the number of priests, both secular and regular, increased rapidly in country in the first half of the eighteenth-century. Thomas Flynn, the parish priest of Cloone in County Leitrim, who was appointed bishop of Ardagh in 1718, was one of the worst offenders in this respect. He was suspended by Benedict XIII in 1729 for indiscriminately ordaining men and he died, aged eighty-eight, just months after his suspension, on 29 January 1730.[120] The large number of secular and regular clergy led to increasing tensions between them and to excessive financial burdens being placed on the poor and dispossessed Catholics. Laurence Richardson reported accurately to Rome in 1750 that the Catholics of the diocese are 'very poor and none of them own even a little land, as the non-Catholics hold the entire countryside. Moreover, all the Catholics are compelled to live in low and wretched dwellings [*humilibus et miseris domunculis*] as are the parish priests'.[121]

The succession of bad harvests between 1726 and 1729 resulted in famine and distress. The wet summer of 1739 and the severe frost of that winter were followed by a cold and dry summer in 1740 and by widespread famine, fever, dysentery and death.[122] People were impoverished and were unable to support the increasing number of priests. It was in 1741, just as the country was emerging from severe famine, that Rome decreed that Irish bishops were to ordain no more than twelve priests during their entire episcopacy. On 18 May 1749 Laurence Richardson, with the backing of the archbishop of Dublin and the bishop of Meath, applied to the Nuncio in Flanders to be exempted from this restriction.[123] The request was turned down at a meeting of Propaganda Fide on 23 September 1749.[124] Undaunted, he applied again for an exemption in July 1752 stating that most of his parish priests were advanced in years and that it was

---

120.   Kelly, 'The Catholic Church in the diocese of Ardagh', pp 73–4. He is buried in Cloone cemetery. See M.J. Masterson, 'Miscellany' in *Ardagh and Clonmacnois antiquarian journal*, ii, 11 (1946), pp 84–5.

121.   *Arch. Hib.*, v (1917), p. 132; O'Connell, *The diocese of Kilmore*, p. 495. The Rev. Philip Skelton, who travelled through County Cavan in 1757, described the 'wretched hovels' people lived in and how, in some instances, the only food people had was a mixture of cow's blood and sorrel 'boiled up together.' See Samuel Burdy, *The life of the late Rev. Philip Skelton, with some curious anecdotes* (Dublin, 1792), p. 124. John Cradock, the Church of Ireland bishop of Kilmore, wrote in 1758, just one year after he was appointed to Kilmore, that 'very lately … dearth, scarcity, distress and inclement seasons made their menacing appearance among us'. See *A sermon preached in Christ-Church, Dublin; on Friday Feb. 17, 1758* (Dublin, 1758), p. 10.

122.   For bad harvests and famine conditions in Ireland in the 1730s to 1750s see L.M. Cullen, 'Economic development, 1691–1750' in *A new history of Ireland*, iv, pp 146–7.

123.   APF, *Acta*, 119, ff. 228v-234v; APF, *SOCG* 742, f. 153v; Moran (ed.), *Spic. Ossor.*, iii, pp 161–2.

124.   Fenning, 'Laurence Richardson', p. 149, n. 38.

impossible to find replacements for priests who were sick. Propaganda Fide relented this time and allowed him to ordain a further six priests.[125]

The ongoing tensions between the regular and secular clergy peaked during the episcopacy of Laurence Richardson and, notwithstanding his position as bishop of Kilmore, he sided with the regulars in several disputes throughout Ireland and was labelled by Patrick MacDonagh, the bishop of Killaloe, as the 'protector of the Franciscan and Dominican orders'.[126] He supported the Augustinians when he wrote to Patrick Brullaughan in Rome in 1747 recommending that a convent of Augustinian nuns, headed by Susana Fallon, be established in Athlone[127] and three years later he attested to the general good character of friars and nuns in Ireland.[128] He intervened in a dispute over the Franciscan friary in Wexford and his letters to Nicholas Sweetman, the bishop of Ferns, on the matter have been described as 'politely offensive'.[129] Following the appointment of Michael O'Reilly, the Kilmore-born bishop of Derry, as archbishop of Armagh in January 1749, the Roman authorities moved quickly and granted the vacant See of Derry to John Brullaughan, the parish priest of Coleraine who was widely regarded as being unsuitable because of his irregular lifestyle. Michael O'Reilly complained to Rome about their decision and Cardinal Corsini wrote to Laurence Richardson asking him to reply to him quickly with 'a sincere, clear and final exposé of the evidence needed to settle the dispute'.[130] Laurence Richardson overstepped the mark, declared himself an apostolic delegate and set up a formal inquiry before sending seventy pages of sworn testimony to Rome on 21 October 1749.[131] This evidence could not be used since Richardson had no mandate for what he did. A single letter to Rome from Daniel O'Reilly, the bishop of Clogher, achieved what Richardson's large file could not, and Brullaughan was forced to renounce all claims to the See of Derry.

There were a number of zealous reformers in Ireland who were intent on sorting out the ongoing disputes between the regular and secular clergy in the country. The most notable of these reformers were Michael O'Reilly, the archbishop of Armagh who declared in

---

125.   APF, *Acta*, 122, ff. 235–6; APF, *SOCG* 753, ff. 212–3.

126.   Cathaldus Giblin, 'Ten documents relating to Irish diocesan affairs 1740–84 from Franciscan Library, Killiney' in *Coll. Hib.*, 20 (1978), p. 76.

127.   SCAR, Codex iv, doc. 106a; Hugh Fenning, 'The diocese of Elphin 1747–1802: documents from the Roman archives' in *Arch. Hib.*, xxxvi/xxxvii (1994/1995), pp 159–61.

128.   SCAR, Codex iv, doc. 172.

129.   Fenning, 'Laurence Richardson', p. 150.

130.   APF, *CP* 110, f. 30.

131.   Ibid., ff. 29–74.

December 1750 that there 'will never be peace so long as regulars are named bishop'[132] and John Murphy, a Dublin born priest, who Laurence Richardson had unjustly described in 1748 as 'a man of no learning and I fear, a man of ostentation'.[133] In the spring of 1750 John Murphy, claiming to represent the four archbishops of Ireland, went to Rome and prevailed on Propaganda Fide to issue two decrees which they hoped would bring about the much-needed reform in the Irish church.[134] Despite protestations from Laurence Richardson who claimed that there were 'certain ecclesiastics who are persecuting the regular clergy more severely than did Queen Elizabeth'[135] the Roman decrees stood. These decrees, which subjected the regulars to the bishops of Ireland and forbade the reception of novices in the country, came into force in early 1751. It was a devastating blow for Laurence Richardson who had fought the cause of the regulars for many years.

Two years later, on 29 January 1753, Laurence Richardson died after a long illness at the relatively young age of fifty-two. He had stipulated in his will that he be 'buryed in the most private manner at twelve o'clock at night and with as little expence as possible'.[136] His wishes were carried out and he was buried in the Trimleston family vault in St James's church in Dublin.[137] As his predecessor had done he left his 'grey mare and dun horse' to Patrick Masterson, the parish priest of Urney and Annagelliff and he left sixty pounds as a burse for six clerical students ('apprentices'), two of whom were to be from Leitrim and four from Cavan.[138]

Dominican Priests

Between the years 1728 and 1753 the diocese of Kilmore was administered by two Dominican bishops, Michael MacDonogh (1728-46) and Laurence Richardson (1747-53). Michael MacDonogh had managed to establish a small Dominican convent in the parish of Drumlane and

132.   Fenning, 'Documents of Irish interest in the *Fondo Missioni*', p. 11.
133.   Fenning, 'Letters from a Jesuit in Dublin', pp 147–8. For Fr John Murphy, see *An account of the life and character of the late Rev. John Murphy D.D., taken from authentic memoirs and original papers, by the living testimonies of his fellow students and contemporaries* (Dublin, 1753); Toby Barnard, 'A saint for eighteenth-century Dublin? Father John Murphy' in Ryan & Tait (eds), *Religion and politics in urban Ireland*, pp 225–48; Fenning, *The undoing of the Friars*, pp 161–7.
134.   It transpired that John Murphy only represented the views of the archbishops of Armagh and Dublin and not those of Cashel or Tuam.
135.   AGOP, IV 217, p. 120.
136.   Carrigan, 'Irish episcopal wills', p. 184.
137.   *Pue's Occurrences*, 30 January 1753; Brady, *Catholics and Catholicism*, p. 81. A portrait of Laurence Richardson was in the possession of the Dominican sisters of Drogheda. Its whereabouts is not now known.
138.   Carrigan, 'Irish episcopal wills', p. 184.

a number of men from Kilmore joined the Dominicans during this period and ministered in the diocese and elsewhere after ordination. One of the first Kilmore men to join the Dominican Order after Michael MacDonogh's appointment to the diocese was John Maguire, a native of Knocknniny. By 1732 he was already ordained a priest although he only began to study philosophy in San Sisto in Rome in September of that year and he remained there for approximately six years.[139] Having completed his theological studies he taught in Holy Cross College in Louvain for a period in the mid 1740s and then returned to Ireland where he was prior of Gola and parish priest in Aghalurcher in the diocese of Clogher.[140] He died sometime between the years 1777 and 1781 and was buried in Aghalurcher.

Thomas Fitzsimons, another Kilmore native, was in Louvain and already a Dominican priest by May 1745. He returned to Ireland and was parish priest of Drumlane in 1750 and was preacher general for the convent of Gola. In 1756 he was listed as the prior of Cavan convent, and he died there sometime between 1769 and 1773.[141] Patrick Sheridan was the Dominican parish priest of Ballintemple in 1750 and remained in that position for a considerable period after that.[142] The Dominican Patrick Backahan was a curate in Kinawley for at least a decade before his death in 1775.[143] John O'Neill, who was 'a son of Cavan convent', went to Rome to study and was ordained there on 8 June 1754. In 1761, having finished his studies in San Sisto College, he returned to Ireland and was transferred to Drogheda on 12 October 1765. He died in 1774.[144]

Andreas Smith baptised a number of children in the combined parishes of Killinkere and Mullagh in the autumn of 1767 and spring of 1768 and was, it appears, a native of Killinkere.[145] He was fifty years old in 1767 and he died in the Dominican 'convent of Cavan' sometime before 1773.[146] Bernard Brady, a 'son' of the Dominican

139.   For his time in Rome see AGOP, iv, 214, p. 69; AGOP, xi, 3600 & iv, 217, pp 12, 34.
140.   De Burgo, *Hibernia Dominicana*, p. 333.
141.   For Thomas Fitzsimons see Fenning, *The Irish Dominican province*, pp 192, 198, 216, 329, 609; De Burgo, *Hibernia Dominicana*, p. 288; APF, CP, 137, f. 284.
142.   *Arch. Hib.*, v (1917), pp 133–4.
143.   MacKiernan, *Diocese of Kilmore*, pp 164, 165, 167; Terence P. Cunningham, 'The 1766 religious census, Kilmore and Ardagh' in *Bréifne*, i, 4 (1961), p. 361. Patrick Backahan was sixty years old in 1767 and was said to be prior of Cavan Dominican convent in that year. See *Report on the houses of the Irish Dominican province* (2 Sept. 1767) in *Coll. Hib.*, 8 (1965), pp 93–4.
144.   Fenning, *The Irish Dominican province*, p. 362, n. 24; *Coll. Hib.*, 8(1965), p. 92.
145.   See the baptismal register of the combined parishes of Killinkere and Mullagh at 4 Sept. 1767, 10 Mar. 1768, 25 Mar. 1768, 27 Mar. 1768 and 31 Mar. 1768; Traynor, 'More Kilmore clergy lists', p. 215; Fenning, *The Irish Dominican province*, pp 262, 614.
146.   *Report on the houses of the Irish Dominican province*, p. 94.

convent of Cavan was ordained in Louvain in 1756. He taught in Holy Cross College in Louvain until he returned to Ireland in 1769. He was appointed parish priest in Derryvullen and vicar-general of the diocese of Clogher.[147] John O'Reilly was a priest-student at Holy Cross College in Louvain in July 1750 when he was given permission to return to Ireland to sell property at 'Lackan', in County Cavan in order to give the proceeds to the Dominican convent of Cavan. He was based in Newbridge in Kildare for much of his time in Ireland and he died there sometime before 1773.[148] It is possible that there may have been a tradition of members of the O'Reilly family joining the Dominicans because among the sons of 'Thomáis mc Seaghain' O'Reilly is listed one 'Phillip an bráthair d'Ord St Dominic'.[149]

The diocese of Kilmore had Dominicans bishops for the twenty-five year period between 1728 and 1753. The parish of Drumlane had Dominican priests for considerably longer than that, apparently from *c*.1700 to *c*.1770. During this time the priest's house in Drumlane was referred to as 'the convent of Cavan' and it was dedicated to the Virgin Mary. This Dominican 'convent of Cavan' struggled to survive and to get official recognition and with the death of Laurence Richardson in 1753 all hope of its survival had vanished. However, the Dominican presence in the diocese, which had peaked in the middle decades of the 1700s, continued until the beginning of the 1800s and Dominican priests such as Anthony Fay and Ross MacCabe, both natives of Kilmore and nominally linked to the convent of Cavan, ministered in the parish of Naul in County Dublin into the early years of the nineteenth-century.[150] The Dominicans made their mark on the diocese, particularly in the middle decades of the 1700s, and the two Dominican bishops, despite being resident in Dublin, had re-established the episcopacy in Kilmore and adequately administered an impoverished diocese in the final years of the penal persecutions.

---

147.   Hugh Fenning, 'Bernard Brady, O.P., parish priest of Derryvullen, 1770- *c*.1800' in *Clogher Record*, vi, 2 (1967), pp 394–5.
148.   AGOP, iv, p. 118; *Coll. Hib.*, 8(1965), p. 100.
149.   Carney (ed.), *A genealogical history of the O'Reillys*, p. 35.
150.   Luke Tierney, 'Dominicans serving in Dublin parishes' in *Reportorium Novum*, iii, 1 (1962), pp 158, 161.

Chapter 16

Divisions and Diversity: 1750–1770

Patrick Masterson, the vicar-general of Kilmore, called a meeting of the priests of the diocese on 29 January 1753, just days after Bishop Laurence Richardson had died. Masterson had been vicar-general for the two Dominican bishops of the diocese, Michael MacDonogh and Laurence Richardson, and both of them had, he said, shown 'him 'extraordinary marks of friendship'.[1] In their wills both bishops had left their horses to Masterson, though it seems likely that they were only given to him in a caretaker capacity so that he might present them to the succeeding bishop of the diocese.[2] It was decided at that meeting of the Kilmore clergy not to recommend anyone for the vacant See, since such recommendations had carried no weight in the previous two appointments. Instead Patrick Masterson took the precaution of writing to Patrick Brullaughan, the Irish power broker who was based in the Dominican church of *Sancta Maria supra Minervam* in Rome, advising him of the stance taken by the Kilmore clergy and asking him to ignore any other letters claiming to represent the Kilmore priests' views on who should be their next bishop.[3]

Archbishop Michael O'Reilly, who previously had to cope with a disastrous nomination to the See of Derry, showed none of the reticence of Patrick Masterson. He wrote to Lord Lismore recommending his cousin Philip O'Reilly, the parish priest of Drogheda, for the bishopric of their native diocese of Kilmore and he advised Philip O'Reilly to apply for the mensal parish of Annagh, which had been left vacant by the death of Laurence Richardson.[4] He also persuaded about half of the parish priests of the diocese to recommend both Philip O'Reilly and John O'Reilly, the parish priest of Crosserlough, for the vacant See. The influential Cardinal Corsini recommended

---

1. *IER*, xi (Oct. 1874), p. 102.
2. Michael MacDonogh, in his will, left 'a 2 year old filly to Mr Patrick Masterson of Cavan with the injunction led on him in my separate direction' - presumably a direction to give the horse to whoever succeeded him as bishop of Kilmore. See Carrigan, 'Irish episcopal wills', p. 183.
3. SCAR, codex 1, vol. i, f. 151r.
4. Fenning, 'Laurence Richardson' p. 156. Annagh was a mensal parish at this time.

James Matthew Brady, the superior of the Irish College in Paris , for Kilmore.[5] Among the other names being suggested were Nathaniel MacDonnell,vicar-general of Derry, Andrew Campbell, archdeacon of Armagh and James Madden, the parish priest of Armagh. Although the tide had turned against the regular priests at this time, three very capable candidates, the Franciscans John MacMullan and Francis Maguire, and the Dominican, Bernard MacHenry, were also recommended for Kilmore during the year 1753.[6]

Francis Maguire, a Franciscan native of the diocese of Kilmore, had the backing of some of the leading Franciscans in the country at this time. They wrote to Rome stating that Maguire, who had a doctorate in theology, was a man of noble ancestry and lawful birth, a man of integrity and humility, had all the requisite qualities to be appointed bishop of Kilmore. The letter was signed by eight leading Franciscans, including Bernardine O'Reilly,[7] the minister provincial who would in 1754 be appointed guardian of Cavan friary, and John MacMullan, who had previously been mentioned for Kilmore.[8] Significantly, he also had the support of ten Kilmore priests from the parishes of north-Leitrim, west-Cavan and south-Fermanagh and of thirteen priests from the diocese of Clogher.[9] Their letter of recommendation was certified by John MacMullan who had also acted as notary for the Franciscan letter on behalf of Francis Maguire.[10] These letters to Rome expose a deep divide in the diocese with the Cavan-based priests supporting Archbishop Michael O'Reilly's candidates and the remaining priests of the diocese supporting Francis Maguire. Nicholas White, a Dublin priest and former student of the Collegio Urbano in Rome, also threw his hat in the ring, recommending himself for Kilmore.[11] The issue was resolved quickly. Laurence Richardson was less than ten weeks dead when, on 3 April 1753, Andrew Campbell, a priest from the archdiocese of Armagh, was appointed bishop of Kilmore.[12] He was ordained bishop on 3 June 1753 by Archbishop Michael O'Reilly who was assisted by Stephen MacEgan of Meath and Augustine Cheevers of Ardagh and Clonmacnois.

5.   For James M. Brady, see MacKiernan, *Diocese of Kilmore*, p. 162. He was appointed bishop of Ardagh in 1758.
6.   APF, *CP* 133, ff. 152–3, 174. Bernard MacHenry was well respected and a capable administrator and, having ministered in the diocese, would have been a suitable bishop for Kilmore.
7.   Mooney, 'Some Cavan Franciscans', pp 20–1.
8.   Cathaldus Giblin, 'Miscellaneous papers' in *Arch. Hib.*, xvi (1951), pp 90–1.
9.   Ibid., pp 92–3.
10.   The dating of this letter, 6 September 1753, poses a problem since Andrew Campbell had already been ordained bishop of Kilmore three months earlier.
11.   APF, *SC Irlanda* 10, ff. 402–3.
12.   Giblin, 'Miscellaneous papers', pp 94–5.

Andrew Campbell

Andrew Campbell was born in Claristown, in the parish of Dunany (now Togher) in County Louth in 1711 to Richard Campbell and Mary Hullen.[13] Little is known of his early years except that he went to study for the priesthood in Spain.[14] In the registers of the English College of Saint Gregory in Seville it is recorded that 'Don Andrés Cambel' received tonsure on 18 September 1733, sub-diaconate on 18 September 1734 and the diaconate on 5 March 1735.[15] Andrew Campbell was accepted into the Jesuit order in Seville because 'of his talent and competence'. However, things did not go smoothly there and he was dismissed from the Order because 'he was tested in his vocation' and was 'an instigator of intrigue in the novitiate'.[16] This dismissal from the Order forced him to continue his studies elsewhere. He studied arts and philosophy for three years and theology for one year in Saint Gregory's College in Seville before continuing his studies in the Irish College in Alcalá de Henares, a seminary which was not controlled by the Jesuits.[17]

Andrew Campbell was ordained a priest in 1736 and the following year he applied to the king of Spain for the *viaticum* or royal grant to help defray the costs of his returning to Ireland, where he hoped to 'preach the gospels and to defend the catholic faith against the heretics'.[18] The *viaticum* was refused and Campbell remained in Spain, where he continued to study theology before being awarded a doctorate in *alia parva universitate*, possibly in the University of Siguenza.[19] Andrew Campbell's fortunes improved considerably in 1740 when Maria and Margarita Lawless, sisters of the prestigious Captain-General Patricio Lawless, the governor of the Balearic Islands who died in 1739,

---

13.   A report compiled in 1763 states that 'Domus Andreas Campbell … promotusque fuit ad episcopatum 3 April 1753, aetatis suae circiter 45'. See Giblin, 'Miscellaneous papers', pp 94–5. However, the inscription on the Campbell tombstone states that he was fifty-eight when he died in 1769.

14.   Some accounts mistakenly state that he had studied in Rome. See L.P. Murray, 'The piper-bishop from Togher: Dr Andrew Campbell, Bishop of Kilmore, 1753–69' in *The Examiner*, 3 January 1931; O'Connell, *The diocese of Kilmore*, p. 502. Fr L.P. Murray, in a letter to Patrick Lyons, the bishop-elect of Kilmore in the summer of 1937, a short time after Philip O'Connell's history of the diocese was published, stated that 'O'Connell's account of Campbell is full of errors. I am unfortunately to blame –as he lifted most of them from an account that I wrote in *The Examiner* fifteen or sixteen years ago'. See KDA, PL, 7.5. My thanks to Tom McKiernan for this reference.

15.   John Silke, 'The Irish College, Seville' in *Arch. Hib.* xxiv (1961), p. 127; Micheline Walsh, 'Andrew Campbell, Bishop of Kilmore, 1753–1769, student days in Spain' in *JCLAS*, xviii, 4 (1976), p. 298.

16.   Luis Valderas to William Clarke, 24 September 1737. For translation of this letter see Walsh, 'Andrew Campbell', p. 300.

17.   Giblin, 'Miscellaneous papers', pp 94–5; Patricia O'Connell, *The Irish College at Alcalá de Henares 1649–1785* (Dublin, 1997), pp 58, 79, 115.

18.   Andrew Campbell to King Philip V. For translation see Walsh, 'Andrew Campbell', p. 299.

19.   Giblin, 'Miscellaneous papers', p. 95.

appointed him to act as their 'full and absolute agent' in Madrid.[20] A few months later he applied once more to the king of Spain for the *viaticum* and this time William Clarke, a Scottish Jesuit and confessor to King Philip V, glossed over the details of Andrew Campbell's early departure from the Jesuit College in Seville by stating that he was then 'in poor health and that the climate did not suit him'.[21] On 19 September 1741 'Don Andrés Cambel' was granted the *viaticum* of one hundred ducats and presumably returned to Ireland shortly afterwards.

Michael O'Reilly, the Kilmore-born parish priest of Drogheda, was appointed bishop of Derry in 1739 and he was succeeded by Philip O'Reilly. The fact that Andrew Campbell's name appears in the Drogheda parish register in November 1752, when he acted as sponsor at two baptisms, probably led to the mistaken conclusion that he had ministered as either the parish priest or curate in Drogheda.[22] He was appointed bishop of Kilmore on 3 April 1753 and went to live with his family on their large farm in Claristown, becoming parish priest of his native Dunany and Port, a parish situated on the Irish Sea coastline, halfway between Drogheda and Dundalk. Just as his two predecessors had done, Andrew Campbell lived on the east coast of Ireland and from there tried to administer a diocese which stretched to the west coast of Ireland, touching the sea at the southern tip of County Donegal. Philip O'Connell carried out important research on the life of Andrew Campbell by locating his tombstone in Port cemetery in 1929 and by gathering some of the oral traditions relating to him.[23] O'Connell claimed that Campbell, disguised as a piper, travelled on foot throughout the diocese of Kilmore for three months each summer where he 'laboured most zealously for his flock and visited every part of his extensive diocese regularly'.[24] The parish registers of Munterconnacht and Castlerahan, which began in 1752, Lurgan which began in 1755 and Killinkere and Mullagh which began in 1766, all carry evidence that he visited these east-Cavan parishes. However, he may not have been

20.   Walsh, 'Andrew Campbell', pp 298, 301. Andrew Campbell's mother, Mary Hullen, had previously been married to Patrick Lawless who died after just one year of marriage. They had one son, Patrick, who, in later years, married Margaret Campbell. See Murray, 'The piper-bishop from Togher', p. 4. So it is possible that Andrew Campbell was related to the sisters Maria and Margarita Lawless, though I have not been able to establish such a connection.
21.   William Clarke to the Philip V's secretary, 13 July 1740. Translated in Walsh, 'Andrew Campbell', p. 302.
22.   KDA, P/L, 7.5; Patrick J. Campbell, 'Andrew Campbell, bishop of Kilmore, 1753–1769' in *JCLAS*, xviii, 4 (1976), p. 297.
23.   See Philip O'Connell, 'The tomb of Bishop Andrew Campbell' in *The Breifny Antiquarian society journal*, iii, 2 (1929–30), pp 284–6.
24.   O'Connell, *The diocese of Kilmore*, pp 505–6.

Figure 16.1: Chalice of Bishop Andrew Campbell (1761) and detail on the base.

so diligent in visiting the parishes in west-Cavan and north-Leitrim because, following his death in 1769, a letter which 'the vicar forane and parish priests of the lower deanery in the diocese' wrote to Rome stated that Bishop Campbell had never 'visited the largest part of his diocese, as a result of which were born many abuses and the non-observance of discipline'.[25] Bishop Denis Maguire, who was bishop of Kilmore from 1770 to 1798, stated that his 'predecessors visited the diocese perhaps once a year for an annual conference'.[26]

Philip O'Connell states that according to tradition Andrew Campbell's appointment 'was at first unpopular with some of the clergy of the diocese' – no doubt a reference to the priests of the north-western part of the diocese who had proposed Francis Maguire for Kilmore.[27] It is possible that their letter to Rome, which was dated 6 September 1753, was an ill-advised attempt to unseat the newly appointed bishop and, despite

25.   APF, *CP*, vol. 137, f. 214.
26.   APF, *Acta*, xii, ff. 58–9.
27.   O'Connell, *The diocese of Kilmore*, footnote on p. 504.

O'Connell's assertion that Andrew Campbell became 'extremely popular with priests and people', it is clear that the clerical divisions in the diocese persisted throughout his episcopate.

In 1751 the long serving Archbishop Christopher Butler of Cashel complained about priests 'covered with a dirty and tattered alb and vestment, approaching to an altar decked with foul rags, [and] a pewter chalice'.[28] No doubt similar problems existed in Kilmore and Andrew Campbell tried to bring about some reform by encouraging the priests of the diocese to replace the old pewter chalices with more appropriate silver ones. He gave good example himself by having a chalice made in 1761 which bore the inscription *Orate pro Andrea Campbell episcopo Kilmorensis qui me fieri fecit An D. 1761.*[29] See Figure 16.1. Peter Maguire, the parish priest of Denn, followed suit with a chalice in 1762 and Bartley MacCabe, the parish priest of Mullagh/Killinkere, did likewise in 1768.[30] The parish of Castlerahan began keeping a marriage register in 1751 and a baptismal register in 1752, both being in place before Andrew Campbell was appointed to Kilmore. Campbell must have encouraged this practice, however, because the Lurgan parish register began in 1755, Castletara in 1763 and Killinkere/Mullagh in 1766. The establishing of parish registers and the commissioning of silver chalices was confined to a small group of parishes situated to the east of Cavan town, the area of the diocese nearest to, though still a considerable distance away from, Bishop Campbell's residence on the County Louth coastline.

There seems little doubt but that the tradition that Andrew Campbell travelled around disguised as a highland piper is true. This tradition resulted in the commissioning of a posthumous portrait of him dressed in highland garb and holding a set of bagpipes, a portrait that was completed about one hundred years after his death.[31] (See Fig. 16.2).This disguise seems strangely anachronistic and unnecessary, since neither Andrew Campbell nor his predecessor, Laurence Richardson, suffered any persecution. It is true that Bishop Nicholas Sweetman of Ferns was arrested in 1751 and Archbishop Michael O'Reilly in 1756 but both were released without delay and without charge.[32] However, the bishops did fear the return of active persecution and were anxious to keep a low profile.

28.   Quoted in John Brady & Patrick Corish, 'The Church under the Penal Code' in Corish (ed.), *A history of Irish Catholicism*, 4, ii, p. 52.
29.   This chalice has survived and is held in the cathedral of Saints Patrick and Felim in Cavan.
30.   *Breiffne Antiquarian and historical society journal*, iii, 2 (1929–1930), p. 248.
31.   This portrait is in the Pastoral Centre in Cavan. It was painted by a 'Mr Harman'. See O'Connell, *The diocese of Kilmore*, p. 508.
32.   O'Brien (ed.), *Catholic Ireland in the eighteenth century, collected essays of Maureen Wall*, pp 37, 58; Corish, *The Catholic community*, p. 119.

Figure 16.2: Posthumous portrait of Andrew Campbell, bishop of Kilmore (1753-1769).

When Andrew Campbell met with the bishops of Armagh, Clogher, Meath, Derry, Raphoe and Kildare at the home of Lord Trimlestown in County Meath in 1757 it was said that they all arrived 'clad in frieze, like farmers' in order to conceal their real identity.[33] The main purpose of their meeting was to give assurances to the government that they saw no contradiction between being a good Catholic and a loyal subject of King George II. In Trimlestown they drew up a document directing all the clergy in Ireland to offer up prayers each Sunday and holy day asking

33.   O'Connell, *The diocese of Kilmore*, p. 509.

Figure 16.3: Title page of Bishop Andrew Campbell's Roman missal with, presumably, his own handwriting.

God to 'bless our good and gracious sovereign King George and his royal family'.[34] Charles O'Conor's *Dissertations on the antient history of Ireland*, which was first published in 1753, was designed to promote the civil rights of Catholics and, like the bishops, to give assurances that Catholics were loyal subjects of the king even though they did not recognise him as the head of their Church.

The Penal Laws were still on the statute books in the mid 1700s but those affecting the Catholic clergy were either being intermittently and half-heartedly imposed or, more likely, not being imposed at all. Neither the war which began between France and England in 1744 nor the rebellion in Scotland following the arrival there in 1745 of the young Pretender, Charles Edward, had sparked off any trouble in Ireland and the defeat of the Jacobites at Culloden in April 1746 eased the fears of Protestants living in Ireland. The sense of relief was obvious in the address which Joseph Story, the Church of Ireland bishop of Kilmore, gave to his clergy in Cavan just over two months after the battle at Culloden. He stated:

> We have had our Fears and Terrors in this Kingdom where the Papists are much more numerous, and we doubt not very great numbers would be ready to rise and join our enemies on very slight encouragement; tho' during this late Rebellion, they have behaved peaceably beyond our hopes and expectations.[35]

Four months later, John Madden, the dean of Kilmore and vicar of Kilmore and Ballintemple, preached a sermon in St Anne's church in Dublin, thanking God that 'for above fifty years past, we have enjoyed a most blessed calm, such as this island probably never enjoyed for so long a time together, since it was inhabited'.[36] From the mid-century onwards both the Protestant

---

34.   O'Brien (ed.), *Catholic Ireland in the eighteenth century, collected essays of Maureen Wall*, p. 59.

35.   Story, *The bishop of Kilmore's charge to the clergy of his diocese*, p. 9. Bishop Story died on 22 September 1757 and is buried at Kilmore. See Leslie, *Kilmore clergy*, p. 863.

36.   John Madden, *A sermon preached at St Anne's, Dublin on Thursday the 9th October, 1746 being the day appointed for a General Thanksgiving to Almighty God for the suppression of the late unnatural Rebellion* (Dublin, 1748), p. 8. John Madden died on 7 November 1751 and was buried in the church where he had preached this sermon. See Leslie, *Clergy of Kilmore*, p. 659. It is not clear what the connection between St Anne's church and County Cavan was. Theophilus Lord Newtown-Butler, who had extensive lands in Cavan and Fermanagh, left in his will dated 20 February 1721, '£13 per annum for ever to [the] minister and churchwardens of parish of St Ann's, Dublin in trust to buy five shillings worth of bread to be had in good loaves and distribute the same amongst the poor every Sabbath at the parish church of St Ann's aforesaid.' See P. Beryl Eustace (ed.), *Registry of deeds, Dublin, abstracts of wills*, i, 1708–1745, (Dublin, 1956), p. 125.

fears of a Jacobite inspired rebellion in Ireland and the Catholic fears of further persecution were on the wane. Andrew Campbell's travelling around disguised as a piper was a matter of choice rather than of necessity though it does suggest that after the persecution of Catholic clergy had ceased there was a period when bishops and other ecclesiastics dared not draw attention to themselves in case the Penal Laws, which were still on the statute books, were rigorously enforced once more. Bishop Campbell's missal, which carries the hand-written inscription *Ex libris Andrea Campbell, Episcopi Kilmors, An.D.1761* on the title page, has survived and is held in the Kilmore diocesan archive. See Figure 16.3.

Bishop Campbell inherited the family farm in Louth following the death of Richard, his father, in June 1762. His father had instructed him how he was to dispose of it and the bishop, in his own will, stated 'I confirm and ratifie, in as much as [in] me lieth, my father's last will and testament' and he directed that the 'lands, corn and chatles' be divided between his half brother Patrick Lawless and his nephew Andrew Magrane. Nicholas Magrane, another nephew, was to be excluded 'from this and every other legacy'. Unlike his two predecessor in Kilmore, Andrew Campbell makes no reference in his will to the diocese of Kilmore and the only clue the will gives of his clerical status was that he left five pounds to Philip Levins, the parish priest of Ardee, to be distributed 'amongst the poor and most indigent Roman Catholicks of the parish of Dunany and Port'.[37] Bishop Andrew Campbell died in 1769. He was buried in the family plot in Port cemetery. The grave slab carries the inscription:

> Here lies the Body of the Revd. Docto
> Andrew Campbell Bishop of Kilmore
> Who died decem. 1. 1769 aged 58 yrs.[38]

Non-Conformist Denominations

The religious landscape of the diocese of Kilmore continued to change throughout the eighteenth-century with the fragmentation of Presbyterianism - caused principally by the setting up of Seceder congregations - and the arrival of evangelical Moravian and Methodist preachers from *c.*1750 onwards. Presbyterians, unlike some members of the Church of Ireland, were not large landowners and consequently they, along with their Catholic neighbours, suffered during the harsh economic climate

---

37. Carrigan, 'Catholic episcopal wills', pp 185–6.
38. O'Connell, 'The tomb of Bishop Andrew Campbell' pp 284–6; Campbell, 'Andrew Campbell, bishop of Kilmore, 1753–1769', pp 296–7; Patrick Mallon and Noel Ross, 'Gravestone inscriptions in Port' in *JCLAS*, xxi, 2(1986), p. 208.

of the early eighteenth-century.[39] Some Presbyterians sought to escape from the economic and religious climate that prevailed in Ireland by deciding to cross the Atlantic to the New World. This emigration, which began to increase from 1718 onwards, peaked in the years 1725 to 1729. Poverty, mainly caused by poor harvests and rising rents, was the main cause of this emigration although the *Address of Protestant Dissenting Ministers to the King*, which was written in 1729, claimed that the sacramental test was also a major issue for Presbyterians. This test obliged any person holding public office to produce a certificate proving that they had received the sacrament of the Lord's Supper 'according to the usage of the Church of Ireland'. The obligation to pay tithes to ministers of the Established Church weighed heavily on Presbyterians as well as Catholics and convinced quite a few of them that they should emigrate to the Americas where they hoped they would enjoy greater prosperity and the religious freedom that was denied to them in Ireland.

Seceder Congregations

The Presbyterians also had to cope with a split within their own ranks. In 1733 four Scottish ministers separated from the main church body and formed the 'Associate Presbytery' and soon they became known as Seceders. As Eoin Magennis has pointed out 'south Ulster became a fertile ground' for the Seceders and by the mid-1740s Seceder preachers were being invited over from Scotland to provide supply preaching or else to replace ministers that the locals were unhappy with.[40] In March 1751 almost 200 people signed a petition for the Scottish Seceder minister, Thomas Clark, to come to Cahans/Ballybay to be their new minister.[41] His uncompromising approach, his criticism of other Presbyterian ministers who read their sermons and his refusal to take an oath or 'kiss the book [Bible] after the Popish style'[42] created enemies for himself, particularly within the Presbyterian community. Clark was harassed and arrested and eventually, on 10 May 1764, he and 300 of the Cahans/Ballybay congregation set sail from Warrenpoint hoping to find a better life in America.[43]

39. Jonathan Bardon, *A history of Ulster* (Belfast, 1992), pp 174–5.
40. Magennis, 'Belturbet, Cahans and two Presbyterian revolutions', pp 143–4.
41. David Stewart, *The Seceders in Ireland with annals of their congregations* (Belfast, 1950), pp 290–4.
42. Quoted in Lindsay T. Brown, 'The Presbyterian dilemma, a survey of the Presbyterians and politics in Counties Cavan and Monaghan over three hundred years' in *Clogher Record*, xv, 2 (1995), p. 35.
43. David Nesbitt, *Full Circle* (Ballybay, 1999); Magennis, 'Belturbet, Cahans and two Presbyterian revolutions', p. 146. A similar exodus had taken place in County Longford in 1729. See Thomas J. Barron, 'A Presbyterian exodus from County Longford in 1729' in *Bréifne*, v, 18 (1977–78), pp 253–8.

Corraneary congregation was the first Secession community to be set up in Kilmore diocese.[44] The Presbyterian congregation there had complained about the unorthodox ideas of their minister and John Craig replaced him in 1759. John Craig also took services for the Seceder congregation in Bailieborough every third Sabbath. He was replaced by Francis Carlisle in 1794. Carlisle lived in Bailieborough and ministered to both the Corraneary and Bailieborough congregations. After his death in 1811 Bailieborough became a separate congregation and his widow, Anne Jane Carlisle, became involved in the temperance movement, cooperating with Father Theobald Matthew and others in a temperance crusade.[45] The Seceder congregation in Cootehill had George Mairs as their first minister following his ordination at Cootehill on 14 April 1789. He married Sarah McFadden, a local woman, and ministered in Cootehill until 1793. Both he and John Craig, the Seceder minister for Corraneary and Bailieborough, emigrated to America in 1793, a move triggered by the ferocity of the Defender disturbances in east Cavan at this time. John Marshall, who was ordained on 25 September 1795, succeeded John Craig and ministered in Cootehill until his death in 1820.[46] The fourth and final Seceder congregation in Kilmore was established at Seafin in the parish of Killinkere in 1827 when William Bell, the Seceder minister in Bailieborough, opened a mission station there.[47] James Clarke, who was ordained on 29 November 1831, was appointed to Seafin and ministered there until 1869.[48] The four Seceder churches which were established within a fifteen mile radius of each other in east-Cavan divided the Presbyterian communities in this area and resulted in two parallel Presbyterian communities in the towns of Cootehill and Bailieborough.

Hearts of Oak

Presbyterians and Catholics resented having to pay, not only tithes to the Church of Ireland clergy, but also 'small dues' for baptisms, marriages, churchings and funerals, even though these services were carried out in their own churches and by their own clergy. They also objected to the local cess or taxes they had to pay for the building of roads and bridges, some of which seemed to be built more for the private benefit of landlords than for the public good. It was reported from Ulster in 1729 that:

44.   Armstrong, 'Cavan and the Presbyterian frontier', p. 234.
45.   Stewart, *The Seceders in Ireland*, p. 307; Leslie McKeague, *Anne Jane Carlile 1775–1864, temperance pioneer* (Belfast, 2015); idem, *Trinity Presbyterian Church Bailieborough* (Bailieborough, 2013), pp 25–6.
46.   Stewart, *The Seceders in Ireland*, p. 306.
47.   Ibid., p. 377.
48.   Ibid.

The Presbiteirin ministers have taken their shear of pains
to seduce their poor Ignorant heerers, by Bellowing from
their pulpits against the Landlords and the Clargey, calling
them Rackers of Rents and Scruers of Tythes.[49]

From the mid-1750s onwards many Presbyterian ministers and 'some
rambling ministers of several different denominations'[50] became more
vocal in their criticisms of the landed gentry and the clergy of the Established Church and by the end of June 1763 very large crowds of people,
who called themselves 'Hearts of Oak' or 'Oakboys', were gathering in
mid-Ulster to protest against the local cess and small dues they were expected to pay. The crowds, 'distinguished by oak boughs in their hats',[51]
visited the landlords and forced them to take an oath saying that they
would no longer demand any of the local taxes which had been agreed
at the assizes. However, their 'vengeance was chiefly against the clergy'
and many of the Church of Ireland clergy were badly treated, humili-
ated and forced to swear publicly that they would no longer collect the
small dues.[52] By 18 July 1763 James Hamilton reported from Monaghan
that huge numbers of Oakboys were 'driving throughout all parts of this
and the neighbouring county [Cavan], compelling all Magistrates, Clergy,
Tythe farmers and Constables to take the oath'.[53]

For the first few weeks of this popular rising the Hearts of Oak went
about their business unchallenged. However, before the middle of July
Charles Coote, the Cootehill-based magistrate, was ready to go on the
offensive. He and his party of Dragoons clashed with the Oabkboys
in Castleblayney. They killed McDonald, one of the Oakboy leaders, injured others and arrested several more.[54] For the next ten days,
following his success in Castleblayney, Coote pursued the Oakboys
in the Cootehill, Redhills and Belturbet areas of County Cavan. The
Oakboys had planned to raid the military barracks in Belturbet for
arms and, having failed in this, were driven from the town. Some
of their members were arrested in Redhills and a final showdown
between Coote and the Oakboys took place at Wattlebridge where seven
of the rebels were killed, many others wounded and eleven were taken

49. Quoted in Bardon, *A history of Ulster* (Belfast, 1992), p. 178.
50. *A second letter to the people of Ireland on the subject of tythes, with a particular address to the dissenters...* (Dublin, 1758), pp 5–6.
51. *A genuine account of the progress of Charles Coote, Esq, in pursuing and defeating the Oakboys in the Counties of Monaghan, Cavan and Fermanagh* (Dublin, 1763), p. 6.
52. Ibid., p. 4.
53. PRONI, T/3019/4645; *Faulkner's Dublin Journal*, 26–30 July 1763.
54. Eoin Magennis, 'A Presbyterian insurrection? Reconsidering the Hearts of Oak disturbances of 1763' in *IHS*, xxxi, 122 (Nov. 1998), p. 171; *A genuine account*, pp 6–9.

prisoner.[55] Four of these prisoners, all Presbyterians from Scotshouse, were indicted at the Cavan assizes.[56] There were probably some Catholic and Church of Ireland people involved in the Oakboy disturbances of 1763, however, Thomas Waite, writing on 23 July 1763, was of the opinion that the Oakboys 'consist of people of all religions but are mainly Presbyterians'.[57] The decisive actions of Charles Coote discouraged the Oakboys from any further action in the area and he was awarded a knighthood for his 'laudable services'.[58]

Moravians

The United Brethren or Moravian Church began in the central European province of Moravia in the fifteenth -century. A group of Moravians who had come to London in the 1730s made such and impression on John Cennick that he joined their church and later became their most effective missionary in Ireland.[59] Brother Brampton, a Moravian minister, preached in Cootehill on 13 January 1751, having been invited there by a group of people who had heard him preach in Dublin. Bishop Boehler, another Moravian minister, preached in Cootehill the following year to 'mostly Irish people or (Papists)'.[60] John Cennick first visited the town in 1752 preaching twice on 13 February and twice the following day to large crowds of 'Church people, Presbyterians and Quakers'.[61] His preaching made a deep impression and many of his hearers were moved to tears. A contemporary (hostile) account describes the manner in which the Moravian ministers preached, appealing to the heart rather than the head:

> They frequently strengthened their insinuations by familiar
> accounts they would give of themselves, which they would
> artfully usher in and mingle with their private discourses;

55. *A genuine account*, p. 15; James S. Donnelly, 'Hearts of Oak, Hearts of Steel' in *Studia Hibernica*, xxi (1981), p. 19.
56. Magennis, 'A Presbyterian insurrection?', p. 175.
57. PRONI, T/3019/4655.
58. *Calendar of Home Office Papers*, 1760–1765, p. 337. Coote was twenty-five years old in 1763. See John Coleman, 'Charles Coote MP [earl of Bellamont] (1738–1800) and the suppression of the Oak Boys in Counties Cavan, Fermanagh and Monaghan, July 1763' in *Bréifne*, xiv, 52 (2017), p. 148.
59. For the Moravian Church in Cavan see Patrick Cassidy, 'The Moravian Church in County Cavan 1751–1924' in *Bréifne*, x, 39 (2003), pp 21–44; idem, 'Non-conformist religious denominations in County Cavan in the seventeenth and eighteenth centuries' in Cherry & Scott (eds), *Cavan history and society*, pp 209–13.
60. J.H. Cooper (ed.), 'Extracts from the Journal of John Cennick: Moravian evangelist' in *The Moravian history magazine* (Belfast, 1996), p. 2.
61. Ibid., p. 52.

Figure 16.4: John Wesley (1703–1791).

telling that for many years they were in darkness themselves and inclined to all manner of evil; till they had heard such and such a holy Brother preach. Then they would recount all the temptations they underwent, their struggles between the Flesh and the Spirit, between Satan and the Word, till at length they found their hearts opening and hungering to receive it … To strengthen all this they frequently shewed them several parts of St Paul's writings … which they took care to interpret, after their own manner, to the ignorant wavering person.[62]

This new preaching style brought results. Following a meeting between Cennick and some Cootehill business people in 1752, plans were made to build a chapel on a site given by Matthew Read, a linen draper, in the townland of Corbeagh, and by 1755 a new chapel, capable of accommodating 400 people was built. John Wesley described the new

62.   John Roche, *Moravian heresy wherein the principal errors of the doctrine as taught … by Mr Cennick and other Moravian teachers, are fully set forth, proved and refuted …* (Dublin, 1741), p. 71.

establishment in 1758:

> I walked afterwards to the German house, about as large as the chapel at Snowfields. They have pitched upon a delightful situation, laid out a garden by it, planted trees around the ground and every way approved themselves wise in their generation.[63]

A small number of celibate Moravians lived in community beside the chapel, though the numbers in the congregation, which was formally established in 1765, remained small. They earned money by lace-making and in the linen industry by spinning and weaving. The Moravian community in Cootehill varied in size from time to time. George Smith, their Moravian minister from 1769–1773 wrote that 'The brethren here are loved and respected by their neighbours. There is a good harmony between Brother Smith and the single Brethren. There live few in the house and there are out of the house but very few who can be looked upon as Society members'.[64] It was reported that there were 109 members in 1773, though this had dwindled to twenty-one by 1792.

A Moravian society was established in Arvagh in 1755 and the Moravian chapel which was built there in the late 1750s was said to be the first stone building in the town.[65] Brother Archibald McKinstry and Sister McKinstry ministered to the small Moravian community there and they were assisted by Brother Lochman, the minister in Cootehill. The last known Moravian minister at Arvagh was Brother Waugh and the society was always a small one, having only four married couples and seven single members in 1778. When Brother and Sister Barnes travelled from Cootehill to Arvagh on 22 October 1792 they were disappointed to find 'so little spiritual life' in the community and it died out shortly afterwards. The Cootehill congregation fared better. It experienced a revival in 1826 and survived until the early 1900s.[66] Judging by the surnames of the families attending the Moravian church in Cootehill in the 1760s it appears that the majority, though not all, of its members were of English or Scottish descent.[67] The enthusiastic Moravian preachers caused a stir in the diocese when they first arrived in the early 1750s and a decade earlier the Church of Ireland bishop of Kilmore, Josiah Hort, was concerned enough to order

---

63.   Nehemiah Curnock, *The journal of John Wesley*, iv (London, 1938), p. 266.
64.   Quoted in Cassidy, 'Non-conformist religious denominations', p. 211.
65.   Ibid., p. 212.
66.   Cassidy, 'The Moravian church in County Cavan', pp 35–43.
67.   Ibid., Appendix I, p. 44.

six advance copies of John Roche's book on the Moravian 'heresy'.[68] In the end the Moravians had little overall impact on the diocese having established only two small communities in it, one lasting approximately fifty years and the other 150 years.

Methodism

John Wesley arrived in Ireland for the first time on 9 August 1747. A Methodist society had already been formed in Dublin earlier that year and his visit was intended to encourage the young society and to ensure that his Christian revivalist movement would get a foothold in Ireland as it had already done in England and Wales. Within a few years of Wesley's first visit to Ireland, Methodist preachers were zig-zagging their way across the diocese of Kilmore, creating a stir, gathering followers, setting up Methodist societies and generally posing a threat to the Christian churches already established there.[69] John Wesley had been ordained a priest of the Church of England in 1728. He and his brother Charles were members of the 'Holy Club' at Oxford which met regularly to study theology, read the Bible, pray, to visit the prisons and pray for the poor. They were noted for their strict discipline and their methodical approach and so were called 'Methodists' by those who were critical of their ways. John Wesley had a conversion experience at Aldersgate in May 1738 and the following year he left the security of pulpit and parish and set out as a travelling preacher ignoring the traditional boundaries and structures of the Anglican Church.

Thomas Kead was one of the first Methodist preachers in Ireland and by the beginning of the year 1758, several months before Wesley first visited the town, he was preaching in Cootehill with considerable success.[70] One of his first converts in Cootehill was John Smith, a native of County Armagh who was living in the town. When John Wesley first visited Cootehill on 22 May 1758 he appointed Smith as the leader of the Methodist class there. Some months later the fledgling Methodist class in Cootehill began to experience persecution:

> Members of the different churches in the town began to oppose the little band … Their malice was chiefly directed against John Smith … as the most zealous of the Methodists …

68.   Roche, *The Moravian heresy*, p. 3.
69.   For Methodism in the diocese of Kilmore at this time see Liam Kelly, 'The growth of Methodism in Leitrim and Cavan: 1750–1800' in *Bréifne*, x, 38 (2002), pp 455–93.
70.   Francis J. Cole, *Cootehill Methodism* (1946), p. 2; Robert H. Gallagher, *Pioneer preachers of Irish Methodism* (Belfast, 1965), pp 1–3; Dudley L. Cooney, The *Methodists in Ireland, a short history* (Dublin, 2001), p. 125.

> They collected mobs, surrounded the place of meeting, seized the worshippers, knocked them down, beat and even dragged them through cess-pools and sewers.[71]

Despite the opposition, John Smith converted several people to Methodism in Cootehill and remained there until 1766 when he went to work as an itinerant preacher in Tyrone, Armagh and Fermanagh. Many of the early Methodist preachers met violent opposition and John Smith was attacked and badly beaten near Clogher in County Tyrone in 1774, dying some weeks later from his injuries.[72] One of Smith's converts in Cootehill was John Bredin, a Tullyvin-based Catholic school-teacher who had become addicted to drink and had fallen on hard times. He gave up the drink and became a Methodist preacher and in 1769 was appointed to the Castlebar circuit. Despite being plagued by ill-health he worked as a Methodist missionary for more than fifty years in England, Scotland, Jersey and Ireland. He died on 2 November 1819.[73]

Methodism flourished in Cootehill. John Wesley visited there in 1758, 1760 and 1762 and then did not return to the town until 1778 – despite being in County Cavan several times in the intervening years. Perhaps he decided that Methodism had a firm foothold in Cootehill and other places needed him more. The 1778 trip was Wesley's seventeenth visit to Ireland. He was, by then, a venerable seventy-five year old and was generally received well wherever he went. Wesley was allowed to preach in the Presbyterian meeting-house in Cootehill on 23 May 1778 and was amazed at the diversity of religions present: 'I had a very extraordinary congregation. To many church people were added Seceders, Arians, Moravians and what not'.[74] After Wesley's time the Rev. Thomas Coke, a Welshman and ordained Anglican priest, visited Cootehill regularly as a Methodist preacher. He met the earl of Bellamont in 1795 and described him as 'a pattern of politeness'.[75] The earl showed him the site he had given for the erection of a Methodist 'preaching house' and later he donated twenty guineas towards the cost of building it. This preaching house was built in 1797 and the support given by the Coote family to the linen workers of the area, irrespective of their religion, helps to explain the great diversity of religions in Cootehill at this time.

71.   C.H. Crookshank, *History of Methodism in Ireland* (London, 1886), ii, pp 93–4.
72.   Gallagher, *Pioneer preachers*, pp 9–12.
73.   For Bredin see Robert H. Gallagher, *John Bredin, Roman Catholic school master and Methodist preacher* (Belfast, 1960).
74.   Curnock, *The Journal of John Wesley*, vi, p. 193.
75.   Crookshank, *History of Methodism in Ireland*, ii, pp 93–4.

Swanlinbar

John Wesley visited Swanlinbar, a town famed for its mineral waters, on eight occasions between 1760 and 1785. He liked the people he found there and said they were 'as simple and artless as if they had lived on the Welsh mountains'.[76] Each of Wesley's visits to the town took place in the early summer months when the population was swollen by the many visitors coming for the spa waters – so when he preached there he was guaranteed a good audience. Wesley preached in the open air at the town's end on 4 May 1769 but was frustrated by the hold the priests had over the Catholic population:

> The very Papists appearing as attentive as the Protestants; and I doubt not thousands of these would soon be zealous Christians were it not for their wretched priests, who will not enter the Kingdom of God themselves, and diligently hinder those that would.[77]

Wesley found the Methodists in Swanlinbar to have more vitality and enthusiasm than those in the surrounding towns of Manorhamilton, Enniskillen or Belturbet. When he visited the west Cavan town on 6 June 1771 he found that 'the people were all alive, full of faith and love … The congregation in the evening refreshed me much by their spirit as well as their number … I have heard no such [singing] voices since we left Cork, nor seen so earnest a people since we left Limerick'.[78]

James Creighton was the Church of Ireland curate in Swanlinbar and it appears that he met Wesley for the first time in May 1773. Creighton was at first opposed to Wesley and may have resented the fact that his brother Robert and his two sisters who lived at Kilmore had already become Methodists.[79] However, following an exchange of letters with Wesley and a conversion experience, Creighton became a Methodist preacher. Angel Anna Slacke, one of the leading female Methodists in Ireland at this time, knew James Creighton when he was curate in her parish of Kiltubrid in County Leitrim and, following his conversion to Methodism, went to hear him preach in Ballinamore.[80] She was amazed at how much both he and his preaching style had changed. She wrote in her diary: 'I had known him

76.   Curnock, *The Journal of John Wesley*, v, p. 205.
77.   Ibid., p. 315.
78.   Ibid., pp 415–6.
79.   Kelly, 'The growth of Methodism', pp 469–70.
80.   For Angel Anna Slacke see Liam Kelly, 'A leading woman of early Methodism – Angel Anna Slacke (1748–1796)' in *Bulletin of the Wesley Historical Society* (Irish branch), i, 4 (Winter, 1987), pp 23–8; idem, *The face of time* (Dublin, 1995), pp 12–19.

before he gave up all for Christ and was astonished to hear him preach extempore. His sermon was excellent and contained much information'.[81] In his 1778 address to 'the inhabitants of Kinawly' – the parish in which Swanlinbar is located – James Creighton warned them to be on the lookout for false prophets who may preach well 'with an audible, clear, articulate voice; and yet it may have no effect on the hearers, it may not be sent home to their Hearts by the Spirit of God'.[82]

The Methodist preachers used simple language and spoke with enthusiasm and conviction. Their meetings were dramatic and emotional and when John Wesley preached in Swanlinbar on 20 May 1773 he reported that 'the hearts of the people were as wax melting before the fire'.[83] James Creighton continued as curate in Swanlinbar for some months but, to the consternation of some of his clerical colleagues, he ignored parish boundaries and began visiting neighbouring parishes and counties to preach in the evangelical style of the Methodist preachers. This brought him into conflict with his rector and his bishop with the result that the curacy was taken from him and given to John Cooksey. In 1784, at the invitation of John Wesley, James Creighton went to work in England and remained there until his death in 1819.

The success of Methodism in Swanlinbar reduced the Church of Ireland community there. John Jebb, who was appointed the Church of Ireland curate in Swanlinbar in July 1799, stated that there were many Wesleyan Methodists among his parishioners and even though he never concealed his differences with them, they got on well together.[84] Despite the growth of Methodism in the town, there was still a sizeable Church of Ireland population there. Writing in May 1800, John Jebb stated that his congregation was:

> For the most part of the lower order; [they were] very decent, regular and attentive. I almost regret that the arrival of water-drinkers is so near. I think I could preach more usefully to

81. Angel Anna Slacke's unpublished diary, p. 4. A copy of this diary is held in Ballinamore library.
82. James Creighton, *A caution against false prophets addressed to the inhabitants of Kinawly in the diocese of Kilmore* (Dublin, 1791), p. 14. Creighton also wrote long rambling poems of rhyming couplets. One of his poems was a tribute to Elizabeth Percy of Garadice in County Leitrim who was an early Methodist. See *Poetic miscellanies, written occasionally and addressed to the author's relatives and particular friends, by Rev. J. C.* (London, 1791), pp 13–20 and 57–70.
83. Curnock, *The Journal of John Wesley*, v, p. 507.
84. John Jebb was ecumenical in his outlook and related well to Catholics while rector of Abington in County Limerick. He was appointed bishop of Limerick in 1822. For John Jebb, see Desmond McCabe, *DIB*, iv, pp 960–2.

my own poor but respectable audience; they are in general about 150 in number, sometimes, much more.[85]

The Established Church had survived in the parish despite the trauma of the previous decades when it lost a curate and a sizeable portion of its members to Methodism. However, Methodism continued to flourish in Swanlinbar during the period 1750 to 1800 – more so than in any other location in the diocese of Kilmore.

Other Methodist Centres

John Wesley was not impressed with Belturbet when he visited there on 14 June 1760. He said that this military base, was 'a town in which there is neither Papist nor Presbyterian; but to supply that defect there are Sabbath-breakers, drunkards and common swearers in abundance'.[86] He had a more positive experience when he preached in Belturbet town hall on 29 May 1775. His final visit to the town was on 22 May 1778 when he preached in the 'Armoury, a noble room, to a very large and serious congregation'. He described Belturbet on this visit as being 'once populous, now greatly decayed'.[87] Charles Graham and Gideon Ouseley, Methodist missionary preachers, visited Belturbet on 8 July 1800 and preached in the market house to a large crowd among whom was 'a considerable sprinkling of ladies and gentlemen'.[88] Eleven years later Graham reported that 'here [in Belturbet] we have a very respectable society'.[89] Charles Graham was born near Dromahair in 1750. He worked as a local preacher on the Sligo circuit before being accepted as a general missionary in 1789. He was a fluent Irish speaker and became known as 'the apostle of Kerry' because of his great success among the Irish-speaking people there.

Manorhamilton also became an important Methodist centre although a 'young gentlewoman' laughing incessantly during John Wesley's first sermon there on 5 May 1769 did not bode well for his chances there. Despite this, he felt that there was 'a general love of the gospel here'.[90] In all, Wesley visited Manorhamilton on seven different occasions and during his 1785 visit he stayed with a Mr Bradham who was described as 'one of the earliest and most influential Methodists of this neighbourhood' and

85.   Charles Forster (ed.), *Thirty years correspondence between John Jebb D.D. … and Alexander Knox* (Philadelphia, 1835), i, p. 4. My thanks to Desmond McCabe for this reference.
86.   Curnock, *The Journal of John Wesley*, iv, p. 389. This small town had both a brewery and a distillery. See Ordnance Survey map (1836).
87.   Ibid. vi, pp 192–3.
88.   Rev. W.G. Campbell, *The apostle of Kerry … being the Life and Labours of the Rev. Charles Graham* (Toronto, 1869), pp 104–5.
89.   Ibid., p. 177.
90.   Curnock, *The Journal of John Wesley*, v, pp 315–6.

while there Wesley preached in the courthouse.[91] Adam Averell, another Methodist preacher, visited the town on 29 June 1797 and stated that 'there is in this town a preaching house, neatly fitted up and about fifty in society amongst whom is much of the life and love of God'.[92] Averell returned to Manorhamilton in the spring of 1798 and the preaching house being too small, he spoke in the sessions house to about four hundred people who, he said, 'seemed to be the most solemnly affected hearers I had met on my tour'.[93] Manorhamilton became the head of a Methodist circuit and a Methodist chapel was built there in 1812.[94]

Unlike the Moravian church, which was confined to just two centres in County Cavan, the evangelical Methodists made inroads into many areas of the diocese. Apart from the centres mentioned above, John Wesley also preached in Ballyconnell, Florencecourt, Killeshandra, Kilmore, Ballyhaise and Cavan town. When Charles Graham and Gideon Ouseley went on their grand tour of the diocese in 1799 and 1800, they caused quite a stir. Their approach was so high-powered that when they preached in Bailieborough they alarmed even the Methodists there 'who had never seen mission work on this fashion'.[95] Charles Graham described their visit to Cavan town:

> It was a fair day. We were as wet as we could be, but neither of us dried or refreshed ourselves until we preached in the fair. A lady who saw us through her window wept all the time. The people remained uncovered all through the rain and were bathed in tears. They entreated us to preach that night in the court-house and they would come to hear, which we did. We also visited the prisoners in jail.[96]

There were quite a few converts to Methodism in Killeshandra parish, both in the town and later in the rural townland of Corlisbrattan. Trinity College had purchased the advowson or right to appoint the rectors to Killeshandra parish in 1763 and, in 1787, William Hales, the professor of Hebrew and oriental languages in the college, was appointed rector of Killeshandra. The success of Methodism in his parish spurred him to

91.   Ibid., vii, p. 83.
92.   Alexander Stewart & George Revington (eds), *Memoir of the life and labours of the Rev. Adam Averell* (Dublin, 1848), p. 119.
93.   Ibid., p. 191.
94.   Kelly, 'The growth of Methodism', pp 483–4.
95.   Charles Graham to Thomas Coke, November 1799.
96.   Campbell, *The apostle of Kerry*, p. 91.

write *Methodism Inspected* in 1802 and another critical pamphlet of the same name in 1805.

It is difficult to estimate how many people from the diocese became Methodists between 1750 and 1800. A report which states that there were 875 Methodists in Ballyconnell and 580 in Cavan town in 1790 seems wide off the mark.[97] It would appear that the numbers in the Methodist societies throughout the diocese were considerably smaller and these figures may represent the total number in particular circuits rather than in individual towns. The Manorhamilton society had fifty members in 1797 and chances are that Swanlinbar Methodist community was larger than that. However, it seems certain that the number of Methodists in the diocese at the end of the 1700s can be counted in hundreds and not thousands. In 1750 there were virtually no Methodists in the diocese and the fact that there were several hundreds of them fifty years later is a result of, not just the energy and skill of John Wesley, but of all the other local, circuit and general preachers who endured bad roads, inclement weather and much opposition as they went about their work. By 1800 Methodism was the fourth largest religious denomination in Kilmore. The religious landscape had changed considerably between 1750 and 1800. The Methodist and, to a lesser extent, the Moravian preachers had made their mark.

97.   *Minutes of some late conversations between Rev. Thomas Coke and others* (Dublin, 1790), p. 8.

Chapter 17

Decades of Revolution: 1770–1800

On 9 December 1769, just eight days after the death of Bishop Andrew Campbell, the Kilmore cathedral chapter met and elected Patrick Masterson vicar capitular of the diocese. This decision, it was claimed, had the approval of the clergy of the diocese and was confirmed by the archbishop of Armagh, Anthony Blake, on 30 December 1769. The letter informing Rome of this development was signed by the archbishop of Armagh and thirty-two priests representing every area of Kilmore diocese.[1] John Ward, the parish priest of Templeport, who had been rector of the Irish College in Alcalá de Henares and returned to Ireland in 1767, acted as notary.[2]

This letter gives a false impression of unity among the clergy of the diocese, however. Less than two weeks after it was sent to Rome the nuncio in Brussels wrote to Cardinal Castellini stating that Patrick Masterson had convened only four members of the cathedral chapter and that their decision to elect him vicar capitular 'was not generally pleasing to the clergy of that diocese'.[3] He mentioned the blood brothers, Thomas and Francis Nettervill, both Dominicans, as suitable candidates for the vacant See of Kilmore. He also suggested that Patrick Brady, the Franciscan guardian in Prague[4] and 'a member of an ancient family in Ireland … who founded the episcopal See of Kilmore' as another possible candidate for Kilmore. He proposed that Philip O'Reilly, the bishop of Raphoe, since 'the diocese of Raphoe is one of the poorest in the country and hardly sufficient to give a decent living', be translated to Kilmore. Significantly, he also felt it his duty to recall the merits of the Kilmore-born Franciscan Bishop of Dromore (Denis Maguire) stating that the Sacred Congregation 'considers him worthy of the kindest comments'.[5]

1. APF, *CP* 137, f. 283rv; *Bréifne*, iv, 14(1971), pp 221–4.
2. For John Ward see O'Connell, *The Irish College at Alcalá de Henares*, p. 44; MacKiernan, *Diocese of Kilmore*, p. 169. John Ward was a native of Killeshandra. Another Killeshandra priest, Charles MacKiernan, was rector of the Irish College in Alcalá de Henares from 1768–70.
3. APF, *CP* 137, ff. 253v-255r.
4. Parez & Kucharová, *The Irish Franciscans in Prague*, p. 179.
5. Ibid.

The priests of the diocese recommended a number of people for the vacant See, including Patrick Masterson, Thomas Sheridan, the parish priest of Annagh and former rector of Alcalá de Henares, Anthony Smith parish priest of Laragh and Charles Magauran, the parish priest of Drung. Patrick Masterson's chances of being appointed to Kilmore were scuppered by a letter from the vicar forane[6] and 'parish priests of the lower deanery', stating that Masterson had secretly travelled the diocese canvassing 'the people of voice' to vote in his favour. This critical letter claimed that Masterson was a man of low birth and little education. It claimed that if he was appointed bishop there would be trouble among the clergy and that he would be despised by the gentry and would not be able to carry out the duties of a bishop since 'he was so weak from paralysis that he could barely write his own name'.[7] The letter added that 'neither the deceased bishop [Andrew Campbell] nor his vicar-general [Patrick Masterson] had ever visited the largest part of his diocese, as a result of which were born many abuses and the non-observance of discipline'.[8]

There were deep divisions within the clergy of the diocese, perhaps an inevitable result of three successive bishops choosing to reside on the east coast of the country. Despite their best intentions the parishes to the north and west of the diocese felt isolated and neglected by these bishops and by Patrick Masterson, the vicar-general to all three who resided in Cavan town.[9] Because of the disunity within the diocese Propaganda Fide decided that it could not make a case for Patrick Masterson or any of the other candidates proposed by the chapter but would instead 'defer the election until such time as there are presented more suitable candidates, of which there is no shortage either in the diocese or in foreign lands'.[10] Their decision was not deferred for long. On 20 March 1770, it was decided that Denis Maguire, the bishop of Dromore, would be translated to Kilmore and that Patrick Brady, another Franciscan native of Kilmore, would replace him in Dromore.[11]

Denis Maguire

Denis Maguire was born in 1721 in the parish of Killesher – a Kilmore parish in County Fermanagh. He belonged to the aristocratic Maguire

6.   The vicar forane, sometimes known as the dean or archpriest of a deanery, is appointed by the bishop.
7.   Ibid., ff. 213r-216r.
8.   Ibid.
9.   Writing from Antwerp on 3 February 1747, Fr Dan O'Reilly stated that Patrick Masterson was from 'a low and ignoble family … who advanced himself by his suppleness to comply with his late Lordships's [Michael MacDonogh's] measures to the dignity of Dean and Vicar General of the said diocese.' See Fagan, *Ireland in the Stuart papers*, 1743–65, p. 56.
10.   Ibid.
11.   APF, *CP*, 137, f. 216.

family of that county, a family that had provided patrons and priests for the church from medieval times.[12] The family had strong links with the Franciscan friary at Lisgoole and several members of the family, including Denis Maguire, became Franciscans. Denis Maguire studied in Louvain where he presented a thesis in 1746 on the 'Chronology and geography of the early books of the bible' and two years later he was awarded an S.T.L. for his thesis on the 'Theology of God and the Most Holy Trinity'.[13] He taught Philosophy in Louvain before moving to Prague where he taught both philosophy and theology. He was then appointed guardian, firstly of St Isidore's College in Rome and then of St Anthony's in Louvain.[14] He was already back working in Ireland when he was appointed bishop of Dromore on 10 February 1767, a position he held for just over three years before being appointed to Kilmore. Denis Maguire, just like his three predecessors, opted to live outside the diocese, staying with his brother in Enniskillen.[15] However, he was living only ten miles away from the nearest parish in Kilmore and the parishes in the north and west of the diocese, which had previously felt neglected, could be easily reached from his base in Enniskillen. Unlike his predecessors, he was a native of the diocese and a member of a re-spected aristocratic family, and yet, despite these advantages, he was to experience considerable opposition in Kilmore especially during the first half of his episcopacy.

If he had not known it before he was appointed to Kilmore, Denis Maguire soon learned that there were factions and serious divisions among the clergy of the diocese.[16] Some of these factions consisted of family or kinship groups among the clergy and others were the inevitable result of a succession of absentee bishops and the difficulties of travel and communication in an elongated diocese. The newly-appointed bishop adopted a more 'hands on' approach than his predecessors and was determined to establish his authority and to improve both clerical discipline and the standard of preaching. The election of Patrick Masterson as vicar capitular by a diocesan chapter of just four people,

12.   For Denis Maguire see Francis G. Duffy, 'Denis Maguire O.F.M Bishop of Kilmore 1770–98' (unpublished MA thesis NUIM, 1996); idem, 'Denis Maguire OFM, Bishop of Kilmore 1770–98' in *Bréifne*, viii, 33 (1997), pp 739–81. Any subsequent references to Francis Duffy's research will be to his thesis and not to the article in *Bréifne*. See also Parez & Kucharová, *The Irish Franciscans in Prague*, p. 188.
13.   Ignatius Fennessy (ed.), 'Canon E. Reusen's list of Irish Franciscan theses in Louvain', 1620–1738' in *Coll. Hib.*, 48 (2006), pp 45–6.
14.   Peter Kelly to Sir James Caldwell, 21 September 1765, in CDA, 3/17/40.
15.   Duffy, 'Denis Maguire', p. 17.
16.   The diocese of Dromore was also riven by divisions at this time. See Patrick Kearns, 'James Pulleine, an 18th century Dean of Dromore' in *Seanchas Ard Mhacha*, xi, 1 (1983–4), p. 77.

Figure 17.1: Portrait of Denis Maguire, Franciscan bishop of Kilmore (1770–1798).

in December 1769, suggests that the chapter was dysfunctional. Early in his episcopacy Denis Maguire discovered that two of his parish priests, John MacKiernan, the parish priest of Carrigallen, and John Ward, the parish priest of Templeport, had assumed the title of chancellor and treasurer of the chapter, without his knowledge or consent. Some of the priests had written to Rome complaining that Denis Maguire had not filled vacancies which had arisen in the chapter and in his reply to Propaganda Fide on 20 July 1773 the bishop suggested that in order to put the matter beyond controversy 'let the chapter be canonically erected, or let it be authoritatively stated that no chapter exists' because 'if chapters are invented it is the end of proper jurisdiction and rule'.[17] Bishop Maguire was anxious to avoid a repeat of the irregular behaviour of the chapter in 1769 and his preference was to establish a properly constituted cathedral chapter, even if there was no Catholic cathedral in the diocese. He wrote:

> A few of those who boast they are canons would not agree to anything that could take away from their dignity whether real or imaginary. I said many times that it would be more honourable for the diocese and more in accordance with the established procedures when the see happens to be vacant to have a chapter that could not be questioned and [which would have] a sufficient number of canons .[18]

The dispute rumbled on for a time and in the end no chapter was established.[19] Maguire had learned from the divisions that had preceded his own appointment to Kilmore and in order to avoid similar problems in the diocese after his own death, he requested, and was granted in 1793, a coadjutor bishop who would automatically take over from him.[20]

An Impoverished Diocese

The absence of both a residence and a sufficient income for the Catholic bishop of Kilmore are among the reasons put forward by four successive bishops choosing to live outside the diocese – residing instead with either their families or religious communities. From medieval times bishops of the diocese had tried in a variety of ways and with limited success to supplement their small income. The effects of both the Reformation, which resulted in the parish churches and tithes going to the state church, and the Penal Laws which resulted in Catholics losing their lands, further impoverished an already poor diocese. Bishop Maguire reported that:

---

17.   APF, *Acta*, xii, ff. 58–9.
18.   Ibid.
19.   Duffy, 'Denis Maguire', p. 39.
20.   APF, *Fondo di Vienna*, xxviii, f. 133r.

> Parents are often lax in sending their children to the
> churches where they can be taught the catechism; they
> blame poverty and lack of clothes for this failure. I am
> bound to say parents are not telling lies when they make
> this excuse. It is poverty too which deprives the young
> people of schooling. In this matter these parish priests do
> what they can, as their position or duty allow, but they can-
> not do all they wish.[21]

During the episcopacy of Michael MacDonogh the income of the bishop
of Kilmore was paltry and things had improved only slightly by the
time Denis Maguire became bishop in 1770.[22] He wrote to Propaganda
Fide on 20 July 1773 stating that his income was inadequate to fund the
cost of his many journeys around the diocese and requesting permission
to ask the priests of the diocese to give him one and a half sovereigns
per annum rather than the one sovereign which was the current practice.
He admitted that he got a 'middling income' from his mensal parish but
went on to say 'I have to keep a servant and two horses. I have neither
sheep nor money in places where I could get interest. That is my state'.[23]
He was, he argued, doing much more work in the diocese than his
predecessors and the priests could afford the extra half sovereign:

> The parish priests can do this much more easily now than
> a generation ago, when praise the Lord, the number of the
> faithful in these times is greater than it was then. In addition,
> it is well known (and my opponents are forced to admit) that
> I do twice as much work in frequent journeys throughout
> the diocese to be present at practically all the conferences
> … (although the venues are very far apart) from the month
> of March to October inclusively. My predecessors visited
> the diocese perhaps once a year for an annual conference.
> Everyone can see that I have daily expenses, for example on
> animals for travel.[24]

Bishop Maguire had opponents both within the diocese and outside
it and his most formidable opponent outside the diocese was James
Matthew Brady, a native of Kilmore, who had been appointed bishop

21.   *Relatio status* of Denis Maguire, *Acta*, xvii, ff. 188–9 (18 November 1794).
22.   Thomas Brennan to Michael Fitzgerald (10 Jan. 1747); *AICR*, Liber xxvi, ff. 149–50.
23.   APF, *Acta*, xii, ff. 58–9.
24.   Ibid; Duffy, 'Denis Maguire', p. 41.

of Ardagh in 1758. Denis Maguire suspected that Brady was trying to prevent him getting an increased income and he concluded his letter by saying 'I suspect that a certain confrere involves himself too much in my affairs. I do not cast my sickle into another man's harvest'.[25]

It seems likely that Denis Maguire was not granted the extra half sovereign from his parish priests in order to increase his *cathedraticum* because seven years later, on 28 July 1780, he again wrote to Propaganda Fide, this time asking that he be granted the parish of Annagh as a second mensal parish. He explained that in his diocese:

> There are few or no Catholics from whom he could hope for support and that what he gets is from one very poor [mensal] parish to which he had always hoped to add another but he got no suitable opportunity these ten years. But labouring with apostolic patience he bore up without an adequate salary. Since now the parish of Annagh is vacant and which can conveniently and without damage be joined to his parish, he begs your eminence to confer on him the said parish.[26]

Annagh had been a mensal parish while the Dominicans, Michael MacDonogh and Laurence Richardson, were bishops of the diocese, but this ceased following the death of Richardson in 1753. Denis Maguire wrote to Rome once more, asking that in view of his 'extraordinary labours and frequent journeys' which he undertook at great expense that he be granted the second mensal parish.[27] He discovered to his consternation that Rome had appointed James Matthew Brady, 'a bishop who is so hostile to me' to head up a commission of inquiry into the affair.[28] He seemed paranoid about the bishop of Ardagh, though not without reason. Bishop James M. Brady continued to meddle in the affairs of his native diocese and may have managed to prevent Denis Maguire getting the increased incomes he had sought. Denis Maguire continued to struggle financially and in 1793, following a bout of scruples, he wrote to Propaganda Fide asking forgiveness for having accepted money when issuing marriage dispensations.[29] Bishop Maguire made several complaints to Rome about James M. Brady interfering in the affairs of Kilmore and yet Maguire himself was guilty of meddling

25.   Ibid.
26.   APF, *Acta*, xiv, f. 361; Duffy, 'Denis Maguire', p. 42.
27.   Ibid., f. 362.
28.   Ibid., f. 326.
29.   Hugh Fenning, 'The Udienze series in the Roman archives of Propaganda Fide, 1750–1820' in *Arch. Hib.*, xxxxviii (1994), pp 101–2.

in the affairs of the neighbouring diocese of Clogher when, in 1793, he supported his kinsman, Hugh Maguire of Tempo, in a patronage dispute with Bishop Hugh O'Reilly over the right to appoint priests to the parish of Enniskillen.[30]

Troublesome Priests

Denis Maguire also had opponents within the diocese, most notably Eugene Brady, a diocesan priest and a relation of James M. Brady, the bishop of Ardagh. Eugene Brady had studied in Louvain and after his ordination *c*.1756 remained on the continent until *c*.1767 when he returned to Ireland and was appointed to the parish of Crosserlough.[31] From 1773 onwards Eugene Brady was on a collision course with his bishop who suspected that the bishop of Ardagh, the 'companion and associate'[32] of Eugene Brady was 'from the outset, to a large extent, if not the author at least the promoter of this rebellion'.[33] Denis Maguire, in a letter to Rome dated 28 October 1780, accused Eugene Brady of 'a great number of scandals and … intolerable abuses … committed in my diocese over a period of time, resulting in the destruction of very many from the faith'.[34] He first suspended Brady, but all to no avail. Eugene Brady, armed with letters of recommendation from the bishop of Ardagh, was given a curacy in Dublin diocese. However, when John Carpenter, the archbishop of Dublin, learned about Brady's record he banished him from Dublin diocese.

Three years later, on 20 March 1783, Denis Maguire wrote to Rome once more outlining the misdeeds of Eugene Brady, his rebellious priest. This time the charges he made were more specific and related to Brady's activities in Cavan parish:

> Eugene Brady was in open rebellion in speaking against and hindering by every unlawful means the building of a new church for the convenience of the people of Cavan parish … He administers the sacrament of penance sacrilegiously, assists at clandestine marriages that are invalid … he usurps the rights of the local parish priest Hugh O'Reilly whom we had canonically appointed to run the parish of Cavan with proper legal title.[35]

30.   See Anselm Faulkner, 'The right of patronage of the Maguire's of Tempo' in *Clogher Record*, ix, 2 (1977), pp 167–86; W.A. Maguire, 'The Maguires of Tempo: vicissitudes of a County Fermanagh family' in Murphy & Roulston (eds), *Fermanagh, history and society*, pp 159–61.
31.   Nilis, 'Irish students at Leuven University', p. 216; MacKiernan, *Diocese of Kilmore*, p. 169.
32.   APF, *Acta*, xiv, f. 326.
33.   Ibid., xv, f. 443.
34.   Ibid.
35.   Ibid., xiv, f. 329.

It appears that the new church referred to here was the one which was built in 1774 at Skelton's ford in Cavan town and which later became the site of the old cathedral.[36] Eugene Brady failed to prevent the construction of this church and so he set up his own unofficial chapel, possibly at Drumcrave or more likely in Annagelliff, where he gathered a considerable number of followers. Denis Maguire claimed that if people refused to attend Eugene Brady's chapel he 'threatened them with death and burning them out of their homes'. Brady's activities brought him into direct confrontation with Hugh O'Reilly the parish priest of Cavan. Bishop Maguire reported that:

> On Christmas day last [1782], Eugene Brady, persuaded by the devil, no doubt and in the presence of a big number of people spat in the face of the parish priest, Hugh O'Reilly, at the spot where the latter had arrived to say Mass. John Brady, a brother of Eugene committed the same crime at the same time. A noble pair of brothers.[37]

Denis Maguire asked Propaganda Fide to remove Eugene Brady from the diocese if for no other reason than Brady had threatened to kill him. The danger was very real. Two years later Maguire wrote to Rome about Brady:

> To crown all his evil deeds, this priest either personally or through some followers that he has seduced, on 14 July past [1784], at dead of night, slaughtered in a most cruel manner my two horses (all my worldly possessions), near the spot where I had confirmed some of the faithful the day before. Three days before the house of the parish priest where I was staying after giving confirmation the day before, was set on fire around midnight. And if the house-keeper by some good fortune had not wakened, everyone in bed in the house would have perished.[38]

These attacks increased the stakes dramatically and Denis Maguire did not feel safe in the areas of his diocese where Brady had most support.

36.   Liam Kelly, *Churches of the diocese of Kilmore* (Belfast, 2005), p. 19.
37.   Ibid.
38.   APF, *Acta*, xv, ff. 564–5. Laurence Taaffe, a priest of Armagh diocese, wrote to Cardinal Antonelli in Propaganda Fide and stated, incorrectly, that these attacks in Kilmore occurred as a result of tensions between the Franciscan and secular priests of the diocese. See APF, SC *Irlanda*, xv, f. 543; Fenning, *The undoing of the friars*, pp 52–3.

He informed Rome that 'it should be clear the dangers that await me if I visit a neighbourhood where such scoundrels are waiting to take my life and my goods. The unfortunate priest has threatened to kill me, but I trust in God'.[39] Denis Maguire had excommunicated Brady, but to no effect. Rome appointed Hugh O'Reilly, the bishop of Clogher, to investigate the matter and make a decision on it. He did so and reported to Propaganda Fide on 13 February 1786 that Eugene Brady was incorrigible and that he had made the decision to excommunicate him. Bravely or foolishly the bishop of Clogher decided to go to Brady's church 'so that no one could think … that I was afraid of him'. He wrote to Rome: 'I went with the hope that I might bring back to the fold of their own shepherd those who through fear or false zeal or unfortunate error were supporting the priest. But sad to say, I escaped with difficulty from the hands of him and a few of his followers'.[40] Eugene Brady died in 1792 and, even though the dispute with his bishop appears to have abated somewhat after 1786, nevertheless, it was a dispute that had dragged on for approximately fifteen years and had cast a dark shadow on more than half of Denis Maguire's episcopacy.

John McKiernan, the parish priest of Carrigallen, was also in dispute with his bishop, though the scale of this dispute was significantly less than the one between Eugene Brady and Denis Maguire. McKiernan had claimed to be either chancellor or treasurer (it is not clear which) of the dysfunctional cathedral chapter which was in place when Denis Maguire was appointed to the diocese. By questioning the validity of the old chapter and then ignoring it Maguire had alienated McKiernan and the others who claimed that they were canons. In 1782 the bishop intervened in a dispute between John McKiernan and his curate, John Reilly, which resulted in a written agreement being signed stating that the parish priest would pay his curate an annual salary of twenty guineas. The salary was paid for one year only, the parish priest reneging on the payment because, McKiernan claimed, his curate was spreading rumours about him, stating that he had an inappropriate relationship with his housekeeper.[41] The bishop and the curate had the backing of other priests in the area but John McKiernan 'continued to put his own opinion before that of wiser men'.[42] Denis Maguire wrote to Propaganda Fide on 22 December 1784 outlining the details of this dispute. He was in a dilemma about what action to take, knowing that he should suspend

---

39.   Ibid.
40.   APF, *CP* xvi, f. 8.
41.   Duffy, 'Denis Maguire', p. 35.
42.   Ibid.

him and yet aware that the suspension would achieve nothing because the priest 'is stubborn and ... ignorant rather than learned' and will not abide by the suspension. John McKiernan outlived his bishop by three years, dying in 1801.[43]

Education of Priests

It is difficult to be precise about what percentage of the priests ministering in Kilmore during the episcopacy of Denis Maguire had the benefit of a continental education, though it seems possible that as many as half of them had studied abroad. Salamanca was the most popular destination for Kilmore students and at least eleven of the priests who ministered during Maguire's episcopacy had studied there. A further six studied in Alcalá de Henares, three in Paris and three in Louvain with one each in Nantes, Douai and Rome.[44] Francis Duffy, in his study of Denis Maguire, has estimated that about fourteen Franciscans ministered in the diocese at this time and chances are that most or all of them, like Denis Maguire himself, had studied in Louvain.[45] A continental education did not guarantee competence and it was said (by a hostile witness) that Patrick Masterson, who had studied in Salamanca, had never graduated 'in any science or juridical discipline or theology'.[46] John O'Reilly was a student in Antwerp and was ordained a priest sometime before he was sent to Maynooth when the seminary opened there in 1795. However he was 'called to mission' early because 'of his inability to follow the college lectures'.[47] Denis Maguire, who had described John McKiernan as 'ignorant rather than learned', seemed to think that there were others like him in the diocese. In his *Relatio Status* report of 1794 Maguire stated:

> The parish priests cannot be found fault with for any great neglect. But there are some (as happens in all walks of life) who are more diligent than others. The parish priests do not entirely neglect the preaching to the people as the opportunity arises and taking the distance between places into account.[48]

43.   MacKiernan, *Diocese of Kilmore*, p. 174.
44.   Luke Moynagh, the parish priest of Kilmore, was one of the priests educated in Alcalá de Henares. He died on 23 October 1781 when he was thrown from his horse near Ballinagh and drowned in a roadside drain. See *Hibernian Journal*, 31 October 1781; MacKiernan, *Diocese of Kilmore*, p. 167; O'Connell, *The Irish College at Alcalá de Henares*, p. 70.
45.   Duffy, 'Denis Maguire', Appendix I, p.64.
46.   APF, *CP*, 137, ff. 213–6.
47.   MCA, 84/10/1.
48.   APF, *Fondo di Vienna*, xxviii, ff. 188–9.

This underwhelming endorsement of the priests of the diocese points to deficiencies in preaching and the bishop used the monthly conferences of priests, which were held between March and October each year, to further 'the instruction and discipline of my parish priests'[49] and to advise them on 'cases of conscience'.[50] After a shaky start, Bishop Maguire appears to have got on well with his priests and halfway through his time in Kilmore he wrote 'thank God, apart from that notorious rebel Eugene Brady and the unpredictable parish priest, John McKiernan, the rest of the priests, parish priests and curates, show due reverence and do not reject discipline'.[51]

Converts to the Church of Ireland

In the forty year period from 1760 to 1800 a total of sixty-six Catholic priests throughout the country became members of the Church of Ireland. The Amending act of 1709 (8 Anne, c. 3), which strengthened the provisions of the Registration act of 1704 (2 Anne, c.7), stated that 'every Popish priest being approved of as a convert ... and conforming himself to the Church of Ireland as by law established and having taken the oaths ... such converted priests shall receive twenty pound yearly'. The act required that the priests recant their 'Romish faith' and 'publickly read the liturgy of the Church of Ireland' in a church nominated by the bishop of the diocese. It appears that no priest from the diocese of Kilmore joined the Church of Ireland at this time.[52] However, Denn parish church, which was situated in the townland of Carrickaboy, made the national news when, on 26 March 1770, Patrick Sweeney, a priest of the diocese of Ardagh and parish priest of Bornacoola in County Leitrim, read his recantation and publicly embraced the Protestant religion in it.[53] Why the parish church of Denn was chosen can only be guessed at. Perhaps it was hoped that by doing so in a quiet country church both publicity and trouble could be avoided. Six weeks later John Gallagher, a schoolmaster from Virginia read his recantation and embraced the Protestant religion in the parish church of Lurgan.[54] In early July 1771 Patt M'Kearnan, an apothecary from Belturbet, embraced the Protestant religion in the parish church of Belturbet.[55] However, the number of Catholics converting to the Church

---

49.   APF, *Acta*, xiv, f.362.
50.   APF, *Acta*, xii, ff. 58–9.
51.   APF, *Acta*, xv, ff. 564–5.
52.   See 'List of convert priests 1703–1838 with dates of enrolment' in Eileen O'Byrne (ed.), *The Convert Rolls* (Dublin, 1981), pp 299–31.
53.   *Dublin Chronicle*, 31 March 1770; *Sleator's Public Gazetteer*, 31 March 1770.
54.   Ibid., 5 May 1770.
55.   *Hibernian Journal*, 8 July 1771; Brady, *Catholics and Catholicism*, p. 144.

of Ireland at this time was relatively small in the diocese and from 1789 the numbers dropped sharply throughout the country.[56]

Franciscan Parish Priests

The Franciscans remained longer than any of the other religious orders in the diocese of Kilmore. The Augustinians and the Premonstratensians who had a presence in the diocese throughout the late medieval period had left by 1600 and the Dominicans were only in the diocese for a period of about sixty years following the appointment of the Dominican bishop, Michael MacDonogh, in 1728. During medieval times the Franciscan friary in Cavan was the only one situated in the diocese although Creevelea friary, located in Ardagh and on the border with Kilmore, had a big impact on Kilmore. The friaries of Lisgoole and Jamestown were also influential, though to a lesser extent, in the Kilmore parishes of Fermanagh and south-Leitrim. These friaries continued to have guardians long after the friars had ceased to live conventually and the 1766 religious census, which lists nine friars in Kilmore, shows them to be well scattered in parishes throughout the diocese.[57]

Between the years 1728 and 1753 the Franciscan and Dominican clergy in Kilmore received good support from the two Dominican bishops of the diocese. However, from 1751 onwards the tide was turning against the regular clergy, not just in Kilmore but throughout the country and when Andrew Campbell became bishop in 1753 he proved to be less sympathetic to the friars than his two predecessors had been. The Roman decrees of 1751, which forbade the friaries to receive or profess new members, had a devastating effect on the friars in Ireland. In the seventeen years between 1750 and 1767 the number of Franciscan friars in the country dropped by 44 % and the number of Dominicans by 16%. Besides, the age-profile of those who remained had increased considerably.[58] The situation was so grave that in 1768 most of the bishops of the country petitioned Rome to revoke or moderate the 1751 decrees and allow the regulars to receive novices once more. Andrew Campbell, unlike virtually all of the other bishops in Connacht and Ulster and perhaps in loyalty to his deceased friend and neighbour, Archbishop Michael O'Reilly,[59] continued to oppose any easing of the 1751 decree.[60] With the appointment of

56.   O'Byrne, *The convert rolls*, p. xiv.
57.   NAI, MS 2476; Cunningham, 'The 1766 religious census', pp 358–9. At least one of the friars listed in the survey, Patrick Backahan, the curate in Kinawley, was a Dominican.
58.   Fenning, *The undoing of the Friars*, p. 278.
59.   Archbishop O'Reilly, who died in 1758, had lived in Dromiskin, not far from where Andrew Campbell was based in County Louth.
60.   APF, *SOCG* 825, f. 343.

Denis Maguire to Kilmore in 1770, the regular clergy in the diocese had a sympathetic ear once more. However, he was careful not to be partial to the Franciscans. Michael O'Reilly, the parish priest of Kilmore, stated in 1817 that the 'venerated and venerable Doctor Maguire … tolerated no divisions, no parties'[61] and in 1796 Maguire demonstrated his impartiality when he did not hesitate to discipline James MacGowan, a Franciscan priest, who was ministering in the diocese of Kilmore.[62]

The decision by Propaganda Fide in 1751 to prohibit the friaries in Ireland from receiving novices marked the beginning of the end for the Franciscans in Kilmore. By a strange contradiction, the Franciscans had survived all of the post-Reformation persecutions and their terminal decline in the diocese began just as the penal law restrictions were being eased. The Franciscans continued to minister in parishes in Kilmore both as curates and parish priests and during the episcopacy of Denis Maguire the concentration of friars was greatest in the parishes towards the centre of the diocese with Franciscans ministering in Innismagrath, Oughteragh and Drumreilly in Leitrim, Killesher, Kinawley and Knockninny in Fermanagh and Templeport and Kildallan in west Cavan. There were no Franciscans in the seven most northerly parishes in Leitrim and there were Franciscans in only five of the seventeen most easterly parishes in Cavan.[63]

The appointment of Franciscans to parishes may, at first glance, seem to favour them since this would give them an income. However, these appointments had a negative effect, resulting in the breakdown of Franciscan morale and in all semblance of community life. Patrick Maguire, a native of Kinawley and the Franciscan parish priest of Templeport, was Bishop Farrell O'Reilly's choice for his coadjutor in 1817. There was considerable resistance to Patrick Maguire's appointment, not because he was a Franciscan but rather because it was seen as an attempt by the O'Reilly priests 'to perpetuate their influence in the diocese by having someone appointed who would be beholden to them'.[64] Despite this opposition Patrick Maguire was appointed coadjutor bishop in 1818, though he was destined never to succeed Farrell O'Reilly as he died three years before him, on 25 April 1826.[65] The number of Franciscans in the diocese continued to decline during the early decades of the 1800s and the deaths of Ambrose Cassidy, the

61.   Copy of Franciscan pamphlet in KDA, JB/11, pp 4–5.
62.   APF, *Fondo di Vienna*, xxviii, ff. 278r-279r.
63.   For distribution of Franciscan priests in Kilmore see map in Duffy, 'Denis Maguire', p. 10.
64.   Gallogly, *The diocese of Kilmore 1800–1950*, p. 6.
65.   Ibid., pp 6–12.

parish priest of Innismagrath, in 1824, and that of Maurice Cassidy, the parish priest of Killinagh, in 1827, brought to an end the Franciscan involvement in Kilmore. By that time the Franciscans had been ever-present in the diocese for more than 500 years.

Relief for Catholics

From *c*.1750 onwards, even though the legal position of Catholics had not changed, the relations between Catholics and Protestants were less strained than they had been although Catholics still treaded warily in case a policy of persecution might be pursued once more.[66] The report from 1787 in *Faulkner's Dublin Journal* on the setting up of a multi-denominational school at Crossdoney by Michael Reilly, the parish priest of Kilmore, is a sign of this new atmosphere:

> We learn from Cress-stoney, in the county Cavan, that a Sunday school has been instituted there by the Rev. Michael Reilly, priest of that parish; and that there are regularly every Sunday upwards of four hundred children of every denomination, instructed in their catechisms, reading, writing etc. What redounds very much to Mr Reilly's honour is that he himself hired persons of opposite profession to instruct the children in their respective religions, and sent to Dublin for a vast number of proper books, which he distributed by his own hand among them, and enoyned them at the same time to abide by such precepts as they contained.[67]

The 1782 Relief act allowed Catholics to be educated, provided they received a licence from the Protestant bishop.[68] Presumably Michael O'Reilly had availed of this clause and was granted a licence from Bishop George Lewis Jones who lived nearby. However, this development in the parish of Kilmore seems to have been the exception rather the rule at this time, which may explain why it was reported in a Dublin newspaper.

The Catholic Committee, which first met in Dublin in March 1760, was set up by Charles O'Conor and other Catholic gentry in order to assure the king of their loyalty and to remove some of the restrictions Catholics were labouring under. The committee, although largely ineffective, continued in existence until 1793. The Catholic relief act of

---

66. Corish, *The Catholic Community*, pp 118–9.
67. *Faulkner's Dublin Journal*, 12 May 1787; Brady, *Catholics and Catholicism*, p. 253.
68. Corish, *The Catholic Community*, p. 131.

1778, which enabled Catholics to take leases for 999 years and to inherit in the same way as Protestants, was passed because of the financial crisis, the fear of mass emigration from Ireland and the necessity of keeping Ireland loyal during a time of war.[69] Another Catholic relief act in 1782 allowed Catholics to acquire land, though not in parliamentary boroughs.[70] These acts, which appeared to bring some relief to Catholics, merely served to highlight a host of other inequalities they were labouring under. Attempts were made by members of the Catholic Committee to make common cause with the Ulster Presbyterians and following meetings of Catholics in Jamestown on 23 August 1791 and Elphin on the following day, a letter was sent to the Ulster Volunteers expressing support for their cause. The Volunteer Companies of Belfast met in the Linen Hall on 4 October 1791 and drafted a reply. The letter, signed by William Sinclair, stated:

> We shall be exceedingly happy to cultivate a correspondence with you on every occasion where our joint efforts may tend to restore to Irishmen their long lost rights … Differing in our religion as we differ in our faces, but resembling each other in the great features of humanity; let us unite to vindicate the rights of our Common Nature.[71]

On 27 December 1791 the leadership of the Catholic Committee passed from a conservative group led by Lord Kenmare to John Keogh and other more radical, middle-class Catholics. By July 1792 Theobald Wolfe Tone was appointed agent and secretary of the committee and the following month he and John Keogh met with Richard O'Reilly, the archbishop of Armagh and seven other Ulster bishops in order to win their support for the Convention and to make common cause with Ulster (Presbyterian) radicals. Denis Maguire was not present at this meeting though it seems likely that he supported the holding of the Convention since several members of the extended Maguire clan represented Fermanagh at the Convention.[72] Bishop Maguire was

69.   Wall, 'The quest for Catholic equality, 1745–1778' in O'Brien (ed.), *Catholic Ireland in the eighteenth century, collected essays of Maureen Wall*, pp 126–7.
70.   Moody, Martin & Byrne (eds), *A new history of Ireland*, viii, p. 280. There were also relief acts for Presbyterians. The sacramental test was removed in 1780 and two years later marriages by Presbyterian minsters were declared valid.
71.   NAI, R.P.620/19/28.
72.   Theobald Wolfe Tone, 'Journals, notes, letters [1789–95]' in Thomas Bartlett (ed.), *Life of Theobald Wolfe Tone* (Dublin, 1998), p. 143; Eamon O'Flaherty, 'The Catholic Convention and Anglo-Irish politics, 1791–3' in *Arch. Hib.*, 40 (1985), p. 23; C.J. Woods, 'The personnel of the Catholic Convention, 1792–3' in *Arch. Hib.*, 57 (2003), p. 58.

by this time in his early seventies and possibly in poor health since just three months previously Charles O'Reilly had been appointed coadjutor bishop of Kilmore. Tone was satisfied with the meeting, writing 'All well on the Catholic question. The matter of the North now settled' and he described the bishops as 'all very pleasant, sensible men'.[73]

The Catholic Convention

The Catholic Committee took the decision to hold a Convention in Dublin and, in a bid to make it more democratic, decided that it would consist of elected representatives from every county in Ireland.[74] Myles Keon, a Catholic landowner from Keonbrook in County Leitrim, devised a plan whereby two electors would represent each parish and these would in turn vote for the county members.[75] By the end of November 1792 all of the delegates had been elected and they assembled in Dublin on 3 December 1792. Edward Dowell, from Killeshandra and Patrick Dowell, an apothecary with an address in Abbey Street in Dublin, were two of Cavan's representatives at the Convention. Patrick O'Reilly from Granard, Hugh Reilly, a linen dealer and brewer from Cavan, and James Palles, a wholesale merchant living in Dublin, were the other Cavan representatives. Myles Keon from Keonbrook and his brother in law, Hugh O'Beirne from Jamestown, represented County Leitrim as did John O'Donnell from Larkfield, Robert Dillon, a woollen-draper based in Dublin, and John Keogh, one of the Convention leaders, who qualified to represent Leitrim because he owned land in the county.[76] The Convention met for a week and at the end the delegates drew up a petition addressed to the king, asking him for complete emancipation. Five delegates, including John Keogh, were delegated to bring the petition to London and present it to King George III. The resultant Relief act, which was passed in April 1793, fell far short of the complete emancipation the Catholic Convention had hoped for.

The Catholic relief acts and the renewed activity of the Catholic Committee raised fears among the Protestant population of the diocese that even more changes were on the way. When the Grand Jury of County Cavan met for the summer assizes of 1792 they resolved:

73. Tone, 'Journals notes, letters', p. 143.
74. Calling this gathering a 'convention' was evidence that Irish Catholics were catching the 'French disease'. Ominously, the National Convention, which was held in Paris in September 1792, had resulted in war and the deposition of the king. See Corish, *The Irish Catholic experience*, p. 145.
75. Tone, 'Memoirs' in Bartlett, *Life of Theobald Wolfe Tone*, p. 54. For Myles Keon see C.J. Woods, 'Miles Keon' in *D.I.B.*, v, pp 152–3.
76. TNA, H.O.100/38/35 and 100/38/318; Woods, 'The personnel of the Catholic Convention, 1792–3', pp 45, 47, 54, 55, 63, 65, 67, 68.

> That we do entirely concur in principle, opinion and determination, and that we will so operate to the utmost extent with the respective bodies of our Protestant fellow-subjects who have declared their settled resolution to maintain and preserve the Protestant Ascendacy in Church and State.

This resolution was printed at regular intervals in the *Freeman's Journal* over a six week period in the months of September and October 1792 and this intransigence may have contributed, at least in part, to the rise of Defenderism in the county a few months later.

Defenderism

Sectarian tensions and strife between the Protestant Peep O'Day Boys and the Catholic Defenders, both secret agrarian societies, had been brewing in the linen triangle in County Armagh since 1785 and by late 1792 Defenderism was spreading rapidly in east Cavan. Defender makers were travelling around, usually in pairs, administering the Defender oath. Their task was made easy by the desperate poverty of the majority of the Catholics. In the first weeks of 1793 large numbers of Defenders gathered and, in nocturnal raids on the houses of the gentry, took all the weaponry they could find.[77] On 24 January 1793, George Holdcroft, a postmaster and magistrate based in Kells reported that:

> Several of the Protestant and Presbyterian gentlemen in this neighbourhood and the neighbourhood of Ballyborro and Kingscourt had their houses attacked at the silent and unprepared hour of midnight and robbed of their arms by the Defenders known to be Roman Catholic peasantry and farmers.[78]

Lord Farnham learned that money had been collected at the chapels after Mass in County Cavan and suspected that this money was being gathered, with the support of the priests, to help arm the rebels.[79] However, the priests were not involved with the Defenders and it seems more likely that the money collected was intended for the Catholic Committee. The earl of Bellamont, who spoke as 'Governor

77. For the Defender disturbances in Kilmore see Liam Kelly, *A flame now quenched, rebels and Frenchmen in Leitrim 1793–1798* (Dublin, 1998), pp 19–46; idem, 'A turbulent decade: County Cavan in the 1790s' in Cherry & Scott (eds), *Cavan history and society*, pp 251–91.
78. Holdcroft to Hobart, TNA, H.O. 100/42/196.
79. *Freeman's Journal*, 16 February 1793.

of the county [Cavan]' in the House of Lords on 11 February 1793, stated 'My Lords, the Roman Catholic Clergy have been supposed to have had an influence in this insurrection – I rather attribute it to their want of influence'.[80] Patrick Joseph Plunkett, the Catholic bishop of Meath, chaired a meeting of his clergy which reaffirmed their allegiance 'to the best of Kings' and then pleaded with the Defenders:

> To repair to your peaceful homes; resume your former industry; be reconciled to your neighbours of every religious persuasion; and we venture to assert that you will soon see an end to grievances of every kind, to that poverty and wretchedness which give pain to the beholder.[81]

The Defenders were concerned with local grievances relating to food and wages, the small dues and tithes paid to the Church of Ireland clergy, the rent paid to the landlords and the dues paid to the Catholic priests. By May 1793 the Defender riots had spread to County Leitrim and the rebels had by then added the new Militia act to their long list of grievances. The landlords and the clergy of every persuasion were unpopular with the Defenders. Some Catholic chapels were boarded up and the priests were threatened. Angel Anna Slacke, the Methodist leader from Annadale in County Leitrim, wrote in her diary on 19 May 1793 that 'We hear of great disturbances. The priests are threatened by their own parishioners'.

The following Defender catechism found in the pocket of a man hanged in Carrick-on-Shannon in April 1795 is one of the better-known examples:

> Are you concerned? I am. To what? To the National Convention. What do you design by that cause? To quell all nations, dethrone all kings and plant the true religion that was lost since the Reformation. What do you fall by? Sin. What do you rise by? Repentance. Where did the cock first crow that all the world heard? In France.[82]

A similar Defender catechism and other documents were found in Cavan town in June 1795.[83] The strange blend of ideas culled from

80.   Ibid.
81.   Anon., *A candid and impartial account of the disturbances in the County Meath in the years 1792, 1793 and 1794, by a County Meath freeholder* (Dublin, 1794), pp 49–50.
82.   NAI, R.P.620/22/19.
83.   TNA, H.O. 100/58/201 and 100/58/203–5.

revolutionary France and Roman Catholicism found in these documents made little sense to those sworn into the secret society and would have made even less sense to the revolutionaries in France where much of their ire was directed against the Catholic Church.

The Defender uprisings in the diocese, which began at the end of December 1792 and continued sporadically until May 1795, were brutally suppressed by the military. However, Catholics were greatly encouraged when Lord Fitzwilliam, the new viceroy, arrived in Ireland on 4 January 1795 and immediately declared himself in favour of further reform. There were hopes that the restriction on Catholics entering parliament would be lifted and that a new national seminary would be established. Wolfe Tone and the United Irish movement he had helped to establish wanted Catholics and radical Presbyterians to come together and in the spring of 1795 it seemed that there was considerable support among the Presbyterians in Cavan for the Catholic relief bill introduced in the House of Commons by Henry Grattan on 12 February 1795. However, the support from the Presbyterians was not universal and on 3 May 1795 the Presbyterians from Crosserule, near Ballyjamesduff, wrote to the king stating that:

> We beg leave to assure your Majesty that nothing can be more repugnant to our ideas than such a measure, a measure which we conceive to be equally unwarranted by past experience and present observation. And we hope that your Majesty will not recommend to your parliament any further alteration in the laws respecting Catholics.[84]

A similar letter was sent to the king two weeks later from the Presbyterians of the nearby townland of Croaghan.[85] By then Grattan's Catholic relief bill had been defeated and Fitzwilliam recalled to London.

A National Seminary

The 'Act for the better education of persons professing the popish or Roman Catholic religion', which was introduced to parliament on 23 April 1795, was passed and was given royal assent on 5 June 1795.[86] This bill resulted in the establishment of a seminary in Maynooth in the autumn of 1795. It was intended to replace the Irish seminaries on the continent which had been closed following the outbreak of war on 1 February 1793. Patrick O'Reilly (Killann) and John O'Reilly (Drumgoon), who had been students in Antwerp, were sent

84.   TNA, H.O. 100/58/17.
85.   Ibid., 100/58/13–14.
86.   Patrick J. Corish, *Maynooth College, 1795–1995* (Dublin, 1995), p. 10.

to Maynooth when the seminary first opened in 1795.[87] Denis Keany (Glenfarne?) and Peter Rodaghan (Fenagh) both entered Maynooth as Kilmore students in 1798. Denis McCabe (Drumgoon) joined them in 1799. Three more Kilmore men, Francis Thally (?), Felix McCabe (Drumgoon) and Eugene O'Reilly (?), entered Maynooth in 1800 and they were joined by Roger Maguire (Killasnett) in 1801.[88] All of these nine Kilmore students in Maynooth were in their mid to late twenties when they entered the college, all were ordained and four of them – Denis Keany, Peter Rodaghan, Eugene Reilly and Roger Maguire, were dead by 1810.[89] Thomas Clancy (1748-1814), a Leitrim-born Franciscan who was ordained in Rome in 1772, having taught theology in Prague, returned to Ireland in the early 1790s and was appointed the first professor of Scripture in Maynooth College in 1795. He resigned his position two years later and returned to Prague where he lived out the remainder of his life.[90]

Ten clerical and seven lay-students were expelled from Maynooth College on 12 May 1798 because of their support for the United Irishmen and it is possible that one of the expelled lay-students was a Cavan man named Nicholas Brady.[91] On 27 May 1798 Henry Clements, writing from 'Forthenry, near Cavan' reported that Nicholas Brady had made his escape from Maynooth College and had come to his relations in 'a mountainous part of this country … to inflame the minds of the people'.[92] Patrick O'Reilly, who had studied in Antwerp and was already ordained before he entered Maynooth in 1795, had his studies cut short in June 1798 because 'his conduct was not thoroughly satisfactory'.[93] It is possible that his expulsion was connected to the United Irish rebellion which was raging in Leinster at that time although the college authorities struggled to maintain discipline when young seminarians were studying alongside ordained priests who were in their mid-twenties or older. Because of this it was decided in 1799 that no

---

87.   MCA, B4/10/1; Patrick Hamell, *Maynooth students and ordinations index, 1795–1895* (Maynooth, 1982), p. 153.

88.   T.P. Cunningham & Francis J. MacKiernan, 'Maynooth archives – Maynooth students' in *Arch. Hib.*, 43 (1989), p. 27; Hamell, *Maynooth students and ordinations*, pp 30, 87, 100, 155.

89.   MacKiernan, *Diocese of Kilmore*, pp 176–7.

90.   Corish, *Maynooth College*, p. 445. See also Jennings & Giblin (eds), *Louvain papers*, p. 536; Parez & Kucharová, *The Irish Franciscans in Prague*, pp 148–9, 156–7, 180.

91.   *A letter from the Rev. Peter Flood … relative to the Pamphlet entitled 'A Fair representation of the present political state of Ireland' by Patrick Duigenan …* (Dublin, 1800), pp 8–9; Corish, *Maynooth College*, p. 19.

92.   NAI, R.P. 620/381/69. Henry Clements thought that Nicholas Brady was a teacher in Maynooth College though it seems more likely that he was a lay student there. It is possible that this is the same Nicholas Brady who became a Kilmore clerical student in Maynooth in 1808 and was ordained in 1813.

93.   MCA, 84/10/1. He died as parish priest of Urney and Annagelliff in 1843. See MacKiernan, *Diocese of Kilmore*, p. 176.

more priest-students would be admitted to Maynooth, bringing to an end the long-standing tradition of Irish men being ordained before their seminary education was completed.[94]

Barn Churches: 1770–1800

The twenty-eight year episcopacy of Denis Maguire (1770-1798) was marked by the building of many modest and mostly single-cell, thatched chapels throughout the diocese.[95] From the 1750s onwards there was a growing confidence among Catholics and as a result the Mass rocks gradually gave way to these 'Mass-houses' which were tolerated by the authorities provided they did not have either bell or steeple.[96] There was, in some parishes, an interim period between the Mass rock and stone-walled chapel, which saw the erection of a *scalán*[97] or *seal foscaid* - a wickerwork and thatched shelter which gave some shelter to the priest but not always to the congregation. Sometimes these wattled or mud-walled shelters were longer structures with an open gabled end, thus giving shelter to at least some of the congregation. The *scalán* in the townland of Leginn in Knockninny in Fermanagh was different. 'It was built of mud and stones, thatched with rushes and open at both ends. Against the back wall was raised a little altar of sods'.[98] From *c*.1770 onwards, the newly-built chapels were generally barn churches with rubble stone walls, although the chapel erected in the townland of Cornaghy in Carrigallen parish in 1770 was mud-walled and it survived until 1839.[99] The chapel near Tullaghan on the Atlantic coast was more substantial and even had a carved stone which carried the inscription 'All you who pass pray for Rev. Eugene McGowan, the founder of this chapel in the year of the Lord 1770'.[100] Most of the chapels built in this period were not unlike elongated vernacular thatched dwelling houses. The verse composed about a chapel in the townland of Loonogs in the parish of Denn, gives an indication of its dimensions:

> From East to West in length it ran
> Full twenty yards and two a span.
> Its width in feet was twenty three

94.   Corish, *Maynooth College*, p. 35.
95.   Gallogly, *The diocese of Kilmore*, p. 369.
96.   F.H.A. Aalen, Kevin Whelan & Matthew Stout (eds), *Atlas of the Irish rural landscape* (Cork, 1997), p. 192; Corish, *The Catholic Community*, p. 131.
97.   Sometimes spelled *scathlán*.
98.   John O'Donnell (ed.), *St Mary's Church, Teemore 1893–1993* (Teemore, 1993), p. 8.
99.   Kelly, *Churches of the diocese of Kilmore*, p. 48.
100.   Ibid., p. 103; P. Ó Gallachair, 'A forgotten Penal-day Church in Kinlough' in *Bréifne*, i, 1 (1958), pp 28–9.

Figure 17.2: Holy Trinity barn church at Kildoagh, near Bawnboy.

> The measures marked in memory.
> The height from floor up to the eve
> A six-foot man his hand could leave.[101]

These chapels, which were built in the last decades of the 1700s, generally remained in use for less than fifty years and were replaced in the decades before the Great Famine because they were dark, damp and too small to accommodate a fast-growing population. Dernasmallan chapel in Aughnasheelin, which was built in 1790, had a shorter life-span than most and was closed in 1833. Holy Trinity church in Kildoagh, a barn church which was erected in the parish of Templeport in 1796, was larger than many of the other late eighteenth-century churches in the diocese and although not in use since 1979 it has survived relatively intact making it one of the best examples of an Irish vernacular church from this era. It is a single cell chapel with two doors and two galleries, one for women and the other for men. The altar was in the middle of the long south wall which meant that the women and men faced each other from either end of the chapel. There was just

---

101.   This verse was collected by Úna Lynch in the 1930s from an old man named John Deane and it was included in the folklore gathered by Crosskeys National School for the Folklore Commission. For full text of poem see Liam Kelly, *St Matthew's Church, Drumavaddy* (Cavan, 2013), Appendix iv, pp 128–9. The chapel in Loonogs was T-shaped. See Ordnance Survey map (1836).

one seat directly opposite the altar on the long north wall and it was seldom used except during funerals when the coffin was placed on it.[102] (See Fig. 17.2). Other barn churches were single cell buildings with the altar at one gable end and the main door and gallery at the other.[103]

These chapels were originally barn-like, without furnishings, statues or sacred images and were, in many instances, used as schools on weekdays. They were also regularly used as threshing-barns. Brian Ó Mórdha has recorded the oral tradition relating to the chapel in the townland of Drumurray and parish of Kilsherdany which was built in 1769:

> It was thatched … The walls were built of stone only to a height of some feet and were clay-built from there to the roof. In its final days at least it was in a rather dilapidated condition and holes in the eastern gable were stuffed with whins … It was used for a variety of purposes and was swept each Saturday night in preparation for the following Sunday morning Mass; this was particularly necessary in winter time because the church would appear to have been used as a kind of communal threshing centre.[104]

The chapels were also used as meeting places for such groups as the Defenders and the United Irishmen. Angel Anna Slacke, in an undated letter, apparently written sometime in 1795 to her friend Mrs Fleming, noted that the Defenders' 'place of consultation is the Mass-house'[105] and according to tradition a number of Aughnasheelin men attended Mass in the chapel in Crimlin before joining the French soldiers on their way to Ballinamuck in early September 1798.[106]

The United Irishmen

The Defender revolt which erupted in the diocese of Kilmore in early January 1793 and continued sporadically for two and a half years, was suppressed by the summer of 1795. By then many who had taken the Defender oath were being sworn into the more radical United Irishmen. The misbehaviour of the over-zealous military when supressing the

102.   William Garner, 'Kildoagh Catholic Church, Co. Cavan, in *Architecture in Ireland*, i, 10 (Winter 1979–80), pp 39–41; *An introduction to the architectural heritage of County* Cavan, pp 42–3; Elgy Gillespie, 'Kildoagh Barn Church' in *The Irish Times*, 2 December, 1975.
103.   Gallogly, *The diocese of Kilmore*, p. 370.
104.   Brian Ó Mórdha, *Kilsherdany: Its history and people* (Cavan, 1977), p. 35.
105.   Kelly, *A flame now quenched*, p. 31.
106.   Information gathered from Thady Prior, Callowhill, *c.*1968.

Defender uprisings and the arrival of many Catholic refugees from Armagh and other neighbouring counties into west Cavan and Leitrim following the battle of the Diamond in September 1795 meant that the task of the United Irish oath-makers was made easy. Large numbers joined the United Irishmen and in east Cavan many Presbyterians joined their ranks. Henry Clements, writing from Cootehill on 20 April 1797, reported that 'the houses for swearing in these United Irishmen are as public as whiskey houses, particularly one at the end of Bridge Street, Cootehill, where Stewart, the Presbyterian Parson … or his daughter constantly attend for that purpose'.[107] Rev. Moore, the Presbyterian minister in Kingscourt was also said to be an active supporter of the United Irishmen. Robert Montgomery, the minister for the Presbyterian congregation in Corglass who had rebuilt their meeting house[108] in 1795, was also a supporter of the United Irishmen, as were virtually all of his congregation.[109]

The large numbers who joined the United Irishmen, their parading and their attacks on the big houses for arms caused consternation among the landed gentry. Charles Broderick, the Church of Ireland bishop of Kilmore, wrote to General John Knox on 20 May 1797 stating that he thought it 'absolutely necessary' for more soldiers to be sent to the area because 'disturbances have been gradually approaching upon us'.[110] Dr William Hales, the Church of Ireland clergyman in Killeshandra, wrote a similar letter two days later from 'this sequestered nook of Ulster' recommending that the Killeshandra infantry and cavalry corps be given money and ammunition to help secure the region.[111]

The tithes payable to the Church of Ireland clergy was an issue which preoccupied the Defenders in 1795. Angel Anna Slacke, although a devout and enthusiastic Methodist, continued to attend the service of the Church of Ireland in Kiltubrid parish in County Leitrim. On 16 March 1795, she wrote to her friends Mrs Fleming stating that:

> The common people are very much burdened to support Bishops and Rectors in luxury, nor do I think it just that they should be oppressed for clergy who they receive no benefit from either in public or in private. And almost every person in this parish [Kiltubrid] have declared that they will not pay any more tythes and that they will not

107.   NAI, R.P.620/29/219.
108.   *An introduction to the architectural heritage of County Cavan*, p. 45.
109.   Kelly, 'A turbulent decade', pp 269–70.
110.   NAI, R.P.620/30/120.
111.   NAI, R.P.620/30/190.

oppose the proctors when they take pledges for same, but would let their cattle go to pound peacefully, and when the day of sale comes they will murder any who may attempt to buy them. They have given notice of their intention by putting up papers on the Church and Chapel doors.[112]

Eighteen months later the United Irishmen of east Cavan were concerned with similar issues. On 21 August 1796 a gentleman (possibly a clergyman) from County Cavan who called himself *Amicus Patria* described how 'in one parish neighbouring to mine a paper was put up on the Church gate with violent threats against the clergyman if he did not lower his tithes and the rent of his Glebe lands and threatening death to any man who should dare to take down the warning'. The letter writer described how in another neighbouring parish the rebels had 'entirely destroyed the Clergyman's garden' and then 'erected a gallows and threatened to hang up his tithe-manager'.[113] The writer feared for this clergyman's life if he remained in the area. The man referred to here may have been James Young, a magistrate and Church of Ireland curate based in Killinkere, who had taken part in several military operations against the rebels of the area, even though it was reported on 9 May 1797 that he and his family had moved to Dublin as they were not 'safe any longer in Bailieboro'.[114] The opposition of the United Irishmen in east Cavan to the tithes took different forms to that adopted by the Defenders of County Leitrim. George Holdcroft wrote on 11 May 1797 that:

> In the vicinity of Bailieboro … the general cry … is half rent and no tythes. And to show that they will not suffer themselves to be compelled to pay rent they are levelling all the pounds in the country. On Thursday night the pound of Bailieboro was levelled to the ground and last night the pound of Virginia.[115]

112.   Unpublished letter of A. A. Slacke.
113.   NAI, R.P.620/24/137.
114.   NAI, R.P.620/30/49. James Young was also a curate in the parish of St Nicholas Without in Dublin at this time. See Leslie, *Clergy of Kilmore*, p. 929. Carncross Cullen (1753–1807), the vicar of Cloonclare, also took an active military role against the Defenders in north Leitrim. It was said that the 'county of Leitrim is indebted [to him] for its internal peace' and that along with the Clare Militia he was 'active in apprehending the Defenders and lodging them daily in [Manorhamilton] gaol'. See *Faulkner's Dublin Journal*, 5 May 1795.
115.   NAI, R.P.620/30/49.

The following day the cattle pound in Mullagh was destroyed.[116] These actions caused alarm among the Church of Ireland clergy and the landed gentry. Rev. William Hales wrote from Killeshandra on 22 May 1797 stating that 'I much fear we are on the eve of some tremendous explosion of great extent and magnitude … they [the United Irishmen] are carrying on with a rapidity and political contrivance that is both frightful and amazing'.[117] However, from this time onwards the military were getting the upper hand throughout the diocese and the United Irishmen were in decline fifteen months before General Humbert and his French soldiers would race through County Leitrim on the way to their inevitable defeat at Ballinamuck.

When the anonymous *Amicus Patria* wrote from Cavan to Dublin castle on 21 August 1796 he recommended that some concessions should be made to the Catholics. He suggested that 'an additional Member [of Parliament] should be returned for each County and that this member should be a Catholic'. He also suggested that some way should be devised 'for providing for the Catholic Clergy'. He hoped that these measures would 'dissolve the party of united Irishmen by detaching from it thro' jealousy many of the Leaders of the Dissenters'.[118] Judging by the names of the United Irishmen arrested for destroying the cattle pounds in east Cavan it would seem that the Presbyterians were at the heart of the anti-tithe activities in the area.[119] However, the Government policies and the sectarian nature of the rebellion which began in Leinster on 23 May 1798 had the effect of detaching Presbyterians from the United Irishmen. George Holdcroft, writing from Kells on 26 June said that he was 'happy to report that the inhabitants of Bailieboro are dividing' and that 'the neighbourhood remains perfectly quiet'.[120]

The diocese of Kilmore, which had large-scale disturbances earlier in the decade, remained quiet throughout the early summer rebellions in Leinster and the Ulster counties of Antrim and Down. The arrival of Humbert's French expeditionary force and their Irish allies into Dromahair on 6 September 1798 and their subsequent rapid march through County Leitrim caused quite a stir in the north western part of the diocese. They were greeted joyfully according to the poem *Cumhaidh Na Cléire* which was written in County Leitrim shortly afterwards, though the

116.   Ibid., 620/30/77.
117.   Ibid., 620/30/190.
118.   Ibid., 620/24/137.
119.   Kelly, 'A turbulent decade', p. 279.
120.   Ibid., p. 280.

numbers who joined them were quite small.[121] In general the Catholic priests steered clear of them, though Ambrose Cassidy, the County Derry-born Franciscan parish priest of Ballinaglera, befriended them and, according to a note added to the manuscript containing *Cumhaidh Na Cléire*, he was 'persecuted at the time of the French'.[122] He died as parish priest of Innismagrath on 22 November 1824 and was buried in Corrus cemetery.[123]

The victories of the military over the rebels in the summer of 1798, especially the more local victories at Granard and Ballinamuck in early September, brought a relative calm to the diocese once more. On 12 September 1798, four days after the battle at Ballinamuck, Rev. William Hales called a special public vestry meeting in Killeshandra. At that meeting it was resolved that:

> A SOLEMN THANKSGIVING be offered on Sunday next, to THE LORD OF HOSTS for the defeat of the Gallic invasion and domestic rebellion in the heart of the kingdom, at Ballinamuck, in the County Longford, on Saturday last – and for the special deliverance of this church and town from the horrors of war and battle.[124]

The Church of Ireland clergy and the landed gentry could heave a sigh of relief that the sporadic violence which had affected the diocese for the previous five and a half years was coming to an end.

The Catholic clergy, especially the hierarchy, were opposed to the activities of the United Irishmen and at the beginning of June 1798, about ten days after the rebellion had erupted in Leinster, Denis Maguire and his coadjutor Charles O'Reilly, together with many other bishops and prominent lay Catholics, were signatories to a letter which pleaded with the 'deluded people now in rebellion' to desist from violence. This letter, which was published in *The Times*, made no impression on the rebels.[125] Denis Maguire was seventy-seven years old at this time and

---

121.   RIA, MS 23042, f. 38r. The author of this poem is not known. It was dictated by the north Leitrim poet Theophilus O'Flynn and collected by James Hardiman in 1835. See Séamus P. Ó Mórdha, 'Cumhaidh Na Cléire, a '98 poem from north Leitrim' in *Bréifne*, i, 1 (1958), pp 34–40.

122.   RIA, MS 23042, f. 38v.

123.   Clancy & Forde, *Ballinaglera and Innishmagrath*, pp 42–3.

124.   John Jones, *An Impartial Narrative of the most important engagements that took place between his Majesty's forces and the insurgents during the Irish Rebellion in 1798* (Dublin, 1798), ii, p. 278.

125.   *The Times* [London], 2 June 1798.

in poor health. He died seven months later, on 23 December 1798.[126] He had been bishop of the diocese for almost twenty-nine years and was succeeded by Charles O'Reilly, a native of Drumgoon, who had been his coadjutor since 23 April 1793.

Charles O'Reilly was born *c*.1750 and went to study in the University of Louvain where he graduated with a Licentiate of Arts in in 1773.[127] He was ordained *c*.1775 and returned to Ireland sometime before he was appointed parish priest of his native parish of Drumgoon in 1781, a position he held until his death in 1800.[128] Four months after O'Reilly was made coadjutor, Denis Maguire wrote to Cardinal Antonelli in Propaganda Fide thanking him for appointing O'Reilly as his coadjutor and saying that the appointment 'brought joy both to the whole diocese as well as to me'. He described his coadjutor as 'a very competent theologian, an excellent philosopher and [he] has a good memory'.[129] When Charles O'Reilly became bishop he made Drumgoon a mensal parish and continued to live there, residing in the town of Cootehill.[130] Charles O'Reilly was the first bishop to reside in the diocese since the death of Eugene MacSweeney in 1669. However, Charles O'Reilly was bishop for only fifteen months. He died on 5 March 1800 and was buried in his family plot in Kilsherdany cemetery. His tombstone carries the O'Reilly coat of arms and a Latin inscription.[131]

In 1817 Michael O'Reilly, the parish priest of Kilmore who had established the multi-denominational school in his parish, spoke highly of both Denis Maguire and Charles O'Reilly at a meeting of clergy in Cavan. In oratorical style he referred to Denis Maguire as the 'venerated and venerable Doctor Maguire' and as 'a Prince of Bishops'. He said that when Charles O'Reilly died in 1800 the 'diocese sustained an incalculable loss … had he lived he would have imitated, nay equalled the virtues of his worthy, his almost matchless predecessor'.[132] Denis Maguire, despite residing outside the diocese, had been diligent

126.   He was buried in Devenish and ordered that a 'decent tombstone, not a very expensive one' be placed over his grave. Carrigan, 'Catholic episcopal wills', pp 187–8.
127.   Nilis, 'Irish students at Leuven University', p. 243.
128.   MacKiernan, *Diocese of Kilmore*, pp 14, 55, 169.
129.   APF, *Fondo di Vienna*, xxviii, f. 81rv.
130.   Drumgoon remained a mensal parish until 1843.
131.   Gallogly, *The diocese of Kilmore*, pp 3–4. The inscription on Charles O'Reilly's horizontal gravestone reads: *Hoc monumentum erectum fuit in memo/riam Illustrissimi D.D. Caroli O'Reilly, Episco/pi Catholici Kilmorensis qui in Domino/ obdormivit die quinto Martii 1800 Anno/ aetatis Quinqagesimo. Requiescat in pace.*
132.   KDA, JB/11. Michael O'Reilly died in 1818. He was buried in Holy Trinity Island. The inscription on his headstone reads: *I.H.S./Sacred to the memory of the Revd Michl O'Reilly pastor/ of the parish of Kilmore for 33 years departed this life/1818 aged 80 years. Requiescat in pace. Amen.*

and thorough in carrying out his duties and Charles O'Reilly, even though he was bishop for a very short time, had carried on in the manner of his predecessor and had pointed the way forward by residing in the diocese. However, it was not until another quarter of a century had passed, after James Browne was appointed bishop of Kilmore in 1829, that root and branch reforms were carried out and that the structures of the modern diocese of Kilmore were put in place.

Bibliography

Manuscript Sources

Belfast:

Public Records Office of Northern Ireland
> DIO 4/24/1–28; 4/24/2/1; 4/24/2/23.
> D. 1449.
> T/3019/4655.
> Wynne papers, MIC/666/D/3/1–11.

Brussels:

Bibliotéque Royale
> MS 4190–4200, f.129.

Cavan:

Archive of Cavan County Library
> BC2, M3571.

Kilmore Diocesan Archive
> JB/11. P.L. 7.5.

Dublin:

Dublin Diocesan Archives
> Emilio Ranuzzi, *Sfoglio dei volume per obitum dell archivio segreto Vaticano per le diocese d'Irlanda*, ii, (1630).

Irish Jesuit Archive
> Jesuit annual letter 1617 (MacErlean transcripts).

National Archives of Ireland
> Rebellion Papers 620/19/28; 620/22/19; 620/24/137; 620/30/49; 620/30/77; 620/30/190.

National Library of Ireland
> Farnham papers, D.20433, 20438.
> MSS 2685, 2865, p. 151; MS. 8014/X.
> Smythe of Barbavilla papers, MS. 41, 575/15.

Royal Irish Academy
> MSS 23A, 15, ff. 275–354; 23042, f. 38r.

Trinity College

MSS 3, 69, 77, 550, 747, 808 (5), 832, 833, 1188, 1391, 1419,

London:

British Library

Egerton MS 107; 1781, f. 128v.

Additional MS 18, 205.

The National Archives, Kew

SP, 60/1/9; 61/2/63.

H.O.100/38/35;   100/38/318;   100/42/196;   100/58/17;   100/58/201; 100/58/203–5.

MPFi/81.

Maynooth:

Maynooth College Archive

MS 84/10/1.

Monaghan:

Clogher Diocesan Archive

MS 3/17/40.

Oxford:

Bodleian Library

Rawlinson MS A. 237; B 484, f.18; B.513; C.98, f.20.

Rome:

Vatican Archive

Fondo Borghese, 124C, f. 78rv.

Acta Camerarii, ix, ff. 10v, 193.

Vatican Library

MSS *Barberini Latini*, 2867, ff. 77v-78r; 2869, f. 9v; 2879, f. 188rv.

Irish College Archive

Liber, xxvi, ff. 149–50.

Propaganda Fide Archive

Acta Consistorialia, xii, ff. 58–9; xiv, f.362; xvii, ff.188–9; cxix, ff. 228v-234v; cxxii, ff. 235–6.

Fondo di Vienna, xii, ff. 57r-58v, 142r; xiii, ff. 386r, 436rv-439v, 442rv, 454r-461v, 489r, 498r, 499v; xiv, ff. 31rv, 192r-195v; xxvii, ff. 89r-90r; xviii, ff. 133r, 188r -189v, 278r-279r.

Processus Datariae, ii, ff. 146v-151v; iv, ff. 299r-304r; vii, ff. 211r-216v, 223r-233v.

Scritture originali riferite nelle congregazioni generali, 140, ff.159rv, 160rv, 168rv; 467, f.235; 742, f.153v;

Scritture riferite nei Congressi (Irlanda), 2, f.102r; 7, ff. 492–3, 506, 521–2; 9, ff. 238, 543–6, 596–7; 10, ff. 306–7, 314r-5v, 402–3, 503; 15, f. 543

San Clemente Archive
Codex 1, vol. i, ff. 151, 168; Codex IV, doc. 106a.

Rolls Series, Calendars, Annals

Brewer, J., & W. Bullen (eds), *Calendar of the Carew manuscripts preserved in the archepiscopal library at Lambeth*, i (London, 1868).

Calendar of State Papers and manuscripts relating to English affairs existing in the archives and collections of Venice, xi, 1607–1610.

Calendar of State papers, Domestic series, 1678.

Calendar of State papers relating to Ireland (London, 1860 -).

Calendar of entries in the papal registers relating to Great Britain and Ireland, 20 vols (London, 1893 -).

Calendar of patent rolls, Richard II, iv, 1389–1392 (London, 1902).

Calendar of Irish patent rolls of James I (Dublin, 1966).

Freeman, A.M. (ed.), *Annála Connacht, the annals of Connacht, A.D.1224–1544* (Dublin, 1944).

Hamilton, Hans Claude, *Calendar of the State papers relating to Ireland, 1509–1573* (London, 1860).

Hennessy, William M. (ed.), *The annals of Loch Cé* (London, 1871).

    & B. McCarthy (eds), *Annála Uladh: annals of in Irish and English*, 4 vols (Dublin, 1887–1901).

Morrin, James (ed.), *Calendar of the Patent and close rolls of chancery of Ireland in the reigns of Henry VIII, Edwards VI and Elizabeth*, i (Dublin, 1861).

Calendar of the patent and close rolls of Chancery in Ireland in the reign of Charles I (Dublin, 1863).

Murphy, Denis (ed.), *The Annals of Clonmacnoise* (Dublin, 1896).

O'Donovan, John (ed.), *The annals of the Kingdom of Ireland by the Four Masters from the earliest period to the year 1616*, 7 vols (Dublin, 1856).

Williams, Bernadette (ed.), *The 'Annals of Multyfarnham': Roscommon and Connacht provenance* (Dublin, 2012).

Round, J. Horace, *Calendar of documents preserved in France illustrative of the history of Great Britain and Ireland*, i (London, 1899).

Sweetman, H.S., (ed.),*Calendar of documents relating to Ireland, 1171–1251* (London, 1875).

Calendar of documents relating to Ireland 1285–1292 (London, 1879).

    & G.F. Handcock, (eds), *Calendar of documents relating to Ireland 1302–1307* (London, 1886).

The Irish Fiants of the Tudor Sovereigns, vols i, ii (Dublin, 1994).

Newspapers

Pue's Occurrences, 30 January 1753.

Faulkner's Dublin Journal, 26–30 July 1763.

Dublin Chronicle, 31 March 1770.

Sleator's Public Gazetteer, 31 March 1770.

Hibernian Journal, 31 October 1781.

Freeman's Journal, 16 February 1793.

The Times (London), 2 June 1798.

Irish Examiner, 23 November 1863.

Anglo Celt, 21 August 1937.

Irish Press, 28 November 1961.

Irish Times, 2 December, 1975.

Primary Sources

Allingham, Hugh, & Robert Crawford (eds & trans.), *The Spanish Armada, Captain Cuellar's adventures in Connacht and Ulster A.D.1588* (London, 1897).

Anon, *Another tract of Severall Letters from Ireland* … (London, 1643).

The Answere and vindication of Sir William Cole … (London, 1645).

Last speeches of three priests that were executed for religion, Anno Domini 1679 (London, 1679).

A list of the names of the Popish parish priests throughout the several counties in the Kingdom of Ireland … (Dublin, 1705).

An account of the life and character of the late Rev. John Murphy D.D., taken from authentic memoirs and original papers, by the living testimonies of his fellow students and contemporaries (Dublin, 1753).

A collection of the Epistles and works of Benjamin Holme (London, 1753).

A second letter to the people of Ireland on the subject of tythes, with a particular address to the dissenters … (Dublin, 1758).

Minutes of some late conversations between Rev. Thomas Coke and others (Dublin, 1790).

A candid and impartial account of the disturbances in the County Meath in the years 1792, 1793 and 1794, by a County Meath freeholder (Dublin, 1794).

A genuine account of the progress of Charles Coote, Esq, in pursuing and defeating the Oakboys in the Counties of Monaghan, Cavan and Fermanagh (Dublin, 1763).

Letters written by His Excellency Hugh Boulter, D.D. Lord Primate of All Ireland to Several Ministers of State … (Oxford, 1770).

'Report of Bishop McDonagh, 1741' in *Bréifne*, ii, 8 (1966).

'Kilmore Clergy list of 1723 in *Bréifne*, iii, 11 (1968).

'Letters from a Jesuit in Dublin on the Confraternity of the Holy Name 1747–1748' in *Arch. Hib.*, xxix (1970).

Collegium Hibernorum De Urbe, an early manuscript account of the Irish College, Rome,1628–1678 (Rome, 2003).

Archdall, Mervyn, *Monasticon Hibernicum* (Dublin, 1786).

Boran, Elizabethanne (ed.), *The correspondence of James Ussher*, 3 vols, (Dublin, 2015).

Burke, William P., *The Irish priests in the Penal times, 1660–1760* (Shannon, 1969).

Carney, James (ed.), *Poems on the O'Reillys*, (Dublin, 1950).

    (ed.), *A genealogical history of the O'Reillys written in the eighteenth century by Eóghan Ó Raghallaigh and incorporating portion of the earlier work of Dr Thomas Fitzsimons …* (Cavan, 1959).

Carrigan, William, 'Catholic episcopal wills' in *Arch. Hib.*, i (1912).

Chart, D.A., (ed.), *The register of John Swayne, archbishop of Armagh and primate of Ireland 1418–1439* (Belfast, 1935).

Cooper, J.H., (ed.), 'Extracts from the Journal of John Cennick: Moravian evangelist' in *The Moravian history magazine* (Belfast, 1996).

Costello, M.A. , *De Annatis Hiberniae* (Dundalk, 1909).

Cradock, John, *A sermon preached in Christ-Church, Dublin, on Friday Feb. 17, 1758* (Dublin, 1758).

Creighton, James, *A caution against false prophets addressed to the inhabitants of Kinawly in the diocese of Kilmore* (Dublin, 1791).

    Poetic miscellanies, written occasionally and addressed to the author's relatives and particular friends, by Rev. J. C. (London, 1791).

Cromwell, Oliver, *The letters and speeches of Oliver Cromwell with elucidations by Thomas Carlyle* (London, 1904).

Curnock, Nehemiah, *The journal of John Wesley*, 8 vols (London, 1938).

De Burgh, Ulick John, *The Memoirs and letters of Ulick, Marquis of Clanricarde* (London, 1757).

Edmundson, William, *A Journal of the life, travels, sufferings and labour of love in the work of ministry of … William Edmundson* (London, 1774).

Forster, Charles (ed.), *Thirty years correspondence between John Jebb D.D. … and Alexander Knox* (Philadelphia, 1835).

Hamilton, Frederick, *The information of Sir Frederick Hamilton, Knight and Colonel, given to the Committees of both Kingdoms …* (London, 1645).

Hanly, John J., (ed.), *The letters of Saint Oliver Plunkett 1625–1681* (Dublin, 1979).

Harrison, Richard, *Irelands misery since the late cessation: sent in a letter from a gentleman in Dublin, to his brother in law, now residing in London, sometime living in the county of Cavan …* (London, 1644).

Hennessy, William & D.H. Kelly (eds), *The Book of Fenagh* (Dublin, 1875).

Henry, William, *An account of Lough Lheichs, Anglice: The Lake of cures in the County of Cavan, in a letter to the Right Reverend Josiah Hort, Lord bishop of Kilmore and Ardagh …* (Dublin, 1736).

Herity, Michael (ed.), *Ordnance survey letters, Londonderry, Fermanagh, Armagh-Monaghan, Louth, Cavan-Leitrim* (Dublin, 2012).

Jennings, Brendan & Cathaldus Giblin (eds), *Louvain papers 1606–1827* (Dublin, 1968).

Jones, Henry, *A Remonstrance of divers remarkable passages concerning the church and kingdome of Ireland* (London, 1642).

A Remonstrance of the beginnings and proceedings of the rebellion in the County of Cavan … (London, 1642).

Jones, John, *An Impartial Narrative of the most important engagements that took place between his Majesty's forces and the insurgents during the Irish Rebellion in 1798* (Dublin, 1798).

Jones, Rufus (ed.), *George Fox – an autobiography* (London, 1908).

Keating, Geoffrey, *Foras feasa ar Éireann: the history of Ireland*, 4 vols, ed. by D. Comyn & P.S. Dineen, (London, 1902–14).

Knowler, William (ed.), *The Earl of Strafforde's letters and dispatches* (London, 1739).

Liebler, Kaspar, *Annales Conventus SS. Auxiliariorum extra muros Hammelburgenses OFM Recollectorum* (Hammelburg, 1648–80).

Madden, John, *A sermon preached at St Anne's, Dublin on Thursday the 9th October, 1746 being the day appointed for a General Thanksgiving to Almighty God for the suppression of the late unnatural Rebellion* (Dublin, 1748).

Massari, Dionisio, 'My Irish campaign' in *The Catholic bulletin and book review*, vii (1917), viii (1918), ix (1919).

McNeill, Charles (ed.), *Registrum de Kilmainham: register of chapter acts of the hospital of St John of Jerusalem in Ireland* (Dublin, 1932).

Milne, Kenneth & Paddy McNally (eds), *The Boulter letters* (Dublin, 2016).

Moigne, Thomas, *A True copy of all the rents, procurations, tithes and pensions as belong to the two united bishoprics of Kilmore and Ardagh* (1622).

Ó Cléirigh, Micheál , *The Martyrology of Donegal*, ed. & trans. by John O'Donovan (Dublin, 1864).

O'Ferrall, R., & R. O'Connell, *Commentarius Rinuccinianus de sedis … per annos 1645–9*, 6 vols, ed. by S. Kavanagh, (Dublin, 1932–49).

O'Mahony, Francis, 'Brevis synopsis provinciae Hiberniae FF. Minorum' in *Anal. Hib.*, vi (1934).

Plummer, Charles (ed.), *Bethada Náem nÉrenn* (Oxford, 1922).

Plunkett, Oliver, *Jus Primatiale, The ancient right and preheminency of the see of Armagh* (London, 1672).

Richardson, John, *A short history of the attempts that have been made to convert the Popish natives of Ireland to the Established Religion with a proposal for their conversion* (London, 1712).

  A proposal for the conversion of the Popish natives of Ireland to the Establish'd Religion (London, 1712).

  A Sermon preached at the Consecration of St James's Church at Coot-Hill: July the 25th 1715 by John Richardson, rector of the parish of Annah … (Dublin, 1716).

  The true interest of the Irish Nation: in a sermon preached in the Church of Belturbet on Sunday 23rd of October, 1715, on the occasion of Captain Bryan Reily's Renunciation of the errors of the Church of Rome (Dublin, 1716).

  The great Folly, superstition and idolatry of pilgrimages in Ireland, especially of that to St Patrick's purgatory … (Dublin, 1727).

Richardson, Laurence, *An essay on the Rosary of the B.V.M.* (Dublin, 1736).

  The impossibility of salvation outside the Roman Catholic Church (Dublin, 1742).

  The manner of hearing Mass with prayers before Confession and Communion (Dublin, 1746).

An appendix to the manner of hearing Mass (Dublin, 1748).

A letter to the R.C. clergy of the diocese of K[ilmore] (Dublin, 1749).

Shirley, E.P., *Original Letters and papers* (London, 1851).

Shuckburgh, E.S., *Two biographies of William Bedell* (Cambridge, 1902).

Smith, Brendan (ed.), *The register of Milo Sweteman archbishop of Armagh 1361–1380* (Dublin, 1996).

The register of Nicholas Fleming archbishop of Armagh 1404–1416 (Dublin, 2003).

Stokes, George T., (ed.), *Pococke's tour in Ireland in 1752* (Dublin, 1891).

Story, Joseph, *The Bishop of Kilmore's charge to the Clergy of his Diocese at his ordinary visitation held at Cavan June 26, 1746* (Dublin, 1747).

Sughi, Mario A., (ed.), *Registrum Octaviani, the register of Octavian de Palatio Archbishop of Armagh 1478- 1513*, (Dublin, 1999).

Teate, Faithful, *Souldiers commission, charge … in a sermon preached in Christ-Church Dublin, May 14, 1642 … by Faithfull Teate DD.* (Dublin, 1658).

Todd, J.H., & W. Reeves (eds), John O'Donovan (translator), *The Martyrology of Donegal* (Dublin, 1864).

Treadwell, Victor (ed.), *The Irish Commission of 1622* (Dublin, 2006).

Secondary Sources

Aalen, F.H.A., Kevin Whelan & Matthew Stout (eds), *Atlas of the Irish Rural Landscape* (Cork, 1997).

Anon, *An account of the Charity Schools in Great Britain and Ireland* (London, 1714).

An account of the Charity Schools in Ireland (Dublin, 1730).

Acts and statutes made in a Parliament begun at Dublin the twenty first day of September, Anno Dom. 1703, in the Second year of the reign of our Most Gracious sovereign Lady Queen Anne … (Dublin, 1710).

An abstract of the sufferings of the people call'd Quakers … from the year 1660 to the year 1666, iii (London, 1738).

A compendious view of some extraordinary sufferings of the people called Quakers … in the Kingdom of Ireland from the year 1655 … (Dublin, 1751).

Fourth report of the Royal Commission of historical manuscripts (London, 1874).

A letter from the Rev. Peter Flood … relative to the Pamphlet entitled 'A Fair representation of the present political state of Ireland' by Patrick Duigenan … (Dublin, 1800).

Report on Franciscan manuscripts preserved at the convent, Merchant's Quay, (Dublin, 1906).

'Commonwealth records' in *Arch. Hib.* vii (1918–21).

'Very Rev, Hugh Canon Brady' in *Breifny Antiquarian Journal*, i, 3 (1922).

Father Luke Wadding commemorative volume (Dublin, 1957).

Report on the houses of the Irish Dominican province (2 Sept. 1767) in *Coll. Hib.*, 8 (1965).

The 1608 Royal Schools celebrate 400 years of history (Armagh, 2007).

An introduction to the Architectural heritage of County Cavan (Dublin, 2013).

Antry, T.J., & C. Neel, *Norbert and early Norbertine spirituality* (Mahwah, 2007).

Armstrong, Robert, 'Cavan and the Presbyterian frontier in the early eighteenth century' in Cherry & Scott (eds), *Cavan: history and society* (2014).

    & Tadhg Ó hAnnracháin (eds), *Community in early modern Ireland* (Dublin, 2006).

Backmund, P. Norberto, *Monasticon Premonstratense*, 3 vols, (Straubing, 1952).

Ball, J.T., *The Reformed Church of Ireland, 1537–1886* (London, 1886).

Bardon, Jonathan, *A history of Ulster* (Belfast, 1992).

    'The plantation and the Royal Schools, Ulster before 1608' in *The 1608 Royal Schools celebrate 400 years of history* (2007).

    'Revd John Richardson (*c*.1669–1747): County Cavan rector and Irish-language enthusiast' in Cherry & Scott (eds), *Cavan: history and society* (2014).

Barnard, T.G., & W.G. Neely (eds), *The clergy of the Church of Ireland, 1000–2000* (Dublin, 2006).

    A saint for eighteenth-century Dublin? Father John Murphy' in Ryan & Tait (eds), *Religion and politics in urban Ireland, c.1500-c.1750: essays in honour of Colm Lennon* (Dublin, 2016).

Barron, T.J., 'A Presbyterian exodus from County Longford in 1729' in *Bréifne*, v, 18 (1977–78).

    'The exodus of Protestant settlers from County Cavan in 1642', *The Heart of Bréifne*, iii (1980).

Barry, John, & Hiram Morgan (eds), *Great deeds in Ireland* (Cork, 2013).

Bartlett, Thomas (ed.), *Life of Theobald Wolfe Tone* (Dublin, 1998).

Beattie, Gordon, *Gregory's Angels, a history of the abbeys, priories, parishes and schools of the monks and nuns following the rule of St Benedict* (Herefordshire, 1997).

Bergin, John, Eoin Magennis, Lesa Ní Mhunghaile & Patrick Walsh (eds), *New perspectives on the penal laws* (Dublin, 2011).

Beirne, Francis (ed.),*The Diocese of Elphin* (Dublin, 2000).

Berresford Ellis, Peter, *Hell or Connaught, the Cromwellian colonisation of Ireland, 1652–1660* (Belfast, 1975).

Bermingham, Helen, 'Priest's residences in later medieval Ireland' in Fitzpatrick & Gillespie (eds), *The parish in medieval and early modern Ireland* (2006).

Bernard, Nicholas, *The life and predicions of the Rev. James Ussher* (London, 1656).

Berry, Henry F. (ed.), *Statute Rolls of the Parliament of Ireland, reign of King Henry the sixth* (Dublin, 1910).

    (ed.), 'Probable early students of Trinity College, Dublin (being wards of the crown), 1599–1616' in *Hermathena*, xvi (1911).

Bhreathnach, Edel, Joseph MacMahon & John McCafferty (eds), *The Irish Franciscans, 1534–1990* (Dublin, 2009).

Bickley, Francis (ed.), *Report on the manuscripts of the late Reginald Hastings*, iv (London, 1947).

Binasco, Matteo, & Vera Orschel, 'Prosopography of Irish students admitted to the Irish College, Rome, 1628–1798' in *Arch. Hib*. lxvi (2013).

Borlase, Edmund, *The history of the Irish rebellion* (Dublin, 1743).

Bracken, Damian, & Dag Ó Riain-Raedel (eds), *Ireland and Europe in the Twelfth century, reform and renewal* (Dublin, 2006).

Bradley, John, 'The Irish Barn Church' in *Seanchas Ard Mhacha*, 21/22 (2007–08).

Bradshaw, Brendan, *The dissolution of the religious orders in Ireland under Henry VIII* (Cambridge, 1974).

'The Edwardian Reformation in Ireland, 1547–53' in *Arch. Hib.*, xxxiv (1977). & Dáire Keogh (eds), *Christianity in Ireland: revisiting the story* (Blackrock, 2002).

Brady, Ciaran, 'The O'Reillys of east Bréifne and the problem of surrender and re-grant' in *Bréifne*, vi, 23 (1985).

'The end of the O'Reilly lordship, 1584–1610' in David Edwards (ed.), *Regions and rulers in Ireland, 1100–1650* (2004).

Brady, John, *Catholics and Catholicism in the eighteenth century press* (Maynooth, 1965).

& Patrick Corish, 'The Church under the Penal Code', in Corish (ed.), *A history of Irish Catholicism*, 4, ii (1971).

Brady, Richard, 'Thomas MacBrady, Bishop of Kilmore (1480–1511)' in *Breifny Antiquarian and Historical Society Journal*, iii, I (1927).

Breathnach, Diarmuid, 'Sirideánaigh éirimlúla Chábháin' in the *Irish Press*, 28 November 1961. Brenan, M.J., *An ecclesiastical history of Ireland* (Dublin, 1814).

Brockliss, L.W.B. & Patrick Ferté, 'Prosopography of Irish clerics in the Universities of Paris and Toulouse' in *Arch. Hib.*, lviii (2004).

Brown, Lindsay T., 'The Presbyterian dilemma, a survey of the Presbyterians and politics in Counties Cavan and Monaghan over three hundred years' in *Clogher Record*, xv, 2 (1995).

Browne, Martin, & Colmán Ó Clabaigh (eds), *The Irish Benedictines, a history* (Dublin, 2005).

Soldiers of Christ, the Knights Hospitaller and the Knights Templar in medieval Ireland (Dublin, 2016).

Burdy, Samuel, *The life of the late Rev. Philip Skelton, with some curious anecdotes* (Dublin, 1792).

Burnet, Gilbert, *The life of William Bedell, DD, bishop of Kilmore in Ireland* (London, 1685).

Burton, Janet & Karen Stober (eds), *The Regular Canons in the medieval British Isles* (Belgium, 2011).

Butler, James, 'Why Jamestown was fortified' in *Journal of Ardagh & Clonmacnoise Antiquarian Society*, i, 5 (1935).

Caball, Marc, *Poets and politics: continuity and reaction in Irish poetry, 1558–1625* (Cork, 1998).

'Solid divine and worthy scholar: William Bedell, Venice and Gaelic culture' in Kelly & Mac Murchaid (eds), *Irish and English: essays on the Irish linguistic and cultural frontier, 1600–1900* (Dublin, 2012).

'A star of the first magnitude: William Bedell (1571–1642)', Cherry & Scott (eds), *Cavan: history and Society* (Dublin, 2009).

Campbell, Patrick J., 'Andrew Campbell, bishop of Kilmore, 1753–1769' in *JCLAS*, xviii, 4 (1976).

Campbell, W.G., *The apostle of Kerry … being the Life and Labours of the Rev. Charles Graham* (Toronto, 1869).

Candon, Anthony, 'Power, politics and polygamy: women and marriage in late pre-Norman Ireland' in Bracken & Ó Riain-Raedel (eds), *Ireland and Europe* (Dublin, 2006).

Casey, Denis, 'Tigernán Ua Ruairc and the Book of Kells' in Katharine Simms (ed.), *Gaelic Ireland, c.600-c.1700* (Dublin, 2013).

Cassidy, Patrick, 'The Quakers of Cootehill' in *Bréifne*, x, 38 (2002).

'The Moravian Church in County Cavan 1751–1924' in *Bréifne*, x, 39 (2003).

'The Quakers of County Cavan 1655–1900' in *Bréifne*, xii, 45 (2009–10).

'Non-conformist religious denominations in County Cavan in the 17th and 18th centuries' in Cherry & Scott (eds), *Cavan: history and society* (Dublin, 2014).

'The origins and growth of the Presbyterian Church in County Cavan' in *Bréifne*, xii, 47 (2012).

Casway, Jerrold, 'The Belturbet Council and election of March 1650' in *Clogher Record*, xii, 2 (1986).

'The last Lords of Leitrim: The sons of Sir Teigue O'Rourke', *Bréifne*, vii, 26 (1988).

Chart, D.A., (ed.), *A preliminary survey of the ancient monuments of Northern Ireland* (Belfast, 1940).

Cherry, Jonathan, 'The Maxwell family of Farnham, County Cavan: an introduction' in *Bréifne*, xi, 42 (2006).

'The indigenous and colonial urbanization of Cavan town, *c.*1300-*c.*1641' in Scott (ed.), *Culture and society in early modern Bréifne/Cavan* (Dublin, 2009).

& Brendan Scott (eds), *Cavan: history and society* (Dublin, 2014).

Clancy, Eileen, & Patrick J. Forde, *Ballinaglera and Inishmagrath, the history and tradition of two Leitrim parishes* (Leitrim, 2003).

Ballinaglera parish, Co. Leitrim, aspects of its history and traditions (Dublin, 1980).

Clancy, Peter, *Historical notices of the parish of Inishmagrath* (Ballinaglera, 1956).

Clarke, Aidan, 'The 1641 depositions' in *Treasures of the Library, Trinity College Dublin* (Dublin, 1986).

The Old English in Ireland, 1625–42 (Dublin, 2000).

'The '1641 massacres' in Ó Siochrú & Ohlmeyer (eds), *Ireland: 1641* (2013).

Cleary, Gregory, *Father Luke Wadding and St Isidore's College, Rome* (Rome, 1925).

Clogy, Alexander, *Memoir of the life and episcopate of Dr William Bedell*, ed. by W. W. Wilkins (London, 1862).

Clyne, Miriam, 'Archaeological excavations at Holy Trinity Abbey, Lough Key, Co. Roscommon' in *PRIA*, 105C, 2 (2005).

'Medieval Irish Premonstratensian monasteries and their European context', unpublished PhD thesis (NUIG, 2010).

'The founders and patrons of Premonstratensian houses in Ireland' in Burton & Stober (eds), *The Regular Canons in the medieval British Isles* (2011).

Cochrane, Robert, *Creevelea abbey Co. Leitrim, National Monument No. 69* (Dublin, n.d.).

Cogan, A., *The diocese of Meath, ancient and modern*, ii, (Dublin, 1867).

Cole, Francis J., *Cootehill Methodism* (1946).

Coleman, John, 'Charles Coote MP [earl of Bellamont] (1738–1800) and the suppression of the Oak Boys in Counties Cavan, Fermanagh and Monaghan, July 1763' in *Bréifne*, xiv, 52 (2017).

Colgan, John, *Acta sanctorum* (Louvain, 1645).

Columcille, Fr, 'Seven documents from the old abbey of Mellifont' in *JCLAS*, xiii, 1 (1953).

Comey, Martin, 'The monastery at Slanore' in *The Breifny Antiquarian Journal*, i, 2 (1921).

Conlan, Patrick, *Franciscan Ireland*, (Dublin, 1988).

Connolly, S.J., *Religion, law and power, the making of Protestant Ireland,1660–1760* (Oxford, 1992).

(ed.), *Oxford companion to Irish history*, (Oxford, 1998).

Conway, Dominic, 'Guide to documents of Irish and British interest in Fondo Borghese, series ii – iv' in *Arch. Hib.*, xxiv (1961).

Cooney, Dudley L., The *Methodists in Ireland, a short history* (Dublin, 2001).

Cope, Joseph, 'The experience of survival during the 1641 Irish rebellion' in *The Historical Journal*, xxxxvi, 2 (2003).

Corish, Patrick J., 'The origins of Catholic Nationalism' in Corish (ed.), *A History of Irish Catholicism*, iii, 8 (Dublin, 1968).

'The rising of 1641 and the confederacy, 1641–5' in Moody, Martin & Byrne (eds), *A new history of Ireland*, iii (Oxford, 1976).

The Catholic Community in the seventeenth and eighteenth centuries (Dublin, 1981).

The Irish Catholic Experience, a historical survey (Dublin, 1985).

'The Irish martyrs and Irish history' in *Arch. Hib.*, xlvii (1993).

Maynooth College, 1795–1995 (Dublin, 1995).

Cosgrave, Art , 'Irish Episcopal temporalities in the thirteenth century' in *Arch. Hib.* 32 (1974).

& Donal McCartney (eds), *Studies in Irish history presented to R. Dudley Edwards* (Dublin, 1979).

Costecalde, Claude, & Brian Walker (eds), *The Church of Ireland, an illustrated history* (Dublin, 2013).

Cotter, Eamonn, 'The archaeology of the Irish Hospitaller preceptories of Mourneabbey and Hospital in context' in Browne & Ó Clabaigh (eds), *Soldiers of Christ* (2016).

Cregan, Donald F., 'The Confederation of Kilkenny: its organisation, personnel and history', (unpublished PhD thesis, UCD, 1947).

'The Confederate Catholics of Ireland: the personnel of the Confederation, 1642–9' in *IHS*, xxix, 116 (1995).

'The social and cultural background of a Counter-Reformation episcopate, 1618–60' in Cosgrave & McCartney (eds), *Studies in Irish history presented to R. Dudley Edwards* (1979).

Creighton, Anne, 'The Remonstrance of December 1661 and Catholic politics in Restoration Ireland' in *IHS*, xxxiv, 133 (May 2004).

Cronin, J.M., 'The other Irish martyr of the Titus Oates plot' in *Blessed Oliver Plunkett: historical studies* (Dublin, 1937).

Crookshank, C.H., *History of Methodism in Ireland* (London, 1886).

Cullen, L. M., 'Economic development, 1691–1750' in Moody & Vaughan (eds), *A new history of Ireland*, iv (Oxford, 1986).

Cunningham, Bernadette, *The world of Geoffrey Keating, history, myth and religion in seventeenth-century Ireland* (Dublin, 2000).

'The Ó Duibhgeannáin family of historians and the Annals of the Four Masters' in *Bréifne*, xi, 44 (2008).

The Annals of the Four Masters, Irish history, kingship and society in early the early seventeenth century (Dublin, 2010).

'John Colgan as historian' in Gillespie & Ó hUiginn (eds), *Irish Europe 1600–1650, writing and learning* (Dublin, 2013).

'Catholic intellectual culture in early modern Ireland', Ó hAnnracháin & Armstrong (eds), *Christianities in the early modern Celtic world* (2014).

& Raymond Gillespie, 'The purposes of patronage: Brian Maguire of Knocknin-ny and his manuscripts' in *Clogher Record*, xiii, 1 (1988).

'The Lough Derg pilgrimage in the age of the Counter-Reformation' in Éire-Ireland, 39: 3 & 4 (2004).

'Muirgheas Ó Maoilchonaire of Cluain Plocáin: an early sixteenth-century Connacht scribe at work' in *Studia Hibernica*, 35 (2008–9).

Cunningham, Terence P., 'The 1766 religious census, Kilmore and Ardagh' in *Bréifne*, i, 4 (1961).

& Francis J. MacKiernan, 'Maynooth archives – Maynooth students' in *Arch. Hib.*, 43 (1989).

Cusack, Danny, *Kilmainham of the woody hollow* (Kilmainhamwood, 1998).

Daly, Edward & Kieran Devlin, *The clergy of the diocese of Derry, an index* (Dublin, 2009).

Davies, Oliver, 'The churches of County Cavan' in *Bréifne*, xiii, 48 (2013).

'Killinagh church & Crom Cruaich' in *Bréifne* xiii, 48 (2013).

'Old churches in the parish of Rossinver, Co. Leitrim' in *Bréifne*, xiii, 48 (2013).

Day, Angélique & Patrick McWilliams (eds), *Ordnance Survey memoirs of Ireland*, iv (Dublin, 1990).

Ordnance survey memoirs of Ireland, parishes of Fermanagh 1834–5 (Belfast, 1990).

Davies, Richard G., 'The episcopate and the political crisis in England of 1386–1388' in *Speculum*, li, 4 (Oct. 1976).

Devlin, Ciarán, 'Some episcopal lives' in Jefferies & Devlin (eds), *History of the diocese of Derry from earliest times* (Dublin, 2000).

The making of medieval Derry (Dublin, 2013).

'Ecclesiastical appointments in the province of Tuam, 1399–1477' in *Arch. Hib.*, 33 (1975).

Doherty, Richard, *The Williamite war in Ireland 1688–1691* (Dublin, 1998).

Donnelly, J.S., & Kerry Miller (eds), *Irish popular culture 1650–1850* (Dublin, 1999).

Donnelly, Philip, 'Church policy in the diocese of Derry after the Reformation' in *Clogher Record*, xix, 2/3 (2007/08).

Dudley Edwards, R., 'Papal provision in fifteenth century Ireland' in *Medieval Studies presented to Aubrey Gwynn* (1961).

Duffy, Eamon, *The stripping of the altars: traditional religion in England, 1400–1580* (London, 1992).

The voices of Morebath (London, 2001).

Duffy, Francis G., 'Denis Maguire O.F.M Bishop of Kilmore 1770–98' (unpublished M.A. thesis NUIM, 1996).

'Denis Maguire OFM, Bishop of Kilmore 1770–98' in *Bréifne*, viii, 33 (1997).

Duffy, Seán (ed.), *Medieval Dublin, VII* (Dublin, 2006).

    Princes, prelates and poets in medieval Ireland (Dublin, 2013).

Faulkner, Anselm, 'Thomas Magauran O.F.M. (*c.*1640–1715)' in *Bréifne*, iv, 13 (1970).

Flanagan, P.J., 'The diocese of Clogher in 1714' in *Clogher Record*, i, 3 (1955).

Fleming, John, *Gille of Limerick (c.1070–1145): Architect of a medieval church* (Dublin, 2001).

Davies, Oliver, 'A summary of the archaeology of Ulster, Part II' in *UJA*, xii (1949).

De Burgo, Thomas, *Hibernia Dominicana* (Kilkenny, 1762).

Doherty, Charles, 'The transmission of the cult of St Máedhóg' in Ní Chatháin & Richter (eds), *Ireland and Europe in the early middle ages* (2002).

Donnelly, J.S., & Kerry Miller (eds), *Irish popular culture 1650–1850* (Dublin, 1999).

Duffy, Seán (ed.), *Princes, prelates and poets in medieval Ireland* (Dublin, 2013).

Earley, Joseph E., & Leonard Boyle, 'Conflict over the rectory of Cinéal Luacháin during the 15th century', in *Bréifne*, ix, 35 (1999).

Earley, Joseph E., 'Saving the medieval building on Church Island in Garadice Lake' in *Bréifne*, xi, 41 (2005).

    & Diarmuid Ó Seaneacháin, 'The medieval island church in Lough Garadice' in *Bréifne*, xiii, 50 (2015).

Edwards, David (ed.), *Regions and rulers in Ireland 1100–1650* (Dublin, 2004).

    & Padraig Lenihan, Clodagh Tait (eds), *Age of atrocity, violence and political conflict in early modern Ireland* (Dublin, 2007).

Elliott, Marianne, *The Catholics of Ulster* (London, 2000).

Ellis, Steven G., *Ireland in the age of the Tudors 1447–1603* (London, 1998).

Empey, Adrian, 'Irish clergy in the high and late Middle Ages' in Barnard & Neely (eds), *The clergy of the Church of Ireland, 1000–2000* (2006).

    (ed.), *Early Stuart Irish warrants, 1623–1639, The Falkland and Wentworth administrations* (Dublin, 2015).

Erck, John C., *An account of the ecclesiastical establishment subsisting in Ireland as also an ecclesiastical register of the names of the dignitaries and parochial clergy …* (Dublin, 1830).

Etchingham, Colmán, *Church organisation in Ireland AD 650 to 1000* (Maynooth, 1999).

    & Catherine Swift, 'Early Irish church organisation: the case of Drumlease and the Book of Armagh' in *Bréifne*, ix, 37 (2001).

Eustace, P. Beryl (ed.), *Registry of deeds, Dublin, abstracts of wills*, i, 1708–1745, (Dublin, 1956).

Fagan, Patrick, *The diocese of Meath in the eighteenth century* (Dublin, 2001).

    Ireland in the Stuart Papers, 1743–65 (Dublin, 1995).

Falvey, Jeremiah, 'The Church of Ireland episcopate in the eighteenth century: an overview' in *Eighteenth century Ireland*, viii (1993).

Faulkner, Anselm, 'The right of patronage of the Maguire's of Tempo' in *Clogher Record*, ix, 2 (1977).

    'Philip O'Reilly, O.F.M. (*c.*1600–1660)' in *Breifne*, v, 19 (1979).

Fennessy, Ignatius, 'Richard Brady, OFM, Bishop of Kilmore 1580–1607' in *Bréifne*, ix, 36 (2000).

'Two letters from Boetius (Augustine) MacEgan OFM, on the death of Archbishop Florence Conroy, OFM, 1629' in *Coll. Hib.*, 43 (2001).

'Canon E. Reusen's list of Irish Franciscan theses in Louvain', 1620–1738'in *Coll. Hib.*, 48 (2006).

Fenning, Hugh, 'Michael MacDonogh, O.P., Bishop of Kilmore 1728–46' in *IER*, cvi, 3 (Sept.1966).

'Bernard Brady, O.P., parish priest of Derryvullen, 1770-c.1800' in *Clogher Record*, vi, 2 (1967).

'Laurence Richardson, O.P., Bishop of Kilmore, 1747–53' in *IER*, cix (Mar.1968).

'A guide to Eighteenth-century reports on Irish dioceses in the archives of Propaganda Fide' in *Coll. Hib.*, 11 (1968).

'Letters from a Jesuit in Dublin on the Confraternity of the Holy Name, 1747–1748' in *Arch. Hib.*, xxix (1970).

The undoing of the Friars of Ireland (Louvain, 1972).

The Fottrell papers, 1721–39 (Belfast, 1980).

'Irishmen ordained at Lisbon 1587–1615, 1641–60' in *Coll. Hib.*, 31/32 (1989).

The Irish Dominican Province, 1698–1797 (Dublin, 1990).

'The Udienze series in the Roman archives of Propaganda Fide, 1750–1820' in *Arch. Hib.*, xxxxviii (1994).

'Documents of Irish interest in the *Fondo Missioni* of the Vatican archives' in *Arch. Hib.*, xxxxix (1995).

'The diocese of Elphin 1747–1802: documents from the Roman archives' in *Arch. Hib.*, xxxvi/xxxvii (1994/1995).

'Irishmen ordained at Rome, 1572–1697' in *Arch. Hib.*, lix (2005).

Finan (ed.), Thomas, *Medieval Lough Cé, history, archaeology and landscape* (Dublin, 2010).

Finnegan, Rachel, 'Fraternising with Papists: an Anglican clergyman abroad', in Brendan Leahy & Salvador Ryan (eds), *Treasures of Irish Christianity*, iii (Dublin, 2015).

Fitzmaurice, E.B., & A.G. Little (eds), *Materials for the history of the Franciscan province in Ireland*, (Manchester, 1920).

Fitzpatrick, Elizabeth, & Raymond Gillespie (eds), *The parish in medieval and early modern Ireland* (Dublin, 2006).

Flanagan, Marie Therese, *The transformation of the Irish Church in the twelfth century* (Suffolk, 2013).

'St Malachy, St Bernard of Clairvaux, and the Cistercian order' in *Arch. Hib.*, lxviii (2015).

Flanagan, P.J., 'The diocese of Clogher in 1714' in *Clogher Record*, i, 2 (1954).

Flanagan, Rachel, 'A voyage to see scenes of Our Saviour's life and passion: Richard Pococke's eastern journey (1737–41) in Leahy & Ryan (eds), *Treasures of Irish Christianity*, iii (2015).

Letters from abroad: the grand tour correspondence of Richard Pococke and Jeremiah Milles (Kilkenny, 2013).

Flower, Robin, *Irish Manuscripts in the British Library*, ii (Dublin, 1992).

Flynn, Laurence J., 'Hugh MacMahon Bishop of Clogher 1707–15 and Archbishop of Armagh 1715–37' in *Seanchas Ard Mhacha*, vii, 1 (1973).

Flynn, Thomas S., *The Irish Dominicans 1536–1641* (Dublin, 1993).

Foley, Claire, & Colm Donnelly, *Parke's Castle, Co. Leitrim: archaeology, history and architecture* (Dublin, 2012).

Foley, Claire & Ronan McHugh, *An archaeological survey of County Fermanagh* (Belfast, 2014).

Foley, Ronan, 'Therapeutic landscapes in Cavan' in Cherry & Scott (eds), *Cavan history and society* (2014).

Ford, Alan, 'The Reformation in Kilmore' in Gillespie (ed.), *Cavan: essays on the history of an Irish County* (1995).

The Protestant Reformation in Ireland 1590–1641 (Dublin, 1997).

Ford, Alan, J. McGuire & K. Milne (eds), *As by law established, the Church of Ireland since the reformation* (Dublin, 1995).

Forkan, Kevin, 'Inventing an Irish Protestant icon: the strange death of Sir Charles Coote, 1642' in Edwards, Lenihan & Tait (eds), *Age of Atrocity* (2007).

Forrestal, Alison, *Catholic Synods in Ireland, 1600–1690* (Dublin, 1998).

Franks, Lyn, 'The Maxwell family, barons and sometimes earls of Farnham, County Cavan – a genealogy' in *Bréifne* xiv, 52 (2017).

Freeman, Martin (ed.), *The Compossicion booke of Conought* (Dublin, 1936).

Gallagher, Robert H., *John Bredin, Roman Catholic school master and Methodist preacher* (Belfast, 1960).

Pioneer preachers of Irish Methodism (Belfast, 1965).

Gallogly, Dan, 'Brian of the Ramparts O'Rourke (1566–1591)' in *Bréifne*, ii, 5 (1962).

'Brian Oge O'Rourke and the Nine Years war' in *Bréifne*, ii, 6 (1963).

'Bréifne and its chieftains 940–1300' in *Bréifne*, 26, vii (1988).

'1641 Rebellion in Leitrim' in *Bréifne*, ii, 8 (1966).

Sliabh an Iarainn slopes (Monaghan, 1991).

The diocese of Kilmore 1800–1950 (Cavan, 1999).

Garner, William, 'Kildoagh Catholic Church, Co. Cavan' in *Architecture in Ireland*, i, 10 (Winter 1979–80).

Gibbons, Luke, & Kieran O'Conor (eds), *Charles O'Conor of Ballinagare, life and works* (Dublin, 2015).

Giblin, Cathaldus, 'Miscellaneous papers' in *Arch. Hib.*, xvi (1951).

(ed.), *Liber Lovaniensis, a collection of Irish Franciscan documents 1629–1717* (Dublin, 1956).

'Ten documents relating to Irish diocesan affairs 1740–84 from Franciscan Library, Killiney' in *Coll. Hib.*, 20 (1978).

Gilbert, John T., *A Contemporary history of affairs in Ireland from 1641–1652* (Dublin, 1880).

(ed.), *History of the Irish Confederation and the war in Ireland, 1641–1643* (Dublin, 1882).

(ed.), *Chartularies of St Mary's abbey, Dublin*, 2 vols (Dublin, 1884).

Gillespie, Raymond, 'The Presbyterian revolution in Ulster, 1660–1690' in William J. Shiels & Diana Wood (eds), *The Churches, Ireland and the Irish* (Oxford, 1989).

'Destabilizing Ulster, 1641–2' in Brian Mac Cuarta (ed.), *Ulster 1641: aspects of the Rising* (1993).

(ed.), *Cavan, essays on the history of an Irish county* (Dublin, 1995 repr. 2004).

Devoted people: belief and religion in early modern Ireland (Manchester, 1997).

'Popular and unpopular religion: a view from early modern Ireland' in Donnelly & Miller (eds), *Irish popular culture 1650–1850* (Dublin, 1999).

'A sixteenth-century saint's life: the second Irish life of St Maedoc' in *Bréifne*, x, 40 (2004).

'The Church of Ireland clergy, *c.*1640: representation and reality' in Barnard & Neely (eds), *The Clergy of the Church of Ireland* (2006).

Seventeenth century Ireland (Dublin, 2006).

'Saints and manuscripts in sixteenth-century Bréifne' in *Bréifne*, xi, 44 (2008).

'The making of O'Rourke, 1536' in Scott (ed.), *Culture and society in early modern Bréifne/Cavan* (2009).

'The Irish Franciscans 1600–1700' in Bhreathnach, MacMahon & McCafferty, *The Irish Franciscans, 1534–1990* (2009).

'Traditional religion in sixteenth-century Ireland' in Ó hAnnracháin & Armstrong, *Christianities in the early modern Celtic world* (2014).

& Gerard Moran (eds), *Longford, essays in county history* (Dublin, 1991).

& Ruairi Ó hUiginn (eds), *Irish Europe 1600–1650* (Dublin, 2013).

& Salvador Ryan, Brendan Scott (eds), *Making the Book of Fenagh, context and text* (Cavan, 2016).

Given-Wilson, Chris, *The Royal household and the king's affinity: service, politics and finance in England, 1360–1413* (New Haven, 1986).

Gogarty, Thomas (ed.), 'Documents concerning Primate Dowdall' in *Arch. Hib.*, i (1912).

Goode, Starr, *Sheela na gig, the dark goddess of sacred power*, (Rochester, 2016).

Grattan, W.H., 'The episcopal succession in the diocese of Kilmore, 1356–1560' in *The Breifny Antiquarian Society's Journal*, i, 1 (1920).

Grattan Flood, W.H., 'The episcopal succession in the diocese of Kilmore, 1560–1910' in *Breifny Antiquarian and Historical Society Journal*, iii, 1 (1927).

Greenwood, E.M., 'The Ulster cycle and the place of Armagh in the tradition' in Hughes & Nolan (eds), *Armagh history and society* (2001).

Gribbin, Joseph A., *The Premonstratensian Order in late medieval England* (Suffolk, 2001).

Grose, Francis, *The antiquities of Ireland*, 2 vols,(London, 1791).

Gumley, Walter, 'Provincial priors and vicars of the English Dominicans, 1221–1916' in *The English Historical review,* xxxiii, 130 (Apr. 1918).

Gwynn, Aubrey, 'Archbishop Cromer's register' in *JCLAS*, x, 3 (1943).

The medieval province of Armagh, 1470–1545 (Dundalk, 1945).

'The origins of the diocese of Kilmore' in *Bréifne*, i, 4 (1961).

The twelfth century reform (Dublin, 1968).

The Irish Church in the eleventh and twelfth centuries, ed. by Gerard O'Brien (Dublin, 1992).

& R. Neville Hadcock, *Medieval Religious houses in Ireland* (Dublin, 1970).

Gwynn, Lucius (ed. & trans.), 'Beatha Lasrach' in Éiriu, v (1911).

Hagan, J., 'Miscellanea Vaticano-Hibernica 1420–1631, in *Arch. Hib.*, iv (1915).

(ed.), 'Relationes Status' in *Arch.Hib.*, v (1916).

'Miscellanea Vaticano-Hibernica' in *Arch. Hib.*, vi (1917).

Hall, Dianne, *Women and the church in medieval Ireland, c.1140–1540* (Dublin, 2003).

Hall, Thomas , 'Killan old church, County Cavan' in *JRSAI*, xxxviii, 4 (Dec.1908).

Halton, Thomas, 'Timothy Godwin, Bishop of Kilmore' in *Bréifne*, iii, 11 (1968).

Hamlin, Ann, 'Two cross heads from County Fermanagh: Killesher and Galloon' in *UJA*, 43 (1980).

Hamell, Patrick, *Maynooth students and ordinations index, 1795–1895* (Maynooth, 1982).

'Saint Oliver Plunkett 1625–1681' in Hughes & Nolan (eds), *Armagh history and society* (2001).

Hardiman, James, *Tracts relating to Ireland* (Dublin, 1843).

Haren, Michael J., 'The religious outlook of a Gaelic lord: and new light on Thomas Óg Maguire' in *IHS*, xxv, 98 (Nov., 1986).

Harris, Walter (ed.), *The whole works of Sir James Ware concerning Ireland* (Dublin, 1739).

(ed.), *Hibernica: or Some Antient Piecese relating to Ireland* (Dublin, 1757).

Hartnett, P.J., 'Rossinver church and graveyard, Co. Leitrim' in *JRSAI*, 84, 2(1954).

Hayton, David, 'Did Protestantism fail in early eighteenth-century Ireland? Charity schools and the enterprise of religious and social reformation, *c.*1690–1730' in Ford, McGuire & Milne (eds), *As by law established* (1995).

Hennessy, William (ed.), *Chronicum Scotorum, a chronicle of Irish affairs from the earliest times to A.D. 1135* (London, 1866).

Hickson, Mary, *Ireland in the seventeenth century or the Irish massacres of 1641–2*, i (London, 1884).

Hourihane, Colum, *Gothic art in Ireland 1169–1550* (Yale, 2003).

Howlett, J.A., 'The Benedictines in Ireland' in *The Irish Monthly*, vol. 19, no. 219 (Sept. 1891).

Hughes, A.J., & William Nolan (eds), *Armagh history and society* (Dublin, 2001).

Hunter, R.J., 'An Ulster plantation town – Virginia' in *Bréifne*, iv, 13 (1970).

The Ulster plantation in the counties of Armagh and Cavan, 1608–1641 (Belfast, 2012).

'Sir William Cole, the town of Enniskillen and plantation County Fermanagh' in Murphy & Roulston (eds), *Fermanagh history and society* (Dublin, 2004).

Iske, Basil, *The Green Cockatrice* (Dublin, 1978).

Jefferies, Henry A., 'The Irish parliament of 1560: the Anglican reforms authorised' in *IHS*, 26 (1988).

Priests and prelates of Armagh in the age of Reformations 1518–1558 (Dublin, 1997).

'Erenaghs in pre-plantation Ulster: an early seventeenth-century account' in

Arch. Hib., liii (1999).

'The Armagh registers and the re-interpretation of Irish church history on the eve of the Reformations' in *Seanchas Ard Mhacha*, xviii, 1 (1999–2000).

'The early Tudor reformations in the Irish Pale' in *The Journal of ecclesiastical history*, lii, 1 (Jan. 2001).

(ed.), *History of the diocese of Clogher* (Dublin, 2005).

The Irish church and the Tudor reformations (Dublin, 2010).

'Why the Reformation failed in Ireland' in *IHS* (2016), 40 (158).

& Ciarán Devlin (eds), *History of the diocese of Derry from earliest times* (Dublin, 2000).

Jennings, Brendan (ed.), 'Brussels MS. 3947: Donatus Moneyus de Provincia Hiberniae S. Francisci' in *Anal. Hib.*, vi (Nov. 1934).

'Miscellaneous documents I, 1588–1634' in *Arch. Hib.*, xii (1946).

'Miscellaneous documents III' in *Arch. Hib.*, xv (1950).

Wadding papers 1614–38 (Dublin, 1953).

'Irish preachers and confessors in the archdiocese of Malines' in *Arch. Hib.*, xxiii (1960).

'Fr John Colgan's Acta Sanctorum' in Ó Muraíle (ed.), *Mícheál Ó Cléirigh, his associates and St Anthony's College, Louvain* (2008).

'Micheál Ó Cléirigh, chief of the Four Masters, and his associates' in Ó Muraíle (ed.),

Micheál Ó Cléirigh, his associates and St Anthony's College, Louvain (2008).

Jones, Frederick M., 'The Counter-Reformation' in Corish (ed.), in *A history of Irish Catholicism*, iii (1967).

Kearns, Patrick, 'James Pulleine, an 18th century Dean of Dromore' in *Seanchas Ard Mhacha*, xi, 1 (1983–4).

Kelly, Eamonn P., *Sheela-na-gigs, origins and functions* (Dublin, 1996).

Kelly, James, 'The Catholic church in Kilmore, 1580–1880' in Gillespie (ed.), *Cavan, essays on the history of an Irish county* (1995).

'The impact of the penal laws' in James Kelly & Dáire Keogh (eds), *History of the Catholic diocese of Dublin* (Dublin, 2000).

& Ciarán Mac Murchaid (eds), *Irish and English: essays on the Irish linguistic and cultural frontier, 1600–1900* (Dublin, 2012).

Kelly, Liam, 'A leading woman of early Methodism – Angel Anna Slacke (1748–1796)' in *Bulletin of the Wesley Historical Society* (Irish branch), i, 4 (Winter, 1987).

The face of time (Dublin, 1995).

A flame now quenched, rebels and Frenchmen in Leitrim 1793–1798 (Dublin, 1998),

'The growth of Methodism in Leitrim and Cavan: 1750–1800' in *Bréifne*, x, 38 (2002).

Churches of the diocese of Kilmore (Belfast, 2005).

St Matthew's Church, Drumavaddy (Cavan, 2013).

'A turbulent decade: County Cavan in the 1790s' in Cherry & Scott (eds), *Cavan history and society* (2014).

& Brendan Scott, 'Fenagh in 1516: the social and religious context for the Book of Fenagh' in Gillespie, Ryan & Scott (eds), *Making the Book of Fenagh, context and text* (2016).

Kenny, Michael, 'Irish secular silver, 1600–1750' in Ó Floinn (ed.), *Franciscan faith: sacred art in Ireland* (2011).

Kerney Walsh, Micheline, 'Archbishop Magauran and his return to Ireland, October 1592' in *Seanchas Ard Mhacha*, xiv, 1 (1990).

Kilroy, Phil, 'Bishops and ministers in Ulster during the primacy of Ussher, 1625–1656' in *Seanchas Ard Mhacha*, viii, 2 (1977).

King, Heather A. (ed.), *Clonmacnoise studies* (Dublin, 1998).

Krasnodebska-D'Aughton, Malgorzata, 'Franciscan chalices, 1600–50' in Bhreathnach, MacMahon & McCafferty (eds), *The Irish Franciscans 1534–1990* (2009).

Lacey, Brian, *Medieval and monastic Derry, sixth century to 1600* (Dublin, 2013).

Lanigan Wood, Helen, 'Ecclesiastical sites in County Fermanagh from the early Christian period until the end of the medieval period' in Foley & McHugh, *An archaeological survey of County Fermanagh* (2014).

Lawlor, H.J., 'A calendar of the register of Archbishop Fleming' in *PRIA*, 30 (1912–13).

Leahy, Brendan, & Salvador Ryan (eds), *Treasures of Irish Christianity*, iii (Dublin, 2015).

Leask, H.G., *Irish churches and monastic buildings* (Dundalk, 1955).

Lennon, Colm, 'The Nugent family and the diocese of Kilmore in the sixteenth and early seventeenth centuries' in *Bréifne*, ix, 37 (2001).

    Sixteenth century Ireland (Dublin, 2005).

    'Bishops in contention: secular and ecclesiastical politics in later sixteenth-century Clogher' in *Clogher Record*, xix, 1 (2006).

Leslie, J.B., revised & edited by D.W.T. Crooks, *Clergy of Kilmore, Elphin and Ardagh, biographical succession lists* (Belfast, 2008).

Lewis, Samuel, *Topographical dictionary of Ireland* (London, 1837).

Loeber, Rolf, 'A gate to Connacht: the building of the fortified town of James-town, County Leitrim, in the era of plantation' in *The Irish Sword*, xv, 60 (Summer 1983).

Logan, John, 'Tadgh O Roddy and two surveys of Co. Leitrim' in *Bréifne*, iv, 14 (1971).

Logan, Patrick, 'Leitrim priests in penal times' in *Ardagh and Clonmacnois Antiquarian Society Journal*, ii, 11 (1946).

    'Medieval hospital system in Bréifne' in *Bréifne*, iv, 13 (1970).

Lynch, Anthony, 'The administration of John Bole, Archbishop of Armagh, 1457–71' in *Seanchas Ard Mhacha*, xiv, 2 (1991).

    'A Calendar of the reassembled register of John Bole, Archbishop of Armagh, 1457–71' in *Seanchas Ard Mhacha*, xv, 1 (1992).

Lynch, John (ed.), *De Praesulibus Hiberniae* (Dublin, 1944).

Lyons, Mary Ann, *Church and society in County Kildare, c.1470–1547* (Dublin, 2000).

    'Lay female piety and church patronage in late medieval Ireland', in Bradshaw & Keogh (eds), *Christianity in Ireland* (2002).

'The role of St Anthony's College, Louvain in establishing the Irish Franciscan college network, 1607–60' in Bhreathnach, MacMahon & McCafferty (eds), *The Irish Franciscans 1534–1990* (2009).

'St Anthony's College, Louvain' in Gillespie & Ó hUiginn (eds), *Irish Europe 1600–1650* (2013).

& Thomas O'Connor, (eds), *The Ulster Earls and Baroque Europe* (Dublin, 2010).

Lysaght, Patricia, 'Hospitality at wakes and funerals in Ireland from the seventeenth to the nineteenth century' in *Folklore*, 114 (2003).

MacAtasney, Gerard, *The plantation of County Leitrim: 1585–1670* (Leitrim, 2013).

Mac Cathmhaoil, Oliver P., unpublished 'Survey of Magherintemple ecclesiastical enclosure, commonly known as Maghera fort and graveyard' (2001).

MacCotter, Paul, *Medieval Ireland, territorial, political and economic divisions* (Dublin, 2008).

'Túath, manor and parish: the kingdom of Fír Maige, cantred of Fermoy' in *Peritia*, 22–23, (2011).

'Parish, pastoral care and tuath in the diocese of Limerick c.1201' in *JRSAI*, (2012).

A history of the medieval diocese of Cloyne (Dublin, 2013).

'The early history and sub-divisions of the kingdom of Bréifne' in Cherry & Scott (eds), *Cavan: history and society* (2014).

Mac Craith, Mícheal, 'Creideamh agus athartha: idé-eolaíocht pholaitíochta agus aos léinn na Gaeilge i dtús an seachtú haois déag' in M. Ní Dhonnachadha (ed.), *Nua*-léamha: gnéith de chultúr, stair agus *polaitíocht na hÉireann, c.1600-c.1900* (Dublin, 1996).

'Collegium S. Antonii Lovanii, quod Collegium est unicum remedium ad conservandam Provinciam' in Bhreathnach, MacMahon & McCafferty (eds), *The Irish Franciscans 1534–1990* (2009).

Mac Cuarta, Brian (ed.), *Ulster 1641: aspects of the Rising* (Belfast, 1993).

'Leitrim plantation papers' in *Bréifne*, ix, 35 (1999).

'The plantation of Leitrim, 1620–41' in *IHS*, 32, no. 127 (2001).

Catholic revival in the north of Ireland 1603–41 (Dublin, 2007).

'Religious violence against settlers in south Ulster, 1641–2' in Edwards, Lenihan &Tait (eds), *Age of Atrocity* (2007).

'Catholic revival in Kilmore diocese, 1603–41' in Scott (ed.), *Culture and society in early modern Bréifne/Cavan* (2009).

'The Catholic Church in Ulster under the plantation, 1609–42' in Ó Ciardha & Ó Siochrú (eds), *The plantation of Ulster, ideology and practice* (2012).

'Irish Government lists of Catholic personnel, c.1613' in *Arch. Hib.*, lxvii (2015).

MacCurtain, Margaret, *Tudor and Stuart Ireland* (Dublin, 1972).

MacKiernan, Francis J., 'Father Michael Smith, candidate for the bishopric of Kilmore' in *Bréifne*, i, 4 (1961).

Diocese of Kilmore, bishops and priests, 1136–1988 (Cavan, 1989).

St Mary's abbey Cavan (Cavan, 2000).

'Thomas Fitzsimons (1614–80)' in *Bréifne*, ix, 37 (2001).

'Diocese of Kilmore (1678–1728)' in *Bréifne*, x, 38 (2002).

Mac Murchaidh, Ciarán, 'Dr James Gallagher, alumnus Kilmorensis: bishop of Raphoe (1725–37) and Kildare and Leighlin (1737–51)' in *Bréifne*, x, 40 (2004).

'Text and translation of James Gallagher's 'A sermon on the assumption of Our Blessed Virgin Mary' (1736)' in *Arch. Hib.*, lxii (2009).

'My Repeated Troubles' in Bergin, Magennis, Ní Mhunghaile & Walsh (eds), *New perspectives on the Penal Laws* (2011).

Mac Muirí, Seosamh, *Tadhg Ó Rodaighe, an scolaidhe treitheach* (Baile Átha Cliath, 2014).

Mac Niocaill, Gearóid, 'Cairt Ó Mhaolmhordha Ó Raghallaigh, 1558' in *Bréifne*, i, 2 (1959).

(ed.), 'Dán do Chormac Mág Shamhradháin Easpag Ardachaidh 1444–1476' in *Seanchas Ard Mhacha*, iv, 1 (1960–61).

(ed.), *Notititae as Leabhar Cheanannais* (Cló Morainn, 1961).

Magennis, Eoin, 'A Presbyterian insurrection? Reconsidering the Hearts of Oak disturbances of 1763' in *IHS*, xxxi, 122 (Nov. 1998).

'Belturbet, Cahans and two Presbyterian revolutions in South Ulster, 1660–1770' in *Seanchas Ard Mhacha*, xxi/xxii (2007–08).

Maginn, Christopher & Gerald Power (eds), *Frontiers, states and identity in early modern Ireland and beyond: essays in honour of Steven G. Ellis* (Dublin, 2016).

Maguire, Noel, 'Inscriptions in Kinawley cemetery' in *Clogher Record*, i, 4 (1956).

Maguire, W.A., 'The Maguires of Tempo: vicissitudes of a County Fermanagh family' in Murphy & Roulston (eds), *Fermanagh, history and society*, (2004).

Mallon, Patrick & Noel Ross, 'Gravestone inscriptions in Port' in *JCLAS*, xxi, 2(1986).

Manning, Conleth, *Clogh Oughter Castle, Co. Cavan, archaeology, history and architecture* (Dublin, 2013).

Mannion, Joseph, 'As trew Englishe as any man borne in Myddlesex': Sir Francis Shane, 1540–1614' in Christopher Maginn & Gerald Power (eds), *Frontiers, states and identity in early modern Ireland and beyond: essays in honour of Steeven G. Ellis* (Dublin, 2016).

Mant, Richard, *The Church of Ireland from the Reformation to the Revolution* (London, 1840).

Margey, Annaleigh, 'Surveying and mapping plantation in Cavan *c*.1580–1622' in Scott (ed.), *Culture and society in early modern Bréifne/Cavan* (2009).

Martin, F.X., 'The Irish Augustinian reform movement in the fifteenth century' in Watt, Morrall & Martin (eds), *Medieval Studies presented to Aubrey Gwynn* (1961).

Masterson, M.J., 'The Jamestown declaration with notes and addenda' in *Journal of Ardagh and Clonmacnoise Antiquarian Society*, i, 5 (1935).

Masterson, Rory, 'The alien priory of Fore, Co. Westmeath, in the middle ages' in *Arch. Hib.*, 53 (1999).

'The diocese of Kilmore and the priory of Fore: 1000–1540' in *Bréifne*, x, 39 (2003).

Medieval Fore, County Westmeath (Dublin, 2014).

Mayhew, George P., 'Jonathan Swift's Prefermts of Ireland, 1713–1714' in *Huntington Library Quarterly*, xxx, 4 (Aug. 1967).

McBride, Ian, 'Catholic politics in the penal era' in Bergin, Magennis, Ní Mhunghaile & Walsh (eds), *New perspectives on the penal laws* (2011).

McCabe, Brian, 'An Elizabethan prelate: John Garvey (1527–1596) in *Bréifne*, vii, 26 (1998).

McCarthy, Daniel (ed.), *Collections on Irish church history: from the MSS of the late V. Rev. Laurence Renehan* (Dublin, 1861).

McCaughey, Terence, *Dr Bedell and Mr King: the making of the Irish bible* (Dublin, 2001).

McCoy, Charlene & Micheál Ó Siochrú, 'County Fermanagh and the 1641 Depositions' in *Arch. Hib.*, lxi (2008).

McCready, David J.W., 'Cavan Royal school' in *Bréifne*, xi, 43 (2007).

McDermott, J.J., & Kieran O'Conor, 'Rosclogher castle: A Gaelic lordship centre on Lough Melvin, County

Leitrim' in *Bréifne*, xiii, 50 (2015).

McEnery, M.J., & Raymond Refaussé, *Christ Church Deeds* (Dublin, 2001).

McInerney, Luke, *Clerical and learned lineages of medieval Co. Clare* (Dublin, 2014).

McKeague, Leslie, *Trinity Presbyterian Church Bailieborough* (Bailieborough, 2013).

  First Bailieborough Presbyterian Church (Bailieborough, 2014).

  Anne Jane Carlile 1775–1864, temperance pioneer (Belfast, 2015).

McKenna, Elizabeth, 'The gift of a lady: women as patrons of the arts in medieval Ireland' in Meek (ed.), *Women in Renaissance and early modern Europe* (2000).

McNamee, James J., 'Ardacha Dominicana' in *Journal of Ardagh & Clonmacnois antiquarian society*, 12 (1951).

  History of the diocese of Ardagh (Dublin, 1954).

Meagher, John J., 'Proclamation against Patrick MacGowan, priest, 16 July 1583' in *Coll. Hib.*, 25 (1983).

Meehan, C.P., *The Confederation of Kilkenny* (Dublin, 1846).

  The Rise and fall of the Irish Franciscan monasteries (Dublin, 1872).

Meehan, Joseph B., 'Termon or Hospital land in Cavan, 1590' in *Breifny antiquarian Society Journal*, i, 2 (1921).

Meehan, Patrick F., *Blessed Charles Meehan, OFM, 1645–1679* (Portlaoise, *c*.1990).

Meek, Christine (ed.), *Women in Renaissance and early modern Europe* (Dublin, 2000).

Mhág Craith, Cuthbert, *Dán na mBráthar Mionúr, nótaí* (Baile Átha Cliath, 1980).

Middleton, Kathleen, 'John Richardson at Belturbet: demographic change and evangelistic opportunity in South Ulster, 1690–1727' in *Eighteenth century Ireland/Iris an dá chultúr*, xxviii (Dublin, 2013).

Millett, Benignus, 'Archbishop Edmund O'Reilly's report' in *Coll. Hib.*, ii (1959).

  The Irish Franciscans 1651–1665 (Rome, 1964).

  'Catalogue of Irish material in fourteen volumes of the *Scritture originali riferite nelle congregazioni generali*' in *Coll. Hib.*, x (1967).

  'Survival and Reorganization 1650–95' in Corish (ed.), *A History of Irish Catholicism*, iii (1968).

  'Calendar of Irish material in vols 12 & 13 (ff. 1–200) of *Fondo di Vienna* in Propaganda archives' in *Coll. Hib.*, xxiv (1982).

'Calendar of Irish materials' in *Arch. Hib.*, xxiv (1982).

'Dioceses in Ireland up to the 15th century' in *Seanchas Ard Mhacha*, xii, 1 (1986).

'The Irish Franciscans and education in late medieval times and the early Counter-Reformation, 1230–1630' in *Seanchas Ard Mhacha*, xviii (2001).

'A report from the president of Munster, Sir William Drury, 24 March 1577' in *Coll. Hib.*, 46/47 (2004/2005).

'The beatified martyrs of Ireland: Bishop Patrick O'Healy, OFM and Conn O'Rourke, OFM' in *Irish Theol. Quart.*, lxiv (1999).

'Patrick O'Healy, OFM and Conn O'Rourke, OFM: two Irish martyrs' in *Bréifne*, xii, 46 (2011).

Monahan, John, *Records relating to the dioceses of Ardagh and Clonmacnoise* (Dublin, 1886).

Moody, T.W., F.X. Martin & F.J. Byrne (eds), *A new history of Ireland*, iii (Oxford, 1976).

Mooney, Canice, 'The Franciscan friary of Jamestown' in *The Journal of Ardagh and Clonmacnois antiquarian society*, ii, 11 (1946).

'The Ven. Charles Meehan, OFM' in *Franciscan College Annual* (1952).

'Franciscan architecture in pre-Reformation Ireland' in *JRSAI*, lxxxv, 2 (1955).

'Father Francis Magruairk, OFM' in *Seanchas Ard Mhacha*, ii, 2 (1957).

'Some Cavan Franciscans of the past' in *Bréifne*, i, 1 (1958).

'Some Leitrim Franciscans of the past' in *Bréifne*, i, 4 (1961).

'Further light on Father Charles Meehan, OFM' in *Coll. Hib.*, 6 & 7 (1963–64).

Irish Franciscans and France (Dublin, 1964).

'The first impact of the Reformation' in Corish (ed.), *A history of Irish Catholicism*, iii, 2 (Dublin, 1967).

'The Irish sword and the Franciscan cowl' in *The Irish Sword*, i, 2.

'St Anthony's College, Louvain' in Ó Muraíle (ed.), *Mícheál Ó Cléirigh, his associates* (2008).

Moore, Eoghan, 'Captain Hugh O'Reilly of Lisgannon' in *Breifne*, xiii, 51(2016).

Moore, Michael J., *An introduction to the architectural heritage of County Leitrim* (Dublin, 2004).

Moran, Patrick F., *Memoirs of the Most Rev. Oliver Plunkett* (Dublin, 1861).

History of the Catholic Archbishops of Dublin (Dublin, 1864).

(ed.), *Spicilegium Ossoriense*, 3 vols (Dublin, 1874, 1878, 1884).

Morley, Henry (ed.), *Ireland under Elizabeth and James the First* (London, 1890).

Moss, Rachel, 'The old portal and cathedral of Kilmore' in *Bréifne*, xii, 46 (2011).

(ed.), *Art and architecture of Ireland*, i, *Medieval c.400-c.1600* (Dublin, 2014).

& Colmán Ó Clabaigh, Salvador Ryan (eds), '*Art & devotion in late medieval Ireland* (Dublin, 2006).

Moynes, Vera (ed.), *Irish Jesuit annual letters 1604–1674* (Dublin, 2017).

Muhr, Kay, 'The place-names of County Fermanagh', in Murphy & Roulston (eds), *Fermanagh history and society* (2004).

Mullarkey, Paul, 'The shrine of St Caillín of Fenagh' in Gillespie, Ryan & Scott (eds), *Making the Book of Fenagh* (2016).

Murphy, Denis (ed.), 'On an ancient MS. Life of St Caillín of Fenagh and on his shrine' in *PRIA*, 17 (1889–91).

The Annals of Clonmacnoise (Dublin, 1896).

Murphy, Eileen M., & William J. Roulston (eds), *Fermanagh history and society* (Dublin, 2004).

Murray, Griffin, 'A note on the provenance of the Breac Maodhóg' in *JRSAI*, 135 (2005).

'The crosier of the O'Bradys' in *Bréifne*, xii, 47 (2012).

'The Breac Maodhóg: a unique medieval Irish reliquary in Cherry & Scott (eds), *Cavan history and*

society (2014).

Murray, L.P., 'Father Brian MacHenry, O.P., Drogheda' in *JCLAS*, vi, 4 (1928).

'Archbishop Cromer's register' in *JCLAS,* vii, 4 (Dec.1932).

Nesbitt, David, *Full Circle* (Ballybay, 1999).

Ní Chatháin, Próinséas, & Michael Richter (eds), *Ireland and Europe in the early middle ages* (Dublin, 2002).

Ní Dhonnachadha, M., (ed.), *Nua-*léamha: gnéith de chultúr, stair agus polaitíocht na hÉireann, c.1600-c.1900 (Dublin, 1996).

Nicholls, K.W., 'Rectory, vicarage and parish in the western Irish dioceses' in *JRSAI*, 101 (1971).

'The Register of Clogher' in *Clogher Record*, vii, 3(1971/72).

'Medieval Irish Cathedral Chapters' in *Arch. Hib.*, 31 (1973).

Nicholson, Helen J., 'A long way from Jerusalem: the Templars and Hospitallers in Ireland, *c.*1172–1348' in Browne & Ó Clabaigh (eds), *Soldiers of Christ* (2016).

Nickalls, John (ed.), *The journal of George Fox* (Cambridge, 1952).

Ní Ghabhláin, Sinéad, 'Church and community in medieval Ireland: the diocese of Kilfenora' in *JRSAI*, cxxv (1995).

Ní Ghrádaigh, Jenifer, 'But what exactly did she give? Derforgaill and the nun's church at Clonmacnois' in King (ed.), *Clonmacnoise studies* (1998).

Nilis, Jeroen, 'Irish students at Leuven University, 1548–1797' in *Arch. Hib.*, lx (2006–07).

O'Byrne, Eileen (ed.), *The convert Rolls* (Dublin, 1981).

O'Brien, A.F., 'Episcopal elections in Ireland *c.*1254–72' in *PRIA*, 73 (1973).

O'Brien, Gerard (ed.), *Catholic Ireland in the eighteenth century, collected essays of Maureen Wall* (Dublin, 1989).

O'Callaghan, Seán, *To Hell or Barbados* (Dingle, 2000).

Ó Catháin, Diarmaid, 'Some account of Charles O'Conor and literacy in Irish in his time' in Gibbons & O'Conor (eds), *Charles O'Conor of Ballinagare, life and works* (2015).

Ó Ciardha, Eamonn, *Ireland and the Jacobite cause, 1685–1766* (Dublin, 2002).

Ó Canann, Tomás G., 'A poem on the rights of the Coarb of Saint Molaisse' in *Clogher Record*, xv, 1 (1994).

Ó Clabaigh, Colmán, *The Franciscans in Ireland, 1400–1534, from reform to reformation* (Dublin, 2002).

The Friars in Ireland 1224–1540 (Dublin, 2012).

& Martin Browne (eds), *The Irish Benedictines, a history* (Dublin, 2005).

& Martin Browne (eds), *Soldiers of Christ, the Knights Hospitaller and the Knights Templar in medieval Ireland* (Dublin, 2016).

Ó Cléirigh, T., *Aodh Mac Aingil agus an scoil Nua-Ghaedhilge i Lobháin* (Dublin, 1985).

O'Connell, Patricia, *The Irish College at Alcalá de Henares 1649–1785* (Dublin, 1997).

O'Connell, Philip, 'Moybolge and its ancient church' in *The Journal of the Breiffne Antiquarian Society*, ii, 2 (1924).

'St Ultan' in *The Journal of the Breiffne Antiquarian Society*, iii, 2 (1929–30).

'The tomb of Bishop Andrew Campbell' in *The Journal of the Breiffne Antiquarian Society*, iii, 2 (1929–30).

The diocese of Kilmore, its history and antiquities (Dublin, 1937).

The schools and scholars of Bréifne (Dublin, 1942).

O'Connell, W.D., 'The Cahill Propositions, 1629' in *IER*, 5, lxii.

O'Connor, Thomas, 'The Irish College, Rome in the age of religious renewal' in *Collegium Hibernorum De Urbe, an early manuscript account of the Irish College, Rome 1628–1678* (2003).

Irish voices from the Spanish Inquisition, migrants, converts and brokers in early modern Iberia, (Basingstroke, 2016).

& Mary Ann Lyons (eds), *The Ulster Earls and Baroque Europe* (Dublin, 2010).

O'Conor, Charles, 'Charles O'Conor of Belangare' in *Studies*, xxiii, 89 (Mar. 1934).

Ó Corráin, Donnchadh, *The Irish Church, its reform and the English invasion* (Dublin, 2017).

O'Doherty, Denis J., 'Students of the Irish College Salamanca (1595–1619)' in *Arch. Hib.*, ii (1913).

Ó Doibhlin, Diarmaid, 'Penal days' in Jefferies & Devlin (eds), *History of the diocese of Derry* (2000).

O'Donnell, John (ed.), *St Mary's Church, Teemore 1893–1993* (Teemore, 1993).

O'Donnell, Terence, *Franciscan abbey of Multyfarnham* (Multyfarnham, 1951).

'Father Donagh Mooney, OFM: the Franciscan convent of Donegal' in O'Donnell (ed.), *Father John Colgan OFM 1592–1658* (1959).

(ed.), *Father John Colgan OFM 1592–1658* (Dublin, 1959).

O'Donoghue, Fergus, 'The Jesuits come to Ireland' in *Studies*, lxxx, 317 (Spring, 1991).

O'Donovan, Patrick F., *Archaeological inventory of County Cavan* (Dublin, 1995).

Ó Droma, Micheál, & Marcella Loughman, 'Archaeological investigations at the Town Hall, Belturbet, County Cavan' in *Bréifne*, xiii, 50 (2015).

Ó Dufaigh, Seosamh, 'Lasair of Aghavea' in *Clogher Record*, xviii, 2 (2004).

Ó Duigneáin, Proinnsíos, 'Hugh O'Donnell of Larkfield – patron of Gaelic literature (1691–1754)' in *Bréifne*, vi, 24 (1986).

Dromahaire, story and pictures (Manorhamilton, 1990).

Ó Fiaich, Tomás, 'Edmund O'Reilly, Archbishop of Armagh, 1657–1669' in *Father Luke Wadding commemorative volume* (1957).

Oliver Plunkett, Ireland's new saint (Dublin, 1975).

Ó Fiannachta, Pádraig, 'Do Chlainn tSiomuinn' in *Bréifne*, ix, 37 (2001).

O'Flaherty, Eamon, 'The Catholic Convention and Anglo-Irish politics, 1791–3' in *Arch. Hib.*, 40 (1985).

Ó Floinn, Raghnall, 'The Soiscél Molaisse' in *Clogher Record*, xii, 2 (1989).

'Irish Franciscan church furnishings in the pre-Reformation period' in Ó Floinn (ed.), *Franciscan faith: sacred art in Ireland AD 1600–1750* (2011).

'Irish goldsmith's work of the later middle ages' in *Irish arts review yearbook*, xii (1996).

(ed.), *Franciscan faith: sacred art in Ireland AD 1600–1750* (Dublin, 2011).

Ó Gallachair, P., 'A missing Maguire chalice' in *Clogher Record*, i, 3 (1955).

'A forgotten Penal-day Church in Kinlough' in *Bréifne*, i, 1 (1958).

O'Gorman, Thomas, *The genealogy of the very ancient and illustrious House of O'Reilly formerly princes and dynasts of Brefny O'Reilly now called the County of Cavan in the Kingdom of Ireland* (Dublin, c.1789).

Ó Háinle, Cathal, 'Registers of a midland parish 1791–1810: Ballinahown, County Offaly and County Westmeath' in *Arch. Hib.*, lxv (2012).

Ó hAnnracháin, Tadhg, & Robert Armstrong, *Christianities in the early modern Celtic world* (London, 2014).

Ó h-Innse, Seamus (ed. & trans.), *Miscellaneous Irish Annals (AD 1114–1437), Fragment iii* (Dublin, 1947).

O'Keefe, Tadhg, *Ireland's Round Towers* (Stroud, 2004).

'Augustinian Regular Canons in twelfth and thirteenth-century Ireland: history, architecture and identity' in Burton & Stober (eds), *The Regular Canons in the medieval British Isles* (2011).

Medieval Irish Buildings 1100–1600 (Dublin, 2015).

& Pat Grogan, 'Building a frontier? The architecture of the military orders in medieval Ireland' in Browne & Ó Clabaigh (eds), *Soldiers of Christ* (2016).

Ó Maolagáin, Padraig, 'An Early History of Fermanagh' in *Clogher Record*, ii, 2 (1958).

Ó Mórdha, Brian, *Kilsherdany: Its history and people* (Cavan, 1977).

Ó Mórdha, Eoghan, 'The Uí Briúin Bréifni genealogies and the origins of Bréifne' in *Peritia*, 16 (2002).

Ó Mórdha, Séamus P., 'Cumhaidh Na Cléire, a '98 poem from north Leitrim' in *Bréifne*, i, 1 (1958).

'Hugh O'Reilly (1581?-1653): A reforming primate' in *Bréifne*, iv, 13 (1970) & *Bréifne*, iv, 15 (1972).

'Heber MacMahon, soldier-bishop of the Confederation of Kilkenny' in *Clogher Record*, iii, *Clogher Record album: a diocesan history* (1975).

'Some aspects of the literary tradition of the Bréifne-Fermanagh area' in *Bréifne*, vi, 21 (1982).

Ó Muráile, Nollaig, 'The Barony-names of Fermanagh and Monaghan' in *Clogher Record*, ii, 3 (1984).

(ed.), *Irish leaders and learning through the ages* (Dublin, 2003).

'Séamus Mág Uidhir, a scribe of Bréifne, and his work' in *Bréifne*, xi, 42 (2006).

(ed.), *Micheál Ó Cléirigh, his associates and St Anthony's College, Louvain* (Dublin, 2008).

'Keeping the embers alive: Charles O'Conor and Irish manuscripts – his own and others' in Gibbons & O'Conor (eds), *Charles O'Conor of Ballinagare* (2015).

O'Neill, Michael, 'The medieval parish churches in County Meath' in *JRSAI*, cxxxii (2002).

    'Irish Franciscan friary architecture: late medieval and early modern' in Bhreathnach, MacMahon & McCafferty (eds), *The Irish Franciscans 1534–1990* (2009).

Middleton, Kathleen M., 'Religious revolution and social crisis in southwest Scotland and Ulster, 1687–1714' (unpublished PhD thesis), TCD, 2010.

Ó'Raghallaigh MacBradaigh, Seán, 'Teallach Cearbhuill: the genealogy of Macbradaigh of Cúil Brighde in Cavan' in *Bréifne*, v, 17 (1976).

O'Reilly, J.J., *The history of Bréifne O'Reilly* (New York, 1975).

O'Reilly, Myles, *Memorials of those who suffered for the Catholic faith in Ireland in the sixteenth, seventeenth and eighteenth centuries* (London, 1868).

Ó Riain, Pádraig, *A dictionary of Irish saints* (Dublin, 2011).

    'Caillín of Fenagh' in Gillespie, Ryan & Scott (eds), *Making the Book of Fenagh, context and text* (2016).

Ó Ríordáin, John J., *Early Irish Saints* (Dublin, 2001).

Ó Siochrú, Micheál, & Jane Ohlmeyer (eds), *Ireland: 1641 contexts and reactions* (Manchester, 2013).

Ó Suilleabháin, Pádraig, 'Thomas Fitzsimons and the Primer of the Blessed Virgin Mary' in *Bréifne*, iv, 13 (1970).

O'Sullivan, Aidan, *The archaeology of lake settlement in Ireland* (Dublin, 1998).

O'Sullivan, Benedict, 'The Dominicans in medieval Dublin' in *Dublin Historical Record*, ix, 2 (June-Aug. 1947).

    Medieval Irish Dominican studies, ed. by Hugh Fenning (Dublin, 2009).

O'Sullivan, Catherine Marie, *Hospitality in medieval Ireland, 900–1500* (Dublin, 2004).

O'Sullivan, Harold, 'The Franciscans in Dundalk' in *Seanchas Ard Mhacha*, iv (1960–1).

Otway-Ruthen, A.J., 'The partition of the de Verdon lands in Ireland in 1332' in *PRIA*, 66 (1967/68).

Parez, Jan & Hedvika Kucharová, *The Irish Franciscans in Prague 1629–1786* (Prague, 2015).

Parker, Ciaran, 'The O'Reillys of east Breifne *c.*1250 - *c.*1450' in *Breifne*, viii, 2 (1991).

    'Cavan, a medieval border area' in Gillespie (ed.), *Cavan, essays on the history of an Irish county* (1995).

    'The diocese of Tir Brun (Kilmore) in the middle ages' in *Bréifne*, viii, 33 (1997).

Patterson, T.G.F., & Oliver Davies, 'Ecclesiastical remains in Co. Cavan', repr., *Bréifne*, xiii, 48 (2013).

Perceval-Maxwell, M., *Scottish migration to Ulster* (London, 1973).

Perros-Walton, Helen, 'Church reform in Connacht' in Duffy (ed.), *Princes, prelates and poets* (2013).

Petrie, George, *The ecclesiastical architecture of Ireland, an essay on the origin and uses of the Round Towers of Ireland* (Dublin, 1845).

Pochin Mould, Daphne D.C., *The Irish Dominicans* (Dublin, 1957).

Prendergast, John P., *The Cromwellian settlement of Ireland* (Dublin, 1922).

Quane, Michael, 'Cavan Royal School' in *JRSAI*, c, 1 (1970).

Quigley, W.G.H., & E.F.D. Roberts (eds), *Registrum Johannis Mey, the register of John Mey Archbishop of Armagh, 1443–1456* (Belfast, 1972).

Quinn, D.B., & K.W. Nicholls, 'Ireland in 1534' in Moody, Martin & Byrne (eds), *A new history of Ireland*, iii (1976).

Rafferty, Oliver P., *Catholicism in Ulster 1603–1983* (South Carolina, 1994).

Robson, Michael, 'Franciscan bishops of Irish dioceses active in medieval England' in *Coll. Hib.*, 38 (1997).

Roche, John, *Moravian heresy wherein the principal errors of the doctrine as taught … by Mr Cennick and other Moravian teachers, are fully set forth, proved and refuted …* (Dublin, 1741).

Rogan, Edward, *Synods and catechesis in Ireland, c.445–1962* (Rome, 1987).

Ronan, Myles V., *The Reformation in Ireland under Elizabeth, 1558–1580* (London, 1930).

Rooney, Dominic, *The life and times of Sir Frederick Hamilton 1590–1647* (Dublin, 2013).

Roulston, William, 'The Scots in plantation Cavan, 1610–42' in Scott (ed.), *Culture and society in early modern Bréifne/Cavan* (2009).

&Terence Reeves-Smyth, *Lakeland Heritage, antiquities of Fermanagh* (Belfast, 2013).

Round, J.H., & Muiris P. Mac Síthigh, 'Cairteacha Meán-aoiseacha do Mhainistir Fhohbair (XII –XII Céad)' in *Seanchas Ard Mhacha*, iv, no. 1 (1960–61).

Rowan, Alistair, *The buildings of Ireland, north west Ulster* (Dublin, 1979).

Ryan, Salvador, 'Wily women of God in Bréifne's late medieval and early modern devotional collections' in Scott (ed.), *Culture and society in early modern Bréifne/ Cavan* (2009).

& Colman Ó Clabaigh, Rachel Moss (eds), *Art & devotion in late medieval Ireland*, (Dublin, 2006).

& Brendan Leahy (eds), *Treasures of Irish Christianity*, iii (Dublin, 2015).

& Clodagh Tait (eds), *Religion and politics in urban Ireland, c.1500-c.1750: essays in honour of Colm Lennon* (Dublin, 2016).

& Raymond Gillespie, Brendan Scott (eds), *Making the Book of Fenagh, context and text* (2016).

Saul, Nigel, *Richard II* (New Haven, 1997).

Schlegel, Donald M., 'The Sheridans untangled' in *Bréifne*, xiii, 51 (2016).

Scott, Brendan, 'Dissolution of religious houses in the Tudor diocese of Meath' in *Arch. Hib.*, lix (2005).

Religion and Reformation in the Tudor diocese of Meath (Dublin, 2006).

Cavan, 1609–1653, Plantation, war and religion (Dublin, 2007).

'Reporting the 1641 rising in Cavan and Leitrim' in Scott (ed.), *Culture and society in early modern Breifne/Cavan* (2009).

'Accounts of the Battle of Cavan town, 1690' in Scott (ed.), *Cavan Town, 1610–2010 – a brief history* (2010).

(ed.), *Cavan Town, 1610–2010 – a brief history* (Cavan, 2010).

Farnham images from the Maxwell estate, County Cavan (Dublin, 2010).

'Accusations against Murtagh King, 1638' in *Arch. Hib.*, lxv (2012).

'The Knights Hospitaller in Tudor Ireland: their dissolution and attempted revival' in Browne & Ó Clabaigh (eds), *Soldiers of Christ* (2016).

'The 1622 Royal visitation of the Church of Ireland in Ulster' in Scott & Dooher (eds), *Plantation, aspects of seventeenth-century Ulster society* (2013).

& John Dooher (eds), *Plantation, aspects of seventeenth-century Ulster society* (Belfast, 2013).

& Jonathan Cherry (eds), *Cavan history and society* (Dublin, 2014).

Scully, Siobhán, 'Medieval parish churches and parochial organisation in Muintir Eolais' unpublished MA thesis (NUIG, 1999).

Seymour, St John D., 'The coarb in the medieval Irish church' in *PRIA*, 41 (1932–4).

'Drumreilly and its clergy' in *JRSAI*, v, 2 (Dec. 1935).

Sharpe, Richard, 'Churches and communities in early medieval Ireland: towards a pastoral care model' in J. Blair & R. Sharpe (eds), *Pastoral care before the parish* (Leicester, 1992).

Sheridan, Don, 'The Sheridan family, a study in the interplay between fact and romantic myth' in *Bréifne*, xi, 43 (2007).

Sherlock, Rory, 'The other Burren – archaeology and landscape in north-west Cavan' in Cherry & Scott (eds), *Cavan history and society* (2014).

Shiels, William J., & Diana Wood (eds), *The Churches, Ireland and the Irish* (Oxford, 1989).

Silke, John, 'The Irish College, Seville' in *Arch. Hib.* xxiv (1961).

Simms, J.W., 'The restoration, 1660–85' in Moody, Martin & Byrne (eds), *A new history of Ireland*, iii (1976).

Simms, Katharine, 'Gaelic lordships in Ulster in the later Middle Ages' (unpublished PhD thesis, TCD, 1976).

'Guesting and feasting in Gaelic Ireland' in *JRSAI*, cviii (1978).

'The O'Reillys and the kingdom of east Bréifne' in *Bréifne*, v, 19 (1979).

'The origins of the diocese of Clogher' in *Clogher Record*, x, 2 (1980).

'*Gaelic Ireland (c.600-c.1700): politics, culture and landscapes* (Dublin, 2013).

Smith, Brendan, 'The adventures of Milo Sweteman archbishop of Armagh 1361–1380' in *History Ireland*, iv, 4 (Winter, 1996).

Smyth, William J., *Map-making, landscapes and memory* (Cork, 2006).

'A Cultural geography of the 1641 rising/rebellion' in Ó Siochrú & Ohlmeyer (eds), *Ireland: 1641 contexts and reactions* (Manchester, 2013).

Stalley, Roger, 'Sailing to Santiago: medieval pilgrimage to Santiago de Compostela and its artistic influences in Ireland' in John Bradley (ed.), *Settlement and society in medieval Ireland, studies presented to F.X. Martin*, (Kilkenny, 1988).

'The Irish medieval pilgrimage to Santiago de Compostela' in *History Ireland*, 3 (Autumn, 1998) 6. Stewart, Alexander & George Revington (eds), *Memoir of the Life and Labours of the Rev. Adam Averell* (Dublin, 1848).

Stewart, David, *The Seceders in Ireland with annals of their congregations* (Belfast, 1950).

Stubbs, William, *Registrum Sacrum Anglicanum, an attempt to exhibit the course of Episcopal Succession in England from the records and chronicles of the church* (Oxford, 1858).

Sughi, Mario A., 'The appointment of Octavian de Palatio as archbishop of Armagh, 1477–8' in *IHS*, xxxi, 122 (Nov.1998).

Swords, Liam, 'Patrick O Donnelly, 1649–1719, bishop of Dromore' in *Seanchas Ardmacha*, 15, 2(1993).

The diocese of Achonry 1689–1818, a hidden church (Dublin, 1997).

'Fr John Farrelly, Doctor of the Sorbonne (1657–1736)' in *Bréifne*, ix, 35(1998).

A people's church, the diocese of Achonry from the sixth to the seventeenth century, (Dublin, 2013).

Tait, Clodagh, 'Art and the cult of the Virgin Mary in Ireland, *c*.1500–1660' in Moss, Ó Clabaigh & Ryan (eds), *Art and devotion in medieval Ireland* (2006).

'The wills of the Irish Catholic community, *c*.1550–*c*.1660' in Armstrong & Ó hAnnracháin (eds), *Community in early modern Ireland* (Dublin, 2006).

'The just vengeance of God: reporting the violent deaths of persecutors in early modern Ireland' in Edwards, Lenihan, & Clodagh Tait (eds), *Age of atrocity* (2007).

Tierney, Luke, 'Dominicans serving in Dublin parishes' in *Reportorium Novum*, iii, 1 (1962).

Tone, Theobald Wolfe, 'Journals, notes, letters [1789–95]' in Thomas Bartlett (ed.), *Life of Theobald Wolfe Tone* (Dublin, 1998).

Traynor, Owen F., 'Kilmore clergy list of 1723' in *Bréifne*, iii, 11 (1968).

'More Kilmore clergy lists', *Bréifne*, iv, 14 (1971).

Treadwell, Victor, *Buckingham and Ireland 1616–1628*, (Dublin, 1998).

Tynan, Michael, *Catholic instruction in Ireland 1720–1950* (Dublin, 1985).

Vallancey, Charles, *Collectanea De Rebus Hibernicis* (Dublin, 1786).

Veach, Colin T., 'A question of timing: Walter de Lacy's seisin of Meath 1189–94' in *PRIA*, 109C (2009).

& Freya Verstraten Veach, 'William Gorm de Lacy: chiefest champion in these parts of Europe' in Duffy (ed.), *Princes, Prelates and poets* (2013).

Wall, Maureen, *The Penal Laws, 1691–1760* (Dundalk, 1976).

Catholic Ireland in the eighteenth century (Dublin, 1989).

Walsh, Micheline, 'Andrew Campbell, Bishop of Kilmore, 1753–1769, student days in Spain' in *JCLAS*, xviii, 4 (1976).

Walsh, Paul, 'The Ua Maelechlainn kings of Meath' in Ó Muráile (ed.), *Irish leaders and learning through the ages* (Dublin, 2003).

Walsh, Peter, *The history and vindication of the loyal formulary or Irish Remonstrance…* (London, 1674).

Ware, James, *The antiquities and history of Ireland* (London, 1705).

Watt, John, 'English law and the Irish church: the reign of Edward I' in Watt, Morrall & Martin (eds), *Medieval Studies presented to Aubrey Gwynn* (1961).

The Church in medieval Ireland (Dublin, 1972).

Watt, J.A., J.B. Morrall & F.X. Martin (eds), *Medieval studies presented to Aubrey Gwynn* (Dublin, 1961).

White, Newport B., *Extents of Irish monastic possessions, 1540–1541* (Dublin, 1943).

Wight, Thomas & John Rutty, *A history of the rise and progress of the people called Quakers in Ireland from the year 1653 to 1700* (London, 1800).

Wightman, W.E., *The Lacy family in England and Normandy, 1066–1194* (Oxford, 1966).

Zucchelli, Christine, *Sacred stones of Ireland* (Cork, 2016).

Index

Kilmore Upper, townland, 31

Kilnacross, 178

Kilnacrott, 67

Kilnavart, 92, 221, 249

Kilronan, 249

Kildrumferton, 76, 87, 149, 190, 353, 415

Kilsallagh, 317

Kilsherdany, parish, 46, 47, 59, 76, 77, 87–8, 121, 169, 247, 289, 353, 478, 483

Kilsherdany, vicar of, 135, 136, 416

Kilsherdany, vicarage of, 125

Kiltoghert, 287

Kiltubrid, 303, 328, 365, 449, 479

Kiltyclogher, 377

Kinawley, church,146, 150, 159, 181

Kinawley, parish, 92, 167, 170, 177, 221, 312, 318, 376, 428, 468

Kinawley, vicar of, 127, 297, 308

Kinawley, vicarage of, 87, 287

Kingscourt, 472, 479

Kinnypottle, river, 66

Knight, Richard, 415

Knights Hospitaller, 41–2, 111

Knights Templar, 41

Knockbride, curate of, 151

Knockbride, parish, 35, 76, 92, 188, 287, 292, 308, 315, 319, 416

Knockninny, 150, 170, 221, 251, 395, 396, 428, 468, 476

Knox, John, 479

L

Lacey, Hugh, 198

Laggan, 364

Laighne, saint,159, 169

Lake, Thomas, 245

Lambert, Oliver, 238

Lane–Fox estate, 397

Laois, county, 361

Laragh, parish, 46, 76, 84, 87, 89–90, 91–2, 100, 102, 119, 121, 124, 128, 169, 252, 292, 310, 314, 317, 353, 375, 380, 415, 456

Larkfield, 375, 396

Lasair, saint, 87, 159, 166–7, 170

Laud, William, 274, 275, 276, 286, 290

Laurence, saint, 171

Lavey, parish, 46, 76, 121, 162, 163, 178, 248, 250, 290, 292, 310, 390–1, 392, 416

Lawless, Margarita, 433

Lawless, Maria, 433

Lawless, Patricio, 433

Lawless, Patrick, 440

Leackmogue, 180

Leac Mhaedóc, 179

Lee, Fergus Laurence, 354

Leginn, 476

Leigh, Michael, 415

Leighlin, 197–8, 383, 402, 408, 421

Leitrim, castle, 175

Leitrim, county, 21, 74, 76, 77, 108, 144, 160, 168, 172, 177, 199–204, 206, 211, 232, 235–40, 241, 246, 249, 250, 252, 258, 262, 263, 265, 269, 279, 287–8, 291, 297, 300–1, 304, 306, 312–3, 323, 328, 330,335, 339, 341–2, 343–4, 345, 358, 365, 335, 339, 341–2, 343–4, 345, 358, 365, 368, 376, 378–80, 389, 392, 396, 402, 410, 415, 425, 427, 432, 435, 449, 466, 467, 468, 471, 473, 475, 479–89, 481

Leitrim, village, 230

Lemakevoge, 179

Lennon, Colm, 190

Leo XIII, 371

Leth Chuinn, 71

Levins, Philip, 440